Teaching English Abroad

Talk your way around the world!

Teaching English Abroad

Talk your way around the world!

Susan Griffith

Distributed in the U.S.A. by Peterson's Guides, Inc.,
202 Carnegie Center, Princeton, N.J. 08543
Web site http://www.petersons.com

Published by Vacation Work, 9 Park End Street, Oxford
Web site http://www.vacationwork.co.uk

First published 1991
Fourth edition 1999

TEACHING ENGLISH ABROAD
by Susan Griffith

Copyright © 1999

ISBN 1 85458 207 0

Cover Design
Miller Craig & Cocking Design Partnership

Illustrations by John Taylor

Map by Andrea Pullen

Publicity: Roger Musker

Imageset and Printed by Unwin Brothers Ltd., Old Woking, Surrey

Contents

PART I INTRODUCTION

PART II COUNTRY BY COUNTRY GUIDE

PART III APPENDICES

Acknowledgments

The new revised edition of *Teaching English Abroad* would not have been possible without the help of scores of world travellers and ELT teachers who have generously shared their information, insights and anecdotes. As well as all the people who helped with the three previous editions, I would like to thank the following for their contributions, some of them substantial, to the research and writing of this updated edition. I owe a special debt of gratitude to my assistant, Geneviève Séguin, who combined efficiency and enthusiasm in equal measure.

Germany	Nathan Edwards
Greece	Jain Cook
Portugal	Sam Dunlop, Maggie Milne
Spain	Brian Farrelly, Joanna Mudie
Slovenia	Adam Cook
Eastern Europe	Marisa Wharton
Czech Republic	Brian Farrelly
Hungary	Steve Anderson
Poland	Heidi Rothwell-Walker
Romania	Michael Frost
Russia	Robert Jensky
Estonia	Sarah Wadsworth
Latvia	Rhys Sage
Lithuania	John Morgan, Alan Reekie
Azerbaijan	Richard McGeough
Oman	Sandeha Lynch
Saudi Arabia	Carl Hart, Morris Jensen
Yemen	Mary Hall
Turkey	Brian Komyathy, Eugene Tate
Tunisia	Roger Musker
China	William Hawkes
Hong Kong	Jane Harris, Andrew Monks
Japan	Deborah Cordingley, Nathan Edwards, Robert Mizzi, Bridgid Seymour-East
Korea	Gary Downs, Patrick Edgington, Tim Leffel, William Naquin, Kathy Panton
Nepal	Giles Freeman
Sri Lanka	Simon Rowland
Taiwan	Peter McGuire
Thailand	Richard Guellala, Annette Kunigagon, Helen Welch
South America	Nick Branch

Telephone area code changes: On April 22nd 2000 there are to be a number of changes to certain area telephone code prefixes in the UK. The most important of these is that the current 0171- and 0181- prefixes for London will both be replaced by the prefix 020-, followed by 7 for current 0171 numbers and 8 for current 0181 numbers. Also affected will be Cardiff (numbers will begin 029 20), Portsmouth (023 92), Southampton (023 80) and Northern Ireland (028 90 for Belfast); contact directory enquiries for other numbers in Northern Ireland.

NOTE: While every effort has been made to ensure that the information contained in this book was correct at the time of going to press, details are bound to change, especially those pertaining to visa requirements for teachers, exchange rates and the conditions offered by the schools listed in the country directories. Readers are invited to write to Susan Griffith, Vacation Work, 9 Park End Street, Oxford OX1 1HJ, with any comments or corrections. The best contributions will be rewarded with a free copy of the next edition or any other Vacation Work title of their choice.

Preface

Every morning and every evening, the streets of Seville and Skopje, Santiago and Seoul are thronged with people rushing to their English lessons. Children and adolescents are motivated by an eagerness to participate in popular culture; businessmen and women want to forge deals with partners in America; everybody wants to use the internet.

Those of us who speak English as a first language tend to take for granted how universally dominant it has become. English is the language of pop songs, computer games and air traffic control. Even the French have been forced to admit its supremacy: the French Prime Minister recently conceded in a speech that 'we need a world language; and since it won't be Esperanto, it will probably be English'. It is no wonder that the demand for instruction is increasing exponentially around the world. Within the next ten years, the number of people who communicate in English as a subsidiary language will overtake the number who speak it as a native. Despite global financial turmoil, especially in the Far East, Russia and Brazil, the market for English is still miraculously vigorous.

An ability to teach the English language is surely the most globally mobile skill there is. The teaching industry which services the world demand continues to mushroom: private language institutes have opened in areas of the world once closed to EFL teachers from Kazakhstan to Caracas, Shanghai to Chiang Mai. Mediating agencies match job-seeking teachers with teacher-seeking employers. The number of training centres worldwide which offer validated courses in the teaching of English as a foreign language has increased dramatically since the last edition of this book. The proliferation of candidates with an English language teaching (ELT) qualification has made it more important to obtain training to be able to compete.

There is no average profile of the travelling teacher. For this fourth edition of *Teaching English Abroad*, I have received enthusiastic feedback from a man who spent the summer between school and university teaching English in rural Sri Lanka, an Irish woman who offers advice to job-seeking foreigners at her guest house in northern Thailand, a politics graduate whose Hungarian surname prompted him to spend time in central Europe, an American freelance travel journalist who acquired a TEFL Certificate and taught in Korea, an advertising executive who took a short sabbatical to teach English in North Africa, an Oxford postgrad in biochemistry who spent a year teaching in Bogota, a nurse working for an international aid agency in the Middle East, a civil servant with an interest in Romania, an Australian school leaver teaching as a volunteer in Nepal, and a sculptor from Wales who accepted a lucrative teaching contract in Oman. The beauty of English teaching is that it is accessible to so many.

Interwoven with the actual experiences of people who have taught English abroad, is specific job vacancy information. Five hundred language schools around the world submitted details of their teaching vacancies for this edition, and in addition the addresses of hundreds of other schools are provided. My aim has been to make the information in this book as concrete as possible, to cut the waffle. Unlike other books in this field, this one does not rely exclusively on information supplied by the ELT establishment. What is just as valuable for the potential job-seeker is the unofficial word-of-mouth information, for example whether or not the Korean embassy is likely to reply to letters of enquiry about teaching, whether a certain organisation might sometimes hire people without paper qualifications, how hard it is to get a working visa in Moscow or St. Petersburg, and so on.

Teaching English Abroad tries to maintain a fine balance. On the one hand, it is not aimed primarily at the career EFL teacher who already has access to a wide range of information on working abroad. Neither is it intended to encourage layabouts and illiterates to masquerade as teachers, nor to bluster their way into jobs abroad on the insufficient grounds that they are native speakers of the language. But between these two extremes, there is a huge pool of people who have the appropriate background and personality to become successful teachers of their native language. It remains the case that the majority of TEFL teachers leave the profession after a couple of years, poised to succeed in any workplace where thinking on your feet is required.

Like every enterprise, teaching English in foreign cultures has its specific rewards and risks which I have attempted to identify, in the hope of easing the path for those who are tempted but remain hesitant. This book can be the stepping stone to a brilliant year or two abroad.

Susan Griffith
Cambridge
December 1998

PART I

Introduction

**Training
Finding a Job
Preparation
Problems**

Introduction

One billion people will speak or be trying to speak English as a first, second or foreign language, by the dawn of the new millennium, according to figures published by the British Council. It is not clear who has counted them all, but it has been said that 300 million people are learning English at the present time. Estimates have been made that 90% of the world's electronically stored information is in English and that a majority of the 50 million Internet users communicate in the language you are reading at this moment. Mind-boggling statistics aside, the demand for instruction at all levels by people who happen to speak English as their mother tongue is enormous and set to continue increasing for the forseeable future.

For whatever historical and economic reasons, English has come to dominate the world, the late twentieth century sequel of colonialism. When the newly liberated nations of Eastern Europe sloughed off Russian, they turned in very large measure to English rather than to the other main European languages. Countries as far-flung as Cambodia, Namibia and Algeria are busy making English one of the keystones of their educational systems. English is the international language of science, of air traffic control and to a very large extent of trade and export. This is bad news for all those Germans, Swedes and French Canadians who would like to market their language skills in order to fund a short or long stay abroad. But it is English speakers, mainly from Britain, Ireland, North America and Australia/New Zealand who accidentally find themselves in possession of such a sought-after commodity.

Some Definitions

The commonly used acronyms ELT, TEFL, TESL and TESOL can be confusing, especially since they are often used interchangeably. ELT, which stands for English Language Teaching, has come to be the mainstream expression in the UK (preferred by such august bodies as the University of Cambridge and by the publishers of the main journal in the field). But most people still refer to TEFL (pronounced 'teffle'), Teaching English as a Foreign Language. TESL stands for Teaching English as a Second Language, and TESOL means Teaching English to Speakers of Other Languages. English is learned as a *foreign* language by people who may need the language for certain purposes such as business or tourism but who live in countries where English has no official status. English is learned as a *second* language when it will have to be used for day to day life, for example by emigrants to the UK and the USA or by inhabitants of ex-colonies where English retains official status and may well be the medium of instruction in schools. (English is the official or joint-official language in 75 countries.)

Because this book is for people who want to travel abroad to teach, the term TEFL is mainly used as well as ELT. Teachers of ESL are normally involved with multicultural education. In the US, the vast majority of English language teaching is of ESL because of the huge demand for English among foreigners who have emigrated to the US. Therefore the term ESL dominates in American contexts, even when (technically) EFL is meant.

The acronym TESOL covers both situations, yet it is not widely used apart from in institutions which favour the Trinity College qualifications known as the Certificate and Licentiate Diploma in TESOL (see Training section later) and also in the context of the American organisation TESOL Inc., which is the largest English teachers' organisation in the world claiming more than 16,000 members.

There is no shortage of other acronyms in the world of TEFL. One of the main ones is ESP which means English for Specific Purposes. ESP aims to match language teaching with the needs of various professions such as business, banking, tourism, medicine, science and technology, secretaries, etc. Business English is probably the most important in this category (and 'English for Shopping' as sometimes offered in Japan is the least important). Because a great many learners are motivated by a desire to use English at work, they want their teachers to adopt a functional rather than a structural approach. In other words they want to have lessons in which they can pretend to be telephoning a client, recommending, advising, agreeing, complaining and so on. They are certainly not interested in the subjunctive.

EAP stands for English for Academic Purposes, i.e. English at an advanced level taught to students who are normally planning to study at foreign universities. EAP is largely in the hands of government-funded programmes, such as those run by the British Council.

Note that the acronym TOEFL can cause confusion. The Test of English as a Foreign Language is a US-based standardised test administered to language learners. Passing a TOEFL exam is widely held to be a reliable indicator of how well an individual can communicate in English. The focus of many language schools abroad is to prepare candidates for the exam, and so may advertise for teachers with 'TOEFL' experience.

SCOPE OF OPPORTUNITIES

The range of locations and situations in which English is in demand covers an enormous spectrum. If TEFL is booming in Laos and Cambodia, there can be few corners of the world to which English has not penetrated. English has been called a 'barometer of Western influence' and there is only a handful of countries in the world which have rejected Western influence outright (like Bhutan and Iraq) and which therefore have no call for EFL teachers. More important nations with their own native English-speaking population (like India) are also not promising destinations for the aspiring teacher.

With the arrival of the single European market in 1992, Europe has become an even greater consumer of English than ever before. There has been an enormous increase in demand especially from companies and professionals eager to participate in an integrated Europe. The field of teaching English to young children is especially flourishing in Mediterranean countries. The attraction of European Union countries for British and Irish teachers is even greater since they have the legal right to work.

The kinds of people who want to learn English are as numerous as the places in which they live. The economic crisis in the Far East and Russia has prompted a decline in the number of 'leisure students', people attending English classes simply for pleasure. The those countries hit hardest by recession (like Thailand and Korea), the amount of work available teaching in companies has diminished as well. The area of the industry which seems to be booming almost everywhere is the teaching of children (known as Young Learners in the trade). Kids as young as three are being sent to private English classes to enhance their career prospects.

People around the world can think of a dozen reasons why they need to sign up for private English lessons. A Taiwanese student dreams of studying at UCLA. The wife of the Peruvian ambassador in Islamabad wants to be able to speak English at official functions. A Greek secondary school student has to pass her English exams in order to proceed to the next year and, like most of her classmates, attends a private tutorial college for English lessons. A Siberian worker associates English with the language of freedom and liberalism. A Turkish youth wants to be able to flirt with tourists from northern Europe. A Mexican waiter wants to get a job in the Acapulco Hilton. A Saudi engineer has to be able to read reports and manuals in English for his job. The list is open-ended, and prospects for hopeful teachers are therefore excellent. There are also hundreds of international schools throughout the world where English is the medium of instruction for all subjects and there may be specific EFL vacancies. These will be of most interest to certified teachers who wish to work abroad.

But the situation is not all rosy for the prospective teacher. As the profile of the English language has risen, so has the profile of the profession which teaches it, and the number of qualified and experienced English teachers has increased along with the rise in demand. The phenomenal explosion in the availability of training courses means that a much higher proportion of job-seekers has a TEFL certificate than was the case a decade ago, and (quite rightly) foreign language schools are becoming more selective when hiring staff.

People who cruise into a country expecting to be hired as an EFL teacher simply on the basis of being a native speaker are in most cases (though not quite all) in for a nasty shock. Employers at all levels will ask for evidence of the ability to teach their language or at least a university degree as proof of a sound educational background. Certainly without a degree, a TEFL qualification or any relevant experience, the scope of opportunities shrinks drastically.

Who is eligible to teach?

Anyone who can speak English fluently and has a lively positive personality has a fighting chance of finding an opening as a teacher somewhere. Geordies, Tasmanians and Alabamans have all been known to be hired as English teachers (not to mention Norwegians and North Africans), though most employers favour native speakers of English without a heavy regional accent. Depending on the economic and cultural orientation of a country, schools will prefer British English (what the Director-General of the British Council likes to call 'standard English') or North American English. For obvious geopolitical reasons Europe and Africa incline towards Britain while Latin America and the Far East incline towards the US. Many countries have no decided preference, for example Indonesia and Turkey. Clear diction is usually more important than accent.

English language teaching is an industry which is seldom regulated, giving rise to a host of cowboy schools, which are mentioned (usually disparagingly) throughout this book. The other side of the coin is the proliferation of cowboy *teachers*, who have no feel for language, no interest in their pupils and no qualms about ripping them off. The issue of qualifications must be considered carefully. It is obviously unwise to assume that fluency in English is a sufficient qualification to turn someone into an EFL teacher. Many experienced teachers of English come to feel very strongly that untrained teachers do a disservice both to their pupils and to their language. Certainly anyone who is serious about going abroad to teach English should turn to the relevant chapter to consider the training options.

Among the army of teachers-cum-travellers, there are undoubtedly some lazy, spiritless and ungrammatical native speakers of English who have bluffed their way into a teaching job. Most books and journals about language teaching are unanimous in their condemnation of such amateurs. Yet there are some excellent teachers who have learned how to teach by practising rather than by studying. For certain kinds of teaching jobs, a background in business and commerce might be far more useful than any paper qualifications in teaching. Therefore we have not excluded the unqualified teacher-traveller from our account. As long as they take their responsibilities seriously and bear in mind that their pupils have entrusted them with significant quantities of time and money to help them learn, they need not bring the EFL profession into disrepute. Some untrained teachers we talked to during the research for this book found the responsibility so unnerving that they promptly enrolled in a TEFL course before unleashing themselves on an unsuspecting language-learning public.

Non native speakers should not asssume that their services will not be in demand outside their home countries. Richard Ridha Guellala was born in Holland, raised in Tunisia and partly educated in England, and now has one of the most highly respected qualifications in TEFL, the Cambridge Diploma. At present he is teaching in Thailand:

> *Most non-native speakers think that a position as an EFL teacher is impossible for them. However I came to the conclusion that even unqualified non-native speakers are often hired by Asian schools, as long as they project a professional image during the interview, speak clearly, are well-groomed, know the basics of English grammar and are fluent in the language. Scandinavians and Dutch are sometimes even more successful in finding teaching jobs at top schools than native speakers. True, we non-native speakers possess a rather 'heavy' or 'funny' accent but, believe it or not, some Asian employers favour our accents to the native speaker's because we speak more slowly and use very simple basic vocubulary.*

At an extreme opposite from the casual teacher-traveller is the teacher who makes ELT a career. Only a minority of people teaching English abroad are professional teachers. Career prospects in ELT are in fact not very bright. After teachers have achieved a certain level of training and experience, they can aspire to work for International House and then for the British Council. From there, they might become a director of studies at a private language institute, though are unlikely to become a director unless their primary interest is business and administration or unless they have some capital to invest in order to buy and run their own school.

An increasing number of early-retired and other mature people are becoming interested in teaching English abroad for a year or two. Although it may be true that in certain contexts, language institutes are more inclined to employ a bright young graduate, if only for reasons of image, there are plenty of others who will value maturity, especially the growing number of establishments which specialise in teaching young children. Recently there has been a noticeable shift in the market of English learners to the younger age groups, with whom hopeful teachers fresh from university are often poorly equipped to cope.

What employers are looking for

Between the dodgy operators and the British Council is a vast middle ground of respectable English teaching establishments. Many would prefer to hire only qualified staff, yet they are not always available. On the whole these schools are looking for teachers with a good educational background, clear correct speech, familiarity with the main issues and approaches to TEFL and an outgoing personality. A BA and/or TEFL certificate is no guarantee of ability as Marta Eleniak observed in Spain where she taught during her 'gap' year (after doing a one-week introductory TEFL course):

> *I've seen graduate teachers make such a mockery of the enterprise that it's almost criminal. TEFL is creative teaching. Forget about your educational experiences. In*

TEFL you have got to be able to do an impression of a chicken, you've got to be a performer. And you have to be flexible. If the pupils are falling asleep, conduct a short aerobics class and change tack to something more interesting. A good teacher builds a rapport with the class, and is enthusiastic, patient, imaginative and genuinely interested in the welfare of the pupils.

A sophisticated knowledge of English grammar is not needed, since in most cases, native speakers are hired to encourage conversation and practise pronunciation, leaving the grammar lessons to local teachers. On the other hand, a basic grasp is necessary if only to keep up with your pupils.

MOTIVES FOR TEACHING ENGLISH

There are perhaps five main types of individual to be found teaching English from Tarragona to Taipei: the serious career teacher, the student of the prevailing language and culture who teaches in order to fund a longer stay, the long-term traveller who wants to prolong and fund his or her travels, the philanthropic or religious person sponsored by an aid organisation, charity or mission society, and finally the misfit or oddball, perhaps fleeing unhappiness at home.

In many countries, English teaching is the most easily attainable employment, in fact the *only* available employment for foreigners. Anyone who wants to transcend the status of mere tourist in a country like Thailand, Peru or Japan will probably be attracted to the idea of teaching English. The assumption behind some thinking at the snobbish end of the EFL spectrum is that people who do it for only a year or two as a means to an end (e.g. learning Chinese, studying Italian art, eating French food) are necessarily inadequate teachers.

There are small pockets of people (mainly in the Far East) whose sole ambition is to earn as much money as possible to pay off debts or fund further world travels. These are seldom good teachers if only because they take on so many hours of teaching that they can't possibly prepare properly for their lessons. But for most teachers, making a lot of money is not a priority or, if it was at the outset, they are soon disillusioned.

Salaries in popular tourist destinations (like Paris, Barcelona, Chiang Mai) may actually be lower than in less appealing neighbouring towns, even though the cost of living is higher. Pay scales are relatively meaningless out of context. For example the high salaries paid in Japan are usually eaten up (at least in the first year) by high rents and other expenses. When converted into sterling a salary in Brazil or Turkey might sound reasonable, but chronic inflation and currency devaluations could soon alter the picture. In some countries like the Ukraine and Kenya, a TEFL salary may not be enough to fund anything beyond a very spartan lifestyle, and savings from home are essential to fund any travelling. Yet the majority of people who spend time abroad teaching English are able to afford to live comfortably and have an enjoyable time without feeling pinched, but end up saving little.

RED TAPE

The European Union consists of the UK, Ireland, Netherlands, Belgium, Luxembourg, Denmark, Sweden, Finland, Austria, France, Germany, Italy, Greece, Spain and Portugal, the latter six of which have enormous EFL markets. Within the EU the red tape should be minimal for all nationals of member states who wish to work in any capacity (though the relevant sections of the country chapters make it clear that this is not always the case). Anyone who intends to stay for more than three months requires a residence permit, which may be a bureaucratic hassle to obtain but should not be cause for anxiety, once you have a teaching job.

Outside the EU, legislation varies from country to country. In theory there is also 'free reciprocity of labour' within the European Economic Area. The EEA takes in those Western European countries which have decided to stay outside the Union, viz. Iceland, Liechtenstein, Norway and Switzerland.

All of this means that British and Irish nationals have a significant advantage over Americans, Canadians, Australians and New Zealanders when job-hunting in Europe.

Although not impossible for other nationalities, it is very difficult for them to find an employer willing to undertake the task of proving to the authorities that no EU national is available or able to do the job. Brian Komyathy from Long Island New York was pleasantly surprised at how easy it was to arrange a job in Hungary, but then correspondingly disappointed when he made enquiries about moving to an EU country the following year:

> *European walls of regulations do not exactly bespeak, 'Americans welcome aboard'.*
> *I'm technically eligible to acquire Irish and hence EU citizenship through my*
> *grandparents, so as soon as various documentary records are located and processed*
> *I'll not have the problems I do now. A slew of phone calls convinced me of the*
> *necessity of taking this course. Greece will be my last resort since it was the only place*
> *which didn't (figuratively) hang up on me when they recognised the origin of my*
> *accent.*

International exchange organisations may be able to assist. For example the Council on International Educational Exchange (205 East 42nd Street, New York, NY 10017) runs work abroad programmes for students in a number of countries and arranges for temporary work permits to be issued. With offices in France, Germany, Italy and Spain, Council might seem an obvious contact for Americans seeking to teach English in Europe, however the time limits of the programme (three to six months) make participants unattractive to employers who normally want teachers to stay for the nine or ten months of the academic year.

Other US-based organisations (InterExchange for instance) cooperate with partner organisations in various countries like the Czech Republic, Jamaica, China and many others, to place native speaker teachers in schools or institutes, often as volunteers. For particulars, see the chapter *Finding a Job: Opportunities for North Americans.*

The immigration authorities of many countries accord English teachers special status, recognising that their own nationals cannot compete as they can for other jobs. Other countries may lack the mechanism for granting work visas to English teachers and so will often turn a blind eye to those who teach on tourist visas, since everyone knows that locals are not being deprived of jobs, rather they're being given an advantage by having the chance to learn English.

The President of a major language school group Bénédict makes a useful suggestion in his standard reply to enquiries from job-seekers:

> *If you are looking for a teaching job you must remember that the present crisis makes*
> *it often difficult for foreigners to obtain the necessary authorisations. In such cases it*
> *may be useful to seek a study-and-teach solution. Such an exchange is frequently*
> *possible for short-term or long-term periods.*

Teachers who fix up a job before leaving home can usually sort out their visas or at least set the wheels in motion before arrival, which greatly simplifies matters. The majority of countries will process visas only when they are applied for from outside the country. Otherwise it may be necessary to go to your chosen country on a tourist visa, find a job, then leave the country to apply for the work visa. The restrictions and procedures for obtaining the appropriate documentation to teach legally are set out in *Part II* of this book country by country. Prospective teachers should contact the relevant Consulate for the official line (addresses in *Appendix 2*). If there is any doubt, ring the embassy a second time to confirm the original information. It is amazing how inconsistent such sources of information can be. Always enlist the help of your employer who should be familiar with procedures (assuming he or she has hired foreign teachers before) and who should be willing to help defray the often considerable costs.

If you do get tangled up in red tape, always remain patient with consular officials. If things seem to be grinding to a halt, it may be helpful to pester them, provided this is done with unfailing politeness.

REWARDS AND RISKS

The rewards of teaching abroad are mostly self-evident: the chance to become integrated in a foreign culture, the pleasure of making communication possible for your students, the interesting characters and lifestyles you will encounter, a feeling of increased self-reliance, a better perspective on your own culture and your own habits, a base for foreign travel, a good suntan ... and so on. Good teachers (e.g. those who enjoy doing impressions of chickens?) often find their classes positively fun and place a high value on the relationships they form with their students. Teaching is a lot of fun when it's done right. One-to-one teaching can also be enjoyable since you have a better chance to get to know your students or clients. (By the same token, it can be a miserable experience if you don't get on, since there is no escape from the intimacy of the arrangement.) Off-site teaching provides glimpses into a variety of workplaces and private homes, perhaps even resulting in hospitality and friendship with your students.

As competition for jobs has increased, working conditions have not improved. There is a growing tendency for EFL teachers to be offered non-contract freelance work, with no guarantee of hours, making it necessary for them to work for more than one employer in order to make a living. Job security is a scarce commodity. Part-time workers of course miss out on all the benefits of full-time work such as bonuses, holiday pay, help with accommodation in some cases and so on.

Uninitiated teachers run the risk of finding themselves working for a shark or a cowboy who doesn't care a fig about the quality of teaching or the satisfaction of the teachers, as long as pupils keep signing up and paying their fees. 'Client satisfaction' is their only criterion of success; business takes complete precedence over education. Exploitation of teachers is not uncommon since the profession is hampered by a lack of both regulation and unionisation.

The job of teaching English is demanding; it demands energy, enthusiasm and imagination, which are not always easy to produce when confronted with a room full of stonily silent faces. Instead of the thrill of communication, the drudgery of language drills begins to dominate. Instead of the pleasure of exchanging views with people of a different culture, teachers become weighed down by sheafs of photocopies and visual aids. Like most jobs when done right, teaching English is no piece of cake and is at times discouraging, but invariably it has its golden moments. It offers opportunities for creativity, learning about other cultures and attitudes, making friends and of course travelling. Not a bad job in many ways.

Roberta Wedge writes amusingly on a possible spin-off from a teaching contract abroad:

> TEFL is one of the most sex-balanced job fields I know (though the Director of Studies is usually a man) and, for those who are interested, the possibilities of finding your one true love appear to be high. 'Thrown together in an isolated Spanish village, eating tapas in the bar, hammering out lesson plans together—we found we have so much in common.' And a year later they were married. (A true story.)

THE VALUE OF ELT QUALIFICATIONS

Training in teaching English as a foreign language is not absolutely essential for successful job-hunting; but it makes the task easier by an order of magnitude. Anyone with the Cambridge/RSA Certificate (CELTA) or the Trinity Certificate in TESOL (discussed in detail below) is in a much stronger position to get a job in any country where English is widely taught. These Certificate courses provide a rigorous introduction to teaching English in just one month full-time (admittedly at considerable expense), and so anyone interested in spending some time teaching abroad should seriously consider enrolling in a Certificate course. There are numerous other kinds of qualifications available, some obtainable after a weekend course and others after years of university study; many are described briefly in the *Directory of Training Courses* below.

However, the Cambridge and Trinity Certificates should not be thought of as a magical passport to work. Increasingly, even Certificate-holders are having to struggle to find a decent job, mainly because so many more people now have the qualification than five or ten years ago. Many language schools, especially in France and Germany, will not want to hire a novice teacher and are unlikely to be tempted to take on anyone who does not present a dynamic and energetic image. Still, the four-week Certificate training continues to give applicants an important edge over the competition.

Increasing your marketability is not the only reason to get some training. The assumption that just because you can speak a language you can teach is simply false. There may be plenty of people who have a natural flair for teaching and who can do an excellent job without the benefit of a Certificate or any other English Language Teaching (ELT) qualification. (As mentioned earlier, the term ELT has come to be preferred to TEFL in many contexts.) There are, however, many other people who, when faced with a class full of eager adolescents, would not have a clue where to begin. Doing a TEFL course cannot fail to increase your confidence and provide you with a range of ideas on how to teach and (just as important) how not to teach. Even a short introductory course can usually illustrate methods of making lessons interesting and of introducing the range of teaching materials and approaches available to the novice teacher. What is needed more than theory or academic attainment, is an ability to entertain and to dramatise, but not without a framework into which your classroom efforts can be placed.

A perpetual problem which a TEFL course solves is the general level of ignorance of grammar among native speakers. Native-speaker teachers often find that their pupils, who are much better informed on English grammar than they are, can easily catch them out with questions about verb tenses and subjunctives, causing embarrassment all round. Some training courses can also introduce you to the cultural barriers you can expect to encounter and the specific language-learning difficulties experienced by various nationalities (many of which will be touched on in the country chapters).

Some go so far as to see training almost as a moral obligation. Completely untrained teachers may end up being responsible for teaching people who have paid a great deal of money for expert instruction. This is of special concern in countries which have been inundated with 'tourist-teachers', while the Ministries of Education may be struggling to create all-graduate teaching professions. If you happen not to be a natural in the classroom, you may well fail to teach anything much to your pupils, whether they be young children in Hong Kong or businessmen in Portugal.

Not satisfied that a one-week course was enough to qualify him as a teacher, Ian Abbott went on to do the Cambridge/RSA Certificate at International House in Rome and summarises his view of TEFL training:

> *I wouldn't recommend teaching English as a foreign language without investing in a course first. You've got to remember that the people coming along to your lessons are desperate to learn your language and it is costing them a small fortune. It is only fair that you know what you are doing and can in the end take that money without guilt, knowing you haven't ripped them off to increase your travel funds.*

One of the practical advantages of joining a TEFL course is that many training centres have contacts with recruitment agencies or language schools abroad and can advise on, if not fix up, a job abroad for you at the end of the course. Training centres differ enormously on how much help they can offer. If the 'after-sales service' is important to you, shop around before choosing which training course to patronise.

Even in countries where it may be commonplace to work without a formal TEFL qualification (for example Thailand and Japan), teachers who lack a specific grounding in TEFL will often be at a disadvantage, since the jobs they are likely to get will be with schools at the cowboy end of the market who may in turn be more likely to offer exploitative conditions. In some countries (such as Turkey) a TEFL certificate is a prerequisite for a work visa, which is yet another justification for doing some formal training before setting off.

RANGE OF COURSES

There is a bewildering array of courses available, at vastly different levels and costs, so it is wise to carry out some careful research before choosing. A comprehensive guide to the courses on offer both in the UK and abroad is contained in the annual *ELT International Careers Guide* which includes tables comparing duration, cost, location and starting dates of training courses at all levels. It explains the differences among the various certificates, diplomas and MAs on offer as well as introductory and correspondence courses in more detail than the scope of this book allows. It is available from large bookshops or directly from the same address as that of the monthly journal *EL Gazette*, Dilke House, 1 Malet St, Bloomsbury, London WC1E

7AJ (0171-255 1969). The ninth edition (1998/9) costs £12.95/US$24.95 (plus postage).

The British Council Information Centre (Bridgewater House, 58 Whitworth St, Manchester M1 6BB; 0161-957 7755) publishes a free information leaflet *How to Become a Teacher of English as a Foreign Language* and distributes lists of Academic Courses in TEFL, Cambridge/RSA Certificate and Diploma courses and Trinity College Certificate and Licentiate Diploma courses, all described below.

If you need help funding a training course, you may be eligible for a Career Development Loan. CDLs are bank loans covering up to 80% of the cost of a vocational course lasting less than two years. Payment can be deferred until three months after the course finishes, whereupon repayments have to be made. The participating banks are Barclays, the Cooperative and the Clydesdale. Write for details to CDL (Freepost, Newcastle upon Tyne X, NE85 1BR; 0800 585505). Note that tax discounts have been introduced which will allow people over the age of 30 who qualify to set the cost of training courses against tax; this could mean a saving of more than £100, depending on circumstances. Ask your prospective course provider for details.

When choosing a course, it is worth asking certain questions which will indicate how useful the qualification will be at the end of it, such as, is there any external validation of the course and how much opportunity is there for teaching practice? Also find out what size a class you will be in (10-12 is much better than 15-20) and what qualifications and experience the tutors have.

The *Directory of Training Courses* in this chapter organises the courses available under various headings. The 100+ hour Certificate courses externally validated by the University of Cambridge and Trinity College Longon, 'Academic and Other Recognised Courses' which are primarily full academic courses offered at universities (this list is far from comprehensive), a few 'Distance Learning' courses, 'Short Introductory Courses in the UK' and, finally, a selection of courses offered worldwide 'Training Courses Abroad'.

CERTIFICATE COURSES

The most useful qualification for anyone intending to spend a year or more abroad as an English teacher is a Certificate in English Language Teaching validated by one of the two examination bodies active in the field of ELT, the University of Cambridge Local Examinations Syndicate (UCLES) and Trinity College London. The Certificate qualification is acquired after an intensive 100-120 hour course offered full-time over one month or (increasingly) part-time over several months.

Most centres expect applicants to have the equivalent of university entrance qualifications, i.e. three GCSEs and two A levels and some require a degree. Admission to the course is at the discretion of the course organiser after a sometimes lengthy selection process. Places on courses at the well-established centres may be difficult to get because of high demand, especially in summer, so early application is advised.

Applicants must be able to demonstrate a suitable level of language awareness and convince the interviewer that they have potential to develop as a teacher. Past academic achievement is less important than aptitude; even a PhD does not guarantee acceptance. Most schools will send you a task sheet or grammar quiz as part of the application. Sample questions might be 'how would you convey the idea of regret to a language learner?' or 'describe the difference in meaning between *I don't really like beetroot* and *I really don't like beetroot*?

Courses are not cheap but should be viewed as an investment and a potential passport to a worthwhile profession in many different countries. In fact, prices have come down somewhat over the past two years, with many centres trying to survive amidst keen competition. The range is about £650 to £1,000 for a full-time course with an average half between those two figures. Most centres include the validation body's fee, variously called assessment, moderation or examination fee, which is roughly £70.

Many colleges of further education offer the Trinity or Cambridge Certificate part-time and these are normally less expensive, as low as £300. If the Further Education Funding Council acts on recent recommendations, prices in the FE sector could fall dramatically.

Timetables for part-time courses vary, but the norm is to attend classes one or two evenings a week for one or two terms of the academic year plus occasional full days for teaching observation and practice. Some universities and colleges have language institutes which run intensive TEFL courses at various levels on a commercial basis, and fees at these institutions are often equivalent to private training courses.

Once accepted onto a Certificate course, you will normally be given a pre-course task to familiarise yourself with some key concepts and issues before the course begins. Full-time courses are very intensive and 100% attendance is required, so you need to be in a position to dedicate yourself completely to the task in hand for four weeks. The standard of teaching is high, the course rigorous and demanding and the emphasis is on the practice of any theory taught. One of the requirements is that participants teach a minimum of six hours of observed lessons to real live English language students.

 UNIVERSITY *of* CAMBRIDGE
Local Examinations Syndicate

RSA/Certificates and Diplomas in English Language Teaching

THE CERTIFICATES AND DIPLOMAS ARE:

- distinguished by the quality of the training provided by 270 established centres in over 40 countries worldwide

- more widely accepted by employers in the UK and overseas than any other international ELT qualification.

For further information please contact:

Helen Rose, The CILTS Unit, University of Cambridge Local Examinations Syndicate, 1 Hills Road, Cambridge, CB1 2EU, UK

Tel: +44 (0)1223 553789   Fax: +44 (0)1223 460278
e-mail: cilts@ucles.org.uk   http://www.edunet.com/ciltsrsa/

Cambridge/RSA

The Cambridge/RSA CELTA (Certificate in English Language Teaching to Adults) was previously known as the CTEFLA and before that as the Prep.Cert. The syllabus and assessment have been revised after a lengthy period of piloting and consultation with course providers and professionals in the field. The revised scheme became fully operational two years ago and includes a job placement service (described below). The course is administered and regulated by the University of Cambridge Local Examinations Syndicate or UCLES (Syndicate Buildings, 1 Hills Road, Cambridge CB1 2EU; 01223 553789/e-mail cilts@ucles.org.uk). The RSA part of the name and logo stands for Royal Society of Arts which has had no role in administering the scheme for many years.

Pass certificates are awarded by the University of Cambridge to successful candidates. The grades are Pass, Pass 'B' and Pass 'A'. The pass rate is normally an encouraging 90% or over, simply because UCLES/RSA requires that course providers take a great deal of care in selecting candidates in the first place.

The CELTA is very widely recognised in the international field of English language teaching. A summary of the CELTA course content includes language awareness and knowledge; understanding adult learners; the roles of teachers and learners; the principles and practice of effective teaching (including classroom management, lesson planning approaches and techniques for teaching language and skills in the classroom); using materials and resources; and professional development. A new course offered by the Cambridge/RSA is the CELTYL (Certificate in English Language Teaching to Young Learners). Further information about the content of the courses and methods of assessment are available from the CILTS Unit at UCLES, together with a list of the more than 180 centres both in Britain and abroad where the courses are offered. (CILTS stands for Cambridge Integrated Language Teaching Schemes.)

A free job placement service has been introduced at the request of course providers and applicants. This allows candidates who have been accepted onto a CELTA course access to a freephone number on which they can arrange to be interviewed by job placement officers either locally or in London. Contingent on passing the course, the placement office will attempt to match candidates with jobs worldwide.

Cambridge/RSA courses are offered in a surprising number of locations from San Francisco to Sydney. In fact there are 89 overseas centres. The British Council run a few Certificate courses, for example in Milan, Naples, Istanbul, Cairo, Oman, Hong Kong and Kuala Lumpur, while International House offer Cambridge/RSA Certificate courses in a number of overseas centres such as Barcelona, Lisbon, Kraków, Rome and Cairo. Other foreign venues are listed in the information from UCLES including 16 centres in Australia and five in New Zealand. The CELTA is going from strength to strength in North America where US-based employers are steadily becoming more aware of it. There are now 13 Cambridge-recognised centres in North America.

Possible advantages of doing a Cambridge/RSA Certificate abroad are that you may already be teaching or living in that country and want to upgrade your qualifications locally; the course and cost of living may be cheaper than in England (Istanbul, Cairo and Bangkok are especially favoured for this reason); and course participants would almost certainly be put in touch with local employers, making it much easier to land a job than if applying from home. A further advantage is that when you are living in a non-English speaking environment, you might become more sensitive to the difficulties faced by language learners and more attuned to the importance of cultural differences.

Trinity College

The main alternative to the Cambridge/RSA CELTA is the Certificate in TESOL awarded by Trinity College London (16 Park Crescent, London W1N 4AP; 0171-323 2328/fax 0171-323 5201; e-mail info@trinitycollege.co.uk; http://www.trinitycollege.co.uk). When job details in this book and elsewhere say 'Cambridge/RSA or equivalent', they are referring primarily to the Trinity College qualifications which are regarded as having equal academic standing. The Trinity College Certificate has continued to enjoy tremendous success with a constantly increasing list of centres which offer the courses both in Britain and abroad (including South America).

Trinity College stipulates a minimum of 130 tuition hours offered intensively over four weeks or part-time. Some have a distance-learning component but this cannot count towards the minimum hours. A summary of the course content includes language awareness, teaching and learning methodologies, classroom management, hands-on experience of teaching aids (from blackboards to computers), introduction

to the learning of an unknown language (in which trainees receive s
Arabic or whatever), lesson planning and a minimum of six hours of o
practice and at least four further hours observing experienced teache
Trinity have also introduced a Certificate in Teaching English to Y
(TEYL) which is aimed primarily at practising primary teachers. 1
planning to introduce special short add-on-courses for those wishing to t
one.

The Trinity course is just as strenuous as its competitor, as Jayne Nash describes:

> *My TESOL course in Coventry was certainly very intensive, with a wide variety of*
> *tasks, tutoring sessions, projects and seminars. We covered English grammar,*
> *language teaching, the use of teaching aids, classroom management... We were*
> *marked on a student profile (four one-to-one sessions with a designated English*
> *language learner), a language learning diary (10 hours of Mandarin Chinese lessons,*
> *giving us the idea of how it feels to be a learner), 4 live teaching practices, 3 with*
> *foreigners at the College and the other in a local primary school teaching Asian*
> *children, and 7 observations (4 video and 3 live). We also had a grammar/phonetics/*
> *linguistics exam and a short project presentation (I put together a teaching pack with*
> *visual aids for teaching in Africa).*

Even after such a wide-ranging practical course, Jayne goes on to say that 'no amount of training can prepare you for the real thing,' though it did make her realise what a challenging occupation TEFL is.

Choosing a Certificate Course

It is up to prospective trainees to weigh up the pros and cons of the courses available to them and to establish how rigorously the course he or she is considering is monitored. One reservation that a few employers abroad have expressed is that the proliferation of Certificate courses has made it more difficult to maintain a uniform standard, especially since so much of the assessment of candidates is subjective. The general decline in standards of literacy in Britain and North America has also prompted some to complain of a decline.

When it comes to work load, trainees in both Certificate courses complain of a punishing schedule. But most come away claiming that the course elements are superb. At the time, participants sometimes feel as though they are drowning in information, but realise that the course has to pack a great deal of material into four brief weeks. The majority who go on to teach abroad are very grateful for the training it gave them, as in the case of Andrew Sykes teaching in Bordeaux:

> *As for the Certificate course that I did at Leeds Metropolitan University, it was*
> *certainly one of the most stimulating, challenging and interesting things I have ever*
> *studied for. Initially I felt a bit out of place—I had a background of science A levels,*
> *a maths degree and 2½ years as a (failed) accountant. The course was professionally*
> *run and there were good teacher-student relations. Most people had never taught*
> *anybody anything before in their life, but we were gradually eased into teaching by*
> *the supportive teaching staff who were refreshingly (and diplomatically) critical when*
> *required to be. A criticism which some students had was that there wasn't enough*
> *feedback about what was expected to gain a pass, let alone achieve an A or B. The best*
> *recommendation for the course is perhaps that I would never have felt comfortable*
> *teaching without it.*

So even if your social life disappears for a month and all you can talk about at weekends is gerunds and infinitives, the consensus is that it is worthwhile.

The University of London Institute of Education offers a Certificate in English Teaching for practising teachers outside the UK. It can be studied in modular form and is taught locally by approved course directors. Certification counts towards the Institute of Education's Diploma in TESOL. For further details contact Anne Rickwood (ULCET), Edexcel International, 32 Russell Square, London WC1B 5DN (0171-331 4021).

Beyond the Certificate is the Diploma. Whereas the Certificate is considered a pre-service qualification, the Diploma (as distinct from any old diploma with a lower case) is an in-service course which is followed by practising EFL teachers. The Cambridge/RSA Diploma in English Language Teaching to Adults (DELTA) and the Trinity Licentiate Diploma (LTCT TESOL) are high-level qualifications normally open to graduates who have at least two years of recent ELT classroom experience. The Diploma course is offered intensively over 12 weeks but more usually part-time over several months or a year. The fees of over £1,000 are sometimes subsidised by employers.

Increasingly, universities (especially the former polytechnics) from Brighton to Belfast offer their own Certificate or Diploma in TEFL. Most are one or two year courses, full or part-time, and are more academic than Cambridge/RSA and Trinity courses. It is important to do some research before committing yourself to a course so that you are sure that the qualification you obtain will be recognised by employers both in the UK and overseas. Once again find out if there is some form of external assessment and whether the course includes a reasonable amount of teaching practice. The British Association of TESOL Qualifying Institutions (BATQI, School of Education, University of Leeds LS2 9AJ) is the relevant regulatory body for state providers of TEFL training courses.

A number of undergraduate institutions offer TESL as part of an undergraduate course; the weighty *UCAS Handbook* lists all university courses in the UK and can be consulted in any careers or general library. The highly respected PGCE (Post Graduate Certificate in Education) in TESOL was abolished in the early 1990s and trainee teachers are now able to study TESOL only as a subsidiary subject. The Graduate Teacher Training Registry (Fulton House, Jessop Avenue, Cheltenham, Gloucestershire GL50 3SH; tel: 01242 225868) will send the annual PGCE *Guide for Applicants* from which can be extracted information about the few centres which offer a TESOL component in the PGCE (viz. the University College of Wales at Aberystwyth, Edge Hill College of Higher Education, Leeds University, Leicester University, Manchester Metropolitan University and Manchester University). The Teacher Training Agency (01245 454454) might also offer advice.

MA courses in ELT and Applied Linguistics are offered at dozens of universities and colleges. Some (like Aston University) offer a Master's by distance learning in collaboration with the British Council. Arguably, there is a world oversupply of MAs, since there is a relative scarcity of high level posts which require an MA; for example the British Council has only ten or so positions a year.

Introductory Courses

Although the Cambridge and Trinity Certificates are sometimes referred to as 'introductory courses', there are many cheaper, shorter and less rigorous introductions to the subject. With the dramatic rise in the popularity of Certificate courses there has been a decline in what might be considered as more amateurish courses, though these do have a role to play, for example for school leavers who would not be accepted onto a Certificate course or for the curious who do not want to commit themselves to a month-long course nor pay £700 or £800.

Because there are so many commercial enterprises and 'cowboy' operators cashing in on the present EFL boom, standards vary and course literature should be studied carefully before choosing. Most people who have done a TEFL training course claim that the most worthwhile part is the actual teaching practice, preferably to living breathing foreigners rather than in mock lessons to fellow participants. The fact is that most short introductory courses do not allow for much chance to do teaching practice. Many schools looking for teachers have expressed the view that peer-teaching is of little value.

The more upmarket introductory courses often present themselves as an opportunity to sample the field to see whether you want to go on to do a Certificate

at a later stage. Others make their course sound as if it alone will be suffi
doors worldwide. It would be unreasonable to expect a weekend or five-day
equip anyone to teach, but most participants do find them helpful.

The majority of residential courses last one week (i.e. five days) and cost betw
£125 and £190, not counting accommodation. Almost all will issue some kind c
certificate which can sometimes be used to impress prospective employers. Anyone
who wants a job after doing a short course should aim to do it in the spring when the
majority of jobs are advertised for the following academic year. Many people who
complete an introductory or 'taster' course go on to do an intensive certificate, often
at the same centre.

A number of private language centres offer their own short courses in TEFL which
may focus on their own method, developed specifically with the chain of schools in
mind (for example Berlitz and Linguarama), or may offer a more general introduction.
Anyone who wishes to specialise in the highly marketable field of business English
should enquire about specialist courses such as those offered by Linguarama. The
London Chamber of Commerce & Industry (LCCI) validates a certificate in teaching
English for business.

Distance Learning Courses

Some practising teachers of English who want to obtain a qualification are attracted
to the idea of self-study by correspondence partly because it will be much cheaper than
a conventional course and because it can be done in the candidate's own time. As a
part of the general move within the profession to monitor standards and offer
assurances of quality, the Accreditation Council for TESOL Distance Education
Courses (ACTDEC) was set up, to which a handful of course providers belong. A copy
of their code of practice can be requested from the Secretary, 21 Wessex Gardens,
Dore, Sheffield S17 3PQ (fax 0114 236 0774/e-mail t-link@vip.solis.co.uk). Typically,
distance courses at the professional end of the spectrum involve at least 200 hours of
home study. Some offer distance learning in combination with a residential
element.

People considering this route to TEFL training should be cautious. The most
obvious disadvantage is the lack of face-to-face teaching practice, though some do
provide opportunities for blocks of teaching practice. If you are not satisfied with the
course but have paid your money (typically £400+ for a certificate course), you have
little recourse. Although Katherine Dixon didn't find fault with the content of the
course, she was not impressed with the level of efficiency of the accredited distance
course in which she decided to enrol while teaching English in Japan:

> *I registered in August for a distance course which they claim can be completed in six*
> *to nine months. I am supposed to to be receiving packets weekly, but only once did*
> *that happen. Since August, the intervals between packets have been eight weeks, nine*
> *weeks and 13 weeks. In October, I phoned England twice to enquire about the delay.*
> *Both times I was assured that the next packet had been sent but when it finally*
> *arrived, the postmark revealed that it had been sent after my call. Since it is no longer*
> *possible for me to complete the course in the time allowed, I have written twice asking*
> *for a refund. I have received no response whatsoever.*

Of the range of distance courses and qualifications on offer, some offer professional
courses of quality. One or two are sound but provide relatively short basic
programmes, yet frequently lead to a so-called Diploma. Many however have a
definite credibility gap; even their course information and covering letters are riddled
with spelling and grammatical mistakes. Be especially cautious if the organisation
operates from a PO Box and/or provides no telephone number.

Details of introductory and distance training courses both in Britain and abroad are
provided at the end of the *Directory of Training Courses* which follows.

Training in the US

Most TESL training in the US is integrated into university degree courses in Applied

g in the US 23
ent to open
course to
een

...undergraduate and graduate levels. Until the beginning of the ...ually no short intensive courses in TEFL available in North ...y changed. In addition to the eight Cambridge/RSA centres in ...nber of independent TEFL training organisations offering four-...s (see *Directory of Training Courses* below). The major providers ...Teachers, Transworld and Worldwide Teachers are well connected ...s abroad (particularly in Latin America and the Far East). Their ...tters contain lots of quotations from ex-trainees who have found ...e world, so their emphasis is on assisting with job placement. Compe... ...:n, and prices fairly consistent at about $2,000 for a four-week course.

There are a few one-semester courses in TESL offered at American colleges and universities. Increasingly American universities are offering intensive TESL training. If you cannot afford to do a course but want to learn about TEFL, it may be possible to audit such a course. One resource for finding a programme of study in the field of TESOL within North America is the *Directory of Professional Preparation Programs in TESOL in the United States and Canada.* This is the most comprehensive listing available, containing information about graduate, PhD and certificate programmes. Each entry lists contact information, course descriptions, faculty information and tuition costs. The 1999-2001 edition costs US$44.95 plus 12% postage (or $29.95 plus postage for TESOL members; see *Finding a Job*). A useful companion is *The Handbook of Funding Opportunities in the Field of TESOL* for US$14.95 plus $4.50. The *Career Counsel* is a free newsletter that gives basic information about the profession. All of these publications are available from TESOL (Teachers of English to Speakers of Other Languages, Inc.), 1600 Cameron St, Suite 300, Alexandria, VA 22314 (703-836-0774/fax 703-836-7864; e-mail: tesol@tesol.edu/Web-site: http://www.tesol.edu).

It is easier to get practical experience of teaching English (without a qualification) by joining one of the many voluntary ESL programmes found in almost every American city, run by community colleges, civic organisations and literacy groups. Literacy Volunteers of America operate in most states and offer volunteer tutors an 18-hour pre-service training programme. The Contact Literacy Center (PO Box 81826, Lincoln, NE 68501-1826) acts as a clearinghouse of information but does not arrange its own training courses. Laubach Literacy Action offers a 12-hour tutor training workshop for their volunteers.

The equivalent of the US directory mentioned above in Australasia is *Teacher Training in TESOL: A Directory of Courses in Australia and New Zealand* which costs A$30 within Australia and A$35 to overseas addresses (surface post). Write to Australian TESOL (PO Box 296, Rozelle, NSW 2039) for order details.

DIRECTORY OF TRAINING COURSES

Cambridge/RSA Certificate (CELTA) Courses in the UK

All courses last four weeks full-time unless otherwise stated. The fees quoted (which should be taken merely as a guide) include the CELTA examination fee of £68.65 unless otherwise stated.

AMERSHAM & WYCOMBE COLLEGE, High Wycombe Campus, Spring Lane, Flackwell Heath, High Wycombe, Bucks. HP10 9HE. Tel: 01494 735555. Fax: 01494 735577. Offers Cambridge/RSA CELTA part-time. 20 weeks from September to March; Tuesdays from 9:30am to 4:30pm. £500. Help given with job placement. Applications must be sent by the end of July.
ANGLIA POLYTECHNIC UNIVERSITY, East Road, Cambridge CB1 1PT. Tel: 01223 363271. Fax: 01223 352933. E-mail: m.l.baker@anglia.ac.uk. Full-time in July and August only. 9.30am-6pm. Includes 6 hours of teaching practice and 8 hours of observation of experienced teachers. £950 (including examination fee).

Accommodation can be arranged in APU halls of residence. Information is supplied about jobs.

ANGLO-CONTINENTAL TEACHER TRAINING CENTRE, 29-35 Wimborne Road, Bournemouth BH2 6NA. Tel: 01202 557414, ext 282. Fax: 01202 556156. E-mail: english@anglo-continental.com. Full-time (125 hours) 3 courses per year. £862. Part-time courses over 6 months proposed. Accommodation can be arranged.

ANGLOSCHOOL, 146 Church Road, Upper Norwood, London SE19 2NT. Tel: 0181-653 7285. Fax: 0181-653 9667. E-mail: english@angloschool.co.uk. 4 week courses 4 times a year. £820. Video and booklet on basic teaching techniques available.

BARNET COLLEGE, Wood Street, Barnet EN5 4AZ. Tel: 0181-440 6321. Fax: 0181-441 5236. E-mail: stsald@barnet.ac.uk. Intensive courses January-February, April-May, June-July, September-October and November. Part-time evening course September-June. £750. Possibility of short-term accommodation.

BASIL PATERSON EDINBURGH LANGUAGE FOUNDATION, Dugdale McAdam House, 22-23 Abercromby Place, Edinburgh EH3 6QE. Tel: 0131-556 7696. Fax: 0131-557 8503. E-mail: courses@bp-coll.demon.co.uk Internet: http://www.basilpaterson.co.uk 12 courses per year. £999. Accommodation service available. Early application advised.

BEDFORD COLLEGE, Enterprise House, Old Ford End Road, Bedford MK40 4PF. Tel: 01234 271492. Fax: 01234 364272. E-mail: gp67@dial.pipex.com. Part-time course October-February. £770. Also offer part-time introductory course.

BELL TEACHER TRAINING INSTITUTE, Hillscross, Red Cross Lane, Cambridge CB2 2QX. Tel: 01223 247242. Fax: 01223 412410. E-mail: info@bel-schools.ac.uk. Full-time and part-time courses all year round. Part-time DELTA course also offered.

BELL LANGUAGE SCHOOL, NORWICH, Bowthorpe Hall, Norwich NR5 9AA. Tel: 01603 745615. Fax: 01603 747669. E-mail: Sarah@bellbow.demon.co.uk. Full-time courses offered 6 times per year. £990. 8 week DELTA course also offered (£1,250).

BELL LANGUAGE SCHOOL, SAFFRON WALDEN, South Road, Saffron Walden, Essex CB11 3DP. Tel: 01799 522918. Fax: 01799 526949. E-mail: info@bell-schools.ac.uk. Full-time DELTA course.

BLACKBURN COLLEGE, Gateway Centre, Feilden St, Blackburn BB2 1LH. Tel: 01254 292929 (student services enquiries). Part-time course over academic year (September-June); one day per week. £298. Covers EFL and ESOL with particular focus on teaching adults in Britain. Advice and guidance on job-finding.

BRASSHOUSE CENTRE, 50 Sheepcote Street, Birmingham B16 8AJ. Tel: 0121-643 0114. Part-time once a year (October-March). £850.

BROMLEY SCHOOL OF ENGLISH, 2 Park Road, Bromley, Kent BR1 3HP. Tel: 0181-313 0308. Fax: 0181-313 3957. Full-time course offered 6 times a year. £495 for over 30s, £620 under 30s. Accommodation in family (half-board) or self-catering residence available. Information, advice and references given for jobs.

BROOKLANDS COLLEGE, Heath Road, Weybridge, Surrey KT13 8TT. Tel: 01932 797797. Full-time course in July only. Part-time daytime courses September-February and February-July. £750.

CILC (Cheltenham International Language Centre), Cheltenham & Gloucester College of Higher Education, Francis Close Hall, Swindon Road, Cheltenham, Glos. GL50 4AZ. Tel: 01242 532925. Fax: 01242 532926. E-mail: cilc@chelt.ac.uk. Cambridge/RSA centre offering full-time (5 weeks) CELTA courses throughout the year. One-day taster courses also offered. Homestay accommodation can be arranged.

CITY OF BATH COLLEGE, Avon Street, Bath BA1 1UP. Tel: 01225 312191. Fax: 01225 444213. E-mail: bulld@eng.citybathcoll.ac.uk. Full-time and part-time courses. Accommodation can be arranged with local families.

CITY OF BRISTOL COLLEGE, Languages Dept., Brunel Centre, Ashley Down, Bristol BS7 9BU. Tel: 0117 904 5178. Fax: 0117 904 5180. E-mail: alicoris@sbristol.tcom.uk. Part-time courses (2 days per week for 10 weeks) starting September, January and April. £950. Accommodation can be arranged. Help also given with job placement. Early application recommended since courses usually over-subscribed.

CLARENDON COLLEGE, International Language Centre, 11 Queen Street, Nottingham NG1 2BL. Tel: 0115 955 3100. Fax: 0115 950 6546. Part-time 10-week courses begin Sept, Jan and April (day courses), £718. Part-time 16-week courses begin Sept and Feb (evening courses), £718. Full-time 5-week course July-August, £710. Offer unlimited observation of EFL classes and 5 levels of classes for practice teaching.

CONCORDE INTERNATIONAL STUDY CENTRE, 22/24 Cheriton Gardens, Folkestone, Kent CT20 2AT. Tel: 01303 256752. Fax: 01303 220538. Full-time courses between April and October. £668. Some self-catering accommodation or with local families. Offers summer placements in UK to spring graduates.

CROYDON CONTINUING EDUCATION & TRAINING SERVICE (CETS), English and Bilingual Skills, South Norwood Centre, Sandown Road, South Norwood, London SE25 4XE. Tel: 0181-656 6620. Fax: 0181-662 1828. Part-time course over 25 weeks from September to May. 2 half-day sessions a week. £650. Also offer an ESOL component for teaching minority groups in this country. Annual vacancies in large ESOL department at CETS.

DEVON SCHOOL OF ENGLISH, The Old Vicarage, 1 Lower Polsham Road, Paignton, Devon TQ3 2AF. Tel: 01803 559718. Fax: 01803 551407. E-mail: english@devonschool.co.uk. Full-time once or twice a year. Accommodation with host families or self-catering.

DUNDEE COLLEGE, Blackness Road, Dundee DD1 5UA. Tel: 01382 834898. Fax: 01382 322286. E-mail: dic@dundeecoll.ac.uk. Full-time courses 3 times a year starting September, January and May. £795. Accommodation can be arranged. No help with job placement.

EASTBOURNE SCHOOL OF ENGLISH, 8 Trinity Trees, Eastbourne, East Sussex BN21 3LD. Tel: 01323 721759. Fax: 01323 639271. E-mail: english@esoe.co.uk.
ELT BANBURY LTD, 49 Oxford Road, Banbury, Oxfordshire OX16 7EQ. Tel: 01295 263502/263480. Fax: 01295 271658. E-mail: elt_banbury@compuserve.com. Full-time 6 times a year. £150+ per week. Accommodation can be arranged for £77 per week. ELT also functions as a recruitment agency for EFL teachers.
FILTON COLLEGE, Filton Avenue, Bristol BS12 7AT. Tel: 0117-931 2121. Fax: 0117-909 2373. Part-time September to May/June.

FRANCES KING TEACHER TRAINING, 5 Grosvenor Gardens, Victoria, London SW1W 0BB. Tel: 0171-630 8055. Fax: 0171-630 8077. E-mail: sean@fkse.ac.uk. Internet: www.fkse.ac.uk. 4-week intensive courses throughout the year. £799 with possible tax relief for over 30s. Help with accommodation. Jobs noticeboard (which can be used after course) and contact with range of employers/agencies.
GEOS ENGLISH ACADEMY, 55-61 Portland Road, Hove, East Sussex BN3 5DQ. Tel: 01273 735975. Fax: 01273 732884. Intensive course throughout the year. Accommodation can be arranged.
GLOSCAT (Gloucester College of Arts & Technology), Park Campus, 73 The Park, Cheltenham, Glos. GL50 2RR. Tel: 01242 532129. Full-time (6 weeks) several times a year. Part-time (6 months) January-June.
GREENHILL COLLEGE, Temple House Site, 221-225 Station Road, Harrow, Middlesex HA1 2XL. Tel: 0181-869 8805. Fax: 0181-427 9201. E-mail: enquiries@harrow.ac.uk. Part-time offered over 2 or 3 terms (Tuesdays 9.30am-5pm). £458 plus exam fee. 2 courses have EFL focus, one has ESOL focus. Help given with accommodation via a local accommodation centre. Large number and range of classes. Also offer one-week introductory course in July and one or two day taster and refresher courses.

HAMMERSMITH & WEST LONDON COLLEGE, Gliddon Road, London W14 9BL. Tel: 0181-563 0063. Fax: 0181-748 5053. Full-time starting September, November, January, March, May, July and August; or part-time September-March (evenings). £695. Also offer Cambridge/RSA DELTA (£695).

HANDSWORTH COLLEGE, Soho Road, Birmingham B21 9DP. Tel: 0121-551 6031. E-mail: l.webster@handsworth.ac.uk. Part-time once a year (36 weeks, 1 day per week). £370 or possibility of no-fees-policy if funding available. Emphasis on ESL as well as EFL.

HARROW HOUSE INTERNATIONAL COLLEGE, Harrow Drive, Swanage, Dorset BH19 1PE. Tel: 01929 424421/422852. Fax: 01929 427175. 6 courses per year. £875 inclusive. Alternatives include course plus host family full-board accommodation for £1,195 or course plus on-site full-board accommodation in single study bedroom for £980. Extensive sporting facilities available to trainees. Trainees have 24 hour access to multi-media self-access centre which has computers, videos, audio equipment and library facilities. Maximum 10 trainees per course.

HILDERSTONE COLLEGE, Broadstairs, Kent CT10 2AQ. Tel: 01843 869171. Fax: 01843 603877. E-mail: info@hilderstone.ac.uk. Several full-time courses per year. Accommodation can be arranged with a local family on self-catering or half-board basis, or in guest house.

HUDDERSFIELD TECHNICAL COLLEGE, New North Road, Huddersfield, West Yorkshire HD1 5NN. Tel: 01484 536521. Fax: 01484 511885. Full-time and part-time (16 weeks). £750; remission of fees arranged if in receipt of benefit. Accommodation can be arranged if necessary. Guidance offered with jobs.

INTERNATIONAL HOUSE HASTINGS, White Rock, Hastings, East Sussex TN34 1JY. Tel: 01424 720100/720104. Fax: 01424 720323. E-mail: training@ilcgroup.com. Monthly. £799. Self-catering accommodation approximately £45 a week. Also offers Cambridge Diploma (DELTA), 2-week course on teaching young learners and a wide range of other 2-week and 5-day specialist courses. Helps with recruitment in their 35 summer schools in Britain, Ireland, France, USA and Canada.

INTERNATIONAL TEACHER TRAINING INSTITUTE (INTERNATIONAL HOUSE), 106 Piccadilly, London W1V 9FL. Tel: 0171-491 2598. Fax: 0171-409 0959. E-mail: teacher@dial.pipex.com. Full-time (4 weeks) offered monthly, or part-time: Tuesday and Thursday evenings for 11 weeks plus 5 Saturdays. Part-time course offered 6 times a year. IH is a pioneering organisation in the TEFL field and now one of the largest and best known organisers of Cambridge/RSA courses. Several IH schools abroad offer CELTA courses (see advertisement). Also offer Cambridge/RSA Diploma course and range of specialist courses. For a complete list of International House training courses request the ITTI Training booklet from the above address. IH has about 110 affiliated language schools in 30 countries, and recruits between 300 and 350 teachers a year, many of whom are IH graduates.

INTERNATIONAL HOUSE NEWCASTLE UPON TYNE, 14-18 Stowell St, Newcastle upon Tyne NE1 4XQ. Tel: 0191-232 9551. Fax: 0191-232 1126. Full-time CELTA courses offered all year round. Apply early. Accommodation can be arranged. Help with job hunting given.

INTERNATIONAL LANGUAGE INSTITUTE, County House, Vicar Lane, Leeds LS1 7JH. Tel: 0113 242 8893. Fax: 0113 234 7543. E-mail: 101322.1376@compuserve.com. Full-time 5-6 times per year. Half-board accommodation available. Self-catering can be arranged in the summer term. Trinity Cert. course and one-week introductory course also offered.

LANGUAGE CENTRE, York College of Further & Higher Education, Tadcaster Road, York YO2 1UA. Tel: 01904 770366. Fax: 01904 770363. Part-time evening course over 22 weeks from September. Approx. £700. Contact with schools abroad for job placement. VSO-sponsored.

LANGUAGE LINK TRAINING, 181 Earls Court Road, London SW5 9RB. Tel: 0171-370 4755. Fax: 0171-370 1123. New part-time CELTA course offered over three months of the summer (£850) as well as Trinity Certificate and others.

LEEDS METROPOLITAN UNIVERSITY, Centre for Language Study, Beckett Park Campus, Leeds LS6 3QS. Tel: 0113 283 7440 (+44 113 274 7440 from outside the UK). Fax: 0113 274 5966 (+44 113 274 5966 from outside the UK). E-mail: cls@lmu.ac.uk. Internet: http://www.lmu.ac.uk/cls/ 4-week course offered 9 times per year. £670-£870. Additional modules available to upgrade to Postgraduate Certificate. Accommodation available for £78 per week with host families, £45 in halls of residence. Also offer Trinity Certificate and MA Language Teaching (see listings).

LOUGHBOROUGH COLLEGE, Radmoor, Loughborough LE11 3BT. Tel: 01509 215831. Fax: 01509 232310. Part-time (2 days per week for 16 weeks), September-January and February-June. Suitable only for those within commuting distance. Once or twice a year.

MID-KENT COLLEGE, Oakwood Park, Tonbridge Road, Maidstone ME16 8AQ. Tel: 01622 691555. Fax: 01622 695049. Part-time over 2 semesters; evenings twice a week and daytimes once a week. £600.

MORAY HOUSE ENGLISH LANGUAGE CENTRE, Holyrood Road, Edinburgh EH8 8AQ. Tel: 0131-558 6332. Fax: 0131-557 5138. E-mail: elc@mhie.ac.uk. Full-time courses.

NEWCASTLE COLLEGE, Rye Hill Campus, Scotswood Road, Newcastle-upon-Tyne NE4 5BR. Tel: 0191-200 4000. Part-time twice a year (15 weeks starting in September and February). Database of potential employers.

NEWHAM COLLEGE OF FURTHER ED., East Ham Campus, High Street South, East Ham, London E6 3AB. Tel: 0181-257 4000. Fax: 0181-257 4307. 2½ days per week for 14 weeks includes teacher observation and practice. Offered twice a year (autumn and spring terms). Also offer City & Guilds 9281 Initial Teacher Certificate in ESOL and basic skills.

NEWNHAM LANGUAGE CENTRE, 8 Grange Road, Cambridge CB3 9DU. Tel: 01223 311344. Fax: 01223 461411. E-mail: info@nlc.co.uk. 4 times per year. £935. Bed and breakfast accommodation can sometimes be arranged with host families for £55-57 per week.

NORTH TRAFFORD COLLEGE, Talbot Road, Stretford, Manchester M32 0XH. Tel: 0161-872 3731. Fax: 0161-872 7921. 28 weeks part-time from September.

OXFORD BROOKES UNIVERSITY, International Centre for English Language Studies, School of Languages, Headington, Oxford OX3 0BP. Tel: 01865 483725/483874. Fax: 01865 483791. E-mail: icels@sol.brookes.ac.uk. 2 part-time courses per year (2 full days and 1 evening per week).

OXFORD COLLEGE OF FURTHER EDUCATION, Oxpens Road, Oxford OX1 1SA. Tel: 01865 269268. Fax: 01865 240574. E-mail: adwilliams@oxfe.ac.uk. Intensive course in July. Part-time over two terms, October to March. 2 evenings January to June. Cost: part-time £830, intensive £880. Also offers DELTA.

PILGRIMS, Pilgrims House, Orchard Street, Canterbury, Kent CT2 2BF. Tel: 01227 762111. Fax: 01227 459027. E-mail: clientservices@pilgrims.co.uk. Courses held on University campus, 5 times a year. Self-catering accommodation in 5-bedroom on-campus house. Private room in college residence with full board also available. Pilgrims invite groups of students from abroad specifically for Cambridge/RSA teaching practice. Offer more teaching practice time than prescribed minimum. Steady stream of job offers from Europe, Asia, etc.

REGENT LONDON, 12 Buckingham Street, London WC2N 6DF. Tel: 0171-872 6620. Fax: 0171-872 6630. Web-site: http://www.regoxford.demon.co.uk. 7 times a year. £825. Accommodation can be arranged in host families or hostels.

REGENT OXFORD, Teacher Training, 90 Banbury Road, Oxford OX2 6JT. Tel: 01865 515566/512538. E-mail: info@regoxford.demon.co.uk. 12 courses a year. £828 + VAT + registration fee. Offers more hours of input (mornings and afternoons) than most other centres. Help given with job-finding, based on files of reports from ex-trainees and teachers. Opportunities for unobserved teaching at 4 levels.

SAXONCOURT TEACHER TRAINING, 59 South Molton Street, London W1Y 1HH. Tel: 0171-499 8533. Fax: 0171-499 9374. E-mail: tt@saxoncourt.com. CELTA courses run throughout the year (£719). Cambridge/RSA CELTYL (Young Learners) courses in July/August and at Easter. Advice given on financing courses. Accommodation can be arranged (self-catering or with families). Over 300 jobs available around the world through Saxoncourt Recruitment (see *Finding a Job*).

SKOLA TEACHER TRAINING, 21 Star St, London W2 1QB. Tel: 0171-724 2217. Fax: 0171-724 2219. E-mail: maie.skola@easynet.co.uk Full-time 10 times a year. £650. Also offer a two day course in grammar for English Language Teaching and the Cambridge CELTA Extension course in Teaching Young Learners.

SOAS (School of Oriental and African Studies), University of London, English Language Unit, Thornhaugh St, Russell Square, London WC1H 0XG. Tel: 0171-580 8272/637 2388. Fax: 0171-631 3043. E-mail: english@soas.ac.uk. Full-time in summer. £880. University accommodation service can advise.

SOUTH DEVON COLLEGE, Newton Road, Torquay, Devon TQ2 5BY. Tel: 01803 386338. Fax: 01803 386333. E-mail: chadfiel@sdc.ac.uk. Intensive course and part-time September-April.

SOUTH THAMES COLLEGE, 50 Putney Hill, London SW15 6QX. Tel: 0181-918 7354. Fax: 0181-918 7347. 8-week course (daytime classes) offered in May/June, part-time evening course (20 weeks September-March) and full-time course in summer. £600 plus exam fee. Bed & breakfast list may be available. Trainees receive some tuition in a foreign language. May be able to match students to individual job vacancies.

SOUTH TRAFFORD COLLEGE, Manchester Road, Altrincham, Cheshire WA14 5PQ. Tel: 0161-952 4720. Fax: 0161-952 4672. E-mail: c3@stcoll.ac.uk. 30-week CELTA course beginning in September. £625. Also offer 15-week CENTRA Foundation Certificate in TEFL twice a year, beginning September and January (£95). Good contacts for job placement.

SOUTHWARK COLLEGE, EFL Section, Waterloo Centre, The Cut, London SE1 8LE. Tel: 0171-815 1682. Fax: 0171-261 1301. 5-week CELTA course. £695 including moderation fee and pre-course distance learning component. Also offer Trinity CTESOL (20 weeks part-time, £685) and CEELT (10 weeks part-time, £345).

ST GILES COLLEGE, 51 Shepherd's Hill, Highgate, London N6 5QP. Tel: 0181-340 0828/9207. Fax: 0181-348 9389. E-mail: lonhigh@stgiles.u-net.com. Full-time courses held monthly. £920. Accommodation can be arranged with local families. Job counselling service.

ST GILES COLLEGE, 3 Marlborough Place, Brighton, Sussex BN1 1UB. Tel: 01273 682747. Fax: 01273 689808. E-mail: stgiles@pavilion.co.uk. 10 times a year (between September and June). £920 full-time. Accommodation can be arranged with local families for £74 a week. Job counselling service.

STANTON TEACHER TRAINING, 167 Queensway, London W2 4SB. Tel: 0171-221 7259. Fax: 0171-792 9047. Monthly. £684. Bed and breakfast in local homes or hostels can be arranged.

STEVENSON COLLEGE, Bankhead Avenue, Sighthill, Edinburgh EH6 4PL. Tel: 0131-535 4700. Fax: 0131-535 4666. Part-time evening course September-December. Full-time course also offered. Accommodation can be arranged with host families.

STOKE-ON-TRENT COLLEGE, Cauldon Campus, Stoke Road, Shelton, Stoke-on-Trent ST4 2DG. Tel: 01782 208208. Fax: 01782 603504. E-mail: dston@stokecoll.ac.uk. Part-time (2 afternoons and 2 evenings per week for one term) offered three times a year (starting September, January and March).

STUDIO SCHOOL, 6 Salisbury Villas, Station Road, Cambridge CB1 2JF. Tel: 01223 369701. Fax: 01223 314944. E-mail:studio.cambridge@dial.pipex.com. CELTA courses in March, May and September. £880. Accommodation can be arranged. Successful candidates may be offered temporary contracts.

THAMES VALLEY UNIVERSITY, The School of English Language Education, Walpole House, 18-22 Bond St, Ealing, London W5 5AA. Tel: 0181-579 5000 (Learning Advice Centre). E-mail: celtaenq@tvu.ac.uk. 6-week full-time courses start in April and June. Part-time course starts in October. £700 (with possible tax rebate). Also offer MA in English Language Teaching.

TORBAY LANGUAGE CENTRE, Conway Road, Paignton, Devon TQ4 5LH. Tel: 01803 558555. Fax: 01803 559606. Full-time once or twice a year. £750 plus exam fee. Accommodation available in school-owned hotel or host families. Guarantee summer employment for all successful candidates.

UNIVERSITY OF DURHAM LANGUAGE CENTRE, Elvet Riverside, New Elvet, Durham, DH1 3JT. Tel: 0191-374 3716. Fax: 0191-374 7790. Intensive courses offered at Easter, in July, August and September. £875. Accommodation can be arranged from £35 p.w. for self-catering.

UNIVERSITY OF GLASGOW EFL UNIT, Hetherington Building, Bute Gardens, Glasgow G12 8RS. Tel: 0141-330 4220. Fax: 0141-339 1119. E-mail: mmc@arts.gla.ac.uk. Part-time once a year (4 months).

UNIVERSITY OF STRATHCLYDE, English Language Teaching Division, Room 110, Livingstone Tower, 26 Richmond St, Glasgow G1 1XH. Tel: 0141-548 3065. Fax: 0141-553 4122. E-mail: eltd.les@strath.ac.uk. Full-time (5 weeks) 3 times a year February, July and August. Part-time October to January. Approx. £900.

WALTHAM FOREST COLLEGE, Forest Road, London E17 4JB. Tel: 0181-527 2311. Fax: 0181-531 2349. E-mail: efl@waltham.ac.uk. 1 intensive course per year (June/July) and part-time from September to March (2 evenings per week). £450 plus £200 for moderation, materials and Centre expenses. Also offer part-time DELTA.

WEST HERTS COLLEGE, Cassio Campus, Langley Road, Watford WD1 3RH. Tel: 01923 812049/812055. Fax: 01923 812480. 20 weeks part-time (Sept-March). Twice a week: one evening and one daytime. £690. Also offer introduction to TEFL.

WESTMINSTER COLLEGE, Peter St, London W1V 4HS. Tel: 0171-437 8536. Fax: 0171-287 0711. Full-time 7 times a year September-June. Very large state sector ESOL school with 1,500 adult students learning English in any one term.

WIGAN & LEIGH COLLEGE, PO Box 53, Parsons Walk, Wigan, Lancashire WN1 1RS. Tel: 01942 761563. Fax: 01942 501572. 12 week course offered twice a year. £500 plus UCLES registration. Fee remission for unemployed in receipt of benefit. Also offer Cambridge/RSA Diploma and 4 week Introduction to TESOL.

WOOLWICH COLLEGE, Villas Road, Plumstead, London SE18 7PN. Tel: 0181-488 4800. Fax: 0181-488 4899. Full-time 5 times a year. Part-time evening course once a year. £550 (£170 for people receiving benefit). Accommodation isn't provided but college gives advice and guidance. Students get support from the Student Union and the College Trust for funds (eg. books and bus passes). Some successful trainees are hired for summer ESOL courses.

Cambridge/RSA Certificate (CELTA) Courses Abroad

The following centres, listed alphabetically by country, offer the Cambridge/RSA Certificate course.

Australia

AUSTRALIAN CENTRE FOR LANGUAGES, PO Box N556, Grosvenor Place, The Rocks, Sydney, NSW 2000. Tel: 2-9742 5277. Fax: 2-9252 3799. Full-time and part-time (15 weeks). Accommodation can be arranged.

AUSTRALIAN TESOL TRAINING CENTRE, Level 6, 530 Oxford Street (PO Box 82), Bondi Junction, NSW 2022. Tel: 2-9389 0249. Fax: 2-9389 7788. E-mail: gs@ace.edu.au. Full-time (4 weeks) and part-time (12 weeks). A$2,090. Longest established and largest Cambridge/RSA Centre in Australia. Also offers 1-week introductory courses.

HOLMESGLEN LANGUAGE CENTRE, Holmesglen Institute of TAFE, PO Box 42, Chadstone, Victoria 3148. Tel: 3-9564 1820. Fax: 3-9564 1712. E-mail: larryf@holmesglen.vic.edu.au. Full-time courses offered 6 times a year and part-time (18 week) 3 times a year. A$1,890. DELTA offered once a year over 8 months; A$3,200. Also offers 1-week introductory and refresher TEFL courses on demand. Accommodation can be organised with homestay families or help can be given to find short-term rental accommodation. Help is given with job placement.

HOLMES INSTITUTE TEACHER TRAINING, 185 Spring Street, Melbourne, Victoria 3000. Tel: 3-9662 2055. Fax: 3-9639 0904. E-mail: holmes@world.net. Web-site: http://www.edunet.com/holmes. 9 full-time CELTA courses a year. A$1,895. City centre location. Accommodation available.

INSEARCH LANGUAGE CENTRE, University of Technology Sydney, Level 3, 10 Quay St, PO Box K1206, Haymarket, Sydney, NSW 2000. Tel: 2-281 4544. Fax: 281 4675. E-mail:enquiries@ilc.nsw.edu.au. Web-site: http://www.uts.edu.au/oth/ilc Full-time 6 times a year and part-time twice. A$2,370. Homestays can be arranged. Has centres in Chiang Mai, Medan, Osaka, Shanghai and Kuwait.

INSTITUTE OF CONTINUING & TESOL EDUCATION (ICTE), The University of Queensland, Brisbane 4072. Tel: 7-3365 6565. Fax: 7-3365 6599. E-mail: icte@mailbox.uq.edu.au. CELTA course given 3 times a year (Jan/Feb, May/June, October/Nov) over 4 weeks. A$2,500 per course (including assessment fee). Accommodation can be arranged on request. Information given on where to obtain assistance with job placement.

INTERNATIONAL HOUSE QUEENSLAND, English Language College, Box 7368, 130 McLeod St, Cairns, Queensland 4870. Tel: 70-313466. Fax: 70-313464. E-mail: ihqcnsinfo@internetnorth.com.au. Full-time course every 4 months. Homestays from $150 per week.

INTERNATIONAL HOUSE SYDNEY (WARATAH), Level 6, 58 York Street, Sydney NSW 2000. Tel: 2-9262 2886. Fax: 02-9262 2872. E-mail: nrendall@ihsydney.com. Web-site: www.ihsydney.com. Full-time in January and July. Part-time (20 weeks) starting February and August. $A2,300. Homestay accommodation can be arranged. A job club helps with CVs, contacting schools and giving advice.

LA TROBE UNIVERSITY LANGUAGE CENTRE, Bundoora, VIC 3083. Tel: 3-9479 1722. Fax: 3-9479 3676. E-mail: languagecentre@latrobe.edu.au. Web-site: http://www.latrobe.edu.au. Full-time 5-6 times a year. A$1,890.

MILNER INTERNATIONAL COLLEGE OF ENGLISH, 379 Hay St, Perth, Western Australia 6000. Tel: 8-9325 5444. Fax: 8-9221 2392. E-mail: milner@wantree.com.au. Full-time courses 5 times a year. A$2,250. Flats available for A$160-200 a week, homestays for A$150 a week.

RMIT UNIVERSITY, Centre for English Language Learning, 480 Elizabeth St, Melbourne, Victoria 3000. Tel: 3-9639 0300. Fax: 3-9663 8504. E-mail: cell@rmit.edu.au. Web-site: http://www.training.rmit.edu.au. Full-time 6 times a year, part-time (16 weeks) twice a year. A$1,950. Homestays can be arranged.

ST. MARK'S INTERNATIONAL COLLEGE, 375 Stirling St, Perth, WA 6000. Tel: 8-9227 9888. Fax: 8-9227 9880. E-mail: smic@iinet.net.au. Part-time (12 weeks) 4 times a year. A$2,250.

SOUTH AUSTRALIAN COLLEGE OF ENGLISH (SACE), 254 North Terrace, Adelaide, SA 5000. Tel: 8-8232 0335. Fax: 8-8223 7206. E-mail: sacecoll@camtech.net.au. Full-time and part-time courses. A$2,050.

TASMANIAN COLLEGE OF ENGLISH, 322 Liverpool Street, Hobart, Tasmania 7000. Tel: 3-6231 9911. Fax: 3-6231 9912. E-mail: sacetas@tassie.net.au. Full-time 3 times a year. $A2,000 all inclusive. Accommodation must be arranged independently. Small classes. College housed in heritage mansion.

Austria

bfi VIENNA, Vocational Training Institute Vienna, Kinderspitalgasse 5, A-1090 Vienna. Tel: 1-404 35 114. Fax: 1-404 35 124. E-mail: anmeldung.bat@bfi-wien.or.at. Full-time (September) and part-time (February-May). AS18,000. Accommodation available on request.

Bahrain

THE BRITISH COUNCIL, BAHRAIN, P.O. Box 452, Manama, Bahrain. Tel: 261555. Fax: 258689. E-mail: marystansfeld@bc-bahrain.sprint.com. CELTA offered 3 times a year, part-time over 11-12 weeks. 640 dinars.

Canada

COLUMBIA COLLEGE, 500-555 Seymour Street, Vancouver, British Columbia V6B 6J9. Tel: 604-683-8360. Fax: 604-682-7191. Intensive (4 weeks) 6 times a year. C$2,500.

INTERNATIONAL LANGUAGE INSTITUTE, 5151 Terminal Rd. 8th Fl, Halifax, Nova Scotia B3J 1A1. Tel: 902-429-3636. Fax: 902-429-2900. E-mail: study@ili-halifax.com. Web-site: URL http://www.ili-halifax.com. Full-time, four times a year and part-time (22 weeks) once a year. C$1,800 or US$1400.

KWANTLEN UNIVERSITY COLLEGE, 1266 72nd Ave. Surrey, British Columbia V3W 2M8. Tel: 604-599-2693. Fax: 604-599-2716. E-mail: martyn@kwantlen.bc.ca. 3 150-hour CELTA courses offered part-time over 5, 8 or 12 weeks. C$2,500. Homestay accommodation can be arranged. Help given with job placement. Courses held at the Richmond Campus, a 25-minute drive from downtown Vancouver.

LANGUAGE STUDIES CANADA, 124 Eglinton Avenue West, Suite 400, Toronto, Ontario M4R 2G8. Tel: 416-488-2200. Fax: 416-488-2225. E-mail: celta@tor.lsc-canada.com. 8 intensive courses offered a year. C$2,150 plus texts. Accommodation co-ordinator assists with homestay and accommodation in residences or apartment hotels. Notice boards, addresses and contacts provided. Wheelchair accessible. Most graduates gain immediate employment.

UNIVERSITY OF WINNIPEG, Division of Continuing Education, 346 Portage Avenue, Winnipeg, Manitoba R3C 0C3. Tel: 204-982-1171. Fax: 204-944-0115. E-mail: eliz@coned.uwinnipeg.ca. Full-time twice a year. From C$2,000. Accommodation can be arranged in homestay or residence with affiliated colleges. No placement programme, but resource bank available.

Czech Republic

INTERNATIONAL HOUSE PRAGUE, Lupacova 1, 130 00 Prague 3. Tel: (2) 697 4513/900 02 685. Fax: (2) 231 8584. E-mail: ilhprague@telecom.cz. Two four-week courses a year (May/June and July), one five-week course (Nov/Dec), one part-time (Jan-May). Fees (1998): 32,550 crowns for 4-week course, 38,200 crowns for 5-week course, 24,675 crowns for part-time course. Accommodation can be arranged for full-time courses at an additional cost.

Egypt

AMERICAN UNIVERSITY IN CAIRO, PO Box 2511, Cairo. Tel: 2-357 6840. Fax: 2-355 7565. US enquiries to 420 Fifth Avenue, 3rd Floor, New York, NY 10018-2729 (212-730-8800/fax 212-730-1600/e-mail: aucegypt@aucnyo.edu). Full-time CELTA course. Also offer MA in Teaching English as a Foreign Language (MA/TEFL).

INTERNATIONAL LANGUAGE INSTITUTE (ILI), 2 Mohamed Bayoumi St, Off Merghany St, Heliopolis, Cairo. Tel: 2-291 9295/418 9212. Fax: 2-415 1082. E-mail: ili@ritsec.com.eg. Affiliated to International House. 7 full-time courses a year. Accommodation in shared flats can be arranged.

France

ILC/IH PARIS, 13 Passage Dauphine, 75006 Paris. Tel: 1-44 41 80 20. Fax: 1-44 41 80 21. 4-week intensive (130 hours) courses held 8 times a year. Prices on application.

Germany

MUNCHNER VOLKSHOCHSCHULE, Fachgebiet Englisch, Postfach 80 11 64, 81611 München. Fax: 89-480 06 252. 5 week intensive course offered once a year in April-May. DM2,300. Accommodation not available. Small groups. General advice given on jobs. Opportunity for some successful trainees to work in Munich on a freelance basis. Information sent out from October preceding the course. Also offers one-week introductory Preliminary Certificate course.

Hong Kong

THE BRITISH COUNCIL, HONG KONG, 3 Supreme Court Road, Admiralty, Hong Kong. Tel: 2913 5581 (Rebecca Ho). Fax: 2913 5588. E-mail: nick.florent@bc-hongkong.spring.com. Semi-intensive course: intensive first week followed by 8 weeks part-time (Wednesday evenings and Saturday mornings). Starting dates at end of August, November, February and May. HK19,600. Also offer Certificate in English Language Teaching to Young Learners (CELTYL). Twice a year starting November and May. 3 day intensive followed by 8/9 weeks part-time. HK$19,600.

Hungary

INTERNATIONAL HOUSE LANGUAGE SCHOOL, Teacher Training Institute, Bimbó út 7, 1022 Budapest. Tel: 1-212 4010. Fax: 1-316 2491. E-mail: ttraining@ih.hu. Web-site: www.ih.hu. Full-time courses starting June, July and August; part-time course (3 evenings per week) from end of September and beginning of March. Also offer DELTA.

India

THE BRITISH COUNCIL NEW DELHI, English Language Teaching Centre, 17 Kasturba Gandhi Marg, New Delhi 110001. Tel: 11-371 1401. Fax: 11-371 0717. E-mail: emma.levy@bc-delhi.bcindia.sprintsmx.ems.vsnl.net.in
CELTA given over 4-5 weeks 2-3 times a year. £800. Course participants are responsible for finding their own accommodation (advice given). Part-time work for successful course participants.

Indonesia

THE BRITISH INSTITUTE (TBI), Plaza Setiabudi 2, Jalan Rasuna Said, Kav 61-62, Jakarta 12920. Tel: 21-525 6750. Fax: 21-520 7574. E-mail: unisad@ibm.net. 2 intensive courses a year. Assistance can be provided to find local guest house accommodation.

Ireland

LANGUAGE CENTRE OF IRELAND, 45 Kildare St, Dublin 2. Tel: 1-671 6266. Fax: 1-671 6430. E-mail: langcntr@indigo.ie. Full-time and part-time (9 weeks) 3 times a year.

LANGUAGE CENTRE, UCC, The National University of Ireland, Cork. Tel: 21-902043/903225. Fax: 21-903223. 4-week intensive and 10-12 week part-time courses. IR£850. Homestay/residence available during summer intensive course, accommodation lists and advice in other cases. Noticeboard of vacancies. Part-time DELTA also available, IR£1,600.

Italy

THE CAMBRIDGE SCHOOL, Via San Rocchetto 3, 37121 Verona. Tel: 45-800 3154. Fax: 45-8014900. E-mail: info@cambridgeschool.it. Full-time and part-time CELTA courses throughout the year.

INTERNATIONAL HOUSE—ROME, Viale Manzoni 22, 00185 Rome. Tel: 06-704 76 894. Fax: 06-704 97 842. Full-time (July, September, February) and semi-intensive (October to January and March to May). L2,600,000. Hotels from L75,000 per night and homestays for L700,000 for 4 weeks. Also run CELTYL and DELTA courses.

Kuwait

THE BRITISH COUNCIL, KUWAIT, PO Box 345, 13004 Safat. Tel: 251 5512. Fax: 255 1376. E-mail: britcoun@kuwait.net. Part-time course over 15 weeks, offered twice a year (September and January/February). 510 Kuwaiti dinars. Places are offered to people already resident in Kuwait because of strict visa regulations.

Malaysia

THE BRITISH COUNCIL, KUALA LUMPUR, The Language Centre, 3rd & 4th Floors, Wisma Hangsam, 1 Jalan Hang Lekir, 50000 Kuala Lumpur. Tel: 3-230 6304. Fax: 3-232 9448. E-mail: bclc@po.jaring.my. Web-site: www.britcoun.org.my/malaysia/mallang. Full-time courses (5 weeks) start in July and August. Part-time courses (10 weeks) start in January, April and October. Course fee each session: 4,000 ringgits.

Malta

NSTS ENGLISH LANGUAGE INSTITUTE, International Teacher Training Centre, 220 St. Paul Street, Valletta VLT 07. Tel: 33 61 05. Fax: 23 03 30. E-mail: nststrav@kemmunet.net.mt. Intensive courses August and November. Semi-intensive course over 14 weeks starts January. 567 Maltese pounds (£896). Low-cost self-catering accommodation and other accommodation available.

Netherlands

BRITISH LANGUAGE TRAINING CENTRE, Oxford House, N.Z. Voorburgwal 328 e, 1012 RW Amsterdam. Tel: (20) 622 36 34. Fax: (20) 626 49 62. E-mail: bltc@bltc.nl. 4-week full-time course offered once a year, and 12-week part-time course twice a year. 3,700 guilders. Wide mix of approaches, including business and one-to-one sessions. Advice on job-finding.

New Zealand

AUCKLAND LANGUAGE CENTRE, PO Box 105035, Auckland. Tel: 9-303 1962. Fax: 9-307 9219. 4 full-time courses per year. Homestays can be arranged.

CAPITAL LANGUAGE ACADEMY, PO Box 1100, Wellington (Street address: Level 9, The Breeze Plaza, 57-65 Manners Mall, Wellington). Tel: 4-472 7557. Fax: 4-472 5285. E-mail: 100245.13@compuserve.com. 4 times a year. NZ$2,700. Homestay accommodation can be arranged.

ILA SOUTH PACIFIC LTD., PO Box 25-170, Christchurch (Street address: 21 Kilmore St). Tel: 3-379 5452. Fax: 3-379 5373. E-mail: staffch@ila.co.nz. 5 courses a year (January, February, June, October and November). Homestay or bed & breakfast accommodation can be arranged.

LANGUAGES INTERNATIONAL, 27 Princes St (PO Box 5293), Auckland 1. Tel: 9-309 0615. Fax: 9-377 2806. E-mail: success@langsint.co.nz. Web-site: www.langsint.co.nz. 5 times a year. NZ$2,900. Also offers DELTA course.

UNIVERSITY OF WAIKATO LANGUAGE INSTITUTE, PO Box 1317, Waikato Mail Centre, Hamilton. Tel: 7-838 4193. Fax: 7-838 4194. E-mail: language@waikato.ac.nz. Full-time 2-3 times a year (mid-June to mid-July and mid-November to mid-December). NZ$2,850. Hostel accommodation available on campus (though course is run off-campus). Employment session at end of course. University also offers postgraduate MA and Diploma of Second Language Teaching.

Oman

BRITISH COUNCIL, PO Box 73, Postal Code 115, Medinat Sultan Qaboos. Tel: 600548 ext 221. Fax: 698018. E-mail: 100656.2511@compuserve.com. Intensive course (5 weeks) and semi-intensive course (3 days a week for 10 weeks), 2-3 times a year.

POLYGLOT INSTITUTE, PO Box 221 (Postal Code 112), Ruwi. Tel: 701261. Fax: 794602. Part-time (10 weeks) twice a year. Accommodation can be arranged.

Poland

ELS-BELL SCHOOL OF ENGLISH, ul. Polanki 110, 80-308 Gdansk, Poland. Tel/fax: 58-554 8382. 4 weeks in June/July. Approx. £700. Part-time DELTA also available October-May. £900. Accommodation can be arranged on request. Help given with job placement.

INTERNATIONAL HOUSE/CJO WROCLAW, Teacher Training Centre, ul. Ruska 46a, 50-079 Wroclaw. Tel/fax: +48 (71) 72 36 98. E-mail: ttcentre@id.pl; Web-site: http:// www.silesia.top.pl/~ihih/katowice. 4-week CELTA course offered in August. £740 plus accommodation (approx. £150). Job opportunities at IH schools for successful candidates. Flight reimbursement possible if employed by IH/CJO schools (Wroclaw, Katowice, Opole, Bielska-Biala). Also offer 2-week Cambridge/RSA CELTYL extension courses three times a year (£420) and 1-week Teaching Business English course four times a year (£190). 9-week DELTA course offered once in summer (£1,065).

Portugal

CAMBRIDGE SCHOOL, Avenida da Liberdade 173-4°, 1250 Lisbon. Tel: 1-352 7474. Fax: 1-353 4729. Intensive courses offered in the summer. Successful candidates normally offered a job in one of the group's schools in Portugal. Assistance with accommodation.

INTERNATIONAL HOUSE LISBON, Rua Marquês Sá da Bandeira 16, 1050 Lisbon. Tel: 1-315 14 96. Fax: 1-353 00 81. E-mail: ihlisbon@mail.telepac.pt. CELTA and CELTYL courses 8 times a year. 210,000 escudos. Also part-time DELTA course (300,000 escudos) and other courses including TEFL introduction courses and Business English (see listing).

Singapore

THE BRITISH COUNCIL SINGAPORE, Holland Village, 362 Holland Road, Singapore 278696. Tel: 463 5525. Fax: 463 2970. Part-time: 2 full days per week for 10 weeks. £1,000. No accommodation or help with job placement. 20 hour introductory course also offered.

South Africa

LANGUAGE LAB INTERNATIONAL HOUSE, 54 De Korte Street, Braamfontein, Johannesburg 2001. Tel: 11-339 1051. Fax: 11-403 1759. E-mail: langlab@icon.co.za Full-time 3 times a year. R6,400 (increases expected as rand loses value). Accommodation can be provided.

Spain

THE BRITISH LANGUAGE CENTRE, Calle Bravo Murillo 377-2°, 28020 Madrid. Tel: 91-733 07 39. Fax: 91-314 50 09. Full-time and part-time (15 weeks) starting most months of the year. 140,000 pesetas. Help given with accommodation (approximately 40,000 pesetas a month). Also offer Cambridge/RSA Diploma course and intro courses (see listings).
CAMPBELL COLLEGE, Teacher Training Centre, Calle Pascual y Genis 11, pta 3, 46002 Valencia. Tel/fax: 96-352 4217. 4-week courses run in summer and autumn. Assistance in finding suitable accommodation. Can assist in finding jobs locally after course.
CLIC INTERNATIONAL HOUSE, SEVILLE, Teacher Training Department, Calle Santa Ana 11, 41002 Seville. Tel: (95) 438 4703. Fax: (95) 437 1806. E-mail: clic1@arrakis.es. 4-week intensive CELTA courses offered about 6 times a year. About £650. Accommodation arranged by school. Personal help and advice given on job placement. Interviewing takes place at new premises at Calle Albareda 19, 41001 Seville (95-450 2131/fax 95-456 1696/e-mail: clic@arrakis.es).
INTERNATIONAL HOUSE BARCELONA, Trafalgar 14 entlo, 08010 Barcelona. Tel: 93-268 4511. Fax: 93-268 0239. E-mail: training@bcn.ihes.com. Full-time 9 times a year and one part-time course. 170,000 pesetas. Help given with accommodation. Access to the internet and e-mail available.

INTERNATIONAL HOUSE MADRID, C/ Zurbano 8, 28010 Madrid. Tel: (91) 310 1314. Fax: (91) 308 5321. E-mail: ttraining@ihmadrid.es. Full-time CELTA courses offered June, July, August and September; part-time courses starting October and January. 150,000 pesetas. Also offers part-time DELTA and Spanish lessons.
YORK HOUSE, English Language Centre, Muntaner 479, 08021 Barcelona. Tel: 93-211 32 00. Fax: 93-418 58 66. Full-time twice a year (July and September). Single rooms available.

Switzerland

THE BELL SCHOOL, GENEVA, 12 Chemin des Colombettes, 1202 Geneva. Tel: 22-740 20 22. Fax: 22-740 20 44. Full-time in Geneva and Zurich. Part-time courses also offered.
VOLKSHOCHSCHULE, ZURICH, Splügenstrasse 10, 8002 Zurich. Tel: 1-205 84 84. Fax: 1-205 84 85. Part-time throughout the year.

Thailand

ECC (THAILAND), 430/17-24 Chula Soi 64, Siam Square, Bangkok 10330. Tel: 2-255 1856-9. Fax: 2-254 2243. E-mail: rsa@eccthai.com. www.eccthai.com. Internet: www.eccthai.com. 5 full-time courses per year. US$1,200. Central Bangkok guest houses cost 400-700 Baht per night. CELTA graduates are offered full-time teaching contracts with ECC at one of their 50 branches in Bangkok and throughout the country. ECC offers other short courses: Teaching English to Young Learners and Teaching Business English.

Turkey

THE BRITISH COUNCIL, IZMIR, Teachers' Centre, 1374 Sokak No. 18, Selvili Is Merkezi K3, 35210 Cankaya-Izmir. Tel: 232-446 0131. Fax: 232-446 0130. E-mail: steve.darn@bc-izmir.sprint.com. Four week full-time course from mid-June, £900 including exam fee.
INTERNATIONAL TRAINING INSTITUTE, Istiklal Cad., Kallavi Sokak 7-9, Kat. 4, Galatasaray, Istanbul, Turkey. Tel: 212-243 2888. Fax: 212-245 3163. E-mail: tomitithom@arti.net.tr. 1 intensive course per year, 2 part-time courses over 10 weeks. £800. Possibility to stay in a shared flat. Help given with job placement. Also offer Introduction to TEFL, CELTYL and DELTA.

United Arab Emirates

THE BRITISH COUNCIL, ABU DHABI, PO Box 46523, Abu Dhabi. Tel: 2-659300. Fax: 2-664340. Intensive (4 weeks) once or twice a year. No accommodation.

USA

CENTER FOR LANGUAGE, EDUCATION & DEVELOPMENT (CLED), Georgetown University, 3607 O Street NW, Washington, DC 20007. Tel: 202-687-4400. Fax: 202-337-1559. 2 full-time courses in summer. Accommodation on campus. Trainees get double teaching practice.
EMBASSY CES, The Center for English Studies, 330 Seventh Avenue, New York, NY 10001. Tel: 212-629-7300. Fax: 212-736-7950. E-mail: cesnewyork@cescorp.com. 10 full-time courses per year. $2,225. Accommodation in student residences and bed and breakfasts. Job counselling given.
ENGLISH INTERNATIONAL, 655 Sutter St, Suite 200, San Francisco, CA 94102. E-mail:TeflUSA@compuserve.com. Web-site: www.english-international.com. Full-time 4-week course offered monthly (except December). $2,750. Job guidance. Graduate credit recommendation of 6 semester hours towards MA TESOL.

INTERNATIONAL HOUSE—TEACHER TRAINING USA, 200 SW Market Street, Suite 111, Portland, OR 97201. Tel: 503-224-1960. Fax: 503-224-2041. Also IH Teacher Training USA, 320 Wilshire Blvd, Third Floor, Santa Monica, CA 90401. Tel: 310-394-8618. Fax: 310-394-2708. E-mail: celta@ih-portland.com. Full-time 4-week CELTA courses run January to November. $2,500. Half-board homestay accommodation arranged for $140 per week (Portland) or $180 (Santa Monica). Applications for both locations should be sent to the Portland centre.

ST GILES LANGUAGE TEACHING CENTER, One Hallidie Plaza, Suite 350, San Francisco, CA 94102. Tel: 415-788-3552. Fax: 415-788-1923. E-mail: sfstgile@slip.net. Web-site: www.stgiles-usa.com. Full-time (4 weeks) 5 times a year. $2,550. Assistance with accommodation. Free information seminars held 5 times a year.

Trinity College Certificate (TESOL) Courses

All courses last four weeks full-time unless otherwise stated. The Trinity College moderation fee is fixed by individual course providers, though is usually £70.

ABERDEEN COLLEGE, Gallowgate, Aberdeen AB25 1BN. Tel: 01224 612000. Fax: 01224 612001. Part-time September-March; 6-9 hours per week. £385.

BASINGSTOKE COLLEGE OF TECHNOLOGY, Worting Road, Basingstoke, Hants. RG21 8TN. Tel: 01256 54141. Direct line to Languages Dept: 01256 306350. Fax: 01256 306444. E-mail: annabel.stowe@bcot.ac.uk. Intensive course once a year in July. Part-time from September/October for 6 months, either one day a week or two evenings a week. £550. Accommodation with host families if necessary. Links with local firms requiring ESP and local summer schools for EFL.

BLACKPOOL & THE FYLDE COLLEGE, Ashfield Road, Bispham, Blackpool, Lancashire FY2 0HB. Tel: 01253 352352. Fax: 01253 356127. E-mail: visitors@blackpool.ac.uk. Part-time once a year: 3 hours a week for 29 weeks. £850. Access to job offers received in Study Unit.

BOLTON COLLEGE, Manchester Road, Bolton BL2 1ER. Tel: 01204 531411. Fax: 01204 380774. Part-time from September to June. £475 plus moderation fee of £70. Four levels of language classes for teaching practice.

BRACKNELL & WOKINGHAM COLLEGE, Montague House, Broad Street, Wokingham, Berks. RG40 1AU. Tel: 0118 978 2728. Fax: 0118 989 4315. E-mail: colette.galloway@bracknell.ac.uk. Part-time (32 weeks, over a third of which is observation and practice teaching of EFL students on-site). £610 (including exam fee). Also, part-time Trinity College Diploma course over 22 weeks; £395 (excluding exam fee).

BRADFORD & ILKLEY COMMUNITY COLLEGE, English Language Centre, Great Horton Road, Bradford BD7 1AY. Tel: 01274 753207. Fax: 01274 741553. E-mail: elainet@bilk.ac.uk. Full-time offered 5 times a year (February, May, July, October and November); also part-time evening courses October-May. £600. Trinity Diploma also offered part-time (£1,000).

BURY COLLEGE, Market Street, Bury, Lancs. BL9 OBG. Tel: 0161-280 8280. Fax: 0161-280 8228. E-mail: information@burycollege.ac.uk. Web-site: http://www.burycollege.ac.uk. Part-time evening course (Thursdays 6-9pm) September to June or part-time evening course with independent learning January-June. Approx. £375 plus moderaion fee of £70.

CALDERDALE COLLEGE, Francis Street, Halifax, West Yorks. HX1 3UZ. Tel: 01422 399319. Fax: 01422 399320. Part-time once a year (one 3-hour session per week). £650. Teaching practice with Russian groups among others. Extra ESP component in course. Choice of unknown language is Japanese, Chinese or modern Greek.

CICERO LANGUAGES INTERNATIONAL, 42 Upper Grosvenor Road, Tunbridge Wells, Kent TN1 2ET. Tel: 01892 547077. Fax: 01892 522749. E-mail: cicero@pavilion.co.uk. 4-week courses in February, March, May, September, October and November. Half-board accommodation with local families. Links with language schools abroad, e.g. in Latvia.

CITY COLLEGE MANCHESTER, Fielden Centre, 141 Barlow Moor Road, West Didsbury, Manchester M20 2PQ. Tel: 0161-957 1660. Fax: 0161-434 0443. Part-time course over 18 weeks. Also offer full-time courses abroad (Mallorca, Kalamata, Zagreb). Help given with job search.

COLCHESTER INSTITUTE, Sheepen Road, Colchester, Essex CO3 3LL. Tel: 01206 718186/718713. Fax: 01206 763041. E-mail: efl1@colch.inst.uk. 2 intensive 9-week courses held a year plus 4 weeks distance learning. Accommodation can be arranged in Colchester.

COVENTRY TESOL CENTRE, Coventry Technical College, Butts, Coventry CV1 3GD. Tel: 01203 526742. E-mail: c.fry@covcollege.ac.uk. Full-time 8 times a year; part-time over the academic year. Accommodation can be arranged through college accommodation office. Also offer Trinity Cert. courses in Czech Republic, Spain, Poland and Turkey. Same fee plus £300 for accommodation overseas.

DARLINGTON COLLEGE OF TECHNOLOGY, Cleveland Avenue, Darlington, Co. Durham DL3 7BB. Tel: 01325 503050. Fax: 01325 503000. Part-time (36 weeks starting in January). £198 plus moderation fee. List of local homestays/flats available. Japanese language offered as part of course.

ENGLISH WORLDWIDE, The Italian Building, Dockhead, London SE1 2BS. Tel: 0171-252 1402. Fax: 0171-231 8002. E-mail: info.eww@pop3.hiway.co.uk. Licentiate Diploma offered by distance learning (in cooperation with Sheffield Hallam University, see below). Candidates are mainly ELT teachers working abroad. Also offer the LCCI Certificate in Teaching English for Business. EWW is primarily a recruitment agency and so can help graduates find jobs (see chapter *Finding a Job*).

FARNBOROUGH COLLEGE OF TECHNOLOGY, Manor Park, Aldershot, Hampshire GU12 4JN. Tel: 01252 307 407. Part-time over $2\frac{1}{2}$ terms, once a year. £475.

GATESHEAD COLLEGE, Durham Road, Gateshead NE9 5BN. Tel: 0191-490 0300. Fax: 0191-490 2313. Internet: www.gateshead.ac.uk. Part-time September to May (evenings).

GOLDERS GREEN COLLEGE, 11 Golders Green Road, London NW11 8DE. Tel/fax: 0181-905 5467/455 6528/442 0101. E-mail: ggcol@easynet.co.uk. 5 week course offered 10 times a year; includes 1 week pre-TESOL course. Also part-time over 13 weeks starting March and September. £645 plus moderation fee. Bed and breakfast available for £65-£70 per week, half-board for £80-£90.

GROVE HOUSE LANGUAGE CENTRE, Carlton Avenue, Greenhithe, Kent DA9 9DR. Tel: 01322 386826. Fax: 01322 386347. 8 or 9 times a year. Accommodation arranged.

HART VILLAGES CENTRE, Robert May's School, West Street, Odiham, Hampshire RG29 1NA. Tel: 01256 703808. Fax: 01256 703012. Part-time over 32 weeks; Friday mornings plus teaching practice (day or evening).

HOPWOOD HALL COLLEGE, St. Mary's Gate, Rochdale OL12 6RY. Tel: 01706 345346/freephone 0800 834297. Fax: 01706 41426. E-mail: enquiries@hopwood.ac.uk. Web-site: http://www.hopwood.ac.uk. Part-time (30 weeks) once a year. £540.

HULL COLLEGE, School of Humanities, Languages & EFL, Park Street Centre, Hull HU2 8RR. Tel: 01482 329943. Fax: 01482 598989. E-mail: dwilson@hull-college.ac.uk. 16 hours a week for 10 weeks plus 1 reading week offered termly. £250.

INLINGUA TEACHER TRAINING & RECRUITMENT, Rodney Lodge, Rodney Road, Cheltenham, Glos. GL50 1JF. Tel: 01242 253171. Fax: 01242 253181. E-mail: recruitment@inlingua-cheltenham.co.uk. Internet: http://www.inlingua-cheltenham.co.uk. Full-time 5 week courses offered year round, and part-time course. £850 (reductions possible for over 30s). Applicants are interviewed in person. Most successful applicants find work through inlingua's recruitment service which places teachers in schools worldwide (see *Finding a Job*).

INTERNATIONAL LANGUAGE INSTITUTE/ILI, County House, Vicar Lane, Leeds LS1 7JH. Tel: 0113 242 8893. Fax: 0113 234 7543. E-mail: 101322.1376@compuserve.com. 5-week full-time course offered once a year from November. £874. Half-board accommodation available. More than half of 130 hour course consists of teaching practice. Also offers CELTA course.

INTERNATIONAL TRAINING NETWORK, Exchange Buildings, Upper Hinton Road, Bournemouth, Dorset BH1 2HH. Tel/fax: 01202 789089. Intensive 5-week course offered 7 times a year. Family accommodation with half-board can be arranged. Specifically train Christians who want to go into the mission field as TEFL teachers. Assistance with job placement given.

ITS ENGLISH SCHOOL, HASTINGS, 43-45 Cambridge Gardens, Hastings, Sussex TN34 1EN. Tel: 01424 438025. Fax: 01424 438050. E-mail: itsbest@its-hastings.co.uk. Intensive course offered 7 times a year, 4/5 weeks or in two blocks of a fortnight each. £495 plus moderation fee. Family accommodation from £77 per week. Also offer Trinity Diploma, part distance learning, part attendance (£695 plus exam fee). Short introductory course and 2-week certificate course in teaching at primary and secondary schools also offered (see listings).

JOSEPH PRIESTLEY COLLEGE, Alec Beevers Centre, Burton Avenue, Leeds, W. Yorks. LS11 5ER. Tel: 0113 271 1994. Fax: 0113 288 0525. E-mail: tesol@jpc.ac.uk. 3 courses per year: full time (6 weeks) in June/July, semi-intensive (12 weeks starting in March) and part-time (20 weeks starting September).

KENT SCHOOL OF ENGLISH, 3 Granville Road, Broadstairs, Kent CT10 1QD. Tel: 01843 868207. Fax: 01843 860418. E-mail: kse@adept.co.uk. Intensive twice a year. £650. Host family or guest house accommodation can be arranged.

LANGSIDE COLLEGE GLASGOW, 50 Prospecthill Road, Glasgow G42 9LB. Tel: 0141-649 4991/2256. Fax: 0141-632 5252. E-mail: tfoster@perseus.langside.ac.uk. Part-time over academic year. £500 plus moderation fee. Also offer part-time Trinity Diploma (£500 plus exam fee). Help with job placement. Also offer part-time introduction to TESOL. Non-graduates accepted onto course, provided they show good language awareness and well-developed interpersonal skills.

LANGUAGE LINK TRAINING, 181 Earls Court Road, London SW5 9RB. Tel: 0171-370 4755. Fax: 0171-370 1123. Intensive courses held monthly. £723 plus moderation fee. Teaching practice in small groups. Can help place successful candidates in posts in Central and Eastern Europe (see Recruitment Organisation entry). Also offers part-time CELTA, 1-week Introduction to TEFL and 1 or 2-week booster course for non-native English teachers 3 times a year.

THE LANGUAGE PROJECT, 78-80 Colston Street, Bristol BS1 5BB. Tel: 0117 927 3993/Fax: 0117 907 7181. E-mail: administration@langproj.demon.co.uk. Trinity Diploma in TESOL October-December and March-May. 10 weeks full-time or 2 blocks of 10 weeks part-time. Accommodation can be arranged with a family or in a hotel. Also offer Introduction to TEFL/TESL.

LEEDS METROPOLITAN UNIVERSITY, Centre for Language Study, Beckett Park Campus, Leeds LS6 3QS. Tel: 0113 283 7440 (+44 113 274 7440 from outside the UK). Fax: 0113 274 5966 (+44 113 274 5966 from outside the UK). E-mail: cls@lmu.ac.uk. Internet:http://www.lmu.ac.uk/cls/ Part-time once a year £380. Additional modules available to upgrade to Postgraduate Certificate. Also offer CELTA and MA Language Teaching (see listings).

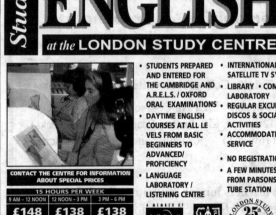

LONDON STUDY CENTRE, 676 Fulham Road, London SW6 5SA. Tel: 0171-731 3549/736 4990/731 8298/384 2734. Fax: 0171-731 6060/731 1498. E-mail: english_ language@compuserve.com. Web-site: http://www.londonstudycentre.com. Full-time (5 weeks) throughout the year and part-time (15 weeks) starting January, May and October. £750 full-time, £780 part-time. Course and career counselling. Accommodation advice available.

MANCHESTER ACADEMY OF ENGLISH, St Margaret's Chambers, 5 Newton St, Manchester M1 1HL. Tel: 0161-237 5619. Fax: 0161-237 9016. E-mail: english@manacad.u-net.com. 4-week intensive course offered 6 times per year. £795 including moderation fee. Accommodation available if required: homestay with full board for £85 per week or (summers only) in student residence for £60-£65 per week (self-catering).

MANCHESTER COLLEGE OF ARTS AND TECHNOLOGY, Department of Language Studies, Lower Hardman St. Manchester M3 3ER. Tel: 0161-953 2266. Fax: 0161-953 2259. E-mail: deba1@mcr1.poptel.org.uk. Part-time September to May (Tuesday and Thursday evenings 6-8pm). £575. Course run in established FE college with many foreign students. Help given with job placement.

MIDDLESBROUGH COLLEGE, Kirby Campus, Roman Road, Linthorpe, Middlesebrough, Teesside TS5 5PJ. Tel: 01642 333333. Fax: 01642 333310. Part-time course once a year (3 hours a week).

NORTHAMPTON COLLEGE, Military Road, Northampton NN1 3ET. Tel: 01604 734 170/2. Fax: 01604 734 183. Part-time once a year September to June (Tuesday evenings 6pm-9pm plus 4 Saturdays). £468 plus moderation fee (approx. £75).

NORTHBROOK COLLEGE SUSSEX, Modern Languages Department, Littlehampton Road, Goring-by-Sea, West Sussex BN12 6NU. Tel: 01903 830057. Fax: 01903 606207. Full-time starting January, March, June, July and October; part-time (Thursday evenings 6-9pm) starting September, January and April. £512 including moderation fee. College also offers preparatory courses (see listing in Introductory Courses).

OAKLANDS COLLEGE, Oaklands Campus, Hartfield Road, St Albans, Herts. AL4 0JA. Tel: 01727 737152. Fax: 01727 855677. E-mail: efl@oaklands.ac.uk. Intensive courses (5 weeks), semi-intensive (10 weeks) and part-time evening courses (36 weeks). Cost £595 including moderation fee. Also offer Licentiate Diploma £495 excluding examination fee. Accommodation service available.

OXFORD HOUSE COLLEGE, 3 Oxford St, London W1R 1RF and 28 Market Place, London W1N 7AL. Tel: 0171-580 9785. Fax: 0171-323 4582. E-mail: oxhc@easynet.co.uk. Web-site: www.oxford-house-college.ac.uk. Large Trinity College validated centre offering CTESOL courses full-time (4 weeks) or part-time (13 or 22 weeks). 4 week course offered in London, and locations abroad, currently Barcelona, Budapest, Istanbul and Tuscany. The Trinity Diploma course (for experienced teachers only) is also offered, by distance learning or part-time in London (13 weeks). Jobs board shows job vacancies. 'Alumni' of the college are given discounts on further courses and free membership of the Oxford House Club, which organises monthly seminars in London on English language teaching.

PARK LANE COLLEGE, Park Lane, Leeds LS3 1AA. Tel: 0113 244 3011. Fax: 0113 244 6372. Part-time (September-June); 1 afternoon per week. £330 plus moderation fee.

PLYMOUTH COLLEGE OF FURTHER EDUCATION, Goschen Centre, Saltash Rosas, Plymouth PL1 2BD. Tel: 01752 305277. Fax: 01752 305065. E-mail: ggodfrey@pcfe.plymouth.ac.uk. Part-time September to June. £998.75. Accommodation can be arranged if required. Advice and references are also given to help with job hunting.

POLYGLOT LANGUAGE CENTRE, Bennett Court, 1 Bellevue Road, London SW17 7EG. Tel: 0181-767 9113. Fax: 0181-767 9104. Also: 214 Trinity Road, London SW17 7HP. 6 times a year. £800. Accommodation can be arranged from £60 a week. Also offer introductory courses.

QUEEN'S UNIVERSITY OF BELFAST TEFL CENTRE, Belfast BT7 1NN, Northern Ireland. Tel: 01232 335373. Fax: 01232 335379. E-mail: tefl@qub.ac.uk. Full-time (5 weeks) in July and August and part-time (4 months) from October to February. £795. Also offer DELTA (£1,100) and MA (see *Academic Courses*). Accommodation can be arranged in university residences for £49 per week. Help is given with job placement.

THE REGENCY SCHOOL OF ENGLISH, Royal Crescent, Ramsgate, Kent CT11 9PE. Tel: 01843 591212. Fax: 01843 850035. Twice a year (April and November). £700. Accommodation can be arranged for £85 per week half-board. Also offer 5-day introductory course.

REGENT EDINBURGH, 29 Chester Street, Edinburgh EH3 7EN. Tel: 0131-225 9888. Fax: 0131-225 2133. 4-week intensive offered monthly. £897. Host family/college residence accommodation. High pass rates to date.

RICHMOND ADULT & COMMUNITY COLLEGE, Clifden Centre, Clifden Road, Twickenham, Middlesex TW1 4LT. Tel: 0181-891 5907. Fax: 0181-892 6354. Full-time in July/August and part-time over 36 weeks (one afternoon per week). £820. Mature students welcome.

ST BRELADE'S COLLEGE, Mont Les Vaux, St. Aubin, Jersey JE3 8AF. Tel: 01534 41305. Fax: 01534 41159. Twice a year (March and September). £700 plus exam fee. Bed & breakfast accommodation for £55 per week. 2-month distance learning and 4 weeks residential course.

ST GEORGE'S SCHOOL OF ENGLISH, 76 Mortimer St, London W1N 7DE. Tel: 0171-299 1700. Fax: 0171-299 1711. Web-site: www.stgeorges.co.uk. Intensive course offered monthly. £695. Can offer contracted employment overseas to successful trainees.

SANDWELL COLLEGE, Crocketts Lane, Smethwick, West Midlands B66 3BU. Tel: 0121-556 6000 (ext. 6233). Fax: 0121-253 6322. One part-time course per year. £700 (concessions if unwaged).

SHEFFIELD HALLAM UNIVERSITY TESOL CENTRE, School of Education, Collegiate Crescent Campus, Sheffield S10 2BP. Tel: 0114 225 2240. Fax: 0114 225 2280. E-mail: tesol@shu.ac.uk. Website: http://www.shu.ac.uk/schools/bus/sbscentr/tesol. 12 weeks distance learning plus 4 weeks intensive full-time study block, plus further 8 weeks post-course essay. 8-9 times a year. £950.

SIDMOUTH INTERNATIONAL SCHOOL, May Cottage, Sidmouth, Devon EX10 8EN. Tel: 01395 516754. Fax: 01395 579270. E-mail: sdmthint@mail.zynet.co.uk. Full-time twice a year (October and March). Accommodation can be arranged. Teaching practice includes 6 hours group teaching and 4 hours one-to-one.

SOUTH EAST ESSEX COLLEGE, Carnarvon Road, Southend-on-Sea, Essex SS2 6LS. Tel: 01702 220400. Fax: 01702 432320. Part-time once a year. £465. Also offer part-time Diploma course.

SOUTHWARK COLLEGE, EFL Section, Waterloo Centre, The Cut, London SE1 8LE. Tel: 0171-815 1682. Fax: 0171-261 1301. CTESOL courses offered part-time over 20 weeks between January and June. £685. Also offer CELTA (5 weeks, £695) and CEELT (10 weeks part-time, £345).

STRANMILLIS COLLEGE, Stranmillis Road, Belfast BT9 5DY, Northern Ireland. Tel: 01232 381271. Fax: 01232 664423. Full-time course each September. £795. Accommodation available in halls of residence, if required. Central location. Informal advice given with job placement.

STUDENTS INTERNATIONAL LTD., 158 Dalby Road, Melton Mowbray, Leicestershire LE13 OBJ. Tel: 01664 481997. Fax: 01664 563332. 6 full-time courses. £795. Host family accommodation for £90 a week half board. Unknown language is Arabic.

SURREY LANGUAGE CENTRE, 39 West Street, Farnham, Surrey GU9 7DR. Tel: 01252 723494. Fax: 01252 712927. E-mail: stbltd@compuserve.com. Full-time offered monthly. £690. Local accommodation can be arranged.

SURREY YOUTH & ADULT EDUCATION SERVICES (SYAES), Elmbridge Area, Esher Green Centre, 19 Esher Green, Esher, Surrey KT10 8AA. Tel: 01372 465374. Fax: 01372 463696. Part-time (22 weeks from October/November to May). Job placement bulletin available.

SUTTON COLLEGE OF LIBERAL ARTS, St. Nicholas Way, Sutton, Surrey SM1 1EA. Tel: 0181-770 6902. Fax: 0181-770 6933. Part-time (32 weeks) September to July.

THURROCK COLLEGE, Woodview, Grays, Essex RM16 2YR. Tel: 01375 391199. Fax: 01375 376703. E-mail: efl@thurrock.ac.uk. 4-week intensive course plus pre-course reading, offered twice a year starting February and November. £749. Self-catering or half-board accommodation can be arranged.

UNIVERSAL LANGUAGE TRAINING (ULT), The Old Forge, Ockham Lane, Ockham, Woking, Surrey GU23 6NP. Tel: 01483 210083. Fax: 01483 211185. Intensive courses offered year round and 2 part-time courses over 16 weeks. Host families available. Job contacts. 4-week courses also held in Zamora, Spain in April, August and November.

UNIVERSITY OF LUTON, Park Square, Luton, Bedfordshire LU1 3AJ. Tel: 01582 734111. Fax: 01582 489014. E-mail: andrew.russell@luton.ac.uk. 4-week full-time Certificate programme in July. £750.

UNIVERSITY OF ST ANDREWS

ENGLISH LANGUAGE TEACHING

Trinity College, London CertTESOL

- 30 hours Distance Learning component + 5 weeks full time study
- Accommodation available

Enrolment forms and further details may be obtained from:

English Language Teaching, University of St. Andrews
Butts Wynd, St. Andrews, Fife KY16 9AL

Phone: 01334 462255   Fax: 01334 462270   e-mail elt@st-and.ac.uk

---

UNIVERSITY OF ST. ANDREWS, English Language Teaching, Butts Wynd, St. Andrews, Fife KY16 9AL. Tel: 01334 462255. Fax: 01334 462270. E-mail: emgh@st-and.ac.uk. 5-week full-time plus 1 week distance learning, offered twice a year. £830 (tuition only). Self-catering accommodation can be arranged. Access to jobs through university's Careers Advisory Service. Opportunities to observe academic English courses, ESP and general English courses. Also offer 30 hour introductory TEFL course.

UNIVERSITY OF WESTMINSTER, English Language Section, School of Languages, 9-18 Euston Centre, London NW1 3ET. Tel: 0171-911 5000. Fax: 0171-911 5007. E-mail: patersk@westminster.ac.uk. 5-week courses 6 times a year.

UNIVERSITY OF WOLVERHAMPTON, School of Languages & European Studies, Stafford Street, Wolverhampton WV1 1SB. Tel: 01902 322484. Fax: 01902 322739. E-mail: sles-enquiries@wlv.ac.uk. Part-time (one evening a week). £790 plus moderation fee.

WALTHAM FOREST COLLEGE, Forest Road, London E17 4JB. Tel: 0181-527 2311. Fax: 0181-523 2376. E-mail: efl@waltham.ac.uk. One intensive course (5 weeks) in June/July and one part-time course September to March (1 day, 1 evening per week).

WINDSOR SCHOOLS GROUP, 21 Osborne Road, Windsor, Berkshire SL4 3EG. Tel: 01753 858995. Fax: 01753 831726. Full-time offered monthly and part-time (4 months or 1 academic year). £799 (incl. VAT). Also offer Trinity Diploma course (£900 plus exam fees). Accommodation can be arranged for £70-£95 per week. Associated English schools for teaching practice in UK and placement in schools in Europe (especially Spain and Italy). Cert TESOL also offered in Barcelona.

WIRRAL METROPOLITAN COLLEGE, The English Language Unit, IBMC, Europa Boulevard, Conway Park, Birkenhead, Wirral L42 9QD. Tel: 0151-551 7088/ 7114. Fax: 0151-551 7001. E-mail: harriet.parker@wmc.ac.uk. Part-time over 30 weeks (January-June). £630. In-house teaching practice. Local accommodation can be found if required. Bilingual trainees welcome with proficiency level of English. Comprehensive student support available.

Argentina

CENTUM, SERVICIOS DE IDIOMAS, Bartlomé Mitre, 4th floor, 1036 Buenos Aires. Fax: 1-328-5150/328-2385/328-8572. Part-time over 12 weeks (summer) or 36 weeks (academic year). 140 hours total. Emphasis on teaching Business English. Specialist 50-hour course in Teaching English for Business offered. Also offer Licentiate Diploma course. Accommodation not provided.

Cyprus

FORUM LANGUAGE CENTRE, P.O. Box 5567, Nicosia 1310, Cyprus. Tel/fax: 2-497766. E-mail: forum1@cytanet.com.cy. Part-time: 2 half-days per week for 5 months. £730.

Italy

BC ENGLISH LANGUAGE TRAINING, CP 685, 59100 Prato, Italy. Tel/fax: 0574-20487. E-mail: bcelt@texnet.it. Intensive course offered in conjunction with Oxford House College, London. £800. Distance Learning Cert in conjunction with Sheffield Hallam University. L2,800,000. Help is given for accommodation and job placement.

New Zealand

INTERNATIONAL ACADEMY OF LANGUAGES, Dominion Road (PO Box 10222), Auckland, New Zealand. Fax: 9-366 4422. Intensive course 8 times a year. Part-time (3 months). NZ$2,800 (full-time), NZ$3,000 (part-time). Many graduates find teaching contracts in Asia Pacific region.

INTERNATIONAL PACIFIC COLLEGE, Institute of TESOL, Private Bag 11 021, Palmerston North, New Zealand. Tel: 6-354 0818. Fax: 6-354 0935. 4-weeks full-time plus pre-course distance learning component. Offered 4 times a year. NZ$2,800. Help can be given in finding accommodation. Emphasis on intercultural awareness.

SEAFIELD SCHOOL OF ENGLISH, 99 Seaview Road, (PO Box 18516), New Brighton, Christchurch, New Zealand. Tel: 3-388 3850. Fax: 3-388 4970. E-mail: succeed@seafield.co.nz. 3 months of distance learning followed by a 4-week intensive course, offered 4 times a year. NZ$2,600. Also Trinity LTCL (TESOL) Diploma, 9 months distance learning in conjunction with Sheffield Hallam University, followed by a 2 week intensive course. NZ$4,550.

Portugal

THE BRITISH COUNCIL, PORTO, Rua do Breiner 155, 4050 Porto, Portugal. Tel: 2-207 30 60. Fax: 2-207 30 68. E-mail: liam.vint@britcounpt.org. TESOL Certificate course runs part-time once a year (duration of an academic year). Local job opportunities.

Spain

NEXT TRAINING ESPANA, Rocafort 241-243, 6°-5a, 08029 Barcelona, Spain. Tel: 0034 93 322 02 00. Fax: 0034 93 322 34 95. E-mail: next.training@bcn.servicom.es. Website: www.next.edu. Intensive 4-week course offered 8 times per year. £725 includes course and moderation fees, accommodation, post-course 5-day Spanish intensive course. Comprehensive job-finding service for Spain; job offers made to successful graduates. Social and activity programme available. Trinity Diploma courses offered full-time, part-time and distance learning.
THE LANGUAGE INSTITUTE, Calle Oliva 11-2D, Pontevedra, Galicia, Spain. Tel: 986-862461. Fax: 986-871978. Intensive course (130 hours) offered July/August. Accommodation can be arranged for 25,000-30,000 pesetas per month. Help with job-finding.

Uruguay

LIGHTHOUSE ENGLISH INSTITUTE, Sarandi y Ventura Alegre, Torre Maldonado Shopping Centre, Maldonado, Uruguay. Tel: 4-21361. Part-time April-

December (Saturdays 10am-3pm). Teaching practice takes place in October. Job placement in local schools.

Academic and Other Recognised Courses

This represents a small selection of university courses in TEFL/TESL in the UK.

ASTON UNIVERSITY, Language Studies Unit, Department of Languages and European Studies, Aston Triangle, Birmingham B4 7ET. Tel: 0121-359 3611 ext. 4236. Fax: 0121-359 2725. E-mail: isu@aston.ac.uk. 4-week Certificate in TEFL aimed at recent graduates. Held in August. £745. Self-catering accommodation in halls of residence available for £60 per week. Also Advanced Certificate in TEFL for experienced teachers of any discipline: 6 months by distance learning (from January). Also Master's in TESOL/TESP for experienced graduates. 1 year full-time from October, or 2-5 years by distance learning, or combination of in-house and Distance Learning study.

ENGLISH WORLDWIDE, The Italian Building, Dockhead, London SE1 2BS. Tel: 0171-252 1402. Fax: 0171-231 8002. E-mail: info.eww@pop3.hiway.co.uk. 2-week Certificate in Teaching English for Business validated by the London Chamber of Commerce and Industry (LCCI). Offered on demand. £650 plus VAT. Assistance with accommodation. Help given with job placement since EWW is an educational consultancy and TEFL recruitment agency.

KING'S COLLEGE, LONDON, English Language Centre, Campden Hill Road, London W8 7AH. Tel: 0171-333 4075. Fax: 0171-333 4066. E-mail: elc@kcl.ac.uk. MA in ELT and Applied Linguistics. 2 years part time. Approx. £1,300 per academic year. Graduates can enter MA on fast-track basis, missing out 2 course units. Also offer DELTA part-time (1 evening a week for a year). £850 plus £175 UCLES examination fee.

LEEDS METROPOLITAN UNIVERSITY, Centre for Language Study, Beckett Park Campus, Leeds LS6 3QS. Tel: 0113 283 7440 (+44 113 274 7440 from outside the UK). Fax: 0113 274 5966 (+44 113 274 5966 from outside the UK). E-mail: cls@lmu.ac.uk. Internet: http://www.lmu.ac.uk/cls/ 1 year full-time or part-time modes. Weekend or block study periods enable distance learning. Focus on reflective practitioner and research applied to teaching/learning context. Also offer CELTA and Trinity Cert TESOL (see listings).

LONDON GUILDHALL UNIVERSITY, The English Language Centre, Old Castle Street, London E1 7NT. Tel: 0171-320 1251. Fax: 0171-320 1253. E-mail: kramer@lgu.ac.uk. LCCI Certificate in Teaching Business English offered twice a year in January and July (and on demand for groups). Course lasts 2 weeks. £550. Accommodation available in halls of residence.

MIDDLESEX UNIVERSITY, School of Modern Languages, Queensway, Enfield, Middlesex EN3 4SF. Tel: 0181-362. Fax: 0181-805 0702. Introduction to TEFL. Part-time (48 class hours) February-June. Part of academic course but can be taken on its own. £200. Also offer undergraduate degrees with a TEFL minor (6 15-week modules).

MULTI LINGUA, Administration Centre, Abbot House, Sydenham Road, Guildford, Surrey GU1 3RL. Tel: 01483 535118. Fax: 01483 534777. E-mail: mail@multi-lingua.co.uk. Full-time 4-week Certificate course (ML Cert. TEFL) held monthly or part-time starting January and September (2 evenings a week for 6 months). £840 plus £65 moderation fee. Accommodation with host families at £100 per week, or hall of residence or hotels (accommodation booking fee of £45). Job opportunities through associated schools. Also offer 5-day introductory course.

QUEEN'S UNIVERSITY OF BELFAST, TEFL Centre, Belfast, Northern Ireland BT7 1NN. Tel: 01232 335373. Fax: 01232 335379. E-mail: tefl@qub.ac.uk. MA in English Language Teaching. 1 year full-time. £2,400 for EU students, £6,730 non-EU. Accommodation available in university residences for £49 per week. Also offer the Trinity Certificate (TESOL) and RSA/Cambridge DELTA.

THAMES VALLEY UNIVERSITY, School of English Language Education, Walpole House, 18-22 Bond St, Ealing, London W5 5AA. Tel: 0181-579 5000 and ask for The Learning Advice Centre. E-mail: celtaenq@tvu.ac.uk. MA in English Language Teaching. Also offers CELTA.

UNIVERSITY OF BRIGHTON, The School of Languages, Falmer, Brighton, East Sussex BN1 9PH. Tel: 01273 643337. Fax: 01273 690710. E-mail: slweb@bton.ac.uk. Offers Diploma and MBA in TEFL; full-time September-June or 2 years part-time. Applicants are normally graduates or qualified teachers.

UNIVERSITY OF CENTRAL LANCASHIRE, Department of Languages, Preston, Lancashire PR1 2HF. Tel: 01772 893136. Certificate in TEFL. Full-time for 4 weeks in July/August. £658 plus £50 per week if accommodation is required.

UNIVERSITY OF ESSEX, EFL Unit, Department of Language & Linguistics, Wivenhoe Park Campus, Colchester, Essex CO4 3SQ. Tel: 01206 872217. Fax: 01206 873107. E-mail: dilly@essex.ac.uk. Diploma in TEFL (3 terms), Certificate in Teaching English as a Foreign Language/CTEFL (1 term), Certificate in English for Language Teaching/CEFLT (1 term) and CEELT Preparation Course (3 weeks).

UNIVERSITY OF EXETER, School of Education, Heavitree Road, Exeter EX1 2LU. Tel: 01392 264838. Fax: 01392 264810. B.Phil.(Ed) and M.Ed. (one year); and Certificate in Advanced Professional Studies in ELT (one term); Ed.D in TEFL (taught doctorate), 2 years full-time or 4 years part-time. Majority of students are teachers from overseas.

UNIVERSITY OF MANCHESTER, Centre for English Language Studies in Education, School of Education, Oxford Road, Manchester M13 9PL. Tel: 0161-275 3467 (+44-161-275 3467 from abroad). Fax: 0161-275 3480. E-mail: CELSE@man.ac.uk. url: http://www.man.ac.uk/CELSE. Foundation Certificate in TESOL. Full-time (4 weeks) in June/July. £780. University accommodation available.

CELSE

Centre for English Language Studies in Education

MEds at Manchester

Choose from the following courses:

Distance

MEd ELT A distance/summer modular course offering a wide choice of course components. Distance start dates every October, January and April; 6 week summer block every July/August

MEd in Educational Technology and ELT As the MEd ELT, but with an emphasis on the role of educational technology in ELT. Also available world wide fully distance if you have internet access

On-site

MEd TESOL The full-time (also available locally part-time) version of the MEd ELT

MEd in Educational Technology and TESOL The full-time version of

For further details please contact:
The Secretary, CELSE, School of Education, University of Manchester, Oxford Road, Manchester M13 9PL, UK Tel: 0161-275 3467 Fax: 0161-275 3480 Email: celse@man.ac.uk
URL: http://www.man.ac.uk/CELSE/

UNIVERSITY OF READING, Centre for Applied Language Studies (CALS), Whiteknights, PO Box 241, Reading RG6 6WB. Tel: 0118-931 8511. Fax: 0118-975 6506. E-mail: CALS@reading.ac.uk. MA in the Teaching of English as a Foreign Language. Full-time on campus, October to June; or by distance study starting May and November and lasting between 2 and 5 years. Tuition fees for campus-based course are £4,635 (EU) or £7,490 (non-EU). Distance study fees are in three parts, £1,685, £1,265 and £1,265. Campus accommodation available. Flexible programme of study combining different modes.
UNIVERSITY OF STIRLING, Centre for English Language Teaching, Stirling FK9 4LA. Tel: 01786 467934. Fax: 01786 466131. Undergraduate and graduate degrees in TEFL/TESOL and in CALL (Computer Assisted Language Learning) & TESOL.
UNIVERSITY OF WARWICK, Centre for English Language Teacher Education, Coventry CV4 7AL. Tel: 01203 523200. Fax: 01203 524318. E-mail: CELT@warwick.ac.uk. BA in TESOL, MA in ELT/ESP/ELTYL. Also offer 10 week course in ELT, ESP and Teaching Young Learners (January to March).

Distance Learning Courses

INTESOL, 19 Lower Oakfield, Pitlochry, Perthshire PH16 5DS, Scotland. Tel/fax: 01796 474199. Website: http://www.yell.co.uk/sites/intesol/. Distance Learning Preliminary Certificate in TESOL. £195 UK, £210-£230 overseas. Certificate of Educational Studies in TESOL (accredited by ACTDEC) £275 UK, £295-£305 overseas. Also offer option to combine 2 weeks home study with 2 weeks residential £795 inclusive of accommodation and meals. Work closely with recruitment agency to place trainees.
LANGUAGE 2 ASSOCIATES, 25 Woodway Crescent, Harrow, Middlesex HA1 2NH. Tel: 0181-907 2618. Fax: 0181-909 1885. E-mail: langtwo@dircon.com Distance learning courses for teachers and intensive courses validated by the College of Teachers.

LONDON TEFL BUREAU, Suite 401, 302 Regent St, London W1R 5AL. Tel: 0171-580 4242. Intensive TEFL Certificate and Diploma courses: 8 weeks for £175, 4 weeks intensive for £220. Diploma course takes 6 or 12 weeks (£260 or £310). Also offer courses in teaching Business English and Young Learners.

PH GROUP, 8a Summerley Street, London SW18 4ET. Tel/fax: 0181-947 6397. E-mail: Abhod43@aol.com. Providing a staged approach to TEFL training through a combination of seminars and/or distance learning. Students can build full TEFL qualifications as time and finances allow.

ROBACO GLOBAL, 8 Nesburn Road, Barnes, Wearside SR4 7LR. Tel/fax: 0191-551 9102. E-mail: Robaco@dial.pipex.com. Internet: http://www.tefl.com/Robaco. Office in Middle East: Box 8416 SWCC, Jubail 31951, Saudi Arabia. Certificate, diploma, MA courses by distance and/or internet learning. From £425 including moderation, certification, teaching practice at Bournemouth school. Recruitment for posts abroad.

Short Introductory Courses

BEDFORD COLLEGE, Enterprise House, Old Ford End Road, Bedford MK40 4PF. Tel: 01234 271492. Fax: 01234 364272. E-mail: gp67@dial.pipex.com. Part-time introductory course. Also offer CELTA.

BERLITZ (UK) LTD., 9-13 Grosvenor St, London W1A 3BZ. Tel: 0171-915 0909. Fax: 0171-915 0222. Do not run open TEFL training courses. Compulsory method training course for all employees, lasting 1-2 weeks. Normally course is taken at hiring centre.

CILC (Cheltenham International Language Centre), Cheltenham & Gloucester College of Higher Education, Francis Close Hall, Swindon Road, Cheltenham, Glos. GL50 4AZ. Tel: 01242 532925. Fax: 01242 532926. E-mail: cilc@chelt.ac.uk. CELTA centre which offers one-day taster courses.

DUNDEE COLLEGE, Blackness Road, Dundee DD1 5UA. Tel: 01362 834 898. Fax: 01362 322 286. E-mail: dic@dundeecoll.ac.uk. 2-day introductory courses in TEFL 3 times a year (October 28/29, February 24/25 and May 19/20). Accommodation can be arranged.

GLOBE ENGLISH CENTRE, 31 St. David's Hill, Exeter, Devon EX4 4DA. Tel: 01392 71036. Fax: 01392 427559. Part-time intro course; 10 weeks (Thursday evenings 7-9pm) September-December. £125.

GREENHILL COLLEGE, Temple House Site, 221-225 Station Road, Harrow, Middlesex HA1 2XL. Tel: 0181-869 8805. Fax: 0181-427 9201. E-mail: enquiries@harrow.ac.uk. CELTA centre which offers 1-week TEFL Introductory course in July, £170. 1 or 2 day taster days and refresher courses also given, £30 a day. Help with accommodation can be given.

INTERNATIONAL HOUSE HASTINGS, White Rock, Hastings, East Sussex TN34 1JY. Tel: 01424 720100/720104. Fax: 01424 720323. E-mail: training@ilcgroup.com. Various 2-week specialist courses for TEFL teachers. Self-catering accommodation approx. £45 a week. Also offers CELTA and DELTA.

INTERNATIONAL LANGUAGE INSTITUTE/ILI, County House, Vicar Lane, Leeds LS1 7JH. Tel: 0113 242 8893. Fax: 0113 234 7543. E-mail: 101322.1376@compuserve.com. CELTA/Trinity centre which offers one-week (25 hours) intro course, £135. Accommodation with a family can be arranged. Suitable for anyone considering taking up TEFL at UK summer schools or overseas. Practice teaching in peer groups.

INTESOL, 19 Lower Oakfield, Pitlochry, Perthshire PH16 5DS. Tel/fax: 01796 474199. Website: http://www.yell.co.uk/sites/intesol/. Distance learning organisation which offers two 2-week residential courses in Scotland per year (February and November). Combined with 2 weeks of home study. £795 includes accommodation and meals. Close contacts with recruitment agent.

I TO I INTERNATIONAL PROJECTS LTD., One Cottage Road, Headingley, Leeds LS6 4DD. Tel: 0113 217 9800. Fax: 0113 217 9801. E-mail: travel@i-to-i.com. Website: www.i-to-i.com. Intensive TEFL courses. 20-hour weekend courses held at venues nationwide. Extensive guidance on work opportunities abroad (see entry for *i to i* in *Finding a Job*). 20-hour optional home study grammar module available. Fees: £195 waged, £155 un-waged.

ITS ENGLISH SCHOOL, HASTINGS, 43-45 Cambridge Gardens, Hastings, Sussex TN34 1EN. Tel: 01424 438025. Fax: 01424 438050. E-mail: itsbest@its-hastings.co.uk. Trinity centre which offers 5-day short Certificate in Teaching Practice. Times by arrangement. £185. Accommodation with local families from £60 per week half board.

LANGSIDE COLLEGE GLASGOW, 50 Prospecthill Road, Glasgow G42 9LB. Tel: 0141-649 4991/2256. Fax: 0141-632 5252. E-mail: tfoster@perseus.langside.ac.uk. Introduction to TESOL one evening per week for 10 weeks, given 3 times a year. £80 including materials. Also offer Trinity Certificate and Diploma.

LANGUAGE LINK TRAINING, 181 Earls Court Road, London SW5 9RB. Tel: 0171-370 4755. Fax: 0171-370 1123. One-week pre-TESOL introductory courses according to demand. Includes observation in Language Link schools. Also offer Trinity TESOL Cert. and part-time CELTA (see listings).

THE LANGUAGE PROJECT, 78-80 Colston Street, Bristol BS1 5BB. Tel: 0117 927 3993. Fax: 0117 907 7181. E-mail: administration@langproj.demon.co.uk. Web-site: www.langproj.demon.co.uk. Introduction to TEFL/TESL. One-week intensive course offered monthly. Introduction to every aspect of practical classroom teaching. £130. Accommodation can be arranged with a family or in a hotel. Also offers Trinity Diploma.

LINGUARAMA, New Oxford House, 16 Waterloo St, Birmingham B2 5UG. Tel: 0121-632 5925. E-mail: birmingham@linguarama.com. Also 28-32 Princess St, Manchester M1 4LB; tel: 0161-228 3983/fax: 0161-236 9833. E-mail: manchester@linguarama.com. Chain of over 40 language schools which offers its own 5½ day introductory courses in Birmingham and Manchester throughout the year. Fees are £275 non-residential. Possibility of a placement in a Linguarama school abroad (mainly Germany, Finland, France, Spain, Italy and Central Europe) on successful completion of the course. Specialist course in teaching business English also available.

MULTI LINGUA, Administration Centre, Abbot House, Sydenham Road, Guildford, Surrey GU1 3RL. Tel: 01483 535118. Fax: 01483 534777. E-mail: mail@multi-lingua.co.uk. 5-day TEFL Preparatory course (or 5 consecutive Saturdays) held monthly. £215. Also one-week Teaching English for Business course 6 times a year. £390. Family accommodation arranged for £100. Also offer 4-week ML Certificate course (see listing under 'Academic and Other Recognised Courses').

NEWHAM COLLEGE OF FURTHER EDUCATION, East Ham Campus, High Street South, East Ham, London E6 3AB. Tel: 0181-257 4000. Fax: 0181-257 4307. Initial Teacher Cert. ESOL & Basic Skills (City & Guilds 9281). 5 hours p.w. for 14 weeks. Twice a year in autumn and spring terms. Also offers part-time CELTA.

NORTHAMPTON COLLEGE, Military Road, Northampton NN1 3ET. Tel: 01604 734170/2. Fax: 01604 734183. Introduction to TEFL. Part-time over 10 weeks (daytimes) plus 1 Saturday. Once a year April to June. Approx. £45. Basic introduction offering a taste of TEFL. Also offers the Trinity Cert. TESOL.

NORTHBROOK COLLEGE SUSSEX, Modern Languages Department, Littlehampton Road, Goring-by-Sea, West Sussex BN12 6NU. Tel: 01903 830057. Fax: 01903 606207. Pre-TESOL Preparatory course. 4 weeks (full-time) 6 times a year. Part-time evening class offered three times a year. £148 full-time (£98 concessions), £85 part-time (£55 concessions). Accommodation can be arranged for £70-£75 per week. Also offer Trinity Cert.

OXFORD INTENSIVE SCHOOL OF ENGLISH, 13-15 High St. Oxford OX1 4EA. Tel: (01865) 247 272. Fax: (01865) 723 648. Web-site: http://www.oise.co.uk. 2½ week in-house training courses to graduates who are native speakers of English. To teach one-to-one for OISE in Oxford. 2 times a year, March and June. £75. Course participants who pass final exam guaranteed up to 6 hours a day of teaching in July/August. Potential OISE tutors need to have suitable room for teaching within 1½ miles of central Oxford.

PH GROUP/H & L Associates, 8a, Summerley Street, London SW18 4ET. Tel/fax: 0181 947 6397. E-mail: abhod43@aol.com or hlassocs@aol.com. Run one-day seminars called 'Open up a Teacher' and Introductory Certificate in TEFL. £90. Held in various locations around Britain and Spain (Malaga, Granada, Alicante).
SHEFFIELD HALLAM UNIVERSITY, TESOL Centre, School of Education, 36 Collegiate Campus, Sheffield S10 2BP. Tel: 0114 225 2240. Fax: 0114 255 2280. E-mail: tesol@shu.ac.uk. Trinity centre which offers intro courses.
SKOLA TEACHER TRAINING, 21 Star St, London W2 1QB. Tel: 0171-724 2217. Fax: 0171-387 7575. E-mail: maie.skola@easynet.co.uk CELTA centre which offers two-day courses every month in Grammar for English Language Teaching. £85.

TEFL TRAINING, Freepost, Stonesfield, Witney, Oxon. OX8 8BR. Tel: 01993 891121. Fax: 01993 891686. 20-hour weekend seminar plus 80 hours of self-study. Monthly in London and other centres. £235 (concessions for students and unemployed).
TEFL TRAINING INTERNATIONAL, 3 Queensberry Place, South Kensington, London SW7 2DL. Freephone 0800 174031. Fax: 01491 411383. One day introductory workshop/taster day (one Saturday every month or so), £35. Grammar Awareness for TEFL (4 Friday evenings, 8 courses a year) and 6-week evening TEFL certificate (Monday and Wednesday evenings or Tuesday and Thursday evenings), £550.
UNIVERSITY OF ST. ANDREWS, English Language Teaching, Butts Wynd, St. Andrews, Fife KY16 9AL. Tel: 01334 462255. Fax: 01334 462270. E-mail: emgh@st-and.ac.uk. 30-hour introductory course 3 times a year. Also offer Trinity College Certificate.
WEST HERTS COLLEGE, Cassio Campus, Langley Road, Watford WD1 3RH. Tel: (01923) 812 049/812 055. Fax: (01923) 812 480. Introduction to Teaching English as a Foreign or Second Language runs in June each year. 4 evenings (7-9pm). From £50. College facilities.

WIGAN & LEIGH COLLEGE, PO Box 53, Parsons Walk, Wigan, Lancs. WN1 1RS. Tel: 01942 761563. Fax: 01942 761572. Introduction to TESOL over 4 weeks. Variable dates, £80. Also offer CELTA and DELTA.

Training Courses Abroad (Non-Cambridge/Non-Trinity)

Australia

AUSTRALIAN TESOL TRAINING CENTRE, Level 6, 530 Oxford Street (PO Box 82), Bondi Junction, NSW 2022. Tel: 2-9389 0249. Fax: 2-9389 7788. E-mail: gs@ace.edu.au. CELTA centre which offers several one-week intro courses throughout the year. A$395. Homestay accommodation can be arranged.

ENGLISH LANGUAGE AND LITERACY SERVICES (ELLS), Adelaide Institute of Training and Further Education (Government Department of Education, Training and Employment), 5th Floor, Renaissance Centre, 127 Rundle Mall, Adelaide, South Australia 5000. Tel: 8-8224 0922. Fax: 8-8232 1826. E-mail: kwatson@adel.tafe.sa.edu.au. Web-site: www.tafe.sa.edu.au/institutes/adelaide/ells/ tesolplus. Intensive 4-week Certificate in TESOL course (5 days a week). Part-time course (daytime or evenings over 3 months).

HOLMESGLEN LANGUAGE CENTRE, Holmesglen Institute of TAFE, PO Box 42, Chadstone, Victoria 3148. Tel: 3-9564 1820. Fax: 3-9564 1712. E-mail: larryf@holmesglen.vic.edu.au. 1-week Introductory Course in English Language Teaching offered and 1-week Refresher Course in English Language Teaching (on demand). One-day Professional Development Workshops for ESL Teachers (on demand). Highly trained and experienced staff with strong overseas knowledge. Modern facilities.

Austria

BUSINESS LANGUAGE CENTRE, Charles La Fond & Co. KEG, Trattnerhof 2, 1010 Vienna. Tel: 222-533 7001-0. Fax: 222-532 8521. London Chamber of Commerce (LCCI) Certificate for Teaching English for Business.

Canada

ATLANTIC OVERSEAS TEACHING INSTITUTE, 1106 Barrington St, Halifax, Nova Scotia B3H 2R2. Tel: 902-423-4767. Fax: 902-422-4724. E-mail: aoti@istar.ca. TEFL Certificate Programme includes placement assistance and ongoing follow-up. 3 formats available each month except December. Evenings over 2 weeks, one-week intensive (full-day sessions) or 5 consecutive Saturdays. C$550. Special weekly accommodation rates provided.

CANADIAN GLOBAL TESOL TRAINING INSTITUTE, PO Box 41081, Edmonton, Alberta, Canada T6J 6M7. Tel: (403) 438-5704. Fax: (403) 435-0918. E-mail: tesol@cdnglobalinst.com. Web-site: www.cdnglobalinst.com. 5 day, 45 hour intensive TESOL Certification course, in class or by correspondence worldwide. Inclusive prices are C$450 in Canada, US$450 in other countries. Other courses offered by correspondence include Teaching Business English (US$250), Teaching TOEFL Preparation (US$250) and Teaching Comprehensive Grammar (US$200). 50 courses per year in 20 cities across Canada. Accommodation can be arranged. Contacts with recruiters and language schools for employment.

LANGUAGES INTERNATIONAL (TORONTO) INC., 330 Bay Street, Suite 910, Toronto, Ontario M6H 2S8. Tel: (416) 361-2411. Fax: (416) 361-2403. E-mail: litoront@istar.ca. 4-week Introductory TESL Certificate course every 2 months. C$595. Homestay and other reasonably priced accommodation arranged near school; university residences available May-August. Refers graduates to recruiters and potential employers. Maintains current job listings. Also offer optional 100-hour practicum (to maximise student contact).

UNIVERSITY OF SASKATCHEWAN, Centre for Second Language Instruction, Extension Division, 326 Kirk Hall, Saskatoon, Saskatchewan S7N 0W0. Tel: (306) 966-5563. Fax: (306) 966-5590. E-mail: extcred@usask.ca. Certificate Program in Teaching English as a Second Language (CERTESL). Part-time distance study plus optional on-campus practicum. Total of 6 courses cost C$333 each.

Czech Republic

ITC INTERNATIONAL TEFL CERTIFICATE, PRAGUE, Spanielova 1292, 163 00 Prague 6. Tel/fax: (2) 301 9784. Voice-mail (2) 96 14 10 14. E-mail: info@itc-training.com. Web-site: www.itc-training.com. US information: San Francisco 415-544-0447. 4-week International TEFL Certificate course. US$1,500 includes registration, course manual, airport greeting, orientation, survival Czech lessons, guaranteed job placement for successful graduates, and lifetime job guidance. Lodging available in private room with shared bath for US$450.

VIA LINGUA, Azalková 12, 100 00 Prague 10. Tel/fax: (2) 758773. 4-week intensive TEFL courses offered year-round. £700 or US$1,100 with accommodation. Job guidance and placement service.

Egypt

AMERICAN UNIVERSITY IN CAIRO, PO Box 2511, Cairo. Tel: 2-357 6840. Fax: 2-355 7565. US enquiries to 420 Fifth Avenue, 3rd Floor, New York, NY 10018-2729 (212-730-8800/fax 212-730-1600/e-mail: aucegypt@aucnyo.edu). MA in Teaching English as a Foreign Language (MA/TEFL). Full-time students can complete the course in two years (fall and spring semester, plus optional summer). Tuition $5,150 per semester. Shared room is $1,320, and single room is $2,140. Programme tries to balance theory and practice. American-style education in an overseas setting. Informal help given with job search.

France

THE AMERICAN UNIVERSITY OF PARIS, 102 rue Saint-Dominique, 75007 Paris. Tel: 1-40 62 07 20. Fax: 1-40 62 07 17. E-mail: CE@aup.fr. Web-site: http://www.aup.fr. TESOL Certificate over 3 months from September (afternoons Monday-Thursday). Teaching practice Tuesday and Thursday evenings or Saturday mornings. FF21,350. University housing assistance possible.
WICE, 20 boulevard du Montparnasse, 75015 Paris. Tel: 1-45 66 75 50. Fax: 1-40 65 96 53. E-mail: wice@club-internet.fr. Web-site: http://www.wice.org. TEFL Certificate in conjunction with Rutgers State University, Newark Campus, New Jersey, USA. One month accelerated (full-time) courses in June and September. Part-time courses (October-May) with choice of morning, afternoon or evening sessions on Tuesdays and Thursdays. F8,300 accelerated and F9,300 year-long; both plus F350 membership fee for WICE. No accommodation.

Germany

MUNCHNER VOLKSHOCHSCHULE, Fachgebiet Englisch, Postfach 80 11 64, 81611 München. Fax: 0049 89 48006 2 52. 1-week Preliminary Certificate in TEFL. Once a year in September. DM270. Information can be sent from May preceding the course. Also offers CELTA.

Greece

CELT ATHENS, 77 Academias Street, 106 78 Athens. Tel/fax: 1-33 02 406. Introductory TEFL course (approx. 90 hours, full-time or part-time). £400. Also offer the Cambridge DELTA and DOTE.
INTERNATIONAL LANGUAGE CENTRE McLAREN, 35 Votsi str. 26221 Patras. Tel: (61) 278 542. Fax: 622 293. Teacher training courses, some for teachers whose first language is not English and some on the island of Kefalonia.
OMIROS TEACHER TRAINING CENTER, 52 Academias St, 10679 Athens. English language centres (see entry in chapter on Greece) which occasionally run introductory and specialised training courses for English teachers.
PROFILE, Professionals in Language & Education, A. Frantzi 4 and Kallirois, 11745 Athens, Greece. Tel: 1-922 2065. Fax: 1-924 1543. E-mail: profile-educinst@ath.forthnet.gr. Cambridge/RSA courses (COTE/DOTE) & in-house methodology training.

Hong Kong

THE BRITISH COUNCIL, 3 Supreme Court Road, Admiralty, Hong Kong. Tel: (852) 2913 5581. Fax: (852) 2913 5588. Certificate in Teaching English to Young Learners (CELTYL). Twice a year starting November and May. 3-day intensive followed by 8 or 9 weeks part-time. HK$19,600.

Hungary

NEW WORLD TEACHERS, 605 Market Street, Suite 800, San Francisco, CA 94105, USA. San Francisco training centre (see contact details and listing below) which offers 4-week TEFL Certificate course in Budapest. Courses also available in the US, Mexico and Thailand.

Indonesia

ITC INTERNATIONAL TEFL CERTIFICATE BALI, Jl. Kartini No. 83a, Denpassar, Bali, Indonesia. E-mail: info@itc-training.com. Web-site: www.itc-training.com. US information: 4-week International TEFL Certificate course. US$1,700 includes registration, course manual, airport greeting, orientation, and lifetime job guidance. Lodging available in private air-conditioned room for US$675.

Ireland

INTERNATIONAL T.E.F.L. COLLEGE OF IRELAND, 6 Merrion Square North, Dublin, 2. Tel/fax: 1-280 7001. 100 or 120 hour TEFL training courses. 4-6 weeks tuition (daytime and evenings). Offered monthly throughout the year. £200-£300. Accommodation available on request. Teaching practice and placement.

UNIVERSITY OF LIMERICK, Plassey Technological Park, Limerick. Tel: 61-202700. Fax: 61-334850. E-mail: Admissions@ul.ie. Internet: http://www.ul.ie/lcs/TEFL. Graduate Diploma in TEFL. One-year from September. Also offers MA in TEFL.

The following centres offer the 100+ hour International Certificate in TEFL validated by the Irish Association for Teacher Training in TEFL (ATT, PO Box 3384, Dublin 6):

Bluefeather School, Montpelier House, 35 Montpelier Parade, Monkstown, Co. Dublin.

Excel International Language Institute, IDA Enterprise Centre, North Mall, Cork.

TEFL Training Institute, 38 Harrington St, Dublin 8.

The Irish equivalent of ARELS, the Recognised English Language Schools Association (RELSA) of Ireland, promotes its own Preparatory Certificate in Teaching English as a Foreign Language, which involves a 70-hour practical course. A list of RELSA schools may be requested from 17 Camden St Lower, Dublin 2 (1-475 3122/fax 1-475 3088). The following member schools offer the course:

Centre for English Studies, 31 Dame St, Dublin 2. Tel: 1-671 4233. Fax: 1-671 4425.

Dublin School of English, 10-12 Westmoreland St, Dublin 2. Tel: 1-677 3322. Fax: 1-679 5454/671 8451. E-mail: Admin@dse.ie

Emerald Cultural Institute, 10 Palmerston Park, Rathgar, Dublin 6.

English Language Institute, 99 St. Stephen's Green, Dublin 2. Tel: 1-475 2965. Fax: 1-475 2967.

Galway Language Centre, The Bridge Mills, Galway. Tel: 91-566468. Fax: 91-564122.

Language & Activity Holidays, 31-32 St. Patrick's Quay, Cork.

Language Centre of Ireland, 45 Kildare St, Dublin 2. Tel: 1-671 6266. Fax: 1-671 6430.

Language & Leisure Ireland, 1 Clarinda Park North, Dun Laoghaire, Co. Dublin.

Westlingua Language School, Cathedral Buildings, Middle Street, Galway. Tel: 91-568188.

Italy

BRITISH INSTITUTES, Monza, Italy. Fax: 039-325056. E-mail: british@askesis.it. Organises short methodology course in the spring with a view to recruiting teachers for its network of language institutes in Italy.

Mexico

ITC INTERNATIONAL TEFL CERTIFICATE PUERTO VALLARTA, c/o 655 Powell St, Suite 505, San Francisco, CA 94108, USA. Tel: (415) 544-0447. Fax: (530) 895-0998. E-mail: info@itc-training.com. Web-site: www.itc-training.com. 4-week International TEFL Certificate course. US$1,700 includes registration, course manual, airport greeting, orientation, and lifetime job guidance. Lodging available in shared room in air-conditioned condominium for US$500.

NEW WORLD TEACHERS, 605 Market Street, Suite 800, San Francisco, CA 94105. San Francisco training centre (see contact details and listing below) which offers 4-week TEFL Certificate course at the University of Guadalajara in Puerto Vallarta. Courses also available in the US, Hungary and Thailand.

WORLDWIDE TEACHERS DEVELOPMENT INSTITUTE, 266 Beacon Street, Boston, MA 02116. Tel: 800-875-5564. Fax: (617) 262-0308. E-mail: bostontefl@aol.com. Intensive TEFL and Cert.TBE (Business English) certificate programs offered in Guadalajara, Mexico, or via Distance Learning. Courses also offered in Boston (see USA).

New Zealand

DOMINION ENGLISH SCHOOLS, 47 Customs St (PO Box 4217), Auckland. Tel: 9-377-3280. Fax: 377-3473. E-mail: english@dominion.school.nz. 3 times a year. NZ$2,750. Homestay accommodation can be arranged for NZ$190 per week, an apartment for NZ$260.

Portugal

INTERNATIONAL HOUSE LISBON, Rua Marquês Sá da Bandeira 16, 1050 Lisbon. Tel: 1-315 14 96. Fax: 1-353 00 81. E-mail: ihlisbon@mail.telepac.pt. Cambridge/RSA centre which offers 2-week introductory course to EFL (70,000 escudos), 1-week Teaching Business English (40,000 escudos) and 2-week Young Learners Extension Course (105,000 escudos).

Singapore

THE BRITISH COUNCIL, 236A Holland Road, Singapore. Tel: 463 5525. Fax: 463 2970. Specific introductory Courses for teaching adults, young learners and home tuition. Intro courses are part-time (2 2-hour sessions per week for 5 weeks, 4 times a year). £200 approx. Also offer part-time CELTA.

Spain

THE BRITISH LANGUAGE CENTRE, Calle Bravo Murillo 377-2°, 28020 Madrid. Tel: 91-733 07 39/733 04 08. Fax: 91-314 50 09. Cambridge/RSA centre which offers Pre-Diploma course (32 hours over 8 weeks) in the autumn. 40,000 pesetas.
ITC INTERNATIONAL TEFL CERTIFICATE BARCELONA, c/o Vahle, c/alta de San Pedro 59 bis 3°1°, 08003 Barcelona. Tel/fax: (2) 301 9784. Voice-mail (2) 96 14 10 14. E-mail: info@itc-training.com. Web-site: www.itc-training.com. US information: San Francisco 415-544-0447. 4-week International TEFL Certificate course. US$1,500 includes registration, course manual, airport greeting, orientation, and lifetime job guidance. Lodging available in private room with shared bath for US$600.

Thailand

NEW WORLD TEACHERS, 605 Market Street, Suite 800, San Francisco, CA 94105, USA. San Francisco training centre (see contact details and listing below) which offers 4-week TEFL Certificate course in Phuket. Courses also available in the US, Mexico and Hungary.

Turkey

INTERNATIONAL TRAINING INSTITUTE, Istiklal Cad., Kallavi Sokak 7-9, Galatasaray, Istanbul. Tel: 212-243 2888. Fax: 212-245 3163. E-mail: tomitithom@arti.net.tr. CELTA centre which runs Introduction to TEFL and CELTYL courses. Accommodation can be arranged in shared flat.

USA

AMERICAN ENGLISH PROGRAMS OF NEW ENGLAND, 17 South Street, Northampton, MA 01060. Tel/fax: (413) 582-1812, toll free 1-800-665-2829 (in USA only). E-mail: info@teflcertificate.com Web-site: www.teflcertificate.com. Intensive 4-week TEFL Certificate courses (140 hours) offered monthly. Optional 1 week add-on certificate in Teaching Business English. Tuition $1800 includes texts and lifetime job assistance. Homestay accommodation available for $100 per week.
HAMLINE UNIVERSITY, TEFL Certificate Program, Graduate School of Education, 1536 Hewitt Avenue, St. Paul, MN 55104, USA. Tel: (651) 523-2853/800-888-2182. Fax: (651) 523-2489. E-mail: bparrish@gw.hamline.edu. Three intensive one-month courses per year (July, August and April). One 10-week semi-intensive (January-March) and 1 evening extensive (September-March). Prices $1,970-$2,295.

On-campus housing available except in August (approximately $600 per month including meals). Focus is on hands-on learning. Ongoing career counselling provided. Graduate credit granted.

LADO INTERNATIONAL COLLEGE, 2233 Wisconsin Avenue NW, Washington, DC 20007, USA. Fax: (202) 337-1118. E-mail: TeacherTraining@ladoent.com. Website: www.LADO.com/Teacher/Home_T.htm. Lado Teaching Certificate Program based on Dr. Robert Lado's own Total Approach Method for teaching English communication skills. Full-time (8 hours per day) for 4 weeks, offered monthly. $1,750. Compulsory 20 hours of teaching practice on-site. Shared accommodation can be arranged. Has links with schools operating in Japan and recruitment companies in Korea.

NEW WORLD TEACHERS, 605 Market Street, Suite 800, San Francisco, CA 94105. Tel (within the USA): 800-644-5424. Tel (from overseas): 415-546-5200. Fax: 415-546-4196. E-mail: teacherssf@aol.com. Web-site: www.goteach.com. Intensive TEFL Certificate courses (4 weeks, $2,200) or part-time (10 weeks, ($1,950) offered year-round. Courses emphasise teaching American English. Specialised workshops on teaching EFL to young learners also available. Accommodation in the school's own guest house in San Francisco. Courses also available in Mexico, Hungary and Thailand. Extensive job placement assistance including personal counselling, database of international employers and internet access to network of TEFL graduates around the world.

SCHOOL OF TEACHING ENGLISH AS A SECOND LANGUAGE, Seattle University School of Education, 2601 NW 56th Street, Seattle, WA 98107. Tel: 206-781-8607. Fax: 206-781-8922. E-mail: hasegawa@seattleu.edu. Web-site: www.seattleu.edu/soe/stesl. 4 week intensive course offered monthly. Credits from Seattle University can be graduate-status. Applicants must have BA though waivers are possible. $2,160. Housing, employment information and counselling.

TRANSWORLD SCHOOLS, 701 Sutter Street, 2nd Floor, San Francisco, CA 94109. Tel: 415-928-2835. Fax: 415-928-0261. E-mail: transwd@aol.com. Web-site: www.transworldschools.com. Certificate in Teaching English as a Foreign Language, offered full-time (3 weeks) or part-time (9 weeks), $1,400. Also offer Advanced Certificate TEFL (1 week full-time or 3 weeks part-time, $600) and Certificate in Teaching Business English (2 weeks full-time, 6 weeks part-time), $1,700. Combined CTEFL and Advanced CTEFL: 4 weeks intensive or 12 weeks part-time, $1,600. Accommodation within 5 minutes walk of school in downtown San Francisco; $170 per week, $260 with meals. Job placement assistance given throughout course and lifetime access to job files. Course includes Computer Assisted Language Learning, video use, teaching children, teaching Business English and ESP, Cambridge Proficiency and TOEFL. Facilities include multi-media computer lab with ESL software library.

UNIVERSITY OF CALIFORNIA EXTENSION, PO Box 6050, Irvine, CA 92716-6050. Tel: 714-824-8196. Fax: 714-824-8065. Accelerated Certificate in TESL offered over 5 months. Tuition from $4,000.

WORLDWIDE TEACHERS DEVELOPMENT INSTITUTE, 266 Beacon Street, Boston, MA 02116. Tel: 800-875-5564. Fax: (617) 262-0308. E-mail: bostontefl@aol.com. Intensive TEFL and Cert. TBE (Business English) certificate programs offered in Boston or via Distance Learning. Harvard University Club or other accommodation. (PDP) Mass. Dept. of Education. Course also offered in Guadalajara (see Mexico).

Finding a job

Teaching jobs are either fixed up from home or sought out on location. Having a job arranged before departure obviously removes much of the uncertainty and anxiety of leaving home for an extended period. It also allows the possibility of preparing in appropriate ways: sorting out the right visa, researching the course books in use, etc. Others prefer to meet their employer and inspect the school before signing a contract. It is always an advantage to meet other teachers and learn about the TEFL scene in that particular place firsthand before committing yourself, rather than accepting a job in complete ignorance of the prevailing conditions. But of course this is not always feasible.

Employers normally choose their staff several months before they are needed, so most schools advertise between April and July for jobs starting in September. If you want to fix up a job in person, you will either have to go on a reconnaisance mission well in advance of your proposed starting date or take your chances of finding a last-minute vacancy.

There are three ways of fixing up a teaching job in advance: by answering an advertisement, using a recruitment agency (which includes the large international English teaching organisations like International House) or conducting a speculative job search, i.e. making contact by e-mail or letter with all the schools whose addresses you can find in books, lists or on the internet.

ADVERTISEMENTS

Luckily for the job-seeking teacher in the UK, two publications have a virtual monopoly on TEFL adverts. The two places to look are the Classified Adverts of the *Education Guardian* every Tuesday and the *Times Educational Supplement* published on Fridays but available in newsagents throughout the week. Outside the peak recruiting time (Easter to August), advertisements for TEFL training courses outnumber actual job vacancies but it is always worth having a look.

The monthly *EL Gazette* is a good source of news and developments in the ELT industry for all interested individuals, though it is pitched at the professional end of the market. Single issues of the journal cost £2.20/$5.50 while an annual subscription costs £25.50 (UK), £30 (Europe) and £34.50/US$75 worldwide. Contact *EL Gazette,* Dilke House, 1 Malet St. Bloomsbury, London WC1E 7JN (0171-255 1969) or in the US: PO Box 61202, Oklahoma City, OK 73146 (fax 405-557-2538).

EL Prospects is the monthly employment supplement which is sent free to *EL Gazette* subscribers. It can also be subscribed to separately; the current rate is £9.95 for six issues/US$9.95 for four. Each issue provides the number of teaching positions by region, e.g. 99 positions in the Pacific Rim, 3 in South America, and so on. Quite a high percentage of the listings are with VSO and the British Council, and many also provide only an e-mail address. The e-mail address of the journal is elprospects@worldnet.att.net.

Relevant adverts occasionally appear in other places such as *Overseas Jobs Express,* the *Guardian Weekly, The Times* (on Wednesdays), the *Graduate Post,* etc. but these are insignificant in comparison.

The best source of job ads for qualified TEFL teachers is TESOL's *Placement Bulletin.* The magazine includes ESL/EFL job listings and articles about employment in ESOL. A subscription is US$35 by e-mail or $30 by regular mail and is available from TESOL (Teachers of English to Speakers of Other Languages, Inc.), 1600 Cameron St, Suite 300, Alexandria, VA 22314 (703-836-0774/fax 703-836-7864; e-mail: tesol@tesol.edu/Web-site: http://www.tesol.edu).

Another American publication in the field of overseas education is *The International Educator* (PO Box 513, Cummaquid, MA 02637, USA; and 102A Pope's Lane, London W5 4NS; 0181-840 2587/e-mail: tie@capecod.net/www.tieonline.com). It concentrates on jobs in international English-medium schools, most of which follow an American curriculum, British curriculum or the International Baccalaureate (IB). The schools which advertise in *TIE* mainly employ qualified primary and secondary teachers of all subjects. The EFL/ESL jobs that are advertised are normally open to EFL teachers with experience of teaching children and not just adults. The journal is published four times a year (October, December, February and April) plus a Jobs Only Supplement is produced in June. An annual subscription costs £23 ($30 for residents of the US & Canada), while membership which includes various extras (discounts, travel insurance, etc.) costs £36/$50.

Yet another publication of interest to international job seekers is the *International Employment Gazette* (423 Townes Street, Greenville, SC 29601, USA; 1-800-882-9188) which is published every two weeks and contains details of ELT vacancies and recruitment organisations in North America. A three-month subscription costs $35 in the US ($45 foreign).

Various newsletters and publications contain lists of international schools which normally do not relate to actual vacancies. Given that any good library (public or careers) should have a copy of one of the Directories of International Schools (like the ones available from ECIS in the UK or ISIS in Princeton), it may be superfluous to purchase separate lists.

Education Information Services (EIS) (PO Box 620662, Newton, MA 02162-0662; 781-433-0125/fax: 781-237-2842) publishes every six weeks a list of about 150 openings in international and American schools of interest primarily to US-certified teachers. They publish lists with names and addresses of American overseas and international schools in all countries of the world. They are also building up lists of the leading language schools in many countries which hire EFL teachers.

Other sources of addresses of mainstream schools abroad (as opposed to language schools) include the *Bulletin of Overseas Teaching Opportunities* which costs $42 per year (Oveseas Academic Opportunities, 72 Franklin Ave, Ocean Grove, NJ 07756; tel/fax 732-774-1040). It lists about 30 vacancies each month, a few of which hire EFL teachers. Country-by-country lists of international and US curriculum schools are available from Friends of World Teaching, PO Box 121049, San Diego, CA 92112-1049; 619-224-2365 ($20 for three countries).

The internet offers an increasingly useful medium for EFL recruiters and teachers alike. For schools, a web-site offers a means of publicity and also an international advertising medium for reaching potential teaching staff. It is far quicker and cheaper for schools in, say, Thailand, Ecuador or Russia to post vacancy notices on the internet than it would be to place an advert in a foreign newspaper. Teachers looking for employment can use search engines to look for all pages with references to EFL, English language schools and recruitment. CVs can be e-mailed quickly and cheaply to advertising schools, who can then use e-mail themselves to chase up references. This presupposes a degree of IT awareness and access but it is certainly a useful supplement to traditional jobsearch methods. Already there are some schools which advertise solely on the internet. One site which is frequently recommended is Dave Sperling's ESL Café http://wwwpacificnet/-sperling/jobcenter.html. Relevant web sites are mentioned throughout this book.

Interpreting Adverts

Jobs are listed year round, though schools which advertise in February or October are often advertising a very urgent vacancy, e.g. 'to start immediately, good salary, air fares, accommodation'—but these are exceptional.

Almost all adverts specify TEFL training/experience as a minimum requirement. But there is always a chance that this is merely rhetorical. Those who lack such a background should not feel defeated before they begin, since a TEFL background may turn out not to be essential. A carefully crafted CV and enthusiastic personality (not to mention a shortage of suitable applicants) could well persuade a school that they don't really have to insist on a Cambridge or Trinity Certificate after all.

The *Times Educational Supplement* (or *TES*) includes two relevant headings. 'Overseas Appointments' primarily (but not exclusively) lists jobs in English-medium schools, while 'English as a Foreign Language' is for TEFL jobs outside Britain. Although there is no guarantee that schools which use the hallowed pages of the British educational press for their siren songs of employment will be reasonable employers, most are established schools which go to the trouble and expense of recruiting abroad.

Advertisements will often include a contact name or company in the UK to which enquiries should be addressed for posts abroad. This may be a TEFL training centre or a language school in the UK which is in contact with language schools abroad or it may just be an ex-employee who has agreed to do some recruitment for a commission fee. When discussing terms and conditions with an agent, bear in mind that the agent may be more interested in collecting his commission for finding someone to fill the vacancy than he is in conveying all the facts.

Occasionally cases crop up of misleading or even fraudulent ads. The most recent case resulted in a headline in the *Times Educational Supplement*: 'Thousands conned by Botswana job hoax.' A conman placed adverts for teaching jobs in a fictitious school in Botswana, sent a letter of acceptance to all who applied and a request for $100 as a visa processing fee. Even if this sort of bare-faced fraud is rare, it is best to be skeptical when interpreting ads, including on the internet where promises of earning huge salaries are usually pie-in-the-sky.

Apart from newspapers, there are a few other places where vacancies abroad might be mentioned. ELT training centres often have numerous links with foreign schools and may have a notice board with posted vacancies (as in the case of International House in Piccadilly). Unless you are a trainee at the relevant centre, it will probably be tricky consulting such a notice board, but a cooperative secretary might not mind a *potential* trainee consulting the board. University careers offices may also have contacts with schools abroad to which their graduates have gone in the past, so if you have a university connection, it is worth making enquiries.

THE BRITISH COUNCIL

Among the heaviest advertisers of all is the largest ELT (English language teaching) employer in the world. The British Council represents the elite end of the English language teaching industry, running its own Teaching Centres (formerly known as Direct Teaching Outlets or DTOs) in 56 countries. These offer the highest quality language teaching available in those countries and employ the best qualified teachers, so it is important to understand that the British Council will not welcome applications from very inexperienced or unqualified teachers. The British Council is a very professional organisation and jobs with them tend to come with attractive terms and conditions.

Council offices abroad are normally well-informed about opportunities for English language teaching locally. Most maintain a list of private language schools (while making it clear that inclusion does not confer recognition), which is often a useful starting point for a job search. Whether they will send it in advance or give a copy to enquirers is at the discretion of staff. Some British Council offices even publish informal leaflets about teaching possibilities.

The Council publishes an *Address Book* of its offices worldwide which is updated quarterly. A copy can be requested from the Council's Information Centre (Bridgewater House, 58 Whitworth St, Manchester M1 6BB; 0161-957 7755). While researching the current edition of this book, each of these offices was written to and any relevant responses have been included in the country chapters.

The charter of the British Council defines its aims as 'to promote Britain abroad, providing access to British ideas, talents and experience in education and training, books and periodicals, the English language, the arts, the sciences and technology.' It is non-profit-making and works non-politically in more than 100 countries. It employs about 7,500 staff in all, divided between Britain and abroad, a good percentage of whom are involved with the teaching of the English language in some capacity. Other work which the Council carries out includes the running of libraries, the organisation of cultural tours and exchanges, etc. But language teaching and teacher recruitment remain one of its central concerns.

A useful starting place for qualified teachers is to request their recruitment literature which is available free of charge from the Teaching Centre Recruitment Unit, formerly CMDT or Central Management of Direct Teaching (10 Spring Gardens, London SW1A 2BN; 0171-389 4931/www.britcoun.org/english).

Structure of the British Council

The British Council is a large and complex institution with two headquarters: one at 10 Spring Gardens London SW1A 2BN (0171-930 8466) and the other at Bridgewater House, 58 Whitworth St, Manchester M1 6BB (0161-957 7000). Telephone callers who do not know exactly which department they need should contact the Council's Information Unit in Manchester (0161-957 7755).

Here is a layman's guide to the sections and departments of possible interest to prospective teachers:

Educational Enterprises, 10 Spring Gardens, London SW1A 2BN. Tel: 0171-389 4931. Fax: 0171-389 4140. E-mail: calice.miller@britcoun.org.
Educational Enterprises is the new name for the department which oversees the Council's 127 Teaching Centres including 97 main centres around the world. The recruitment unit is responsible for the bulk of the hiring of contract teachers. Each Teaching Centre employs between 3 and 200 teachers, many of whom are qualified to Diploma level, though some centres will consider applications from people with a certificate level qualification and experience.

Teaching Centres recruit both through London and locally. Qualified teachers who are planning to move to a location where there is a British Council Teaching Centre would be welcome to apply direct to the Teaching Centre Manager for information on opportunities for local contracts. At the time of writing, the Teaching Centre Recruitment Unit anticipated hiring about 250 teachers (more than twice as many as four years ago) in the coming year, as well as 25 middle managers and 30 managers, many of whose posts are filled through internal transfer. The Recruitment Unit regularly advertises in the national press. It also has its own web-site with a vacancy list www.britcoun.org/english/engvacs.htm. They especially welcome applications from teachers with experience or an interest in specialist areas such as Young Learners, Business English, skills through English, IT/CALL, etc.

Contracts are normally for two years and renewable. Recruitment goes on year round though the majority of vacancies are still for September/October starts. Interviews for these posts are held in London between April and August. Although terms and conditions vary from centre to centre, the terms of employment with the British Council are very favourable. Teachers recruited through Educational Enterprises usually have their air fares paid, an allowance for shipping their belongings and an attractive salary package. Many teachers value all the intangible benefits such as the security of working for an established institution, and encouragement of professional development with possible perks such as receiving a subsidy to study for a Diploma qualification or other training grants. Once you have secured one job with the Council, it is possible to move to other jobs in other places, since the Council regularly notifies its network of all vacancies. Last year about a third of British Council teaching posts were filled through internal transfer.

Overseas Appointments Service/OAS, Bridgewater House, 58 Whitworth St, Manchester M1 6BB; 0161-957 7384.
The Overseas Appointments Service recruits personnel for posts abroad in universities, teacher training colleges, ministries of education, etc. The majority of educational vacancies are related to ELT but by no means all, since the Council is often asked to provide technical experts for educational establishments abroad.

A substantial part of OAS's work is on behalf of the UK government's Department for International Development (Abercrombie House, Eaglesham Road, East Kilbride, Glasgow G75 8EA) formerly the Overseas Development Administration (ODA). Large display adverts bearing both logos can occasionally be seen in the *Times Educational Supplement* and the *Guardian*. Anyone who is sufficiently qualified to be eligible for these positions can submit an application which will be kept active for a calendar year.

Information Centre, Bridgewater House, 58 Whitworth St, Manchester M1 6BB; 0161-957 7755/fax 0161-957 7762.
The Information Centre distributes two information packs to members of the public: *How to Become a Teacher of English as a Foreign Language* which includes lists of TEFL courses, and *British Council Accredited English Language Schools in the UK.*

RECRUITMENT ORGANISATIONS

Major providers of ELT and teacher placement organisations of various kinds may be able to assist prospective teachers in English-speaking countries to find teaching jobs. Some are international educational foundations; some are voluntary organisations like VSO or charities; some are major chains of commercial language schools; and others are small agencies which serve as intermediaries between independent language schools abroad and prospective teachers. The companies and organisations listed in this chapter have been assigned to the following categories (though there is some blurring of distinctions): International ELT Organisations (including the major language school chains); Commercial Recruitment Agencies; Voluntary and Religious Organisations (including gap year placements), North American Organisations which cater primarily (though not exclusively) to citizens of the US and Canada; and, finally, Placement Services for British and American state-qualified teachers. Note that agencies and organisations which operate only in one country or one region are described in the country chapters in the second part of this book.

It is hardly worthwhile for a family-run language school in northern Greece or southern Brazil to pay the high costs which most agencies charge schools just to obtain one or two native speaker teachers. Vacancies that are filled with the help of agencies and recruitment consultants tend to be at the elite end of the ELT market. Jobs advertised by agencies are usually for specialised or high level positions, for example in corporations with in-house EFL programmes or foreign governments.

Agencies make their money by charging client employers; the service to teachers is normally free of charge. By law in the UK, no fee can be charged to job-seekers either before or after placement, except if a package of services is sold alongside (e.g. insurance, visas, travel, etc.) Note that different rules apply in other countries, so that placement fees are the norm in the US. Some of the best recruitment organisations to deal with are ones which specialise in a single country, such as English Educational Services in Madrid or Cambridge Teachers Recruitment in Athens (see Spain and Greece chapters). They tend to have more first-hand knowledge of their client schools.

On the other hand, the use of an intermediary by foreign language institutes is no guarantee of anything. Particularly in the American context, small independent recruiters are sometimes trying to fill vacancies that no one in the country who is familiar with the employer would deign to fill. As the American Rusty Holmes said of his employer in Taiwan, 'The school was so bad it had to recruit from America.' If you are in any doubt about the reliability of an agency or the client he/she represents, it is a sensible precaution to ask for the name of one or more previous teachers whom you can ask for a first-hand account. It is a bad sign if the agency is unable or reluctant to oblige.

The hiring of teachers for chain schools abroad is done either at a local level (so direct applications are always worthwhile) or centrally, especially if the affiliated school has trouble filling vacancies on its own.

One way in which recruitment agencies work is to create a database of teachers' CVs and to try to match these with suitable vacancies as they occur. In order to be registered with such an agency it is normally essential to have a relevant qualification, often at least the Cambridge/RSA or Trinity Certificate. When applicants outnumber vacancies, it is not surprising to hear that most agencies are unwilling to register non-nationals without superior qualifications. Recruitment agencies in the UK may find it difficult to cope with applications from the US since it is difficult to translate qualifications; one mentioned that because of anti-discrimination legislation, American applicants do not always mention their age or sex, which most language school directors want to know.

Smaller agencies may have fewer vacancies on their books but they can often offer a more personal service. It is a legal requirement for agencies to obtain references from any client to which it wants to send teachers. A good agency will provide a full briefing and information pack on the school in particular and the country in general, and will make sure that the contract offered is a reasonable one. If a job doesn't work out, the agency should provide a back-up service and make itself available to sort out misunderstandings and (if appropriate) offer an alternative placement. Marisa Wharton describes the support an agency should provide when things go wrong:

> *When our employers in the Czech Republic broke the contract and behaved like mafiosos, IPG were very helpful. They found my husband a different job in Poland, so at least one of us has been placed. At the moment they are trying to sort out some sort of compensation for us.*

International ELT Organisations

The Bell Educational Trust in Cambridge, occasionally recruits teachers for ELT posts in its own and associated schools in Thailand, Poland, Hungary and the Czech Republic. It hires only those with advanced qualifications and experience, particularly of teaching younger learners.

Bénédict Schools, PO Box 270 (rue des Terreaux 29), 1000 Lausanne 9, Switzerland. Tel: (21) 323 66 55. Fax: (21) 311 02 29. Have over 80 business and language schools in Europe, Africa, South and North America on a franchise basis. Each school hires its own TEFL-qualified teachers, but some also run in-house training courses. A list of addresses is available from the Swiss headquarters. Bénédict Schools work in association with International Language Academies which have centres in 24 cities in the UK, two in the USA and two in New Zealand, and are related to Nord Anglia listed below.

Berlitz UK, 9-13 Grosvenor Street, London W1A 3BZ. Tel: 0171-915 0909. Fax: 0171-915 0222. Berlitz Inc., 400 Alexander Park Drive, Princeton, NJ 08540-6306, USA. Tel: (609) 514-9650. Fax: (609) 514-9672. Berlitz is one of the biggest language training organisations in the world with about 330 centres in 33 countries. It is also one of the oldest; Berlitz celebrated its 120th anniversary in 1998. The company's core business is language and cultural training, and teacher vacancies occur most often in Latin America, Spain, Italy, Germany, France and Korea. All Berlitz teachers are native-fluent speakers and university graduates who are trained in the 'Berlitz Method,' a direct teaching approach that does not rely on translation. Berlitz is known for supervising their teachers' techniques very closely, and deviation from the method is not permitted. When Berlitz has urgent vacancies to fill, usually in Spain and Italy, it places an advertisement in British newspapers inviting any interested university graduates to attend interviews in London, Manchester, Edinburgh or Dublin. Normally, however, Berlitz schools abroad employ teachers directly, usually after they have completed a two-week training course.

British Council—see section above.

Central Bureau for Educational Visits & Exchanges, 10 Spring Gardens, London SW1A 2BN. Tel: 0171-389 4004. Fax: 0171-389 4426. Also offices in Scotland (3 Bruntsfield Crescent, Edinburgh EH10 4HD) and Northern Ireland (1 Chlorine Gardens, Belfast BT9 5DJ). Administer various exchange programmes for certified teachers and language assistant placements to help local teachers of English in many countries of the world from France to Venezuela. Applicants must be aged 20-30 with at least two years of university level education normally in the language of the destination country. In some countries (especially in Latin America and Eastern Europe) posts are of particular interest to graduates interested in a career in TEFL.

C*f*BT Education Services

C*f*BT Education Services is a leading supplier of educational resource management and consultancy services world-wide. We manage a range of EFL/EAP/Computer/Subject teaching opportunities every year in established and new projects overseas, including Brunei, Oman and Turkey.

C*f*BT
Education Services

Experience guidelines and qualifications will vary, but there is a minimum qualification of first degree, RSA/Trinity Certificate and 2 years teaching experience. In some cases a PGCE or Masters in Applied Linguistics/Language is required.

Consultancy: individuals with experience beyond teaching e.g. teacher training, materials writing, curriculum development may be considered for short or long term positions on aid-funded projects.

International Database: individuals are encouraged to register with C*f*BT for future posts.

Details of the minimum requirements for any current projects are available. Please submit your Curriculum Vitae in digital format on 3.5 disc/email in Word or Wordperfect format/or through out website to:

C*f*BT Education Services, International Recruitment, 1 The Chambers, East Street, Reading, RG1 4JD, Fax: (+44) (0)118 952 3924, E-mail: Intrecruit@cfbt-hq.org.uk http://www.cfbt.com

Country-by-country details are available from the Assistants Department (0171-389 4169/fax 0171-389 4594). Application forms are available from October; the deadline is December of the preceding year.

CfBT Education Services, 1 The Chambers, East Street, Reading RG1 4JD. Tel: (0118) 952 3900. Fax: (0118) 952 3924. E-mail: intrecruit@cfbt-hq.org.uk. Web-site: www.cfbt.com. Recruits and manages EFL/EAP/ESP/Primary/Secondary teachers and instructors for its own projects and a diverse range of public and private sector clients overseas and in the UK. In addition they recruit educational consultants for aid work in developing countries with regional bases in Africa, South East Asia, Eastern Europe, the Gulf and the Caribbean.

Council on International Educational Exchange, 52 Poland St, London W1V 4JQ. Tel: 0171-478 2000. Fax: 0171-734 7322. E-mail: InfoUK@ciee.org. Web-site: www.ciee.org. Council administers the Japan Exchange & Teaching (JET) and Teach in China Programmes (see respective chapters). Have occasional smaller scale programmes, too, for example placing teachers of business English in the Lebanon. The US headquarters are listed under *Opportunities for North Americans* below.

EF English First, Teacher Recruitment, Kensington Cloisters, 5 Kensington Church Street, London W8 4LD. Tel: 0171-878 3500. Fax: 0171-795 6635/6615. Web-site: http://www.ef.com/EFWeb/EF1/English_First.htm. EF has schools in South and Central America (Ecuador, Colombia and Mexico), Eastern Europe (Lithuania, Poland and Russia), Asia (China and Indonesia) and Morocco. Recruitment of up to 400 teachers from all English-speaking countries takes place year-round. TEFL/TESL and 1-2 years' experience are minimum requirements.

ELS Language Centers, International Division, 5761 Buckingham Parkway, Culver City, CA 90230-6583, USA. Tel: (310) 642-0988. Fax: (310) 649-5231. E-mail: international@els.com. Web-site: http://www.els.com. ELS operate schools in over 50 locations worldwide. The International Division is a clearinghouse of recruitment for ELS's overseas franchises in a range of countries in Latin America, Asia and the Middle East (but not Europe). The minimum requirements to recommend an applicant for overseas placement are a bachelor's degree in any subject and completion of a 130-hour TEFL or TESL certificate programme. Applicants should submit a resumé, cover letter and copies of two letters of recommendation to the above address, marked for the attention of Overseas Recruitment.

Note that ELS is represented in London at 3 Charing Cross Road, London WC2H 0HA. The UK Recruitment Officer is particularly active in recruiting teachers for ELS-affiliated schools in Korea (see chapter). New ELS Language Centers are scheduled to open in China and the Middle East in the coming year (see chapter on the Middle East for regional details).

ELT Banbury, 49 Oxford Road, Banbury, Oxon. OX16 9AH. Tel: (01295) 263480/ 263502. Fax: (01295) 271658. E-mail: elt_banbury@compuserve.com. Maintains Teacher Directory for worldwide recruitment. CELTA or Trinity Certificate is minimum requirement. Recruits for its own centres in 14 countries (Europe, Far East and Middle East) and on behalf of other institutions.

English Worldwide, The Italian Building, Dockhead, London SE1 2BS. Tel: 0171-252 1402. Fax: 0171-231 8002. E-mail: info.eww@pop3.hiway.co.uk. This specialist educational recruitment agency founded in 1984 places EFL teachers in posts in Europe, the Middle East, Latin America and the Far East. Also places qualified primary and secondary teachers in international schools worldwide. Maintains a permanent database of CVs. EFL applicants must have at least a Cambridge/RSA or Trinity Certificate. EWW has offices in Milan and Oman as well.

ILC (International Language Centres), International House, White Rock, Hastings, East Sussex TN34 1JY. Tel: (01424) 435491. Fax: (01424) 720102. E-mail: ilc@compuserve.com. Web-site: http://www.ilcgroup.com. Although ILC Recruitment no longer operates, ILC does recruit for vacancies within the ILC Group (which has associated schools in France, Czech Republic, the Middle East and Japan). It is most active in recruiting teachers for its oil company contract work in Kuwait and for its vacation courses in 30 locations, mostly in Britain and Ireland.

inlingua Teacher Training & Recruitment, Rodney Lodge, Rodney Road, Cheltenham, Glos. GL50 1JF. Tel: 01242 253171. Fax: 01242 253181. E-mail: recruitment@inlingua-cheltenham.co.uk.   Internet   http://www.inlingua-cheltenham.co.uk. Has more than 300 centres worldwide (operating as separate businesses) for which it recruits over 200 teachers annually. The majority are for schools in Spain, Italy, Germany, Russia, Poland, Turkey and Singapore. Opportunities also exist in France, Korea, Thailand, Indonesia, Venezuela and other destinations. The minimum requirement is a Trinity Certificate in TESOL or a CELTA. Interested applicants should send in a CV. (Note that inlingua offer the Trinity Certificate course; see *Training*).

International Certificate Conference (ICC), Secretariat, Hansaallee 150, D-60320 Frankfurt, Germany. Tel: (69) 56 02 01 66. Fax: (69) 56 01 01 68. E-mail: icc_europe@csi.com. Umbrella organisation for 13 adult education associations (e.g. *Volkshochschulen* or folk high schools) cooperating on the learning and teaching of foreign languages in Europe. Can provide enquirers with a list of member organisations and contact names.

International House, 106 Piccadilly, London W1V 9FL. Tel: 0171-491 2598. Fax: 0171-491 0959. E-mail: ih_staffunit@compuserve.com IH is the largest independent British-based organisation for teaching English, with 110 schools in 30 countries. Through the Staffing Unit, IH recruits more than 350 teachers and senior people for its schools overseas. The minimum requirement is the Cambridge/RSA CELTA. Interviews are held in London. Teachers sign contracts before departure and travel expenses to the destination are paid. On arrival teachers have an orientation period before starting teaching. All schools give educational support and are well resourced.

IH operates a Transfer System whereby teachers can move from school to school and country to country. IH offers solid career routes and opportunities to move up the career ladder. At the present time the majority of vacancies are in Eastern and Central Europe although recruitment is for all IH schools and affiliates worldwide. The large format Recruitment Programme brochure is useful for prospective teachers, since it provides a description of individual schools and their environs and in some cases the terms of contract (salary, hours, housing, etc.) The new edition comes out in spring in time for the busy recruitment season. International House in Piccadilly also has a notice board on which many other organisations advertise their vacancies.

International Placement Group (IPG), Jezkova 9, 130 00 Prague 3, Czech Republic. Tel/fax: (2) 2272 0237/279568. UK headquarters: 72 New Bond St, London W1Y 9DD. Tel: 0181-682 1309. E-mail: ipgcz@mbox.vol.cz. EFL teacher recruitment firm specialising in Eastern Europe. Client schools in Poland, Czech Republic, Slovakia, Russia, Estonia, Lithuania and also in Uruguay, Peru and Guatemala with plans to add Slovenia, Finland and Colombia in the coming year.

Language Link, 21 Harrington Road, London SW7 3EU. Tel: 0171-225 1065. Fax: 0171-584 3518. E-mail: languagelink@compuserve.com. Training and recruitment agency which places qualified (including newly qualified) teachers in its network of affiliated schools in Slovakia, Poland, Russia, Czech Republic, Germany, the Ukraine, Vietnam, Colombia, etc. Interested teachers should ring to arrange an interview, and then send CV and photo. (See Training chapter for details of Language Link's regular Trinity Certificate courses.)

Linguarama, Group Personnel Department, Oceanic House, 89 High St, Alton, Hampshire GU34 1LG; 01420 80899/fax: 01420 80856. E-mail: personnel@linguarama.com. Web-site: http://www.linguarama.com/jobs. Linguarama's motto is 'Language Training for Business' and their short teacher training course reflects this emphasis. Applicants for jobs in Linguarama language schools abroad must have at least a degree and a Linguarama qualification or Cambridge/Trinity

Certificate. Linguarama have two offices in London (for teacher interviews, visa services, etc.) as well as the above address which deals with vacancies at over 40 European centres in Finland, Germany, France, Spain, Italy and Central Europe.

Nord-Anglia International Ltd. Overseas Recruitment Department, 10 Eden Place, Cheadle, Stockport, Cheshire SK8 1AT. Tel: 0161-491 8415. Fax: 0161-491 4410. Specialises in EFL vacation courses throughout the UK, but runs a recruitment service which is open not only to their own summer school teachers. Vacancies worldwide in teaching English to adults, teens and juniors on business and general courses. Degree and EFL qualifications required. EFL experience preferred. Apply March-June for UK summer work and year round for overseas positions. Last minute vacancies being advertised in September were in Spain, Poland, Kiev, Taiwan and Portugal.

Overseas Placing Unit—part of the European Employment Service Network (EURES). Occasionally language school vacancies are registered with the OPU. Access to this vacancy information is available through local Jobcentres only.

Saxoncourt Recruitment, 59 South Molton St, London W1Y 1HH. Tel: 0171-491 1919. Fax: 0171-499 3657. E-mail: recruit@saxoncourt.com. Web-site: www.saxoncourt.com. Recruit over 300 teachers each year for schools in Southeast Asia (especially for the partner Shane Schools in Japan, etc.), Western and Eastern Europe, Latin America and the Middle East. Applications are welcome from candidates holding the CELTA (offered by Saxoncourt Teacher Training at the same address), Trinity College Cert. TESOL or equivalent course of over 100 hours. Interested candidates should send a CV and covering letter. Coordinate 'Job shops' held in various UK cities over the summer (e.g. Birmingham, Edinburgh and Sheffield).

University of Cambridge Local Examinations Syndicate (UCLES), Syndicate Buildings, 1 Hills Road, Cambridge CB1 2EU. A new feature of the course Certificate in English Language Teaching to Adults (CELTA) administered by UCLES is a free job placement service for candidates in the UK (see description of Cambridge/RSA Certificate Courses in the *Training* chapter).

Wall Street Institute International, Rambla de Catalunya 2-4, Planta Baixa, 08007 Barcelona, Spain. Tel: (93) 412 00 14. Fax: (93) 412 38 03. Web-site: www.educate.com. Expanding chain of 250 commercial language institutes for adults which employ approximately 750 full-time EFL teachers in Europe (Spain, Switzerland, Portugal, Italy, France and Germany) and Latin America (Mexico, Chile, Venezuela). For details about employment in a specific centre or country, contact individual centres or the country's 'Master Center' which in some cases acts as a clearinghouse for vacancies. The minimum requirements for teachers are: native speaking, university degree, professional attitude and appearance, and ability to work within the framework of a well-defined method and system, developed by WSI and using a combination of interactive multimedia laboratory study and classes with native speakers. WSI is now part of Sylvan Learning Systems Inc.

Commercial Agencies

Anyone with a TEFL background should write to relevant agencies with a CV and covering letter, preferably enclosing a self-addressed envelope or (if overseas) international reply coupons. Agencies which specialise in a single country are not included in this chapter, but are mentioned in the country chapters.

Anglo-Pacific (Asia) Consultancy, Suite 32, Nevilles Court, Dollis Hill Lane, London NW2 6HG. Tel: 0181-452 7836. Educational consultancy which specialises in recruitment in Thailand, Taiwan, China and Russia with occasional vacancies in Indonesia and European countries (e.g. Austria) year round. They welcome approaches from graduates (or people with HND/equivalent higher qualifications) who have a recognised TEFL Certificate. Place teachers at all levels in the public and private sectors. Aim to provide teachers with background information about their destination country including teaching tips and cultural information.

ESS, Macmillan House, 96 Kensington High St, London W8 4SG. Tel: 0171-937

3110. This agency (English & Spanish Studies) occasionally advertises vacancies in Spain (Catalonia) and Russia.

Eurotemp (Employment Agency)—seen advertising in Tuesday *Guardian* for EFL teachers for France, etc., but did not reply to requests for further details. The advertised address was PO Box 20, Stratford-upon-Avon, Warks. CV37 8YL.

i to i International Projects Ltd, One Cottage Road, Headingley, Leeds LS6 4DD. Tel: 0113 217 9800. Fax: 0113 217 9801. E-mail: travel@i-to-i.com. Web-site: www.i-to-i.com. Independent TEFL training organisation which recruits teachers (many of them graduates of the i to i courses) for a group of schools in Izmir, Turkey, and for language schools in Greece (cost of the scheme from £100 excluding training). Must have some TEFL training, e.g. recognised Certificate or i to i's own certificate (see *Training: Introductory Courses*).

Also place self-funding volunteers as teachers in a range of countries as part of their 'i venture' programme. Volunteers work on school projects teaching English in Sri Lanka, India, Bolivia, Russia, Uzbekistan and possibly Cuba. Placements are flexible and last 1-12 months. Placement fees vary from about £900 for Uzbekistan to £1,300 for India and South America; this includes TEFL training weekend and in-country orientation/support. Flights, insurance and visas are extra. i to i publish a free quarterly magazine called *Inspired*.

Langstar Educational Services, 105 Hundred Acres Lane, Amersham, Bucks. HP7 9BN. Tel: (01494) 727590. Fax: (01494) 724454. Recruit teachers mainly for Poland, Turkey, Italy, Spain (as of next year) and occasionally elsewhere in Europe. Keep teachers' CVs on file. As a rule, minimum requirement is a recognised TEFL Certificate though experience not always needed.

LANGUAGE MATTERS

To School Directors/Proprietors:
Our aim is to provide the quality of staff *you* need in a prompt cost-efficient manner. We also offer a range of educational services including University placements. Consultancy on setting up courses, in-house training etc.

To Prospective Teachers:
Graduates with TEFL Certificates and experience of teaching are invited to send their CVs.

Write or Fax to: Language Matters, 34 Beckhampton Road, Oldfield Park, Bath BA2 3LL. Tel/Fax: 44 + (0)1225 352026

Language Matters, 34 Beckhampton Road, Oldfield, Bath BA2 3LL. Tel/fax: 01225 352026. Agency recruits qualified and experienced teachers for a wide range of countries including Europe and the Far East.

Skola Recruitment, 21 Star St, London W2 1QB. Tel: 0171-402 0416. Fax: 0171-724 2219. Email: emaie.skola@easynet.co.uk. CELTA course providers which also does recruitment. About 150 teachers placed per year, the majority of whom are for Greece via Skola/Teachers in Greece. Also recruit for other countries and for UK summer schools. Candidates must have a Cambridge CELTA or Trinity TESOL, and be able to attend an interview in London (though occasionally telephone interviews suffice).

Teaching Abroad, Gerrard House, Rustington, West Sussex BN16 1AW. Tel: (01903) 859911. Fax: (01903) 785779. E-mail: teaching_abroad@garlands.uk.com. Web-site: www.teaching-abroad.co.uk. About 250-300 volunteers recruited each year to work as English language teaching assistants for short or longer periods in Ukraine, Russia (Moscow, St. Petersburg and Siberia), India, Ghana, Brazil, Mexico and China. No TEFL background required. Packages cost from £895 (excluding air fares).

TEFLNet Recruitment, Yapham Grange, Yapham Mill, York YO42 1PB. Tel: (01904) 784440. Fax: (01759) 305586. E-mail: teflnet@langwork.demon.co.uk. ALP/TEFLNet is an independent recruitment service which matches the requirements of

EFL schools, colleges and training organisations with the qualifications, experience and preferences of EFL teachers and trainers. Placements are available for newly qualified teachers through to specialists. About two-thirds of positions require a degree and most require a Trinity or Cambridge TEFL Certificate. Main destinations are Asia (especially Thailand) and Eastern Europe (especially Poland). The majority of vacancies have a September start.

Teacher Recruitment International (Aust), PO Box 177, Tumby Bay, South Australia 5605, Australia. Tel: (8) 8688 4260. Fax: (8) 8688 4222. E-mail: tri@camtech.net.au. Places mostly Australian and New Zealand teachers of ESL/EFL in language institutes and colleges in Asia and the Middle East. Candidates must have a CELTA and in most cases an Honours degree in English or Applied Linguistics.

Voluntary and Religious Organisations

Two organisations which collate information about vacancies within both religious and secular organisations are:

Christians Abroad, 1 Stockwell Green, London SW9 9HP. Tel: 0171-346 5950. Fax: 0171-346 5951. E-mail: projects@cabroad.org.uk. Web-site: www.cabroad.org.uk. Ecumenical charity which provides information and advice to people of any faith or none who are thinking of working overseas, whatever their circumstances, whether short or long term, voluntary or paid. A free information booklet lists a variety of voluntary organisations in the UK and overseas, some of which are looking for EFL teachers. For qualified people, *Opportunities Abroad,* a monthly listing of vacancies through around 40 agencies, is available on subscription (£2.50 for a single issue, £25 for ten) and a database of skilled personnel is kept and searched on behalf of agencies looking for staff. Christian professional EFL and English teachers are often sought for Africa and the Far East. At the time of writing, Christians Abroad was recruiting EFL teachers for Japan, China and Hong Kong.

Christian Vocations, Holloway St West, Lower Gornal, Dudley, West Midlands DY3 2DZ. Tel: 01902 882836. Publishes a directory of short-term opportunities with Christian agencies; the *STS Directory* costs £5 (including postage). They also annually publish *Jobs Abroad* in the spring for Christians looking for more long term openings, which includes a section on vacancies in TEFL.

The most important voluntary agency in the UK recruits EFL teachers as well as many other kinds of volunteer.

VSO (Voluntary Service Overseas), 317 Putney Bridge Road, London SW15 2PN. Contact VSO Enquiries Unit on 0181-780 7500 (with answerphone out of office hours). Fax: 0181-780 7576. E-mail: Enquiry@VSO.org.com.uk. Regular advertisements in Tuesday *Guardian* and *EL Gazette & Prospects.* Most postings are for two years but there are some one year renewable contracts for trained, experienced TEFL teachers. Requirements vary, but most placements need people with a minimum of a degree and the CELTA or Trinity TESOL. VSO sends people aged 21-70 to over 50 countries in Africa and Asia. For TEFL/ELT posts, large programmes include: China, Vietnam, Mongolia, Laos, Indonesia; Mozambique, Tanzania, Eritrea, Ghana, Nigeria. VSO is opening a new programme in March 1999 in Rwanda.

VSO offers a good package including: return airfare, full medical cover, a pension scheme, NI contributions, a pre-departure equipment grant of £500, a mid-tour grant and a re-settlement grant of £1,500. Whilst overseas, the local employer provides accommodation and a basic but adequate salary. VSO also provides pre-departure training in adapting TEFL/ELT skills and in-country language training.

VSO has a separate initiative for Eastern Europe called East European Partnership, Carlton House, 27A Carlton Drive, London SW15 2BS (see chapter on Eastern Europe).

A number of UK organisations make it possible for school-leavers in their gap year to work for six months abroad, and many of these placements are in schools where volunteers teach English. The following are involved in this field:

Gap Challenge, Black Arrow House, 2 Chandos Road, London NW10 6NF. Tel: 0181-961 1122. Fax: 0181-961 1551. E-mail: welcome@world-challenge.co.uk. Web-site: www.world-challenge.co.uk. Provides gap year students and graduates aged 18-25 with 3 and 6 month voluntary work placements in a range of countries. Departures are in September and January each year. Teaching positions available in India (Manali and Goa), Nepal (Kathmandu and Pokhara), Tanzania (Zanzibar), Malawi and (from 1999) Malaysia and Peru. Inclusive placement fees £1,500-£2,500 including airfares.

GAP Activity Projects, 44 Queen's Road, Reading, Berks. RG1 4BB. Tel: (0118) 959 4914. Fax: (0118) 957 6634. E-mail: volunteer@gap.org.uk. Web-site: www.gap.org.uk. Positions for school leavers, including many as teaching assistants, in Latin America (Argentina, Brazil, Chile, Ecuador, Mexico and Paraguay), Asia (China including Hong Kong, India including working with Tibetan refugees, Japan, Malaysia and Vietnam), the Middle East (Jordan and Israel), North Africa (Morocco) and Central Europe (Czech Republic, Hungary, Poland, Romania, Russia and the Slovak Republic). Posts are for between four and eleven months (six is average) and cost the volunteer £490 plus air fares and insurance, while board, lodging and (sometimes) pocket money are provided. A one or two week TEFL course costing £120-£190 is mandatory for those undertaking to teach English.

Involvement Volunteers UK, 7 Bushmead Ave, Kingskerswell, Newton Abbot, Devon TQ12 5EN (01803 872594). Main IV address: PO Box 218, Port Melbourne, Victoria 3207, Australia. Tel: (3) 9646 9392. Fax: (3) 9646 5504. E-mail: ivimel@iaccess.com.au. European office: IV Deutschland, Naturbadstr. 49, 91056 Erlangen (tel/fax 91-358075). A few of their many projects for paying volunteers worldwide involve teaching spoken English at village schools.

The Project Trust, The Hebridean Centre, Ballyhough, Isle of Coll, Argyll PA78 6TE. Tel: (01879) 230444. Fax: (01879) 230357. E-mail: projecttrust@compuserve.com. Satellite office in London office: 5 St. John St, London EC1M 4AA (0171-490 8764/ fax: 0171-490 8759, but it's best to correspond with HQ. An educational charity which sends British school-leavers aged 17-19 overseas for a year starting between July and September. About two-thirds of all 200+ placements are made to English-teaching projects in schools in a great many countries: Botswana, Brazil, Chile, China, Cuba, Egypt, Guyana, Honduras, Hong Kong, Indonesia, Japan, Jordan, Malaysia, Namibia, Pakistan, Peru, Sri Lanka, Thailand, Uganda, Vietnam and Zimbabwe. Volunteers are required to fund-raise a proportion of the cost of their year abroad, which in 1999/2000 is £3,250. Applications can be processed between 8 and 17 months prior to departure to allow time for pre-service training to take place.

Students Partnership Worldwide (SPW), 17 Dean's Yard, London SW1P 3PB. Tel: 0171-222 0138/967 8070. Fax: 0171-233 0008/963 1006. E-mail: spwuk@gn.apc.org. Web-site: www.spw.org. Overseas teaching placements for school leavers, undergraduates and graduates aged 18-25 in Zimbabwe, Tanzania, Uganda, Namibia, South Africa (former homelands of Ciskei and Transkei), India and Nepal. Programme costs are £2,000-£2,500 which include travel, insurance, living expenses, administration and in-country support by SPW staff. Pre-departure briefings in London are advisable; in-country training (3-6 weeks) is obligatory. Basic language and TEFL training is given.

Charities and mission societies which occasionally require EFL teachers include:

Christian Mission Society, Partnership House, 157 Waterloo Road, London SE1 8UU. Tel: 0171-928 8681. Fax: 0171-401 3215. Overseas Experience Placements programme assigns Christian volunteers to projects in Africa, Asia, the Middle East and Eastern Europe including TEFL (duration 6-18 months). Longer term teaching appointments for example in Sri Lanka, Taiwan and Thailand.

Concern Worldwide, 52-55 Lower Camden St, Dublin 2, Ireland. Tel: 1-475 4162. UK office: 248-250 Lavender Hill, London SW11 1LJ (0171-738 1033/fax 0171-738 1032). Recruits mainly primary school certified teachers (B.Ed, Cert.Ed or PGCE) for many countries including Bangladesh, Cambodia, Ethiopia, Mozambique, Rwanda, Tanzania and Uganda. Focus is on curriculum development and teacher training rather than classroom teaching.

International Cooperation for Development (ICD), Unit 3, Canonbury Yard, 190a New North Road, London N1 7BJ. Tel: 0171-354 0883. Fax: 0171-359 0017. ICD, the overseas technical assistance programme of CIIR (Catholic Institute for International Relations) recruits professionally qualified and experienced people to work in the developing world. ICD occasionally has teaching positions in one of its programmes in Dominican Republic, Ecuador, El Salvador, Haiti, Honduras, Namibia, Nicaragua, Peru, Somalia/Somaliland, Yemen and Zimbabwe.

Interserve, 325 Kennington Road, London SE11 4QH. Tel: 0171-735 8227. Fax: 0171-587 5362. E-mail: isewi@isewi.globalnet.co.uk. Web-site: http:// www.interserve.org. Teaching posts for self-funded Christian volunteers in India, Pakistan, Nepal, Mongolia, Central Asian Republics and North Africa. Also short-term placements (4-9 months) for church-going school leavers in Asia; programme costs about £1,500.

OMS International, 1 Sandileigh Avenue, Manchester M20 3LN. Tel: 0161-283 7992. Fax: 0161-283 8981. (US headquarters: PO Box A, Greenwood, IN 46142-6599.) An evangelical mission organisation which provides English lessons through local churches in 17 countries worldwide. Opportunities for self-funded Christian volunteers include 3 weeks in Korea, 3 months in Ecuador, 1 year in Hungary and up to 5 years in Brazil or elsewhere.

Scottish Churches World Exchange, 121 George Street, Edinburgh EH2 4YN. Tel: 0131-225 8115. 10-12 month placements in Africa, Asia, Latin America, etc. with community organisations and projects linked to churches. (See China chapter for example of programme.) Most volunteers are expected to contribute towards the cost of their placement, e.g. from £2,350 including travel and training expenses. The Church of Scotland World Mission at the same address (0131-225 5722/fax 0131-226 6121/e-mail: kirkwrldlnk@gn.apc.org) send English language teachers (who are practising Christians) to various countries including Jordan and Romania.

United Nations Volunteers, Palais de Nations, CH-11211 Geneva 10, Switzerland. Some of their 2-year professional postings are for voluntary English teachers.

Wycliffe Bible Translators, Horsleys Green, High Wycombe, Bucks. HP14 3XL. Tel: (01494) 482521. Fax: (01494) 483297. Many opportunities for qualified and experienced Christian teachers for missionary schools worldwide, especially in Indonesia, Papua New Guinea, French-speaking Africa and Kenya. Out of 50 openings for teachers, about 5 are specifically ESL. Volunteers must support themselves.

Opportunities for North Americans

Although the companies, agencies and charities listed here are based in the US and cater primarily to North Americans, some may be in a position to help overseas applicants. Recruitment agencies in the United States have stronger links with Latin America and the Far East than with Europe. As in Britain, some organisations are involved primarily with English-medium international schools following an American curriculum and are looking to recruit state-certified teachers; these are listed separately at the end of this section. It should be noted that unlike in Britain, recruitment agencies are permitted to charge the candidate a substantial fee for successful placement.

The most important organisations for Americans looking for employment opportunities in the field of TEFL are:

TESOL (Teachers of English to Speakers of Other Languages, Inc.), 1600 Cameron St, Suite 300, Alexandria, Virginia 22314. Tel: (703) 836-0774. Fax: (703) 836-7864. E-mail: tesol@tesol.edu. Web-site: http://www.tesol.edu. A key organisation for English language teachers, TESOL is a non-profit organisation which offers various services to members (who number about 16,500 at present) including a placement service. Basic membership is $47 ($41 for students). Of immediate interest to the job-seeker is TESOL's Placement Services which includes a subscription to the TESOL *Placement Bulletin,* a listing of job vacancies worldwide published 10 times a year and costing US$35 by e-mail or $30 by regular mail. TESOL's Placement Services also organises

an Employment Clearinghouse, (ESL/EFL job fair) at TESOL's annual convention and exposition held every March. Jobs are posted, and interviews and hiring are conducted on-site.

Peace Corps, Room 803E, 1111 20th Street NW, Washington, DC 20526. Tel: 1-800-424-8580. Web-site: http://www.peacecorps.gov/. TEFL has historically been one of the major programme areas of the Peace Corps which has English teaching programmes in about 70 countries. Volunteers, who must be US citizens, over age 18 and in good health, are sent on two-year assignments. Peace Corps volunteers teach at both secondary and university level while some become involved with teacher training and curriculum development. It can take up to a year between application and departure.

USIA (United States Information Agency), English Language Programs Division, 301 4th St SW, Washington, DC 20547. Tel: (202) 485-2869/619-5869. Runs network of overseas offices (called USIS, US Information Services) to promote US culture, and therefore (broadly speaking) the counterpart of the British Council. Provides English language instruction at 200 cultural centres (which are administered directly by USIS) and at binational centres (locally run) in about 100 countries. Most teachers for binational centers (which are mainly located in developing countries) are hired directly by the centre in question, however USIA acts as a clearinghouse for requests. It also operates the English Teaching Fellow Program which places TESL/TEFL graduates in language centres abroad including binational centres. Qualified candidates who want to teach in USIS Cultural Centers should obtain the official federal application form (171) and submit it to the English Teaching Specialists Department, Room 523, at the above address.

The USIA **Fulbright Senior Scholar Program** provides grants for teaching English in over 30 countries. A doctorate is usually required, although a Master's degree is sufficient in some countries. Applicants must be US citizens. Application information is available from the Council for International Exchange of Scholars (3007 Tilden St NW, Suite 5L, Washington, DC 20008-3009; 202-686-7877/e-mail: apprequest@cies.iie.org).

WorldTeach Inc., Harvard Institute for International Development, 14 Story Street, Cambridge, MA 02138. Tel: (617) 495-5527/800-4-TEACH-0. Fax: (617) 495-1599. E-mail: info@worldteach.org. Web-site: www.worldteach.org. Private, non-profit organisation founded iin 1986 which places several hundred volunteers as teachers of EFL or ESL in countries which request assistance. Currently, WorldTeach provides college graduates for one-year contracts to Costa Rica, Ecuador and Namibia. 6-month opportunities available in China (Yantai) where volunteers teach adults, and in Mexico and Honduras where volunteers teach English to nature guides. Also Summer Teaching Programme at a language camp for Chinese high school students in Shanghai. All participants pay a programme fee (from $3,800) which covers training, airfares, orientation and insurance, and are provided with housing and a stipend based on local rates of pay. Applicants accepted year round. Participants do not have to be US citizens, but must have a BA (for 12-month programmes).

World University Service of Canada, 1404 Scott St, PO Box 3000, Ottawa, Ontario, Canada. Fax: (613) 798 0990. E-mail: recruit@wusc.ca. Canadian ESL teachers to range of countries including Laos and Vietnam.

The following commercial language providers and volunteer recruitment agencies may be able to assist EFL job-seekers:

EF Center Boston, Teacher Recruitment, One Education Street, Cambridge, MA 02141. Web-site: http://www.ef.com/EFWeb/EF1/English_First.htm. Largest number of vacancies in Russia, Indonesia, China, Poland and Morocco. Recruitment takes place year-round.

English for Everybody, 655 Powell Street, Suite 505, San Francisco, CA 94108 (415-789-7641/fax 530-895-0998) and Spanielova 1292, 163 00 Prague 6 (tel/fax 42-2-301 9784/e-mail: EFE@itc-training.com (Subject EFE). Teacher placement agency for the Czech Republic and Central/Eastern Europe. Applicants should have TEFL Certification and/or EFL/ESL experience. College degree preferred. Assistance for

US$450 includes guaranteed job, airport greeting, pre-arranged housing, orientation and follow-up.

Fandango, 1613 Escalero Road, Santa Rosa, CA 95409. Tel/fax: (707) 539-2722. Consultancy involved in some placement of EFL teachers in Eastern Europe and Far East. No recent confirmation received.

Global Routes, 1814 Seventh Street, Suite A, Berkeley, CA 94710. Tel: (510) 848-4800. Fax: (510) 848-4801. E-mail: mail@globalroutes.org. Offer 12-week voluntary internships to students who teach English and other subjects in village schools in Kenya, Ecuador, Costa Rica and Thailand, as well as on a Navajo reservation in the US. There are no specific requirements apart from a knowledge of Spanish for Ecuador and Costa Rica. The programme fee is $3,550 for the summer and $3,950 for the spring and autumn (excluding air fares). Academic credit is available.

Global Volunteers, 376 East Little Canada Road, St. Paul, MN 55117-1628. Tel: 800-487-1074. Two or three week placements as English conversation assistants in southern Spain, southern Italy and Greece, as well as a range of developing countries. Fees from $2,000 plus travel.

The following consultancies and exchange organisations may be able to guide students towards a range of overseas options including teaching English:

Council, Council on International Educational Exchange, 205 East 42nd Street, New York, NY 10017. Tel: (212) 661-1414/toll-free 1-888-268-6245. E-mail: info.ciee.org. Web-site: http://www.ciee.org. Administers Teach China programme in the US (see China chapter). Also, runs work abroad programmes for students in France, Germany, Costa Rica and other countries. Participants are given visas which allow them to work at any job for the time allowed. Council has offices in Paris and other cities which will advise on English teaching opportunities.

InterExchange Inc., 161 Sixth Avenue, New York, NY 10013. Tel: (212) 924-0446. Fax: (212) 924-0575. E-mail: interex@earthlink.net. Web-site: www.interexchange.org. Arrange teaching assistantships in Czech Republic, Hungary and Bulgaria (see country chapters). New programmes planned for Spain and Russia. Placement fees $400-$450.

Alliances Abroad, 409 Deep Eddy Ave, Austin, TX 78703. Tel: 1-888-6-ABROAD. E-mail: info@alliancesabroad.com. Web-site: http://www.alliancesabroad.com/alliances. English teaching placement programme in Latin America, South America, French-speaking Africa and China. Fees average $750 per month which includes insurance and orientation. Language tutors placed in Germany, Italy and Spain. Participants live as members of a family for 1-3 months and provide tutoring for 10-12 hours a week in exchange for room and board. Placement fees are $1,000-$1,700.

Taking Off, PO Box 104, Newton Highlands, MA 02161. Tel: (617) 630-1606. Fax: (617) 630-1605. E-mail: Tkingoff@aol.com. Clients are given access to database with over 2,500 opportunities worldwide, including some in the field of EFL. Offer a personal service for an hourly rate of $150 or for ongoing assistance there is a flat fee of $1,000.

Centre for Interim Programs, PO Box 2347, Cambridge, MA 02238. Consultancy which advises high school leavers and others on programmes abroad including voluntary English teaching placements. Consultation fees start at $1,500.

Certified Teachers

Certified primary and secondary teachers who want to work in mainstream international schools abroad should be aware of the following agencies and organisations which match up qualified candidates with vacancies. Most of the hiring for primary and secondary schools abroad (often referred to in the American context as K-12—kindergarten to grade 12) is done at recruitment fairs included on the list below. The files of job-seekers are added to a database which can be consulted by recruiters who then choose whom they want to interview. Candidates who successfully land a job abroad with the help of a US agency may have to pay a placement fee of $300-$600, though in some cases the employer underwrites this expense.

ECIS (European Council of International Schools), 21 Lavant St, Petersfield, Hants. GU32 3EL. Tel: 01730 268244. E-mail: staffingservices@ecis.org. Assists only teachers who have a B.Ed. or PGCE with at least two years' teaching experience. They publish a new edition of the *International Schools Directory* every year; the 1998/9 edition costs £35/$57.

Gabbitas Educational Consultants, 126-130 Regent Street, London W1R 6EE. Fax: 0171-437 1764. Venerable institution which maintains a register of qualified and experienced teachers available for long-term teaching posts in South America, the Middle East and Africa, including some English language teaching jobs.

WES/Worldwide Education Service, Canada House, 272 Field End Road, Eastcote, Middlesex HA4 9NA. Tel: 0181-582 0317. Fax: 0181-429 4838/582 0320. E-mail: wes@weswoldwide.com. Educational consultancy which recruits mostly qualified teachers for full-time posts with British and international schools worldwide. WES maintains a register of qualified teachers.

Central Bureau for Educational Visits and Exchanges, 10 Spring Gardens, London SW1A 2BN. Tel: 0171-389 4665 (or 0131-447 8024 in Scotland). Short or year-long exchanges for modern languages teachers organised in Austria, France, Germany, Spain and Switzerland.

League for the Exchange of Commonwealth Teachers, Commonwealth House, 7 Lion Yard, Tremadoc Road, Clapham, London SW4 7NQ. Placements abroad for experienced teachers in Commonwealth countries, Barbados to South Africa.

Q.T.S. Quality Services for Teachers and Schools, 36 High Ash Drive, Leeds LS17 8RA. Tel: (0113) 269 6636. Fax: (0113) 266 1977. Teacher recruitment worldwide, with emphasis on the Middle East. Fully qualified, British-trained infant, junior and secondary teachers,

International Schools Services, PO Box 5910, Princeton, NJ 08543, USA. Tel: (609) 452-0990. Fax: (609) 452-2690. E-mail: edustaffing@iss.edu. Web-site: www.iss.edu. Teaching opportunities for educators and certified teachers in private American and international schools around the world. ISS candidates attend annual US-based International Recruitment Centers (IRCs) where headteachers of overseas schools interview potential staff. Applicants must have a bachelor's degree and two years of current relevant experience. IRC registration materials are provided upon approval of application.

Ohio State University (College of Education Placement Services), 110 Arps Hall, 1945 N. High St, Columbus, OH 43201-1172. Tel: (614) 292-2741. Fax: (614) 688 4612. Teacher recruitment fair held in February.

Queen's University Placement Office, Faculty of Education, Kingston, Ontario K7L 3N6, Canada. Tel: (613) 545-6201. Fax: (613) 545-6691. Web-site: http://educ.queensu.ca/-placment. Host an annual recruiting fair in February for international schools. Registration costs C$100. Teacher certification required plus at least two years' K-12 teaching experience.

Search Associates, PO Box 168, Chiang Mai 50000, Thailand. Tel/fax: (53) 244322. US address: PO Box 636, Dallas, PA 18612. Advice, information and placement assistance for teachers with mainstream school experience (pupils aged 3-18) seeking 2 or 3 year contracts with international schools. Registration fee is £75. Teacher/school job fairs are organised in Oxford, Düsseldorf, Dubai, Kuala Lumpur, Australia/New Zealand and various North American locations.

Teacher Recruitment International (Aust), PO Box 177, Tumby Bay, South Australia 5605, Australia. Tel: (8) 8688 4260. Fax: (8) 8688 4222. E-mail: tri@camtech.net.au. Place teachers in secondary school (English curriculum) posts in international schools in Asia and the Middle East. Prefer Australian and New Zealand candidates.

University of Northern Iowa, Overseas Placement Service for Educators, UNI, Cedar Falls, Iowa 50614-0390. Tel: (319) 273-2083. Fax: (319) 273-6998. E-mail: overseas.placement@uni.edu. Web-site: http://www.uni.edu/placemnt/student/internat.html. Educators must hold current certification in elementary or secondary education. A comprehensive service includes the annual UNI Overseas Recruiting Fair in February/March.

SPECULATIVE JOB HUNT

Only a small percentage of language schools advertise in the foreign press or use an agency. The vast majority depend on local adverts, word of mouth, personal contacts and direct approaches. Therefore a speculative job search probably has a better chance with TEFL jobs than in many other fields of employment. For a successful campaign, only two things are needed: a reasonable CV and a list of addresses of potential employers.

Applying in Advance

Entire books and consultancy companies are devoted to showing people how to draw up an impressive curriculum vitae (or resumé as it is called in the USA). But it is really just a matter of common sense. Obviously employers will be more inclined to take seriously a well presented document than something scribbled on the back of a dog-eared envelope. Obviously any relevant training or experience should be highlighted rather than submerged in the trivia about your schooling and hobbies. If you lack any TEFL experience, try to bring out anything in your past which demonstrates your 'people skills', such as voluntary work, group counselling, one-to-one remedial tutoring, etc. and your interest in (and ability to adapt to) foreign countries. If you are targeting one country, it would be worth drawing up a CV in the local language; Judith Twycross was convinced that her CV in Spanish was a great asset when looking for teaching work in Colombia. If you get the job, however, be prepared for your new employer to expect you to be able to speak the vernacular.

Attitudes and personality are probably just as important as educational achievements in TEFL, so anything which proves an aptitude for teaching and an extrovert personality will be relevant. Because this is difficult to do on paper, some eager job-hunters have gone so far as to send off a video of themselves, preferably a snippet of teaching. This is not worth doing unless (a) a school has expressed some interest and (b) you can make a good impression on an amateur video. A cheaper alternative might be to send a photo and a cassette of your speaking voice, again assuming this will be a help rather than a hindrance.

The other essential ingredient is a list of addresses. Each of the country chapters in this book provides such a list and recommends ways of obtaining other addresses, for example by contacting a federation of language schools (if there is one) or the British Council in your destination country. It is always worth writing to or even phoning the local British Council office, since they may be prepared to offer a general assessment of the local TEFL scene as well as provide a list of selected language schools in their region (for the benefit of enquiries from local language learners). The degree of their helpfulness will be at the discretion of the English Language Adviser or her/his secretary. Americans can try requesting a similar list from the relevant USIS offices which may also be able to offer general advice about language teaching in that country.

The book in your hand provides a good starting place for gathering a list of addresses, by including entries for about 500 institutes and organisations. Their teacher requirements were all checked and updated in 1998. At the end of each country chapter are lists of other school addresses (more than 1,000 in total). Although they did not confirm their requirements, possibly because they did not want a small number of vacancies to be widely publicised, it is still worthwhile for qualified candidates to approach them.

Note that telephone numbers included throughout this book do not include the international access codes (00 from Britain, 011 from the US) nor the country code. These can be found listed at the front or back of telephone directories. The numbers quoted do give the area codes minus the prefix 0 which should be used if dialling within the country rather than from abroad.

The most comprehensive source of addresses in most cases is the Yellow Pages which you should be able to consult in advance at large reference libraries, and possibly also at the country's Consulate or Chamber of Commerce (if there is one) in

London or New York, though these are not always very helpful. If you have a contact in your proposed destination city you could impose on them to photocopy the relevant pages.

Of course it has to be stressed that it is difficult, and increasingly so, to set up a firm job offer simply by correspondence. A language school would have to be fairly desperate to hire a teacher they had never met for a vacancy that had never been advertised. It is a good idea to follow up any hint of interest with a phone call. The best time to phone language school directors is six or seven weeks before the beginning of term. Perhaps the school has a contact in your country who would be willing to conduct an informal interview on their behalf. Perhaps the school will be content with a telephone interview.

If your credentials are not the kind to wow school directors, it might still be worth sending off a batch of warm-up letters, stating your intention to present yourself in person a couple of weeks or months hence. Even if you don't receive a reply, such a strategy may stick in the mind of employers, as an illustration of how organised and determined you are.

Interviews

Schools which advertise in foreign journals often arrange for candidates to be interviewed either by their own representative or by a proxy, such as a previous teacher or an appointed agent. Interviews can take place in strange and unlikely places including private homes. As a woman Roberta Wedge felt that she had to be cautious. Once she was stuck in a seedy pub at the end of a tube line at 9pm looking eagerly at every man who came through the door, and then the Director of Studies stood her up. Take along a friend if you are nervous.

Sometimes large organisations like Berlitz arrange open days and invite anyone who wants to be interviewed to come along. Chances are that British job-seekers will have to travel to London for an interview. Whether you are interviewed at home or abroad, slightly different rules apply. For example smart casual dress, neither flashy nor scruffy, is appropriate in Britain, while something a little more formal might be called for in certain cultures. Even if all your friends laugh when you pack a suit before going abroad, you may find it a genuine asset when trying to outdo the competition. As Steven Hendry, who has taught English both in Japan and Thailand with none of the usual advantages apart from traveller's canniness, says: you may not need a tailor-made suit but you definitely need to be able to present a conservative and respectable image.

As with the CV, so at interview. Highlight anything that is remotely connected with teaching even if it has nothing to do with the English language, and do it energetically and enthusiastically. Yet keenness will seldom be sufficient in itself. You do not have to be an intellectual to teach English; in fact the quiet bookish type is probably at a disadvantage. An amusing illustration of this is provided by Robert Mizzi's description of his interview for the JET Programme in the Japan chapter.

Without a TEFL background you should do a certain amount of research, e.g. acquaint yourself with some of the jargon such as 'notional','communicative-based', etc. It is not uncommon for an interviewer to ask a few basic grammar questions. To help you deal with this eventuality you might turn to the list of recommended reading in the chapter on *Preparation*. By visiting the ELT section of a bookshop, you can begin to familiarise yourself with the range of materials on offer. Always have some questions ready to ask the interviewer, such as 'Do you use Cambridge or Streamline?', 'What audio materials do you have?' 'Do you encourage the use of songs?' or 'Do you teach formal grammar structures?' If you are looking for an opening in a business context, you might pick up a few tips from the section on Interviews in the chapter on Germany.

You will certainly be asked how long you intend to stay and (depending on the time of year) nothing less than nine months will be considered. They will also want to know whether you have had any experience. With luck you will be able to say truthfully that you have (at least) taught at a summer school in Britain (again, see chapter on

Preparation). Some applicants who are convinced that they can do a good job make a similar claim, untruthfully, knowing that at the lower end of the TEFL spectrum this will never be checked. Similarly some candidates claim to have done a TEFL course and pretend to have left the certificate at home. A certain amount of bluffing goes on in all interviews, so you'll just have to decide how far you are prepared to go. Bear in mind that the true depths of your ignorance could easily be plumbed ('Ah, so you've used Cambridge. Why do you prefer it to Streamline?').

Another of your skills you may be tempted to exaggerate is your knowledge of the local language. Philip Dodd was hired by a language teaching agency in Madrid on the understanding that he could speak fluent Spanish and was sent out on his first assignment, to give English lessons to a young child living in a wealthy suburb. He was greeted at the door by the mother who wished to make sure of a few things before she entrusted her precious offspring to this stranger. Not able to follow her voluble stream, Philip nodded affably and said 'si' whenever he guessed it was appropriate. After one of his affable 'si's', the woman's face turned grey and she ordered him out of her house. He still doesn't know what he said that was so shocking. On the other hand, a certain inflation of your abilities may be expected, and will be met with distortions of the truth from the employer as you both decide whether you are going to hit it off.

Pretending to speak the language can get you into hot water

Of course many applicants will be able to avoid potential embarrassment at interview by having prepared themselves for a stint as a teacher. If you have done a TEFL course of any description, be sure to take along the certificate, however humble the qualification. Even schools in farflung places are becoming increasingly familiar with the distinctions between various qualifications and are unlikely to confuse a Cambridge/RSA Certificate with an anonymous correspondence 'certificate'. In Asia especially, nothing short of the original will do, since there are so many counterfeit copies around.

If you have a university degree, be sure to take the certificate along. Even if the interviewer is prepared to take your word for it, the school administration may need the document at a later stage either to give you a salary increment or to obtain a work permit. Adam Hartley, who taught English in China, hadn't realised that his MA would have earned him a higher salary; although he arranged for two separate copies to be sent from Britain, neither arrived and he had to be content with the basic salary. Americans should take along their university transcripts; any school accustomed to hiring Americans will be familiar with these. Also take along any references; something written on headed paper will always impress, even if your previous jobs were not in teaching.

Once the interviewer indicates that you are a strong contender, it is your turn to ask questions. Ask about the details of pay, hours and conditions and take notes (see the section on Contracts below). Often there are disappointing discrepancies between what is promised in the early stages and what is delivered; at least if these things have been discussed at interview, you will be in a stronger bargaining position if the conditions are not met.

If you are offered a job by an agent and are worried about what kind of employer the school will be, you could phone the local British Council office to find out whether the school enjoys a good local reputation. Occasionally an embassy or consulate will assist, as in the case of the US Embassy in Seoul which keeps a file of language schools about which they have received persistent complaints. More commonly, someone will have set up a web-page where this kind of inside information can be obtained (again, common in Korea).

ON THE SPOT

It is almost impossible to fix up a job in advance in some countries, due to the way the TEFL business operates. For example, written applications to the majority of language schools in Bangkok (assuming you could compile a list of addresses) are a waste of time since the pool of teacher-travellers on the spot is appropriate to the unpredictable needs of Thai schools. Even in countries like Spain and Germany for which adverts appear in the UK, the bulk of hiring goes on on-the-spot.

When you arrive in a likely place, your initial steps might include some of the following: transcribing a list of schools from the Yellow Pages consulted in the telephone office, reading the classified column of the local newspapers including the English language papers, checking notice boards in likely locations such as the British Council, USIS, universities, TEFL training centres, English language bookshops (where you should also notice which EFL materials are stocked), or hostels which teacher-travellers frequent.

A reconnaisance trip is a good idea if possible. For example Fiona Paton wanted to teach English in France. On her way back from a summer holiday in Spain, she jumped off the train in Vichy for long enough to distribute her CV to several language schools. To her surprise, a letter arrived from one of them once she was at home offering her a job for the academic year, which she subsequently accepted and greatly enjoyed.

After obtaining a list of potential employers and before contacting them, get hold of a detailed map and guide to the public transport network so you can locate the schools. Phone the schools and try to arrange a meeting with the director or director of studies (DOS). Even if an initial chat does not result in a job offer, you may learn something about the local TEFL scene which will benefit you at the next interview, especially if you ask lots of questions. You might also be able to strike up a conversation with one of the foreign teachers who could turn out to be a valuable source of information about that school in particular and the situation generally. It is very common to have to begin with just a few hours a week. Make it clear that you are prepared to stand in at short notice for an absent teacher. The longer you stay in one place, the more hours will come your way and the better your chances of securing a stable contract.

This gradual approach also gives you a chance to discover which are the cowboy schools, something which is difficult to do before you are on the scene. The British Council has called for an EU-wide recognition scheme for language schools, to force rogue schools out of business. But this is a long way off, and in the meantime disreputable schools flourish in Europe just as they do in other parts of the world. It is not always easy to distinguish them, though if a school sports a sign 'Purrfect

Anglish' you are probably not going to need an MA in Applied Linguistics to get a job there. Working for a cowboy outfit may not be the end of the world, though it often spells trouble, as the chapter *Problems* will reveal. But without many qualifications you may not have much choice.

Cowboy schools abound

FREELANCE TEACHING

Private English lessons are usually more lucrative than contract teaching simply because the middle man has been cut out. Learners may prefer them as well, not only because of the more personal attention they receive in a private lesson but because it costs them less. As a private tutor working from your own home or visiting pupils in theirs, you can undercut the big schools with their overheads. But at the same time you deprive yourself of the advantages of working for a decent school: access to resources and equipment, in-service training, social security schemes and holiday pay. The life of a freelance teacher can be quite a lonely one. Normally teachers working for a school take on a small amount of private teaching to supplement their income, provided this is allowed in their contracts. Most employers do not mind unless your private teaching is interfering with your school schedule or (obviously) if you are pinching potential clients from your employer.

In order to round up private pupils, you will have to sell yourself as energetically as any salesman. Turn to the section on Freelance Teaching in the Spain chapter for some ideas which have worked in Spain but could work anywhere. It might be possible to persuade companies to pay you to run English classes for employees during the lunch hour or siesta (if appropriate), though you would have to be a confident teacher and dynamic salesperson to succeed. You are far more likely to find one or two pupils by word of mouth and build from there.

Self-promotion is essential. Steven Hendry recommends plastering neatly printed bilingual notices all over town, as he did to good effect in Chiang Mai in northern Thailand. Meanwhile Ian McArthur in Cairo made a large number of posters (in Arabic and English) and painstakingly coloured in the Union Jack by hand in order to attract attention. (Unfortunately these were such a novelty that many posters were pinched.) Putting a notice up on appropriate notice boards (in schools, universities, public libraries, popular supermarkets) and running an advertisement in the local paper are good ideas for those who have the use of a phone or an e-mail address (since few people would reply by post to such an advert). Some have gone so far as to hire a paging device so that they can be contacted anytime. These methods should put you in touch with a few hopeful language learners. If you are any good, word will spread and more paying pupils will come your way, though it can be a slow process.

To counterbalance the advantages of higher pay and a more flexible schedule, freelance teaching has many disadvantages. Everyone, from lazy Taiwanese teenagers to busy Barcelona businessmen, cancels or postpones one-to-one lessons with irritating frequency. People who have taught in Latin countries complain that the problem is chronic. Cancellations among school and university students especially escalate at exam time. It is important to agree on a procedure for cancellations which won't leave you out of pocket. Although it is virtually impossible to arrange to be paid in advance, you can request 24 hours notice of a cancellation and mention politely that if they fail to give due warning you will insist on being paid for the missed lesson. But you can't take too tough a line, since your clients are paying above the odds for your flexibility. Another consideration is the unpaid time spent travelling between clients' homes and workplaces.

If you are less interested in making money than integrating with a culture, exchanging conversation for board and lodging may be an appealing possibility. This can be set up by answering (or placing) small ads in appropriate places (the American Church in Paris notice board is famous for this). Hannah Start, a school leaver in Merseyside, put up a notice at her local English language school indicating that she wanted to exchange English conversation for accommodation in Paris; a businesswoman on an intensive English course contacted her and invited her to stay with her.

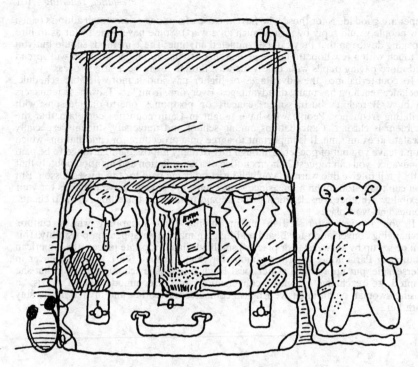

Preparation

The preceding chapters on ELT training and job-hunting set out ways in which you can make yourself more attractive to potential employers. One of the best ways in which to prepare for a stint of teaching abroad is to teach English locally. Relevant experience can usually be gained by volunteering to tutor immigrants in your home town; this is particularly feasible in the US where literacy programmes take place on a massive scale. It might also be a good idea to contact the director of a local commercial language school and ask to sit in on some lessons to see what it's all about and to talk to teachers. A polite note expressing your interest in TEFL would probably meet with a positive response. EFL teachers are like everyone else; they are experts at what they do and don't mind sharing that knowledge with interested outsiders.

More prolonged exposure to TEFL can best be gained by working at a language summer school. This not only provides a chance to find out whether you will enjoy English teaching for a longer period, but may put you in touch with people who are well-informed on overseas possibilities.

UK SUMMER SCHOOLS

Language summer courses take place throughout the British Isles, especially in tourist areas. The short-term nature of the teacher requirements means that schools sometimes have difficulties finding enough qualified staff, though with a recent decrease in the number of language learners coming to Britain, there are fewer jobs floating around. Wages are higher than for most seasonal summer jobs and as a result it is harder to get a job teaching English in Torquay than in Taipei. You may have to use the same wiles as described above in the section on interviews in order to be hired.

It is estimated that there are 600-800 English language schools in operation in Britain during July and August, mainly catering for foreign students, especially from France, Spain and Italy, but increasingly from further afield (e.g. Eastern Europe and Turkey). Many of these schools advertise heavily in the spring, e.g. 'Teach English on the English Riviera'. Quality varies dramatically of course. The more established schools are usually members of ARELS, the Association of Recognised English Language Services, which is trying to raise standards and whose staff are less likely to be novice teachers. The organisation is located at 2 Pontypool Place, Valentine Place, London SE1 8QF (0171-242 3136) and will send a list of its 200+ members to enquirers. The counterpart in the state sector is BASELT (British Association of State English Language Teaching, Cheltenham & Gloucester College of H.E., Francis Close Hall, Swindon Road, Cheltenham, Glos. GL50 4AZ.)

At the other end of the spectrum are the entrepreneurs who rent space (possibly ill-suited to teaching) and will take on almost anyone to teach. Teachers are thrown in at the deep end with little preparation and few materials. Marta Eleniak was not very happy with her employer:

> *I have got nothing good to say about my employer. We were expected to do nearly everything including perform miracles, with no support and pathetic facilities. I can only liken it to being asked to entertain 200 people for 4 hours with a plastic bowl. The pupils got a raw deal too because of false promises made to them.*

She does admit that it was on the basis of this three-week job that she got a job in a Madrid language school.

Schools at both extremes are listed in the Yellow Pages and advertise in the national press. They are located throughout the UK, but are concentrated in London and the South-East, Oxford, Cambridge and resorts like Bournemouth and Blackpool. Recruitment of summer teachers gets underway in the new year and is usually well advanced by Easter. The average starting salary for teachers is £170-£200 per week, though Certificate-qualified teachers should earn £250-£300. Residential schools may pay less if they are providing board and lodging, though some pay the same because the hours are so much longer. Since most schools are located in popular tourist destinations, private accommodation can be prohibitively expensive and the residential option attractive. Without any TEFL background it is easier to get taken on as a non-teaching sports and activities supervisor which at least would introduce you to the world of TEFL. EFL teachers must expect a number of extracurricular activities such as chaperoning a group of over-excited adolescents to a West End theatre or on an art gallery visit.

Here is a short list of major language course organisations which normally offer a large number of summer vacancies:

Abbey Colleges, 53 Wells Road, Malvern Wells, Worcestershire WR14 4JF. Summer courses in Malvern and London employ about 25 teachers plus activity staff .

Anglo Continental Educational Group, 33 Wimborne Road, Bournemouth BH2 6NA 901202 557414/fax 01202 556156). Up to 100 EFL teachers for adult summer courses and 20 for adolescents.

Anglo-European Study Tours, 8 Celbridge Mews, Porchester Road, London W2 6EU (0171-229 4435/fax 0171-792 8717). 200+ at centres throughout the UK. No accommodation.

Concorde International Summer Schools, Arnett House, Hawks Lane, Canterbury, Kent CT1 2NU (01227 451035/fax 01227 762760).

EF Language Travel, Cherwell House, 3rd Floor, London Place, Oxford OX4 1AH (01865 200720). 1,000 group leaders and teachers needed for centres in Hastings, Brighton, London, Cambridge and Oxford.

Elizabeth Johnson Organisation, West House, 19/21 West St, Haslemere, Surrey GU27 2AE. With 35 centres around the UK.

Embassy Study Tours, 44 Cromwell Road, Hove, East Sussex BN3 3ER (01273 207481). English language activity programmes throughout UK and Ireland.

English Language & Cultural Organisation, Lowlands, Chorleywood Road, Rickmansworth, Herts. WD3 4ES (01923 776731/fax 01923 774678). 20-30 EFL teachers to work at several locations in the south of England.

International Language Centres (ILC Vacation Courses), White Rock, Hastings, East Sussex TN34 1JY (01424 720100). Hire 300-500 teachers (minimum Cambridge/ Trinity Certificate) for 40 summer schools in London, Edinburgh, Dublin, Oxford, Bath and many other cathedral and coastal cities.

International Quest Centres, 9 Stradbroke Road, Southwold, Suffolk IP18 6LL (01502 722648/fax 01502 722645). 200 EFL teachers. Wage of £9 per hour.

International Study Programmes, The Manor, Hazleton, Nr. Cheltenham, Glos. GL54 4EB (01451 860379).

Kingswood Group, Linton House, 164-180 Union St, London SE1 0LH (0171-922 1234). Summer camps run in Normandy as well as southern England.

Living Language Centre, Highcliffe House, Clifton Gardens, Folkestone, Kent CT20 2EF (01303 258536/fax 01303 851455).

Nord-Anglia, 10 Eden Place, Cheadle, Stockport, Cheshire SK8 1AT (0161-491 8477/ 491 8415/fax 0161-491 4409). 300+ EFL teachers for more than 80 centres around Britain, especially the North.

OISE Youth Language Centres, OISE House, Binsey Lane, Oxford OX2 0EY (01865 792799/fax 01865 792706). 500 summer and Easter vacancies in dozens of locations. OISE offer their own training course to tutors.

Passport Language Schools, 37 Park Road, Bromley, Kent BR1 3HJ (0181-466 5925). Employ about 150 teachers for 20 schools (mainly Kent, South Coast, Oxford, Derby and Swansea).

SUL Language Schools, Beech Holm, 7 Woodland Avenue, Tywardreath, Par, Cornwall PL24 2PL (01726 814227/fax 01726 813135).

TASIS England American School, Coldharbour Lane, Thorpe, Surrey KT20 8TE. Of special interest to American EFL teachers who want to teach in Britain from late June to late August; only suitably qualified Americans are eligible for work permits.

Thames Valley Cultural Centres, 15 Park St, Windsor, Berks. SL4 1LU (01753 852001/ fax 01753 831165)

YES Education Centres, 12 Eversfield Road, Eastbourne, East Sussex BN21 2AS (01323 644830/fax 01323 726260). EFL teachers for summer courses in Abingdon, Brighton, Hastings, Oxford, Seaford and Maidenhead.   Roberta Wedge found that working for a large summer school organisation was not only good preparation for a teaching contract in Italy, but was fun for its own sake:

> *The big language mills in Britain are a good way to see the country. I signed up with OISE in Exeter because I wanted to tramp the moors. It's possible to spend the whole summer jumping around fortnightly from contract to contract, all arranged ahead of time through the same organisation. Make sure you know what to do about accommodation, though; I have a tent in reserve.*

WHILE YOU'RE WAITING

After you have secured a job, there may be a considerable gap which will give you a chance to organise the practicalities of moving abroad and to prepare yourself in other ways. If you are going to a country which requires immigration procedures (the majority of cases unless you're an EU national planning to work in another member state) you can start the visa procedures. In addition to deciding what to take and how to get to your destination, you should think about your tax position and health insurance, plus find out as much as you can about the situation in which you will find yourself.

Many teachers take out a subscription to the *Guardian Weekly* (164 Deansgate, Manchester M60 2RR; 0161-832 7200) to guarantee access to world news, though you might prefer to wait until you arrive to see what newspapers are available. A one-year subscription costs £58 in Europe and North America, £66 elsewhere. Also contact BBC English, the English language teaching arm of BBC World Service, Bush House, London WC2B 4PH (e-mail: bbc.english@bbc.co.uk). Comprehensive information about BBC English can be found on the internet http://www.bbc.co.uk/worldservice/ BBC_English. Copies of their 'Learning English' leaflet which lists BBC English programme details with scheduled times and frequencies are available free. They also have a pamphlet called 'English Language Teaching'.

Alternative English language broadcasting organisations are Voice of America, Radio Canada International (PO Box 6000, Montreal, Canada H3C 3A8) and Swiss Radio International (SBC, CH-3000 Bern 15, Switzerland), all of which will send information about their services. SRI publish a monthly magazine *Swiss World* in English and other languages which would be useful to teachers in Germany and elsewhere in Europe.

ELT professionals should consider joining the International Association of Teachers of English as a Foreign Language (IATEFL, 3 Kingsdown Park, Whitstable, Kent CT5 2FL; 01227 276528/fax 01227 274415/e-mail: IATEFL@compuserve.com/Web-site: http://www.iatefl.org). Membership, which costs £30 to individuals or £90 to institutions, entitles teachers to various services including six newsletters annually and access to special interest groups, conferences, workshops and symposia.

The more information you can find out about your future employer the better. Kathy Panton thinks that she would have been a more effective teacher in her first year in the Czech Republic if she had asked more probing questions beforehand:

> Now that I have a better idea of what to teach I think I could handle it, but a first year teacher should ask a lot of questions; such as, what books the students have used, teacher continuity, very detailed report of what the students can do (as opposed to what they have studied), and most of all what they will be expected to accomplish during the school year. If the report is vague, I don't think anyone should take the job unless they are really confident that they'll be able to develop the framework themselves. I would look for a school that said something like, 'You'll guide the students through Hotline 1 textbook, and also give them extra vocabulary and speaking exercises to supplement the text. You'll also work with a phonics text for a few weeks, because these students have poor pronunciation. You'll probably find it useful to bring some old magazines but the school has several ESL textbooks already.' This would show that the school takes both curriculum and organisation seriously.

An invaluable source of information is someone who has taught at the school before; ask your employer for a couple of addresses. Past teachers will be in a position to pass on priceless minutiae, not only recommending pubs, bakeries, etc. but (if the accommodation is tied to the job) they can advise you to arrive early and avoid the back bedroom because of the noisy plumbing.

Contracts

This is the point at which a formal contract or at least an informal agreement should be drawn up. Any employer who is reluctant to provide something in writing is definitely suspect. Horror stories abound of the young unsuspecting teacher who goes out to teach overseas and discovers no pay, no accommodation and maybe even no school. For this reason it is not only very important to sign a contract, but also to have a good idea as to what it is letting you in for.

The following items should be covered in a contract or at least given some consideration:

1. Name and address of employer.
2. Details of the duties and hours of the job. (A standard load might be 24 contact teaching hours a week, plus 3 hours on standby to fill in for an absent teacher, fill all the board markers in the staff room, etc.)
3. The amount and currency of your pay. Is it adequate to live on? How often are you paid? Is any money held back? Can it be easily transferred into sterling or dollars?

What arrangements are there if the exchange rate drops suddenly or the local currency is devalued?

4. The length of the contract and whether it is renewable.

5. Help with finding and paying for accommodation. If accommodation is not provided free, is your salary adequate to cover this? If it is, are utilities included? Does the organisation pay for a stay in a hotel while you look for somewhere to live? How easy is it to find accommodation in the area? If it is unfurnished what help do you get in providing furniture? Can you get a salary advance to pay for this and for any rent deposits?

6. Your tax liability.

7. Provisions for health care and sick pay.

8. Payment of pension or national insurance contributions.

9. Bonuses, gratuities or perks.

10. Days off, statutory holidays and vacation times.

11. Paid flights home if the contract is outside Europe, and mid-term flights if you are teaching for 2 years.

12. Luggage and surplus luggage allowance at the beginning and end of the contract.

13. Any probationary period and the length of notice which you and the employer must give.

14. Penalties for breaking the contract and circumstances under which the penalties would be waived (e.g. extreme family illness, etc.)

Obviously any contract should be carefully studied before signing. It is a wise precaution to make a photocopy of it before returning to avoid what happened to Belinda Michaels whose employer in Greece refused to give her a copy when she started to dispute some points. In some cases the only contract offered will be in a foreign language (e.g. Arabic) and you will either have to trust your contact at the school for a translation or consider obtaining an independent English translation.

Health and Insurance

Increasingly, the immigration authorities abroad will not grant a teacher a work permit until they have provided a medical certificate. Many countries now insist on an HIV test and various other health checks including for syphilis and TB. GPs will charge for carrying out these tests, whether you do it before you leave home or after arrival.

Reputable schools will make the necessary contributions into the national health insurance and social security scheme. Even if you are covered by the national scheme, however, you may find that there are exclusion clauses such as dental treatment, non-emergency treatment, prescription drugs, etc. Or you may find that you are only covered while at work. Private travel insurance is very expensive (not less than £200 for 12 months) so it is important to clarify the position before departure. Specialist expatriate policies might be worth investigating. A policy endorsed by American Citizens Abroad (3ter Chemin Thury, PO Box 321, 1211 Geneva 12, Switzerland) is available from Abrams Insurance (1051 North George Mason Drive, Arlington, VA 22205). The following UK companies are familiar with insuring expats including EFL teachers:

Bone & Company, 69a Castle Street, Farnham, Surrey GU9 7LP (01252 724140).

Dove Insurance Brokers, Green Tree House, 11 St. Margaret's St, Bradford-on-Avon, Wilts. BA15 1DA (01225 864642).

Our Way Travel, Foxbury House, Foxbury Road, Bromley, Kent BR1 4DG (0181-313 3900).

If you are British and intending to work in the European Union (Germany, France, Italy, Spain, Portugal, Greece, Austria, Denmark, Sweden, Finland, Netherlands, Belgium, Luxembourg and Ireland), you should acquire form E-111, which is a certificate of entitlement to medical treatment within the EU. The leaflet T6 contains the application form and is available from British post offices. Even if your employer will be paying into a health scheme, cover may not take effect immediately and it is as well to have the ordinary tourist cover for the first three months. An E-111 provides cover for up to 12 months; after that the appropriate form is E-106. Council in New York (address in *Finding a Job* chapter) offers an International Teachers' Identity Card (like a student card) for $20, which includes cover for emergency repatriation.

If your destination is tropical, consult an up-to-date book on health such as *Travellers' Health: How to Stay Healthy Abroad* by Richard Dawood (OUP, £7.99) or the excellent and highly readable general guide *The Tropical Traveller* by John Hatt. British Airways has set up a network of travel clinics throughout the UK which will give advice on specific destinations, administer jabs and prescribe the correct anti-malarials, etc. Telephone advice on immunisations and malaria is available from MASTA (Medical Advisory Service for Travellers Abroad), Keppel St, London WC1E 7HT. The Travellers' Health Line operates on 0891 224100; after callers leave details of their itinerary, dates of arrival and expected living conditions, a basic MASTA Health Brief will be sent to them, though the call on this premium rate line will cost £2-£3. If a more personalised Health Brief is required, travellers should telephone 01705 553933 to find out the cost, according to the depth of detail required.

If you are heading off to central Africa or any other place where the incidence of HIV is high, you will be understandably worried about the standards of health care in general and the quality of blood and syringes in particular. Sterile medical packs containing hypodermic needles, intravenous drip needles, etc. are available from MASTA.

Americans should obtain the booklet 'Health Information for International Travel' which includes information on vaccination requirements, malaria prophylactics, etc. The US Public Health Service updates it annually; to obtain a copy of this document, contact the Superintendent of Documents, US Government Printing Office, Washington, DC 20402-9325 and enquire about the current cost.

National Insurance Contributions and Social Security

If you are a national of a European Economic Area country working in another member state, you will be covered by European Social Security regulations. Advice and the free information leaflet SA29 'Your Social Security Health Care and Pension Rights in the European Community plus Iceland, Liechtenstein and Norway' may be obtained from the Contributions Agency International Services, Longbenton, Newcastle-upon-Tyne NE98 1YX (06451 54811, local rate call). The leaflet explains that payments made in any EEA country count towards benefit entitlement when you return home. The UK also has Social Security agreements with other countries including Croatia, Cyprus, Israel, Jamaica, Malta, Slovenia, Switzerland, Turkey, USA and republics of the former Yugoslavia. If you are going to teach in any of these countries, contact International Services for the appropriate leaflet.

In countries where no Social Security agreement exists, the leaflet NI38 'Social Security Abroad' gives an outline of the arrangements and options open to you. If you fail to make National Insurance contributions while you are out of the UK, you will forfeit entitlement to benefits on your return. You can decide to pay voluntary contributions at regular intervals or in a lump sum in order to retain your rights to certain benefits. Unfortunately this entitles you only to a retirement/widow's pension, not to sickness benefit or unemployment benefit. Since teachers abroad are seldom in a pension scheme, it is usually worth maintaining your right to a UK state pension.

Tax

Calculating your liability to tax when working outside your home country is notoriously complicated so, if possible, check your position with an accountant. Everything depends on whether you fall into the category of 'resident', 'ordinarily resident' or 'domiciled'. Most EFL teachers count as domiciled in the UK since it is assumed that they will ultimately return. From October 1998, new legislation removed the 'foreign earnings deduction' for UK nationals unless they are out of the country for a complete tax year. Since most teaching contracts operate from September, this means that the vast majority of EFL teachers, including teachers on high salaries in the

Middle East or on the Japan Exchange and Teaching scheme which were formerly tax-free, will now be liable to UK tax. If you are out of the country for a tax year, you will be entitled to the exemption provided no more than 62 days (i.e. one-sixth of the year) are spent in the UK.

If the country in which you have been teaching has a double taxation agreement with Britain, you can offset tax paid abroad against your tax bill at home. But not all countries have such an agreement (Sweden for example) and it is not inconceivable that you will be taxed twice. Keep all receipts and financial documents in case you need to plead your case at a later date.

Inland Revenue leaflets which may be of assistance are IR20 'Residents and non-residents: Liability to tax in the UK' and IR139 'Income from Abroad? A guide to UK tax on overseas income.' IR120 lists the relevant contact offices within the Inland Revenue. General tax enquiries may be addressed to the Inland Revenue Financial Intermediaries & Claims Office (Non-Residents), St. John's House, Merton Road, Bootle, Merseyside L69 9BB (0151-472 6214/5/6). The Inland Revenue also has an EC Unit: G.17 Strand Bridge House, 138-142 Strand, London WC2R 1HH (0171-438 6051). General enquiries are dealt with in Somerset House: Room G1, West Wing, Somerset House, Strand, London WC2R 1LB (0171-438 6420/5). A possible source of further information on tax is the annually revised book *Working Abroad* published by Kogan Page in conjunction with the *Daily Telegraph*.

If US citizens can establish that they are resident abroad, the first $80,000 (from the year 2000) of overseas earnings is tax-exempt in the US.

Travel

London is the cheap airfare capital of the world and the number of agencies offering discount flights to all corners of the world is seemingly endless. To narrow the choice you should find a travel agency which specialises in your destination. Those who know their way around the web can find lots of useful information. Start with www.cheapflights.co.uk which allows users to log onto a destination and see a list of prices offered by a variety of airlines and agents. It also has links to other travel-related topics (exchange rates, weather forecast, health advice). Compare the prices posted on www.travelocity.com.

Alternatively, consult specialist travel magazines such as *TNT* (which is free in London) plus *Time Out* and the Saturday edition of the *Independent* or other national papers. By ringing a few of the agencies with advertisements you will soon discover which airlines offer the cheapest service. STA and Campus Travel with branches in most university towns can usually be relied on to come up with the best flight options to suit your needs.; STA's telephone sales numbers are 0171-361 6161 for Europe, 0171-361 6262 worldwide (http://www.statravel.co.uk) while Campus can be contacted on 0171-730 3402 (Europe), 0171-730 8111 (worldwide) and on the internet www.campustravel.co.uk.

In North America, the best newspapers to scour for cheap flights are the *New York Times* (the Sunday edition has a section devoted to travel with cut-price flights advertised), the *LA Times, San Francisco Chronicle-Examiner, Miami Herald, Dallas Morning News, Chicago Sun Times,* the *Boston Globe* and the Canadian *Globe & Mail*. Recommended agencies include Council Travel Services (part of the Council on International Educational Exchange) with branches in most major university towns, and STA with 100 offices worldwide including 15 in the US. If your dates are flexible, contact Airtech, 584 Broadway, Suite 1007, New York, NY 10012 (212-219-7000) which advertises its fares by saying, 'if you can beat these prices, start your own damn airline'. One-way transatlantic fares start at $179 from the east coast and $279 from the west. Travel CUTS in Canada sell discounted fares and have offices overseas (e.g. in London at 295a Regent St, London W1R 7YA).

Within Europe, the railway is often the preferred way of travelling, especially since the months of September and June when most teachers are travelling to and from their destinations are among the most enjoyable times to travel. Good discounts are available to travellers under 26; details are available from Eurotrain (see Campus address above) or Wasteels Travel (0171-834 7066).

Good maps and guide books always enhance one's anticipation and enjoyment of going abroad. If you are in London, visit the famous map shop Edward Stanford Ltd., (12-14 Long Acre, Covent Garden, WC2E 9LP) which also sends maps by post. The Map Shop (15 High St, Upton-on-Severn, Worcestershire WR8 0HJ; 01684 593146) does an extensive mail order business and will send you the relevant list of their holdings. Daunt Books for Travellers (83 Marylebone High Street, London W1M 4DE) organises its holdings according to region, shelving practical guides next to relevant travel literature.

In the US a good travel bookstore is the Travellers Bookstore (75 Rockefeller Plaza, 22 W 52nd St, Lobby, New York, NY 10019; toll-free 800-755-8728; fax 212-397-3984). They produce a detailed catalogue on most countries as well as a quarterly newsletter, and do most of their business by mail order.

Browsing in the travel section of any bookshop will introduce you to the range of travel guides. The Rough Guides series is generally excellent, and the very detailed books published by Lonely Planet are very popular. If you want a detailed historical and architectural guide, obtain a *Blue Guide* or a *Michelin Green Guide*.

Learning the Language

Even if you will not need any knowledge of the local language in the classroom, the ability to communicate will increase your enjoyment many times over. After a long hard week of trying to din some English into your pupils' heads, you probably won't relish the prospect of struggling to convey your requests to uncomprehending shopkeepers, neighbours, etc. A failure at least to try to learn some of the local language reflects badly on the teacher and reinforces the suspicion that English teachers are afflicted with cultural arrogance.

If there is time before you leave home, you might consider enrolling in a part-time or short intensive course of conversation classes at a local college of further education or using a self-study programme with books and tapes. This will have the salutary effect of reminding you how difficult it is to learn a language. There are a great many teach-yourself courses on the market from the BBC, Berlitz and so on. A course consisting of a couple of course books and a couple of tapes will cost in the region of £30. Linguaphone (0800 282417) which is one of the biggest (and most expensive) recommends half an hour of study a day for three months.

If you are heading for a remote place, take a language course with you, since tapes and books (including a good dictionary) may not be available locally and your enthusiasm to learn may be rekindled once you are on-location. Of course it is much easier to learn the language once you are there. Some employers may even offer you the chance to join language classes free of charge; if you are particularly interested in this perk, ask about it in advance.

In a few cases, it is a positive disadvantage to speak the language as Jamie Masters discovered in Crete:

> *About speaking Greek. Well, no one told me. I assumed that they'd be quite pleased to have a Greek-speaking English teacher, best of both worlds. It's useful for discipline; the kids can't talk about you behind your back; you can tell when they're cheating on their vocab tests; and, I stupidly thought, you can explain things more clearly, really get them to understand... Well, I was wrong, and was laboriously reprimanded for it when they finally worked out what I was doing. But by that time it was too late: the kids knew I could understand Greek, and so they knew they didn't have to make the effort to speak to me in English. No amount of my playing dumb worked.*

WHAT TO TAKE

The research you do on your destination will no doubt include its climate, which will help you choose an appropriate range of clothing to take. But there is probably no need to equip yourself for every eventuality. EFL teachers normally earn enough to afford to buy a warm coat or boots if required. Be sure to pack enough smart clothes to see you through the academic year; blue jeans are rarely acceptable in the classroom.

Even though you are expecting to earn a decent salary, you should not arrive short of money. It is usual to be paid only at the end of the first month. Plus you may need sizeable sums for rent deposits and other setting-up expenses.

A generous supply of passport photos and copies of your vital documents (birth certificate, education certificates, references) should be considered essential. Recreational reading in English will be limited, so you should take a good supply of novels, etc. It could take time to establish a busy social life, leaving more time for reading than usual. In such circumstances, having access to the World Service can be a godsend. You will need a good short-wave radio with several bands powerful enough to pick up the BBC. 'Dedicated' short-wave receivers which are about the size of a paperback start at £65. If you are travelling via the Middle East or Hong Kong, think about buying one duty-free. A further advantage of having access to the BBC is that you can tape programmes for use in the classroom.

If possible find out from recently returned travellers what items are in short supply or very expensive (e.g. deodorant in Greece, cigarette papers in Scandinavia). Some items which recur on teachers' lists are vitamin tablets, a deck of cards, ear plugs and thermal underwear.

Teaching Materials

Try to find out which course your school follows and then become familiar with it. Depending on the circumstances, there may be a shortage of materials, so again enquire in advance about the facilities. (For example, English texts being used in a few places in Cambodia dated from 1938 and contained such useful sentences as, 'I got this suit in Savile Row'.) If you are going to have to be self-reliant, you may want to write to the major EFL publishers, primarily Oxford University Press, Cambridge University Press, Longman, Heinemann, Penguin and Phoenix to request details of their course books with a sample lesson if possible, and the address of their stockist in your destination country.

Before leaving home, you should visit a good ELT department of a bookshop or obtain a detailed catalogue of ELT materials from a specialist EFL bookshop. KELTIC is a major specialist EFL bookshop and international mail order service offering an extensive range of materials, information and a free catalogue *The KELTIC Guide to ELT Materials* to teachers and schools worldwide. The London shop is at 25 Chepstow Corner, Chepstow Place, London W2 4XE (tel: 0171-229 8560; fax: 0171-221 7955; e-mail: shop@keltic-london.co.uk) and the KELTIC International Order Department is at 39 Alexandra Road, Addlestone, Surrey KT15 2PQ (tel: 01932 820485; fax: 01932 854320; e-mail: keltic@keltic.co.uk. Web-site: http://www.keltic.co.uk).

Another major stockist is BEBC the Bournemouth English Book Centre (Albion Close, Parkstone, Poole, Dorset BH12 3LL; 01202 715555/fax 01202 739609/www.elt.co.uk) which also supplies books by mail order to teachers all over the world. Orders of more than 15 books are sent post-free within the EU. Dillons (82 Gower St, London WC1E 6EQ; ELT enquiry number 0171-636 1577 ext 231/293; fax 0171-580 7680; e-mail: arts@dillons.org.uk) also annually publish a handy ELT catalogue. For a list of recommended titles, see the following section. Waterstone's in Manchester is strong in the north of England (91 Deansgate, Manchester M3 2BW; 0161-834 7055). GBG Direct is an overseas mail order bookshops from which you can order English language books once you are abroad (24 Seward St, London EC1V 3GB; 0171-490 9900).

Here is a list of items to consider packing which most often crop up in the recommendations of teachers of conversation classes in which the main target is to get the students talking. Teachers expecting to teach at an under-resourced school might think about taking some of the following: good dual language dictionary, picture dictionary, cassettes (including pop music with clear lyrics such as Pink Floyd, Beatles, Simon & Garfunkle, Tracy Chapman, early Billy Bragg), blank tapes (and a cassette recorder if necessary with spare batteries), games and activities book; illustrated magazines like *National Geographic* or unusual publications like old comic books, teen mags or *The Big Issue* (interesting to many language learners in former communist countries); maps (for example of London), tourist guides to your home country, travel brochures, blank application forms, flash cards (which are expensive if bought commercially; home-made ones work just as well); grammar exercise book; old Cambridge exam papers (if you are going to be teaching First Certificate or Proficiency classes). Postcards, balloons, stick-on stars and photos of yourself as an infant have all been used to good effect. If you know that there will be a shortage of materials, it might even be worth taking general stationery such as notebooks, carbon paper, Blutack, plastic files, large pieces of paper, coloured markers, etc. Most employers would be willing to pay the postage costs if you don't want to carry it all in your luggage. (If you are entering a country without a pre-arranged work visa, bear in mind that teaching aids in your luggage will alert customs officers that you intend to work.)

Richard McBrien, who taught English in China, recommends taking a collection of photos of anything in your home environment. A few rolls shot of local petrol stations, supermarkets, houses, parks, etc. can be of great interest to pupils in far-off lands. It may of course be difficult to anticipate what will excite your students' curiosity. The anthropologist Nigel Barley, who writes amusing books on his fieldwork, describes being enlisted to attend an impromptu English conversation club in a remote corner of Indonesia in his book *Not a Hazardous Sport*:

I answered questions about the royal family, traffic lights and the etiquette of eating asparagus, and gave a quick analysis of the shipbuilding industry. At the end of the evening, I fled back to the hotel.

EFL teachers cannot escape so easily, so you should be prepared to be treated like a guru of contemporary British or American culture.

Bibliography

There is such a plethora of books and materials that the choice can be daunting to the uninitiated. One valuable resource for English language teachers working abroad is TESOL's *More Than a Native Speaker: An Introduction for Volunteers Teaching Abroad* by Don Snow. The book covers classroom survival skills and includes a 'Starter Kit for Course Planning.' The book also addresses adapting to life in a new culture and ways to teach listening, speaking, reading, writing, grammar, vocabulary and culture. The book costs $29.95 plus 12% postage (or $24.95 plus postage for TESOL members). Orders may be ordered directly from TESOL Inc., 1600 Cameron St, Suite 300, Alexandria, VA 22314 (703-836-0774/fax 703-836-7864; e-mail: tesol@tesol.edu/ Web-site: http://www.tesol.edu).

Every teacher should have a basic manual of grammar handy, such as one of the following:

The Heinemann English Grammar, by D. Beaumont & C. Granger (Heinemann). A reference-cum-practice book at intermediate level. £8.95.

Practical English Grammar, by A. J. Thomson & A. V. Martinet (OUP, 1990) £6.35. Has built-in exercises.

Using English Grammar, by Edward Woods & Nicole McLeod (Phoenix) £9.95.

English Grammar in Use, by Raymond Murphy (CUP). Second edition, £7.75. Plus *Supplementary Exercises,* £4.45.

Advanced Grammar in Use, by Martin Hewings (CUP, 1999).

English Grammar, (Collins, Gem). £2.99. Genuinely pocket-sized. (Dubbed by at least one novice, 'the Teacher's Friend'.)

Practical English Usage, by M. Swan (OUP). Second edition, £12.90.

A Practical Handbook of Language Teaching, David Cross (Phoenix). £15.95. Do-it-yourself guide for teachers with poor resources.

Here is a selected list of recommended books and teaching aids which you could consider; obviously you won't want to buy all of them.

Collins Cobuild English Dictionary (Collins) £15. Collins publish a range of dictionaries for the language learner.

Cambridge International Dictionary of English (CUP, 1995). £12.55 paperback.

Grammar Games & Activities, by Peter Watcyn-Jones (Penguin) £21. Other titles by the same author include *Pair Work, Vocabulary Games* and *Fun and Games.*

Grammar Workbooks 1 and 2 for Beginners and Pre-Intermediate (Penguin) £3.75 each.

More Grammar Games, by M. Rinvolucri and P. Davis (CUP) £13.25. Includes activities for all levels.

Recipes for Tired Teachers, edited by Christopher Sion (Addison-Wesley/Longman) £17.95.

The Practice of English Language Teaching, by Jeremy Harmer (Longman) £13.95. Part of the Longman Handbooks for Language Teachers Series which aim to provide practical classroom guidance. The new title from the same author is *How to Teach English* aimed at people new to the profession (£12.50).

An Introduction to English Language Teaching, by John Haycraft (Longman) £11.95. Aimed at unqualified/inexperienced people and less taxing than many EFL books.

Source Book for Teaching English as a Foreign Language, by Michael Lewis and Jimmie Hill (Heinemann, 1993). £13.15. Practical guide for those with little formal training.

The Standby Book, edited by Seth Lindstromberg (CUP, 1997). £11.95 paperback, in the Cambridge Handbooks for Language Teachers series.

Lessons from Nothing, by Bruce Marsland (CUP, 1998). £9.50. From the Cambridge Handbooks for Language Teachers series.

Young Learners, by Phillips, *Storytelling With Children* by A. Wright, *Conversation* by

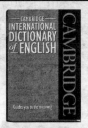
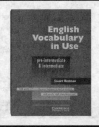

Nolasco & Arthur and *Role Play* by Porter Ladousse, all part of OUP's series *Resource Books for Teachers* at £10.10 each.

Challenge to Think, C. Frank, M. Rinvolucri, and M. Berger (OUP). Good for unexpected fill-in lessons and as course book supplement. £9.15

The Lexical Approach. by Michael Lewis (£14.50).

Anyone who is likely to be teaching young children might like to request the catalogue of Ladybird's Books for English Learning, since the well known children's publisher has an inexpensive series *English for Beginners* for children (Ladybird Books, Beeches Road, Loughborough, Leics. LE11 2NQ; 01509 234672).

Problems

Potential problems fall into two broad categories: personal and professional. You may quickly feel settled and find your new setting fascinating but may discover that the job itself is beset with difficulties. On the other hand the teaching might suit but otherwise you feel alienated and lonely. Those who choose to uproot themselves suddenly should be fairly confident that they have enough resources to rely on themselves, and must expect some adjustment problems. Only you can assess your chances of enjoying the whole experience and of not feeling traumatised. Women may encounter special problems in countries where women have little status. A book which will introduce you to potential difficulties and includes chapters on most of the countries of the world is called *More Women Travel*.

PROBLEMS AT WORK

Anyone who has done some language teaching will be familiar with at least some of the problems EFL teachers face. Problems encountered in a classroom of Turkish or Peruvian adolescents will be quite different from the ones experienced teaching French or Japanese businessmen. The country chapters attempt to identify some of the specific problems which groups of language learners present.

Although you are unlikely to be expected to entertain 200 people for four hours with a plastic bowl, there may be a fairly complete lack of facilities and resources. The teacher who has packed some of the teaching materials listed above will feel particularly grateful for his or her foresight in such circumstances. Some schools, especially at the cowboy end of the spectrum go to the other extreme of providing very rigid lesson plans from which you are not allowed to deviate and which are likely to be uncongenial and uninspiring. Even when reasonable course texts are provided, supplementary materials for role play and games can considerably liven up classes (and teachers). You can obtain extra teaching aids after arrival from the nearest English language bookshop or make them yourself, for example tape a dialogue between yourself and an English speaking friend or cut up magazines or use postcards to make flashcards. If the missing facilities are more basic (e.g. tables, chairs, heating, paper, pens) you will have to improvise as best you can and (if appropriate) press the administration for some equipment.

Problems with Pupils

A very common problem is to find yourself in front of a class of mixed ability and incompatible aims. How do you plan a lesson that will satisfy a sophisticated businessman whose English is fairly advanced, a delinquent teenager and a housewife crippled by lack of confidence? A good school of course will stream its clients and make life easier for its teachers. But this may be left to you, in which case a set of commercially produced tests to assess level of language acquisition could come in very handy. Alternatively you can devise a simple questionnaire for the students to describe their hobbies, studies, family or whatever. This will not only display their use of English but also give you some clues about their various backgrounds. One way of coping with gross discrepancies is to divide the class into compatible groups of pairs and give tasks which work at different levels. Sub-dividing a class is in fact generally a good idea especially in classes which are too large.

In classes of mixed ages, you may have trouble pleasing everyone

In some places you may even have to contend with racial or cultural friction among pupils, as Bryn Thomas encountered in Egypt:

> *One of the problems I found in the class was the often quite shocking displays of racism by the Egyptians towards their dark-skinned neighbours from Somalia. Vast amounts of tact and diplomacy were required to ensure that enough attention was*

given to the Somalis (who tend to be shy, quiet and highly intelligent) without upsetting the sometimes rowdy and over-enthusiastic Egyptians.

Your expectations of what teaching is supposed to achieve may be quite different from the expectations of your students. Foreign educational systems are often far more formal than their British or American counterparts and students may seem distressingly content to memorise and regurgitate, often with the sole motivation of passing an exam. But this doesn't always operate. Many teachers have had to face a class who don't seem to care at all about learning any English and merely want to be entertained.

In many countries free discussion is quite alien, whether because of repressive governments or cultural taboos. It is essential to be sensitive to these cultural differences and not to expect too much of your pupils straightaway. The only way of overcoming this reluctance to express an opinion or indeed express anything at all is to involve them patiently and tactfully, again by splitting them into smaller units and asking them to come up with a joint reply.

Discipline is seldom a serious problem outside Europe; in fact liberal teachers are often taken aback by what they perceive as an excess of docility, an over-willingness to believe that 'teacher is always right'. In some cases, classes of bored and rebellious European teenagers might cause problems (especially on Fridays), or children who are being sent to English lessons after school simply as an alternative to babysitting for working mothers. Unfortunately, a couple of troublemakers can poison a class. You may even have to contend with one or two downright uncontrollable students as Jamie Masters did in Crete:

> *At least two of my pupils were very malevolent. There was one, Makis, who used to bring a 'prop' to every lesson, some new way of disrupting the class—an air pistol, a piece of string with a banknote tied to it, a whistle, white paint. He used to slap my cheeks, hug me and lift me off the floor, was quite open about not wanting to work... and then claimed I was picking on him when I retaliated. Well, call me a humourless unfeeling bastard, but...*

One teacher in Turkey found the majority of his students 'bouncy, bright, enthusiastic and sharp' but with one class he was always amazed that they walked upright when they got out of their chairs. It often turns out that each class develops a certain character. Some months after Jamie Masters returned home to London, he confessed:

> *Even now you only have to say the words 'D class Mastamba' to strike terror into my heart. But the A class in the same school was a joy to teach: rowdy, yes, but I had a lot of time for them. Within a class there are different personalities of course but they tend to get subsumed into the personality of the group. So I had good classes and bad classes in all the places I taught. When I left, some classes cheered; others wept and drew hearts all over their vocab tests. The main line of demarcation may in fact be age rather than income: the younger students more or less accept that they have to work; the older ones are beginning to rebel.*

Marta Eleniak, who taught in Spain, recommends taking a hard line:

> *Be a bitch at the start. The kids can be very wicked and take advantage of any good nature shown. Squash anyone who is late, shouts, gossips, etc. the first time or it'll never stop. The good classes make you love teaching. The bad make you feel as if you want to go back to filing.*

Each level and age group brings its own difficulties. Anyone who has no experience of dealing with young children may find it impossible to grab and hold their attention, let alone teach them any English. A lack of inhibition is very useful for teaching young children who will enjoy sing-songs, nursery rhymes, simple puzzles and games, etc. A firm hand may also be necessary if Aine Fligg's experience in Hong Kong is anything to go by. She was bitten on the ankle by one of her less receptive students. When the headmaster came in and remonstrated (with Aine!) the child bit him on the nose. The brat was then incarcerated in a cupboard, and emerged somewhat subdued.

Beginners of all ages progress much more rapidly than intermediate learners. Many teachers find adolescent intermediate learners the most difficult to teach. The original fun and novelty are past and they now face a long slog of consolidating vocabulary and structures. (The 'intermediate plateau' is a well-known phenomenon in language acquisition.) Adolescents may resent 'grammar games' (which are a standard part of EFL) thinking that games are suitable only for children.

The worst problem of all is to be confronted with a bored and unresponsive class. This may happen in a class of beginners who can't understand what is going on, especially a problem if you don't speak a word of their language. It can be extremely frustrating for all concerned when trying to teach some concept or new vocabulary without being able to provide the simple equivalent. If this is the case, you'll have to rely heavily on visual aids. Whole books have been written to show EFL teachers how to draw, for example *1000+ Pictures for Teachers to Copy* by Wright from CUP (£15.50). For a very low-level class, you may need to resort to your bilingual dictionary for lesson plans. On the other hand some teachers enjoy the challenge: 18 year old Hannah Bullock found teaching her class of Czech beginners good fun 'because each lesson was like an invigorating game of charades.' Many new teachers make the mistake of doing all the talking. During his year of teaching in Slovenia, Adam Cook, like many others before him, came to the conclusion that silence is one of the teacher's most effective tools.

The best way to inject a little life into a lethargic class is to get them moving around, for example get them to do a relaxation exercise or have them carry out a little survey of their neighbours and then report their findings back to the class. A reluctance to participate may be because the pupils do not see the point of it. In many countries foreign teachers come to feel like a dancing bear or performing monkey, someone who is expected to be a cultural token and an entertainer. If the students are expecting someone to dance a jig or swing from the chandelier (so to speak) they will be understandably disappointed to be presented with someone asking them to form sentences using the present perfect. At the other extreme, it is similarly disconcerting to be treated just as a model of pronunciation, and you may begin to wonder whether your employer might be better off employing a tape recorder.

Problems with Yourself

Of course lessons which fizzle or never get off the ground are not always the fault of the students. One of the most common traps into which inexperienced teachers fall is to dominate the class too much. Conversational English can only be acquired by endless practice and so you must allow your pupils to do most of the talking. Even if there are long pauses between your questions and their attempts to answer, the temptation to fill the silences should be avoided. Pauses have a positive role to play, allowing pupils a chance to dwell on and absorb the point you have just been illustrating. Avoid asking 'do you understand?' since the answer is meaningless; it is much more useful to test their comprehension indirectly.

A native speaker's function is seldom to teach grammar, though he or she should feel comfortable naming grammatical constructions. You are not there to help the students to analyse the language but to use it and communicate with it. It has been said that grammar is the highway code, the catalogue of rules and traffic signs, quite useless in isolation from driving, which gets you where you want to go. Grammar is only the cookery book while talking is cooking for other people to understand/eat. Persuading some students, whose language education has been founded on grammar rather than communication, that this is the priority may be difficult, but try not to be drawn into detailed explanations of grammatical structures.

This is probably not a very great temptation for many teachers who can barely distinguish prepositions from pronouns. Being utterly ignorant of grammar often results in embarrassing situations. You can only get away with bluffing for so long ('Stefan, I don't think it matters here whether or not it's a subjunctive') and irate pupils have been known to report to school directors that their teachers are grammar-illiterate. One useful trick suggested by Roberta Wedge is to reply, 'very good question—we're going to deal with that in the next class.' Normally it will suffice to have studied a general grammar handbook such as *Practical English Grammar* or *Practical English Usage* (see Bibliography above). If you contradict yourself between one lesson and the next, and an eager student notices it, take Richard Osborne's advice and say 'Ah yes, I'm sorry about that. You see, that's the way we do it at home. Bizness is always spelled with a z in Canada.'

The worst fate which can befall a teacher is to run dry, to run out of ideas and steam completely before the appointed hour has arrived. This usually happens when you fail to arrive with a structured lesson plan. It is usually a recipe for disaster to announce at the beginning of the lesson 'tonight let's talk about our travels/hobbies/animals' or whatever. Any course book will help you to avoid grinding to a halt. Supplementary materials such as songs and games can be lifesavers in (and out) of a crisis. If you are absolutely stuck for what to talk about next, try writing the lyrics of a popular song on the board and asking the class to analyse it or even act it out (avoiding titles such as 'I Want Your Body'). Apparently songs which have worked well for many teachers include George Michael's 'Careless Whispers', the Beatles' 'Here Comes the Sun' and 'When I'm 64' and 'Perfect Day' by Lou Reed. Another way of stepping outside the predictability of a course book might be to teach a short poem which you like, or even a short story (e.g. by Saki) if the class is sufficiently advanced.

Get the class to act out the title of a popular song

A very popular way to structure a lesson is in 'notions'; you take a general situation like 'praising' or 'complaining', teach some relevant vocabulary and structures and then have the class put them into practice in role-play situations. Unfortunately repetition is the key to language learning, though you have to avoid boring drills which will kill any interest in the language.

Culture shock is experienced by most people who live in a foreign country in whatever circumstances (see below), but can be especially problematic for teachers. Unthinkingly you might choose a topic which seems neutral to you but is controversial to them. A little feature on the English pub for example would not be enjoyed in Saudi Arabia. A discussion about whaling might make a class of Norwegians uncomfortable. Asking questions about foreign travels would be tactless in many places where few will be able to afford international travel.

One of the hardest problems to contend with is teacher burn-out. If you invariably arrive just as the class is scheduled to begin, show no enthusiasm, and glance at the clock every 90 seconds, you will not be a popular teacher. Getting hold of some new authentic materials might shore up your flagging enthusiasm for the enterprise. If not, perhaps it is time to consider going home (bearing in mind your contractual commitments).

Problems with Employers

All sorts of schools break their promises about pay, perks and availability of resources. The worst disappointment of all, however, is to turn up and find that you don't have a job at all. Because schools which hire their teachers sight unseen often find themselves let down at the last moment, they may over-hire, just in the way that airlines overbook their flights in the expectation of a certain level of cancellation. Even more probable is that the school has not been able to predict the number of pupils who will enrol and decides to hire enough teachers to cover the projected maximum. Whatever the reason, it can be devastating to have the job carpet whipped from under your feet. Having a signed contract helps. It may also be a good idea to maintain contact with the school between being hired and your first day of work. If the worst does happen, you could try losing your temper, threatening to tarnish their good name, and demand a month's pay and your return airfare. Or you could try playing on the guilt of the director and ask him or her to help you get a last-minute job in another school.

Just because a school does not belong to the EFL establishment does not mean that teachers will be treated badly (and vice versa). However the back street fly-by-night school may well cause its foreign teachers anxiety. The most common complaints revolve around wages—not enough or not often enough or both. Either you will have signed a contract (possibly in ignorance of the prevailing conditions and pay levels) or you have nothing in writing and find that your pay packet does not correspond with what you were originally promised. It is probably not advisable to take up a confrontational stance straightaway since this may be the beginning of a year of hostility and misery. Polite but persistent negotiations might prove successful. Find out if there is a relevant teachers union, join it and ask them for advice (though EFL is notorious for being non-unionised). As the year wears on, your bargaining clout increases, especially if you are a half-decent teacher, since you will be more difficult to replace mid-term.

One recourse is to bring your employer's shortcomings to the attention of the British Council or in extreme cases of exploitation, your Embassy/Consulate. If you are being genuinely maltreated and you are prepared to leave the job, delivering an ultimatum and threatening to leave might work. Remember that if there are cowboy schools, there are also cowboy teachers. Many honest and responsible employers have fallen victim to unreliable and undisciplined individuals who break their promises, show up late and abuse the accommodation they are given. Try not to let your employer down unless the provocation is serious.

Language schools must function as businesses as well as educational establishments and in some case the profit motive overtakes everything else. In those cases, teachers soon realise that they matter less to the people in charge than the number and satisfaction of students. You may be asked to conduct a conversation class in a room not much smaller than the Albert Hall. Some employers leave you entirely to your own devices and even look to you for teaching ideas. Others interfere to an annoying degree; we've heard of one school director in Spain who bugged the classrooms to make sure the staff were following his idiosyncratic home-produced course outlines. Jayne Nash worked for a chain of schools in France which use their own method; clients learned basic phrases and words for everyday situations parrot fashion:

> *The courses were aimed at local business people, therefore students learned mostly spoken English to introduce themselves, their company or product, language for meetings, telephone conversations, etc. The method seemed very effective, but can prove extremely tedious for the teacher. After you have repeated a word 10-20 times with 10 students, 4 times a day, 5 days a week...*

One of the most commonly heard complaints from teachers concerns their schedule. Eager only to satisfy clients, employers tend to mess around with teachers' timetables, offering awkward combinations of hours or changing the schedule at the last moment, which is extremely stressful. A certain amount of evening work is almost inevitable in private language schools where pupils (whether of school or working age) must study

English out-of-hours. Having to work early in the morning and then again through the evening can become exhausting after a while. It can also be annoying to have several long gruelling days a week and other days with scarcely any teaching at all (but still not days off).

One trick to beware of is to find that the 24 hours a week you were told you would be working actually means 32 45-minute lessons (which is much harder work than teaching 24 one-hour lessons). Even if the number of hours has not been exaggerated, you may have been deluded into thinking that a 24-hour week is quite cushy. But preparation time can easily add half as many hours again, plus if you are teaching in different locations, travel time (often unpaid) has to be taken into consideration.

In some situations teachers may be expected to participate in extra-curricular activities such as dreary drinks parties for pupils or asked to make a public speech. Make an effort to accept such invitations (especially near the beginning of your contract) or, if you must decline, do so as graciously as possible. There might also be extra duties, translating letters and documents, updating teaching materials, etc. for which you are unlikely to be paid extra.

PROBLEMS OUTSIDE WORK

Your main initial worry outside your place of employment will probably be accommodation. Once this is sorted out, either with the help of your school or on your own, and you have mastered the essentials of getting around and shopping for food, there is nothing to do but enjoy yourself, exploring your new surroundings and making friends.

Culture Shock

Enjoying yourself won't be at all easy if you are suffering from culture shock. Shock

Welcome to your conversation class

implies something which happens suddenly, but cultural disorientation more often creeps up on you. Adrenalin usually sees you through the first few weeks as you find the novelty exhilarating and challenging. You will be amazed and charmed by the odd gestures the people use or the antiquated way that things work. As time goes on, practical irritations intrude and the constant misunderstanding caused by those charming gestures—such as a nod in Greece meaning 'no' or in Japan meaning 'yes, I understand, but don't agree'—and the inconvenience of those antiquated phone boxes and buses will begin to get on your nerves. Unless you can find someone to listen sympathetically to your complaints, you may begin to think you have made a mistake in coming in the first place.

Experts say that most people who have moved abroad hit the trough after three or four months, probably just before Christmas in the case of teachers who started work in September. A holiday over Christmas may serve to calm you down or, if you go home for Christmas, may make you feel terminally homesick and not want to go back. Teachers who survive this, often find that things improve in the second term as they cease to perceive many aspects of life as 'foreign'.

The best way to avoid disappointment is to be well briefed beforehand, as emphasised in the chapter *Preparation*. Gathering general information about the country and specific information about the school before arrival will obviate many of the negative feelings some EFL teachers feel. If you are the type to build up high hopes and expectations of new situations, it is wise to try to dismantle these before leaving home. English teaching is seldom glamorous.

Even if you are feeling depressed and disappointed, do not broadcast your feelings randomly. Feeling contempt and hostility towards your host country is actually part of the process of adjusting to being abroad. But not everyone seems to appreciate that it has more to do with their own feelings than with the inadequacies (real or imagined) of the country they are in. So if you feel you have to let off steam about the local bureaucracy or the dishonesty of taxi-drivers or the way one simply cannot walk ten yards down the pavement without people crossing the street for the express purpose of bumping into you, at least have the common courtesy to do it in private, in letters or when there are no local people around.

This is especially important if you have colleagues who are natives of the country. They may find some of the idiosyncracies of their culture irritating too but, unlike you, they have to live with them forever. Some native-speaker teachers have found an unpleasant rift between local and foreign staff, which in some cases can be accounted for by the simple fact that you are being paid a lot more than they are. Sometimes new foreign teachers find their local colleagues cliquey and uncommunicative. No doubt they have seen a lot of foreigners come, and make a lot of noise, and go, and there is no particular reason why they should find the consignment you're in wildly exciting and worth getting to know.

Loneliness

Creating a social life from scratch is difficult enough at any time, but becomes even more difficult in an alien tongue and culture. You will probably find that many of your fellow teachers are lots of fun and able to offer practical help in your first few weeks (especially any who are bilingual). If you find yourself in a one-foreigner village, surely there's another lonely teacher across the mountaintop. You could meet for a drink at the weekend to commiserate and to draw up a charter and call yourselves 'The Wonga Plateau EFL Teachers' Association' (and remember to put yourself down as founder the next time you are revising your CV).

You may want to take some positive steps to meet people and participate in activities outside the world of English language instruction. This may require uncharacteristically extrovert behaviour, but overcoming initial inhibitions almost always pays worthwhile dividends.

If you are tired of conversations about students' dullness or your director of studies' evident lunacy, you might want to try to meet other expatriates who are not EFL teachers. The local English language bookshop might prove a useful source of information about forthcoming events for English-speakers, as will be any newspapers or magazines published in English such as the *Bulletin* in Belgium or the *Athens Daily News* in Greece. Seek out the overseas student club if there is a university nearby (though when they discover what line of work you are in they may well have designs on you). Even the least devout teachers have found English-speaking churches to be useful for arranging social functions and offering practical advice. If there is a bar in town which models itself on a British pub or American bar, you will no doubt find a few die-hards drinking Guinness or Budweiser, who might be more than willing to befriend you.

The most obvious way to meet other foreigners is to enrol in a language course or perhaps classes in art and civilisation. Even if you are not particularly serious about pursuing language studies, language classes are the ideal place to form vital social contacts. You can also join other clubs or classes aimed at residents abroad, for example some German cities have English amateur dramatics groups.

Making friends with locals may prove more difficult, though circumstances vary enormously according to whether you live in a small town or a big city, with some gregarious colleagues or by yourself, etc. The obvious source of social contact is your students and their friends and families (bearing in mind that in certain cultures, a teacher who goes out to a bar or disco with students risks losing their respect). As long as you don't spend all your free time moping at home, you are bound to strike up conversations with the locals, whether in cafés, on buses or in shops. Admittedly these seldom go past a superficial acquaintance, but they still serve the purpose of making you feel a little more integrated in the community. Local university students will probably be more socially flexible than others and it is worth investigating the bars and cafés frequented by students. If you have a particular hobby, sport or interest, find out if there is a local club where you will meet like-minded people; join local ramblers, jazz buffs, etc.—the more obscure the more welcome you are likely to be. You only have to become friendly with one other person to open up new social horizons if you are invited to meet their friends and family.

Make an effort to organise some breaks from work. Even a couple of days by the seaside or visiting a tourist attraction in the region can revitalise your interest in being abroad and provide a refreshing break from the tyranny of the teacher's routine.

Most wages and prices are given in local currencies. For conversion to sterling and US dollars, see *Appendix 1* on page 472.

Embassies and Consulates will normally provide information on working visas to supplement the information provided in this book. A selective list of diplomatic representatives in London and Washington can be found in *Appendix 2* on page 473.

British Council offices abroad are frequently referred to in these chapters. A list of the relevant addresses is provided in *Appendix 3* on page 475.

Schools whose names are italicised in the text are included in the directory of schools which follows each country chapter. Recruitment agencies whose names appear in italics are listed in the appropriate introductory section beginning on page 81.

WESTERN EUROPE

Austria

The attraction to English in Austria is proved by the number of English bookshops (with names like Big Ben and Shakespeare & Co.) and the popularity of the two English language newspapers *Austria Today* and *Vienna Reporter*. The market for ELT in Austria is divided largely between English for children and English for the business community. As in Germany and Switzerland, most private language institutes depend on freelance part-time teachers drawn from the sizeable resident international community. Some schools may be willing to offer a new arrival a few hours of teaching a week but patience will be required before a teaching timetable can be filled. One bonus for British and Irish teachers is Austria's full membership in the EU. Other nationalities may be able to find freelance work without having a work permit which is otherwise very difficult to obtain unless obtained in the home country. (It is generally accepted that as long as the number of hours worked per week does not exceed ten, no work permit is required.)

The British Council in Vienna Austria has a list of 21 English language institutes in Vienna. This list is annotated so that the kind of English tuition in which the company specialises is given, e.g. executive training, conversation classes, etc.

Teachers with a professional profile might find it worthwhile contacting the Austrian Cultural Institute in London (28 Rutland Gate, SW7 1PQ; 0171-584 8653/fax 0171-225 0470). They produce a leaflet which gives the address of the appropriate government department for British teachers interested in teaching in the state sector and can also supply a list headed 'Private Schools in Austria' which are not language institutes but private secondary schools with names like *Gymnasium Sacre Coeur für Mädchen*. Qualified teacher status would be virtually essential for teaching jobs in either sector. The British Council in Vienna also issues a list 'International and Bilingual Schools in Austria' containing 22 addresses.

Most *Volkshochschulen* offer English courses. The coordinating office in Vienna should be able to send you a list of the institutes around Austria (Verband Osterreichischer Volkshochschulen, Weintraubengasse 13, 1020 Vienna).

The Austrian Embassy in Washington distributes a leaflet *Teaching in Austria* which covers official teacher exchanges but not English language teaching. English Language Teaching Assistants from the UK and US are placed in Austrian secondary schools by the Central Bureau in London and the Fulbright Commission (Schmidgasse 14, 1082 Vienna; fax: 1-408 7765). They are looking for graduates in German and qualified teachers, under the age of 30. The deadline for applications is March 1st for the following academic year.

According to an American teacher-traveller Richard Spacer, who taught privately in Vienna for two months, the manager of inlingua in Vienna was very welcoming and informed him that the two-week methods course was offered to promising teachers free of charge. Richard earned AS200 per hour cash-in-hand. Although he remained in Vienna, he gathered that opportunities might have been more numerous in Salzburg and Linz where there is less competition from the dependants of UN employees.

The rate at reputable institutes starts at AS200 per hour, but may be less if the lessons are shorter than an hour. This is none-too-generous when the high cost of living in Vienna is taken into account. Life in the provinces is less expensive of course.

For practical advice on how to cope with life in Vienna, the handbook *Living in Vienna* published by the American Women's Association of Vienna might prove helpful.

Summer Camps

The demand for teachers of children and young people is very strong in Austria as elsewhere in Europe. Summer camps provide scope for EFL teachers, as indicated in the entries for *English for Children, English for Kids* and *Village Camps* of Switzerland. The organisation Young Austria (Alpenstrasse 108a, A-5020 Salzburg; 662-625 75 80) used to recruit about 30 teachers and monitors to work at summer language and sports camps near Salzburg, but no recent confirmation has been received that they continue to do so.

Some foreign young people who work as au pairs in Austria find that their primary task is to help teenage children with their English, which Maree Lakey from Australia found more taxing than she expected:

> *I am basically here to help the four children (aged between 11 and 17) with their English learning, although this is not always easy. On the whole, they have little desire to learn and see their lessons with me as more of a chore than anything else, but I guess that is not so unusual. I've found out how hard it is to try to speak correct English with them and to explain grammar rules which I have forgotten. It's also a bit difficult sometimes, as my Australian English is different from what the children have to learn. The children are of course not sympathetic to my difficulties, insisting that I should be infallable [sic] being a native speaker.*

LIST OF SCHOOLS

AUSTRO-BRITISH SOCIETY
Wickenburggasse 19, 1080 Vienna. Tel/fax: (1) 406 11 41.
Number of teachers: 12-14.
Preference of nationality: British.
Qualifications: TEFL Certificate and/or experience.
Conditions of employment: 2 semester commitment minimum.
Salary: AS210 per hour.
Facilities/Support: teachers choose own methods; course books available. Pupils are of all ages. Advice on accommodation given if possible.
Recruitment: local interview essential.

BERUFSFOERDERUNGSINSTITUT WIEN
Kinderspitalgasse 5, 1090 Vienna. Tel: 1-404 35 114. Fax: 1-404 35 124. E-mail: anmeldung.bat@bfi-wien.or.at
Number of teachers: about 20.
Preference of nationality: English native speakers.
Qualifications: TEFL qualification (CELTA preferred).
Conditions of employment: freelance basis. Students are attending BFI (Vocational Training Institute of Vienna).
Salary: AS250-AS320 per 45 minute unit.
Facilities/Support: no assistance with finding accommodation given.
Recruitment: local interviews essential.

BUSINESS LANGUAGE CENTER
Charles La Fond & Co. KEG, Trattnerhof 2, 1010 Vienna. Tel: (222) 533 7001-0. Fax: (222) 532 8521.
Number of teachers: 15.
Preference of nationality: none, but must be native speaker of English.
Qualifications: university degree, 3-5 years work experience in the business world, CELTA or equivalent and 1-2 years teaching experience required.
Conditions of employment: minimum stay 12 months. Teachers work on freelance basis and must sort out their own visa and tax requirements. No guarantee of fixed number of hours.

Salary: starting fee of AS180 per 40 minute lesson, net of VAT.
Facilities/Support: compulsory pre-service training programme and 3-4 workshops per year. School offers LCCI Certificate in teaching English for Business. No assistance with accommodation.
Recruitment: personal interview necessary.
Contact: Rebecca Chapman, Pedagogical Manager.

ENGLISH FOR CHILDREN
Kanalstrasse 44, Postfach 160, 1220 Vienna. Tel: (222) 282 77 17. Fax: (222) 282 77 177. Also operate as English Language Day Camp/ELDC at same address.
Number of teachers: varies according to need.
Preference of nationality:none, but must be English native speaker.
Qualifications: minimum age 21. Experience of working with children.
Conditions of employment: freelance 10-month contract (Sept-June). Minimum 4 h.p.w. Summer camp run during month of July.
Facilities/Support: need to be resident in Austria. Full training given free of charge before and during contract. All course materials provided.
Recruitment: direct applications, local advertising and interviews.
Contact: Catherine A. Walker.

ENGLISH FOR KIDS
A. Baumgartnerstr. 44/A 7042, 1230 Vienna. Tel: (1) 667 45 79. Fax: (1) 667 51 63. E-mail: magik@e4kids
Number of teachers: 4-5 for residential summer camp.
Preference of nationality: EU or others with work permit for Austria.
Qualifications: CELTA or Trinity Certificate (minimum grade B) and some formal teaching preferred required.
Conditions of employment: 6-8 weeks in July and August. Pupils aged from kindergarten to age 8 at level one and from 9 to 15 at level two. Also run language camp in the UK for pupils aged 15-17. Full-immersion courses with in-house methods following carefully planned syllabus and teachers' manual, supplemented with CD-Roms, etc.
Salary: varies depending on qualifications. From AS20,000 plus full board and accommodation for 6 weeks.
Facilities/Support: good standard of accommodation and full board provided for teachers.
Recruitment: personal interviews essential, sometimes held in UK.
Contact: Irena Köstenbauer, Principal.

ENGLISH LANGUAGE CENTRE HIETZING
In Der Hagenau 7, 1130 Vienna. Tel/fax: (1) 804 18 69. E-mail: elch@xpoint.at
Number of teachers: 3-4.
Preference of nationality: none.
Qualifications: CELTA and degree (preferably in languages/humanities). Experience advantageous especially of children's classes.
Conditions of employment: 10 month contracts September to June. No fixed hours since teachers work on freelance basis.
Salary: AS250-400 per 60 minutes, depending on size of class. Deduction for health insurance and pension contributions if teacher earns more than AS3,830 per month; if less no deduction is made. Teachers responsible for paying their own income tax.
Facilities/Support: no help with accommodation.
Recruitment: personal interview necessary.

LINGUARAMA SPRACHENINSTITUT
Concordiaplatz 2, 1010 Vienna. Tel/fax: (1) 533 0879. E-mail: vienna@ linguarama.com
Number of teachers: 25-70.
Preference of nationality: native speakers only.

Qualifications: university degree or equivalent plus a basic TEFL qualification e.g. CELTA. Experience teaching Business English is preferred, but must have at least a keen interest in business.
Conditions of employment: mixture of contract and freelance teachers. Early morning and evening work.
Salary: depends on experience.
Facilities/Support: all teachers are given an induction course and paid training is held monthly. Help given to contract teachers to find accommodation and obtain permits.
Recruitment: freelancers hired locally; contract teachers normally via Linguarama Group Personnel Department (89 High St, Alton, Hants. GU34 1LG, UK).

SPIDI (Spracheninstitut der Industrie)
Reisnerstrasse 40, 1030 Vienna. Tel: (1) 714 940319. Fax: (1) 714 9405.
Number of teachers: about 50.
Preference of nationality: EU citizens.
Qualifications: minimum CELTA plus 1 year's experience.
Conditions of employment: freelance only. Variable hours. Pupils of all ages.
Salary: AS250-350 per hour, depending on qualifications and experience.
Facilities/Support: no assistance with accommodation. Staffroom has PC and library. Induction course in mid-September. Monthly workshops for teachers.
Recruitment: local interview essential.
Contact: Kitty Loewenstein, Director of Studies.

TALK PARTNERS
Fischerstiege 10/16, 1010 Vienna. Tel: (1) 535 9695. Fax: (1) 533 3073. E-mail: talk.partners@telecom.at
Number of teachers: 50.
Preference of nationality: none.
Qualifications: minimum CELTA, university degree plus business experience.
Conditions of employment: most trainers are freelance. Hours vary.
Salary: minimum rate is AS200 for 45 minutes.
Facilities/Support: assistance with accommodation may be given if necessary.
Recruitment: local adverts in EFL journals and via British Council. Interviews essential; sometimes available in UK.
Contact: Rupert Sage, Director of Studies.

VERBAND WIENER VOLKSBILDUNG/WIENER VOLKSHOCHSCHULEN
Hollergasse 22, 1150 Vienna. Tel: (1) 89 174. Fax: (1) 89 174 65.
Number of teachers: varies according to demand. All teachers are freelance.
Preference of nationality: none.
Qualifications: CELTA or university training, or extensive experience of language teaching in adult education.
Conditions of employment: maximum 11½ lessons a week; minimum commitment 15 weeks. Hours are 9-12am and 6-9pm, including weekends.
Salary: AS215 per 50-minute lesson.
Facilities/Support: workshops and other training available. Library and media facilities available.
Recruitment: courses planned 6 months in advance. Local interview essential.
Contact: Thomas Fritz, Languages Department.

VILLAGE CAMPS
14 rue de la Morache, 1260 Nyon. Switzerland. Tel: (22) 990 9405. Fax: (22) 990 94 94.
Language summer camp at Zell am See, Austria.
Preference of nationality: none.
Qualifications: experience of teaching children required. Also a knowledge of a second

European language needed. Minimum age 21 for language monitors, 23 for teachers.
Conditions of employment: period of work from end of June to mid-August. Additional duties include supervising sports, activities and excursions.
Salary: English teachers earn £175 per week. Room and board and insurance provided.
Recruitment: via adverts, *TESOL Placement Bulletin*, international schools, etc.

Other Schools to Try

Note that these schools did not confirm their teacher requirements for this edition of *Teaching English Abroad*. Upper case entries marked with an asterisk had entries in the last edition (1997); addresses without asterisks have been taken from various sources, such as British Council lists and the *Yellow Pages*.

INTERNATIONAL SCHOOL KAPRUN, Alpine Sports & Ski Racing Academy, Postfach 47, 5710 Kaprun (tel/fax 6547 7106). 10 young graduates to supervise English and sports in exchange for room and board and ski pass.

English Language Services Network, Reichergasse 59/C, 3411 Klosterneuburg

Amerika-Institut, Operngasse 4, 1010 Vienna
Berlitz Sprachschulen, Graben 13, 1010 Vienna
Berlitz Sprachschulen, Rotenturmstrasse 1-3/8, 1010 Vienna
Berlitz Sprachschulen, Mariahilferstrasse 27, 1060 Vienna
Berlitz Sprachschulen, Troststrasse 50, 1100 Vienna
Didactica Akademie f. Wirtschaft und Sprachen, Schottenfeldgasse 13-15, 1070 Vienna
Euro-Languages, Getreidemarkt 17/1/5, 1060 Vienna (fax 004 315 85 327-19)
ILS, Opernring 1, 1010 Vienna
inlingua Sprachschule, Neuer Markt 1, 1010 Vienna
Institut CEF, Strozzigasse 4, 1080 Vienna
Multi Lingua, Hardtgasse 5/2, 1190 Vienna
Sight & Sound Studio, Schubertring 6-8, 1010 Vienna
Sprachstudio J.J Rousseau, Untere Viaduktgasse 43, 1030 Vienna
Super Language Learning, Florianigasse 55, 1080 Vienna

Benelux

BELGIUM

The situation is more hopeful in Belgium with more and better paid opportunities. The list of language schools in the Brussels Yellow Pages runs to four pages, under the heading *Langues (Ecoles de)/Talensholen.* Several language teaching organisations are represented in more than one Belgian city, especially Berlitz which employs upwards of 150 freelance teachers in more than ten branches. The starting pay at most schools is BF550-600 an hour.

As one of the capitals of the European Union, there is a huge demand for all the principal European languages in Brussels. Yet, despite the enormous amount of language teaching in Belgium, there is not really a shortage of teachers. In addition to the many Belgian teachers, there are also well-qualified expatriate spouses who take up teaching. One area in which a shortage does exist, however, is primary teaching in the private sector.

The Education Office of the British Council in Brussels (which is responsible for Luxembourg as well as Belgium) distributes a list of 22 private language schools. If possible, get hold of the special 'Schools Guide' edition published in April by the weekly English language magazine *The Bulletin* (1038 Chaussée de Waterloo, 1180

Brussels). The section called 'Learning the Language' lists most major language schools, but most issues contain some relevant adverts. Occasionally the classified ads include some requests for live-in helpers willing to teach English, or you can of course advertise yourself, though there will be plenty of competition from highly qualified teachers.

The casual teacher will probably steer clear of the schools which undertake to teach senior EU bureaucrats, but there are plenty of other schools. Telephone teaching has caught on in Belgium, especially among French learners of English; see entry for *Phone Languages*.

As throughout continental Europe, children attend summer camps which focus on language learning. Companies like Kiddy & Junior Classes (8 rue du Marteau, 1210 Brussels; 2-217 23 73), Kids' Computer Club (31 avenue René Gobert, 1180 Brussels; 2-374 27 08) and Call International (277 Avenue d'Auderghem, 1040 Brussels; 2-644 9595) organise holiday English courses; the latter company has centres in Waterloo, Antwerp and Tournai (69-22 45 20). One organisation which sometimes advertises in the UK for teachers is *Pro Linguis,* where Philip Dray worked one summer:

> *The school mainly caters for French boys and girls between 12 and 18. They come to Thiaumont for a course of one or two weeks. They sleep in dormitory-like accommodation in somewhat spartan conditions. I am employed in a freelance capacity to work 90 days between April and mid-September. The salary is £60 a day (paid monthly). The hours are very long: 8 per day with sometimes 7 days in a row though you are compensated by the fact that some days you are completely free. Travel is a great incentive in this part of Belgium (although you need a lot of money for the sky-high prices). For my keep (in a sort of hotel room) I have to check the dorms twice a week, which means enforcing an 11pm curfew, which so far has not been too bad since most kids have been cooperative.*

If you intend to stay in Belgium some time, it might be worth contacting your local *commune* (municipal council), which may offer adult education language courses. *Newcomer* is a free bi-annual publication from the publishers of *The Bulletin* which contains information and contact addresses of interest to the newly arrived teacher.

Freelance

The British Council keeps a register of individuals who teach English privately. Private tutors charge about BF900 an hour. In order to be included on their list of private tutors of English, you must provide documentary evidence that you have a CELTA or 100-hour equivalent plus either teacher certification or two years' TEFL experience. (A typical listing would be for a teacher with a BA (Hons) in modern languages, a PGCE and a TEFL qualification from International House. If your past attainments fall short of these, it is quite feasible to put up notices in one of the large university towns (Brussels, Antwerp, Gent, Leuven, Liège, etc.) offering conversation practice.

Almost all foreign teachers who begin to work for an institute do so on a freelance basis and will have to deal with their own tax and social security situation. Officially they should declare themselves *indépendants* (self-employed persons) and pay contributions which usually amount to about one-third of their salary. In fact many English teachers take their gross salary without declaring it, and don't work long enough to risk being caught. Once a teacher has worked black *(en noir/in het zwart)* it is difficult to regularise his or her status, since they then have to declare all previous earnings. Therefore anyone who plans to spend more than a few months teaching in Belgium should consider this question.

ANTWERPSE TALENAKADEMIE C.V.

Karel Govaertsstraat 23-25, 2100 Deurne. Tel: (3) 366 11 92. Fax: (3) 321 93 50.
Number of teachers: 10.
Preference of nationality: none.
Qualifications: any TEFL qualification and relevant experience.

Conditions of employment: courses last from 1 to 30 weeks. Evening hours 7-10pm. Children and adult classes.
Salary: BF500-800 per hour, depending on client.
Facilities/Support: some assistance with finding accommodation and obtaining work permits if necessary.
Recruitment: interviews in Belgium required.
Contact: Rita Stevens.

BERLITZ LANGUAGE CENTERS
Avenue de Tervueren 265, 1150 Brussels. Tel: (2) 763 08 30. Fax: (2) 771 01 70. E-mail: berlitz.method@skynet.be
Number of teachers: varies with demand.
Preference of nationality: British.
Qualifications: university degree.
Conditions of employment: freelance. Trial period of 3 months preceding contract. Flexible hours.
Facilities/Support: no assistance with accommodation. In-house training lasts 13 days.
Recruitment: via adverts and direct applications.
Contact: Joke Van Daele, Method Director.

BRUSSELS LANGUAGE STUDIES (BLS)
Rue du Marteau 8, 1210 Brussels. Tel: (2) 217 23 73. Fax: (2) 217 64 51.
Number of teachers: 20 freelancers.
Preference of nationality: EU nationals only.
Qualifications: teaching experience with children and adults desirable.
Conditions of employment: weekly contracts during holidays. During school year, all work is on freelance basis. Children's courses are 6 h.p.w.; adults are more.
Salary: BF550 per hour.
Facilities/Support: assistance with finding accommodation if necessary.
Recruitment: direct application and contact with universities. Interviews not held in UK.

EURO BUSINESS LANGUAGES
Leuvensesteenweg 325, 1932 Zaventem. Tel: (2) 720 15 10. Fax: (2) 270 25 80.
Number of teachers: 22.
Preference of nationality: none.
Qualifications: university degree and several years of work experience (preferably teaching English to adults) required.
Conditions of employment: all teachers are freelancers. Variable hours between 8am and 6pm or evening classes until 10pm. Students are all business people. Teachers choose their own course books (but need not pay for these). All courses are custom-made; emphasis on role plays relevant to client's profession.
Salary: starting hourly rate of BF750. Travelling allowance paid if course given at client's office.
Facilities/Support: assistance given to teachers who want to establish legitimate freelance status. Can sponsor non-EU applicants for work permit if appropriate. Training given plus three refresher meetings a year.
Recruitment: personal interview necessary.
Contact: F. Valentin, Director.

LANGUAGES UNLIMITED
77 Chaussée de Charleroi, 1060 Brussels. Tel/fax: (2) 534 76 84.
Number of teachers: 5.
Preference of nationality: British or Irish.
Qualifications: university degree or equivalent, experience dealing with people and teaching, good presentation and pleasant personality.
Conditions of employment: freelance. Hours vary from day to day.

Salary: BF700 per hour.
Facilities/Support: no assistance with accommodation. Training given.
Recruitment: CVs, local interviews essential.
Contact: R. Collins, Teacher Training & Recruitment.

MAY INTERNATIONAL TRAINING CONSULTANTS
55 rue de Bordeaux, 1060 Brussels. Tel: (2) 536 06 70. Fax: (2) 536 06 80. E-mail: mayintl@compuserve.com
Number of teachers: approximately 25.
Preference of nationality: none.
Qualifications: TEFL qualification, minimum 1 year's teaching experience with adults.
Conditions of employment: no contracts, but minimum commitment of 1 year. Mostly day-time work, although evening work is available. Pupils are all adults, and mostly in business/professions. ISO 9001 Quality System in operation.
Salary: minimum BF600 per hour.
Facilities/Support: assistance with accommodation. Informal training/assistance given.
Recruitment: local newspaper adverts. Interviews essential, usually local but sometimes held in UK.
Contact: Valerie McConaghy, Director.

PHONE LANGUAGES
Rue des Echevins 65, 1050 Brussels. Tel: (2) 647 40 20. Fax: (2) 647 40 55.
Number of teachers: 80 throughout Belgium (including 20 English teachers).
Preference of nationality: American and English (BBC accent) preferred but others considered.
Qualifications: BA (TEFL).
Conditions of employment: all teachers are freelance and teach in cycles of 10, 30, 50 or 100 half-hour lessons over the phone. Flexible hours of work between 8am-10pm; the favourite times are 8-10am, lunchtime and 5-8pm. Pupils are all adults (usually business people). Teachers must have their own telephone and be prepared to stay in Belgium for at least one year.
Salary: BF600 per hour.
Facilities/Support: no assistance with accommodation. Free training given for 8-10 half-hours. Course books supplied free of charge.
Recruitment: adverts in local press. Local interviews essential.

PRO LINGUIS
6717 Thiaumont. Tel: (63) 22 04 62. Fax: (63) 22 06 88.
Number of teachers: 14 (freelancers).
Preference of nationality: British.
Qualifications: EFL training, BA (Hons) in English or business. Must have excellent spelling.
Conditions of employment: minimum 1 year contracts or 2 month contracts in summer. 7 hours a day, 4-5 days per week.
Salary: BF3,000-3,300 per day plus full board.
Facilities/Support: assistance with accommodation given and help sometimes available for obtaining work permits.
Recruitment: personal contacts. Interviews in Belgium only.
Contact: Christiane Maillart.

Other Schools to Try
Note that these schools did not confirm their teacher requirements for this edition of *Teaching English Abroad*. Upper case entries marked with an asterisk had entries in the last edition (1997); addresses without asterisks have been taken from various sources, such as British Council lists and the *Yellow Pages*.

Berlitz Language Centre, Meir 21, 1st Floor, 2000 Antwerpen
Berlitz Language Centre, Britselei 15, 2018 Antwerpen
inlingua, Frankrijklei 39, 2000 Antwerpen

Amira, 251 Avenue Louise, 1050 Brussels
Berlitz Language Centre, Avenue Louise 306, 1050 Brussels
Berlitz Language Centre, Avenue des Arts 36, 1040 Brussels
Berlitz Language Centre, Place Stéphanie 10, 1050 Brussels
British Commission, rue de la Charité 39, 1040 Brussels
Crown Language Centre, rue du Béguinage 13, 1000 Brussels
Brussels Language Studies and *Kiddy & Junior Classes,* 8 rue du Marteau, 1210
   Brussels
CALL Languages & Training, Av d'Auderghem 277, 1040 Brussels
CCLM, 29 rue Abbé Jean Heymans, 1200 Brussels
CPAB Language School, Galerie de la Toison d'Or, 4th Floor, 29-31 Chaussée
   d'Ixelles, 1050 Brussels
European Language Center, 141 rue Champ du Roi, 1040 Brussels
Fondation 9, 412 Avenue Louise, 1050 Brussels
Kids' Computer Club, 31 Avenue René Gobert, 1180 Brussels
Languages Unlimited, 77 Chaussée de Charleroi, 1060 Brussels
Liren International Institute, 13 rue du Beau-Site, 1000 Brussels
*THE MITCHELL CENTRE, Rue Louis Hap 156, 1040 Brussels (2-734 80 73/fax 2-
   732 63 35). 15 native speakers for centres in Brussels and Antwerp.
Peters School, rue des 2 Eglises 87, 1040 Brussels

Berlitz Language Centre, Kouter 177, 9000 Gent
Inlingua School of Languages, UCO-Toren/6de Verdieping, Bellevue 9/10, 9050 Gent
   (Ledeberg)
Practicum, Reep 24, 9000 Gent
Ski Ten International, Chateau d'Emines, 5080 La Bruyère
Berlitz Language Centre, rue du Pont d'Avroy 2/4, 4000 Liège
GLTT, 2 rue de l'Ecole, 1640 Sint-Genesius-Rode
Ceran Lingua International, 16 Avenue du Chateau, 4900 Spa (87-791545/e-mail
   ceran@mail.interpac.be). 17 freelancers.
Dialogue, 55 Route du Tonnelet, 4900 Spa
Berlitz Language Centre, Leuvenselaan 17, 3300 Tienen
Access bvba Taalbureau, Abdijstraat 40, 2260 Tongerlo
Kasteel van Velm, 32 Halleweg, 8306 Velm

LUXEMBOURG

There is a handful of private language schools in the country, so not much scope for
ELT teachers. *Phone Languages* in Belgium have a network of telephone teachers in
Luxembourg, but run the operation from the Brussels office. Another possibility is the
Centre de Langues Luxembourg (80 Boulevard G. Patton, L-2316 Luxembourg;
403941/fax 403930).

   Informal live-in tutoring jobs are possible. Luxembourg Accueil Information (10
Bisserwee, L-1238 Luxembourg-Grund; 241717) is a centre for new arrivals and
temporary residents. They provide a range of services on their premises, including
language courses, and might be able to advise on teaching and tutoring possibilities.
The British-Luxembourg Society promotes British culture and the English language in
Luxembourg, and they also might be a source of information. The English language
newspaper is the *Luxembourg News* (25 rue Philippe II, L-2340 Luxembourg).

NETHERLANDS

Urban Dutch people have a very high degree of competence in English after they
finish their schooling. Educated Dutch people are so fluent in English that the
Minister of Education once suggested that English might become the main language
used in Dutch universities, a suggestion which caused an understandable outcry. This

is not a country in which any old BA (Hons) has much chance of stepping into an ELT job.

What private language schools there are tend to provide business English and to be looking for teachers with extensive commercial or government experience as well as a teaching qualification. So many British people have settled in the Netherlands, attracted by its liberal institutions, that most schools depend on long-term freelancers. The British Council in Amsterdam maintains a list of more than 50 language institutes throughout the country which prepare candidates for the Cambridge exams. Highly qualified teachers or those with expertise in tutoring in an executive context should contact these language institutes. The British Language Training Centre in Amsterdam (Oxford House, N.Z. Voorburgwal 328e, 1012 RW Amsterdam; 20-622 36 34/fax 20-626 49 62), which offers the CELTA course, can give advice to qualified job-seekers and might even know of other institutes looking for teachers.

One possibility is the network of *Volksuniversiteit*, the northern European institution of 'folk universities'. There are branches in Amersfoort, Delft, Groningen, Haarlem, Hertogenbosch, Hilversum, Leiden, Rotterdam, Utrecht and several others as well as Amsterdam. When Andrew Boyle wrote to a selection of the addresses on the British Council list, the ones that replied were able to offer only the possibility of part-time work.

Outside the mainstream language institutes, it might be possible to arrange some telephone teaching. Village Camps (see chapter on Switzerland) has a language camp operation in the Netherlands which takes on a few English teachers and monitors.

BERLITZ
Rokin 87-89, 1012 KL Amsterdam. Tel: (20) 622 13 75. Fax: (20) 620 39 59.
Number of teachers: 60.
Preference of nationality: British, Irish.
Qualifications: BA and teaching experience preferred but not essential. Professional manner needed. Candidates should already be living in Amsterdam.
Conditions of employment: employee contract with no guarantee of hours. Opening hours: 7.30am-9.45pm weekdays and 9am-12.45pm Saturdays.
Salary: from 20 guilders per 45-minute lesson. Sessions last a minimum of 90 minutes.
Facilities/Support: no assistance with accommodation. 10 day in-house training is compulsory.
Recruitment: through newspaper adverts. Local interviews essential.

A selection of other schools to try (towns in alphabetical order):
Alphen Studiecentrum, Molenvliet 3, 2405 BZ Alphen a/d Rijn
British Language Training Centre, NZ Voorburgwal 328, 1012 RW Amsterdam. Also offer CELTA course.
Linguarama, S. Strawinskylaan 507, 1077 Amsterdam
New School for Information Services, Jan Luykenstraat 98, 1071 CV Amsterdam
The Workshop, Rostocklaan 38, 7315 HM Apeldoorn
English Language Institute, Berkenweg 46, 3741 BZ Baarn
All-English Institute, Iepenlaan 96, 2061 GN Bloemendaal
Secradesk, Postbus 545, 7500 AM Enschede
Dutchess English Language Centre, Schoutenstraat 86, 1623 RZ Hoorn
Albeda College, Heindijk 16, 3079 PM Rotterdam
Taleninstituut Bogaers, Schouwburgring 97, 5038 TK Tilburg
Schoevers Opleidingen, Kromme Nieuwe Gracht 3, 3512 HC Utrecht

France

The French used to rival the English for their reluctance to learn other languages. A Frenchman abroad spoke French as stubbornly as Britons spoke English. But things have changed, especially in the business and technical community. French telephone directories contain pages of language institutes.

Since the 1970s, the law has put pressure on companies to provide on-going training to staff, and therefore many private language institutes cater purely to the business market. In fact a quick browse through the entries in the List of Schools at the end of this chapter will lead you to the conclusion that all adult language training in France is business-oriented, with most of it taking place on site and the rest taking place in business and vocational schools. In this setting the term *formateurs* or 'trainers' is often used instead of English teachers. Private training companies involved with *formation continue* seem to produce very glossy brochures which look more like the annual report of a multinational corporation than an invitation to take an evening course. Many offer one-to-one tuition.

The French government does not neglect the less privileged, either: there is a scheme in place in some regions whereby the unemployed can take free English lessons at private schools. A considerable number of town councils *(mairies)* and *Chambres de Commerce et d'Industrie* (CCI) have their own Centres d'Etude des Langues. The main CCI in Paris (1-55 65 55 65) should be able to refer enquirers to other centres involved in English teaching; contact their Bureau pour l'Information et l'Orientation Professionnelle on 1-47 66 20 00 between 1.30pm and 5.30pm.

Teaching young children is left mostly to French teachers of English, though native speakers might find a freelance opening. Some municipalities have introduced projects to teach English to four-year-olds. The most popular times are Wednesdays (when state schools are closed) and Saturdays. The fashion for telephone teaching, a concept invented by a Parisian yuppie (or so it is said), seems to be waning somewhat.

Prospects for Teachers

Advanced ELT qualifications seem to be less in demand in France than solid teaching experience, particularly in a business context. But an increasing number of schools require a relevant educational background, e.g. B.Ed., PGCE, CELTA or DELTA. Candidates may be asked to provide an *attestation de durée d'études* to show the educational level they have reached. However, anyone who has a university degree and who can look at home in a business situation has a chance of finding teaching work, particularly if they have a working knowledge of French. Having your own transport is a huge advantage as Helen Welch reported in the autumn of 1998. She arrived in the Toulouse area (from Thailand) in August, was offered two jobs almost straightaway and claims that a car is 'absolutely necessary for teaching here'.

In some circles it is fashionable to learn American English which means that, despite the visa difficulties for non-EU nationals, it is possible for Americans to find work. Twice as many schools listed at the end of this chapter claim to have no preference as to the country of origin of their native-speaker teachers as mention EU nationality.

For EU nationals interested in working in the public sector, recent access to certain posts for *professeurs agrégés* and *certifiés* is now possible. To follow the developments in this and to know more about the National Education System, obtain the *Bulletin Officiel du Ministère de l'Education Nationale* from the bookshop of the Centre National de Documentation Pédagogique (CNDP, 13 rue du Four, 75270 Paris Cedex 06; 1-46 34 54 80), which costs F14.

France is such a popular and obvious destination for British and Irish people and also with North Americans that a speculative job hunt from abroad can be disappointing. Major language teaching organisations receive speculative CVs every day and can't promise anything until they meet the applicant.

FIXING UP A JOB

In Advance

The first step that any aspiring teachers should take is to request a copy of the detailed and realistic document *Teaching English as a Foreign Language in France* from the British Council in Paris (1-49 55 73 00). It is full of hard information, though has not been updated for $2\frac{1}{2}$ years. They also produce a list of 'Institutions Offering English Language Tuition in the Paris Area.' Beside each of the 50+ company addresses, it gives the minimum teaching qualification and the courses and exams offered. Unfortunately nearly a third of the addresses are out-of-date.

Neither the British Council in Paris (9-11 rue de Constantine, 75007; 1-49 55 73 00) nor the one in Bordeaux (Université Victor-Segalen, 3 place de la Victoire, 33076 Bordeaux; 5-57 57 19 52) has a Teaching Centre. (Note that the British Council in Lyon is now closed.) The Paris office has a library which actively assists people who are already teaching in France but which cannot offer individual help to job applicants or deal with CVs. The Paris library is open weekdays from 11am to 6pm (till 7pm on Wednesdays): 1-49 55 73 23. In Bordeaux, the British Council is open from Monday to Friday from 11am-1pm and from 2pm-5pm. Both British Council offices are closed between mid-July and early September.

For addresses of other language schools, try the Franco-British Chamber of Commerce (same address as *IAL*). The British Council recommends consulting *Dicoguide de la Formation* published annually by Génération Formation (27 rue du Chemin Vert, 75011 Paris: 01-48-07-41-41). However this is not very practical advice since the book retails for F2,500. A smaller booklet called *Bien choisir son organisme de séjour linguistique* might prove more useful though it is aimed primarily at French people who want to travel abroad to learn a language. The book may be ordered from the Service d'Abonnements de l'Etudiant (3-44 03 42 75) for F69 plus postage.

The *Central Bureau for Educational Visits and Exchanges* (10 Spring Gardens, London SW1A 2BN; 0171-389-4004) sends a large number of university students studying modern languages at British universities to spend a year as language assistants in French secondary schools. Similarly the *Fulbright Commission* sends about 40 Americans to be teaching assistants in France. They receive a stipend of F5,000-F6,000 a month for eight months beginning October 1st.

The *Alliance Française* has centres throughout the world, with more than 60 in the UK and 100 in the US. Anyone who can converse in French might find it useful to make contact before leaving home. Most centres have a notice board where requests for tutors, au pairs, etc. are occasionally posted. In London, the Alliance Française Grande Bretagne is located at 1 Dorset Square, NW1 6PU (0171-224 1865) and in New York at 22 E. 60th Street, New York, NY 14610 (212-355-6100/fax 212-935-4119/e-mail: frinst1@metgate.metro.org; http://www.fiaf.org).

If you want to find the addresses of private language schools, consult the *Pages Jaunes* (Yellow Pages) under the headings *Enseignement: Langues* or *Ecoles de Langues*. As usual it is easier to consult these at reference libraries than at French Consulates abroad. Other federations and associations which might be able to provide contacts to qualified teachers are listed below. If writing to them, be specific in your request:

Fédération française des organisations de séjours culturels linguistiques (FFOSC), 108 bd Péreire, 75017 Paris (1-40 54 86 99).

Séjours linguistiques associés (SELIA), rue de l'Eperon, 75006 Paris (1-44 32 16 86)

L'Union nationale des organisations de séjours linguistiques (UNOEL), 15-19 rue des Mathurins, 75009 Paris (1-49 24 03 61)

L'Union nationale des organisations de séjours longues durée 'a l'étranger (UNSE), 46 rue du Commandant-J.-Duhail, 94120 Fontenay-sous-Bois (1-48 76 65 12).

Adverts for teaching jobs in France seldom appear in the UK press and virtually never in American journals. The only organisation seen advertising vacancies in

France repeatedly gives only a PO Box address and did not reply to enquiries for this book (EuroTemp Employment Agency, PO Box 20, Stratford-upon-Avon CV37 8YL). French newspapers carry a few ads, including *Le Figaro* (1-56 52 56 52) which can be consulted via the internet (www.cadremploi.fr); teaching jobs appear mainly on Monday and Tuesday. Occasionally the Paris edition of the *International Herald Tribune* is useful.

When applying to a training organisation, try to demonstrate your commercial flair with a polished presentation including a business-like CV (omitting your hobbies) preferably accompanied by a hand-written letter in impeccable French. Andrew Sykes felt that he owed the success of his job-hunt to his misguided and unsuccessful accountancy training rather than to his TEFL Certificate:

> I wrote to more or less all the schools from your book in France and elsewhere that didn't stipulate 'experience required' and was fairly disheartenedd by the few, none-too-encouraging replies along the lines of 'if you're in town, give us a call.' Sitting in a very cheap hotel bedroom halfway down Italy in early November feeling sorry for myself and knowing that I was getting closer and closer to my overdraft limit and an office job back in the UK, I rang the schools that had replied and so picked up the phone and rang through to BEST in Tours. 'Drop in,' the voice said, 'and we will give you an interview'. So I jumped on the next train, met the director on Monday and was offered a job on the Tuesday morning, initially on an hour-by-hour basis and then in December on a contract of 15 hours which was later increased to 20 hours a week.
>
> OK, I was very lucky. I have since learned that the school receives several phone calls and letters per week; it's an employer's market. What got me the job was not my TEFL certificate nor my very good French. It was the fact that I was an ex-accountant. I had been one of the thousands enticed by the financial benefits of joining an accountancy firm after graduation. But I hated the job and failed my first professional exams. Ironically the experience gained during those two and a half years of hell was invaluable. Whereas in Italy they want teaching experience, in France they want business experience.
>
> You will in the end be teaching people not objects, and any experience you can bring to the job (and especially the job interview) will help. However ashamed you may be of telling everyone in the pub back home that you were once a rat catcher, it may be invaluable if the school's main client is 'Rent-o-kill'.

The technique of making a personal approach to schools in the months preceding the one in which you would like to teach is often successful. On the strength of her Cambridge/RSA Certificate from International House, Fiona Paton had been hoping to find teaching work in the south of France in the summer but quickly discovered that there are very few opportunities outside the academic year. On her way back to England, she disembarked from the train in the picturesque town of Vichy in the Auvergne just long enough to distribute a few self-promotional leaflets to three language schools. She was very surprised to receive a favourable reply from one of them once she was home, and so returned a few weeks later for a happy year of teaching.

Teaching English in exchange for room and board is very widespread and is normally arranged on the spot, but can also be set up in advance. While looking for something to do in her gap year, Hannah Start was put in touch with a French bank executive who had done an English language course in Hannah's home town and who wanted to keep up her English at home in Paris by having someone to provide live-in conversation lessons. So, in exchange for three hours of speaking English in the evening (usually over an excellent dinner), Hannah was given free accommodation in the 17th *arrondissement*.

On the Spot

The British Council in Paris and Bordeaux have notice boards advertising current teaching vacancies; the one in Paris is located near the library. When you do go along to look at the adverts, take care to look respectable since you will have to get through security. As well as proper jobs with language schools, live-in positions are also occasionally advertised as Julian Peachey discovered:

I got a job via the British Council notice board looking after a little French boy, but lost that job after a couple of months. I got the British Council's list of English language schools and rang up all 68 of them. One school, desperate for a teacher the next morning, gave me a job over the phone. That was my first break and it paid £10 an hour. I slowly got work at other schools and also found a very cheap studio to sub-rent in Pigalle.

Prospective teachers should not automatically head for Paris. Not only is it hard to find work but of course rents are very high in the capital. (A studio flat might cost F3,000 per month exclusive of utilities, though sharing would bring the cost down.) A host of schools may be found in provincial cities. If you do decide to give it a go in Paris, watch for adverts in the *métro* for English language courses, since these are usually the biggest schools and therefore have the greatest number of vacancies for teachers. Certain streets in the 8th *arrondissement* around the Gare St. Lazare abound in language schools.

Berlitz has a sizeable presence in Paris with the French head office located at 15 rue le Louis Grand, 75002 Paris. Linguarama (6 rue de Berri, 75008 Paris; 1-40 76 07 07) and *inlingua* (172 rue de Courcelle, 75017 Paris; 1-46 22 45 85) both have multiple centres.

Non-EU nationals are bound to encounter problems (see section on Regulations) as Beth Mayer from New York found:

I've tried to get a job at a school teaching, but they asked for working papers which I don't have. I checked with several schools who told me that working papers and a university degree were more important than TEFL qualifications.

Freelance

As is increasingly common in many countries, schools are often reluctant to take on contract teachers for whom they would be obliged to make expensive contributions for

If the school's best business client is Rentokil it may be invaluable

social security (19%-22% of gross pay). So there is a bustling market in freelance teachers. Self-employed workers *(travailleurs indépendants)*, however little they earn, are obliged to register at the social security office (URSSAF de Paris, 3 rue Franklin, 93100 Montreuil; 1-49 20 10 10). The hourly fees *(honoraires)* paid to freelance teachers should be significantly higher than to contract workers *(salariés)* since they are free of deductions. It is very difficult to earn a professional living as a freelancer especially in Paris, since competition is ferocious, the market saturated, and taxes and social charges very high.

However at a more casual level, language exchanges for room and board are commonplace in Paris; these are usually arranged through advertisements or word-of-mouth. You can also offer English lessons privately in people's homes, which often pays F100 a session. In addition to the British Council notice board, there are many other *panneaux* which might prove useful to someone looking for private tutoring. This is especially appealing to Americans who do this without worrying too much about visas.

There are expatriate grapevines all over Paris, very helpful for finding teaching work and accommodation. The one in the foyer of the CIDJ at 101 Quai Branly; 1-44 49 12 00 *(métro* Bir-Hakeim) is good for occasional studenty-type jobs, but sometimes there are adverts for a *soutien scolaire en Anglais* (English tutor). It is worth arriving early to check for new notices (the hours are Monday-Saturday 9am-6pm).

The other mecca for job and flat-hunters is the American Church at 65 Quai d'Orsay *(métro* Invalides). The notices posted upstairs are the official ones, issued every day, and mainly for au pair jobs and accommodation. The downstairs board is more chaotic and it will take about half an hour to rummage through all the notices. It does no harm to put up your own notice here, since it is free.

Other notice boards include the one at the American Cathedral (23 ave. George V; *métro* Alma Marceau), and at the two British churches, St. Georges at 7 rue August Vacquerie in the 16th *arrondissement* and St. Michaels at 5 rue d'Aguesseau in the 8th. The latter board carries notices of accommodation both wanted and available, as well as ads for conversation exchanges (e.g. English for French). The church office is open during the week on Monday, Tuesday, Thursday and Friday from 10am till 1pm and 2pm to 5.30pm. Although the notice board at the Alliance Française (101 Boulevard Raspail, 75270 Paris) is for the use of registered students of French at the Alliance, you may be able to persuade a student to look at the adverts for you, many of which are exchanges of a room for some babysitting and/or teaching. The notice board is in the annex around the corner at 34 rue de Fleurus near the *métro* Notre Dame des Champs (1-45 44 38 28/www.alliancefrancaise.fr).

Most of the above expat meeting-places distribute the free bilingual newsletter *France-USA Contacts* or *FUSAC* which comes out every other Wednesday. It can also be picked up at English language bookshops like W.H. Smith near Place de la Concorde. It comprises mainly classified adverts including some for English teachers which are best followed up on the day the paper appears. It is possible to place an ad before your arrival in France. An advert in *FUSAC* costs F110 for 25 words, and can be sent to 3 rue Larochelle, 75014 Paris (1-45 38 56 57/fax 1-45 35 59 41) or in the US to France Contacts, 48 W 12th St, GO, New York, NY 10011-8639 (212-929-2929). Ask to place your ad under the heading 'Work wanted in France'. During Beth Mayer's first year in Paris she found that advertising in *FUSAC* was very effective:

> I placed an ad to teach English and offer editing services (I was an editor in New York City before moving here) and received many responses. I charged F80 per hour but found that after I had spent time going and coming, I earned only F40 an hour. So perhaps it would have been better to have the lessons at your apartment (if centrally located). I not only 'teach' English but offer English conversation to French people who don't need a teacher but more a companion with whom to practise. I've met a lot of nice people this way and earned money to boot.

It may be worth including a reminder here that anyone who advertises their services should exercise a degree of caution when arranging to meet prospective clients.

REGULATIONS

For Britons, the same situation pertains as throughout the EU, and the bureaucratic procedures can be just as protracted as they are in other member states. French bureaucracy is legendary. EU nationals must apply for a residence permit (*carte de séjour de ressortissant de l'Union Européenne*) from the Aliens Department of the police (*Préfecture*) or at the Townhall within three months of arrival or as soon as work is found. This application should be made in the area in which you are living. You are entitled to work as soon as the application has been lodged; the document typically takes six to nine months to come through.

The documents needed to accompany your application for a *carte de séjour* are your passport and birth certificate, either the original or a certified and translated copy (which costs about F100 at the British Embassy in Paris but may be cheaper if you do it before you leave home). You will also need a *Déclaration d'Etat Civil* from your consulate, on presentation of your birth certificate. In some areas you may also be asked to submit the originals of your diplomas or certificates, photographs, three salary slips, rent receipts and a medical certificate, e.g. from the *Médicine du Travail* centre in Paris. If you are applying before you find a job you may have to show proof of adequate funds (F1,000 and a credit card should be enough). A social security number (*sécu*) will be assigned to you so that employers can start paying contributions for you. No claims can be made before working 120 hours in one month or 200 hours in three months, so it is wise to have private insurance initially. Tax is not deducted in your first year of employment but must be paid in arrears from your second year onwards. The tax year runs from February. Most schools estimate that an annual tax bill for a full-time teacher will be the equivalent of between one month's salary and one and a half month's salary.

It is worth pointing out that anyone with a *carte de séjour* may be able to reduce their rent bill significantly, provided their earnings two years prior to applying were low. The benefit is administered by the Caisse d'Allocations Familiales (CAF), as Andrew Sykes explains:

> *If your income two years before applying was low (e.g. if you worked as a campsite courier as I did), a substantial part of your rent (anything up to 65-70%) may be paid by the French government. At first glance, getting hold of all the paperwork may seem a drag (and expensive in the case of official translations of documents) but it is financially beneficial if they decide you are eligible. As an indication of how much they pay out, the rent that I pay for a large town centre studio is F2,300 per month and the benefit I receive is F1,341 (just under 60%).*

In order to apply, it is necessary to furnish the CAF with a signed/stamped declaration from your landlord, a declaration of income for the calendar year preceding the year of benefit, a *Fiche Individual d'Etat Civile* and various other bits and pieces.

Documents published by the CIDJ could be of help when sorting out the paper work as well as when hunting for a job. To obtain the CIDJ catalogue of information leaflets (*fiches*) by post, send four international reply coupons to CIDJ at 101 Quai Branly, 75740 Paris Cedex 15 (1-44 49 12 00). Most *fiches* cost F10 if picked up in person or F20 or 6 IRCs if requested by post, e.g. 5.5702: 'Séjour et emploi des ressortissants de l'Union Européenne'; 5.574: 'Séjour et emploi des étudiants étrangers'; and 3.01: 'Rechercher un emploi'.

Non-EU Nationals

In France, it is bordering on the impossible for Americans, Canadians, Australians and all other non-EU nationalities to get a work permit. Even with a job offer, applicants are not granted work permits unless they are married to a French national. Non-EU nationals must obtain work documents before they leave their home country, either a *carte de séjour temporaire salarié* (valid for one year and specifying where and in what sector they may work) or a *carte de résident* (valid for ten years and for any activity anywhere in continental France). The only way to get either visa is to have a signed contract in hand and to obtain authorisation from the French Department of Employment. A handful of employers are willing to tackle the bureaucracy which involves applying to the *Agence locale de l'Emploi* or the *Office des Migrations Internationales* (44 rue Bargue, 75732 Paris cedex 15; 1-53 69 53 70). The applicants must also undergo a medical examination by an appointed doctor.

Note that the TEFL training organisation WICE (20 Boulevard du Montparnasse, 75015 Paris; 1-45 66 75 50), which is affiliated to Rutgers University in the US, runs occasional information evenings for Americans on how to get working papers. In its standard letter E7, the CIDJ writes in no uncertain terms about the difficulty of obtaining working papers. It might also be worth obtaining fiche 5.5701 *Séjour et emploi des étrangers*. Also, the US Information Service of the American Embassy runs an English Teacher's Resource and Information Centre (2 rue de Constantine, 75001 Paris; 1-43 12 22 22).

One of the language schools which corresponded with this book phrased the situation rather brutally:

> Unless US citizens have priority work or are married to a French national and have French nationality themselves, they will NOT be able to work in France, even if they have a job offer. Those who are looking for a full-time regular job without satisfying those requirements are wasting their time sending CVs to France. It is very unfortunate but it is the LAW.

In fact thousands of Americans (and other nationalities) are teaching English in France on a part-time basis. If they have student status and are registered in the second year of a university course, they are allowed to work for limited number of hours, usually ten but up to 20 in some cases. As mentioned in the introductory chapter 'Finding a Job,' Council (CIEE, 205 East 42nd St, New York, NY 10017) arranges work permits for qualifying US students for up to six months. Similarly Canadian students can enter France as part of the SWAP scheme (CFS, 243 College St, Toronto, Ontario M5T 2Y1). The CIEE office in Paris (1 Place de l'Odéon, Paris 75006; tel: 1-44 41 74 69) is very supportive of participants and issues its own list of potential employers (including 10 language schools) and regularly publishes a 'Work in France Newsletter'. Apparently about 10% of students on the scheme teach English.

One possibility open to some Americans with Irish or Greek ancestry is to obtain an EU passport.

CONDITIONS OF WORK

Teaching 'beeezneezmen' is not everyone's cup of tea, but it can be less strenuous than other kinds of teaching. Provided you do not feel intimidated by your pupils' polished manners and impeccable dress, and can keep them entertained, you will probably be a success. As mentioned above, one-to-one teaching is not uncommon, for which ELT training (including the CELTA or Trinity Certificate) do not prepare you. However, if you develop a rapport with your client, this can be the most enjoyable teaching of all. As mentioned earlier, language schools which offer this facility to clients may well expect you to drive, perhaps even own, a car so that you can give lessons in offices and private homes. Most schools pay between F90 and F115 (gross) per lesson.

Salaried teachers should be covered by a nationally agreed and widely enforced *Convention Collectif* which makes stable contracts, sick pay, holiday pay, etc. compulsory as well as guaranteeing a monthly salary. The annual holiday allowance for full-time teachers is five weeks plus an extra five days.

Telephone teaching is popular for its convenience and anonymity. For many people, making mistakes over the phone is less embarrassing than face-to-face. Apparently this method of teaching is great fun for teachers since the anonymity prompts people to spill out all their secrets. Many have been surprised by the good results. It is not necessary to be able to speak French and possibly even an advantage to be monolingual, so you won't be tempted to break into French in frustration. The standard rate of pay for telephone teaching is about F50 for half an hour plus telephone expenses.

Split shifts between 8am and 8pm are the norm, with the usual average of 24 contact hours per week. An unusual feature in France is that some schools calculate the salary according to a certain number of teaching hours per 9 or 12 months, and will pay overtime for hours worked in excess of this. Obviously the total can't be calculated until the end of the contract, which is a drawback for anyone considering leaving early.

Partly because of France's proximity to a seemingly inexhaustible supply of willing English teachers, working conditions in France are seldom brilliant. Although Andrew Boyle enjoyed his year teaching English in Lyon and the chance to become integrated into an otherwise impenetrable community, he concluded that even respectable schools treated teachers as their most expendable commodity, a view corroborated by the veteran traveller Jayne Nash who lasted only three months in Le Havre:

> *While I was wined and dined at the interview, I was left completely to my own devices after I arrived in Le Havre on a Saturday morning, having only the weekend to find somewhere to live. If I had not had my own vehicle and spoken fluent French, it would have been a nightmare. As it turned out I signed a contract for an apartment which was double the rent paid by my colleagues. Not once did anyone ask if I needed help, advice, a meal.*

> *Thirty plus hour weeks (not including preparation time), irregular hours at any*

The newest concept in English teaching is teaching by telephone

time between 8am and 8pm with last-minute classes to cover for absent colleagues, and classes of mixed ability, soon took their toll. The money wasn't that good either. I felt my employer cared little for his employees. After three months I found myself under so much stress that I was obliged to leave, although I am normally not someone to shun a challenge or responsibility.

Similarly, after spending the better part of a decade teaching English in the Far East, Helen Welch decided against accepting the jobs offered her in France. She too realised that she had been cheated by her landlady and couldn't face starting from scratch again, teaching-wise, in a new country for notoriously low wages.

By contrast, Fiona Paton was well looked after and had no trouble finding a comfortable and affordable flat in Vichy (which is often easy in popular holiday resorts outside the summer season). Her impression was that flat-sharing is not as commonplace in France as in other countries.

Despite some negative reports, the chance to eat and drink and live in France outweighs the disadvantages for a whole range of Francophiles.

LIST OF SCHOOLS

AC3
38 rue du Temple, 75004 Paris. Tel: (1) 40 29 97 40. Fax: (1) 40 29 97 47. E-mail: ac3hbpe@easynet.fr
Number of teachers: 12.
Preference of nationality: none, but no assistance given with permits.
Qualifications: ability to communicate well.
Conditions of employment: 1 year renewable contracts. Varying hours between 8 and 20 p.w.

Salary: starting wage of F100/hr.
Facilities/Support: no assistance with accommodation or work permits. Some training provided.
Recruitment: local interviews essential.
Contact: Mr. Robin Lent, Director.

ANGLESEY LANGUAGE SERVICES (A.L.S.)
1 bis Avenue Foch, 78400 Chatou. Tel: (1) 34 80 65 15. Fax: (1) 34 80 69 91.
Number of teachers: 10.
Preference of nationality: EU.
Qualifications: CELTA plus 2 years' experience preferred but possibilities for trainees.
Conditions of employment: one year contract. 15-25 h.p.w. Pupils are adults and many are taught in their workplaces. Recent expansion, so group lessons at all levels offered in evenings.
Salary: negotiable.
Facilities/Support: some help with accommodation possible. No training provided.
Recruitment: personal contacts or via UK partner organisation: Ditto 93 Ltd., 3 Kingsmead, Lon Towyn Capel, Treaddur Bay, Anglesey, Gwynedd, North Wales (01407 861331).

AUDIO-ENGLISH
44 allées de Tourny, 33000 Bordeaux. Tel: (5) 56 44 54 05.
Number of teachers: 3-4.
Preference of nationality: British preferred, others considered especially foreign students.
Qualifications: BA or equivalent, and good French. No previous experience necessary, but people who have already lived/worked in France, and who hold a clean driving licence are preferred. Pleasant personality, strong motivation and teaching talent important.
Conditions of employment: minimum 6 month contracts, but 10 months or more preferred. Full-time teachers work 34 h.p.w. including preparation and report-writing time. Part-time work also available. Hours of work between 8am-8pm. Teachers expected to work 2 evenings a week. Mostly adults but some classes of young children.
Salary: F6,700-6,800 per month (gross) less 22% in deductions.
Facilities/Support: no assistance with accommodation. Training provided.
Recruitment: through direct application and adverts, e.g. in *TES*. Interviews essential; occasionally held in UK.
Contact: Christian Labat, Director.

AXIEL-R.2001
85 Boulevard Pasteur, 75015 Paris. Tel: (1) 43 21 59 39. Fax: (1) 42 79 89 96.
Number of teachers: fluctuates seasonally.
Preference of nationality: native speakers.
Qualifications: university degree (Education, Psychology or Business) plus TEFL qualification.
Conditions of employment: variable periods of work to suit teachers. Clients are mainly professional people taught in their workplaces.
Salary: high hourly rate less deductions for social security.
Facilities/Support: no help with accommodation.
Recruitment: via British Council and word-of-mouth. Personal interview necessary.

BEST-ISF (Business English Service & Translation)
24 Bd. Béranger, 37000 Tours. Tel: (2) 47 05 55 33. Fax: (2) 47 64 40 27.
Number of teachers: 10.
Preference of nationality: EU only (unless candidates already have a work permit or students signed up for a second year).

Qualifications: BA, CELTA or good teaching experience of professional English.
Conditions of employment: 9 month to 2 year contracts. Starting dates September and January. 15-27 h.p.w. Pupils are mostly aged between 23-50.
Salary: F7,500-9,500 per month.
Facilities/Support: no assistance with accommodation. A small amount of training given.
Recruitment: through adverts in local papers, and direct applications with CVs or personal calls. Interviews essential, possibly in UK in summer.

BRITISH INSTITUTE IN PARIS (UNIVERSITY OF LONDON)
11 rue de Constantine, 75340 Paris Cedex 07.
Number of teachers: 43 tutors.
Preference of nationality: none.
Qualifications: BA, serious TEFL qualification, at least 5 years' experience and experience in teaching French adults.
Conditions of employment: one semester (15 week) contracts. 4-8 hours per week between 8.30am and 8.45pm.
Salary: F265 per hour.
Facilities/Support: no assistance with accommodation or training. Support given for research projects.
Recruitment: local interviews essential.

CAMBRIDGE CENTRE
57 cours George Clemenceau, 33000 Bordeaux. Tel: (5) 56 81 19 19. Fax: (5) 56 01 15 95. E-mail: cambridge.centre@wanadoo.fr
Number of teachers: 5.
Preference of nationality: none.
Qualifications: TEFL.
Conditions of employment: short or long-term contracts available. Hours vary weekly; lessons scheduled between 8am and 7pm.
Salary: F70 per hour.
Facilities/Support: no assistance with accommodation or training.
Recruitment: select from many CVs received. Interviews not essential.
Contact: Anne-Marie Murillo, Director.

CAREL
Centre Audiovisuel de Royan pour l'Etude des Langues, B.P. 219C, 48 Boulevard Franck Lamy, 17205 Royan Cedex. Tel: (5) 46 39 50 00. Fax: (5) 46 05 27 68. E-mail: info@carel.org. Web-site: http://www2.univ-poitiers.fr/carel/
Number of teachers: 12.
Preference of nationality: American, British.
Qualifications: BA/MA, CELTA and experience of teaching business English.
Conditions of employment: 1 year renewable. 18 h.p.w.
Salary: F7,000-F9,000 per month.
Facilities/Support: assistance with accommodation, work permits and training.
Recruitment: word of mouth, spontaneous applications. Telephone interviews possible though personal interviews preferred.
Contact: R. Gendre, Head of School.

CENTRE DE FORMATION DE ST OMER
Centre d'Etude des Langues, B.P. 278, Z.I. du Brockus, 62504 St. Omer. Tel: (3) 21 88 13 03/21 93 78 45.
Number of teachers: 4.
Preference of nationality: none.
Qualifications: BA plus CELTA (or equivalent) or other TEFL qualification.
Conditions of employment: 9 month contracts (September-June). At least 10 h.p.w. between 8am and 8pm. Most clients are adults, but also classes for adolescents and students.

Salary: F130 per hour.
Facilities/Support: informal assistance with accommodation.
Recruitment: through adverts. Local interviews essential.

CITYLANGUES
Paris La Défense 6, 52/54 rue du Capitaine Guynemer, 92400 Courbevoie. Tel: (1) 47 89 38 05. Fax: (1) 49 05 40 57.
Number of teachers: 15.
Preference of nationality: none, but employ only teachers resident in Paris.
Qualifications: degree and TEFL certificate.
Conditions of employment: teaching represents 70% of total paid hours.
Salary: according to profile.
Facilities/Support: no assistance with accommodation. Training available.
Recruitment: local interviews essential.
Contact: Stefan Wheater.

LE COMPTOIR DES LANGUES
63 Rue la Boétie, 75008 Paris. Tel: (1) 45 61 53 53. Fax: (1) 45 61 53 30.
Number of teachers: 45 (English).
Preference of nationality: British, plus American, Canadian and Australian if they have valid working papers.
Qualifications: university degree and at least 2 years' teaching experience in a school.
Conditions of employment: 1 year contracts, 4-6 hours work per day between 8am and 9pm within Paris, between 9am and 8pm in the suburbs. All clients are business executives.
Salary: starting salary is F90 per hour (gross) including paid holiday.
Facilities/Support: no assistance with accommodation. Training provided.
Recruitment: adverts in French and British newspapers. Interviews essential and sometimes held in London.
Contact: Philippa Dralet, Quality Control.

DIRECT ENGLISH
Ferme de Rambure, 76270 Mesniers en Bray. Tel: (2) 35 94 56 26. Fax: (2) 35 94 51 20. Branches also in Rouen and Montdidier.
Number of teachers: 6-8.
Preference of nationality: none.
Qualifications: TEFL qualification essential. Looking to hire non-smokers with own car.
Conditions of employment: permanent contracts. Classes held between 8am and 8pm. 20 teaching hours p.w.
Salary: approximately F7,000 per month (gross).
Facilities/Support: accommodation provided by school during trial period; afterwards assistance given. Some training, though no methods imposed.
Recruitment: adverts in *TES* and locally. Telephone or personal interviews.
Contact: Mrs. Gallagher.

FONTAINEBLEAU LANGUES & COMMUNICATION
15 rue Saint-Honoré, B.P. 27, 77300 Fontainebleau. Tel: (1) 64 22 48 96. Fax: (1) 64 22 51 94. E-mail: flccalv@club-internet.fr
Number of teachers: 18.
Preference of nationality: British; or Australians, Canadians and Americans with EU nationality or French working papers.
Qualifications: TEFL training (e.g. CELTA). Must be dynamic, versatile and able to motivate students.
Conditions of employment: one year minimum. Some teaching takes place in company premises so a car is necessary (transport costs are reimbursed). Variety of teaching

situations including groups, one-to-one lessons and business English. Hours are grouped as much as possible between 9am and 7pm Monday to Friday.
Salary: F102 per hour including 10% holiday pay. Social security deductions about 20%. Possibility of extra health insurance.
Facilities/Support: assistance with finding accommodation (teachers are put up at directors' houses until they find accommodation). Training workshops held regularly. Large resource centre.
Recruitment: interview essential, occasionally held in UK.

IAL
Centre de Formation de la Chambre de Commerce Franco-Britannique, 41 rue de Turenne, 75003 Paris. Tel/fax: (1) 44 59 25 10. E-mail: ial@calva.net
Number of teachers: 35.
Preference of nationality: British, Irish, American, Canadian.
Qualifications: university degree, TEFL or equivalent plus fluent French.
Conditions of employment: variable contracts. Teachers determine the number of hours worked.
Salary: F105-F115.
Facilities/Support: no assistance with accommodation. 3-4 training sessions per year.
Recruitment: CVs received spontaneously. Local interviews essential.
Contact: Claire Oldmeadow, Course Director.

IFG LANGUES
37 quai de Grenelle, 75738 Paris Cedex 15. Tel: (1) 40 59 30 91/40 59 31 32. Fax: (1) 45 78 96 66. E-mail: ifglangues@wanadoo.fr
Number of teachers: 110 for three centres; the other two are located near the World Trade Centre in La Défense and in Marne la Vallée next to Disneyland Paris.
Preference of nationality: EU or others with permission to work in France.
Qualifications: minimum BA, CELTA or equivalent, and experience. Prefer TOEFL or DELTA qualification plus 2 years' experience.
Conditions of employment: minimum number of hours guaranteed by contract is 1,030 per year of which 897 are teaching hours (average 36 h.p.w. of which 23 are contact hours). 6 weeks paid holiday. Students are professional adults from large and small firms, the French civil service, etc.
Salary: from F100 per hour. F103,040 per year (gross) with possibility of extra hours. Luncheon vouchers, health insurance and pension scheme included in package.
Facilities/Support: assistance sometimes given with accommodation. Advisory and administrative staff number 34. Training ongoing.
Recruitment: adverts in *Guardian* and French newspapers. Interviews and demonstration class held in Paris.

INLINGUA PARIS
109 rue de l'Université, 75007 Paris. Tel: (1) 45 51 46 60.
Number of teachers: 30.
Preference of nationality: none.
Qualifications: TEFL plus 2 years' experience.
Conditions of employment: minimum 12 months. Flexible hours.
Salary: F100-138 per hour.
Facilities/Support: assistance with accommodation, work permits and training.
Recruitment: adverts in *Guardian*. Interviews essential in UK or France.
Contact: Marie-France Domzot, Director.

INLINGUA
B.P. 156, F-76144 Petit Quevilly, Cedex. Tel: (2) 35 69 81 61. Fax: (2) 35 69 81 59. E-mail: inlrouen@normandnet.fr
Number of teachers: 30 for centres in Normany and Picardy.
Preference of nationality: none, though non-EU nationals are employed only if they already have a work permit.

Qualifications: recognised TESOL/TEFL qualification. Personal vehicle normally essential.
Conditions of employment: open-ended contract. Average 22 hours p.w.
Salary: F9000 per month (gross).
Facilities/Support: no assistance with accommodation. One week introduction course and on-going training is given.
Recruitment: adverts in *Guardian*, etc. Interviews in Rouen essential.
Contact: Tom Maitland, Director.

INTERNATIONAL LANGUAGE CENTRE
13 Passage Dauphine, 75008 Paris. Tel: (1) 44 41 80 20. Fax: (1) 44 41 80 21.
Number of teachers: 30.
Preference of nationality: must be native speaker.
Qualifications: CELTA or approved equivalent. Experience of business world needed.
Conditions of employment: teaching hours between 8.30am and 7pm. No standard length of contract.
Salary: variable.
Facilities/Support: assistance with accommodation, work permits and training. ILC offers the CELTA course (see *Training* chapter).
Recruitment: spontaneous CVs and local adverts. Interviews in Paris essential.

ISES
104 Avenue Maginot, Tours 37100. Tel: (2) 47 54 76 79. Fax: (2) 47 54 30 67.
Number of teachers: 15.
Preference of nationality: North American, Australian.
Qualifications: minimum DELTA (CELTA not sufficient) or MA in TESOL.
Conditions of employment: variable hours.
Salary: F70-120 per hour less 22% deductions for social security.
Facilities/Support: help with accommodation possible. Training given.
Recruitment: newspaper adverts and word of mouth. Personal interview necessary.

LINGUARAMA
Mini Parc Alpes Congrès, 6 rue Roland Garros, 38320 Eybens. Tel: (4) 76 62 00 18. Fax: (4) 76 25 89 60.
Number of teachers: 15.
Preference of nationality: none.
Qualifications: one-week TEFL certificate plus minimum 1 year's experience or 4-week Certificate plus minimum 3 months' experience. Driving licence essential.
Conditions of employment: full-time teachers work 27 h.p.w. September to June. Part-time teachers work flexible hours. Most teaching is business English, taught in-company and at school.
Salary: F9,000 per month.
Facilities/Support: advice on accommodation given. Training available.
Recruitment: via Linguarama in England and also locally.

LINGUISTIC SERVICES
2 rte. Vierge à la Lisseuse, 33210 Pujols sur Ciron. Tel: (5) 56 76 66 44.
Number of teachers: 15.
Preference of nationality: British.
Qualifications: BA plus teaching qualification or EFL experience.
Conditions of employment: 1 year contracts. 20-25 h.p.w.
Salary: F200 per hour (gross).
Facilities/Support: assistance with accommodation and training.
Recruitment: word of mouth and small adverts. Face-to-face interviews preferred but thorough telephone interviews can suffice.
Contact: Alan Metcalfe, Director of Studies.

METROPOLITAN LANGUAGES
151 rue de Billancourt, 92100 Boulogne. Tel: (1) 46 04 57 32. Fax: (1) 46 04 57 12.
Number of teachers: 20.
Preference of nationality: none.
Qualifications: university degree required but not necessarily TEFL qualification. Candidates with corporate experience most welcome. Teaching professionals only.
Conditions of employment: long-term contracts. Teaching hours between 8am and 8pm plus Saturday mornings.
Salary: between F6,500 and F9,500 per month, depending on individual monthly quotas. No deductions.
Facilities/Support: can provide addresses of *foyers* for accommodation. One-week pre-term training course.
Recruitment: via adverts in *France USA Contacts* magazine or the American Council in Paris. Personal interview necessary.

UNILANGUES
La Grande Arche, 1 le Parvis-Paroi Nord, 92044 Paris la Défense Cedex 41. Tel: (1) 47 78 45 80. Fax: (1) 49 00 03 16. E-mail: info@unilangues.com
Number of teachers: 16.
Preference of nationality: none.
Qualifications: university degree required plus CELTA or TEFL plus 2 years experience. Working knowledge of French required. Clients are adults.
Conditions of employment: open-ended contracts for full-time teachers. 30-60 hours for temporary assignments.
Salary: F95 per hour; increases to F100 after a trial period of 2-3 months and F105 after 2 years.
Facilities/Support: no help with accommodation. Training available.
Recruitment: via notices put up at British Council or British Institute. Personal interview necessary.
Contact: Rennie Tracy, Head of Studies.

VS LANGUES
16 rue Christophe Colomb, 75008 Paris. Tel: (1) 45 49 90 30. Fax: (1) 45 49 90 32.
Number of teachers: 15.
Preference of nationality: none.
Qualifications: university degree and teaching experience required. Must have nice personality.
Conditions of employment: minimum 6 month contracts. Variable hours between 7am and 10pm and weekends.
Salary: approximately F100 an hour (net).
Facilities/Support: no help with accommodation.
Recruitment: personal interview necessary.

Other Schools to Try

Note that these schools (in Paris followed by other towns in alphabetical order) did not confirm their teacher requirements for this edition of *Teaching English Abroad*. Upper case entries marked with an asterisk had entries in the last edition (1997); addresses without asterisks have been taken from various sources, such as British Council lists and the *Yellow Pages*.

Access Langue Speakwell, 35, rue de Ponthieu, 75008 Paris
Action Formation, 4 bis rue Mertens, 92270 Bois-Colombes
ADELE, 5, rue St-Philippe du Roule, 75008 Paris
BUSINESS & TECHNICAL LANGUAGES (BTL), 82 Boulevard Haussmann, 75008 Paris (1-42 93 45 45/fax 1-42 93 99 19). 25 teachers.
Centre de Langues Tomatis, 6 place de la République Dominicaine, 75017 Paris

Cours George V, 7 rue Marbeuf, 75008 Paris
*CPL/ACREA, 12 rue de Port Mahon, 75002 Paris (1-47 42 44 55/fax 1-47 42 45 11). 15 full-time and varying number of freelancers.
Ecole Nickerson, 26 rue de la Tremoille, 75008 Paris
Ecole de Langues de Neuilly, 114 ave. Ch. de Gaulle, 92200 Neuilly
Euro-teclangues, 48 Bld Voltaire, 75011 Paris
*EXECUTIVE LANGUAGE SERVICES, 20 rue Sainte Croix de la Bretonnerie, 75004 Paris. 36 teachers.
PSR, 116 rue Cardinet, 75017 Paris
Quai d'Orsay Language Centre, 67 Quai d'Orsay, 75007 Paris
*REGENCY LANGUES, 1 rue Ferdinand Duval, 75004 Paris (1-48 04 99 97/fax 1-48 04 34 96). 3 teachers.
Sterling International, 12 rue Hippolyte, Lebas, 75009 Paris
Télélangues Systems, 9 rue Maurice, Grandcoing, 94200 Ivry S/Seine
*TRANSFER FORMATION CONSEIL, 18-20 rue Godot de Mauroy, 75009 Paris (1-42 66 14 11). 50 teachers.
*WALL STREET INSTITUTE, 21 Avenue Victor Hugo, 75116 Paris (1-45 00 59 60/fax 1-45 01 22 64). 1 full-time and 3 part-time teachers.
Universal Communication, 52 rue de Flandre, 750019 Paris

Hamilton House, 47 av Lamartine, Arcachon
Centre Multimédia et Formation, 6 av Virecourt, Artigues
Erasmus, 9 rue République, Blanquefort
Pop Corn, 7 rue Neuve, Blaye

Une Autre Langue, 16 rue Esprit des Lois, 33000 Bordeaux
B.L.S., 1 Cours Georges Clemenceau, 33000 Bordeaux
Cabinet Chapman, 3 rue Lafaurie de Monbadon, 33000 Bordeaux
Callan Method School (SARL), 3 rue Lafaurie de Monbadon, 33000 Bordeaux
Centre d'Etude des Langues (CEL), 2 place Bourse, 33076 Bordeaux Cedex
DLVP/CRIFEL, 3 ter pl Victoire, 33076 Bordeaux Cedex
Effective, 6, rue Charles Lamoureux, 33000 Bordeaux
Insermédia Langues, 83 rue Ségur, 33000 Bordeaux
Ligue de l'Enseignement, 22 rue Huguerie, BP 26, 33026 Bordeaux Cedex
M.C.B Langues, 188 av Louis Barthou, 33200 Bordeaux
Mondial Langue, 62 cours Intendance, 33000 Bordeaux
Saint-Augustin Lycée Professionel Privé, 19, rue Paul Courteault, 33000 Bordeaux
Tomatis Langues, 6 rue Guillaume Brochon, 33000 Bordeaux

Germany

The excellent state education system in western Germany ensures that a majority of Germans have a good grounding in English, so very little teaching is done at the beginner level. If German students want exposure to a native speaker they are far more likely to enrol in a language summer course in Britain than sign up for extra tuition at a local institute. Furthermore, many secondary schools in Germany (including the former East) employ native speakers of English to assist in classrooms (programme details below). English is also offered at *Volkshochschulen* or 'folk high schools', where various subsidised adult education courses are run.

The reunification of Germany created a huge demand for English in the eastern *Länder* which has now eased off to some extent. Cities like Leipzig, Dresden and Erfurt are less popular destinations for job-seeking teachers than Munich and Freiburg, and may therefore afford more opportunities. As in the west, many private institutes have an American bias.

The greatest demand for English in Germany continues to come from the business and professional community. The current difficulties in Germany's economy mean that some companies are cutting back EFL programmes, though government incentives are in place to encourage companies to provide training to their employees, with one of the most popular options being English language training. This means that there are many highly paid in-company positions for EFL and ESP teachers, as well as a number of agencies and consultancies which supply teachers to their clients.

The reduction in in-company opportunities has been somewhat offset by the continuing demand from former East Germans, especially those who have migrated to Frankfurt and elsewhere, who view privately paid-for English classes as an important investment in their job futures.

Prospects for Teachers

Any graduate with a background in economics or business who can speak German has a chance of finding work in a German city. A TEFL Certificate and a university degree have less clout than relevant experience, as Kevin Boyd found when he arrived with his brand new Cambridge Certificate in September:

> I was persuaded by a teaching friend to go to Munich with him to try to get highly paid jobs together. As he spoke some German and had about a year's teaching experience, he got a job straightaway. Every school I went to in Munich just didn't want to know as I couldn't speak German and only had four weeks teaching experience. After two days of this I decided to try my luck in Italy.

Experience in business is often a more desirable qualification than an ELT qualification. The question is not so much whether you know what a past participle is but whether you know what an 'irrevocable letter of credit' or a 'bank giro' is. Many schools offer *Oberstufe,* advanced or specialist courses in, for example, Banking English, Business English, or for bilingual secretaries, etc. Full-time vocationally-oriented courses in languages for business and commerce are called *Berufsfachschule* and this is still a buoyant part of the market. For none of these is a Cambridge or Trinity Certificate or even a Diploma the most appropriate training.

Very few schools are willing to consider candidates who can't speak any German. Although the 'direct method' is in use everywhere (i.e. total immersion in English), the pupils will expect you to be able to explain things in German. If the school prepares its students for the Chamber of Commerce exams (known as LCCI), the teacher will be expected not only to understand the syllabus but to interpret and teach it with confidence. Some schools employ the now unfashionable 'contrastive' method, again making a knowledge of conversational German essential.

Wages for teachers (as for most professions in Germany) are very high, which means that there is less turn-over of staff than elsewhere. On the other hand, there is a definite tax advantage for British nationals if they work for less than two years (see *Regulations* below) which frees up vacancies on an on-going basis. One further requirement of many employers is a driving licence, so that teachers can travel easily from one off-site assignment to another.

FIXING UP A JOB

Posts for English-speaking *Helferen* (classroom assistants) are normally reserved for students of German who apply through the Assistants Department of the Central Bureau for Educational Visits & Exchanges (10 Spring Gardens, London SW1A 2BN; 0171-389 4004). Students and graduates aged 20-30 who want to spend a year in a German secondary school should obtain details of the scheme. Although you cannot normally choose your destination, Language Assistants like Sarah Davies (who was sent to a small town in the east) advises against agreeing to teach in a small village where conditions may be primitive and the sense of isolation strong.

Similarly for US graduates, the USIA Fulbright Program (administered by the Institute of International Education, 809 UN Plaza, New York, NY 10017-3580) places 50 teaching assistants *(Padagogischer Austauschdienst)* in German high schools.

Candidates planning to go on to become teachers of German are strongly preferred for this programme, which pays a monthly stipend of DM1,150 in addition to free flights and insurance. For general information about teaching opportunities in Germany, interested Americans should contact the German Academic Exchange Service or DAAD (Deutscher Akademischer Austauschdienst, 950 Third Avenue, 19th Floor, New York, NY 10022).

University students and graduates can often find out about possible employers from their university careers office or local English schools, as happened to Catherine Rogers. She wrote on spec to a number of local language schools to get some experience before working abroad and ended up being interviewed by two British contacts of a government scheme for teaching English to unemployed engineers and secretaries operating in the Dresden area of the former East Germany.

Like so many embassies, the German Embassy in London is not noted for its helpful attitude to aspiring teachers or other job-seekers. The German Information Centre (34 Belgrave Square, London SW1X 8QB) does, however, distribute a short information sheet headed 'Teaching in Germany'. Apart from directing students to enquire about the exchange programme run by the Central Bureau and providing addresses of the state Ministries of Education, it recommends applying to the Zentralstelle für Arbeitsvermittlung, Feuerbachstrasse 42-46, 60325 Frankfurt am Main 1 (tel: 69-71110/fax: 69-711 15 40). This is the Central Placement Office of the Federal Department of Employment, which has a special department for dealing with applications from abroad. A letter addressed to one of the 184 *Arbeitsamter* (job centres) around the country will be forwarded to the Zentralstelle for processing. A personal visit to an *Arbeitsamt* is more likely to produce results, though you are likely to be told that there are far more qualified teachers and translators than there are vacancies.

The five British Council offices in Germany are on the whole efficient and helpful to people enquiring about English teaching work. The Information section of the British Council in Berlin coordinates ELT enquiries on behalf of the offices in Berlin, Hamburg, Köln, Leipzig and Münch, and will send photocopies of local *Sprachenschulen* from the Yellow Pages *(Gelbe Seiten)*. The British Council in Munich also has its own one-page list of about 40 English language schools.

As usual, it is much more difficult to arrange a job by sending written applications and CVs from the UK than by presenting yourself in person to language school directors and training companies, CV in hand. Determination, qualifications, experience and being on the spot are often deciding factors when an employer has to choose between large numbers of similarly qualified applicants.

Most of the major international language school chains are more or less weathering the recession of the late 1990s. Those whose addresses are included in the introductory chapter *Finding a Job* include Berlitz (with more than 30 schools), Bénédict (with 37 German branches), Language Link, inlingua (with 50 schools), Linguarama which specialises in language training for business in eight cities and Wall Street Institutes. In addition to the entry for *Linguarama Deutschland* in Munich in the directory section, Linguarama schools in Germany are as follows:

Atrium Friedrichstrasse, Friedrichstr. 60, 10117 Berlin (30-203 00 50/ fax 30-203 00 515).

Steinstr. 30, 40210 Düsseldorf (211-13 20 80/fax 211-13 20 85).

Linguarama Haus, Geotheplatz 2, 60311 Franfurt am Main (69-28 02 46/fax 69-28 05 56).

Hopfenburg, Hopfensack 19, 20457 Hamburg (40-33 50 97/fax 40-32 46 09).

Marzellenstr. 3-5, 50667 Köln (221-160 99 0/fax 221-160 99 66).

Lipsia-Haus, Barfüssgässchen 12, 04109 Leipzig (341-213 14 64/fax 341-213 14 82).

Leuschnerstr. 3, 70174 Stuttgart (711-22 19 36/fax 711-226 18 82).

Throughout Germany, more than 1,000 *Volkshochschulen* (VHS) teach the English language (among many other courses) to adults. Native speakers with teaching experience might find a role within this institution (see entry for *Deutscher Volkshochschul-Verband e.V*). In addition to their Homepage, they also provide an internet service whereby candidates seeking teaching opportunities can place their résumés and where *Volkshochschulen* can register their vacancies for lecturers and part-time instructors. The Europe-wide International Certificate Conference (ICC) is based in Germany (Hansaallee 150, 60320 Frankfurt) and acts as an umbrella organisation for adult education associations like VHS, working on teaching foreign languages in Europe. The ICC can send a list of the regional addresses of *Volkshochschulen*.

Interviews

Most schools and institutes in Germany cannot under normal operating circumstances hire someone unseen merely on the basis of his/her CV and photo. Applicants should arrange for a face-to-face interview and make themselves available at a moment's notice. Professional presentation is even more important for securing work in the German business world than elsewhere. Vacancies occur throughout the year since businessmen and women are just as likely to start a course in April as in September. Germans tend to be formal, so dress appropriately and be aware of your manners at an interview. Also good references *(zeugnisse)* are essential.

A good starting place is Frankfurt am Main, known to locals as 'Bankfurt' or 'Mainhattan'. Frankfurt has the highest concentration of major banks and financial institutions in the country (nearly 400) and a correspondingly high number of private language schools. It is helpful, though not essential, to have some basic knowledge of German and business experience. In a job interview with a language school director, demonstrating a detailed knowledge of a handful of commonly used textbooks may be more important than business experience. Nathan Edwards, a Canadian who spent two years teaching in dozens of banks and multinational companies, recommends *Build Your Business English* by J. Flower, *The Language of Meetings* by M. Goodale and *International Business English* by L. Jones and R. Alexander.

You can also impress a potential employer by showing some familiarity with current major Germany business news (bank mergers, etc.). This can easily be done by scanning the English language press or listening to the BBC World Business Report on a short-wave radio. Language schools are looking for teachers who can pose intelligent questions to business students about their jobs. There is a considerable demand from the business community for guidance on conducting 'small talk' in English, which is crucial in building rapport with clients and colleagues.

If asked about permits, visas, etc. (especially in the case of non-EU nationals), reassure the interviewer that you are waiting for your paperwork to be finalised.

Freelance Teaching

The majority of native speakers teaching for commercial institutes are not on contracts but are employed as freelancers *(Honorarvertrag)*, who work for between two and 20 hours per week. In some cases deductions are made for tax and social security but in most cases freelance teachers are left to deal with these themselves. Some consider this to be an advantage, while others consider it exploitative. Many freelancers work uninsured in a very grey area, with the law turning a blind eye.

If you want to find private pupils, you could attend a meeting of an Anglo-German club of which there are many. The Deutsch-Englische Gesellschaft meets regularly in most major cities, including Hamburg, Bonn, Düsseldorf and Cologne: details are available from the British Council. Americans might be able to make contact with English teachers at US cultural centres such as the JFK-Haus Library in Darmstadt (Kasinostr. 3, 64293 Darmstadt; 6151-25924).

Upon successful completion of a Trinity TESOL Certificate course in England, Ann Barkett from Atlanta went to Munich to look for freelance work, but found it tough going:

> *During the period December to March, I was putting up flyers for private and group lessons but received no response. I finally answered an ad for a private student whom I taught for a few weeks, but there just wasn't enough work or money coming in and I was tired of trying at that point.*

Many freelance teachers find themselves for the first time required to design an ESP course (English for Specific Purposes), individually tailored to the needs of their businessmen and women students. Nathan Edwards found that he got better at this:

> *Experience has shown me that such a syllabus must be flexible, open to change and short-term adjustment so as to accommodate the complex and evolving needs of students who are also full-time working professionals. Students and their employers must be given the assurance of a clearly structured course outline, but this must be partly generated by an ongoing negotiated process with all the participants. Finally don't forget that the students themselves can be a valuable source of ESP course material such as authentic English fax or e-mail messages, business letters and company brochures from their offices.*

REGULATIONS

EU nationals are free to travel to Germany to look for work but are still subject to the labyrinthine bureaucracy. The first step is to register your address with the local authority *(Einwohnermeldeamt)* or at the local registry office *(Meldestelle),* as German citizens must also do. For this you will need proof that you are living or working locally, e.g. your landlord's or future employer's countersignature.

Only after doing this is it possible to apply for a residence permit *(Aufenthaltserlaubnis)* from the residence office *(Landeseinerwohneramt)* or from the aliens' authority *(Ausländerbehörde)* probably located in the *Rathaus* or the *Kreisverwaltungsreferat* (Area Administration Centre). You may find that you are granted a five-year residence permit immediately, or you may be given three months in the first instance during which time you are expected to find employment. You normally have to surrender your passport for up to six weeks while your application is being processed, though if you have the stamina you can do battle with the bureaucracy and do it in a day or two. Procedures should be standard throughout Germany, though in the eastern *Länder* where fewer foreigners go, it can be more difficult to get definitive advice. Sarah Davies found that even after she found the right building, there was no reception desk or signposts, so to find the right official it was a question of blundering into various offices and finding him or her by trial and error.

American English is strongly in demand in Germany since so many companies have branches or clients in North America, and many students in Germany prefer the American to the British accent. Americans can arrange teaching jobs in Germany more easily than in Spain, Italy or France. Organisations like the *American Language Academy* (see entry), which offers English courses throughout former East Germany, are prepared to assist in the lengthy process of getting work permits, provided they are otherwise short of teachers. An American who finds an employer while still in the US might seek advice on documentation from the Carl Duisberg Society (CDS International, 330 7th Avenue, 19th Floor, New York, NY 10001-5010; 212-497-3500).

As soon as a teacher from outside the EU obtains a promise of employment, he or she should take steps to get the permits. The teacher must first register his or her name and address (as for EU nationals) and then report to the Ausländersamt (foreigners' office). There they must present a contract or letter from a school claiming that you are the best candidate for the job (difficult) or else request a *Freimitarbeiter Urlaubnis,* the freelancer's permit given to *Honorarvertrag* (freelancers) which may need to be backed up by a letter from an employer. Further requirements include a certificate of good conduct (notarised by the US Embassy for a fee), proof of address and health insurance and also a health certificate from a German doctor. If approved, a one-year residence permit will be affixed to the passport, with a hand-written explanation that the bearer is allowed to work as an English teacher in private language schools only. All of this will take between three and six weeks and cost at least DM75, renewable for three years for a further fee.

The American Ann Barkett did not find the procedures in any way straightforward.

After being enrolled in a Berlitz training course by a director who claimed that there was a desperate need for English teachers, Ann thought employment would automatically follow. But despite passing the course, Ann was not given any teaching hours and could not ascertain the reason for this, especially since her fellow trainees were working an absurd 40 hours a week. She wondered whether it had something to do with her non-EU status, though the Arbeitsamt in Munich had told her that freelancers didn't need a work permit.

Unfortunately Canadians, Australians, New Zealanders and other nationalities experience more difficulties since they require a resident visa which has been applied for in their country of origin. If within the three months of their tourist stay they manage to obtain a formal written offer of employment, they must return to their home country in order to apply for a working visa at the German Consulate. The application process takes up to one month and there is always a risk that the application will be refused. Successful applicants are issued with a one-year renewable work visa. Not all employers are willing to wait one month for a new teacher to begin working and may prefer to hire British or Irish teachers in the meantime.

Foreigners working in Germany should obtain a *Lohnsteuerkarte* (tax card) or a *steuernummer* (tax number) from the local *Steueramt*. The earnings threshold for paying tax about is DM12,500; after which the rates of tax are high, at least 30%. However, according to a tax treaty between Great Britain and Germany (DBA1964/70), professors and teachers who teach at a school for less than two years are exempt from tax. However, most will have about 13% deducted for social security contributions.

CONDITIONS OF WORK

You can almost guarantee that you will be teaching adults (since school children receive such a high standard of English tuition at school), and usually before or after office hours. Contracts for full-time work are normally at least a year long, often with a three-month probation period.

Wages are undoubtedly among the highest anywhere. DM20-30 per 45-minute lesson is standard and DM50 not impossible. A working week of 30 hours could consist of 40 45-minute lessons, which would be a very heavy workload. Off-site teaching hours often incur a premium of about DM5 to compensate for travel time.

If you are depending solely on one employer for your income try to find an institute which guarantees a monthly minimum number of hours. Monthly salaries are usually between DM2,500 and DM3,000 gross, with the possibility of paid overtime. Considering that a one-bedroom flat in one of the big cities can easily cost DM1,000 per month, salaries need to be high. Quite a few schools assist with accommodation. Look up *Wohnung* (apartments/flats) in the phone book or try the local *Mitwohnzentralen* which charges a fee (usually one month's rent) for finding flats, though they may charge less if you end up renting a room or flat from owners who are temporarily absent. It is customary to pay your rent directly out of a bank account, so open a basic savings account as early as you can.

Working and living conditions in the former GDR are gradually coming into line with those in the west and are much improved since the early days of reunification when Catherine Rogers went there:

> Accommodation was provided in 'outer Siberia', five miles from the factory where I was teaching. The temperature fell so low that the inside of the window was completely frozen. The wages were very good and I was able to save half my salary. I tried to sort out the red tape but was told by my boss that the local officials were not really geared up for that sort of thing. The students were extremely helpful and generally thrilled to have a native English speaker. They loved grammar and games, but role plays usually fell flat. Success was virtually guaranteed if I put them in teams since they were very competitive. Most of them went to considerable lengths to help me. The hospitality and kindness were amazing. But I still felt isolated because my German is rather basic and there were no other foreigners around.

Some teachers in the new *Länder* have found it difficult to control their classes.

After years of very strict discipline, it is not surprising that pupils are keen to take advantage of the new liberality. But like Catherine Rogers, Sarah Davies met nothing but a friendly welcome in the east (and no reports have been received to indicate that her pessimistic prediction about the future has come to pass):

> *The easterners are different and everyone has been tremendously friendly and supportive. They are used to pulling together as a community. For instance, before my money came through, the teachers at my school literally passed the hat round for me and gave me a present of cash. I know it's inevitable that they will change as soon as they become materialistic; it seems a shame, but that's progress.*

LIST OF SCHOOLS

ACADEMY OF BUSINESS COMMUNICATION (ABC)
Marienstr. 41, 70178 Stuttgart. Tel: (711) 607 49 25. Fax: (711) 607 49 27. E-mail: info@abc-stuttgart.de

Number of teachers: approx. 25. New ABC schools are opening so numbers may increase.

Preference of nationality: none.

Qualifications: teaching experience or business background plus university degree in any subject.

Conditions of employment: mostly freelance; some contracts available. Academy open Monday to Saturday.

Facilities/Support: advice on finding accommodation. Assistance given to non-EU teachers in obtaining permits. Regular training. Teachers can obtain ABC's own teaching certificate if they attend course and pass test/observation (after approx. one year).

Recruitment: adverts in UK and personal recommendations. Interviews preferred and are occasionally available in UK.

Contact: Mrs. Joy Zeller, Director.

AMERICAN LANGUAGE ACADEMY
Charlottenstrasse 65, 10117 Berlin. Tel: (30) 20 39 78 10. Fax: (30) 20 39 78 13.

Number of teachers: 70 freelancers in 5 centres.

Preference of nationality: none (native speakers only).

Qualifications: CELTA, TEFL, TESL, university certification. Also opportunities for native speakers with practical experience, especially of business English (banking, civil engineering).

Conditions of employment: minimum contract period of 10 weeks. Variable hours, generally between 7.30am and 9pm.

Salary: average rate for 45 minute lesson is DM25.

Facilities/Support: library supply of teaching materials.

Recruitment: advertisements. Local interview necessary.

Contact: Angelika Thormann, Academic Director.

BERLIN SCHOOL OF ENGLISH
Dorotheenstrasse 90, 10117 Berlin. Tel: (30) 229 04 55. Fax: (30) 229 04 71.

Number of teachers: from 15.

Preference of nationality: none.

Qualifications: university degree plus TEFL Certificate and minimum one year's experience.

Conditions of employment: minimum one year on freelance basis. Between 16 and 30 h.p.w.

Salary: approximately DM40 for 90 minute teaching session.

Facilities/Support: assistance given with finding accommodation and obtaining work permits. Some training given.

Recruitment: via local interviews.

Contact: Sarah Quinault, Director of Studies.

BERLITZ DEUTSCHLAND GmbH (LEIPZIG)
Petersstrasse 39-41, 04109 Leipzig. Tel: (341) 2 11 48 17. Fax: (341) 2 11 50 10.
Number of teachers: 15-20.
Preference of nationality: EU or American native speakers preferred.
Qualifications: teaching experience and TEF(S)L helpful; academic background and ability to work with people needed.
Conditions of employment: open-ended contract. Flexible hours between 8am and 9.30pm.
Salary: DM22-24 per 45-minute lesson.
Facilities/Support: 1 week intensive training given (materials, methods, teaching aids). Assistance with accommodation and work permits given.
Recruitment: adverts and personal referral.
Contact: W. Schmidt, Language Centre Director.

BERLITZ DEUTSCHLAND GmbH (MAGDEBURG)
Hasselbackplatz 3, 39104 Magdeburg. Tel: (391) 541 46 88. Fax: (391) 541 46 45.
Number of teachers: 5.
Preference of nationality: none (British, American, Canadian, Australian, New Zealand, etc.) as long as native speakers of English.
Qualifications: university degree.
Conditions of employment: freelance only. 30-40 h.p.w.
Salary: DM22-24 per unit.
Facilities/Support: assistance given with accommodation and work permits.
Recruitment: via internet, job centres and universities. Interviews in UK, US and locally.
Contact: Ms. Anne Richter, Director.

CAMBRIDGE INSTITUT
Hildegardstr. 8, 80539 München. Tel: (89) 22 11 15. Fax: (89) 290 47 38. E-mail: cambridge.institute@ibm.net
Number of teachers: 14.
Preference of nationality: British.
Qualifications: PGCE (preferably in modern languages).
Conditions of employment: 11 month contracts, renewable for a further 11 months. 26 h.p.w. Lessons 9-11.40am and 5.30-9.15pm.
Salary: DM3,500 per month less social security payments of about DM740.
Facilities/Support: assistance with accommodation. One-week induction course and ongoing workshops.
Recruitment: interview essential in Germany or sometimes UK.
Contact: Philip Moore, Co-Director.

CONTEXT SPRACHENDIENSTE GmbH
Elisenstr. 4-10, Köln. Tel: (221) 925 45 612. Fax: (221) 925 45 616. E-mail: abecker@contextinc.com
Number of teachers: 15-20.
Preference of nationality: none.
Qualifications: must be native speakers with academic education and experience.
Conditions of employment: freelance basis. Hours vary between 8am and 8pm.
Salary: varies according to qualifications and experience and degree of difficulty of class taught.
Facilities/Support: accommodation and visas are responsibility of teachers. Some training given.
Recruitment: newspaper adverts, followed by local interviews.
Contact: Curt Berryman, Coordinator of Language Department.

DAVID BERRY LANGUAGES
Weinbergsweg 3, 10119 Berlin. Tel/fax: (30) 449 90 25.
Number of teachers: 10-15.

Preference of nationality: none.
Qualifications: TEFL Certificate, business teaching experience needed.
Conditions of employment: freelance.
Salary: DM25+ per hour.
Facilities/Support: no assistance with accommodation. Training provided.
Recruitment: direct application. Local interview essential.
Contact: David Berry, Director of Studies.

DEUTSCHER VOLKSHOCHSCHUL-VERBAND
**Obere Wilhelmstrasse 32, 53225 Bonn. Tel: (228) 975 69 20. Fax: (228) 975 69 30.
E-mail: buero@dvv-vhs.de. Internet Homepage: www.dvv-vhs.de.**
Number of teachers: opportunities in more than 1,000 associated *Volkshochschulen*.
Preference of nationality: British, American, Canadian, any English-speaking nationality.
Conditions of employment: one semester renewable contracts. Most positions are part-time.
Salary: variable hourly rates. Income from part-time teaching will not necessarily cover living expenses.
Facilities/Support: no assistance with finding accommodation. Help can be given with work permits, in the form of a letter testifying that no EU national is equally qualified. Continuing staff training is available through the German Institute for Adult Education (DIE) in Frankfurt.
Recruitment: must apply to individual *Volkshochschulen*. Local interviews required.

ENGLISCHES INSTITUT KOLN
Gertrudenstr. 24-28, 50667 Köln. Tel: (221) 257 82 74/5. Fax: (221) 25 54 50.
Number of teachers: 20-25.
Preference of nationality: none, though ease of obtaining work permit helps.
Qualifications: BA, TEFL Certificate and at least 2 years' EFL experience.
Conditions of employment: part-time and full-time. Courses offered mornings (including Saturdays) and evenings. Some in-company teaching.
Salary: depends on hours contracted. Standard German deductions of about 25% in total.
Facilities/Support: good teacher resources, optional workshops.
Recruitment: direct application.
Contact: D. Sutherland.

ENGLISH FOR EVERYBODY
Theodor-Storm-Str. 1, 22869 Schenefeld. Tel: (40) 830 99 009. Fax: (40) 830 99 019. E-mail: efe.lowe@metronet.de
Number of teachers: 10.
Preference of nationality: none.
Qualifications: TEFL plus experience.
Conditions of employment: one year contracts. Various hours Monday to Friday mornings and evenings.
Salary: DM30 per hour.
Facilities/Support: assistance given with accommodation. No training.
Recruitment: via adverts, agencies and word of mouth.
Contact: Kerstin Lowe, Owner.

EURO-SCHULEN ERFURT
Bahnhofstrasse 44, 99034 Erfurt. Tel: (361) 646 10 90. Fax: (361) 646 10 93. E-mail: ESO-erfurt@t-online.de
Number of teachers: 3
Preference of nationality: none.
Qualifications: TEFL.
Conditions of employment: 26-30 h.p.w.
Salary: according to qualifications.

Facilities/Support: no assistance with accommodation or training.
Recruitment: local interviews only.
Contact: Dr. Thoralf Helel, Director.

EURO FREMDSPRACHENSCHULE
Donaustr. 11, 85049 Ingolstadt. Tel: (841) 17001. Fax: (841) 17193.
Number of teachers: 7.
Preference of nationality: British, American, Canadian.
Qualifications: at least a BA (including German studies). PGCE preferred. At least 5 years experience.
Conditions of employment: permanent contracts. Part-time work possible. 30 h.p.w.
Salary: based on German state salary scale.
Facilities/Support: assistance given with accommodation and work permits.
Recruitment: interview in Ingolstadt necessary.
Contact: Stuart Wheeler.

FOKUS LANGUAGE SCHOOL
Brienner Strasse 48, 80333 München. Tel: (89) 52 31 43 47. Fax: (89) 52 31 47 51.
E-mail: fokussprachen@t-online.de. Also school in Frankfurt: Gartenstrasse 56, 60596 Frankfurt; 69-61 99 03 84/fax 69-61 99 03 85.
Number of teachers: 20-25.
Preference of nationality: none, but no dialects.
Qualifications: university degree plus TEFL.
Conditions of employment: flexible contracts and hours, mornings and evenings.
Salary: DM30-35 per 45 minutes.
Facilities/Support: assistance with accommodation and work permits. No training.
Recruitment: adverts in UK and local interviews.
Contact: Monika Vibert, Director.

GERMAN AMERICAN INSTITUTE TUEBINGEN
Karlstrasse 3, 72072 Tübingen. Tel: (7071) 34071. Fax: (7071) 31873. E-mail: DAI_TUEBINGEN@compuserve.com
Number of teachers: 15.
Preference of nationality: American.
Qualifications: BA or MA from an American university.
Conditions of employment: freelance only. 3-9 h.p.w. Mostly adult students.
Salary: hourly wage.
Facilities/Support: no help with accommodation. Limited training given.
Recruitment: local interview essential.
Contact: Carolyn Murphey Melchers, Language Program Coordinator.

HAMBURG SCHOOL OF ENGLISH
Eppend. Landstr. 112a, 20249 Hamburg. Tel: (40) 480 21 16/9. Fax: (40) 480 73 67.
E-mail: mpayant@compuserve.
Number of teachers: 16-19.
Preference of nationality: none.
Qualifications: university degree plus TEFL Certificate and minimum one year's experience.
Conditions of employment: minimum one year on freelance basis. Between 16 and 30 h.p.w.
Salary: approximately DM40 for 90 minute teaching session.
Facilities/Support: assistance given with finding accommodation and obtaining work permits. Some training given.
Recruitment: via local interviews.
Contact: Bill Cope, Director of Studies.

ICC SPRACHSCHULE
Villa Rosental, Liviastr. 8, 04105 Leipzig. Tel: (341) 980 40 59. Fax: (341) 980 54 74.
E-mail: home/villa_rosental. Web-site: http://home/t-online.de
Number of teachers: 10.
Preference of nationality: none.
Qualifications: CELTA (or one-month equivalent) and/or 6 months TEFL experience.
Conditions of employment: 9 month contracts. 20 h.p.w. including lots of evening courses.
Salary: DM22.50 per hour (45 minute lessons).
Facilities/Support: assistance with accommodation and work permits for non-EU teachers. Monthly training sessions.
Recruitment: walk-ins. Local interview essential.
Contact: James Parsons, Director of Studies.

INLINGUA
Sendlinger-Tor-Platz 6, 80336 München. Tel: (89) 231 15 30. Fax: (89) 260 99 20.
E-mail: muenchen@inlingua.de. http://www.inlingua.de.muenchen
Number of teachers: 30.
Preference of nationality: none.
Qualifications: minimum BA or BSc.
Conditions of employment: long-term contracts only, minimum 3 years.
Recruitment: written applications enclosing short CV.
Contact: Dr. Ines Guettner, Director of Studies.

INLINGUA SPRACHSCHULE
Kaiserstrasse 37, 60329 Frankfurt. Tel: (69) 242 92 00. Fax: (69) 23 48 29.
Number of teachers: 30.
Preference of nationality: none, but must be native speaker.
Qualifications: BA, TEFL qualification.
Conditions of employment: 18 month contracts. 30-35 h.p.w. Pupils aged 18-60.
Salary: approximately DM3,400 per month (gross).
Facilities/Support: assistance with accommodation. Training provided.
Recruitment: direct.
Contact: Dr. Rene Schwarz.

LEIPZIGER SPRACHENSERVICE
Agentur für Sprachen, Paul-List-Str. 8, Leipzig. Tel/fax: (341) 211 12 82.
Number of teachers: varies according to client demand.
Preference of nationality: none.
Qualifications: fluent German, teaching experience.
Conditions of employment: 3-6 month contracts.
Salary: DM20-40 per hour (varies with clients).
Facilities/Support: can advise on accommodation in Leizig.
Recruitment: interviews not essential.
Contact: Jorg Eckhardt, Managing Director.

LERNEN IM ZENTRUM
Lehrinstitut R. Cerny, Sendlinger Strasse 47, 80331 München. Tel: (89) 260 90 34. Fax: (89) 260 52 97.
Number of teachers: 6.
Preference of nationality: British, American.
Qualifications: experience of business including knowledge of technical terms and paedagogical skills. Knowledge of grammar required.
Conditions of employment: variable hours, depending on number of clients.
Salary: DM25-55 for 60 minutes.
Facilities/Support: assistance with finding accommodation.
Recruitment: local interviews necessary.

LINGUA FRANCA
Pfalzburger Strasse 51, 10717 Berlin. Tel: (30) 861 40 56. Fax: (30) 873 15 20. E-mail: lingua_franca@compuserve.com
Number of teachers: 20.
Preference of nationality: none.
Qualifications: university degree plus TEFL experience and/or certificate. Experience in ESP preferred.
Conditions of employment: freelance only. Can generally give good teachers as many lesson hours as they want.
Salary: DM26-DM30 per 45-minute lesson.
Facilities/Support: no help with accommodation. Will write the necessary letter to the employment office to support work permit application. In-house training available.
Recruitment: local interviews.
Contact: Charles Arrigo, Director.

LINGUARAMA SPRACHENINSTITUT DEUTSCHLAND
Rindermarkt 16, 80331 München. Tel: (89) 2 60 70 40/26 85 71. Fax: (89) 260 98 84. E-mail: 106005.1012@compuserve.com
Number of teachers: from 25 in the smaller Linguarama schools to 70 in the larger ones; Linguarama schools located in Berlin, Düsseldorf, Frankfurt, Hamburg, Köln, Leipzig, München and Stuttgart (addresses given in text of chapter).
Preference of nationality: native speakers only.
Qualifications: minimum university degree or equivalent and a basic TEFL qualification (e.g. CELTA). Experience of teaching business English is preferred but at least teachers should have a keen interest in business.
Conditions of employment: mixture of contract and freelance teachers. Freelance teachers work variable hours, usually early mornings and evenings. Contract teachers usually contracted for 1 year, extendable to 2 years, but occasionally shorter contracts available. 20 days paid holiday per 12 month contract.
Salary: depends on experience.
Facilities/Support: contract teachers are given an initial 2 week accommodation entitlement and assistance with finding permanent accommodation. Travel expenses to the city are paid from the UK if recruitment is through head office. Help is given with obtaining a residence permit, etc. All teachers are given an induction course and paid training is held monthly.
Recruitment: normally local interviews for freelance teachers. Contract staff are sometimes recruited locally or via Linguarama Group Personnel Department, Oceanic House, 89 High St, Alton, Hants. GU34 1LG (see introductory chapter *Finding a Job*).
Contact: Rosemary Annandale, General Manager, Linguarama Deutschland.

LINGUS DAS SPRACHINSTITUT
Bertolt-Brecht-Allee 24, 01309 Dresden. Tel: (351) 3199 3080. Fax: (351) 3199 3081. E-mail: lingus@businesspark-dresden.de
Number of teachers: 10.
Preference of nationality: none.
Qualifications: fully trained.
Conditions of employment: freelance. Number of hours depend on courses: 10-20 p.w.
Salary: DM25 per hour (gross) less about 25% deductions.
Facilities/Support: assistance with accommodation if necessary. No training.
Recruitment: direct. Interviews occasionally held in UK.
Contact: Mr. Karsten Uhl, Director of Studies/Owner.

LTC (LANGUAGE TRAINING CENTER)
Grosse Bleichen 32, 20354 Hamburg. Tel: (40) 357 11038. Fax: (40) 357 11049. E-mail: ltc.hamburg@t-online.de
Number of teachers: about 50.

Preference of nationality: none.
Qualifications: CELTA or equivalent and several years of solid experience.
Conditions of employment: freelance. Early mornings, late afternoons and evenings.
Salary: from about DM35 per hour (net).
Facilities/Support: no assistance with accommodation or work permits.
Recruitment: word of mouth. Local interview essential.
Contact: Jean Mönnich, Director of Studies.

MUNCHNER VOLKSHOCHSCHULE

Fachgebiet Englisch, Postfach 801164m 81611 München. Tel: (89) 480 06 165. Fax: (89) 480 06 252.
Number of teachers: 50-70 freelancers, all native speakers.
Preference of nationality: none. Also employ some non-native speakers.
Qualifications: CELTA or equivalent plus some experience or extensive experience and informal training.
Conditions of employment: freelance only. Applications not considered until teachers are resident in Munich area.
Facilities/Support: extensive programme of free seminars and training.
Recruitment: local interview essential.
Contact: Briony Beaven, Director of Studies for English.

DIE NEUE SCHULE

Sprachen und Mehr, Gieselerstrasse 30a, 10713 Berlin. Tel: (30) 873 03 73. Fax: (30) 873 86 13.
Number of teachers: 15-20.
Preference of nationality: British, American.
Qualifications: RSA/Cambridge or TEFL Certificate and teaching experience needed. Mostly adults (ages 25-40) in small groups of no more than 8.
Conditions of employment: open-ended freelance contracts. Variable hours in the mornings (9-12am) and evenings (6-9.15pm).
Salary: DM26 per 60-minute lesson.
Facilities/Support: no help with accommodation.
Recruitment: personal interview necessary.

PLS LERNSTUDIO

Mariahilfstr. 8, 81541 München. Tel: (89) 651 80 54. Fax: (89) 664947. E-mail: plsmuc@aol.com
Number of teachers: 10.
Preference of nationality: none.
Qualifications: experience in teaching English.
Conditions of employment: 1 year or more. Hours between 10am and 7pm.
Salary: DM36 per hour (net).
Facilities/Support: no assistance with accommodation or work permits. In-house training in Superlearning.
Recruitment: local interview essential.
Contact: Brigitte Braun, Manager.

PROFESSIONAL ENGLISH TRAINING (P.E.T.)

Wittelsbacherstrasse 13, 80469 München. Tel: (89) 202 386 55. Fax: (89) 202 386 54.
Number of teachers: 5-10 freelancers.
Preference of nationality: none, though some clients request British or American accents.
Qualifications: personality is of premium importance. TEFL qualification and/or a degree are desirable, as is business experience.
Conditions of employment: all freelance contracts to give in-company courses. To work early mornings and afternoons/evenings.
Salary: DM40-50 per teaching unit (45 minutes).

Facilities/Support: no assistance with accommodation. Materials support given. Teachers' workshops held.
Recruitment: direct applications. Local interviews necessary.

SPRACHSCHUL-CENTRUM DREIEICH
Frankfurter Strasse 114, 63268 Dreieich. Tel: (6103) 34113. Fax: (6103) 34783.
Number of teachers: 4.
Preference of nationality: Irish, British.
Qualifications: TEFL qualification with 2 years' experience.
Conditions of employment: 9 month contracts (October-June). 27 h.p.w. Pupils are all adults, some company courses.
Salary: DM2,400 per month (tax-free).
Facilities/Support: assistance with accommodation. No training given.
Recruitment: through private contacts. Interviews can be given in Ireland.

STEVENS ENGLISH TRAINING
Rüttenscheiderstr. 68, 45130 Essen. Tel: (201) 787091-93. Fax: (201) 793783.
Number of teachers: 18 full-time and 8 part-time.
Preference of nationality: none though most teachers are British.
Qualifications: TEFL Certificate or business experience.
Conditions of employment: 2 year contracts. Hours between 7.30am and 8.45pm Monday to Friday. 80% of teaching is in-company with high element of ESP.
Salary: DM14-DM28.50 per 45-minute session, calculated on a points system.
Facilities/Support: school has fully equipped flats for up to 9 staff. Extensive workshop programme.
Recruitment: interviews essential and are available once or twice a year in London.
Contacts: Sigrid and Michael Stevens, Managing Directors.

TARGET GBR
Türkenstrasse 66, 80799 München. Tel: (89) 280 92 35. Fax: (89) 280 04 16. E-mail: jsydes@aol.com
Number of teachers: 12.
Preference of nationality: none (though most are British and American).
Qualifications: Cert TEFL is essential. Minimum 3 years experience with business English. Diploma preferred.
Conditions of employment: freelance only. Trainers must be prepared to stay for 18 months.
Salary: DM45-60 per 45 minute lesson.
Facilities/Support: advice given on accommodation if necessary. Will contribute up to half fees of external training.
Recruitment: word of mouth and adverts in regional newspapers. Local interview essential.
Contact: John Sydes, Senior Partner.

WALL STREET INSTITUTE GmbH
Humboldtstr. 2, 79098 Freiburg. Tel: (761) 207110. Fax: (761) 207 1120.
Number of teachers: 6.
Preference of nationality: none.
Qualifications: as much experience as possible
Conditions of employment: open-ended contracts. 20-40 h.p.w.
Salary: depends on position (DM1,600-DM3,500 per month).
Facilities/Support: some training given.
Recruitment: local interviews essential.
Contact: Giuseppe Provenzano, Director.

Other Schools to Try (cities and towns in alphabetical order)

Note that these schools did not confirm their teacher requirements for this edition of

Teaching English Abroad. Upper case entries marked with an asterisk had entries in the last edition (1997); addresses without asterisks have been taken from various sources, such as British Council lists, the *Yellow Pages,* etc.

SpracheDirekt, Breite Strasse 69, 56626 Andernach
Saxon College of English, Markt 15, 09573 Augustusburg
Accent Business Languages, Sächsische Str. 7, 10707 Berlin
Akademia fur Fremdsprachen GmbH, Postfach 104, 10663 Berlin
Berlitz, Kurfürstendamm 74, 10709 Berlin
Central English School, Frankenallee 12, 14052 Berlin/Charlottenburg
Dialog Sprachenschule, Uhlandstrasse 63, 10719 Berlin
Didactica, Kaiser-Friedrich Str. 76, 10585 Berlin
Flying English, Bachestr. 3, 12161 Berlin
inlingua Sprachschule Berlin, Ludwigkirchstr. 9A, 10719 Berlin
Logo, Wichertstrasse 67, Berlin
Protea Sprachschule, Klingsorstr. 7, 12167 Berlin

ABC English, Zwickauer 297, Chemnitz
European Language School, Hansastr. 44, 44137 Dortmund
Berlitz, Wilsdruffer Strasse 11, 01067 Dresden
Fremdsprachen Institut Angelika Trautmann, Schweriner Str. 56, 01067 Dresden
Die Sprachwerkstatt, Grossenhainer 99, 01127 Dresden

*INLINGUA SPRACHSCHULE, Künigstrasse 61, 47051 Duisburg (203-30 53 40). 35 British or American teachers with a BA or equivalent and TEFL qualification, on 2 year contracts.
Berlitz-Sprachschle, Markt 11, Erfurt
Euro Schulen Gera, Friedrich Engels 10, 07545 Gera
Albis Sprach-Institut, Colonnaden 18, 20354 Hamburg
Anglo English School, Gänsemarkt 43, 20354 Hamburg
inlingua, Gr. Sandkaul 19, 50667 Köln
Sprachenschule Klisa, Agrippinaufer 6, 50678 Köln
Via Lingua School of English, Balthasarstr. 2/Ebertplatz, Köln

*AMERIKANISCHES SPRACHINSTITUT, Schlossgasse 6-8, 04109 Leipzig (341-211 82 88/fax 341-211 83 75). 10 full-time freelancers, preferably North American.
FAE Sprachschule, Arndtstrasse 63, 04275 Leipzig
inlingua, Nikolaistrasse 36, 04109 Leipzig
S & W Institut für Fremdsprachen, Sternwartenstr. 4-6, 04103 Leipzig

Euro-Schulen-Sachsen Anhalt, Fuchsberg 5, Magdeburg

A.S.S. München, Leopoldst. 62, 08082 München
Berlitz, Carl-Zeiss-Ring 14, 85737 Ismaning
Desk, Blumentstr. 1, 80331 München
*ENGLISH LANGUAGE CENTRE, Bieberer Strasse 205, 63071 Offenbach am Main (69-85 87 87/fax 69-85 72 02). 8 teachers, preferably British, on 2 year contracts.
Wall Street Institute, Köningstrasse 49, 70173 Stuttgart

Greece

The huge ELT industry in Greece predates Greece's full membership in the European Union, and continues to increase. Of all the candidates worldwide who sit the Cambridge First Certificate and Cambridge Proficiency examinations, about one quarter are in Greece, i.e. more than 130,000. English language teaching in Greece has been described as an exam industry. The British Council estimates that there are between 5,000 and 6,000 private language schools (*frontisteria*) in the country, almost all of them teaching children of secondary school age. This creates a huge demand for native speakers. Standards at *frontisteria* vary from indifferent to excellent, but the run-of-the-mill variety is usually a reasonable place to work for nine months, even if *frontisterion* owners are primarily business people rather than educators.

Frontisteria come in all shapes and sizes. In a town of 30,000 inhabitants, it would not be unusual to find ten English *frontisteria*, three or four of which would be big enough to employ one native English speaker. The city of Patras alone has 400. The Greek Ministry of Education imposes a quota on language schools, stipulating that there can be no more than one foreigner for every nine Greek teachers.

Any Greek who has passed the Cambridge Proficiency exam is legally permitted to open his or her own private school. These are often in buildings which were not designed to be schools and facilities can be very basic. Secondary school pupils in Greece are obliged to study 15 subjects, all of which they must pass before being allowed to proceed to the next year. In most areas the teaching of English in state schools is so inadequate that the vast majority of pupils also attend *frontisteria*, and it is not uncommon for a 15 year old to have two or three hours of lessons a day (in other subjects as well as English) in one or more private establishments to supplement the state schooling. Not surprisingly, the students are not always brimming over with enthusiasm; in fact, quite often they are not even awake.

Prospects for Teachers

Towards the end of the 1990s, the employment situation for teachers is no longer booming, due partly to a falling birthrate, high unemployment and an influx of Greek expatriates from around the world who are given priority over other foreigners. Yet prospects for EU nationals with a university degree are still relatively good, particularly outside Athens. An increasing number of *frontisteria* are looking for other teaching qualifications like a Cambridge or Trinity Certificate. Few insist on experience. The government stipulates that in order to obtain a teacher's licence, English teachers must have at least a BA in English language and literature or education, so that all but the most dodgy schools will expect to see a university certificate. Of the schools listed in the Directory at the end of this chapter, about half mention that they are looking for a TEFL certificate (CELTA/TESOL). Having a TEFL qualification, as always, will make the job hunt easier. Given the size of the ELT market in Greece, it is surprising that no training centres offer the CELTA or the Trinity TESOL Certificate in Greece.

Americans and other non-EU nationals will find it difficult to find a school willing to hire them, purely because of immigration difficulties. The government imposes stiff penalities on employers who break the rules, and few will risk it, as Tim Leffel found out:

> We had planned on teaching in Greece, but as Americans, we were not exactly welcomed with open arms in Athens. They told us to try the countryside.

Tim moved on to Turkey instead. A further complicating factor is the high number of Greek emigrés to North America and Australia who have returned (or whose children have returned) to Greece. In many cases, they are virtually native speakers of English but because of their ancestry do not use up the one-in-nine allocation of foreigners mentioned above. Of course there will always be schools prepared to hire Americans and others if well qualified, such as the *Hellenic American Union* which has one of the largest programmes in adult EFL in Athens.

One reason why EU nationals with basic qualifications can expect to land a job in Greece is that wages are not high enough to attract a great many qualified EFL teachers. Greece tends to be a country where people get their first English teaching job for the experience and then move to more lucrative countries. Also, few schools place any emphasis on staff development or provide in-house training, so serious teachers tend to move on quickly.

The majority of advertised jobs are in towns and cities in mainland Greece. Athens has such a large expatriate community that most of the large central schools at the elite end of the market are able to hire well qualified staff locally. But the competition will not be so keen in Edessa, Larissa, Preveza or any of numerous towns of which the tourist to Greece is unlikely to have heard.

FIXING UP A JOB
In Advance

Unless you elect to register with a recruitment agency (all of which deal primarily with Certificate-qualified teachers), it may not be worthwhile trying to fix up a job in advance, since so much in Greece is accomplished by word of mouth. Getting a list of language schools from outside Greece is not easy. A considerable proportion of *frontisteria* belong to the Pan-Hellenic Federation of Language School Owners (PALSO, 2 Lykavitou St & Akadimias St, 106 71 Kolonaki, Athens; 1-364 0792/364 2359). Unfortunately they do not seem able or willing to send a list of their member schools, though anyone in Athens might be able to obtain some assistance from them. The British Council in Athens does not maintain a list of English schools, though the Teaching Centre Director at the British Council in Thessaloniki can send a list of nearly 100 addresses in and around Thessaloniki, transliterated into the English alphabet. If you do manage to get hold of the list of *Frontisteria* from the Yellow Pages, note that you will have to be conversant with the Greek alphabet unless you find the *Athens Blue Pages*, an English version of the Yellow Pages.

Most schools do their hiring for the following academic year between March and June. Obviously the major chains of schools offer the most opportunities, and it is worth sending your CV in the spring to organisations like the *Strategakis Group* with about a hundred schools in northern Greece or the *Omiros Association* with 120 schools.

Adverts for Greek schools continue to appear, especially in the *TES*. Few seem to go in for lavish display adverts, but there is a sprinkling of four-line adverts along the lines of 'English teachers required. Good salary and housing. Fax your CV and a photo to Frontisterion X.' There are also occasional adverts for live-in tutors. The spring is the best time to look, though inevitably some schools who are let down by contracted teachers place rather panicky ads in August and into September.

Fortunately there are several active recruitment agencies which specialise in Greece with offices in Greece and/or Britain. These recruitment agencies are looking for people with at least a BA and preferably a TEFL qualification and/or experience (depending on the client school's requirements). All client employers provide accommodation. Complaints about a lack of back-up are occasionally heard, so do not expect to be nannied along after placement. The following undertake to match teachers (with EU nationality) with *frontisteria* and do not charge teachers a fee:

Anglo-Hellenic, PO Box 263, 201 00 Corinth. Tel/fax: 741-53511. Dozens of posts in wide choice of locations for university graduates from the UK, preferably with a CELTA. Interviews are conducted in London, Athens or Corinth throughout the summer. 9-month contracts pay the going rate of about £350 per month (net) plus bonuses and accommodation in a furnished flat. Accommodation is normally free to qualified and experienced teachers but not to inexperienced graduates. Contract provided by agency (specimen copy available beforehand).

Cambridge Teachers Recruitment, 33A Makryanni St, New Halkidona, 143 43 Athens. Tel/fax: (1) 218 5155. UK contact address of main interviewer during the summer: Andrew MacLeod-Smith, 30 Radcliffe Road, Croydon, Surrey CR0 5QF (0181-686 3733). One of the largest agencies, placing 80-100 teachers per year in vetted schools. Applicants must have a degree and in most cases a TEFL Certificate, a friendly personality and conscientious attitude. Comprehensive interviews are conducted between mid-June and the end of August; applicants can expect to receive a wealth of information about working in Greece.

English Studies Advisory Centre (ESAC), Cosmos Center, 125-127 Kifisias Ave,

11524 Athens. Tel: (1) 69 97 017. Fax: (1) 69 94 618. Mainly nine-month jobs (September to June) but also some summer positions as well. Applicants should enclose CV, recent photo, phone number and international reply coupon. Andrew Boyle (who had no TEFL background) answered one of ESAC's adverts in the *Guardian* and secured a job in Tripolis after one telephone call.

   i to i International Projects, 1 Cottage Road, Headingley, Leeds LS6 4DD. Tel: 0113 217 9800. TEFL training organisation which has links with schools in Greece and can arrange employment.

   NET (Native English Teachers), 160 Littlehampton Road, Worthing, West Sussex BN13 1QT. Tel: (01903) 218638. Agency run by Susan Lancaster, who interviews British teachers for up to 20 vacancies in *frontisteria*. Selection is based on qualifications, merit and good references. (No help can be given to North Americans because of visa restrictions.) Provides orientation which includes information on cheap air fares and on how to show respect for Greek customs.

   SKOLA/Teachers in Greece, 21 Star St, London W2 1QB. Tel: 0171-402 0416. Fax: 0171-724 2219. Teachers with a British passport and university degree placed in all areas of Greece. Couples can be considered.

   When discussing your future post with an agency, don't be lulled into a false sense of security. It is wise to check contractual details for yourself and verify verbal promises. Check to see whether you are entitled to any compensation if the employer breaks the contract and similarly whether you will have to compensate the school if you leave early. Find out if there will be any other native speaker teachers in the area, and ask about the possibility of contacting your predecessor in the job.

On the Spot

So many *frontisteria* rely on agents to find teachers for them, that it can be difficult to walk into a job. After gaining a lot of on-the-ground experience of Greece, Jane McNally from County Derry in Ireland concluded that knocking on school doors can be discouraging, a view corroborated (summer 1998) by Iain Cook who is Director of Studies at the *Koutsantonis School of Languages* in Patras (see entry):

> *There do not seem to be as many vacancies for teachers as there used to be in the Peloponnese. I have interviewed about 15 British teachers in the past few weeks, all of whom have stressed the difficulty of finding work in this area. They were all personable, smartly dressed, well qualified and experienced, but as yet have received no definite job offers.*

The majority of schools have filled all their vacancies by June, so September is normally too late for prospective teachers to be looking for work. One of the best times to look is January. Greece is far less attractive in mid-winter than in summer, and many foreign teachers do not return to their posts after Christmas. Finding work in the summer is virtually impossible; most English language summer courses in resorts or on the islands are staffed by people who have taught for an academic year.

   Yet in the more remote corners of Greece, native speakers can locate jobs on-the-spot and negotiate a position. Sarah Clifford had no trouble lining up part-time work at a *frontisterion* in the Peloponnesian village of Kynoryrias, with 'no experience, no teaching qualification, no degree and no knowledge of Greek'. The catch was that the hourly wage was lower than average, but she enjoyed rural Greece more than cosmopolitan Athens.

   Little can be reliably accomplished by post or even by telephone. Larry Church describes the unpredictable way in which his second teaching contract was arranged:

> *While on a weekend holiday to Athens from Orestiada, my second teaching job (in Alexandroupolis) occurred through a chance meeting on the airplane with a frontisterion owner. The job offer came during a shared taxi ride into Athens. Taking care of business at the last possible minute being a normal procedure in Greece, a contract was signed in June at the airport, ten minutes before our plane was due to take off for our return trip to America for the summer. At the same time my wife was*

promised some part-time hours in the school, although she had no teaching experience.

Although Jamie Masters knew that October was not prime time for job-hunting, that is when he arrived in Heraklion to look for work:

I advertised (in Greek) in the Cretan newspapers, no joy. I lowered my sights and started knocking on doors of frontisteria. I was put onto some guy who ran an English-language bookshop and went to see him. Turned out he was a lynch-pin in the frontisterion business and in fact I got my first job through him. Simultaneously I went to something which roughly translates as the 'Council for owners of frontisteria' and was given a list of schools which were looking for people. The list, it turned out, was pretty much out of date. But I had insisted on leaving my name with the Council (they certainly didn't offer) and that's how I found my second job.

Once you arrange an interview, be sure to dress well and to amass as many educational diplomas as you can. This will create the right aura of respectability in which to impress the potential employer with your conscientiousness and amiability. Decisions are often taken more according to whether you hit it off with the interviewer than on your qualifications and experience. Jamie Masters found that no one cared a fig about his PhD in Latin.

Check the adverts in the English language daily *Athens News* or *Greek News* or the weekly *Hellenic Times* where *frontisteria* sometimes advertise, though they normally ask for qualifications. These papers are probably more useful if you are looking for a more informal arrangement: many Greek families are looking for live-in or part-time tutors for their children. You can read the *Athens News'* Situations Vacant ads on the internet at http://athensnews.dolnet.gr/ or you can place your own 15-word advert in the *Athens News* for dr2,200; contact them at 3 Christou Lada, 102 37 Athens; 1-33 3404/fax 1-322 3746).

When you elicit interest from a language school owner or a family, take your time over agreeing terms. Greece is not a country in which it pays to rush, and negotiations can be carried out in a leisurely and civilised fashion. On the other hand, do not come to an agreement with an employer without clarifying wages and schedules precisely. Make sure you read your contract very carefully so that you are familiar with what you should be entitled to.

Freelance

Private lessons, at least in the provinces, are very easy to find. Some people estimate that between a third and a half of all English language teaching that goes on in Greece takes place privately. The going rate is dr3,000 an hour for First Certificate teaching, dr5,000 for Proficiency. Rates in Athens are more likely to be in the range dr5,000-10,000. Very few teachers declare their private earnings for tax purposes.

Most teachers in *frontisteria* do at least three or four hours a week of private tutoring, since the basic salary is increasingly difficult to live on, at least if you are on your own instead of part of a teaching couple. Private tutoring jobs seem to materialise either from the language schools (whose directors seldom seem to mind their teachers earning on the side) or from conversations in a *kafeneion*.

Trading English lessons for board and lodging is a common form of freelance teaching in Athens and elsewhere. Sometimes contracted teachers are offered free accommodation in exchange for tutoring their boss's children. In Athens, the rich suburbs of Kifissia and Politia are full of families who can afford to provide private English lessons for their offspring. The suburbs of Pangrati and Filothei are also well-heeled as is the more central suburb of Kolonaki. It is also possible to start up private classes for children, provided you have decent accommodation in a prosperous residential area, though this will normally be too expensive if your only source of income is private teaching. Leah White solved her accommodation problem in Athens by approaching managers of blocks of flats to see whether they could arrange for her to have a rent-free flat in exchange for teaching their children. (This way she avoided the problem which plagues live-in tutors, a lack of privacy.)

REGULATIONS

English teachers must first obtain a teacher's licence and then a residence permit, and the bureaucratic procedures involved can be stressful even with a supportive employer. The two documents needed for a teacher's licence are a health certificate and a degree certificate. The Ministry of Education considers a BA or higher degree in English literature or a degree in Education a sufficient qualification though a TEFL Certificate strengthens your application of course. You must have your degree certificate officially translated and notarised, either before you leave home (which is usually cheaper) or in Greece (ask the British Council for advice). The health certificate can be obtained only in Greece, and involves a chest X-ray and in some cases a blood test.

English speakers of Greek ancestry find it much easier to obtain a teacher's licence and are generally more attractive prospects, as explained by Jain Cook:

> *Australian, Canadian, South African and American Greeks are classed as native speakers because English is their first language, but their Greek surnames helps the one-in-ten Greek/foreigner ratio. They do all their own bureaucratic paperwork, have family and relatives in Greece, fewer accommodation and financial problems and are reliable, very rarely leaving for reasons other than pregnancy. Usually they come back after their maternity leave as they have family to look after the baby. Since February I have interviewed over a hundred such teachers, the majority from Canada. Although many have no teaching experience or qualificaitons, they have already obtained a teacher's licence and therefore school owners are more than willing to consider them.*

Many choose to take out citizenship, which involves getting a Greek Identity Card. This entitles them to a teacher's licence valid for life, exempting them from having to renew it annually as other foreigners do.

When the teacher's licence arrives from Athens, the teacher must take it along with his or her passport, photos and a lot of patience to the police station to apply for a residence permit, which should come through in about a month. The health certificate and residence permit must be renewed annually, though if you protest loudly enough you can usually get away with just having a chest X-ray. You will however have to take your IKA book (see below) to renew your residence permit and a form from your employer which shows the length of your term of employment. The first residence permit is normally valid for just six months, subsequent ones for one to three years. Keep photocopies of all forms.

Some teachers simply extend their tourist visa (as long as they can provide plenty of currency exchange slips to prove that they are self-supporting) or leave the country every three months to renew their tourist stamp. Unfortunately this is expensive and time-consuming if you are in a remote corner of Greece. Also the second term is normally longer than three months and if you have to be replaced for the last few weeks of term, you may find that you are not welcomed back.

Frontisteria usually tend to leave all the bureaucratic legwork to the teachers because hiring a foreigner, especially those coming from outside the EU, is extremely complicated. Employers will take on the necessary transactions only if they are convinced that a candidate will be an asset to their school. Non-EU teachers often find that the Ministry of Education delays and even turns down their applications for a teacher's licence. Officially they must obtain a letter of hire from a language school which must be sent to an address outside Greece. The teacher takes the letter to the nearest Greek consulate and applies for a work permit; the procedures take at least two months.

It is mandatory for Greek employers to register employees with the Greek National Health Insurance scheme (IKA) and pay contributions which amount to 15.89% of the salary. Be sure to find out ahead of time whether the salary quoted is before or after the IKA deduction. You should go with your employer to the local IKA office in order to apply for an IKA book 60 days after starting to pay contributions; thereafter you are entitled to free medical treatment and reduced cost prescriptions on production of the book. If you suspect that your employer is not in fact paying contributions on your behalf, ask to see the stamps. If he or she will not show you, threaten to expose him or her to the authorities. (Once you have paid IKA and tax for two consecutive years, you are entitled to unemployment benefit; some teachers have been known to claim over the summer when they are out of the country, though the authorities may clamp down on this.)

CONDITIONS OF WORK

Standards vary enormously among *frontisteria*. Although there is specific legislation which is meant to regulate the operation of language schools, this is seldom enforced. The way to recognise a good *frontisterion* is by its exam results and by its ability to retain staff.

In general the large chains like *Strategakis* are better, probably for no other reason than that they have a longer history of employing native English speakers. Some of the small one-man or one-woman schools are cowboy outfits run by barely qualified entrepreneurs who have had little contact with the English language; their teaching techniques involve shouting (usually in Greek) at their students and getting them to recite English irregular verbs parrot fashion.

The minimum hourly rate of pay is dr1,717 gross, dr1,445. Anyone with some training or experience should be able to ask for at least dr2,000. No teacher should accept less than the legal rate. Depending on the number of holidays (unpaid) in a month, your take-home pay can fluctuate alarmingly and be barely enough to live on, especially in view of the high rents in Greece which usually take up at least a third of a teacher's salary. In theory teachers should be paid for an extra ten hours of marking a month but almost no one receives this.

Always keep a copy of your contract safe in case difficulties arise, as they did in the case of Belinda Michaels while working at a *frontisterion* in Patras:

> *In November, the school owner told me that the students wanted me back after Christmas. On January 29th 1998, she dismissed me with no notice and no holiday pay. Her excuse was that there was low student attendance during the university exam period. The next day the landlady was very rude to me saying that I had left the school. I had to pay dr46,000 for my January electricity bill which I never saw. She also asked for dr13,000 for the water bill and a month's rent in advance. I immediately left the accommodation. When I went into the school to ask for one month's severance pay to which I was legally entitled, the owner started attacking me verbally and ordered me out of the school. She refused to give me a copy of my contract, nor had the UK agent given me a copy.*

The basic salary should be augmented by compulsory bonuses at Christmas, Easter and summer. Teaching unions have negotiated some reasonable conditions, though not all schools offer them. Bonuses, holiday pay and health insurance should all be stipulated, plus employers may not fire teachers during the school year. The majority of employers offer eight or nine month contracts from September and allow two paid fortnight holidays at Christmas and Easter (remember that the Greek Easter is usually later than elsewhere). Bonuses are calculated according to the number of days worked. For every nine days you have worked before Christmas you get one day's pay (i.e. five hours). For every 13 days worked between January 1st and April 30th you get two days pay. This usually approximates to an extra month's pay at Christmas and half a month's pay at Easter.

You also get a lump sum at the end of your contract which is not in fact a bonus. It is two weeks' holiday pay and two weeks' severance pay (both tax-free). Beware of employers who pay for your accommodation out of your gross salary and then try to calculate your bonuses as a percentage of your net salary. This is illegal. Employers who have suffered from staff desertions in the past may hold back some of your monthly pay as a bond *(kratisi)* against an early departure. The indignity of this niggled away at Jamie Masters (plus he needed the dr5,000 per month) until he complained and the practice was discontinued.

The working week in a *frontisterion* is longer than in most countries averaging 28-30 hours per week. Often the contract includes a maximum number such as 30 or even 36 (excluding preparation time). Split shifts are common especially in areas where the state schools operate a shift system where students attend mornings one week and afternoons the next. A *frontisterion* schedule of 9-11am and 5-10pm means late nights and early starts. The state school system is changing gradually, so that in some areas student attend only morning classes, which in turn means that private schools are offering English tuition only in the evenings, thereby cutting down the potential number of hours a teacher can work.

It is not unusual to be expected to teach in two or more 'satellite' sites of the main school in villages up to ten miles away. Local bus services are generally good and cheap but you could find yourself spending an inordinate amount of (unpaid) time in transit and standing around at bus stops.

All areas have a local Workers' Office where you can go if you are in dispute with your employer or fear that you are being ripped off. They are gradually becoming more efficient and are obliged to investigate every complaint.

Pupils

Most native English speakers are employed to teach advanced classes, usually the two years leading to Cambridge exams. Because of the Greek style of education, pupils won't show much initiative and will expect to be tested frequently on what they have been taught. Andrew Boyle found the prevailing methodology of 'sit 'em down, shut 'em up and give 'em lots of homework' was moderately successful.

Another problem is that there is a great deal of pressure to assign pass marks just to retain the students' custom. Some school owners are so profit-motivated, they have drachmas for eyeballs. Students expect to be told the answers and bosses want their teachers to be lenient with the marking so that the students all pass and parents will re-enrol them.

As a consequence of this leniency, discipline can also be a problem. Miss C. Warren-Swettenham from Oxfordshire worked at a *frontisterion* in Trikkala in Northern Greece:

> As regards the teaching, everything is running smoothly, although at the best of times trying to inspire rowdy adolescent Greek kids with totally unsuitable outdated English books is enough to give you a nervous breakdown. Suggesting a possible alternative to my boss is something I have tried, but to no avail. Basically their idea of English is what they have in grammar books, accompanied by dreary written exercises, conjugating verbs. Any attempt to introduce TEFL teaching where the emphasis is on communicaiton falls on deaf ears.

Jamie Masters came to the conclusion that cheating is a national pastime and hated his role as policeman. He expended a lot of energy on outwitting their strategies, when all he wanted to do was to get them to learn something. He had to teach pupils who had been promoted because of parental pressure, notably one girl in a third year class who didn't understand one word of English and yet turned in perfect compositions, done by other people.

Accommodation

Since most schools provide a flat or at least help in finding a flat, teachers are often not too concerned about their living arrangements. Placements arranged by the recruitment agencies listed above all come with accommodation, which at best is spartan (consisting of a bed, chair, table, baby belling and shower) and at worst revolting. Andrew Boyle described his flat in Tripolis as a 'particularly vile, subterranean cavern with an almost non-existent window and stomach-turning plumbing' but found that anything more congenial was ridiculously expensive. Another problem with tied flats is that you may not be consulted over rent increases. If your employer pays your rent directly out of your salary, you may be helpless to object.

If your employer provides your accommodation, it is definitely worth checking in advance about furnishings. Many flats, especially in Athens, are unfurnished which is a serious nuisance for someone on a nine-month contract. Also check which (if any) utility bills are included in the rent. Many people are shocked at how cold Greece gets in the winter, and at how expensive electricity is. The cost of electricity rose again in July 1998 and water and telephone charges are set to increase in 1999. Jain Cook and her husband had a bill of £250 for two months, using only lights, hot water, iron and TV. Make sure you have plenty of warm clothes and a hot water bottle, so that you don't use up your entire budget on heating.

LEISURE

Teachers in Athens should have no trouble constructing a social life. The monthly paper *The Athenian* available from kiosks in Omonia Square among other places contains details of clubs and events of interest to expats. Outside Athens, the social order is still fairly conservative. A further problem is the enormous language barrier in a country where it will take some time to learn how to read the alphabet. Watching Greek television is a good way to learn the language plus Greek lessons are run free of charge in many locations. Larry Church and his wife were among only five native English speakers in Orestiada and the only Americans; at times they felt like the town oddities, but well-loved ones. Most teachers find the vast majority of Greek people to be honest, friendly and helpful and are seldom disappointed with the hospitality they receive.

As anyone who has visited Greece knows, the country has countless other attractions, not least the very convivial and affordable tavernas. Eating out, wine and cigarettes are more or less the only things that have not become expensive. Cafés *(kafeneions)* are a largely male institution in which women teachers may not feel comfortable. Travel, particularly ferry travel, is relatively cheap and a pure delight out of season.

When people think of Greece they automatically think of sun-soaked Mediterranean beaches, but it is quite a different story in the inland towns of northern Greece in the winter. Erica Jolly and Paul Robinson soon exhausted the possibilities of their northern town:

> There were very few facilities other than bars and a few restaurants. The cinema did show undubbed British and American films but was too cold to sit in in winter. Sports facilities were non-existent and adults were not allowed to use the town's swimming pool. Fortunately we had brought our car and were able to see quite a lot of Greece. We even took the car over to Corfu at Easter. Insurance was not cheap but was easily obtainable.

The cost of living is higher than it used to be. All imports are expensive, for example cosmetics, shoes and clothes. Don't expect to have much left out of your £400 or so take-home pay for saving or splurging.

Despite all the hassles, most people enjoy a year in Greece, as Philip Dray did:

> I have many happy memories of working in northeastern Greece, even though we were asked to work 32 hours a week (and that was too much for £90) and had a boss who was out to exploit from the start. But the town was great, the children superb and I also had friendly colleagues.

LIST OF SCHOOLS

ATHANASSOPOULOS LANGUAGE SCHOOLS
6 Einstein St & Nikis, 18 757 Keratsini-Piraeus. Tel: (1) 43 14 921/40 01 226. Fax: (1) 43 18 241. Branch school at 30 & 34 Ipsilantou St, 187 58 Keratsini (1-43 23 947).
Number of teachers: 9-10.
Preference of nationality: British, American, Canadian.
Qualifications: BA (English) or equivalent. Cambridge/RSA Certificate valued.
Conditions of employment: 8 month extendable contracts. Morning and/or afternoon work. Pupils aged 9-24.

Salary: £450 per month plus £450 summer bonus.
Facilities/Support: subsidised accommodation offered. Free British Council seminars arranged.
Recruitment: through newspaper adverts and TEFL training centres. Interviews essential and are held locally or abroad.

HELLENIC AMERICAN UNION
22 Massalias Street, 106 80 Athens. Tel: (1) 362 9886. Fax: (1) 363 3174.
Number of teachers: 45.
Preference of nationality: EU plus American, Canadian, Australian, etc.
Qualifications: MA preferred (50% of their teachers have an MA).
Conditions of employment: most students are adults but also offer EFL courses for children and adolescents.
Contact: Catherine Georgopoulos, Deputy Director of Education.

HERCULES LANGUAGE SCHOOL
L. Saronidas 28-30, 19013 Saronida. Tel/fax: (291) 60707.
Number of teachers: 3.
Preference of nationality: none.
Qualifications: university degree and TEFL Certificate needed; experience an advantage but not essential.
Conditions of employment: 11 month contract from September. Maximum 30 contact hours p.w. (afternoons and evenings).
Salary: dr220,000 per month, gross. Deductions total approximately dr40,000 per month.
Facilities/Support: accommodation provided in one-bedroom furnished flat, 10 minutes walk from school.
Recruitment: adverts in *TES*. Interviews sometimes held in UK as well as Greece.
Contact: Karen Gallo, Director of Studies.

HOMER ASSOCIATION
—See Omiros Association.

KARANTZOUNIS INSTITUTE OF FOREIGN LANGUAGES
41 Epidavrou St, 104 41 Athens. Tel: (1) 514 2397. Fax: (1) 524 5479.
Number of teachers: 5 at 3 schools (Tertipi 31 & Papanastasiou 82, 104 45 Athens; and Odysseus & Troias 17, 121 33 Peristeri).
Preference of nationality: British, American.
Qualifications: BA.
Conditions of employment: 1 academic year contracts from September to June. 25-28 h.p.w. mainly evening work. Pupils aged 8-16.
Salary: dr130,000-150,000 per month.
Facilities/Support: small independent furnished and equipped apartment provided free of charge. Training provided.
Recruitment: interviews in Athens essential.

D. KOUTOUGERA-KORRE FOREIGN LANGUAGES CENTER
4 Smyrnis St, Nea Filadelfeia, 143 41 Athens. Tel/fax: (1) 25 11 657. Tel: (1) 25 18 281/25 20 854.
Number of teachers: 4 (two couples).
Preference of nationality: British, Irish.
Qualifications: BA/Higher diploma in English/TEFL qualification.
Conditions of employment: minimum 8½ month contracts. 25 h.p.w. Pupils aged 8-18.
Salary: dr200,000 per month plus holiday bonuses totalling dr2,000,000.
Facilities/Support: accommodation available: 1 bedroom furnished flat offered to each couple. Training provided.
Recruitment: adverts in *TES*. Interviews sometimes carried out in UK as well as in Athens. Photo and CV necessary.

KOUTSANTONIS SCHOOL OF LANGUAGES
35 Gounari Avenue, 262 21 Patras. Tel: (61) 273925. Fax: 224496.
Number of teachers: 3.
Preference of nationality: British.
Qualifications: BA and Cambridge/RSA Cert.
Conditions of employment: 8 month contracts. 24 contact h.p.w. (mornings and evenings).
Salary: approximately dr200,000 per month gross (dr180,000 net).
Facilities/Support: help with accommodation given.
Recruitment: local advertisements.

LINDA LEE-NIKOLAOU SCHOOL OF FOREIGN LANGUAGES
12 P. Tsaldari St, Xylokastro, 204 00 Korinthias. Tel: (743) 24678/61276.
Number of teachers: 1.
Preference of nationality: British, Irish.
Qualifications: BA/BSc and Cambridge/RSA Certificate or equivalent. Previous experience not essential but an advantage.
Conditions of employment: 1 academic year renewable contracts. 24 contact h.p.w. Hours of work between 3 and 8pm weekdays.
Salary: negotiable, but above standard rates.
Facilities/Support: free flat provided.
Recruitment: adverts in UK newspapers. Interviews usually essential and take place in UK in July.

LORD BYRON SCHOOL OF ENGLISH
104 Tsimiski St, 54622 Thessaloniki. Tel: (31) 278804/268647. Fax: (31) 234598.
Number of teachers: 6.
Preference of nationality: British.
Qualifications: university degree and TEFL certificate.
Conditions of employment: 8 month contracts (October to May).
Salary: varies according to experience and age (dr2,200-dr2,600 per hour).
Facilities/Support: no assistance with accommodation. Training given.
Recruitment: via TEFL training centres. Interviews essential and sometimes available in the UK.
Contact: Harry Nikolaides, Director of Studies.

OMIROS ASSOCIATION
52 Academias St, 106 79 Athens. Tel: (1) 36 22 887. Fax: (1) 36 21 833.
Number of teachers: an average of 10 at each of the Association's 120 schools in Greece.
Preference of nationality: British.
Qualifications: BA and experience of TEFL.
Conditions of employment: 8-10 month contracts. About 20 h.p.w. Pupils range in age from 9-16.
Salary: on application.
Facilities/Support: assistance with accommodation provided in most cases. Teacher training facilities available in Athens (tel: 1-36 33 242).
Recruitment: adverts in Athens newspapers. Local interviews only between early June and the end of August.

M. PERDIKOPOULOU-NEARCHOU SCHOOL OF FOREIGN LANGUAGES
20 Ayiou Eleftheriou, 671 00 Xanthi. Tel: (541) 25055/29454. Fax: (541) 78616.
Number of teachers: 2.
Preference of nationality: British, Irish.
Qualifications: experienced TEFL teachers.
Conditions of employment: 1 academic year contracts from September to May. 28 h.p.w. Pupils range in age from 8-17.
Salary: according to cost of living.

Facilities/Support: furnished flat provided. No training provided.
Recruitment: through *TES*. Interviews not essential.
Contact: M. Perdikopoulou.

STRATEGAKIS SCHOOLS, FOREIGN LANGUAGES AND COMPUTING
24 Proxenou Koromila St, 546 22 Thessaloniki. Tel: (31) 264276. Fax: (31) 228848. Also: 6 George St, Canningos Square, 106 77 Athens. Tel: (1) 36 11 496/36 12 858. Fax: (1) 36 13 251.
Number of teachers: 50 in 100 schools all over northern Greece.
Preference of nationality: British, Irish.
Qualifications: BA/MA, PGCE (or equivalent). TEFL qualifications welcomed but not required.
Conditions of employment: 1 academic year renewable contracts. 28 h.p.w. Pupils mainly aged 9-17 although there are also some adult groups.
Salary: dr210,000-220,000 per month.
Facilities/Support: accommodation arranged; teacher pays rent. Training provided.
Recruitment: through advertising and UK universities and colleges. Interviews essential and are held in UK, usually in April.

SYCHRONO SCHOOL OF ENGLISH
20 Konitsis St, Veria 591 00. Tel/fax: (331) 29384.
Number of teachers: 1 or 2.
Preference of nationality: British, Irish.
Qualifications: BA or BSc with TEFL Certificate. Must be in perfect health and less than 30.
Conditions of employment: 8 month contracts from mid-September to May. 25-30 h.p.w. Also run summer courses in August and September.
Salary: dr2,000 per hour, less 18% deductions.
Facilities/Support: free accommodation provided (bills payable by teacher). Help with working papers.
Recruitment: personal interview necessary.
Contact: Mrs. Helen Bakaloudi, Owner.

EVA TSOPANAKOS-VENIZELOU FRONTISTERIA
19 Yiannitsi St, 341 00 Chalkis. Tel: (221) 77744. Fax: (221) 85523.
Number of teachers: 6.
Preference of nationality: British, American.
Qualifications: degree plus Cambridge/RSA Cert. or equivalent minimum.
Conditions of employment: minimum 2 year contracts. 20-25 h.p.w. Pupils from 7 years.
Salary: negotiable.
Facilities/Support: assistance given with accommodation and training.
Recruitment: adverts. Local interviews essential.

Other Schools to Try
Note that these schools did not confirm their teacher requirements for this edition of *Teaching English Abroad*. Upper case entries marked with an asterisk had entries in the last edition (1997); addresses without asterisks have been taken from various sources, such as British Council lists, the *Yellow Pages*, etc. The majority of the *frontisteria* here are in Thessaloniki (post code beginning with a 5). Many are small privately-owned language schools listed under the owner's name.

*MICHALOPOULOS SCHOOL OF ENGLISH, 30 E. Antistasis, 593 00 Alexandria (333-22890/fax 333-26601/e-mail micheng@compulink.gr). 2 teachers, preferably British.

*C. PETALAS ENGLISH INSTITUTE, 3 Tzanetou St, 471 00 Arta (681-24414). 2 teachers, preferably Australian or Irish.

Agnes Katsianos, 16 Amerikis Street, 163 41 Athens

*ATHENS COLLEGE, PO Box 65005, 15410 Psychico, Athens (1-671 4621/fax 1-647 8156). 30 teachers, Americans preferred. Must have MA/MEd in ESL and at least 3 years' certified teaching experience.
Eva Chryssanthopoulou, 6 Ploutonos and Nisi St, kalamaki, 174 55 Athens (983 10 91/ 931 26 16).

Irene Bassia, Tsontou Varda 29, 731 00 Chania, Crete

*ZOULA LANGUAGE SCHOOLS, A. Andreadi 5, Sanroco Square, 491 00 Corfu (661-39330/35334/fax 661-35894). 15 teachers from UK, Ireland, Canada, US, etc.

*TREHAS LANGUAGE CENTRES, 20 Koundouriotou St, Keratsini (1-43 20 546); also 34 Argostoliou St, 122 41 Egaleo (1-56 17 263). 4-5 teachers, preferably British, Canadian or Australian.

*ZAVITSANOU LANGUAGE CENTRE, 3 Mitropoleos St, 311 00 Lefkada (645-24514/fax 645-24877). From 5 teachers, preferably British.

*A. LYMBEROPOULOS ENGLISH LANGUAGE INSTITUTE, 29 Pindarou St, 322 00 Thebes (262-29191). 2 teachers, preferably British.
Access Professional English Language Training, Egnatia 136, 546 22, Thessaloniki
Bacoglidis, Diagora 82, 543 51, Thessaloniki
Batsila Marianthi, Prochoma Thessalonikes, 570 11, Thessaloniki
Bellos School, Trilofos Thessalonikis, 575 00, Thessaloniki
Christidou Anna, Ippokratous 14-16, 551 34, Thessaloniki
Danatzi Maria, Grigoriou E. 25, 553 37, Thessaloniki

Italy

The decline in the EFL industry in Italy which resulted from the economic recession of the 1990s resulted in the closure of a number of language schools and sharper competition among the ones that survived. But opportunities for teachers are again abundant, especially in towns and cities which cannot boast leaning towers, gondolas or coliseums. Small towns in Sicily and Sardinia, in the Dolomites and along the Adriatic have more than their fair share of private language schools and institutes, all catering for Italians who have failed to learn English in the state system. (English teaching in Italian schools is generally acknowledged to be inadequate.)

Prospects for Teachers

There is a complete range of language schools in Italy, as any Yellow Pages will confirm. At the elite end of the market, there is the handful of schools (just 28) which belong to AISLI, the Associazione Italiana Scuole di Lingue, which is administered from the Cambridge Centre of English in Modena (Via Campanella 16, 41100 Modena). The Secretariat can send a list of AISLI members (e-mail: timp@teleion.it; http://www.eaquals.org/aisli/aisli.htm). Prospective teachers should apply directly to the schools and not to AISLI.

Very strict regulations mean that only ultra-respectable schools are members and by no means all of them have joined. AISLI schools normally expect their teachers to have advanced qualifications and in return offer attractive remuneration packages and conditions of employment.

At the other end of the spectrum, there is a host of schools which some might describe as cowboy operations, though these are decreasing in number. The CELTA is very widely recognised and respected in Italy (unlike in France, for instance). US qualifications are much less well known for the simple reason that work permits are virtually impossible for non-EU citizens to obtain.

Finding a job is difficult, whatever the qualifications you have to offer, especially in the popular cities. Sandeha Lynch describes the change he witnessed while working at a language school in Bologna for five years:

> *As the economic crisis of the early 90s began to bite, we found that we could no longer offer contracts but only occasional freelance work. This meant that few of the teachers who came could afford to stay very long (Bologna is notoriously expensive especially for rent). Year by year we gradually received more and more applications by post, from the UK, Ireland, North America, Australasia and even Japan. Some were highly qualified or at least had some experience. We were receiving more than a hundred applications a year. None of them received a reply. In my experience the ones who make it as English teachers are the lucky ones. There are, I think, too many teachers for the capacity of the market and not enough students, for the schools themselves are often under threat of closure. My own school is due to close this winter.*

Not all reports are as gloomy as this one, and a healthy number of schools wanted their job vacancies to be registered in this book. However it must be said that the prospects for job-seekers in Italy are not as rosy as they once were.

A further problem has been caused by strict employment regulations in Italy which make small companies very reluctant to offer full-time contracts. One expatriate language school owner went so far as to write, 'Unfortunately there are no longer proper jobs in EFL in independent schools as the cost of employment is prohibitive'. Compulsory contributions for social security and expensive perks (such as the compulsory severance pay of one month's pay) make hiring a member of staff very costly. The majority of English teachers in Italy work on a freelance basis with no job security, which is acceptable for those who only want to spend one or two years in the country.

FIXING UP A JOB
In Advance

There is no single compendium of the hundreds of language school addresses in Italy. The British Council offices in Rome, Milan, Naples, Turin and Bologna may be willing to photocopy the relevant Yellow Pages *(Pagine Gialle)*. The Italian Cultural Institute in London (39 Belgrave Square, London SW1X 8NX; 0171-235 1461) should have an up-to-date list of AISLI members.

International language school groups like Benedict Schools (with 19 Italian outlets), Linguarama, Berlitz and inlingua are major providers of English language teaching in Italy. International House has 22 affiliated schools throughout the country. Wall Street Institutes now have about 50 centres in Italy and actively recruit native speakers.

Several Italian-based chains of language schools account for a large number of teaching jobs. But because many of them operate as independent franchises, it is difficult to get a master list of addresses. Chains include the British Schools Group, British Institutes (50 +) and *Oxford Schools* with 14 schools in northern Italy (see entry). If you are in Italy, go into a branch of the student tourist bureau CTS, for example at Via Genova 16 in Rome, and ask for the leaflet listing all the British Institutes in Italy. (Most language schools in Italy seem to incorporate the word British, English, Oxford or Cambridge randomly combined with Centre, School or Institute, which can result in confusion.) Individual schools advertise their own job vacancies in the *Guardian* or *TES* in the spring and summer. For example British Institutes of Monza were recently advertising for prospective teachers to fax their CVs to Italy (fax 0039 39 325056). In the spring they offer a training course and guarantee a job to anyone who passes the course.

An agency you might try in the UK is *English Worldwide* which can place certificate-trained teachers, preferably with some knowledge of Italian, in various Italian schools. A Trinity College training centre in Italy also acts as a recruitment agency for institutes in Italy. Contact BC English Language Training, C.P. 685, 59100 Prato (fax: 0039 0574 20487/e-mail: bcelt@exnet.it). The director, Claudia Beccheroni, interviews teachers in London in July and September.

On the Spot

The heading *Scuole di Lingue* in the Yellow Pages is the best source of possible
employers. There is a useful *English Yellow Pages* but it covers only the north
(including Milan, Rome, Florence and Bologna). When Bruce Nairne and Sue
Ratcliffe went job-hunting in Italy a few years ago, they relied on the Yellow Pages as
a source of potential employers:

> *Rather unimaginatively we packed our bags and made for Italy in the middle of the
> summer holidays when there was no teaching work at all. Nevertheless we utilised the
> Yellow Pages in the SIP telephone office in Syracuse and proceeded to make 30
> speculative applications, specifying our status as graduates who had completed a
> short course in TEFL. By the end of September we had received four job offers
> without so much as an interview.*

Unfortunately the jobs in Bari which they chose to accept never materialised and so
they once again resorted to the Yellow Pages, this time in Milan railway station, where
they managed to secure the interest of three or four establishments for part-time
work.

As mentioned above, part-time work is the best that most can hope for initially.
Often a few hours teaching can gradually be built up into a full-time job by those
willing to say 'Yes'. If you're there when they need you, you can usually get something.
Most find that the longer they stay, the more hours they get, though there is still no job
security working this way. The importance of having a firm base from which to look for
teaching work and to wait for the hours to accumulate is also stressed by Sandeha
Lynch who again is describing the situation in Bologna:

> *Teachers arriving to look for work on the off-chance would camp in tents, hoping that
> the promise of lots of lessons would become a reality. The unlucky ones caught flu
> and returned home in debt. The luckier ones managed to work during the peak
> period of November to February. Those who were taken on temporarily by my school
> were the ones who had already solved the major problem of accommodation and had
> ample funds to tide them over until the work began.*

Although it is difficult to get work without TEFL training it is not impossible.
Laurence Koe visited all the language schools in Como and Lecco, some of them on
several occasions, and was told that he needed a qualification or that he was there at
the wrong time (October). After three weeks of making the rounds he was asked to
stand in for an absent teacher on one occasion, and this was enough to secure him
further part-time work. After a few more weeks he found work teaching an evening
class of adults. He began to attend the weekly English Club and was offered a few
thousand lire to answer questions on the plot after the showing of a James Bond film.
Most towns have an English Club *(Associazione Italo-Britannico)* which may offer
conversation classes and employ native speakers on a casual basis.

Scouring adverts in English language newspapers has worked for some. Try the
fortnightly publications in Rome *Metropolitan* and *Wanted in Rome*, and also the
Italian-language classified ads paper *Porta Portese*. (If you happen to see a request for
'mothers only', this means that they are looking for someone whose mother tongue is
English not a female with small children.)

Freelance Teaching

Another possibility is to set up as a freelance tutor, though a knowledge of Italian is
even more of an asset here than it is for jobs in schools. You can post notices in
supermarkets, tobacconists, primary and secondary schools, etc. In Rome, the notice
board at International House's training centre (Accademia Britannica, Viale Manzoni
22, 00185 Rome) displays requests for teachers. Also in Rome, check out the notice
boards at English language bookshops like the Lion Bookshop on Via Babuina and
the Economy Bookshop on Via Torino, or frequent the right pubs such as Ned Kelly's
near Palazzo Valdassini and Miscellania near the Pantheon. University students
looking for private tuition might consult the notice boards at the Citta
Universitaria.

Porta Portese is also a good forum in which to advertise your availability to offer English lessons in Rome; adverts placed by women should not betray their gender and meetings with prospective clients should not take place in private homes. It cost Dustie Hickey about £15 to advertise in four editions of the free paper in Rimini. As long as you have access to some premises, you can try to arrange both individual and group lessons, though competition is so cutthroat in some places that hourly fees are less than they used to be, starting at about L14,000 and going up to L45,000 an hour in Rome.

Whatever way you decide to look for work, remember that life grinds to a halt in August, just as in France. Competition is keenest in Rome, Florence and Venice, so new arrivals should head elsewhere. Peter Penn recommends Trieste where he was offered two jobs with no experience.

Universities throughout Italy employ foreigners as *lettori* (readers/lecturers) who teach English as well as other subjects such as business and science in English. There are probably around 1,000 *lettori* on yearly contracts (maximum three years) earning about the same as EFL teachers in private institutes. Although personal recommendation often plays a part in getting this work, it may be worth contacting various faculties directly and asking for work, preferably in September/October. Italian universities are notoriously unwilling to accord the same status and benefits to foreign teachers as to Italian ones (directly flouting EU legislation).

REGULATIONS

The bureaucratic procedures for EU nationals have become easier in recent years. Teachers must take their passport and letter of employment to the local *Questura* (police department) to obtain a *permesso di soggiorno* (residence permit). Ideally, they will also obtain a *libretto di lavoro* (work permit) from the local *Ispettorato del Lavoro* and/or *Ufficio Collocamento* which generally involves much queuing and a wait of several months. It is helpful if you have with you your university diploma, Cambridge or Trinity Certificate and birth certificate (originals rather than copies, and preferably authenticated by the Italian Consulate in your home country).

As mentioned above, non-EU citizens have very little chance of getting their papers in order unless they get a firm offer of a job while they are still in their home country. According to the Italian Embassy in Washington (202-328-5555), language teachers from the US need a visa for *lavoro subordinato*. To qualify they must first obtain from their employer in Italy an authorisation to work issued by the Ministry of Labour or a Provincial Office of Labour *(Servizio politiche del lavoro)* plus an authorisation from the local *Questura*. The originals of these plus a passport and one photo must be sent to the applicant's nearest Embassy or Consulate.

Tax is a further headache for long-stay teachers. As soon as you sort out the work documents, you should obtain a tax number *(codice fiscale)*. The rate of income tax *(Ritenuta d'Acconto)* is usually about 20% in addition to social security deductions of up to 10%.

CONDITIONS OF WORK

A good starting salary for a full-time timetable would be about L1,500,000 net per month (roughly £600). Staff on a *contratto di collaborazione* are paid by the hour, normally ranging from L1,800 to L25,000 net. Always find out if pay scales are quoted net or gross, since the two figures are so different. Take-home pay is not as high as might have been expected because of the high cost of compulsory national insurance, social security and pension contributions. Salaries tend to be substantially higher in northern Italy than in the south to compensate for the much higher cost of living. Teachers in Rome, Milan, Bologna, etc. have had to reconcile themselves to spending up to half their salaries on rent.

Only professional teachers will benefit from the *Contratto Collettivo Nazionale del Lavoro* (CCLN) which sets a high salary for a regulation 100-hour working month. Many schools hiring native-speaker teachers claim that they offer a 'British contract,' i.e. one that is not subject to Italian legislation. Because of the high costs of legal employment, there is still a lot of dubious practice in Italy and prospective teachers should try to talk to an ex-teacher before committing themselves, especially if offered a job before arrival.

Few teachers complain about their students. Even when pupils attend English classes for social reasons (as many do in small towns with little nightlife) or are generally unmotivated, they are normally good-natured, hospitable and talkative in class. In contrast to Greece, many language school directors are British rather than native.

LEISURE TIME

Italian culture and life style do not need to have their praises sung here. A large number of teachers who have gone out on short-term contracts never come back—probably a higher proportion than in any other country. While rents are high, eating out is cheap and wonderful and public transport is quite affordable. Women teachers should be prepared to cope with some Mediterranean *machismo*, particularly in the south.

Compared to many languages, Italian is easy to learn, though courses are expensive. It may be possible to swap English lessons for Italian ones, which might lead to further freelance teaching.

LIST OF SCHOOLS

A.L.S. SUPER RAPID ENGLISH
20 Manor Mansions, London NW3 4NB, UK. Tel: 0171-722 7309 (answerphone). Fax: 0171-483 3365. Recruit for 4-5 Italian schools, e.g.: Via Aureliana 53, 00187 Rome (06-482 8278) plus 2 others in Rome, and Via E. Ruffini 9, 20123 Milan (02-481 8846).
Number of teachers: 25.
Preference of nationality: must speak English as mother tonge and with neutral accent.
Qualifications: tertiary education and good sales skills. TEFL not essential. Must be resourceful, energetic, well-presented and have excellent vocal skills.
Conditions of employment: minimum term of 4 months but 6 months or 1 academic year preferred (closed in July/August). Maximum 25 hours of teaching a week.
Salary: competitive. Relocation costs reimbursed.
Facilities/Support: flats and rooms available. Company training given to teach copyright system (Accelerated Language Systems).
Recruitment: via adverts in *Times* and *TES*, or through universities. Interviews regularly conducted in London.
Contact: Elaine Chapman, Managing Director.

ANGLO AMERICAN CENTRE
Via Mameli 46, 09124 Cagliari, Sardinia. Tel: (070) 654955. Fax: (070) 670605. E-mail: anglo@sol.dada.it
Number of teachers: 30.
Preference of nationality: none.
Qualifications: university degree plus CELTA required.
Conditions of employment: contracts last from October to May. 20-28 h.p.w.
Salary: L1,500,000-L2,000,000 per month less deductions of 19%.
Facilities/Support: no assistance with accommodation. Advice given on obtaining work permits. Training available.
Recruitment: direct application and local interviews.
Contact: Bronya Sykes, Director of Studies.

BENEDICT SCHOOLS
Via Crispi 36A, 80122 Naples. Tel/fax: (081) 662672. Also schools at Piazza Primavera, 80038 Pomigliano d'Arco and Via D. Fiore 123, 80021 Afragola.
Number of teachers: 10-15 full-time teachers and freelancers.
Preference of nationality: none (no assistance given with work permits).
Qualifications: university degree, TEFL and minimum 1 year's experience.
Conditions of employment: 9 month contracts. 90-100 h.p.m.
Salary: L800,000 per month, plus free accommodation, Italian course and flight home at end of contract.
Facilities/Support: training in the Benedict method given.
Recruitment: via agency or direct.
Contact: Carmen Elsa Clemente, Manager.

BENEDICT SCHOOL
Via Salara 36, 48100 Ravenna. Tel: (0544) 38199. Fax: (0544) 38399.
Number of teachers: 5 full-time, some freelancers.
Preference of nationality: British but other nationalities considered.
Qualifications: university degree plus CELTA or equivalent required. Minimum 2 years experience.
Conditions of employment: minimum 6 month contracts, renewable. 25-30 h.p.w.
Salary: according to experience and qualifications.
Facilities/Support: assistance with finding accommodation. Training available.
Recruitment: via agencies or training schools in UK or CVs received directly. Interviews necessary and are sometimes held in the UK.
Contact: Mirella Pin, Director.

BRITISH-AMERICAN-DEUTSCHE-GAMMA INSTITUTES
Via Chiaia, 66, 80122 Naples. Tel: (081) 405196. Also Via Crispi 74, 80121 Naples. Tel: (81) 667805.
Number of teachers: 10+
Preference of nationality: American, Canadian, British, Australian.
Qualifications: A levels, bachelor's degree (grade point average 3.5). Must be experienced preparing candidates for TOEFL and teaching ESP courses.
Conditions of employment: 1 year contracts minimum. 5/6 days per week. Hours of work between 7.30am and 10pm.
Salary: approx. L1,250,000 per month or L15,000 per hour. Less 20% *ritenuta d'acconto*.
Facilities/Support: assistance with accommodation and work permits for qualified Americans.
Recruitment: direct application.
Contact: Dr. Gustavo Rossi Santomauro, Director.

THE BRITISH INSTITUTES
Via Aurelia 137, Rome. Tel: (06) 393 75 966 (5 lines). Fax: (06) 393 75 804. E-mail: british@evol.it
Number of teachers: 50 per year (including part-time teachers).
Preference of nationality: none.
Qualifications: university degree plus serious TEFL course and experience. Knowledge of Italian is valuable.
Conditions of employment: minimum one academic year. Lessons offered 8am-9pm Monday-Saturday.
Salary: varies according to experience, normally L15,000-L18,000 per hour net.
Facilities/Support: no assistance with accommodation or work permits. One-week pre-service training course held last week of September or first week of October.
Recruitment: word of mouth. Most candidates are interviewed in person.
Contact: Tina Conte D'Amico, Director.

BRITISH SCHOOL OF MONZA
Via Zucchi 38, 20052 Monza (MI). Tel: (039) 389803. Fax: (039) 230 2047. E-mail: Risales@tin.it
Number of teachers: 5.
Preference of nationality: EU.
Qualifications: university degree plus CELTA required.
Conditions of employment: 10 month UK contracts. 25 h.p.w.
Salary: L1,500,000 per month.
Facilities/Support: assistance with finding accommodation. Training given.
Recruitment: via UK recruitment agency, so interviews can take place in UK as well as locally.
Contact: Richard Sales, Director.

BRITISH s.r.l.
Via XX Settembre 12, 16121 Genoa. Tel: (010) 593591/562621. Fax: (010) 562621.
Number of teachers: 12.
Preference of nationality: EU only.
Qualifications: BA plus CELTA and minimum experience. Italian useful.
Conditions of employment: 25+ h.p.w. between mid-September and mid-June. Most pupils aged 18-30.
Salary: variable according to hours worked.
Facilities/Support: assistance given with accommodation, teaching materials and course programming.
Recruitment: interviews not essential, but usually take place in Italy.
Contact: Karl Matthews.

CAMBRIDGE CENTRE OF ENGLISH
Via Campanella 16, 41100 Modena. Tel: (059) 241004.
Key member of AISLI.
Number of teachers: 8.
Preference of nationality: British.
Qualifications: BA plus TEFL certificate and 2 years' experience.
Conditions of employment: permanent full-time or part-time. Pupils of all ages from 8.
Salary: from L1,600,000 (gross) per month. 14 months pay. 9 weeks paid holiday. Increments for higher qualifications and experience. All social security payments made.
Recruitment: through recommendation and direct application, often via other AISLI schools. Interviews sometimes held in UK.

CAMBRIDGE INSTITUTE
Viale Cappuccini 45, 66034 Lanciano (CH). Tel: (0872) 727175. Fax: (0872) 710291. Also branch at Corso Garibaldi 38, Ortona (085-906 4010).
Number of teachers: 4-7.
Qualifications: TOEFL/TEFL qualification.
Conditions of employment: one year contracts. 15-30 h.p.w.
Salary: L1,500,000 per month net.
Facilities/Support: assistance with accommodation and work permits. Training available.
Recruitment: adverts in *Guardian* and via word of mouth. Interviews can sometimes be arranged in UK, and are not always essential.
Contact: Piazza Sergio, Principal.

CAMBRIDGE SCHOOL
Via Mercanti 36, 84100 Salerno. Tel: (089) 228942. Fax: (089) 252523.
Number of teachers: 5.
Preference of nationality: British.

Qualifications: BA plus CELTA (grade B) plus 12 months' experience.
Conditions of employment: 9-10 month renewable contracts. 25 contact h.p.w. Pupils aged 6-60.
Salary: competitive and augmented with accommodation allowance.
Facilities/Support: assistance with accommodation. Regular in-house training.
Recruitment: direct. Interviews essential.

THE CAMBRIDGE SCHOOL
Via San Rocchetto 3, 37121 Verona. Tel: (045) 800 3154. Fax: (045) 801 4900. E-mail: info@cambridgeschool.it. Http//www.cambridgeschool.it.
Member of AISLI.
Number of teachers: 14+.
Preference of nationality: must have permission to work in Italy.
Qualifications: CELTA, degree and experience.
Conditions of employment: freelance only. Variable hours.
Salary: variable.
Facilities/Support: assistance given with accommodation. School runs CELTA courses. On-going assistance and training.
Recruitment: on presentation at the school.
Contact: Tracey Sinclair, Director of Studies.

CENTRO LINGUISTICO BRITISH INSTITUTES
Corso Umberto I, 17, 62012 Civitanova Marche (MC). Tel/fax: (0733) 816197. E-mail: bidimccm@tin.it
Number of teachers: 6.
Preference of nationality: British.
Qualifications: BA essential (MA preferred) and TEFL Certificate or Diploma.
Conditions of employment: 8 month contracts from October. 20 h.p.w. minimum.
Salary: L1,600,000 per month.
Facilities/Support: assistance with finding accommodation. Training available.
Recruitment: phone interviews are possible.
Contact: Loretta Muzi, Director.

CLM-BELL (Centro di Lingue Moderne/Bell Educational Trust)
Via Pozzo 30, 38100 Trento. Tel: (0461) 981733. Fax: (0461) 981687.
Member of AISLI and EAQUALS.
Number of teachers: 22 (including German, French and Spanish).
Preference of nationality: EU.
Qualifications: university degree, teaching diploma.
Conditions of employment: permanent contracts (full/part-time). 23 contact h.p.w. Pupils aged from 5.
Salary: from £840 per month.
Facilities/Support: assistance given with finding accommodation.
Recruitment: via Bell Language Schools, 1 Red Cross Lane, Cambridge, UK.

ENGLISH CAMPS
c/o Sophie White, 1 De Freville Avenue, Cambridge CB4 1HN, UK. Summer camp held in Potenza, in the Basilicata region of southern Italy; other venues possible.
Preference of nationality: British.
Qualifications: should have experience working with children, a specialist skill (e.g. sports, music, art, drama, foreign language) and good grasp of English.
Conditions of employment: minimum 2 weeks between mid-June and mid-July. Maximum 10 hours per day Monday-Friday. May involve working in different parts of Italy. Long hours of organising activities, lessons, sports and arts events. Half day or full day off p.w.
Salary: L300,000 per week, paid at end of agreed period. Free board and accommodation provided. Accident insurance provided.

Facilities/Support: training day and free group flight to Naples organised in mid-June.
Recruitment: posters around Cambridge. Interviews held in UK.
Contact: Sophie White.

ENGLISH COLLEGE OF C.M.C. srl
Via P. Umberto 102, 96011 Augusta, Sicily. Tel: (0931) 976609.
Number of teachers: 1 or 2.
Preference of nationality: British subject.
Qualifications: university degree plus TESOL.
Conditions of employment: 9 month contracts. 24 h.p.w.
Salary: L1,050,000 per month net plus free accommodation.
Facilities/Support: accommodation provided. No training available.
Recruitment: adverts in *TES*. Telephone interviews given.
Contact: Mr. C. Strano, School Consultant.

ENGLISH INSTITUTE
Piazza Garibaldi 60, 80142 Naples. Tel: (081) 554 8745. Fax: (081) 282900.
Number of teachers: 4.
Preference of nationality: English.
Qualifications: TEFL Cert.
Conditions of employment: 10 month contracts. Timetable between 9am and 9pm, depending on demand.
Salary: L20,000 per hour net.
Facilities/Support: assistance with finding accommodation and obtaining permits. Training available.
Recruitment: direct application with CVs and TEFL Certificates. Interviews essential.
Contact: Al Sacco, Manager.

THE ENGLISH INSTITUTE
Corso Gelone 82, 96100 Siracusa. Tel/fax: (0931) 60875.
Number of teachers: 5.
Preference of nationality: British, American or others with English as mother tongue.
Qualifications: minimum 1 but preferably 2 years' experience in EFL teaching.
Conditions of employment: 8½ months from September/October. 27 h.p.w. mostly in early evening (4-9pm). Some morning work but no weekends. Children's classes (from age 6) and adult classes up to First Certificate level.
Salary: L1,100,000 per month (net).
Facilities/Support: assistance with finding reasonably priced accommodation. Training available.
Recruitment: adverts in *TES*. Phone interviews possible.
Contact: Mr. Armand Giardina, Director.

ENGLISH SCHOOL
Via dei Correttori 6, 89127 Reggio Calabria. Tel/fax: (0965) 899535.
Belongs to British Schools Group.
Number of teachers: 4.
Preference of nationality: none, though procedures are easier for EU nationals.
Qualifications: minimum requirements are degree, CELTA and 1 year's experience.
Conditions of employment: 9-month renewable contracts (October-June). 28 h.p.w. Children, teens and adults divided into 8 different levels.
Salary: approximately £500 per month (net).
Facilities/Support: assistance given with accommodation. No training.
Recruitment: advertisements and recruitment agencies. Interviews are sometimes held in the UK, but are not essential.
Contact: Maria A. Rizzo, Director.

ENGLISH SCHOOL
Via Montesanto 116, , 87100 Cosenza. Tel/fax: (0984) 28075.
Belongs to British Schools Group.
Number of teachers: 3.
Preference of nationality: none, though EU preferred.
Qualifications: minimum requirements are degree, CELTA and 1 year's experience.
Conditions of employment: 9-month renewable contracts (October-June). 25 h.p.w. teaching children, teens and adults.
Salary: approximately £400 per month (net).
Facilities/Support: assistance given with accommodation. No training.
Recruitment: advertisements and recruitment agencies.
Contact: Maria A. Rizzo, Director.

THE ENGLISH SCHOOL
Viale Roosevelt 14, 67039 Sulmona (AQ). Tel/fax: (0864) 55606.
Number of teachers: 3-4.
Preference of nationality: none.
Qualifications: university degree and TEFL certificate required. 1-2 years' experience working abroad.
Conditions of employment: 8-month contracts October to May. Mainly afternoon and evening classes. Students aged 7-70 (mainly adults).
Salary: minimum £6-£7 per hour (net).
Facilities/Support: assistance with finding accommodation. Training available. CD Rom, computers, etc.
Recruitment: adverts in newspaper. Telephone interviews possible.
Contact: Tania Puglielli.

GREYHOUND LANGUAGE SCHOOL
Via Castellani 9, 15100 Alessandria (AL). Tel: (0131) 31 70 19. Fax: (0131 23 47 87.
E-mail: ghound@tin.it
Number of teachers: 2/3.
Preference of nationality: none; must be native speaker.
Qualifications: university degree, CELTA (equivalent or higher).
Conditions of employment: full-time and part-time contracts. Maximum 7 hours per day in 2 of 3 possible blocks. Pupils range from children to adult professionals.
Salary: negotiable (according to experience and qualifications)
Facilities/Support: assistance with accommodation.
Recruitment: via network of contacts. Interviews essential in Italy or UK.
Contact: Robert Hunter, Director.

INTERNATIONAL BRITISH SCHOOL
Via S. Caterina 146, 89100 Reggio Calabria. Tel: (0965) 45555. Fax: (0965) 42618.
Number of teachers: 3.
Preference of nationality: none.
Qualifications: university degree plus CELTA.
Conditions of employment: 9 month contracts; some UK, some Italian contracts. 25 h.p.w.
Salary: L1,350,000 per month (net).
Facilities/Support: assistance with finding accommodation. British School training courses available.
Recruitment: via agency and adverts. Interviews are available in UK.
Contact: Cristina Willauer, Principal.

INTERNATIONAL HOUSE (CAMPOBASSO)
Via Zurlo 5, 86100 Campobasso. Tel/fax: (0874) 63240/481321.
Number of teachers: 10-15 (for summer camp in Campitello in the Apennines).
Preference of nationality: British.

Qualifications: TEFL qualification essential, and experience on summer camps and/or teaching children and teenagers. Interest in sports and outdoor activities valuable asset.

Conditions of employment: contract of 6 weeks from end of June to early August. 4 hours teaching per day plus 2 afternoons per week for activities and evening activities. Pupils aged 8-16.

Salary: approximately £800.

Facilities/Support: accommodation provided with all meals.

Recruitment: through IH London or direct application.

Contact: Mary Ricciardi.

INTERNATIONAL HOUSE (LIVORNO)
Piazza Folgore 1, 57128 Livorno. Tel: (0336) 709682/(0586) 508060. Fax: (0586) 899854.

Number of teachers: 8.

Preference of nationality: British.

Qualifications: DELTA and 2 years' experience essential.

Conditions of employment: 8-12 month contracts. 23 contact h.p.w. Pupils are all adults.

Salary: L1,800,000 per month (net, index-linked).

Facilities/Support: assistance with accommodation and training given.

Recruitment: interviews in Livorno essential.

INTERNATIONAL HOUSE (PALERMO)
Via Gaetano Daita 29, 90139 Palermo. Tel: (091) 584954. Fax: (091) 323965. E-mail: ihpal@gestelnet.it

Number of teachers: 7-8.

Preference of nationality: British; others considered (preferably European passport).

Qualifications: degree and CELTA (minimum grade 'B'). School interested in career teachers only.

Conditions of employment: 9 month contracts. 25 h.p.w. normally 1-9.30pm.

Salary: L1,800,000 (net).

Facilities/Support: assistance with finding accommodation. Weekly seminars and workshops. School will subsidise in-service Diploma course by distance learning for suitable candidates.

Recruitment: via IH London or directly. Interviews essential.

INTERNATIONAL HOUSE (SEREGNO)
Accademia Britannica Srl, Via Gozzano 4/6, 20038 Seregno (MI). Tel: (0362) 230970. Fax: 328278.

Member of AISLI.

Number of teachers: 10.

Preference of nationality: British.

Qualifications: degree and CELTA with 1-2 years' experience minimum. DELTA preferred.

Conditions of employment: 1-2 year renewable contracts. 24 h.p.w. Pupils of all ages. Some in-company teaching (for which driving licence is needed).

Salary: approximately L1,500,000 (net) per month.

Facilities/Support: assistance given with accommodation, though it is expensive and difficult to find. Training given.

Recruitment: via IH London.

Contact: Marcella Banchetti.

INTERNATIONAL HOUSE (TRADINT)
Via Jannozzi 6, 20097 San Donato Milanese (MI). Tel: (02) 527 91 24. Fax: (02) 556 00 324. E-mail: tradint@mv.itline.it. Also IH has a school in central Milan at Piazza Erculea 9, 20122 Milan (02-805 78 25).
Number of teachers: 15 in suburban locations plus 8 in central Milan.
Preference of nationality: none (British, American, Australian, New Zealand and South African all accepted).
Qualifications: university degree, CELTA and at least 2-3 years of experience.
Conditions of employment: 10-11 month contracts from September. 25 h.p.w., especially morning and evening hours.
Salary: L1,650,000 per month on UK contract.
Facilities/Support: assistance with finding accommodation; provide school apartments where possible. Monthly seminars/workshops held and regular observation by Director of Studies.
Recruitment: locally or via IH Staffing Unit in London.
Contact: Stephanie Oliver, Director of Studies.

INTERNATIONAL LANGUAGE SCHOOL
Via Tibullo 10, 00193 Rome. Tel: (06) 68 30 77 96. Fax: (06) 68 69 758. E-mail: ILS@ggg.it
Number of teachers: 20.
Preference of nationality: none.
Qualifications: degree and CELTA.
Conditions of employment: 2 year contracts. Hours of teaching normally 1-9.30pm.
Salary: L1,360,000 per month.
Facilities/Support: assistance given with accommodation if needed. Training given.
Recruitment: by direct application. Interviews sometimes held in UK.
Contact: Giuseppina Foti, Director.

KEEP TALKING
Via Paolo Sarpi 6, 33100 Udine. Tel: (0432) 505016. Tel/fax: (0432) 501525.
Number of teachers: 10 in 2 schools.
Preference of nationality: none but must be native speakers. Limited help given to non-EU teachers in obtaining permits.
Qualifications: university degree and CELTA or equivalent required plus minimum 2 years' experience.
Conditions of employment 9 month contracts (*contratto di collaborazione*). Min. 750 hours per year. 25 h.p.w. Lessons mostly at lunchtimes and evenings till 9.30pm and some Saturday mornings.
Salary: starting hourly wage of L25,000 (net).
Facilities/Support: assistance with finding accommodation. Training seminars given twice a month. Medical contributions paid by employer.
Recruitment: adverts in the *Guardian* followed by interviews in the UK.
Contact: Kip Kelland, Principal.

LIVING LANGUAGES SCHOOL
Via Magna Grecia 2, 89100 Reggio Calabria. Tel/fax: (0965) 330926.
Number of teachers: 7.
Preference of nationality: mother tongue speakers of English.
Qualifications: TEFL, CELTA.
Conditions of employment: 9 month renewable contracts. Teaching hours from 3-9pm Monday to Friday.
Salary: L1,400,000 (net) per month.
Facilities/Support: help given with accommodation.
Recruitment: via adverts. Interviews sometimes carried out in UK.
Contact: Simon Whitaker-Bott, Director of Studies.

LORD BYRON COLLEGE
Via Sparano 102, 70121 Bari. Tel: (080) 523 2686. Fax: (080) 524 1349. E-mail: lordbyron@mail3.clio.it
Number of teachers: 26.
Preference of nationality: British.
Qualifications: should be aged 24-29. Degree plus TEFL Certificate or PGCE needed plus one year's teaching experience abroad and knowledge of a foreign language.
Conditions of employment: 1 or 2 year renewable contracts. $27\frac{1}{2}$ h.p.w. 1,200 students of all ages and levels but mainly aged 19-30.
Salary: approximately L1,600,000 (net) per month.
Facilities/Support: free basic Italian course and free in-house Trinity College TESOL Diploma course. Large self-access centre with videoclub and CD ROM.
Recruitment: adverts in *Guardian* or apply directly with full CV, photo, references, copies of degree/TEFL certificates. Interviews and hiring mainly in June and December.
Contact: John Credico, Director of Studies.

OXFORD INSTITUTE
10/12 Via Adriatica 10/12, 73100 Lecce. Tel: (0832) 390312. Fax: (0832) 390312.
Number of teachers: 10.
Preference of nationality: none.
Qualifications: CELTA required.
Conditions of employment: 10 month contracts September to June. 25 h.p.w.
Salary: L1,100,000 (net).
Facilities/Support: free accommodation provided. Help given with obtaining all necessary documents. Training available.
Recruitment: adverts in *Guardian* and interviews in London.
Contact: Julia Boyd, Senior Teacher.

OXFORD SCHOOL OF ENGLISH s.r.l.
Administrative Office, Via S. Pertini 14, 30035 Mirano, Venice. Tel: (041) 570 23 55. Fax: (041) 570 23 90. Internet: www.oxforditalia.it
Number of teachers: 20-30 for 14 schools in northeast Italy of which 10 are independent franchises (60-70 teachers employed altogether).
Preference of nationality: British.
Qualifications: degree, TEFL and knowledge of Italian needed.
Conditions of employment: 10 month contracts or longer. 21 h.p.w.
Salary: varies according to hours and length of contract. Deductions of 20% for tax.
Facilities/Support: no assistance with accommodation. Training offered if there are enough new teachers.
Recruitment: interviews in London or Italy.
Contact: Philip Panter, Administrator.

OXFORD SCHOOL OF ENGLISH
Vicolo Biscaro 1, 31100 Treviso. Tel/fax: (0422) 544242.
Number of teachers: 3.
Preference of nationality: none.
Qualifications: university degree plus TEFL and 2 years' experience.
Conditions of employment: 8 month contracts. 20-25 h.p.w. mainly afternoon and evening work (5pm-9.30pm) with scattered hours during the day.
Salary: L29,000 per hour less 20% deductions.
Facilities/Support: assistance with finding accommodation and obtaining permits. No training given.
Recruitment: adverts and interviews in Italy or UK.
Contact: Lucia Forte, Director of Studies.

REGENCY SCHOOL
Via dell'Arcivescovado 7, 10121 Turin. Tel: (011) 562 7456. Fax: (011) 541845. E-mail: regency@tin.it. Web-site: www.regency.it
Number of teachers: 30.
Preference of nationality: none.
Qualifications: university degree essential plus CELTA or equivalent or DELTA or equivalent.
Conditions of employment: full-time and part-time contracts. Maximum 7 hours per day in 2 of possible 3 blocks. Pupils range from young children to adult professionals.

Salary: negotiable (according to experience and qualifications).
Facilities/Support: regular seminars and workshops for teachers.
Recruitment: through network of contacts. Interviews essential in Italy or UK.
Contact: John Lewell.

SHENKER INSTITUTE
Via S. Gerardo dei Tintori 1, 20052 Monza. Tel: (039) 386861. Fax: (039) 388905. E-mail: shmonza@tin.it
Number of teachers: 5.
Preference of nationality: none, though prefer those with permission to work in Italy.
Qualifications: good general education, especially in English. TEFL if possible.
Conditions of employment: minimum 1 year. Timetable varies according to needs.
Salary: varies.
Facilities/Support: assistance with finding accommodation. Training available.
Recruitment: local adverts and interviews.
Contact: Pauline Austin, Managing Director.

SUMMER CAMPS
Via Roma 54, 18038 San Remo. Tel/fax: (0184) 506070. E-mail: edu@rosenet.it/ summercamps
Number of teachers: 50+ for both day camps and residential camps.
Preference of nationality: all native English speakers.
Qualifications: minimum age 18. Must have experience working with children and ability to teach English through the use of drama and outdoor activities. A fun-loving personality and genuine interest in children, high moral standards and a flexible attitude to work required.
Conditions of employment: 4, 8 or 12 weeks in summer. May involve working in different parts of Italy. Long hours of organising activities, lessons, sports and arts events. Half day or full day off p.w.
Salary: £400+ per month plus full board and accommodation. Insurance provided. Bonus possible. Travel within Italy paid for.
Facilities/Support: intensive introductory TEFL course provided.
Recruitment: adverts in UK. Interviews held in UK.

WALL STEET INSTITUTE (BERGAMO)
Via Brigata Lupi 6, 24122 Bergamo. Tel/fax: (035) 224531/235442.
Number of teachers: 8-10.
Preference of nationality: EU nationals.
Qualifications: qualified teachers with EFL experience. Business English preferred.
Conditions of employment: October-June. 18 h.p.w. plus minimum 6 hours preparation. Extra hours when required. In-house and in-company teaching between Monday and Saturday morning.
Facilities/Support: assistance with accommodation if needed. One-week teacher training course at beginning of academic year.
Recruitment: casual enquiries, personal recommendation and direct application. Interviews in Bergamo compulsory.
Contact: Emma Roberts.

WALL STREET INSTITUTE (FERRARA)
Piazzetta Combattenti 6, 44100 Ferrara. Tel: (0532) 200231. Fax: (0532) 209597.
Number of teachers: 6-7.
Preference of nationality: British.
Qualifications: CELTA or other TEFL qualification; teaching experience, knowledge of Italian.
Conditions of employment: 9 month contracts (October-June). 25 h.p.w. Mostly adults.
Salary: approx. L1,400,000 per month.
Facilities/Support: assistance with finding accommodation and obtaining working papers. No training.
Recruitment: direct application and recruiting agencies. Interviews in Ferrara necessary.

WALL STREET INSTITUTE (MILAN)/ST LOUIS SCHOOL
Corso Buenos Aires 79, 20124 Milan. Tel: (02) 673 83 311/760 01435/760 06731. Fax: (02) 669 82 447.
Number of teachers: 45.
Preference of nationality: EU countries or those from elsewhere who already have work permits.
Qualifications: CELTA.
Conditions of employment: contracts run until end of June or mid-July. 25 contact h.p.w. teaching adults.
Salary: L1,650,000-L2,400,000 (net) per month.
Facilities/Support: assistance is given finding accommodation. A limited amount of training is available.
Recruitment: through application in person only. Interviews occasionally held in UK.
Contact: Gillian Murray, General Manager.

WASHINGTON SCHOOL
Via del Corso 184, Rome 00186. Tel: (06) 679 3785. Fax: (06) 678 1512.
Number of teachers: 6-25 (depending on demand for company work).
Preference of nationality: British, Irish.
Qualifications: university degree, CELTA or equivalent, 1 year's experience. Basic Italian useful.
Conditions of employment: freelance teachers only, with hours varying from 4 to 25 p.w.
Salary: L17,000-L20,000 per hour (net) depending on location. Teachers are responsible for paying their own social security.
Facilities/Support: no assistance with accommodation.
Recruitment: local interviews essential.
Contact: S. R. Barley, Director of Studies.

Other Schools to Try (cities and towns in alphabetical order)

Note that these schools did not confirm their teacher requirements for this edition of *Teaching English Abroad.* Upper case entries marked with an asterisk had entries in the last edition (1997); addresses without asterisks have been taken from various sources, such as British Council lists, the AISLI list, *Yellow Pages,* etc.
British Institute, Via Isonzo 16, Foggia
Oxford School of Languages, Via Garibaldi 108, 06034 Foligno (Pg)
British Institute, V. XX Settembre 40/9, Genova
British School of Gorizia, Corso Italia 17, 34170 Gorizia (AISLI member)
International House La Spezia, Via Manzoni 64, 19100 La Spezia (AISLI member)
British Institute, Via Leopardi 8, Milan
British School Milano, Via Pantano 6, 20121 Milan (AISLI member)
REGENT ITALIA s.r.l., Via Fabio Filzi 27, 20124 Milan (02-670 70516/fax 02-670

73625). 15 teachers with CELTA (Grade A or B). Summer and part-time contracts also available.

Victoria Language Centre, Via G. Fassi 28, Carpi, 41012 Modena

British School of Monfalcone, Via Duca d'Aosta 16, 34074 Monfalcone (AISLI member)

American Studies Center, 36 V. D'Isernia, Naples

Anglotutor Centro Linguistico Internazionale, 4 V. Croce Rossa (Rione Alto), Naples

CLM Bell Pergine, Viale Dante Alighieri 1, 38057 Pergine Valsugano (AISLI member)

British Institute, Via Ravenna 3/22, Pescara

International House Pisa, Via Risorgimento 9, 56126 Pisa (AISLI member)

British Institute, Via S. Franca 29, Pistoia

British Language School, 73 V. Diaz, Portici (NA)

British Institute, Via Brunelleschi 30, Prato

WALL STREET INSTITUTE (RAVENNA), Viale Baracca 15, 48100 Ravenna (0544-36826/fax 0544-48409). 5 teachers, ESP preferred (e.g. economics, medicine).

British Institute, V. Mons Tondelli 2, Reggio Emilia

British Institute, C. so DiAugusto 144, Rimini

CLM-Bell, Via Canella 14, 38066 Riva del Garda (AISLI member)

British Institute of Rome, Via 4 Fontane 109, 00184 Rome (AISLI member)

RTS EXECUTIVE LANGUAGE TRAINING, Via Tuscolana 4, 00182 Rome (06-702 2730/fax 06-702 1740). 10 teachers for mainly in-company work.

British Institute, Via A. Mario 16, Rovigo

THE ENGLISH CENTRE, Via P. Paoli 34, 07100 Sassari, Sardinia (079-232154/fax 079-232180). 8 teachers on British contracts.

Portugal

Relations between Portugal and Britain have always been warm and the market for English tuition is as buoyant as anywhere in Europe, especially in the teaching of young children. Most schools cater for anyone over the age of seven, so you should be prepared to teach little ones. In fact some schools organise courses in nursery schools for children from the age of four. Furthermore Portugal's economy has taken considerable strides during the 1990s which has created a bigger demand for English for Special Purposes, especially business. One school has even run an 'English for footballers' course.

The vast majority of British tourists flock to the Algarve along the southern coast of Portugal, which means that many Portuguese in the south who aspire to work in the tourist industry want to learn English. Schools like the *Centro de Linguas* in Lagos and *Interlingua* in Portimao cater for just that market. But the demand for English teachers is greatest in the north. Apart from in the main cities of Lisbon and Oporto, both of which have British Council offices, jobs crop up in historic provincial centres such as Coimbra (where there is also a British Council) and Braga and in small seaside towns like Aveiro and Póvoa do Varzim. These can be a very welcome destination for teachers burned out from teaching in big cities or first-time teachers who want to avoid the rat-race. There is also a British Council office in the town of Parede and another in Cascais, the prosperous seaside suburb of Lisbon, where there is a Teaching Centre.

FIXING UP A JOB

Most teachers in Portugal have either answered adverts in the educational press or are working for International House which has nine affiliated schools in Portugal. Outside the cities where there have traditionally been large expatriate communities, schools cannot depend on English speakers just showing up and so must recruit well in advance of the academic year (late September to the end of June). A few schools use recruitment agencies such as *Language Matters* in Bath.

The only two International House schools in Portugal which did not send details of potential vacancies to this book are IH Barreiro (Avenida Alfredo da Silva 57, 2830 Barreiro) and IH Lamego (Rua Macário de Castro 70, Lamego) which are both small. Note that about three-quarters of all IH students in Portugal are children, so expertise with young learners is a definite asset.

Although the *Bristol Schools Group* does claim to be associated with South West English near Bristol, they prefer to handle applications themselves. (This is the only possibility of which we have heard for working in the Azores, so if you want to work in the most isolated islands in the Atlantic Ocean—over 1,000km west of Portugal—this is your chance.)

Small groups of schools, say six schools in a single region, is the norm in Portugal. A number of the schools listed in the directory at the end of this chapter belong to such mini-chains. One of the most well-established is the *Cambridge Schools* group which every year imports up to 100 teachers.

The British Council offices may have lists of local English language schools in their region, but they probably won't be willing to send them to enquirers. Many schools are small family-run establishments with fewer than ten teachers, so sending off a lot of speculative applications is unlikely to succeed.

As is true anywhere, you might be lucky and fix up something on the spot. In addition to calling at the British Council, check the English language weekly newspaper *Anglo-Portuguese News* which occasionally carries adverts for private tutors. In fact the Deputy Editor was himself an English teacher before he turned to journalism.

The Cambridge/RSA CELTA is widely requested by schools and can be obtained both at International House and the Cambridge School in Lisbon. The Trinity College Certificate course specialising in teaching young learners is also available in Portugal at the *Centre for Training Teachers of English* near Oporto.

REGULATIONS

The red tape for EU nationals working in Portugal is refreshingly painless. All that is required (as throughout the EU) is to obtain a residence permit after an initial three month stay by taking a letter of confirmation and duration of employment to the local authorities, i.e. any office of the *Serviço de Estrangeiros e Fronteiras* (SEF) or Aliens Office.

Although Portugal has been a full member of the European Community since 1992, it has also been possible for Americans and other nationalities to work legally in Portugal (unlike in neighbouring Spain). When the American Richard Spacer was encountering red tape difficulties teaching in Greece, he made enquiries at the Portuguese Embassy in Athens and was told that once he secured a teaching job in Portugal he could apply for the appropriate permits locally. However that may be about to change. According to the *American Language Institute* in Lisbon, Portuguese regulations are undergoing many changes at present, and it sounds as though it may become more difficult for non EU nationals to teach in Portugal.

At present a non-EU citizen must take a contract of employment to an SEF (in Lisbon the address is Avenida António Augusto Aguiar 20; tel: 1-523324/523395; fax: 1-714332). The document obtained here is sent off together with the contract of employment to the Ministry of Labour. The final stage is to take a letter of good conduct provided by the teacher's own embassy to the police for the work and residence permit.

Since most teachers working for nine months are working on a freelance basis, they are responsible for paying their own taxes and contributions, which amount to about 20% of gross salary. Tax is paid on a sliding scale and most teachers on nine-month contracts with no other source of income will not necessarily be liable for tax. By law, all employers must insure their employees against work-related accidents. For eventualities outside work, teachers should insure themselves.

CONDITIONS OF WORK

The consensus seems to be that wages are low, but have been improving at a favourable rate in view of the cost of living. On the positive side, working conditions are generally relaxed. The normal salary range is 130,000-175,000 escudos per month. Full-time contract workers are entitled to an extra month's pay after 12 months. Some schools pay lower salaries but subsidise or pay for flights and accommodation. Several provide free Portuguese lessons. Salaries in Lisbon are significantly higher than in the small towns of northern Portugal. Teachers being paid on an hourly basis should expect to earn from 1,500 escudos an hour up to about 2,000 escudos, but they will not be eligible for the thirteenth month bonus or paid holidays.

Contracts are for a minimum of nine months though some are for a calendar year. Several International House schools have flats for their teachers. Flats in small towns can normally be rented for about 40,000 escudos per person in a shared flat. On average this represents about a quarter of the salary, which is quite a favourable percentage. Accommodation in the greater Lisbon area will not be less than 60,000 escudos per person per month.

LIST OF SCHOOLS

AMERICAN LANGUAGE INSTITUTE
Avenida Duque de Loulé 22-1°, 1050 Lisbon. Tel: (1) 315 2535. Fax: (1) 352 4848. E-mail: ali@.telepac.pt
Number of teachers: 10-12.
Preference of nationality: American or Canadian.
Qualifications: MA in TESOL or CELTA; EFL experience preferred.
Conditions of employment: 1 year contracts. 15-20 h.p.w.
Salary: approximate equivalent to US$12 per hour (net).
Facilities/Support: advice given on finding accommodation (e.g. suggesting reputable agencies). In-service training sessions plus observation and feedback. Help given in applying for permits.
Recruitment: via international TESOL conference in US and interviews in Lisbon.
Contact: Suzanne Tavares, Director of Courses.

AMERICAN LANGUAGE CENTER
Rua José Falcão 15-5°Esq, 4050 Oporto. Tel: (2) 205 8127. Fax: (2) 208 5287.
Number of teachers: 7-8.
Preference of nationality: American, Canadian.
Qualifications: minimum CELTA or equivalent plus 2 years' full time teaching experience. MA in TEFL preferred plus experience.
Conditions of employment: 9-month contracts October to June, with possibility of renewing for a second year. Average 18-21 h.p.w. Mostly evenings (5-10pm) with some day work. Pupils from age 16, mostly professional adults.
Salary: about US$17 an hour.
Facilities/Support: informal assistance with accommodation and working papers.
Recruitment: interviews at TESOL convention in the US each spring or on-site interviews.

BRISTOL SCHOOL GROUP
Instituto de Línguas da Maia & Ermesinde, Trav. Dr. Carlos Pires Felgueiras, 12-3°, 4470 Maia. Tel: (2) 948 8803/972 2761. Fax: (2) 948 6460/972 2761.
Comprises a group of 8 small schools: 4 near Oporto, 2 in the Azores and 2 inland (Castelo Branco and Fundão).
Number of teachers: 22.

Preference of nationality: British only.
Qualifications: BA and TEFL qualification. 1 year's experience essential.
Conditions of employment: minimum period of work October-June, 25 h.p.w. Pupils aged from 8 upwards.
Salary: 185,000 escudos net per month plus Christmas bonus of 35,000 escudos and end-of-contract bonus of 120,000 escudos.
Facilities/Support: assistance with accommodation given. No training.
Recruitment: direct application preferred. Also via adverts in *TES* and via South West English, Pill, Bristol BS20 0AA.
Contact: Idalina Meireles, Director.

CAMBRIDGE SCHOOL
Avenida da Liberdade 173, 1250 Lisbon. Tel: (1) 312 4600. Fax: (1) 353 4729. E-mail: cambridge@mail.telepac.pt
Portugal's largest private language school with 8 centres in Lisbon and other major cities.
Number of teachers: 90-110.
Preference of nationality: British only. Other native speakers must have Portuguese residence.
Qualifications: BA plus CELTA, Trinity College TESOL or equivalent.
Conditions of employment: initial contracts for 9 months from 1st October to 30th June.
Facilities/Support: authorised RSA/UCLES CELTA centre. All schools have 2 or 3 senior staff.
Recruitment: adverts in *TES* and *Guardian*. Applicants should send CV, recent photograph, contact telephone number and copies of degree and EFL Certificate. Interviews are usually held in London in early May and possibly other times depending on requirements. Visitors to Portugal can be interviewed in Lisbon by prior arrangement.
Contact: Jeffrey Kapke, General Director of Studies.

CENTRO DE INGLES DE FAMALICAO
Edificio dos Correios, 4° andar, Praça do Bombeiro Voluntário, 4760 V.N. Famalicão. Tel/fax: (52) 374233.
Number of teachers: 4.
Preference of nationality: EU preferred.
Qualifications: degree and CELTA essential; experience an advantage. CELTA grade A or B preferred.
Conditions of employment: 9 month renewable contracts. 24 contact hours p.w.
Salary: 155,000 escudos per month (net).
Facilities/Support: fully-furnished flat near school provided rent-free. Help given with work permit procedures. Lessons are regularly observed and feedback given.
Recruitment: via adverts in the *Guardian*. Interviews essential, normally in London.
Contact: David Mills, Director of Studies.

CENTRO DE LINGUAS DE LAGOS
Rua Dr. Joaquim Tello 32, 1° esq, 8600 Lagos. Tel/fax: (82) 761070.
Number of teachers: 4.
Preference of nationality: none (must be native speaker).
Qualifications: degree in education or arts subject plus a recognised TEFL qualification required.
Conditions of employment: freelance basis. Between 8 and 25 h.p.w. Mainly late afternoons and evenings. Most students work in tourist-related businesses or are school children. Possibility of work on summer courses for children and teenagers.
Salary: 2,050 escudos (£7) per hour.
Facilities/Support: assistance with finding accommodation.
Recruitment: personal interview necessary.
Contact: Maureen McKeeve, Principal.

ENCOUNTER ENGLISH
Av. Fernao de Magalhaes 604, 4300 Oporto. Tel/fax: (2) 567916.
Number of teachers: 14.
Preference of nationality: British.
Qualifications: CELTA plus 1 or 2 years experience.
Conditions of employment: contracts last from 15th September to 30th June. Up to 24 lessons per week lasting 50 minutes. Mostly evenings and Saturday mornings.
Salary: 150,000-180,000 escudos (net) per month.
Facilities/Support: assistance given with finding accommodation. Training available.
Recruitment: via adverts in *Guardian*. Interviews held locally or in England.
Contact: Stephen Cassidy, Director.

INSTITUTO DE LINGUAS DE S. JOAO DA MADEIRA
Largo Durbalino Laranjeira S/N, 3700 S. João da Madeira. Tel: (56) 833906. Fax: (56) 835887.
Preference of nationality: British.
Qualifications: DELTA/COTE plus 2 years experience.
Conditions of employment: 9 month contracts from October.
Salary: depends on qualifications.
Facilities/Support: no help given with accommodation, work permits or training.
Recruitment: interview essential.
Contact: Dr. Helena Borges, Director.

INTERNATIONAL HOUSE (AVEIRO)
Rua Domingos Carrancho 1-1°, 3800 Aveiro. Tel: (34) 26923/384497. Fax: (34) 23983. E-mail: ihaveiro@ilt.mailpac.pt
Also recruit for International House (Ilhavo), Largo do Municipio 16-1° Dto, 3830 Ilhavo. Tel/fax: (34) 325605.
Number of teachers: 15 (some part-time).
Preference of nationality: EU.
Qualifications: BA plus CELTA (Grade 'B') plus 2 years experience.
Conditions of employment: usually 9 month contracts. 24 h.p.w. Pupils aged 7-70, though majority are young learners. Some company teaching and evening teaching.
Salary: from 178,500 escudos.
Facilities/Support: school flats provided (40,000 escudos each in shared flat). In-service training given.
Recruitment: through IH, London and locally.

INTERNATIONAL HOUSE (BRAGA)
Rua dos Chaos 168, 4710 Braga. Tel: (53) 215250. Fax: (53) 61228.
Number of teachers: 9.
Preference of nationality: British.
Qualifications: BA plus CELTA (Grade 'B') and experience with young learners.
Conditions of employment: 9 month contracts. 24 h.p.w. Pupils aged 7-60, with emphasis on young learners.
Salary: 200,000 escudos per month.
Facilities/Support: assistance with finding accommodation. Induction week, observations and workshops.
Recruitment: interviews take place through IH, London.

INTERNATIONAL HOUSE (COIMBRA)
Rua Antero de Quental 135, 3000 Coimbra. Tel: (39) 822971/834009. Fax: (39) 825487. E-mail: ih.coimbra@mail.telepac.pt
Number of teachers: 14.
Preference of nationality: British.
Qualifications: BA, plus CELTA (minimum Grade 'B').
Conditions of employment: 9 month contracts. 22 h.p.w. Pupils from age 7.
Salary: 230,100 escudos per month.

Facilities/Support: assistance with accommodation. Training given. Supervision for DELTA. Distance Training programme.
Recruitment: through IH, London. Interviews required.
Contact: Dave Tucker, Director of Studies.

INTERNATIONAL HOUSE (LAMEGO)
Rua Macário de Castro 70, 1°, 5100 Lamego. Tel: (54) 656360. Fax: (54) 656536.
Preference of nationality: none.
Qualifications: CELTA (minimum Grade 'B').
Conditions of employment: 9 month contracts from October. 20 teaching hours plus 4 hours admin.
Salary: approximately £600 per month less tax (14.5%) and social security (11%).
Facilities/Support: assistance with accommodation. Training given.
Recruitment: through IH, London. Interviews required.
Contact: Isabel de Sousa, Director.

INTERNATIONAL HOUSE (LISBON)
Rua Marquês Sá da Bandeira 16, 1050 Lisbon. Tel: (1) 315 1496/4/3. Fax: (1) 353 0081. E-mail: ihlisbon@mail.telepac.pt
Number of teachers: 18.
Preference of nationality: British.
Qualifications: CELTA minimum.
Conditions of employment: standard length of stay 9 months. Flexible working hours to include evening work. Pupils range in age from 8 to 80.
Salary: 230,720 escudos per month for first year teachers.
Facilities/Support: assistance with accommodation. CELTA and CELTYL courses offered regularly (see *Training* chapter).
Recruitment: through local adverts and by IH, London.
Contact: Colin McMillan, Director.

INTERNATIONAL HOUSE (PORTO)
Rua Dr. Sousa Rosa 38/1°, 4150 Porto. Tel: (2) 617 7641. Fax: (2) 616 9828. E-mail: ihporto@iname.com. Web-site: http://members.xoom.com/ihporto
Number of teachers: 10.
Preference of nationality: none.
Qualifications: CELTA.
Conditions of employment: 9 month contracts. 24 contact h.p.w. mainly afternoons/ evenings.
Salary: 166,000–178,000 escudos (gross) depending on qualifications and experience. Plus Christmas and summer bonuses.
Facilities/Support: some assistance with finding accommodation. Weekly input sessions.
Recruitment: via IH, London.
Contact: Alison Boardman, Director of Studies.

INTERNATIONAL HOUSE (TORRES VEDRAS)
Rua Miguel Bombarda 3-1°, 2560 Torres Vedras. Tel/fax: (61) 24421. E-mail: ihtorresvedras@mail.telepac.pt
Number of teachers: 5.
Preference of nationality: EU.
Qualifications: CELTA (Grade 'A' or 'B').
Conditions of employment: 9 month contracts (October-June). 20 h.p.w. Pupils are children (6-14) and adults.
Facilities/Support: assistance given with accommodation. Regular seminars, observations and help with lesson-planning given. Newly recruited teachers are expected to attend a development course in teaching younger learners. DELTA course offered in alternate years.

Recruitment: via IH, London and locally.
Contact: Diana England, Director of Studies.

INTERNATIONAL HOUSE (VISEU)
Rua dos Casimiros 33, 3510 Viseu. Tel: (32) 420850. Fax: (32) 420851.
Number of teachers: 9.
Preference of nationality: EU passport-holders preferred.
Qualifications: minimum CELTA (grade 'B'), BA/PGCE.
Conditions of employment: 9-12 month contracts. Maximum 24 contact h.p.w. Pupils aged 8-60.
Salary: from 180,000 escudos per month.
Facilities/Support: three school flats available; rent is about 40,000 escudos per person. In-service training provided.
Recruitment: through IH, London. Interviews required.

LANCASTER COLLEGE
Praceta 25 de Abril 35-1°, 4430 Vila Nova de Gaia. Tel: (2) 377 2030. Fax: (2) 377 2039.   E-mail: LancasterCollege@iname.com.   http://welcme.to/ LancasterCollege
Number of teachers: 10-20 in eight schools.
Preference of nationality: EU (British and Irish preferred).
Qualifications: CELTA, Trinity Cert or equivalent (minimum).
Conditions of employment: 9 month contracts. 16-20 contact h.p.w.; 25 hour working week.
Salary: 1,750 escudos per hour (net for first year).
Facilities/Support: assistance given with finding accommodation. Training given when possible.
Recruitment: via internet and EFL press.
Contact: Personnel Manager.

LINGUACULTURA
Apartado 37/Rua Pedro Santarém 150 1°Dto., 2001 Santarém Codex. Tel: (43) 309140. Fax: (43) 309141.
Number of teachers: 50 in 25 schools located in Santarém, Abrantes, Alcanena, Alenquer, Almeirim, Batalha, Bombarral, Cantanhede, Cartaxo, Elvas, Evora, Fátima, Figueira da Foz, Leiria, Loures, Marinha Grande, Montemor-o-Novo, Ourém, Ponte de Sor, Portalegre, Proença-a-Nova, Tomar, Torres Novas and Tramagal.
Preference of nationality: British.
Qualifications: CELTA plus minimum 1 year of TEFL experience.
Conditions of employment: period of work from mid-September to end of June. 21 h.p.w. Hours include morning and late evening work.
Salary: 1,650 escudos per hour plus accommodation allowance.
Facilities/Support: assistance with finding accommodation. Further training with workshops throughout the year.
Recruitment: adverts in *TES*. Interviews held in Portugal and UK.
Contact: Marco Henriques.

MANITOBA INSTITUTO DE LINGUAS
Apartado 184, 4491 Póvoa de Varzim Codex. Tel/fax: (52) 683014.
Number of teachers: 10-12 in 2 schools (other one is in Vila do Conde).
Preference of nationality: American, Canadian, British, Australian, etc.
Qualifications: B.Ed./MA plus TEFL qualifications and experience.
Conditions of employment: 1-2 year contracts. 25 h.p.w. Pupils aged 7-60.
Salary: above average for Portugal.
Facilities/Support: assistance with finding accommodation. Training provided.
Recruitment: applicants should send proof of degrees and other certificates, at least two references and a recent photograph. Interviews not always necessary.
Contact: Isobel Loureiro, Pedagogic Director.

ROYAL SCHOOL OF LANGUAGES
Av. Lourenco Peixinho 92-2° andar & Rua José Rabumba 2, 3800 Aveiro. Tel: (34) 29156/25104. Fax: (34) 382870
Number of teachers: 28–33 in group of 8 schools.
Preference of nationality: British and South African, plus a few Canadians and Americans.
Qualifications: university degree plus TEFL Certificate (Trinity, Cambridge or equivalent).
Conditions of employment: 9 month contracts. 25–27 teaching hours p.w.
Salary: 150,000–170,000 escudos per month less 20% deductions.
Facilities/Support: assistance given with accommodation and working papers. Training given.
Recruitment: via CVs or interviews which sometimes take place in UK.
Contact: Rosa do Céu Ramos Amorim, School Director.

SINTRALINGUA CENTRO DE LINGUAS LDA
Avenida Movimento das Forças, Armada 14-1° Dto, 2710 Sintra. Tel/fax: (1) 923 4941. E-mail: sintralingua@mail.telepac.pt
Number of teachers: 10.
Preference of nationality: British; must be native speaker.
Qualifications: minimum BA plus CELTA and 2 years experience.
Conditions of employment: 10 or 11 month contracts. Part-time hourly work also available. Lots of evening teaching (5.30pm-9.30pm) but other times possible.
Salary: 205,000 escudos per month full-time. 2,100 escudos per hour part-time.
Facilities/Support: assistance given with finding accommodation. Feedback programme and observation.
Recruitment: via adverts in *Guardian* and interviews in UK or locally.
Contact: J. E. Scott, Director.

Other Schools to Try
Note that these schools (in alphabetical order according to town) did not confirm their teacher requirements for this edition of *Teaching English Abroad*. Upper case entries marked with an asterisk had entries in the last edition (1997); addresses without asterisks have been taken from various sources, such as British Council lists and the *Yellow Pages*.

INSTITUTO BRITANICO (BRAGA), Rua Conselheiro Januário 119, 4700 Braga (53-23298). 10 teachers.
Atrio-Centro Linguas, ISLA, Apartado 224, 5300 Bragança
Instituto Bragança, Apartado 38, 5300 Bragança
Chaves English Centre, Av Pedro Alvares Cabral, 5400 Chaves
The English Centre, R Eng. Custodio Guimaraes, 4740 Esposende
Associaçao Luso-Britanica Felgueiras, Praceta Aniceto P Ferreira, 4610 Felgueiras
British Education Europe, R Bombeiros Voluntarios, 4610 Felgueiras
CD-Complemento Directo, Av. Gen. Humberto Delgado 1022, 4420 Gondomar
Instituto Linguas Gondomar Lda, Praça Manuel Guedes, 240-1° Esq, 4420 Gondomar

GREENWICH INSTITUTO DE LINGUAS, Rua 25 de Abril 560, S. Cosme, 4420 Gondorem (tel/fax 2-483 6429). 6 teachers from UK.
Citania Centro de Ingles, Lda, Av Conde Margaride 543, 4810 Guimaraes
Instituto Britanico, Rua Gravador Molarinho 29, 4800 Guimaraes
Linguagem Instituto de Linguas Lda, Pracada Da Portela, Casa Sgt Duarte 1° Esq, 2810 Laranjeiro (tel/fax 1-259 8381; www.linguagem.com).
Berlitz Language Centre, Ave. Conde Valbom 6-4 Andar, 1000 Lisbon.

CIAL CENTRO DE LINGUAS, Av. da Republica, 14-2°, 1000 Lisbon (1-533733/fax 1-352 3096). 9 teachers for Lisbon, 3 for Oporto, 3 for Faro.

New Institute of Languages, Rua Cordeiro Ferreira 19C 1°Dto, 1750 Lisbon (fax 1-759 0770). TEFL experience not essential.
Wall Street Institute Avenidas, Av. Praia de Vitoria, 71 3rd, 1000 Lisbon
Wall Street Institute, Av. da Liberdade 166 R/C, 1250 Lisbon

*IF-INGLES FUNCIONAL, Ap. 303, 2430 Marinha Grande (44-568351/fax 44-560346). 13 teachers.
IPFEL-Centro Estudos, R Barao S Cosme 166-2° Esq, 4000 Oporto

*ISAI (INSTITUTO SUPERIOR DE ASSISTENTES E INTERPRETES), Rua Alvares Cabral 159, 4050 Oporto (e-mail: isai@mail.telepac.pt). 3 teachers.
Royal School of Languages, R Amial 292, 4200 Oporto
Wall Street Institute Oporto, Rua do Campo Alegre 231, 3°, 4100 Oporto
Academia Estudos Paredes, R Dr Jose Cabral, 4580 Paredes
Instituto Linguas Paredes, Av Republica 401-c/v, 4580 Paredes

*INTERLINGUA LANGUAGE INSTITUTE, Lg. 1° de Dezembro 28, 8500 Portimao (82-427690/416030/fax 82-427690). 7 teachers.
Communicate Language Institute, Pcta Joao Villaret 12B, 2675 Póvoa de St Adriao (e-mail: cli@esoterica.pt). Prefer teachers experienced with young learners to teach in suburban Lisbon primary schools.

*THE NEW INSTITUTE OF LANGUAGES, Urb. da Portela Lt. 197-5° B/C, 2685 Sacavém (1-943 5238) 15 British teachers.
Centro Intercontinental Ingles, R Liberdade 29-2°, Salas 9-10, 3700 S. João Madeira
Escola Inglesa, R Visconde, 2097 3700 S. João Madeira

Scandinavia

Certain similarities exist in ELT throughout Scandinavia. The standard of English teaching in state schools is uniformly high, as anyone who has met a Dane or a Swede travelling abroad will know. Yet many ordinary Scandinavians keep up their English by attending evening classes, if only for social reasons. Sweden, Denmark and Norway have excellent facilities for such people, which are variations on the theme of 'folk university', a state-subsidised system of adult education. Classes at such institutions are the ideal setting for enthusiastic amateur teachers.

But as elsewhere in Europe the greatest demand for the English language comes from the business community, particularly in Finland. Enthusiastic amateurs tend to be less in demand in this setting than mature professionals. Yet Scandinavia is not a very popular destination for such teachers, despite its unspoilt countryside and efficient public transport. So there is scope for most kinds of teacher to work in Scandinavia, particularly in Finland, whose language schools sometimes advertise in the British press.

Since Finland and Sweden joined the European Union in 1994, the red tape has become much easier for EU teachers. But even in Norway, whose people voted by a referendum not to join, language institutes occasionally employ foreign teachers.

DENMARK

There is little recruitment of English teachers outside Denmark, apart from the *Cambridge Institute Foundation* which is Denmark's largest EFL institution with 38 branches and which specialises in English for business. The only UK agency seen advertising recent vacancies in Denmark was SLS, 9 Marsden Park, Clifton, York YO30 4GX (fax 01904 691102) which was looking for Certificate-trained teachers with two years' experience to teach general and business English for ten months from early August.

Many schools expect their teachers to speak Danish, and there seems to be almost enough fully bilingual candidates resident in Denmark to satisfy this requirement. It is worthwhile for any native speaker with an appropriate background who is staying in Denmark to enquire about part-time openings. The British Council in Copenhagen has a list of about 15 addresses, though it may not be as reliable as some. A useful starting place is one of the voluntary organisations which run evening classes countrywide:

Arbejdernes Oplysnings Forbund (AOF), Teglvaerksgade 27, 2100 Copenhagen O.
Folkeligt Oplysnings Forbund (FOF), Frederiksborggade 20, 1360 Copenhagen K
Frit Oplysningsforbund (FO), Landsforbundet, Fredriksberggade 21, 1459 Copenhagen K
Hovedstadens Oplysnings Forbund (HOF), Kobmagergade 26, 1150 Copenhagen K
Studieskolen, Antoniagade 6, 1106 Copenhagen K

All wages are set by law and teaching English is no exception. The minimum is about kr120, and that is what most new arrivals earn. Denmark has among the highest taxes in the world, i.e. 50%.

FINLAND

Although Finland's second language is Swedish, English runs a close second. Finns are admirably energetic and industrious in learning foreign languages, possibly because their own language is so impenetrable (belonging to the Finno-Ugric group of languages along with Hungarian and Estonian). English is taught in every kind of educational institution from trade and technology colleges to universities, but especially in commercial colleges *(Kauppaloulu)* and in Civic and Workers' Institutes. Private language schools flourish too and traditionally have not been too fussy about the paper qualifications of their native speaker teachers. Children start their primary education at age seven, and many children between the ages of three and seven are sent to private kindergartens, many of which are English (as well as German, American, etc.) These often welcome a native English speaker with experience of teaching children. (The only skill which concerned one of these nurseries-cum-kindergartens looking to hire a young British graduate was singing.)

Fixing up a Job

The British Council in Helsinki will send a list of 26 private schools, all of them in Helsinki. One of the key organisations in Finland is the Federation of Finnish-British Societies (Puistokatu 1 b A, 00140 Helsinki; tel/fax (+)358-9-629 626) which takes on a substantial number of both experienced and inexperienced staff for its busy teaching centre in Helsinki and for the 14 Finn-Brit societies and clubs throughout the country. Interviews are held in London in April. They offer nine-month contracts (September to May) which include return air fare and pay between about FIM7,000 for a graduate teacher and FIM9,000+ for an experienced teacher with a TEFL qualification. Accommodation is also arranged, which is normally accompanied by access to a sauna. Part of the job at an English club usually consists of participating in regular social evenings, for example giving a talk about British life, or accompanying classes on excursions and ski trips.

Another big player in the provision of English language teaching is *Richard Lewis Communications* with offices throughout Finland as well as in England (see entry). RLC draws most of its students from senior management in both the public and private sector, and also provides cross-cultural training in Finland.

An employer which advertises at regular intervals is Linguarama. Graduates of Linguarama's introductory training courses in Britain are often encouraged to consider Finland for their posting abroad; their head office in the UK (Oceanic House, 85 High St, Alton, Hants. GU34 1LG) handles some recruitment, or you can contact the growing Helsinki operation on (+)358-9-680 32331/fax 603118/e-mail:

linguarama.hki@linguarama. com. There is a sprinkling of adverts for schools outside Helsinki, for example in Tampere and Hameenlinna.

Despite the theoretical range of possibilities, a speculative job search may be discouraging. With an MA in TESOL and years of teaching experience in Europe and the US, Dennis Bricault hoped that he would get at least one favourable reply to the 20 letters he wrote to various language institutes and universities. Instead he got either silence or rejections and came to the conclusion that Finland is a 'wash-out', at least if you write from an American address.

Finland actively encourages trainees to come to Finland for short-term paid work in a range of fields including language teaching. The Centre for International Mobility (CIMO, PO Box 343, SF-00531 Helsinki; (+)358-9-7747 7615/fax 7747 7064; e-mail: young.professionals@cimo.fi/http://www.cimo.fi) coordinates an International Trainee Exchange programme whereby students and graduates work in their field for a named Finnish employer for between one and 18 months. The academic year lasts from the end of August or beginning of September until the end of May. Of course most schools prefer their native speaker teachers to stay for the whole year though one-term positions are possible. Salaries average about FIM6,500 per month.

The formalities are minimal for EU teachers but the programme is also open to other nationalities who are granted work and residence permits. Non-EU teachers must first find an employer who will obtain permission from the local employment office to hire a foreigner, and then complete the application for a work permit and residence permit while still in their countries of residence.

For those who wish to spend the summer (or longer) in Finland but do not intend to become a serious teacher, the Finnish Family Programme also administered by CIMO places young people aged 18 to 25 in families throughout Finland to converse in English and help generally around the house or farm as needed. The pocket money is FIM1,000-2,000 per month.

There is also demand for private tutoring which you could fix up by advertising in the usual way.

Conditions of Work

A teaching unit of 45 minutes is the norm, with less evening work than elsewhere. A number of schools pay travel expenses and arrange furnished accommodation. Wages are high, but so is the cost of living. Teachers paid by the lesson can expect to earn between FIM100 and FIM130 for 45 minutes. Some schools compress the teaching into four days a week, leaving plenty of time for weekend exploration of the country.

Deductions will be significant from a gross monthly salary of FIM8,000. Taxes are high (approximately 25%) and are usually the responsibility of the teacher, whereas contributions should be paid by your employer; social security and unemployment insurance deductions will amount to at least 6% of the salary.

The Finnish Embassy in London distributes a detailed booklet produced by the Ministry of Labour entitled 'Are You Planning to Move to Finland?' which is worth reading. Helsinki has about 35 museums and art galleries plus a high density of sports facilities, ice rinks, etc. The long dark winters are relieved by a wide choice of cheerful restaurants, cafés, bars and clubs in the cities, and saunas almost everywhere.

NORWAY

The trend in Norwegian EFL is similar to that in Denmark, and most schools rely on a pool of native speakers already resident in Norway. Most jobs are for part-time work and of course do not offer accommodation. At least things are easier from an immigration point of view than they used to be. Although Norway is not a member of the EU, it does allow the free reciprocity of labour so that EU nationals are allowed to work in Norway without a work permit.

The British Council in Oslo does not keep a list of language schools, though it has the Yellow Pages for Oslo, Bergen, Stavanger, Trondheim and others. As throughout

Scandinavia, the Folkuniversity of Norway plays an important role in language tuition and hires many native speakers, mostly on an occasional basis. There are branches in Stavanger, Skien, Kristiansand and Hamar. The basic hourly wage starts at kr100, though this can rise by two or three times for high-level business teaching.

Casual opportunities may crop up in unpredictable places. David Moor was simply intending to spend a month on holiday skiing in Norway. However he saw an advert in a local supermarket for a native English teacher and jumped at the chance:

> *A teacher put me up and fed me. I'd intended to stay in the hostel or a cheap hotel, but was finding Norway expensive. I was just working for keep, teaching three days a week, so I had lots of spare time. I had a fantastic time, much better than a normal holiday.*

SWEDEN

The Folkuniversity of Sweden has a long-established scheme (since 1955) by which British teachers are placed for one academic year (nine months) within a network of adult education centres throughout the country. There are five university extension departments (called *Kursverksamheten* or KV, formerly called British Centres) located in Stockholm, Gothenburg, Lund, Uppsala and Umeå, with branches in many small towns. Anyone interested in teaching in Sweden on this scheme should contact the programme coordinator Ulla Nissen at the FU (Rehnsgatan 20, Box 7845, 10398 Stockholm; 8-789 4100/fax 8-166478). For many years the FU was represented in the UK by the Salisbury Language School (36 Fowler's Road, Salisbury, Wilts. SP1 2QU; 01722 331011); however they no longer carry out recruitment.

Originally the teaching at the Folkuniversity consisted of evening classes called a 'Study Circle', an informal conversation session. Circumstances have changed, however, and the range of pupils can be very varied from unemployed people to business executives, as well as people who want to prepare for Cambridge examinations. Paul Greening taught 'coffee and cake classes to housewives' as well as teaching 'teenagers, businessmen, old aged pensioners and out-of-work semi-alcoholics'.

Business people are coming to dominate this varied list, and light-hearted evening 'study circles' have been mostly replaced by hard-headed company courses. According to Andrew Boyle who spent a year in Sundsvall, Northern Sweden on the scheme, the local administration had not really caught up with the changes:

> *Because Sundsvall was not one of the five main FU towns, the administration were not qualified EFL people, which caused some problems. For example the placement testing procedure consisted of a student being asked on the phone by a secretary speaking Swedish what level they were at. 'Intermediate I think' and intermediate it would be. The administration still had the 'coffee and cake' conversation circle ethos while charging companies commercial rates to have their staff learn specific language skills. The FU were behaving as a business on the one hand (legitimately, I think) but administering that business almost as if it were a hobby.*

The FU in Stockholm runs English summer courses from June to August for which it looks to hire teachers and group leaders. Most of these are drawn from native speakers already in Sweden with the FU who would otherwise be idle all summer (or, more likely, looking for work at a summer school in the UK).

Fixing up a Job

With approximately 20 jobs a year, mostly from September but also from January, Folkuniversitetet offers the best chance to anyone aged 22-40 of fixing up work in Sweden. The 'embryonic EFL teacher' is encouraged to apply and is promised that this will be a good career start (which it generally is, though there are few prospects for an open-ended attachment to the FU). Paul Greening found that his interviewer was more concerned to establish that he would be willing to stick it out in northern Sweden for a year than to see his ELT qualifications.

Anyone who does not want to work through the FU will find it more difficult, although it is considerably easier for Britons to square the legal side of things than it used to be before Sweden joined the EU. Advertisements almost never appear in the educational press. Teachers with a solid ELT background might try the main state universities who put on English courses or the language schools listed in the Yellow Pages of Stockholm, Malmö, Gothenburg, Orebro and Uppsala. Charlotte Rosen decided to do a TEFL course in London before going to Sweden to be with her Swedish fiancé:

> *I had visited Sweden several times before going to Gothenburg to work. After I'd been in Sweden for about six weeks, I looked through the Yellow Pages for language schools and sent off my CV in English which wasn't a problem because everyone speaks English really well. I was offered several interviews, including by the British Institute. Many of them said they were interested but the terms only start in September and January so you have to time your applications quite carefully.*

Making a breakthrough as a freelancer is also difficult without a knowledge of the Swedish labour market and a functioning network of contacts. Some FU teachers do teach privately to supplement their incomes, though technically this is forbidden by the terms of their visa.

Conditions of Work

Folkuniversitetet guarantees 720 hours of work (lessons are 45 minutes long) over the nine-month contract. Hours in excess of this figure of approximately 80 hours per month are paid extra and some more lucrative courses are paid at a higher rate. The teaching schedule varies enormously from place to place but is not normally onerous, though it may involve up to four evenings a week and some travelling, perhaps even to neighbouring towns. It may also include some promoting of KV courses to increase enrolment. The journey from Britain to Sweden is paid, as is the return journey at the end of each of the two contract years.

Folkuniversitetet has the reputation of offering low pay-rates, and certainly they are less than elsewhere in Scandinavia. The current Swedish minimum wage of kr11,000 per month gross is reasonable to live on, but makes it difficult to save. Paul Greening found it difficult to make ends meet on his salary:

> *The accommodation which was provided was good but expensive. I always had to think about prices and look for the cheapest. I was able to save money only because I started a large number of teenage courses for which I was paid extra.*

Teachers must pay tax in Sweden on a scale which varies according to the municipality. Swedish income tax is notoriously high, varying between a quarter and a third of gross earnings.

Constructing a lively social life is a challenge. Most find Swedes fairly reserved, a problem that is not helped by the fact that there are few places to meet the locals outside the classroom, since drinking and eating out are so expensive. Ann Hunter points out that it can be difficult to make Swedish friends:

> *The only Swedes you meet regularly are your pupils and the professional relationship can make it awkward to socialise, though after your first term you can get to know ex-pupils quite well. Learning Swedish, if it is possible, is a good way to meet people, though your fellow students are foreigners of course.*

Andrew Boyle had mixed feeling about Sweden and Swedish people:

> *Sweden is a pleasant place to live, if a little dull at times. It is a generally liberal place, although the increasingly multicultural nature of society is causing Swedes to have to face up to their own prejudices. The students are generally of a high level and although initially quiet not unfriendly and even chatty after they know you a little better.*

Still, you have to be independent and comfortable with your own company for long periods to enjoy Sweden, especially in the north of the country during the seven months of the winter when the locals either hibernate or devote all their leisure to skiing. Anyone who enjoys outdoor activities will probably enjoy a stint in Sweden, especially ramblers and hill-walkers, who take advantage of the *Allemannsrätt,* the law which guarantees free access to the countryside for everyone.

LIST OF SCHOOLS

Denmark

CAMBRIDGE INSTITUTE FOUNDATION
Vimmelskaftet 48, 1161 Copenhagen K. Tel: 33 13 33 02.
Number of teachers: 53 in various schools in the Copenhagen area.
Preference of nationality: British, Irish.
Qualifications: BA, TEFL qualification and at least 1 year's TEFL experience abroad.
Conditions of employment: 8 month renewable contracts (October-May). Minimum 20 h.p.w. Students aged 18-70.
Salary: approximately £20 per teaching hour.
Facilities/Support: assistance with accommodation. Training given.
Recruitment: through adverts in UK newspapers.
Contact: Richard Philp, Principal.

EUROPEAN EDUCATION CENTRE APS
Lyngbyvej 72, 2100 Copenhagen O. Tel: 39 27 05 01. Fax: 39 27 05 12.
Number of teachers: 5-10 (seasonal).
Preference of nationality: British, American.
Qualifications: minimum TEFL plus degree or equivalent.
Conditions of employment: freelance, with no guarantee of hours. Lessons offered mostly in-company between 8.15am and 6pm.
Salary: kr120 per 40-minute lesson plus transport time and expenses.
Facilities/Support: no assistance with accommodation. Application forms for work permits available from school. Basic orientation given, though prefer teachers with some experience.
Recruitment: local interviews after receiving CV. Normally interview applicants who have been resident in Denmark for at least a year.
Contact: John Samson, Director.

SANWES SPROGINSTITUT APS
Kokholm 1, 6000 Kolding. Tel: 75 51 74 10. Fax: 75 51 74 90. E-mail: sanwes@sanwes. Also branches at Horsensvej 39C, 7100 Vejle (75 72 46 10) and Fredericia Uddannelsescenter, Mosegardsvej, 7000 Fredericia (75 94 14 11).
Number of teachers: 8-10.
Preference of nationality: British, American, Australian.
Qualifications: should have some business background, be open-minded, cheerful and have lots of initiative.
Conditions of employment: freelance; preferred minimum period 6 months. Daytime hours; total number depends on clients.
Salary: approximately kr130 per hour.
Facilities/Support: no assistance with accommodation. Pre-service training from other teacher. Help given with work permits.
Recruitment: local interviews.
Contact: Lone von der Sandt, Director.

A selection of other schools to try (towns in alphabetical order):
FOF (Folkeligt Oplysnings Forbund), Sonder Allé 9, 8000 Arhus C (86 12 29 55/fax 86 19 54 35). 5 teachers for adult evening classes.
Babel Sprogtraening, Hyldegardsvej 2, 2920 Charlottenlund

Berlitz International, Vimmelskaftet 42A, 1161 Copenhagen
Master-Ling, Sortedam Dossering 83, 2100 Copenhagen O
Sprogklubben, Vendersgade 6, 1363 Copenhagen K
Studieskolen, Antoniagade 6, 11006 Copenhagen K

Elite Sprogcentret, Hoffmeyersvej 19, 2000 Frederiksberg
Babel Sprogtraening, Naverland 2, 10, 2600 Glostrup
AIS Language Training Centre, Kongevejen 115, 2840 Holte
BS Sprogservice, Birkevej 3, 2830 Virum
Lingua Dan, Hotoften 4, 2830 Virum

Finland

AAC—OPISTO OY
Kauppaneuvoksentie 8, 00200 Helsinki. Tel: (+358-9) 4766 7800. www.aac.fi
Number of teachers: 50 in 7 centres (Helsinki: Lauttasaari and Pitäjänmäki, Tampere, Turku (fax +358-2-469 1240), Jyväskylä, Vaasa and Oulu).
Preference of nationality: British, American, Canadian.
Qualifications: MA in English or MBA or BA plus CELTA, or BA plus business background, teaching experience preferred.
Conditions of employment: 9 month contracts. 80-100 hours per month. Students are business people who want to learn business and/or technical English.
Salary: FIM95-100 per lesson.
Facilities/Support: one-way air fare paid, housing arranged. Training provided on different teaching methods and materials.
Recruitment: direct application, newspaper ads, internet.
Contact: Sinikka Teikari.

GREENWICH MERIDIAN TRAINING
Fabianinkatu 5, 00130 Helsinki, Tel: (+358-9) 3487 0456. Fax: (9) 3487 0457. E-mail: jmdallyn@megabaud.fi
Number of teachers: 3-4.
Preference of nationality: none.
Qualifications: CELTA or equivalent.
Conditions of employment: 1 or 2 years. 28 contact h.p.w. Lessons last 45 minutes.
Salary: FIM8,000 per month minimum, according to qualifications and experience, less taxes, social security (4.7%) and unemployment insurance (1.5%).
Facilities/Support: assistance given with accommodation, work permits and training. Chances to become involved in sales and marketing, internet and book publishing and seminar developments.
Recruitment: direct. Telephone and e-mail contact is sufficient.
Contact: Jeremy Dallyn, Director.

INSTITUTE OF MARKETING
Töölöntullinkatu 6, 00250 Helsinki. Tel: (+358-9) 47361. Fax: (9) 241 4794.
Number of teachers: 10 (part-time).
Preference of nationality: British, American, Canadian.
Qualifications: BA plus TEFL qualification (or equivalent) and experience of teaching adults, especially business English.
Conditions of employment: only part-time work available. Hours of work 9am-4pm. Students aged 20-50.
Salary: FIM150-170 per 45-minute lesson.
Facilities/Support: no assistance with accommodation. Training given.
Recruitment: through direct application and personal recommendation. Local interviews essential.

IWG KIELI-INSTITUUTTI LTD

Hämeenkatu 25 B, 33200 Tampere. Tel: (3) 389 1002. Fax: (3) 389 1003.
Number of teachers: 5 (out of 13).
Preference of nationality: British, American.
Qualifications: BA and TEFL qualification.
Conditions of employment: 9-10 month contracts. 5 hours work per day. Pupils aged 6-70.
Salary: FIM 8,000 per month.
Facilities/Support: accommodation provided. No training.
Recruitment: through adverts. Interviews essential and can be held in UK.

KIELIPISTE KAUPPAKAARI OY

Kaisaniemenkatu 4A, 00100 Helsinki. Tel: (+358-90) 622 6190. Fax: (+358-90) 6226 1999.
Number of teachers: 30-40.
Preference of nationality: none.
Qualifications: CELTA or BA/MA in TEFL plus experience teaching adults and preferably a business background. Some positions also open for ESP teachers of legal (EC) English, technical English, etc.
Conditions of employment: freelance work only. Indeterminate number of hours (2-40) between 8am and 8.15pm. Students are all adults.
Salary: FIM112-122 per 45-minute lesson.
Facilities/Support: no assistance with accommodation.
Recruitment: local interview essential (by appointment only).
Contact: Eeva Sallamaa, Tuition Planner.

LINGVA-FORUM KY

WTC, Aleksanterinkatu 17, 00100 Helsinki. Tel: (+358-9) 6969 3020. Fax: (+358-9) 6969 3021. E-mail: marit@lingvaforum.fi
Number of teachers: 6.
Preference of nationality: British.
Qualifications: minimum BA, TOEFL Certificate or Diploma.
Conditions of employment: 3 months' probation plus 6 months. Approx. 22 h.p.w. Half of weekly hours are between 8am and 4pm, and half between 4pm and 7pm. Only adults studying either business English (how to conduct meetings, negotiations, telephoning) or general English.
Salary: FIM8,000-FIM9,000 per month (based on 22 hours) less tax. Institute pays social security and pension contributions.
Facilities/Support: no assistance with finding accommodation. Emphasis on in-house training.
Recruitment: personal interview necessary.
Contact: Marit Harjula, Managing Director.

MARCKWORT OY

Ludviginkatu 3-5A, 00130 Helsinki. Tel: (+358-0) 612 2280. Fax: (+358-0) 6122 2838. E-mail: marckwort@marckwort.fi. www.marckwort.fi
Number of teachers: 6.
Preference of nationality: British, American.
Qualifications: experience in teaching adults; experience of new teaching methods.
Conditions of employment: variable hours between 8am and 6pm. Average of 10 40-minute lessons per week.
Salary: FIM 110-145 per 45 minutes (net).
Facilities/Support: no assistance with accommodation. Training given in suggestopaedia, NLP, and teaching involving music and activities.
Recruitment: interviewees must teach a demonstration lesson.
Contact: Selene Marckwort, Training Manager.

MBK LANGUAGES OY
Mikonkatu 13G, 00100 Helsinki. Tel: (+358-9) 650681. Fax: (+358-9) 650682. E-mail: mbkoy@netlife.fi
Number of teachers: 5.
Preference of nationality: none (British, American, Irish, Australian, etc.)
Qualifications: university degree in any subject and teaching experience.
Conditions of employment: freelance. Variable hours between 8am and 8pm Monday to Friday; average 10 h.p.w.
Salary: from FIM 100 per lesson (net).
Facilities/Support: some training given if necessary.
Recruitment: via newspaper adverts and word of mouth.
Contact: Kirsti Nurmela-Knox, Director.

REFERICON OY
Miniatontie 4 E 23, 02360 Espoo (Helsinki). Tel: (+358-9) 813 3507. Fax: (+358-9) 801 8801. E-mail: raija.ikonen@refericon.fi
Number of teachers: varies.
Preference of nationality: none.
Qualifications: TESOL plus teaching experience abroad.
Conditions of employment: freelance basis; hours vary according to project. Business is involved with developing CD-ROMs.
Facilities/Support: no assistance with accommodation or work permits.
Contact: Raija Ikonen, Managing Director.

RICHARD LEWIS COMMUNICATIONS
Länsituulentie 10, 02100 Espoo (Helsinki). Tel: (+358-9) 4157 4700. Fax: (+358-9) 466 592. E-mail: 101625.2134@compuserve.com. Offices also in Turku, Tampere, Lahti, Oulu, Jyväskylä and Vaasa; and in the UK: Riversdown House, Warnford, Southampton, Hants. SO32 3LH. Tel: 01962 771111.
Preference of nationality: British.
Qualifications: university degree and TEFL preferred.
Conditions of employment: 9 month contracts (September till the third week in June). Possibility of summer work in England.
Facilities/Support: assistance with finding accommodation. New teachers are given training in RLC's methods.
Recruitment: direct application to Michael Gates, Managing Director (mobile phone +358-50-558 7397).

TALK SHOP LTD.
Yliopistonkatu 23A, 20100 Turku. Tel: (+358-2) 234 5100. Fax: (+358-2) 2234 5110. E-mail: Alex.Frost@talkshop.fi
Number of teachers: 3.
Preference of nationality: American, British.
Qualifications: Cert. TEFL and experience, especially in corporate training.
Conditions of employment: open-ended contracts with possibility of becoming long-term. Hours between 8am and 4pm.
Salary: FIM 9,500+ per month, less about 25% deductions.
Facilities/Support: assistance with accommodation if needed. Help given with work permits. Training given.
Recruitment: interviews necessary.
Contact: Alex Frost, Managing Director.

TYOVAEN AKATEMIA/WORKERS' ACADEMY
Vanha Turuntie 14, 02700 Kauniainen. Tel: (+358-9) 5404 2412. Fax: (+358-9) 5404 2444. E-mail: toimisto@akatemia.org. www.akatemia.org
Number of teachers: 1-4.
Preference of nationality: none (must be native speakers).
Qualifications: TEFL diploma.

Conditions of employment: freelancers teach 15-30 lessons per month for 6-12 months.
Salary: FIM100 per lesson.
Facilities/Support: training given in Finnish.
Contact: Ms. Heidi Mäkäläinen, Language Coordinator.

A selection of other schools to try (towns in alphabetical order):
Advance Oy Ltd, Laivurinkatu 33, 00150 Helsinki
Alpha Communications Oy, Kaisaniemenkatu 4 A, 00100 Helsinki
Ammatti-Instituutti, Pitäjänmäki Valimotie 8, Helsinki
Arkadi Oy, Töölönkatu 8, 00100 Helsinki
Bellcrest Language Services Oy, Luotsikatu 1 A, 00160 Helsinki
Berlitz, Kaivokatu 10 A, 00100 Helsinki
Communication Strategies, Itälahdenkatu 9 A, 00210 Helsinki
Europpalainen Kielikoulu, Kalevankatu 44, 00180 Helsinki
FINTRA, PL 341, Munkkisaarenkatu 2, 00151 Helsinki
*HABIL OY HELSINKI, International House, Mariankatu 15 B 7, 00170 Helsinki
  (+358-9-135 7104/fax 135 7881). 5 teachers.
Helsingin Työväenopisto, Helsinginkatu 26, 00530 Helsinki
Josbel Oy, Vuorimiehenkatu 20, 00150 Helsinki
Karavan Kielikoulu Oy, Paasikivenkatu 13, Helsinki
Kieliavain Kieliopisto, Kaisaniemenkatu 3A, 00100 Helsinki
Kieli-instituutti Languista, Annankatu 29 A, 00100 Helsinki
Kielikimara Oy, Mikonkatu 8A, Helsinki
Kielikoulu Small Talk, Annankatu 31-33 B, 00100 Helsinki
Kieliopisto Intensiivi, Punavuorenkatu 2 A, 00120 Helsinki
LinguaBella, Vuorikatu 16 A, 00100 Helsinki
Linguaphone Kieliopisto, PL 100 (Heikkiläntie 6), 00211 Helsinki
Linguarama Kieliopisto, Annankatu 26, 00100 Helsinki (fax +358-9-603118; e-mail
  linguarama.hki@linguarama.com).
Optimi Training Oy, Ludviginkatu 3-5 B 21, 00130 Helsinki
Translingva, Yrönkatu 21 C, 00100 Helsinki

*LANSI-SUOMEN OPISTO, Loimijoentie 280, 32700 Huittinen (+358-2-567866/fax
  566409). 3 EU teachers.

Norway

FOLKEUNIVERSITETET/FRIUNDERVISNINGEN OSLO
Torggata 7 (P.B. 496 Sentrum), 0105 Oslo. Tel: 22 47 60 00. Fax: 22 47 60 01. E-mail: info@fu.oslo.no
Number of teachers: 2 full-time, 15-20 part-time.
Preference of nationality: none.
Qualifications: TEFL experience and qualifications preferred. Prefer native speakers already resident in Norway.
Conditions of employment: no contracts. Students aged 18-65.
Salary: varies from course to course.
Facilities/Support: no assistance with accommodation. Some training given.
Recruitment: local interviews only.
Contact: E. Stang Lund.

DET INTERNASJONALE SPRAKSENTER
Dronningensgt. 32, 0154 Oslo. Tel: 22 33 15 20. Fax: 22 33 69 30. E-mail: intsprak@online.no
Number of teachers: 5-10 on freelance basis.
Preference of nationality: British preferred.
Qualifications: academic record (TEFL), previous experience and pleasant character needed. Teachers should be already resident in Oslo.

Conditions of employment: variable hours between 8am and 10pm.
Facilities/Support: training and promotion possible through parent organisation.
Recruitment: local interviews only.
Contact: Rut Tostrup Anderson, Manager.

LILLEHAMMER OVERSETTING
Postboks 54, 2601 Lillehammer. Tel: 61 26 47 60. Fax: 61 25 61 14.
Number of teachers: 10 (English and other languages).
Preference of nationality: British (and other European native speakers).
Qualifications: some language teaching experience needed.
Conditions of employment: no full-time contracts. Day and evening work. Students aged 15-30.
Salary: negotiable.
Facilities/Support: assistance with finding accommodation if necessary. Training provided.
Recruitment: personal interview necessary.

NORSK SPRAKINSTITUTT
Kongensgt. 9, 0153 Oslo. Tel: 23 10 01 10. Fax: 23 10 01 27. E-mail: snorsk@online.no
Number of teachers: 7 (but varies).
Preference of nationality: British or American without marked accent.
Qualifications: TEFL, etc. and teaching experience. Work experience in other fields such as business is a valuable asset. Must be resident in Oslo.
Conditions of employment: freelance only. Hours vary according to course requirements.
Salary: hourly rate. Holiday pay based on previous year's earnings.
Recruitment: direct contact.
Contact: David M. Smith, Head of English Department.

SPRAKSKOLEN AS
Karl Johansgat. 8, 0154 Oslo. Tel: 22 42 00 87. Fax: 22 42 32 94. E-mail: spraaksk@online.no
Number of teachers: 1 full-time, 5 part-time.
Preference of nationality: none.
Qualifications: preferably TOEFL or other teaching qualification.
Conditions of employment: freelance. Variable hours, usually 10-20 h.p.w.
Salary: kr100-200 per teaching hour less deductions of 20%-36%.
Facilities/Support: no assistance with accommodation. Little formal training.
Recruitment: word of mouth and local interviews.
Contact: Guy Baillie, Head of English.

Other Schools to try (towns in alphabetical order):
Allegro A/S Spraktjenester, Strandkaien 6, 5013 Bergen
Neltec, Moldbakken 17, 5035 Bergen-Sankviken
Atlas Sprakreiser, Postboks 191, Vindern, 0319 Oslo
Berlitz, Lille Grensen 5, 0159 Oslo
International Language School, Markveien 35 B, 0554 Oslo
*KOMMUNIKE SPRAKINSTITUTT, Jacobaalsgt. 17A, 0364 Oslo (22 69 97 10/fax 22 69 26 75). 5 part-time teachers only.
Polaris Institute AS, Dronningen 1, Pb. A, Bygdoy, 0211 Oslo
English Language Centre, Lokkev. 16, 4008 Stavanger
Folkeuniversitetet Rogaland, Kongsg. 58, 4012 Stavanger
Noricom Spraktjenester, Batstadstien 4, 4056 Tananger
Noricom Spraktjenester, Kjopmannsg.11, 7001 Trondheim

THE BRITISH INSTITUTE
Hagagatan 3, 11348 Stockholm. Tel: (8) 341200. Fax: (8) 344192. E-mail: info@britishinstitute.se
Number of teachers: 12.
Preference of nationality: British.
Qualifications: CELTA or Dip TEFL.
Conditions of employment: short-term or permanent contracts. 1,760 hours per year.
Salary: kr12,000-18,000 per month for permanent staff; kr100-220 per lesson for term staff. Deductions of 30-35% for tax and contributions.
Facilities/Support: no assistance with accommodation. Training provided.
Recruitment: local interview essential.
Contact: Michael Eyre, Principal.

ALL-International Language Center AB, Morbydalen 25, Danderyd
Richard Lewis Communications, Norev. 9, Box 3, 182 05 Djursholm
ABC Engelsk o. Amerikanska Sprakundervisning, Säfflegatan 7, 123 44 Farsta
Internationella Skolorna, Box 26210, 100 41 Stockholm
Interlingua, Tyskbagargatan 7, Box 55568, 102 04 Stockholm
Key English Language Services AB, Gamla Brogatan 9, 11120 Stockholm
Language for Business, Ekbackev. 16, 181 46 Lidingo, Stockholm
Pro Linguis, Hammarby fabriksv. 21 A, Box 17039, 104 62 Stockholm
Speak Right AB, Linneg. 6, 114 47 Stockholm

Spain

The decade of the 1980s was one of unprecedented economic growth in Spain as business and industry forged ahead in preparation for European economic unification. The Olympics in Barcelona, Expo 92 in Seville and Madrid as the 1992 City of Culture prodded Spanish schools and businesses into a frenzy of English language learning. Few job interviews would have omitted the question, 'How much English can you speak?'

But the emphasis has shifted to adapt to changing conditions in the market. The majority of language academies are now involved with the teaching of children starting with the pre-school age group. There is a national push to introduce English early; it is compulsory in state schools from the age of nine, and the Spanish Ministry of Education has asked the British Council to recruit experienced EFL teachers to work in nearly 50 participating primary schools. This trend has filtered through to private language providers, some of whom organise summer language camps for adolescents. As in Greece, many children are enrolled in private English lessons to improve their chances of passing school exams. Language centres which dealt more or less exclusively with company personnel for a decade are suddenly asking their teachers to organise sing-songs and games for young children.

Despite a decline in the adult market, there are still thousands of foreigners teaching English in language institutes from the Basque north (where there is a surprisingly strong concentration) to the Balearic and Canary Islands. The entries for language schools occupy about 18 pages of the Madrid Yellow Pages. Almost every back street in every Spanish town has an *Academia de Ingles.* Technically *academias* are privately run and largely unregulated and *institutos* teach children 16 to 18.

Spain has always been a popular destination for EFL teachers. Who can fail to be attracted to the climate, scenery, history and culture? And yet, many new arrivals in

Spain soon realise that Spain and the Spanish people of their imagination bear little relation to what they find, at least in the major cities. All this economic expansion and increased prosperity has not only led to pollution and over-development, but also to greed and corruption at many levels. Due to recession, the ELT business has become cut-throat with academy owners doing their best to squeeze out every last peseta of profit, which can lead to poor working conditions.

Another myth which is soon exploded is that life in Spain is cheap. Although it is still possible to enjoy a three-course meal with wine for a few pounds and to travel on the metro for a few pence, Madrid is considered to be one of the most expensive cities in the world, and Spain as a whole suffers from high inflation and expensive accommodation. Teaching wages rarely allow more than a tolerably comfortable lifestyle. These are points to bear in mind when visions of *paella* and beaches dance before your eyes.

Prospects for Teachers

The days are gone when any native speaker of English without a TEFL background could reasonably expect to be hired by a language academy. Many schools in the major cities echo the discouraging comments made by the director of a well-established school in Barcelona who said that he has found that there is a large supply of well-qualified native English speakers on hand so that his school cannot possibly reply to all the CVs from abroad that they receive as well.

Other schools report that the number of applications from candidates with a TEFL Certificate has soared simply because so many more centres in the UK and worldwide are churning them out. (One claims to have noticed a decline in standards, at least from the level of literacy displayed in CVs and applications.) Opportunities for untrained graduates have all but disappeared in what can be loosely described as 'respectable' schools, though there are still plenty of more opportunistic language academy directors who might be prepared to hire someone without qualifications, particularly part-time. A great many schools fall into this category. To take a random example, the expatriate director of a well-established school in Alicante estimated that of the 20 or so schools in town, only four operate within the law (i.e. keep their books in order, pay social security contributions for their staff, etc.)

Many Britons and Irish people with or without TEFL qualifications set off for Spain to look for work on spec, preferably in early September. A high percentage of schools, especially those which have been termed 'storefront' schools, depend on word-of-mouth and local walk-ins for their staff requirements. Anyone with some experience and/or a qualification should find it fairly easy to land a job this way. With a knowledge of Spanish, you can usually fill one of the many vacancies for teachers of children (with whom the total immersion method is not always suitable). The usual process is to put together a timetable from various sources and be reconciled to the fact that some or all of your employers in your first year will exploit you to some degree. Those who stay on for a second or further years can become more choosy.

The situation for Americans has become almost impossible if they want to work legally (see section on *Regulations* below).

FIXING UP A JOB

Because schools run the whole gamut from prestigious to cowboy, every method of job-hunting works at some level. The big chains like Wall Street Institutes (with 140 academies in Spain), inlingua (with up to 40), Berlitz and Linguarama mostly hire locally, though it may be worth enquiring at their headquarters (see chapter *Finding a Job*). They are probably a good bet for the novice teacher on account of the stability of hours they can offer. Anyone hired by Berlitz receives a free week-long training course in the Berlitz Method. Similarly, Wall Street Institutes (whose head office in Spain is at Rambla de Catalunya 2-4, 08007 Barcelona; 93-412 0014/fax 93-412 38 03) are always looking for teachers, including relatively inexperienced ones whom they train in their own method.

In Advance

The best place to start for a list of language schools is the Education Department of the Spanish Labour Office (20 Peel St, London W8 7PD; 0171-221 0098). As well as sending an outline of Spanish immigration regulations and a one-page handout 'Teaching English as a Foreign Language', it can send a list of the 350 members of FECEI, the national federation of English language schools *(Federación Española de Centros de Enseñanza de Idiomas)*, though they may not always have the most up-to-date list available. Americans can obtain analagous information from the Spanish Education Office at the Consulate General in San Francisco (1405 Sutter St, San Francisco, CA 94109; 415-922-2308).

FECEI is concerned with maintaining high standards, so its members are committed to providing a high quality of teaching and fair working conditions for teachers. In order to become a member, a school has to undergo a thorough inspection. Therefore FECEI schools represent the elite end of the market and are normally looking for well qualified teachers. The presidency of FECEI is a rotating one. At present the contact is Mr. Frank Spain, Calle Miguel Servet 1, 13500 Puertollano, Ciudad Real (926-42 7537). FECEI comprises 16 regional associations integrated in ACADE (Asociación de Centros Autónomos de Enseñanza Privada, Avda. Alberto Alcocer 46, 28016 Madrid; 91-344 0915/fax 91-344 1583).

The book *Teaching English in Spain* by Jenny Johnson (the director of International House in Barcelona) contains a list of about 40 schools but, more usefully, has a lot of detailed information about the job hunt in Spain. The book (published in 1998 in association with International House) can be ordered through bookshops (ISBN 1 873047 12 6) or from the publishers In Print; the price is £11.99.

Otherwise it will be a matter of consulting the Yellow Pages *(Las Paginas Amarillos)* at specialist libraries in your home country (or preferably once you're in Spain). The Madrid Yellow Pages even carries an advert for an EFL teacher recruitment service at Aximedia Idiomes, C/ Uruguay 11 (91-413 8995/fax 91-415 7951). Although fewer jobs are advertised in the British educational press than formerly, there is a good sprinkling.

Most of the regional British Council offices in Spain maintain lists of language schools in their region (which partially duplicates FECEI lists) apart from Madrid which does not keep a register of schools. The Seville office has separate lists for the eight provinces of Andalucia (Seville, Cadiz, Cordoba, Huelva, Malaga, Granada, Jaén and Almeriá). The offices in Bilbao, Barcelona and Palma de Mallorca also produce useful lists.

British or Irish nationals with a TEFL qualification or PGCE might want to make use of a recruitment agency, whether a general one or one which specialises in Spain such as English Educational Services (Alcalá 20-2°, 28014 Madrid; 91-532 9734/531 4783/fax 531 5298). The owner Richard Harrison recommends that candidates with just a degree and CELTA come to Spain in early September and contact his agency on arrival. He works in conjunction with schools all over Spain. Another agency ESS (English and Spanish Studies, Macmillan House, 96 Kensington High St, London W8 4SG; 0171-937 3110) is less active but advertises vacancies in Catalonia and elsewhere from time to time.

On the Spot

Most teaching jobs in Spain are found on the spot. With increasing competition from candidates with the Cambridge or Trinity Certificate (now considered by many language school owners a minimum requirement), it is more and more difficult for the under-qualified to succeed. The best time to look is between the end of the summer holidays and the start of term, normally October 1st. November is also promising, since that is when teachers hand in their notice for a Christmas departure. Since a considerable number of teachers do not return to their jobs after the Christmas break and schools are often left in the lurch, early January is also possible.

The beginning of summer is the worst time to travel out to Spain to look for work since schools will be closed and their owners unobtainable. There are some language teaching jobs in the summer at residential English camps for children and teenagers, but these are usually more for young people looking for a working holiday as camp monitors than for EFL teachers.

If you want a base from which to look for work and some contact with the kinds of Spaniards who are eager to learn English, you might like to consider a live-in position with a family who wants an English tutor for their children. One agency involved in this kind of placement is GIC, Pintor Sorolla 29, Apdo. 1080, 46901 Monte Vedat (Valencia), or alternatively c/o Pilar Garreta, Apdo. 199, 03730 Javea (Alicante).

The experiences of Jon Loop from Hampshire during his successful job hunt in Madrid in October illustrate that persistence is the key:

> *I travelled to Madrid from Bordeaux in October. I had given a few English lessons in France, but basically I had no experience and no qualifications. I copied down lots of addresses from the Madrid Yellow Pages under the heading 'Academias de Enseñanza Idiomas' and just went round all of them leaving my CV. I got three hours a week after 45 schools and a further three hours after number 75. I visited five more then gave up and waited for the two schools to give me more hours.*
>
> *At the interviews, they asked the usual questions about experience, teaching methods (always say you use media materials), etc. I just looked them in the eye and lied. However I was fairly confident that I could teach English. Since I had been to so many schools previously these interviews were easy, and I had managed to build up a very good CV.*

When knocking on doors, bear in mind that most language academies will be closed between 2pm and 4pm when directors are invariably away from their desks. Try to leave a contact telephone number (most pensions won't mind). A serious director will probe into any claims of experience and will soon weed out any bogus stories. Other directors are just checking to see that you are a reasonable proposition or at least not a complete dud.

A more probable scenario for the untrained is that they will elicit some mild interest from one or two schools and will be told that they may be contacted right at the beginning of term and offered a few hours of teaching. Spanish students sign up for English classes during September and into early October. Consequently the academies do not know how many classes they will offer and how many teachers they will need until quite late. It can become a war of nerves; anyone who is willing and can afford to stay on has an increasingly good chance of becoming established. After going a certain distance in looking for a teaching job, the American George Kelly lost his nerve and abandoned the fray:

> *I arrived in September and spent about two weeks in Madrid looking for an English teaching job. I contacted about 40 schools and had received only one firm offer when I left Spain on September 21st. Many schools told me that they would contact me if they ended up needing teachers, and I believe at least a few of them would have called me.*

If in Madrid, try to locate a copy of the Blue Pages, a directory organised by street. It is possible to pick out language schools in selected neighbourhoods this way, i.e. near where you are staying. It also includes a useful grid map of the Madrid metropolitan area. Alternatively, of course, you can simply wander the streets looking for schools. The density is so high that you are bound to come across several.

Other sources of job vacancy information includes the Madrid daily *El Pais* which usually has a few relevant classifieds under the heading *Trabajo—Idiomas*. Also try *Ya, ABC* or *Segundamano,* Madrid's classified ad paper (published Monday, Wednesday and Friday) which usually carries a good selection of relevant ads under the heading *Empleo* (rather than *Idiomas—Inglés*). The free English language monthly magazine *Barcelona Metropolitan* (Provenza 161, Entlo. 2, 08036 Barcelona) seems to carry more 'Job Search' ads than 'Jobs Offered', but it might carry something of interest for instance 'Wanted—Native English speaker to exchange conversation with Spanish native speaker' or 'We are looking for a group of people to speak/practise English with'. The 'Bulletin Board' column of a past issue contained this interesting possibiity:

> *Free language intercambios—Anyone wishing to practise their English, Catalan or Spanish should get along to the Lincoln Pizzeria (Calle Lincoln 17, next to Otto Zutz) every Friday from about 9am to midnight where you will encounter 70-90 people chattering the night away.*

The magazine is distributed through bookshops; as usual English language bookshops sometimes have a notice board with relevant notices. Also look for *La Vanguardia* in Barcelona.

Although the majority of job-seekers head for Madrid or Barcelona, other towns may answer your requirements better. There are language academies all along the north coast and a door-to-door job hunt in September might pay off. This is the time when tourists are departing so accommodation may be available at a reasonable rent on a nine-month lease.

Freelance Teaching

As usual, private tutoring pays better than contract teaching because there is no middle man. According to Glen Williams, the going rate in Granada starts at about pta1,500 for individuals and from pta2,000 for teaching three or four at once. Freelance rates in Madrid are much higher (pta 3,000) but travelling time has to be taken into consideration. Stuart Britton easily found private pupils to supplement his school income in a small town in the untouristy north of Las Palmas de Gran Canaria. However when his employer found out, he was told to drop them or risk being sacked, even over the summer when the school was closed and Stuart had no other source of income. He resented this so much that he advises not bothering with small schools, and simply concentrate on obtaining private students. He goes on to complain that his advertising for private classes proved useless (his notices were often taken down and newspaper adverts produced nothing) which rather detracts from his advice.

As always, it is difficult to start up without contacts and a good knowledge of the language; and when you do get started it is difficult to earn a stable income due to the frequency with which pupils cancel. The problem is particularly acute in May when school pupils concentrate on preparing for exams and other activities fall by the wayside. Spaniards are fond of their *puente*, the bridge between a mid-week fiesta and the weekend.

Getting private lessons is a marketing exercise and you will have to explore all the avenues which seem appropriate to your circumstances. Obviously you can advertise on notice boards at universities, public libraries, corner shops and wherever you think there is a market. Major stores are a good bet, for example Jumbo and Al Campo in Madrid. A neat notice in Spanish along the lines of 'Profesora Nativa da clases particulares a domicilió' might elicit a favourable response. Send neat notices to local state schools asking them to pin it up broadcasting your willingness to ensure the children's linguistic future. Compile a list of addresses of professionals (e.g. lawyers, architects, etc.) as they may need English for their work and have the wherewithal to pay for it. Try export businesses, distribution companies, perhaps even travel agencies. Make the acquaintance of language teachers who will know of openings. Place adverts in free papers (like *El 18*) and in advertising papers (like *Almoneda* in Granada).

Because private classes are so much better paid than institute teaching, they are much in demand, including by contract teachers, most of whom are engaged in some private tutoring. The ideal is to arrange a school contract with no more than 15 or 20 hours and supplement this with private classes which are lucrative though unstable.

REGULATIONS

Patience is required to deal with the paperwork required by EU nationals after starting work. In order to obtain a residence permit *(residencia)*, employees must take a copy of their contract (in Spanish and officially stamped) to the *Oficina de Extrangería* or, if there isn't a local foreigners' registration office, the *Comisaría Provincial de Policia*. It will also be necessary to queue in various offices to obtain a foreigners' identity number (NIE) from the police and a fiscal identity number (NIF) from the tax office *(Hacienda)*. When the *residencia* is eventually granted, it is valid for five years. Many foreigners resort to engaging a specialist lawyer called a *gestoria* to assist.

The immigration situation for people from outside Europe has become increasingly difficult. Most of the schools which once hired large numbers of North Americans are no longer willing to tackle the lengthy procedures involved in obtaining work permits. As the director of one school explained:

> *The Spanish authorities have rejected all the applications we have made in the past year, using Spain's high unemployment rate as their justification. An appeal now takes at least two years and costs a small fortune in legal fees. This means that we will be employing fewer non-European Union citizens in the future. Candidates have to be very qualified for us to consider them in the first place. Many Americans have now caught on to this problem and apply for Irish or Italian nationality if they are eligible.*

This pessimistic view of the chances for Americans and Canadians was voiced by so many schools that it seems almost superfluous to describe the procedures. Briefly, work permit applications must be lodged and collected in the applicant's country of residence. The application must include a formal job offer from an employer in Spain, a recent medical certificate, *antecedents penales* (police certificate of good character), notarised degree certificate and seven passport photographs. The future employer then applies for the work and residence permits.

None of this means that there aren't any Americans or other nationalities teaching in Spain. Jon Loop's fellow teachers in Madrid were mainly Americans who had no permits whatsoever. According to Jon, many post-Hemingway Americans go to Spain for a year to learn Spanish and 'find themselves man' (as opposed to find themselves a man).

Social security *(seguridad social)* contributions are between 4% and 7% of earnings. Under EU legislation, language schools must give contracts and make contributions for all staff, whether full-time or part-time. In practice, this does not always happen. After a few months of teaching for one academy, Jon Loop asked for a contract and was given a special 11-hour contract (though at the time he was teaching 20 hours a week). Contracts for less than 12 hours a week do not require more than minimal social security contributions. Joanna Mudie from the Midlands describes the situation which results from this:

> *There's a great deal of uncertainty and insecurity about all aspects of work: hours, days, rates of pay, insurance, etc. Contracts (if you're lucky enough to get one) are a load of rubbish because employers put down far fewer hours on paper to avoid paying so much insurance, and also to protect themselves if business dwindles... My advice is, forget your English sense of honesty and obeying the law. 'When in Rome...' Relax and simply don't worry about the legalities. It usually seems to work out okay, and if not, well, it's a nice life in the sun.*

Tax deductions are paid in arrears and do not normally affect teachers on nine-month contracts, though in some cases a small percentage is withdrawn at source *(retenciones)*. Technically any person who spends more than 183 days a year in Spain is considered a resident and is liable to pay Spanish tax, though Spain has a double taxation treaty with the UK.

All those schools which sidestep the regulations to maximise profits do not pay contributions to cover their employees' social security. On the other hand, they might well employ non-Europeans and pay cash-in-hand.

Anyone who works on a tourist visa will have to renew it every three months by leaving the country. Weekend trips to France or Portugal can be organised for this purpose.

CONDITIONS OF WORK

Salaries are not high in Spain and have not increased significantly over the last seven years. A further problem for teachers in Madrid and Barcelona is that there is not much difference between salaries in the big cities where the cost of living has escalated enormously and salaries in the small towns. The minimum net salary is about pta100,000 per month, though most schools offer pta120,000 to pta140,000 for a minimum of 25 hours a week. David Bourne found this sufficient in the town of Gijon in Asturias where he taught for nine months:

> *Prices and rents here are not as bad as they are in the big cities like Madrid, Seville and Barcelona, so most schools live quite happily on their take-home wages. I have been able to save pta230,000 without having to live too stringently for example.*

The best paid hourly wage, say pta2,000, is paid to teachers who are sent out to firms or those teaching short courses which are funded by the European Union, typically of unemployed professionals in their 20s.

Spanish TEFL is no different from TEFL in other countries in that there are lots of employers offering low pay, long hours and exploitative conditions. For example teachers have discovered that pay has been deducted when they have been unavoidably absent or that their bonuses have been withheld with no explanation. As always, you can gain an idea of an employer's integrity by talking to other teachers as well as by using your intuition at the interview. Asking lots of questions is a good idea since then you can find out your pay and maximum hours so that you will be in a stronger position to argue should your employer try to mess you around. But realistically, most new arrivals are exploited at least in some respects in their first year. Laura Phibbs was spared the possibility of being exploited, since her promised job evaporated overnight:

> *The Madrid school director rang me to inform me that I had got the job and I was to start nine days later. When, as instructed, I rang to confirm the arrival time of my plane, I was told that there was no job for me after all since the school had gone bankrupt. I think what really made me angry was that I had rung him rather than the other way round. He did not even say sorry or sound in the least remorseful.*

The same school continues to be listed by the Association of Private Language Schools (ACADE) but not in this book, so it may be that pleading bankruptcy was just an excuse in the face of insufficient pupils.

Increasingly schools do not offer full-time work. Those that do tend to work their teachers very hard, expecting them to teach around 30 hours; the legal maximum is 33. Considering that preparation and travelling is extra, this can result in a gruelling schedule. Dennis Bricault refers to the notoriously uncongenial timetable of most EFL teachers (and not just in Spain) as a 'bookend schedule', whereby you might have to teach between 8am and 10am, then again through the evening. Most teachers put up with the late finishing time without too many murmurs because they are not deprived of Spanish nightlife even if they have to work until 10pm.

According to Spanish law, workers are not entitled to paid holiday until they have been working for 12 months, hence the near-universality of nine-month contracts. Most teachers find it impossible to save enough in nine months to fund themselves abroad for the rest of the year. Most pay agreements also take account of bonuses (*pagas extraordinaria*) of which there are two or three a year. Legal schools will pay *finiquito* (holiday pay) at the end of a contract which should work out to be about £50 for every month worked.

If the terms of a contract are being breached and the employer does not respond to the teacher's reminders, recourse can be taken to a *denuncio*, which involves informing the authorities (either in person or via a union, such as the Commissiones Obreros) that your school is not complying with tax and social security rules or fire regulations or whatever. The *denuncio* can effectively close a school if it is taken seriously and if the school does not have the proverbial friends in high places. In fact the procedure is complicated and time-consuming but the mere mention of it *might* improve your working conditions.

The experience of teaching at a summer camp is entirely different. The pay is fairly good (say, pta100,000-120,000 for a four-week stint plus free board and accommodation), though some organisations offer little more than accommodation, meals and pocket money. Glen Williams describes his summer job at a summer language camp in Izarra in the Basque Country:

> *The children learned English for three hours in the morning with one half hour break (but not for the teacher on morning snack duty trying to fight off the hordes from ripping apart the bocadillos). Then we had another three or four hours of duties ranging from sports and/or arts to shop/bank duty. For many of us, inexperienced with dealing with groups of kids, there were a few problems of discipline. It was the kids' holiday and they quickly cottoned on that we English teachers in general were a bunch of hippies.*

Pupils

For reasons which remain obscure, Spaniards have the reputation for being hopeless at languages, possibly as a result of unreasonable expectations. This is more tolerable in the adults who are fairly well motivated, but often hard-going with children (unless you are especially fond of kids). This was one of David Bourne's biggest problems and one which he thinks is underestimated, especially as a higher proportion of English teaching in Spain is now of children and teenagers:

> *I have found that a lot of the younger students only come here because their parents have sent them in order to improve their exam results. The children themselves would much rather be outside playing football. There are days when you spend most of the lesson trying (unsuccessfully in my case) to keep them quiet. This is especially true on Fridays. I have found it very hard work trying to inject life into a class of bored ten year olds, particularly when the course books provided are equally uninspiring.*

In such cases it might be a good idea to change your aim, from teaching them English to entertaining them (and paying your rent). If students don't want to learn, you will only break your heart trying to achieve the impossible.

A good knowledge of Spanish is helpful if not essential when teaching junior classes as Peter Saliba, Director of the Cross School in Malaga, explains:

> *We need teachers with a fluent command of Spanish, not the typical grasp of elementary phrases which may get them by in a social context. On a limited two or three hour per week teaching timetable, there simply is not time for cumbersome English explanations of English grammar and vocabulary. It is worse still with young learners and teens, who will 'run riot' or at the very least run circles round non-Castilian speaking teachers.*

Classes differ enormously as Jon Loop found during his year of teaching at an academy in Madrid:

> *A lot of my groups were civil servants. They were excruciating because they didn't want to be there. The government has to spend its language training budget and picks people at random. I taught other classes of university students who were very enthusiastic and were great to work with. I taught a group of technicians at the meteorological office who were keen because it was directly linked to their work. Then I taught groups from companies who were not very keen to start with, but by the end of the year we were having a great time. It's classes like this that make teaching worthwhile.*

Jon recommends making good use of your students, since so many Spaniards are friendly and eager to help. If you are having trouble with a recalcitrant landlord, perhaps a letter from a trainee lawyer you happen to be teaching might solve the problem. Students may lend you an unoccupied holiday house or put you in touch with friends looking for private English lessons. In Jon's case, a student arranged for him to spend the harvest at a family vineyard and another helped him to fix up work editing technical papers.

Needless to say, Spaniards are a nation of talkers. If things seem to be going awry in your classes, for example students turning up late or being inattentive, don't pussyfoot around. Make your feelings known, just as Spaniards do.

Accommodation

Rents usually swallow up at least a quarter of a teacher's income, more in the big cities. In small towns, it is not uncommon for schools to arrange accommodation for their teachers. Many Spanish students want to live with English students so check university notice boards for flat shares, especially in the *Facultad de Filosofia y Letras* which includes the Department of English. Some teachers even arrange to share a flat rent-free in exchange for English lessons. Try to avoid using a *finca* (property agency) which will charge at least a month's rent. In Madrid many people use the free ads paper *Segundamano;* if you do decide to compete for a flat listed in this paper, get up early since most flats are gone by 8am.

LEISURE TIME

Once you acquire some Spanish, it is very easy to meet people, since Spaniards are so friendly, relaxed and willing to invite newcomers out with them. Of course there is also a strong fraternity of EFL teachers almost everywhere. With luck you will end up socialising with both groups in bars, at parties, *romerías* (pilgrimages), fiestas, etc.

Spain is a good country for wine-drinking film-goers but not so good for gadget-addicts with poor teeth. Eating, drinking, smoking, entertainment and transport (including taxis) are all still cheap, though this advantage is cancelled out for some by the high cost of other things such as clothes, cars and electrical items, not to mention contraceptives, standard chemists' products and dental care. The cost of living gets lower the longer you stay and discover where the locals get their bargains.

If you're looking for traditional Spanish culture, don't go to Madrid, and certainly don't look for it in Barcelona which is not Spanish at all but Catalan. Seville, Granada and Valencia are lovely Spanish cities. While teaching in Andalucia, Joanna Mudie appreciated the chance to learn about the traditional but still very much alive dances of Spain, e.g. Sevillanas, Malagueras and Pasadoble. If you're looking for an idyllic Mediterranean climate don't go to northern Spain in mid-winter. After teaching in Segovia north of Madrid for a year, Eleanor Sedgwick concluded that it rained more there than in Manchester. But most teachers have little fault to find with the climate. Stuart Britton, who paints, was thrilled by the glorious blue light in which to paint historic castles and colourful narrow streets lined with gorgeous balconies.

Glen Williams describes his spare time activities in Madrid, a city he was clearly enjoying to the full:

> *Madrid is a crazy place. We usually stay out all night at the weekend drinking and boogying. During the gaps in my timetable (10-2 and 4-7) I pretend to study Spanish (I'm no natural) and just wander the back streets. I suppose I should try to be more cultural and learn to play an instrument, write poetry or look at paintings, but I never get myself in gear. I think most people teach English in Spain as a means to live in Spain and learn the Spanish language and culture. But there is a real problem that you end up living in an English enclave, teaching English all day and socialising with English teachers. You have to make a big effort to get out of this rut. I am lucky to live with Spanish people (who do not want to practise their English!).*

A few schools offer free or subsidised Spanish lessons as a perk to teachers. Otherwise investigate the government-run *Escuela Oficial de Idiomas.*

There are so many people teaching English in different situations that there is no average profile. Jon Shurlock worked alongside both reformed alcoholics whose lives had fallen apart and the usual middle class 'jolly nice' people taking a year or two out. While one teacher finds the locals cold and hostile and money-grubbing, another finds them warm and supportive. If the idea of teaching in Spain appeals at all, it is almost always a rewarding and memorable way for people with limited work experience to finance themselves as they travel and live abroad for a spell.

LIST OF SCHOOLS

All schools prefer their teachers to have European Union nationality (and most will not consider applicants without it) and to have a university degree, Cambridge/RSA Certificate (or equivalent) and knowledge of Spanish. Although some may be prepared to consider less, especially from candidates with some business experience or experience teaching children, the ever-increasing number of qualified applicants means that the occasions when schools need to do so are diminishing.

The standard negotiated contract is about pta150,000 per month for a full-time teacher, though net salaries tend to fluctuate between pta125,000 and pta160,000 depending on number of hours worked. The average range of hourly wage is pta1,500-2,000, though a few schools still try to pay pta1,000 an hour and pta100,000 a month. Rates are usually a little higher in Madrid and Barcelona. The best plan is to pick out the schools in the city or province which appeals to you, and write off for details enclosing a CV, photograph and international reply coupons. Most schools carry out their selection procedure of new teachers between April and July, though if you arrive in person to look for a job in September at one of the listed schools, your chances of success are reasonable.

Because of the shift from a teachers' to an employers' market over the past ten years, quite a few schools are reluctant to publicise expected job vacancies for fear of being inundated with applications. The following list of schools is divided into the ones which actively encourage TEFL-trained job-seekers to contact them and those others which may have vacancies from time to time. Bear in mind that a personal visit is always more likely to lead to success than an unsolicited CV by post.

Instead of including full entries for the schools, we have provided a skeletal list of names and addresses of schools willing to consider applications, followed in brackets by the number of native speaker teachers which they expect to employ each year and in some cases some brief annotations. Note that the country prefix to Spanish telephone numbers is 34, and as of April 1998 all area codes are preceded by a 9. Schools are listed alphabetically by town or city.

LANGUAGE CENTRE: C/ Convento 5, 46970 Alaquas (Valencia). Tel/fax: (96) 150 6760. Also branch in Aldaya. (3-4). Teachers normally work part-time and earn pta1,300-1,400 per hour plus contract.

EL CENTRO DE INGLÉS: Juego Pelotas 10, 23740 Andújar (Jaén). Tel/fax: (953) 506821. (2-3). Contact: Julia Hetherington. Prefer experience teaching children and teenagers. Mostly evening classes.

THE AVILA CENTRE OF ENGLISH: Bajada de Don Alonso 1, 05003 Avila. Tel: (920) 213719. Fax: (920) 213631. E-mail: ace@avila.net. (6-7). To teach young children.

BRITISH SCHOOL BARCELONA—fax: (93) 893 7656. E-mail: british@abaforum.es. Advertising recently for qualified teachers with 2 years' experience.

INTERNATIONAL HOUSE: Calle Trafalgar 14 entlo, 08010 Barcelona. Tel: 93-268 4511. Fax: 93-268 0239. (15-20). E-mail: ihbarcelona@bcn.ihes.com. Run CELTA course and hire teachers who have passed the CELTA with an A or B. Maximum 20 h.p.w., pta150,000 per month gross.

LEWIS SCHOOL OF LANGUAGES, Gran Via Carlos III, 97 bajos K, 08028 Barcelona. Tel: (93) 339 2608. Fax: (93) 411 1333. (5). pta1,500 per hour (depending on experience).

MERIT SCHOOL, Campo Florido 54-56, 08027 Barcelona. Tel: (93) 408 1550. Fax: (93)408 2453. (30-40).

WALL STREET INSTITUTE SPAIN: Sylvan Learning Systems, Rambla de Catalunya 2-4, 08007 Barcelona. Tel: (93) 412 0014. Fax: (93) 412 3803. Average of 4-5 teachers at 140 centres.

WALL STREET INSTITUTE: C/ Font Vella 50, 08221 Terrassa (Barcelona). Tel: (93) 784 3131. Fax: (93) 784 3322.

SECOND LANGUAGE ACQUISITION: Autonomía 26, 6° A, 48010 Bilbao (94-444 8062. Fax: (94) 444 8066. (20).

INSTITUTE OF ENGLISH: Mendizábal 77, 46100 Burjassot (Valencia). Tel: (96) 363 2881. Fax: (96) 363 5999. E-mail: inst.eng@arrakis.es. (5).

TELC ENGLISH STUDY CENTRE: Av. Andalucia 8, 6°, 11006 Cadiz. Tel: (956)

271097. Fax: (956) 264358. (10). Interviews take place in UK. Looking for teachers with DELTA or LTCL diploma and minimum of 2 years' experience.

BIG BEN COLLEGE: Centro de Idiomas, Plaza del Raso 13, 26500 Calahorra (La Rioja). Tel: (941) 132130. Fax: (941) 146330. (5-8).

NUMBER NINE ENGLISH LANGUAGE CENTRE: C/ Sant Onofre 1, 07760 Ciutadella de Menorca (Baleares). Tel/fax: (971) 384058. (1-2).

PICCADILLY ENGLISH INSTITUTE, C/ Acacias 11, bjo dcha, 14006 Cordoba. Tel: (957) 280205. (3).

ENGLISH INSTITUTE: Carrer La Mar 38, 03700 Denia (Alicante). Tel: (96) 578 1026. E-mail: tei@arrakis.es. (6).

THE ENGLISH COLLEGE: Carrer Empedrat 4, 03203 Elche (Alicante). Tel: (96) 545 8401. Fax: (96) 545 2302. (5).

INSTITUTE OF MODERN LANGUAGES: Puerta Real 1, 18009 Granada. Tel: (958) 225536. Also at Divina Pastora 9, Portal 13 (Bajo), 18012 Granada; tel: 206100. (14).

CAMBRIDGE SCHOOL: Placa Manel Montanyà 4, 1a, 08400 Granollers (Barcelona). Tel: (93) 870 2001. Fax: (93) 879 5111. (30).

SAN ROQUE SCHOOL OF ENGLISH: Paseo San Roque 1, 19002 Guadalajara. Tel: (949) 217445. Fax: (949) 222302. (6 part-time and 2 full-time). Car drivers preferred for on-site teaching.

EUROPEAN LANGUAGE STUDIES: Edificio Edimburgo, Plaza Niña, 21003 Huelva. Tel: (959) 263821/263862. Fax: (959) 280778. (22). New multimedia centre with 16 computers.

ESCUELA DE IDIOMAS DE JAEN: Doctor Sagaz 18, 23001 Jaen.

SAM'S ACADEMY: Dtres. Castroviejo 29 1° Izda, 26003 Logroña (La Rioja). Tel: (941) 259125. (4). CELTA or BA needed.

ACE CONSULTORES DE IDIOMAS: Capitán Haya 21, 28020 Madrid. Tel: (91) 555 0800. Fax: (91) 597 3262. (50). Business experience preferred as well as ELT training/experience.

ALBION ENGLISH CENTRE: Juan de Cardona 3, 28805 Alcala de Henares (Madrid). Tel: (91) 888 7203. (12 in three centres).

AMERICAN LANGUAGE ACADEMY, Rodríguez San Pedro 2, 609, 28015 Madrid. Tel: (91) 445 5511/445 31 96.

BERLITZ LANGUAGE CENTRE: Gran Via 80, 4°, 28013 Madrid. Tel: (91) 542 3586. Fax: (91) 541 2765. (20-40). Summer positions also available. Advertisements asking for university grads placed in *Guardian;* interviews held in London in June and September. 5 other branches in Madrid.

THE BRITISH LANGUAGE CENTRE: Calle Bravo Murillo 377-2°, 28020 Madrid. Tel: (91) 733 07 39. Fax: (91) 314 50 09. Prestigious centre which runs CELTA courses.

CAMBRIDGE HOUSE: Méndez Alvaro 2, 1° A, 28045 Madrid. Tel: (91) 528 1335. Near metro Atocha. Branches also at C/ López de Hoyos, 95-1A, 28002 Madrid (91-519 4603), C/ Federic Gutiérrez 4-1A, 28027 Madrid (91-377 1179) and C/ Bravo Murillo 153-1C, 29020 Madrid (91-450 0551).

CHESTER SCHOOL OF ENGLISH: Jorge Juan 125, Madrid 28009. Tel: (91) 402 5879. Fax: (91) 401 0673/e-mail: chester@servicom.es/ http://www.chester.es/tefl (20).

DANIEL'S CENTRE, Hilados, 14 Post, 28840 Torrejon de Ardoz (Madrid). Tel/fax: (91) 676 2632. (3-4). Interviews in Oxford in July c/o Oxford English Centre, Wolsey Hall, 66 Banbury Road, Oxford OX2 6PR.

LINGUACENTER BUSINESS LANGUAGE SCHOOL, Calle Rafael Calvo 8, 28010 Madrid. Tel: (91) 447 0300. Fax: (91) 447 07 81. (100+). Demo lesson compulsory.

OPEN SCHOOL OF LANGUAGES, Velázquez 30, 28001 Madrid. Tel: (91) 431 8425. Fax: (91) 435 45 64. Branches at P° Castellana 74, 28046 Madrid (91-564 0022), P° Habana 22, 28036 Madrid (91-411 5215) and Marquès de Urquijo 5, 28008 Madrid (91-541 3100).

CROSS IDIOMAS, C/ Esperanto 19-1°, Of. 7, 29007 Málaga. Tel/fax: (95) 228 0148. (2-3). Prefer teachers over 25 with experience of preparing Cambridge exams including the Business English Certificate (BEC). Fluent Spanish needed for teaching children and teenagers.

CENTRO BRITANICO: Avda. Rodríguez Acosta 6 (PO Box 201, 18600 Motril (Granada). Tel/fax: (958) 600937. E-mail: centro.britanico@grx.servicom.es. Also at Canalejas 3, 23700 Linares (Jaén); tel/fax: 699526. (12). Run summer camp in Viznar near Granada.

ALCE (AUDIOVISUAL LANGUAGE CENTRE): Pasaje de los Nogales 2, 33006 Oviedo. Tel: (985 525 4543. E-mail: alce.idiomas@fade.es. (2 -3).

LORD'S LANGUAGE CENTRE: C/ General Elorza 63 1°F, 33002 Oviedo (Asturias). Tel/fax: (98) 522 8438. (5). Must have EU nationality, CELTA or equivalent, and experience of teaching children and teenagers. Salary of pta115,000.

THE SCHOOL (ENGLISH LEARNING CENTRE): C/ Fray Ceferino 26, 1°I, 33001 Oviedo. Tel: (98)522 8838.

YORK IDIOMAS: C/ Muñoz Degrain 9, 33007 Oviedo. Tel/fax: (98) 524 1341. E-mail: yorkschool@fade.es. Also at C/ Mariscal Solís 5, 33012 Oviedo; tel: (98) 527 14 10, and C/ Bermúdez de Castro 19, 33011 Oviedo; tel: (98) 529 42 49. (5). Pupils from age 4.

EL CENTRO INGLES: Apto. de Correos 85, (Ctra. de Fuentebravia, Km. 1), 11500 El Puerto de Santa María (Cádiz). Tel: (956) 850560. Fax: (956) 873804. (20). Teacher certification preferred for teaching pupils from age 2 in this partially English-medium private school. Also employ 'student teachers' on a year out from university or with TEFL to work with small groups.

NELSON ENGLISH SCHOOL: Jorge Manrique 1, 38005 Santa Cruz de Tenerife. Tel: (922) 218919. Fax: (922) 201555. (7). 80% of students are children aged 6-14. Hourly rate is pta1,700.

INLINGUA IDIOMAS: Avda de Pontejos 5, 39005 Santander. Tel: (942) 278465. Fax: (942) 274402. E-mail: inlingua-sdr@nexo.es. http://www.inlingua.com/ Santander.htm. Two centres in Santander and another in Castro Urdiales, 75km away. (6). Occasionally have short summer vacancies at residential camp.

ENGLISH 1: Marques del Nervion 116, 41005 Seville. Tel: (95) 464 2098. E-mail: english1@arrakis.es. (6). On-the-spot interviews given in September. TEFL Certificate plus experience teaching children needed. Minimum pta150,000 per month.

BRITISH SCHOOL: Plaça Ponent 5-2°, 43001 Tarragona. Tel: (977) 211605. Fax: (977) 211605. (7).

MANGOLD INSTITUTE: Av. Marques de Sotelo, Pasaje Rex 2, 46002 Valencia. Tel: (96) 352 7714. Fax: (96) 361 4556. Branch at: Calle Santo Duque 5-1°, 46700 Gandia (Valencia). Tel/fax: (96) 287 3116. Also 4 other branches. (10).

THE ENGLISH CENTRE: Plaza Paradis 2, 08500 Vic. Tel: (93) 8890578. Fax: (93) 889 1969. E-mail: norris@filnet.es. (15). pta134,000 per month for $9\frac{1}{2}$ months plus 1 month holiday pay.

EUROSCHOOLS: Regueiro 2, 36211 Vigo. Tel/fax: (986) 291748. E-mail: euroschool@moriatys.com. Also at Gregorio Espino 4, 36206 Vigo; tel: 378600. (15).

VIGVATTEN NATUR KLUBB: Apartado No. 3253, 01002 Vitoria-Gasteiz. Tel/fax: (945) 281794. (15). Run English language and sports summer camps in the Basque country, Pyrenees and Sierra de Urbion. Monitors receive free board and lodging and pocket money.

OXFORD CENTRO DE IDIOMAS: San Miguel 16, pral., 50001 Zaragoza. Tel: (76) 221810/211120. Fax: (76) 212010. (10-12).

Other Schools to Try (cities and towns in alphabetical order)

Note that these schools did not confirm their teacher requirements for this edition of *Teaching English Abroad*.

CAMBRIDGE SCHOOL IDIOMAS: Dos de Mayo, 26, 46960 Aldaya.
THE ALGINET ENGLISH CENTRE: Reyes Católicos, 52-2a, 46230 Alginet.

STANTON SCHOOL OF ENGLISH: Angel Lozano, 10-3° izq, 03001 Alicante. Tel: (96) 520 7581. Candidates must teach a demonstration class and take a test in English.

ENGLISH CENTRE: College of Languages, C/ José Artés de Arcos 34, 04004 Almeria. Tel: (951) 234551. Fax: (951) 272738. (96-7 British or Americans). Prefer teachers with experience of teaching children.

CAMBRIDGE CENTRE: Avda. Santos Patronos 25, 46600 Alzira (Valencia). Tel/fax: (96) 241 18 79. (5-7). BA plus minimum 2 years experience wanted.

CENTRE CULTURAL: Passeig de 1 Estació 25, 25600 Balaguer. Tel: (973) 445429. (91-2). Knowledge of Catalan or Spanish desirable.

BRIGHTON IDIOMAS: Rambla Catalunya 66, 08007 Barcelona. Tel: (93) 488 3060. Fax: (93) 216 0747. Summer and academic year vacancies in Barcelona and Madrid. BA plus 2 years' experience required.

CIC ESCOLA D'IDIOMES: Via Augusta 205, 08021 Barcelona.

ENGLISH CENTRE: Paseo Manual, Girona 12, 08034 Barcelona.

ENGLISH LANGUAGE INSTITUTE: Via Augusta 59 4t, 08006 Barcelona.

EUROLOG IDIOMES: Plaza Lesseps 4, 080023 Barcelona.

ICL: Av. Joseph Tarradellas 106 2° 3a, 08029 Barcelona.

INSTITUTE MANGOLD: Rambla Catalunya 16, 08007 Barcelona.

INSTITUTE OF NORTH AMERICAN STUDIES: Via Augusta 123, 08006 Barcelona. Tel: (93) 209 2711. Fax: (93) 202 0690. (85-100). Americans and Canadians. MA plus minimum 2 years' overseas experience.

LINGUARAMA: Gran Via de Carlos III 98, 2°, Edificios Trade, 08028 Barcelona.

OPEN ENGLISH INTERNATIONAL GROUP, S.A., Rambla Catalunya 38, 08007 Barcelona. Fax: (93) 215 0671; e-mail: didactic@openingschool.com).

WINDSOR SCHOOL: Av. Diagonal 319, pral, 4a, 08009 Barcelona.

YOUR HOUSE LANGUAGE SCHOOL: Pl. Nova 15, 08570 Torelló, Barcelona. Tel/fax: (93) 859 2704. (5-10).

THE ACADEMY OF LANGUAGES: Paseo Alfonso XIII 47-49, Apdo. 426, 30203 Cartagena (Murcia). Tel: (968) 520942. Fax: 521988. (12). BA minimum. Initial training given to the inexperienced.

SKILLS CENTRO DE IDIOMAS: Trinidad 94-1°, 2002 Castellon. Tel: (964) 242668. (4). Majority of teaching to children.

KENSINGTON CENTROS DE IDIOMAS: Avda. Pedro Muguruza 8, 20870 Elgoibar. Tel/fax: (943) 740236. Also: Errekalde Auzoa 5, 20577 Antzuola. Tel/fax: (943) 787030.

THE ENGLISH HOUSE ACADEMY: C/ Iglesia 36, 2°, 15402 Ferrol. Tel: (981) 354223. (92).

EXETER ENGLISH SCHOOL: C/ Uria 15-1°A, 33202 Gijon (Asturias). Tel: (985) 533 0070. Also at C/ Pérez de Ayala 31, 33208 Gijon; tel: 516 2876, and C/ Fdez. Ladreda 22, 33430 Candas; tel: 587 1702. (10).

EIS ESCOLA D'IDIOMES: Girona (e-mail: tracuceis@grn.es). Must speak Spanish or Catalan and be aged 25-35.

THE ENGLISH SCHOOL: Calle Bacia 7, 17001 Girona.

THE LANGUAGE CENTRE: Girona (fax 972-201401; e-mail: tlc@bbs.grn.es).

DUNEDIN COLLEGE: Recogidas 18-1° Izq. 18002 Granada. Tel: (958) 255018. Also: C/ Rector Marín Ocete 8, 18014 Granada.

TEC ENGLISH CENTRE: C/ Pedro Frances 22A, 07800 Ibiza (Baleares). Tel: (971) 315828. Fax: (971) 191725. Also in Ibiza at C/ del Sol, Es Mercat, Santa Eulalia; tel: (971) 332070, and C/ San Vicente 21 1°, 07820 San Antonio; tel: (971) 345403. (10). Must have university degree and TEFL.

TEN: CENTRO DE INGLES: C/ Caracuel 24, 11402 Jerez de la Frontera (Cadiz). Tel: (956) 324707. (3).

CAMBRIDGE ENGLISH STUDIES: Avenida de Arteijo, 8-1°, 15004 La Coruña. Tel: (981) 277532/277651. Fax: (981) 267625. Also centre in Ferrol. (2-4).

ENGLISH CENTRE FOR LANZAROTE: C/ Canalejas 1-1°, Arrecife, Lanzarote (928-816156). Also C/ Fraternidad 23, Tias, Lanzarote. Tel: (928) 833519.

LANZAROTE LANGUAGE SCHOOL: fax 28-802685. Summer jobs at children's camp and year-long vacancies from October.

TRELAND ANGLO-WORLD: Mayor 15-7°, 48930 Las Arenas (Vizcaya). Tel: (94) 463 1926/464 8989. Fax: (94) 464 2438. (9).

OXFORD SCHOOL: C/ Aleixandre s/n, 33400 Las Vegas (Corvera de Asturias). Tel: (985) 57 75 75. (1).

ACADEMIA VICTORIA: Gran Via 3, 26002 Logroño (La Rioja). Tel: (941) 242038. Fax: (941) 256711. (4).

LA ACADEMIA DE INGLES: Avda. de Moratalaz 139, (Lonja Comercial), 28030 Madrid. Tel: (91) 430 5545. (16 in two centres).

BETA GROUP: Paseo de la Castellana 210-10°5, 28046 Madrid. Business English teachers needed.

CAMBRIDGE HOUSE: C/ Bravo Murillo 153, 1C, 28020 Madrid.

CEE IDIOMAS: C/ Carmen 6, 28030 Madrid.

CENTRO DE IDIOMAS CONCORDE: C/ Gral. Moscardó 12, 28020 Madrid.

COLON: Gran Via 55, Madrid.

THE ENGLISH CENTRE: Calle Nuñez de Balboa, 17 bajo derecha, 28001 Madrid. Tel: (91) 577 9122. (10).

EUROCENTRES: pa Castellana 194, 28046 Madrid.

IBERLENGUA: Torpedero Tucuman 26, 28016 Madrid. Tel: (91) 350 7297. (6-8). Two years' experience and liking for children's classes.

INLINGUA MADRID S.L.: Calle Arenal 24, 28013 Madrid. Tel: (91) 541 3246/7. Fax: (91) 542 8296. (25).

INTER-COM ENGLISH: C/ Fernández de la Hoz, 20 bajo, 28010 Madrid. Tel: (91) 308 2822. Fax: (91) 308 4775. (25-30). 10-15 h.p.w. teaching primary age children in their schools (for which a knowledge of Spanish is needed) as well as adults (mainly in-company business English classes). Compulsory orientation course given in last week of September.

KING'S COLLEGE: Serrano 44, 28001 Madrid.

KURSOLAN: C/ Sandalo 5, 28042 Madrid. Tel: (91) 320 7500. Fax: (91) 320 7136. (40). Runs 2 summer camps outside Madrid for Spanish boys and girls. Teachers work long hours (teaching and activity/sports programme) from mid-June to September.

LANGUAGE HOUSE: Avda. de Brasilia 7, 28028 Madrid. Tel: (91) 726 1844. (1-2).

LANGUAGES STUDIES INTERNATIONAL: Luchana 31, 1°, 28010 Madrid.

LINGUACENTER: C/ Rafael Calvo 8, 28010 Madrid.

LISTEN AND LEARN: C/ Narváez 14, 28009 Madrid.

LIVERPOOL, CENTRO DE IDIOMAS: Libreros 11-1°, 28801 Alcalá de Henares (Madrid). Tel: (91) 881 3184. Fax: (91) 881 35 84. (14). Run summer school programme in Barcelona for which they hire 15 EFL teachers.

JD RAY IDIOMAS: Antonio Lopez 47 1°b, 28019 Madrid.

T.E.C. ENGLISH: Guzmán Bueno 7, 28015 Madrid. Tel/fax: (91) 543 9271. (5). Applications processed in April/May. Minimum requirement is BA/BSc, TEFL qualification and 1 year experience.

THAMESIS, SA: C/ Castelló 24, bajo Dcha, 28001 Madrid. Tel: (91) 575 8949/431 9635. Fax: (91) 575 6597. (25-30).

WALL STREET INSTITUTE: Centro Comercial Cuesta Blanca, Local 12, 2° Planta, la Moraleja, Alcobendas, 28100 Madrid. Tel: (91) 650 7602. Fax: (91) 650 8246. (4). 6-month contracts (renewable). 2 week training course given.

MALACA INSTITUTO: Calle Cortada 6, Cerrado de Calderon, 29018 Malaga. Fax: (95) 229 6316; e-mail: espanol@malacainst.ch.es.

THE AMERICAN CENTER: Manuel Llaneza 26, 33600 Mieres. Tel: (985) 546 1454. Also at Hevia Aza 36, 33630 Pola de Lena; tel: 549 2513, and Plaza de la Iglesia 2, 33670 Moreda; tel: 548 2811. (6).

CENTRO BRITANICO: Pasaje del Comercio 6, 2° (PO Box 201), 18600 Motril (Granada). Run summer camp near Granada.

ACADEMIA MURCIA: fax 968-2346514/e-mail: CATS@arrakis.es

BILINGUE NORMINGTON: Calle Vinadel 11-15, 30004 Murcia. Tel: (968) 213262. Fax: (968) 628439. (1-2).

BUSINESS ENGLISH ACADEMY: Paseo Mutilnova 55, 31192 Navarra (e-mail: richard.lander@pna.servicom.es). Teachers for Pamplona.

ENGLISH LANGUAGE INSTITUTE: Eduardo Dato, 36 Larra 1, Nervión (Seville). Tel: (95) 464 0026. Fax: (95) 464 9503; e-mail: bridget@arrakis.es. Experienced teachers who will enjoy teaching children and teenagers. Other branches in 1 Porvenir, Gines, Triana, Macarena and Tomares.

BRIAN SCHOOL: Magdalena 19, 33009 Oviedo. Tel: (985) 220408. (4).

IDIOMAS BLAZEK: Llinàs 2, 07014 Palma de Mallorca (Baleares). Tel: (971) 457260. Fax: (971) 284674. (1-2).

PROGRESO CENTRO DE IDIOMAS: Plaza del Progreso 12B, 07013 Palma de Mallorca (Baleares). Tel: (971) 734555. Fax: (971) 455604. (3).

LEAP: C/ Iñigo Arista 18 (Entreplanta), 31007 Pamplona. Tel: (948) 277904. Fax: (948) 271572. (9 in three centres).

ENGLISH CENTRE DE PONTEVEDRA: C/ Cruz Gallastegui 2, 36001 Pontevedra (Galicia). Tel/fax: (986) 843652. (5).

NORFOLK SCHOOL IDIOMAS: Aparejador Monzó 11, 46930 Quart de Poblet.

INTERNATIONAL HOUSE: Llovera 47, 43201 Reus (Tarragona). Tel: (977) 343562. Fax: (977) 340021. (7).

ACADEMIA LACUNZA/INTERNATIONAL HOUSE: Urbieta 14-1°, 20006 San Sebastián.

INLINGUA IDIOMAS: Larramendi 23 bajo, 20006 San Sebastián.

THE SMITHS' SCHOOL: Maestro Guridi s/n, 20008 San Sebastián. Tel: (943) 211028. (10).

AULA 57: Paseo de Canalejas 57, 39004 Santander. Fax (942) 282028. Fluent Spanish needed.

SCHOOL OF ENGLISH: Genaro Oraá 6, 48980 Santurce (Vizcaya). Tel: (94) 461 9555. Fax: 461 5723. (5).

KENT IDIOMAS: C/ Tejedores 26, El Carmen, 40004 Segovia. Tel/fax: (921) 434423. (1-2).

ENGLISH 1: C/ Santa Maria Mozzarello s/n, Seville.

ENGLISH SCHOOL MACARENA: Dr. Jimenez Diaz 20, 41009 Seville. Tel: (95) 435 6134. (16).

EPICENTER: Niebla 13, 41011 Seville. Tel: (95) 427 9540. Also at Edif. Sevilla 2, Planta 1, Mod. 16, 41018 Seville; tel/fax: (95) 464 6246, and Dr. Antonio Cortés Lladó 6, 41004 Seville; tel: (95) 441 1312. (15).

ESCUELA UNION PACIFIC: Virgen de Luján 30A, 41011 Seville. Tel: (95) 445 5515. (15). Mostly part-time work in 5 centres located in Madrid (2), Barcelona, Bilboa and Seville.

LINGUARAMA: C/ Luis de Morales 32, Seville.

LONDON CENTRE: C/ Asunción 52, Seville.

APPLE IDIOMAS: C/ Aben Al Abbar 9, 46021 Valencia. Tel: (96) 362 2545. Also at C/ Agüera 2, 30001 Murcia; tel: (968) 211038; fax: 218164. (20).

INLINGUA: C/ Gregorio Fernandez 6, 47006 Valladolid. Tel/fax: (983) 35 86 97. (5-6). Week long training course given in September.

SANTA ANA CENTRO DE IDIOMAS: C/ Pasión 10 1°, 47001 Valladolid. Tel: (983) 358242. (4).

ENGLISH CENTRE: Calle Bruselas 9, 50003 Zaragoza. Tel: (976) 283246. Mostly teaching children.

TECHNICAL COLLEGE OF ENGLISH: C/ Maria Lostal No. 22, 50008 Zaragoza. Tel: (976) 227909. Fax: (976) 233676. (12). Runs summer courses in the Pyrenees (Cerler and Jaca). Spanish to university level and an interest in children and sport required.

Switzerland

Prospects are gloomy for people who fancy the idea of teaching the gnomes of Zürich or their counterparts in other parts of Switzerland. Not only are the immigration regulations exceedingly restrictive (since Switzerland is not a member of the European Union) but also the economy is not as invincible as it was a decade ago. The director of a *Sprachschule* in Basel assesses the situation:

> As a small language school in a country and region currently experiencing severe withdrawal symptoms (from full employment, job and financial security), it is unlikely that we will be recruiting staff from outside Switzerland, especially as there is a large reservoir of potential candidates here in the Basel region and work permits for staff from outside Switzerland are now a rarity.

Even before the economic downturn, very few native speakers were recruited abroad except at a very advanced level. Those schools which do not insist on very advanced qualifications, for example the Ecole Club Migros chain of language schools which can be found in all the major cities, hire only teachers who already have a 'B' residence permit for Switzerland. There are 12 Wall Street Institutes in Switzerland; a list of addresses is available from the master franchisee, WS Institute, Suisse SA, Rue du Simplon 34, 1006 Lausanne. If you are hired by a Swiss language school, wages are high, ranging from SFr30 to SFr60 for a 50-minute lesson.

Regulations

The Swiss Embassy in London sends out a one-page outline of the types of permit which are available. Naturally it makes depressing reading, stating that only people who are filling high-level vacancies which cannot be filled by someone already resident are eligible to obtain a residence permit. The only two possibilities are *Permis A,* reserved for seasonal employment in the building, hotel and holiday industry, or *Permis B* which is valid for a specific job for a year and can be renewed. Even people who have been offered work by private institutes (teaching business English, for example) have failed to be granted a permit, often on the grounds that the employer cannot guarantee a minimum number of hours. The only other visa possibility is the *Frontalier.* To qualify, you must commute from a French or German town within 10km of the Swiss border where you have been resident for at least six months.

One possible avenue to explore is the approved trainee exchange scheme which operates between English-speaking countries and Switzerland. To qualify to become a *stagiaire* (trainee) with a Swiss employer, you must be aged 18-30 and have trained in the field in which you wish to work. The permit is valid for a year but can be renewed for a further six months. Details are available from the Swiss Federal Aliens Office, Sektion Auswanderung und Stagiaires, CH-3003 Bern (31-322 42 02).

Vacation Work

More possibilities for teaching English exist at summer camps than in city language institutes, as can be seen from the three programmes listed in the Directory below. There are a number of international schools in Switzerland, some of which run English language and sports summer schools. The Swiss Federation of Private Schools produces a leaflet called 'Language Courses in Switzerland' which lists the names and addresses of scores of private schools, with a code showing which ones teach English. The *Service Scolaire* (Advisory Office) is unwilling to send this leaflet to job-hunters, so if you do want to request it, it is best to impersonate a rich person looking for a summer language school on behalf of someone else and preferably enclose international reply coupons. The address is Service Scolaire, 16 rue du Mont-Blanc (PO Box 1488), 1211 Geneva 1.

Watch for occasional ads or, if you are in Switzerland, make local enquiries. Susanna Macmillan hitch-hiked from Italy to Crans-Montana in the Swiss Alps in the autumn and within three days had arranged a job as a *monitrice* at the International School there. The job, which was to teach English and sport, came with room and board and paid an additional SFr850 per month.

In addition to the organisations with entries below, the following organisations offer summer language courses between June and September and may need teachers or monitors (or some combination of the two):

Aiglon Summer School, 1885 Chesières.

Beau Soleil Holiday Language Camp, EPTA Organisation, CH-1884 Villars-sur-Ollon.

Institute Le Rosey, Camp d'Eté, Route des Quatre Communes, CH-1180 Rolle. Winter address January-March: CH-3780 Gstaad (30-435 15). Qualified or experienced EFL teachers for co-educational summer camps with sports coaching on Lake Geneva. Teachers must be capable of carrying out boarding school duties.

Institut le Vieux Chalet, CH-1837 Chateau d'Oex.

Institut Monte Rosa, 57 Avenue de Chillon, CH-1820 Montreux.

Leysin American School in Switzerland, CH-1854 Leysin. Tel: (24) 493 37 7. Fax: (24) 494 15 85.

St. George's School in Switzerland, 1815 Clarens/Montreux.

Surval Mont-Fleuri, Route de Glion 56, CH-1820 Montreux 1.

LIST OF SCHOOLS

THE AMERICAN SCHOOL IN SWITZERLAND (TASIS)
Summer Language Programs, 6926 Montagnola-Lugano. Tel: (91) 994 64 71. Fax: (91) 993 1647. E-mail: administration@tasis.ch. US address: 1640 Wisconsin Avenue NW, Washington, DC 20007 (202-965-5800/fax 202-965-5816).
Preference of nationality: American.
Qualifications: university degree required. CELTA preferred.
Conditions of employment: summer school work involves language teaching plus sports, dorm and travel chaperoning; mid-June to mid-August.
Facilities/Support: all meals and accommodation provided.
Recruitment: CVs sent spontaneously. Personal interview not essential.

BERLITZ
Steinentorstr. 45, 4051 Basel.
Number of teachers: 6.
Preference of nationality: must have work permit.
Qualifications: BA or professional experience, e.g. business, banking.
Conditions of employment: no limit on contract length. Flexible hours of work. Pupils are adults whose average age is between 30-40.
Salary: SFr21.80 per 40-minute lesson plus 10-20% supplements for some programmes.
Facilities/Support: no assistance with accommodation. Training provided.
Recruitment: through adverts. Local interviews essential.

ECOLE CLUB MIGROS
rue Hans Fries 4, 1700 Fribourg. Tel: (26) 322 70 22. Fax: (26) 322 70 18.
Number of teachers: about 12, Branches in Neuchatel and La Chaux de Fond.
Preference of nationality: none, provided they have a *Permis B*.
Qualifications: university degree, adult education certification (if possible), experience teaching adults.
Conditions of employment: open-ended contracts. Mostly evening work.
Salary: SFr35-60 per hour depending on classes, levels and specialities.

Facilities/Support: no assistance with accommodation. Training available.
Recruitment: via unsolicited applications and newspaper adverts.
Contact: Daniella Hind, Language Department Counsellor.

HAUT-LAC INTERNAITONAL LANGUAGE AND LEISURE CENTRE
1831 Les Sciernes. Tel: (26) 928 42 00. Fax: (26) 298 42 01. E-mail: haut-lac@usa.net/www.haut-lac.ch
Number of teachers: teacher/monitors needed for summer and winter language camps for adolescents.
Preference of nationality: none.
Qualifications: must have at least two of the following: qualifications and experience in ELT (or German or French), sports coaching qualification, ability to organise outings and events or classes in drama, art, etc.
Conditions of employment: summer (June to August) and winter (January to end of March).
Facilities/Support: board and lodging provided.
Recruitment: send CV and photo. Only suitable applicants will receive a reply.

VILLAGE CAMPS
14 rue de la Morache, 1260 Nyon. Tel: (22) 990 94 05. Fax: (22) 990 94 94.
Language summer camp near Lake Geneva in French-speaking Switzerland.
Number of teachers: 10. Also need German and French teachers.
Preference of nationality: none.
Qualifications: TEFL/TESOL background. For the position of language counsellor, general experience with children is needed.
Conditions of employment: 5-7 weeks at a summer camp for 10-17 year olds. 3 hours teaching per day plus sports, activities and excursions.
Salary: varies with experience. TEFL teachers receive £175 p.w. plus room and board and insurance.
Facilities/Support: thorough training.
Recruitment: via adverts, *TESOL Placement Bulletin*, international schools, etc.

The Rest of Europe

Outside the mainstream European nations, demand for native speakers of English obviously exists though immigration problems often occur. Before turning to this miscellany of European countries, there is one organisation which employs people to tour all over Europe trying to bring the English language alive for Euro-teenagers.

BIG WHEEL THREATRE IN EDUCATION
54 William Street, Oxford OX3 0ER. Tel: (01865) 241527. Fax: (01865) 248041.
Number of teachers: 10 per year to join theatre-in-education workshops touring the continent: Benelux, Germany, Switzerland and Scandinavia.
Preference of nationality: EU national (usually British).
Qualifications: teaching and performance skills. No particular qualifications. Must be able to drive well. Fun and spontaneous personalities.
Conditions of employment: 3-month tours. 40 h.p.w. (early starts).
Salary: £180 p.w. plus all expenses (accommodation and touring allowance).
Facilities/Support: some training provided.
Recruitment: adverts in *Guardian* and *TES*. Interviews in UK essential.

ANDORRA

Andorra lies in the heart of the Pyrenees between Spain and France, and can be seen as an extension of both countries, though it has its own elected government. It is too small to have many language schools, though the one listed here is a possibility.

CENTRE ANDORRA DE LLENGUES
Avgda. Carlemany 91, Escaldes, Andorra. Tel: (376) 22862/24266. Fax: 22472.
Number of teachers: 4.
Preference of nationality: none.
Qualifications: BA plus TEFL qualification or 2-3 years' experience. Should have fair to good knowledge of Spanish or French. Non-smokers preferred.
Conditions of employment: 10 month contracts from October. 27 hours, 5 days a week. 9-11am, 1-2pm and 4-9.30pm.
Salary: £800 per month (plus overtime payments if appropriate).
Facilities/Support: board and lodging available from £150 per month. Obligatory work permit will be arranged.
Recruitment: via adverts and direct application. Send CV and photo.
Contact: Claude Benet.

CROATIA

This republic of the former Yugoslavia is making strides to recover from its recent history and is building on its strong indigenous English teaching infrastructure. Private language schools flourish in Zagreb, Varazdin and Karlovac, as well as in other towns. For many schools, the idea of employing a native speaker teacher is very attractive. However there is little tradition of doing this and teachers who go to work in Croatia may find themselves breaking new ground in their place of employment. Partly because of their novelty value, teachers would be likely to find themselves being made very welcome and treated well. Salaries are quoted in Deutsch marks, the currency to which the Croatian kuna is tied.

The market for private teaching is very strong with few native speakers on hand to supply it. Many authentic materials are available locally. If a job is fixed up ahead of time, the school can send a labour permit to be presented at the Croatian Embassy in London or Washington. But it may also be possible to obtain authorisation after arrival.

The British Council in Zagreb can offer informal assistance to prospective teachers by sending a brief list of contacts including a few private language schools and academic institutions. The Association of Croatian Teachers of English (HUPE) organises teacher development activities but can't help foreign teachers to find jobs; the President of HUPE can be reached c/o the Faculty of Mechanical Engineering, Ivana Lueiaea 5, 10000 Zagreb. The Croatian Ministry of Education has an ELT Adviser for primary and secondary schools: Trg burze 6, 10000 Zagreb (1-45 69 000).

The voluntary placement organisation Services for Open Learning (see *Eastern Europe: Finding a Job* below) sends teachers to Croatia but reports that posts are dependent on a highly unpredictable Ministry. The procedures for acquiring a work permit are complex and take about three months to complete.

LANCON ENGLISH LANGUAGE CONSULTANCY
Kumiciceva 10, 10 000 Zagreb. Tel: (1) 4552631. Fax: (1) 455 5697. E-mail: lmo@lancon.hr. Web-site: http://www.lancon.hr/lancon
Number of teachers: 10.
Preference of nationality: none.
Qualifications: university degree, a TEFL qualification and 2 years' experience. Knowledge of Business English useful.

Conditions of employment: 1 year contracts, renewable. 24 teaching hours (45 minutes) a week.
Facilities/Support: assistance with accommodation and work permits. Weekly training sessions.
Recruitment: via the internet and direct application. Interviews in Zagreb or by telephone.
Contact: Marc Jeffery, Personnel Director.

SKOLA STRANIH JEZIKA KEZELE
Cesarceva 10, 42000 Varazdin. Tel: (42) 215055. Fax: (42) 215036.
Number of teachers: 1.
Preference of nationality: British, Irish. American.
Qualifications: experience of preparing candidates for exams (TOEFL, PET, FCE, CAE).
Conditions of employment: 6 months or one-year contracts. 25 lessons p.w. Teaching all ages from pre-school to teenagers and adults.
Salary: DM1,000 per month.
Facilities/Support: assistance with accommodation given. Training available.
Recruitment: by word of mouth or personal recommendation. Interviews essential.

SKOLA ZA UCENJE STRANIH JEZIKA
L. Bezeredija 41, 40000 Cakovec. Tel/fax: (40) 311625.
Number of teachers: 1
Preference of nationality: none.
Qualifications: college degree.
Conditions of employment: 1 academic year (or less or more).
Salary: DM600-700 (net) plus free accommodation and meals.
Facilities/Support: accommodation provided, training given and full assistance with work permits.
Recruitment: local interviews.

A selection of other Croatian schools to try:
LINGUA CENTAR D.O.O., Miroslava Krleze 4c, 47000 Karlovac; and Davorina Trstenjaka 1, 47000 Karlovac (tel/fax 47-621900/611899).
Linguae, Radiaeeva 4, 51000 Rijeka
Long Foreign Languages, R Strohala 2, 51000 Rijeka
Centar za strane jezike, Trg Republike 2/1, 21000 Split
Langlia, A. Starèeviaea 19b, 23000 Zadar
Centar za Strane Jezike, Vodnikova 12, 10000 Zagreb
Skola Stranih Jezika, Varsavska 14, 10000 Zagreb
VERN LINGUA, Senoina 28, 10000 Zagreb (tel/fax 41-428548).

CYPRUS

A visitor to (Greek) Cyprus will be struck by the similarities with Greece—cuisine, architecture, landscapes and culture—but then surprised at the relative prominence of English. Signs are printed both in Greek and English, many local people even outside the cities speak some English, and the British influence can be noticed everywhere. Because of the longstanding relationship between Cyprus and Britain, the English language is given a much higher profile in the state educational system. As a result the density of *frontisteria* is not as high as it is in Greece, though there are still a considerable number of private institutes preparing children for external examinations.

The ELT Officer at the British Council (which does not have a teaching operation in Nicosia) sends out a rather discouraging circular letter to the many people enquiring about English teaching vacancies, together with a list of private secondary schools but not EFL institutes. If you wish to advertise your services as a tutor in the English language press of Greek Cyprus, contact the *Cyprus Mail* (PO Box 1144, Nicosia) or the *Cyprus Weekly* (PO Box 4977, Nicosia 1306; 2-666047).

There are no private schools or registered institutes in the Turkish Cypriot sector. Since the demand for English is so great in mainland Turkey, it is not obvious why this would not be the case in Turkish Cyprus, except that there is much less need for English to participate in the tourist industry. Since so few English speakers go to northern Cyprus even as tourists, perhaps an enterprising EFL teacher would be able to create a demand, at least for private tuition, provided he or she was willing to compete with the relatively large number of expatriate English speakers who reside in the TRNC.

The majority of native English speakers employed by language schools in Cyprus are expatriates (predominantly British) who have settled in Cyprus permanently. In early 1988, Cyprus commenced negotiations for accession to the EU, though full membership is a very distant prospect at the moment, and all foreign nationals who wish to work in Cyprus need a work permit. Government regulations require that all English teachers, whether Cypriot nationals or not, must have a degree in English literature in order to be employed in state schools. Of course it is possible to be employed without one in the private sector.

One major English institute, Forum Language Centre, which offers English at all levels, now offers the Trinity CTESOL part-time over five months, though they may run a full-time course in the early summer (see entry in *Training* chapter). They are not able to help graduates to find work locally.

MALTA

Although somewhat off the beaten track and although English is the first language of the tiny island, Malta has not escaped the EFL boom and a number of private language schools have opened in the past ten years. Many cater to groups coming from other Mediterranean countries on short courses in the summer and at other times. Their interests are represented by FELTOM, the Federation of English Language Teaching Organisations Malta (Foundation for International Studies, Old University Building, St. Paul St, Valletta VLT 07). The following schools are members of FELTOM (postal addresses given below); in Sliema: English Language Academy, English Communication School c/o Charisma Travel Ltd., inlingua, Institute of English Language Studies, and the International English Language Centre; elsewhere: Languages Plus Sprachcaffe Co. Ltd. (St. Andrew's), A. M. Language Studio (St. Georges Bay), European Centre of English (Ta' Xbiex, Masida), NSTS English Language Institute (Valletta) and Revival English Language Institute (Gzira).

The British Council in Valletta (housed with the British High Commission) can send a list of 25 language schools but does not recruit teachers nor advise on local employment prospects unless a prospective teacher pays a personal call. The problem with working in Malta has always been the difficulty of obtaining a permit, as Philip Dray from Ireland described a few years ago:

> *I tried many times to get a teaching job in Malta but was thwarted by the paranoia surrounding work permits. The annoying thing is that there is a shortage of teachers. However these vacancies are filled normally by 18 year olds with just A level certificates.*

The procedure for obtaining an employment licence is to obtain a signed form from your prospective employer, who must prove that the position cannot be filled by a skilled Maltese national, and send it to the Department for Citizenship and Expatriate Affairs, 3 Castille Place, Valletta CMR 02 (250868/fax 237513). These are normally valid for one year in the first instance. Further details may be requested from the Malta High Commission in London (Malta House, 36-38 Piccadilly, London W1V 0PQ).

The NSTS English Language Institute (220 St. Paul St, Valletta; 244983/e-mail: nststrav@kemmunet.net.mt) markets its English courses in conjunction with sports holidays for young tourists to Malta. NSTS run weekly vacation courses from June to August, and it might be worth approaching them for a job, particularly if you are a water sports enthusiast. NSTS was keen to hire Robert Mizzi from Canada once they learned that he was half Maltese:

> *I was offered a job quite casually when NSTS found out I was volunteering conversational English in the main youth hostel in Valletta. Perhaps one reason they wanted to hire me was they knew the visa would not be a problem. However I was surprised by how relaxed the offer was. It was just mentioned in passing rather than at an actual interview. I guess it is the Maltese way: once you are one of them, then everything is gravy.*

INLINGUA SCHOOL OF LANGUAGES
9 Triq Guzè Fava, Tower Road, Sliema SLM 15. Tel: 336384/313158. Fax: 336419/318903.
Number of teachers: 15 (out of a total of 100).
Preference of nationality: Maltese (or foreigner if work permit is in hand).
Qualifications: 'A' level English and TEFL qualification minimum.
Conditions of employment: casual and freelance employment only.
Salary: depends on qualifications.
Recruitment: local interviews essential.
Contact: K. Cremona.

A selection of Maltese schools to try (towns in alphabetical order):
Students Travel School, c/o St. Aloysius College, B'kara
Revival English Language Institute, Trinity Hall, Taliana Lane, Gzira
Educational English Culture, Villa Monaco, Sliema Road, Kappara SGN 06 (313033/fax 314523). 3 teachers. M£3.25 per hour.
Villa Torregiani, 38 Ta'Xbiex Sea Front, Msida
Kalypso Academy of English Language, 1 St. Joseph Apartments, Qala Road, Qala, Gozo GS 103
Languages Plus, Sprachcaffe Co. Ltd., St. Andrews, STJ 07
A. M. Language Studio, Villa Tiffani, Santu Wistin Street, St. Georges Bay, STJ 09
Elanguest, Keating House, Ross Street, St. Julians
Magister Academy, L-Arkati, Mensija St, St. Julians
MSD International School of English, Alleluia, Parish Hall, Triq it-Torri, St. Paul's Bay
St. Paul's English Language Centre, Streaked Sparus Street, St. Paul's Bay
English Communication School, c/o Charisma Travel Ltd., 10 St. Pius V Street, Sliema SLM15
English Language Academy, 9 Tower Lane, Sliema
Institute of English Language Studies, 'Il-Merill', Matthew Pulis Str., Sliema
International English Language Centre, 78 Tigne Street, Sliema SLM11
Link School of English, Link Court, 27 Victoria Junction, Sliema
European Centre of English, Paolo Court, 9 Call Street, Ta' Xbiex, MSD 14
International School of English, c/o English Department, Floriana, Valletta
La Salle Institute, 105 St. Thomas St, Floriana, VLT 14
The Voice School of English, 'Vipama', St. Anthony Street, Zabbar

SLOVENIA

The former Yugoslav republic of Slovenia remained uninvolved in the Balkan conflict throughout, which allowed its economy to flourish. It is in the group of countries at the head of the queue to join the European Union. As in Croatia, there are a good many private schools and many opportunities can be created by energetic native speakers both as freelance teachers for institutes or as private tutors.

The English Studies Resource Centre at the British Council in Ljubljana has a long list of private language schools throughout the country which it updates constantly; see their web page (http://www.britishcouncil.si/lic/schools.htm). The Council remains closely in touch with language schools and will refer qualified candidates to possible employers. There is also a British Council Resource Centre in Maribor located in the university library.

Wages are no longer quoted in Deutsch marks but rather in Slovenian tolars. The average hourly wage is 1,800 tolars net. According to most schools, it is not essential for foreign teachers to go through the complex and lengthy procedures for obtaining a work permit during their first year in Slovenia. Language assistants on the Central Bureau's scheme are paid the equivalent of £250-£300 per month for teaching 15 hours a week and given free accommodation.

After answering an advert in the *Guardian*, Adam Cook spent a year working at a *Gimnazija* in the town of Ajdovscina. He was hired with a BA plus an introductory TEFL certificate from the Language Project in Bristol (see entry in *Training* chapter).

> *The work is great and Slovenia is a fabulous country: good standard of living, good wages. My contract stipulates 20 hours a week but I work more, to save myself from boredom if nothing else. I'm paid by the Slovene Ministry of Education but am answerable to the British Council who recruited me in the first place. Slovene students are great and I have no discipline problems.*

BERLITZ LANGUAGE CENTER
Gosposvetska 2,1000 Ljubljana. Tel: (61) 133 13 25. Fax: (61) 133 20 42. E-mail: gregor.sergan@berlitz.SI
Number of teachers: 13.
Preference of nationality: none.
Qualifications: sound educational background, good communication skills, professional attitude and appearance.
Conditions of employment: minimum 1 year. 4-8 teaching hours per day.
Salary: 2,000 tolars per unit (40 minutes).
Facilities/Support: try to assist teachers with accommodation. Compulsory training in Berlitz method. Regular support through observations and workshops.
Recruitment: adverts and personal recommendation. Interviews necessary in most cases, occasionally held abroad.
Contact: Sergan Gregor, Director.

GLOTTA NOVA
Koblarjeva 34, 1000 Ljubljana. Tel: (61) 447225. Fax: (61) 447421. E-mail: glotta-nova@siol.net
Number of teachers: 2-3 (part-time).
Preference of nationality: British.
Qualifications: BA English teacher or at least TEFL training certificate.
Conditions of employment: up to 2 years. Hours 9am to 7pm.
Salary: DM20 per school hour.
Facilities/Support: no assistance with accommodation. Advice can be given on work permits.
Recruitment: adverts, interviews, probationary period.
Contact: Tatjana Dragovie, Teacher Trainer.

S.P. JAMEX
Malgajeva 10, 3000 Celje. Tel: (63) 63 443 192. Fax: (63) 443 191. E-mail: jamex@siol.net
Number of teachers: 1 or 2.
Preference of nationality: none.
Qualifications: linguistic and pedagogic competence; teaching children and adults.
Conditions of employment: one year contract, renewable. 10-20 h.p.w.

Salary: 1,800 tolars per hour (net).
Facilities/Support: possible help with accommodation if necessary. Some training in Suggestopaedia given.
Recruitment: normally recruit teachers locally.
Contact: Jasna Dzumhur, Director.

LJUDSKA UNIVERZA KRANJ
Cesta Staneta Zabarja 1, Kranj. Tel: (64) 222 226. Fax: (64) 212 891. E-mail: lj.uni-kranj@guest.arnes.si
Number of teachers: 2.
Preference of nationality: none.
Qualifications: qualified teachers of English sought. Some experience in ELT preferred.
Conditions of employment: 2-3 month contracts. Teaching hours are either mornings (8am-9.30am) or afternoons/evenings (5pm-9pm).
Salary: 1,800 tolars per lesson (net).
Facilities/Support: help teachers to find lodgings. Training and assistance with work permits given.
Recruitment: word of mouth. Local interviews essential.
Contact: Simona Krizaj Pochat, Head of Languages Department.

NISTA LANGUAGE SCHOOL
Kidriceva 44, 6000 Koper. Tel/fax: (66) 271 271.
Number of teachers: 10.
Preference of nationality: none.
Qualifications: BA and TEFL qualification minimum. One year teaching experience and experience of the business world preferred.
Conditions of employment: 10 month contracts. 26 h.p.w. (guaranteed 16 hours).
Salary: 130,000 tolars per month or 1,250 tolars per hour.
Facilities/Support: assistance with accommodation, work permits and training.
Recruitment: adverts in *TES*, etc.
Contact: Ms. Alenka Rajcic, Director.

PANTEON COLLEGE
Vojkova 1, 1000 Ljubljana. Tel: (61) 312 916. Fax: (61) 13 23 149.
Number of teachers: as many as required.
Preference of nationality: none (though no assistance with work permits).
Conditions of employment: freelance basis: contracts, hours and salaries vary according to course demands.
Facilities/Support: no assistance with accommodation.
Recruitment: direct application and interviews.
Contact: Mr. Andres Toporosic, Director.

YURENA
Glavni trg 11, 8000 Novo Mesto. Tel/fax: (68) 372 100. Fax: (68) 372 101.
Number of teachers: 3.
Preference of nationality: British.
Qualifications: university degree in TEFL preferred; otherwise a TEFL/TESOL Certificate.
Conditions of employment: 10 month contracts from September. 26 h.p.w. Mostly afternoon teaching of children and adults.
Salary: approximately £700 per month net.
Facilities/Support: assistance given with accommodation and work permits.
Recruitment: direct.
Contact: Kati Golobic, Director.

234   Country Guide — Europe

Other Schools to Try

Note that these schools (in alphabetical order according to town) did not confirm their teacher requirements for this edition of *Teaching English Abroad*. The majority are taken from the British Council list which included 85 addresses. Upper case entries marked with an asterisk had entries in the last edition (1997).

Europa Bled. d.o.o, Alpska 7, 4260 Bled
Bled, Sola za Tuje Jezike, Breda Vukelj s.p., Kajuhova c. 11, 4260 Bled
Selih Kozelj d.n.o., Studio za Ucenje, Miklosiceva 9, 3000 Celje
Accent On Language d.o.o., Ljubljanska c. 36, 1230 Domzale
Dude d.o.o. English Language Center, Slamnikarska 1, 1230 Domzale
ISCG Domzale, Kolodvorska c. 6, 1230 Domzale
Poliglot d.o.o., Ljubljanska 110, 1230 Domzale
Sibon, Center za Tuje Jezike, Ljubljanska c. 76 II, 1230 Domzale
Speak It, Heintzman and Heintzman, Trubarjeva ul.4, 1230 Domzale
Altera d.n.o., Kettejeva 23, 1241 Kamnik
Little England Club d.o.o., Medvedova ul. 6, 1241 Kamnik
Eurocenter, Lilijana Durdevic s.p., Kidriceva ul. 46, 6000 Koper
Pharmagan d.o.o., Straziska ul. 7, 4000 Kranj
Progress Jezikovni Tecaji d.o.o., Seljakovo n.33, 4000 Kranj
Most d.o.o., Kovinarska ul. 9, 8270 Krsko
Jezikovni Studio Kotar Sonja,s.p., Cesta na Svetino 10, 3270 Lasko

Abis d.o.o., Kantetova ul.2, 1000 Ljubljana
Alpha d.o.o., Brodarjev trg 14, 1000 Ljubljana
Candor Delavnice Tujih Jezikov, Mirje 1, 1000 Ljubljana
Dialog d.o.o. Sola za tuje jezike, Celoska 61, 113 Ljubljana
Gromar d.o.o., Gola Loka 8, 1210 Ljubljana Sentvid
ICM d.o.o., Kadilnikova ul.3, 1000 Ljubljana
Izobrazevalni Center Horizont, d.o.o., Bezenskova ul..35, 1000 Ljubljana
JEZIKOVNI CENTER INTERNATIONAL, Gornji Trg 4, 1101 Ljubljana (61-125 5317/fax 61-226167).
Jezikovni Center Palatin, Dunajska 7, Ljubljana
KRONA PLUS D.O.O., Trzaska Cesta 2, 1111 Ljubljana (61-126 1266; tel/fax 61-218055).
Logos d.o.o., Izanska c.2a, 1000 Ljubljana
Mint d.o.o. Ljubljana, Jeranova ul.1c, 1000 Ljubljana (61-133 8456/fax 61-126 1206). Recruits native speaker teachers for average monthly wage of US$1,000.
Modrin d.o.o., Staniceva ul.21 (and Jesenkova ul.7), 1000 Ljubljana
Pengvin, Popoviceva ul. 16, 1113 Ljubljana
SOLT, Cesta 27. Aprila 31, 1000 Ljubljana
Stratos English Ljubljana, Business English Professional Skilltraining d.o.o., Vegova 2, 1000 Ljubljana

AS Asistent d.o.o., Glavni trg 17B, 2000 Maribor
Cenca p.o., Masarykova c. 18, Ribnisko selo, 2000 Maribor
Dialog d.o.o. Jezikovna Sola, Terceva ul.39, 2000 Maribor
Jezikovni biro Lindic, Cankarjeva ul.10, 2000 Maribor
Multilingua d.o.o., Ulica bratov Hvalic 16, 5000 Nova Gorica
New College d.o.o., Med ogradami 11A, 5000 Nova Gorica
Athena d.o.o., Kolodvorska c. 17, 6230 Postojna
Ontario d.o.o., Miklosiceva ul.5, 2250 Ptuj
Jezikovna Sola Tabula Rasa, TRg svobode 12, 3325 Sostanj
Candor Dominko k.d., Turnovse 19, 1360 Vrhnika

YUGOSLAVIA

Even when the old Yugoslavia was a popular tourist destination, the ELT industry was not highly developed. When the country was ravaged by war, English dropped off most people's agenda. Now that the situation has become stable, many people in Belgrade and other cities in what remains of Yugoslavia, after the former Yugoslav provinces of Bosnia-Hercegovina, Croatia, Slovenia and Macedonia have separated, are once again showing an interest in learning English. The number of language schools has grown so rapidly that it is very difficult for most of them to attract a native speaker.

In order to get a residence/work permit for Yugoslavia, you must submit a contract of employment and a translated copy of your diploma.

ABC CENTAR
D. Obradovica 38, 21205 Sremski Karlovci. Tel: (21) 881 533. Fax: (21) 881 491. E-mail: radmil@eunet.yu
Number of teachers: 1.
Preference of nationality: British.
Conditions of employment: one academic year.
Recruitment: direct.
Contact: Jovanka Radmilovic, Headteacher.

ABC SCHOOL OF ENGLISH
Sultana Ciuk 7, 26300 Vrsac. Tel: (13) 813 144. Fax: (13) 817 370.
Number of teachers: none at present.
Conditions of employment: 6-12 months. 4-6 hours per day.
Salary: hourly rate.
Facilities/Support: assistance with accommodation, work permits and training.
Recruitment: interviews essential.
Contact: Gradimir Duncic, Principal.

ENGLISH WORLD
Ul. Partizanska Br. 36, 11300 Smederevo. Tel: (26) 227 643.
Number of teachers: 1.
Preference of nationality: none.
Qualifications: university degree in English and 5 years' experience in teaching children.
Conditions of employment: 4 year contracts.
Salary: DM800 (£300) per month.
Facilities/Support: no assistance with accommodation.
Recruitment: by advertisement and interview held locally or abroad.
Contact: Ms. Irena Jeremic, Owner.

FORUM
Jna 1, TC 'Trubac' II Sprat, 26000 Pancevo. Tel: (13) 510 492.
Number of teachers: 1.
Preference of nationality: none.
Qualifications: TEFL, one or more years' experience, nice personality.
Conditions of employment: 1 year; shorter contracts possible (September-December or February-June).
Salary: 30% of total income of groups taught by the teacher.
Facilities/Support: assistance with accommodation and permits.
Recruitment: on recommendation. Personal interview not essential.
Contact: Mrs. Nada Dorotevic, Director.

GALINDO SKOLA (SAVA CENTAR)
Milentija Popovica 9, 11070 Novi Beograd. Tel: (11) 311 4568. Fax: (11) 455785. E-mail: galindo@net.yu
Number of teachers: 3 to work at first private language school in the country.
Preference of nationality: none.

Qualifications: BA in English and TEFL, TESL or TESOL qualification. Knowledge of some Serbo-Croatian would be an advantage. Should be active, enthusiastic and responsible.
Conditions of employment: minimum period 3 months during academic year. 6-7 hours per day, 5 days p.w. teaching children, adolescents and executives.
Salary: £280 per month.
Facilities/Support: free accommodation provided.
Recruitment: direct application.
Contact: Nada Gadjanski.

INSTITUT ZA STRANE JEZIKE
Gospodar Jovanova 35, 11000 Beograd. Tel: (11) 623 034/623 022. Fax: (11) 625 525.
Number of teachers: 1 or 2.
Preference of nationality: British, American, Canadian.
Qualifications: teaching experience and university degree.
Conditions of employment: 6-12 months. Hours of teaching normally 6-9pm.
Salary: about DM600 per month (net).
Facilities/Support: help with work permits but not accommodation. Training available.
Recruitment: personal recommendation. Interviews essential.
Contact: Jelena Kovaecevic, Head of Research.

NEW VISIONS SCHOOL
79 Narodnog Fronta, 21000 Novi Sad. Tel/fax: (21) 367 739/368 766.
Number of teachers: 2-3.
Preference of nationality: British, American, Australian.
Qualifications: TESOL qualifications.
Conditions of employment: 1 year. 20-25 h.p.w.
Salary: £500-600 per month.
Facilities/Support: assistance with accommodation, work permits and training.
Recruitment: interviews essential, sometimes held in England.
Contact: Dragana Djurkovic, Principal.

OLYMPOS
Bastinska 16, 2500 Sombor. Tel: (25) 34057. Fax: (25) 34940.
Number of teachers: 1,
Preference of nationality: British, Canadian, Australian, Indian.
Qualifications: BA or higher degree preferred. Lower qualification with experience accepted.
Conditions of employment: 1 year or longer. 20-24 h.p.w.
Salary: £180 per month.
Facilities/Support: assistance with accommodation, work permits (via student employment agency) and training, with access to local British Council seminars.
Recruitment: personal recommendation. Interviews preferred.
Contact: Karlo Hameder, Director of Studies.

RAINBOW
Kolo Srpskih Sestara 8, 21000 Novi Sad. Tel/fax: (21) 363960. E-mail: rainbow@Eunet.yu
Number of teachers: 1-2.
Preference of nationality: none.
Qualifications: TEFL certificate. Experience not essential.
Conditions of employment: one-year contracts. 18 teaching hours p.w. plus 4 on stand-by. Pupils aged from 6 years to adult, mostly teenagers.
Salary: DM500 per month (net).

Facilities/Support: assistance with accommodation and work permits given. Lessons are observed once a week and seminars are held once a month.
Recruitment: adverts in *Guardian*. Interviews not always essential but can be carried out in UK.

SPEAK UP ENGLISH LANGUAGE SCHOOL
ul. Visnjiceva 31, 34000 Kragujevac. Tel: (34) 67472.
Number of teachers: none at present.
Preference of nationality: British.
Qualifications: experience of working with children as well as some teaching experience. Must be reliable and patient with children (aged 5-18).
Conditions of employment: minimum 6 months. 15-20 h.p.w. Opportunities to work at summer schools by the seaside and winter schools at ski resorts.
Salary: DM equivalent of £100 per month. Deductions of about 35% only if teacher requests it.
Facilities/Support: assistance with accommodation and training given.
Recruitment: recommendations from resident native speakers. Interviews essential.
Contact: Mirjana Milovic, Director of Studies.

A selection of Yugoslav schools to try, taken from the British Council's list (which has over 100 addresses in Yugoslavia).
Anglia, Carli Caplina 37 A, 11000 Beograd
Hello, Partizanske avijacije 25, 11070 Novi Beograd
Kent School of English, Hilandarska 29/II, 11000 Beograd
Lingua English Language Services, Vinogradski venac 12/15, 11030 Beograd
Lingva, Njegoseva 59, 11000 Beograd
Oxford Centar, Dobracina 27/III, 11000 Beograd
Polyglot, Jevrejska 2, 11000 Beograd
Robertson, Kondina 11, 11000 Beograd
Sunny Days School, Jurija Gagarina 205/76, 11070 Novi Beograd
Tom & Emma School of English, Petra Martinovica 26/28, 11030 Beograd
YBS Language School, Simina 19/II, 11000 Beograd

English Teaching Centre, Ljubicka 48, 32000 Cacak
ELC Language School, Nikole Pasic 8/52, 34000 Kragujevac
Inlingua, Ratka Pavlovica 13 (Vinogradi), 34000 Kragujevac
Oxford Centar, Vojvode Putnika 48, 34000 Kragujevac

MACEDONIA

LETIKOM PLUS
Bojmija 8, 91000 Skopje, Macedonia. Tel: (91) 126 017.
Number of teachers: none at present.
Preference of nationality: native speakers of English.
Qualifications: university degree.
Conditions of employment: minimum one school year (September to June). 16 h.p.w.
Salary: approximately £50 per week.
Facilities/Support: assistance with accommodation.
Recruitment: interviews essential.
Contact: Slavica Baneva, Director.

Other Schools to Try:
Lili School of English, Ul. AFZ 7b, 91000 Skopje
Lingual, Ograzden 1-1/2, 91000 Skopje

London-City, Aco Karamanov 13, 91000 Skopje
Pro-Lingua, Bul. Jane Sandanski 36/II/22, 91000 Skopje
Queen, Ul. Naroden Front 5/II/5, 91000 Skopje
St George's School of English, Partizanski odredi 3-3/5, 91000 Skopje (91-125280/fax 91-221269/e-mail stevedan@mol.com.mk) 5–6 teachers with TEFL Certificate. Accommodation and return flights to London provided.
Soros International House, Nikola Parapunov bb, 91000 Skopje
Us Fan, Lerinska 38, 91000 Skopje

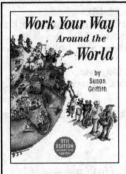

EASTERN EUROPE

The transition to a market economy throughout the vast area of Eastern and Central Europe has resulted in a huge demand for professional assistance at all levels, especially when it comes to improving the skills of communication. The dramatic changes which have taken place in the former Communist Bloc since 1989 mean that in every hotel lobby, office boardroom and government ministry from Silesia to Siberia, deals are being struck, export partnerships forged and academic alliances developed between East and West. The lucky East Europeans benefitting from this new commerce tend to be the ones who have acquired the English language.

While Russia has been wrestling with its political and economic demons, the more stable Central European states of Hungary, Poland, the Czech Republic and Slovakia have gained an increasing level of autonomy from the West. There has been a mild backlash in some quarters against what has been seen as a selling out to the West, especially in the major capitals which are now swarming with foreigners. School directors are now perfectly aware of the English-speaking foreigner who masquerades as a teacher but really intends to indulge in cheap beer and all-night discos. They are suspicious of anyone projecting this hidden agenda, disliking the fact that so many foreigners used the region as an extended party venue early on.

In the years just after the revolution, teachers up and down the countries of Eastern Europe chucked their ancient text books and joyfully embraced the new communicative methodologies. The enthusiasm for learning English was unprecedented. Everybody craved English lessons, assuming that to learn was to earn, parents as well as children and teenagers. Many foreigners, some representing religions like the Mormons and Bahai, arrived and set up schools. The people thought that knowing English would make them happy and rich. It didn't. Furthermore, they learned that learning a language is very difficult, and some of that initial enthusiasm has subsided.

Yet despite having moved past making 'Western' synonymous with 'desirable,' they are still remarkably welcoming to British and American ELT teachers. On most street corners, private language schools employ native speaker teachers. Working in Central and Eastern Europe may not seem as sexy as it did just after the 'revolution', but thousands of Britons and Americans continue to fall under the spell of Prague, Budapest and Kraków. Even those who find themselves in the less prepossessing industrial cities normally come away beguiled by Central European charm.

Even if ordinary people no longer see English as their salvation or even as an automatic passport to higher wages and a better life, they have not stopped wanting to learn it. The English language teaching industry in those countries has grown up, and is now much more likely to hire teachers with proven experience or an appropriate qualification. Massive amounts of money have been invested in Poland, Hungary and the former Czechoslovakia in retraining local teachers for the teaching of English in state schools and these programmes have been largely successful. Demand continues for native speakers in state schools, private language schools and universities, often for native speakers with a sophisticated understanding of linguistic methodology. There is no question now of walking straight into a job in these countries merely because you were born an English-speaker. Yet outside the major centres, the need remains great. Since the fall of Communism in the region, the quality of schooling has fallen sharply, according to a Unicef report published in 1998. While the wealthy elite can afford to pay for extra tuition in English (and other subjects), most citizens must endure smaller education budgets in their local schools and resulting cuts in quality. It is worth bearing these issues in mind when considering where to head to teach EFL, as emphasised by Steve Anderson from Minneapolis who spent two years teaching in Hungary, the first in a well resourced urban school, the second in an impoverished rural one which he found much more fulfilling.

The explosion in the number of training centres for TEFL/TESL teachers in all English-speaking countries means that the pool of available teachers has vastly increased since the early days, and so the balance of supply and demand has shifted. Teachers who can claim to specialise either in teaching young learners or in teaching Business English are especially attractive since both these areas of ELT are booming. Tourism training colleges in Hungary, the Czech & Slovak Republics and the Baltics are especially keen on encouraging conversational English. Failing that, the easiest way to become more employable is to acquire a TEFL qualification which could prove especially useful (and incidentally cheaper) if obtained in Eastern Europe. For example *International House* in Prague, Budapest, Kraków and Wroclaw all offer the CELTA course and both *ITC Prague* and *New World Teachers* have their own 4-week certificate courses (see 'Training Courses Abroad' in the *Training* chapter).

As schools and language training organisations have become more choosy, so too the governments have made visas more difficult to obtain. For example the work visa for teachers in Poland must be obtained in your country of origin and will cost more than £100. Even in countries where English native speakers are sought after, the red tape can be offputting. For example in Russia, visas and residence permits are specific to a given employer. When a pre-arranged job turns out to be less satisfactory than expected, foreign teachers who find a much better job encounter difficulties in switching employers. Officially, it is always necessary to obtain a work visa outside the country though in some cases employers can fix up the red tape after you arrive. In most cases you can enter the country and stay for three months as a tourist.

A future problem which may arise for North Americans is that a few former Eastern bloc countries (viz. Hungary, Slovenia and the Czech Republic) are well on their way to joining the European Union, at which time the immigration regulations will heavily favour English teachers from Britain and Ireland. But this is still several years away. Note that former Yugoslav republics (i.e. Slovenia, Croatia and Macedonia) are included in the previous chapter 'The Rest of Europe', though some placement organisations mentioned here include them as part of Central & Eastern Europe.

One of the first language teaching organisations to break into Eastern Europe has continued to be one of the most active and energetic in the region, International House. Of the 17 countries in which vacancies were being advertised at the time of writing, more than half were countries included in this chapter. In the past few years a number of new International House affiliated schools have opened in Belarus, Macedonia, Lithuania, Ukraine and Poland. The affiliation agreement with all International House schools states that the schools can employ only teachers who have passed the CELTA course. Similarly the British Council was looking for suitable candidates to fill vacancies in its teaching centres in Azerbaijan, Bulgaria, the Czech Republic, Hungary, Poland and Slovakia, among others worldwide.

Local salaries can seem absurdly low when translated into a hard currency. To give one example, the settling-in grant paid by one of the major employers to teachers newly arrived in Kaunas, Lithuania is about £16. A few schools pay a dollar supplement in addition to a local salary; others pay what is usually a generous salary by local standards but which can leave little after paying for food and accommodation. A typical package would include a monthly net salary of between £150 and £400 in addition to free accommodation and possibly some other perks such as a travel stipend. The best paid jobs are for firms which teach in-company courses, especially in Poland.

A host of private language schools which are either independent or part of larger language teaching organisations are represented in Eastern and Central Europe. Most of the Central European schools listed in the Directory are well established and offer above average working conditions. Some mainstream schools in the stable democracies have delegated the task of finding teachers to recruitment agencies. But in the more volatile climate of Russia and former Soviet republics (which are several years behind the Central European nations), schools come and go, and tend to choose their teachers from the pool of native English speakers on the spot, who also come and go. Intrepid travellers visiting the Central Asian Republics with no intention to work are still often invited to stay a while and do some English teaching, as was happening in off-the-beaten track towns in Poland and Czechoslovakia eight or ten years ago.

One interesting option for those who do not wish to commit themselves for a full academic year is to work at one of the many language summer camps which are offered to young people, usually in scenic locations from Lake Balaton in Hungary to Lake Baikal in Siberia.

Conditions of Work

The financial rewards of working in the old Russian Empire are usually so negligible that trained/experienced teachers cannot be enticed to teach there unless they are supported by a voluntary organisation like East European Partnership or the Soros Foundation. The problems attendant on the economic crisis in Russia have been made worse by inflation and sudden price rises which will eat away at a salary that was marginal to begin with. Ironically 'volunteers' with the major agencies are comparatively well off since they benefit from the standard package which includes free travel, insurance and other benefits. Other voluntary programmes arrange for eager but unqualified volunteers in search of a cultural experience who on the whole will be out-of-pocket at the end of a short stint of teaching in the Ukraine, the Baltics, etc. The role of native speaking volunteers is to conduct practical English classes (i.e. conversation classes) to supplement grammar taught by local school staff.

The scarcity of accommodation in the major cities of Eastern Europe is acute. Fortunately many employers of native-speaker teachers supply accommodation, but those who have to depend on the 'open market' (so-called) may experience grave problems. With the new unregulated economic conditions which now pertain, rents are not fixed and as soon as landlords realise that you are not a local, they tend to double or quadruple the rent. If possible, get a local friend to do the negotiations for you in their own language. Be prepared for cramped quarters, perhaps a small room in a student dormitory or family flat.

A certain level of hardship is inevitable, especially for vegetarians, anyone who has forgotten to bring winter boots and those who have breathing problems, since the pollution in many Eastern European cities can be choking. A further problem is the difficulty in communicating, though most people who have spent time in these countries find that they are well looked after by the local people.

It should not be surprising to learn that in the case of some countries and some ELT programmes there is considerable uncertainty and confusion. The dire shortage of English teaching facilities through the past decades cannot be reversed instantaneously. The emergence of these countries into the 'real world' has been attended by problems and pitfalls such as an absence of coordinated educational policies and the possibility of shoddy or exploitative working conditions for teachers, not to mention price rises, unemployment and a dramatic increase in crime.

While opportunities vary from place to place and while the future is uncertain due to the speed of change, it is true to say that there will be a great demand for native English teachers for many years ahead. And though these may not be the best paid EFL jobs in the world, Eastern Europe can offer historic and beautiful cities, genuinely friendly people and a unique chance to experience life in the 'other Europe' before it turns into just another group of free-market democracies.

FINDING A JOB

A range of vacancies in Central and Eastern Europe, particularly in Poland, continue to be advertised in the educational press. A certain number of commercial recruitment agencies are involved with filling vacancies in Eastern Europe, including agencies which charge untrained volunteer teachers a fee for the arrangements to be made on their behalf.

Many British and American programmes that were set up in the wake of the 1989 revolution have now been cancelled, a loss to the state schools in much of Eastern Europe, and also to the many young Britons and Americans who would still be willing to spend a year earning very little. The need for native speakers in state schools hasn't disappeared, but the number of mediating agencies has certainly diminished.

As has been stressed elsewhere, the possibility of creating your own job in this region is very strong. Much of what takes place happens by chance, and protocol is often given a back seat to friendly encounters. Obtaining work often comes down to the right (or wrong) hairstyle or whether you've got any Polish/Lithuanian/Slovak/ Azerbaijani ancestry. Looking professional, being persistent and asking as many questions as you are asked, rather than sitting back on your heels, usually pays off.

But if you want to arrange a position through a mediating organisation, here are the main ones in the UK which continue to recruit teachers for more than one country in the region. (Organisations which deal only with one country are included in the relevant chapter.) Note that a number of general ELT recruitment agencies included in the introductory chapter *Finding a Job* have vacancies in Eastern Europe, such as i to i's *i venture* programme (Russia, Uzbekistan), *EF English First* (Lithuania, Poland, Russia), *Skola Teacher Recruitment* (Ukraine, Russia, Slovenia), *Saxoncourt* (Moscow, Siberia, Belgrade, Warsaw, Kraków, etc.) and so on.

Central Bureau for Educational Visits & Exchanges, Assistants Department, 10 Spring Gardens, London SW1A 2BN. Tel: 0171-389 4169. Graduates who want to spend an academic year in Eastern Europe should obtain the relevant literature from the Central Bureau. Posts are available in Hungary, Slovenia, Romania and Russia, and are at secondary or tertiary level. Compulsory interviews in London.

East European Partnership, Carlton House, 27A Carlton Drive, London SW15 2BS. Tel: 0181-780 7555. Fax: 0181-780 7550. E-mail: depstein@vso.org.uk. EEP is the East European division of Voluntary Service Overseas (VSO). It is a volunteer sending agency which aims to meet the short-term needs for skills in East and Central Europe and Russia. EEP recruits qualified professionals with a minimum of two years post-qualification experience to work in education as well as other sectors. Placements are for one to two years in Albania, Macedonia, Bulgaria, Romania, Slovakia, Czech Republic, former Soviet Union, Latvia and Lithuania. At present they are developing programmes in Kazakhstan and the former Yugoslavia. They offer a salary in line with local salaries, free flights, training and insurance.

International Placement Group/IPG, Jezkova 9, 130 00 Prague 3, Czech Republic. Tel/fax: (2) 2272 0237/279568. E-mail: ipgcz@mbox.vol.cz. Also has office in London: 72 New Bond Street, London W1Y 9DD; tel/fax 0181-885 1994. Teacher recruitment agency which was founded in 1996 and is active in the Czech Republic, Poland (where the majority of vacancies are), Slovakia, Russia, Estonia and Lithuania, as well as worldwide. Frequent interviews arranged in London and recruitment days are held in the summer in North America (e.g. New York and Montreal). IPG accepts applications for about 70 vacancies in Eastern Europe from teachers with at least a CELTA or Trinity (TESOL) Certificate, or teachers with two or more years' full-time professional experience and those with B.Ed/PGCE qualifications. IPG places teachers in everything from daycare to corporate tutoring.

Language Link, 21 Harrington Road, London SW7 3EU. Tel: 0171-225 1065. Fax: 0171-584 3518. E-mail: languagelink@compuserve.com. Mainly active in Russia (see entry) and Slovakia (see entry for *Akademia Vzdelavania*) but also have occasional positions in their network of schools in other parts of East & Central Europe. Accept newly qualified teachers.

Services for Open Learning (SOL), North Devon Professional Centre, Vicarage St, Barnstaple, Devon EX32 7HB. Tel: (01271) 327319. Fax: (01271) 376650. E-mail: sol@enterprise.net. Non-profit-making organisation which annually recruits about 100 graduates (with degree in languages or education or with recognised TEFL Certificate) to teach in schools in the state sector in most Eastern and Central European countries (Belarus, Bosnia, Croatia, Czech Republic, Hungary, Romania and Slovakia). The SOL programme is open to all native speakers of English, though interviews take place only in Britain (March and June) and in Eastern & Central Europe. Contracts are with each school and are for a complete academic year

(September to June), though a handful of posts may arise in January. All posts include free independent housing. Some financial assistance may be available to volunteers going to Romania.

Teachers for Central & Eastern Europe, 21 V 5 Rackovski Blvd, Dimitrovgrad 6400, Bulgaria. Tel/fax: (391) 24787/(391) 23349. E-mail: tfcee_klim@skat.spnet.net or postmaster@haskovo.uspc.bg (attention: Stoitcho Tritchkov, Director). US contact: Bill Morrow (512-494-0392/e-mail: jbmorrow@mail.utexas.edu) and Interexchange in New York (see introductory chapter *Finding a Job*). TFCEE Inc. appoints about 80 native speakers of English a year to teach English (or other disciplines) at English language secondary schools, secondary schools of natural sciences and universities in Bulgaria, Czech Republic, Hungary, Poland and Slovakia (further details about Bulgaria in respective chapter). Most participants are from universities in the US, UK, Canada and Australia. Candidates must send original of transcript/academic record, notarised copies of university diplomas, CV and two letters of academic reference. TEFL certification and experience are not generally required but are strongly recommended. Most appointments are for an academic year, though one semester placements are possible (i.e. mid-September to mid-January, or February to mid-June).

Teaching Abroad, Gerrard House, Rustington, West Sussex BN16 1AW. Tel: (01903) 859911. Fax: (01903) 785779. E-mail: teaching-abroad@garlands.uk.com. Web-site: www.teaching-abroad.co.uk. Recruits volunteers to work as English Language Teaching Assistants for the summer or during the academic year in Russia (Moscow, St. Petersburg and Siberia) and the Ukraine. No TEFL background required. Packages cost from £795 for Ukraine (excluding travel) to £1,495 for Siberia (including travel from UK). Prices include placement, accommodation and back-up. Flexible starting dates and durations for up to three months; extensions can be arranged for a further fee.

Travel Teach, Ellison House, 2 Osborne Road, Newcastle-upon-Tyne NE2 2AA. Tel/fax: 0191-212 0792. Web-site: http://www.travelteach.com. Also have US office, though change of address not known at time of writing. Offer working holiday opportunities, teaching conversational and comprehensive English in two former republics of the Soviet Union: Lithuania and Moldova. English is taught in schools, summer schools and organisations to kindergarten and school children as well as to adults. Flexible periods of teaching from 2 weeks in Moldova/7 weeks in Lithuania to 12 months, including the summer vacation. Open to graduates, undergraduates or gap year students. All-inclusive programme fee includes return air travel, visas, board and lodging throughout with a host family, language learning and organised visits and excursions every three weeks. Orientation, teacher training and materials provided as well as advice on travelling in the region. The programme charge is £450 for Moldova and £499 for Lithuania (with 15% reduction for individuals with a TEFL qualification or Qualified Teacher Status).

For North Americans

Several US organisations are actively involved in teacher recruitment for the region:

Bridges for Education, 94 Lamarck Drive, Buffalo, NY 14226, USA. Tel: (716) 839-0180. Fax: (716) 839-9493. E-mail: jbc@buffalo.edu. Internet: http://wings.buffalo.edu/bfe. Organise international summer peace camps which involve 130 volunteers teaching English for three weeks in July followed by one week of travel in Belarus, Estonia, Hungary, Lithuania, Poland, Romania, Russia, Slovakia and Ukraine. Volunteers trained in basic ESL before departing in a group from North America. Summer teachers often offered longer-term jobs. Participants pay their airfare and programme administration fee.

Central European Teaching Program/CETP, Beloit College, 700 College St, Beloit, WI 53511, USA. Tel: (608) 363-2619. Fax: (608) 363-2449. E-mail: cetp@stu.beloit.edu. Internet: www.beloit.edu/-cetp. CETP places 90 native speakers of any nationality in state schools in Hungary, Romania, Poland and Latvia. Must have university degree, overseas teaching, travel or study experience and/or TEFL/TESL experience. 10 month contracts from September. Monthly salary of $150-$200. Placement fee of $1,200. It was through CETP that Steve Anderson arranged his year of teaching in Hungary, and he was impressed:

> *CETP is a professional yet personal organisation. They maintain in-country contacts for the duration of the contracts and will kindly hammer out any kinks in a teacher's experience (whether it be work-related or otherwise). They purposely keep the directorship in the hands of a young, returning teacher in order to keep administration close to what the organisation actually does.*

Steve goes on to lament the need to introduce such a substantial fee, but recommends it to anyone who can afford it.

English for Everybody, 655 Powell Street, Suite 505, San Francisco, CA 94108, USA; Spanielova 1292, 163 00 Prague. Strong representation in the Czech Republic but operate throughout the region. (See chapter on the Czech Republic).

Interexchange, 161 Sixth Avenue, New York, NY 10013. Tel: (212) 924-0446 ext. 109. Fax: (212) 924-0575. Arrange teaching assistantships in Czech Republic and Hungary, Bulgaria and Poland. Placement fee of $400-$450. Future placements in Russia possible.

Peace Corps, Room 803E, 1111 20th St NW, Washington DC 20526. Tel: (toll-free) 1-800-424-8580. Web-site. http://www.peacecorps.gov/. Provides volunteer teachers on the usual 27 month contracts to the former USSR. Must be US citizen, over 18 and in good health. They recruit people to teach at both secondary and university level and to become involved with teacher training and curriculum development.

Soros Professional English Language Teaching Program (SPELT), University of Montana, Linguistics Program, Missoula, MT 59812. Tel: (406) 243-5164. Fax: (406) 243-2016. E-mail: soros@selway.umt.edu. Since 1991, the Soros Foundation (incorporating the Charter 77 Foundation and Open Society Fund) places instructors in schools in Azerbaijan, Bosnia-Herzegovina, Bulgaria, Croatia, the Czech Republic, Georgia, Hungary, Kazakhstan, Kyrgyzstan, Latvia, Lithuania, Moldova, Romania, Slovakia, Slovenia, Ukraine, Uzbekistan and Yugoslavia. An MA in Applied Linguistics or TESOL is required in most cases though EFL certification will be considered. Prior teaching experience is required. US nationality not necessary.

The rest of this chapter is organised by country. The main six (Bulgaria, Czech Republic, Hungary, Poland, Romania and Slovakia) are followed by Russia and its former satellite states.

Albania barely figures in the literature about ELT in Eastern Europe. Not only does it lack the infrastructure taken for granted in most of Europe, it is considered by many to be downright dangerous. Where once Albanians wanted to learn Italian (in order to understand the illicit Italian television transmitted from across the Adriatic) or French or German, English is now the favoured foreign language and is compulsory from the fifth grade through to university. (There are about 37 English lecturers at the University of Tirana.) There are no private schools in Albania, though English is taught up to 12 hours a week in certain selective schools. There might be a market for private tuition if Albanians had any disposable income, but most do not earn enough to feed and clothe themselves adequately. Many Albanians live in abject poverty, and there is an acute shortage of teaching materials in the country.

The Albanian Youth Club (whose motto is 'We work for a better world for young people') would welcome any voluntary input, whether as teachers of one of their eight classes of children and adults (especially in the summer) or as donors of ELT books and cassettes (hand-me-down photocopiers and computers very welcome...) The Club President, Selami Percja, wrote to say that volunteers do not need to be trained teachers, just ordinary people willing to come at any time of the year. More details are available from the AYC, PO Box 1741, Tirana, Albania.

Bulgaria

Teaching positions for native speakers in Bulgarian state schools are organised by the Ministry of Education & Science. Specialist foreign language secondary schools in Bulgaria employ native speaker teachers on one-year renewable contracts from September. Unfortunately the Central Bureau for Educational Visits and Exchanges in London is no longer involved in the scheme, so direct contact should be made with the Bulgarian Ministry of Education & Science (2A Knjaz Dondoukov, 1000 Sofia; 2-988 0494).

Certainly the Bulgarian educational system could never afford to attract teachers on its own since public expenditure on education in Bulgaria has been reduced by three-quarters since 1989, according to a Unicef report.

The Sofia-based organisation Teachers for Central and Eastern Europe, 21 V 5 Rakovski Boulevard, Dimitrovgrad 6400 (see above for fax, e-mail and contact names in Bulgaria and the US) is most active in Bulgaria. Since 1993 TFCEE has been recruiting native speaker teachers on behalf of the Ministry of Education. With 40 native speaker teachers placed in Bulgarian schools annually, TFCEE is second only to the Peace Corps. Participants are sent to English medium secondary schools or schools of natural sciences in cities of over 50,000 for an academic year, though one-semester placements are possible (i.e. mid-September to mid-January and 1st February to mid-June).

The weekly teaching load is 19 40-minute classes per four-day week. The salary in Bulgarian leva is equivalent to $150 (which is nearly a third higher than that of the host school's principal). Benefits include free furnished accommodation and all utility bills, 60 days of paid holiday, paid sick leave, free Bulgarian language instruction, free health care and free multiple-entry visa and work permit.

In conjunction with the Ministry of Education, English language summer courses are held at mountain and seaside resorts. Teachers can stay from between one and three months. Monthly remuneration exceeds $200 as accommodation is free of charge.

Political change in Bulgaria has been much less dramatic than elsewhere in the former Eastern Bloc, and in fact the Communist party is the elected government. The private sector is still relatively undeveloped, and placement of teachers in state schools is centralised by the Ministry of Education. As a result, there is not much point in contacting individual schools, even if you do obtain a list from the British Council in Sofia. The British Council is responsible for recruiting *lektors* for universities in Bulgaria, who have to have a strong academic background. Most of the main voluntary organisations are active in Bulgaria, including the Soros Foundation and East European Partnership.

One further possibility is to teach conversational English at summer schools in Bulgaria. The Union of Free Students of Bulgaria (c/o 99 Haberdasher St, London N1 6EH) was involved in sending undergraduates and graduates to summer projects, but it was not confirmed that they are still doing this. The British Bulgarian Friendship Society which meets in the basement of Finsbury Library (245 St John St, London EC1V 4NB) might be able (informally) to suggest contacts.

According to the Bulgarian Embassy in London, people who have found employment should apply with a letter from their employer for a multiple entry visa (at a cost of £42) which will be valid for three months. Longer-term work and residence permits can be arranged with the local authorities after arrival.

Writing in *Warwick Network* (the Warwick University graduates' magazine) a few years ago, Bruce Marsland described life in Bulgaria's fourth city Ruse, where he was the city's only Englishman (and where living conditions may well have improved since that time):

Living in a typically grey concrete block, I have to face many of the problems in the same way as the locals. Due to the precarious condition of the nearby nuclear power station, the electricity is cut off for one hour in every four. Romanian industry on the opposite bank of the Danube frequently pollutes the air with chlorine. The regular queues for food such as sheep's milk, cheese and salami (the staple winter diet) have also become part of the routine of survival. Most consumer goods are now available, if at prices too high for the average Bulgarian.

ALLIANCE FOR FOREIGN LANGUAGES
3 Slaveikov Square, Sofia 1000, Bulgaria. Tel: (2) 880238. Fax: (2) 882349.
Number of teachers: no foreign teachers at present.
Preference of nationality: none.
Qualifications: English philology (BA).
Conditions of employment: probationary year, then permanent.
Salary: US$100 per month less 37% deductions.
Facilities/Support: no assistance with accommodation or work permits.
Recruitment: local interview essential.
Contact: Svetla Popova, Teacher Trainer.

PRIVATE SCHOOL FOR BANKING AND BUSINESS
83 Bogomil Street, Plovdiv, Bulgaria. Tel: (32) 68 14 14. Fax: (32) 27 48 80.
Preference of nationality: none.
Qualifications: higher education. Minimum 3 years' experience.
Conditions of employment: 1 year contracts. 31 lessons p.w. (45 minutes each).
Salary: as agreed by state.
Recruitment: interview necessary.
Contact: Fanka Istatkova, President.

Czech Republic

Because of the worldwide increase in the number of trained EFL teachers as well as the popularity of Prague and the Czech Republic, the standard of native speaker teacher has improved. Gone are the days when an English speaker could walk into a school and be offered a position complete with reasonable salary and accommodation, simply by opening his or her mouth. There is still some scope for novices outside Prague. But in Prague, it continues to be difficult to obtain either employment or accommodation because of the competition from so many other foreigners. Some of the smaller Czech towns including some rather uninspiring places in the steel-producing heart of the country and the Moravian capital Brno offer interested teachers much more scope for employment than the tourist-clogged capital.

Teaching private lessons is the most lucrative but the most difficult to fix up for new arrivals. Private lessons now go as high as 300 crowns an hour for businesses, but most earn the teacher about half that. A good way to attract pupils initially is to charge at the lower end of the scale but to teach in groups of three or four.

FIXING UP A JOB
Most schools express no preference for nationality, and prefer a mixture of accents. Americans are still in the ascendancy (it has been estimated that there are between 20,000 and 30,000 in Prague alone), but Canadians, Britons, etc. are all welcome. Australians are generally well received partly because of the large number of Czechs (about 20,000) who emigrated to Australia.

State Schools

Qualified teachers are being recruited to teach in Czech primary and secondary schools, usually on a one-year contract with low-cost or free accommodation and a salary of 6,000-9,000 Czech crowns net per month. In the early days, various institutes and ministries fell over themselves to recruit teachers resulting in much duplication, but now the centralised contact is the *Academic Information Agency (AIA)* in Prague (see entry). AIA is part of the Ministry of Education, and distributes its literature through Czech Embassies abroad. In the UK write to the Cultural Section, Czech Embassy, 26 Kensington Palace Gardens, London W8 4QY; tel: 0171-243 1115/fax: 0171-727 9654.

The AIA assists people interested in teaching English at primary and secondary state schools. Most of the teaching positions are at schools in smaller towns. The school year runs for ten months from September 1st to June 30th, though some vacancies occur in January between semesters. Although the minimum requirement is a BA/MA in English/Applied Linguistics, additional teaching qualifications (TEFL or PGCE) and experience give an applicant priority. Applications should be submitted before the end of April. The AIA simply acts as a go-between, circulating CVs and applications to state schools which have requested a teacher. Schools then contact applicants directly to discuss contractual details.

Kathy Panton is just one of the AIA's satisfied customers: 'I really recommend the AIA; they helped me out of a bad hole when I moved from Liberec to Prague and tried harder than I had any right to expect to get me out of another one, when I was assigned flea-ridden and expensive accommodation.'

Another important Czech organisation for TEFLers is the *Akademie J.A. Komenskeho* which actively recruits native speakers to participate in the Czech adult education programme. Americans should contact *InterExchange* in New York which cooperates with the international exchange organisation APEX in Prague (Pod Juliskou 4, 160 00 Prague 6; tel/fax: 2-311 9158) to place Americans in state schools for the 10-month academic year. The programme is open to graduates who either have a teaching certificate or solid experience of teaching, preferably ESL. The fee is $450 and the deadline is April 15th.

As mentioned in the introduction to this chapter, the organisation based in Bulgaria *Teachers for Central & Eastern Europe* cooperates with the Ministries of Education of the countries in which it is active (including the Czech Republic) in order to place native speakers for an academic year in state schools.

The growth of a free market economy means that the role of voluntary organisations has diminished. Eastern European Partnership (part of VSO) has withdrawn, as has the North American teacher-placement organisation Education for Democracy. Although *SOL* (see introduction to Eastern Europe) is more active in Romania and Hungary, it is able to place EFL teachers in Czech state schools for an academic year, as it did for Brian Farrelly:

> *I taught in two state schools in the Czech Republic and had a really great time in both. I felt really privileged to teach the students there. My first job in a 'gymnazium' secondary school in a small town called Sedlcany south of Prague was arranged by SOL. The staff and students made me tremendously welcome. I also greatly enjoyed the freedom to teach as I saw fit, although I felt initially very daunted by the lack of guidance regarding what I should be doing with the students. My next job was found by the AIA in Prague. After visiting, I was offered a number of schools and I chose another gymnazium in another small town called Jevicko, north of Brno.*

Private Schools

The private sector has matured enormously in the past few years so that there is now a wide range of well established schools offering high standards of instruction. The main international chains of language schools like Linguarama, Berlitz and International House have large established operations in the country. Most teachers are recruited locally, often via notice boards at the British Council or English language bookshops like the Globe. Most schools in Prague can count on receiving plenty of

CVs on spec from which to fill any vacancies which arise. Anyone who is well qualified or experienced should have few difficulties in finding a job on the spot and obtaining a work permit. The Yellow Pages *(Zlaté Stránky)* are an excellent source of addresses under the heading *Jazykove skoly*. Looking at all the glossy ads for English language schools, both Western backed and locally owned, it is hard to believe that just a decade ago, Czechoslovakia was still a Communist country.

Some private recruitment agencies in Britain (such as *Language Link* mentioned in the introduction to this chapter on Eastern Europe) and in the US can place qualified applicants in teaching posts in the Czech Republic. *IPG* based in Prague but with an office in London can be very useful to Certificate-trained ELT teachers. With offices in Prague and San Francisco, the agency *English for Everybody* is in a strong position to match clients with suitable posts in Prague and elsewhere in the Czech Republic. Candidates must have a university degree and either a TEFL Certificate or relevant experience. According to the Director Iva Brozova, newly arrived English teachers in Prague need more than just a job-finding service. They need a practical orientation and someone to turn to with questions and problems, so she maintains regular contact with her clients after they have started work. The assistance fee charged is US$450. English for Everybody may be contacted at 655 Powell Street, Suite 505, San Francisco, CA 94108 (tel: 415-789-7641/fax: 530-895-0998) and Spanielova 1292, 163 00 Prague 6 (tel/fax: 42-2-301 9784/e-mail: EFE@itc-training.com (Subject EFE).

Only very occasionally do Czech schools advertise their vacancies abroad. One school which does advertise every summer in the *Guardian* is the Till English Academy in Northern Moravia (Cs. Armady 10, 710 00 Ostrava; fax 69-226927).

But most people wait until they arrive in Prague before trying to find teaching work, which is what Linda Harrison did:

> The best time to apply is before June. I arrived in September which was too late, but if you persevere there are jobs around. A lot of teaching work here seems to be in companies. Schools employ you to go into offices, etc. to teach English (though not usually business English). After a short job hunt, I was hired by Languages at Work which paid well and provided food and travel vouchers as well as helping with accommodation.

In Prague, keep your eyes open for small notices. M. J. Hinton answered an ad in a coffee shop, phoned up and was invited for an informal interview, which resulted in a good job which involved only seven hours of teaching a week and 11 hours of administration.

Those without qualifications or experience will find it very difficult. Even with a year and a half of teaching experience in a Czech town, Kathy Panton got turned down in Prague because she didn't have a TEFL Certificate. She warns that you can't count on picking up work for at least a month, though living expenses shouldn't be much more than £200 during that time. Unlike state schools, private schools in Prague do not necessarily offer accommodation, and will give preference when hiring to anyone who already has accommodation fixed up.

There are a few advertisements for teaching jobs in the local English press, primarily *The Prague Post* (Na Porici 12, 115 30 Prague 1; fax: 2-248 75 050). Heather Mayes noticed an ad placed here by an American businesswoman looking for EFL teachers to work at a private school in Brno. It may be worth advertising your speciality as an English tutor (e.g. marketing, law, etc.) ahead of time. Kathy Panton suggests enlisting the help of a Czech friend:

> A better way to find work is to get someone (the Czech embassy will probably do it if you catch them on a slow day) to translate 'Native speaker will tutor English to intermediate or advanced students starting... phone/write...' and send it to a newspaper like Mláda Fronta Dnes or Annoncé with a £5 note maybe.

REGULATIONS

Czech embassies distribute clear information about the steps necessary to obtain a work permit and long term residence permit, both of which are supposed to be obtained before you start work in the Czech Republic. The work permit must be obtained from the local employment office *(Urad práce)* by your future employer. They will need a signed form from you plus a photocopy of your passport and the originals or notarised copies of your education certificates. After this has been issued and sent on to you, you must present it along with a number of other documents to the Czech Embassy in your country in order to obtain the Long-Term Residence Permit. You will need confirmation of accommodation (provided by your school), confirmation that you don't have a criminal record, and birth certificate officially translated into Czech (consular staff abroad or your employer will assist). You will also need to obtain a Certificate of Good Conduct from the aliens police.

All of this is quite a palaver and will take between two and three months. The necessity of conforming with these procedures puts some candidates off according to the head of the English Department at the *Státní Jazyková Skola*:

> I must say that quite a lot of teachers inquire about positions available here but what they usually do not like is a long period necessary for arranging the work and residency permits. As a state school we cannot employ anybody illegally. Therefore if the teacher is not in the country, it means a lot of correspondence. All the procedure may take about three months.

The President of APEX (mentioned above) blames the cumbersome red tape for the relatively small number of teacher placements his organisation is able to make, and APEX is lobbying for the Czech government to give official cultural exchange programmes special dispensation so that they can bypass the normal immigration procedures.

It is possible and probably easier to arrange things after arrival in the Czech Republic, though the same time lag will occur, during which you will be working illegally and without state insurance cover. Although some foreigners do teach without worrying about the paperwork, schools can be fined for hiring teachers black. Try to find an employer who is familiar with the procedures and willing to defray some of the expense.

CONDITIONS OF WORK

Most English teachers agree that working conditions in state schools are generally better than in private schools. People teaching at private institutes in Prague where there is a definite glut of foreign teachers, attracted by the cultural chic of the city, have been called the 'sweat shop labourers' of the TEFL world because of the low wages employers can get away with paying. The guaranteed salary at state schools, even if you're sick or there is a holiday, is a definite advantage. If you are lucky enough to be teaching mostly final year students, your working hours in the exam month of June will be minimal. A drawback of state school teaching is the 8am start, but of course there is no evening or weekend work as in private schools.

Compared to the monthly wage in state schools of 6,000-7,000 crowns, private sector wages are normally more like 8,500-10,500 (also net). But this does not include accommodation which will account for between a quarter and third of a teaching salary. Hourly fees start at 75 crowns net, though a more usual wage is 125 crowns less 20%-25% for tax and deductions. A full-time salary should be adequate to live on by local standards but will not allow you to save anything, unless you take on lots of private tutoring.

The majority of private language school clients are adults who are available for lessons after work, so most teaching takes place between 4pm and 8pm Monday to Thursday. (Some schools do specialise in teaching children, for which a basic knowledge of the Czech language is essential.)

Accommodation is generally in very short supply, and housing problems will get even worse if the current laws which regulate the housing market are relaxed. Very little rental accommodation is available on the open market in Prague and, unless you have contacts or your employer undertakes to help you (as many do), you will have severe problems. If you have a friend to translate for you, you can try the accommodation listings in *Annoncé,* the Prague free ads paper. Most employers are prepared to help newcomers to find accommodation, usually a room in a small shared flat or university hostel. Registered students are eligible for very cheap housing and therefore, not surprisingly, it is not at all easy to register as a student. Many teachers in Prague have no choice but to live in a concrete jungle of soulless *paneláks* (monolithic apartment buildings) a long commute away (where the suicide rate is triple the national average).

Students are reported to be 'a delight to teach, alert, intelligent, fun-loving, keen and interested'. Although textbooks are now widely available, teachers would be well advised before setting out to check on the availability of supplementary materials in the school where they are going to teach and to take along their own favourites. Many English teachers avail themselves of the excellent resource centres run by the British Council in Prague (where the joining fee is 300 crowns), Brno, Ceske Budejovice, Olomouc, Ostrava, Pardubice, Plzen and Usti nad Labem.

One of the strongest motivations among secondary school *(Gymnazium)* students to learn English is the prospect of the 'Maturity' exam. At the beginning of the year they are given 25 topics (e.g. the British Royal Family, the influence of the media) and at the end of the year they must talk in English about one topic (chosen at random) for 15 minutes. This is a very good incentive for class participation.

Leisure Time

The cost of living continues to creep up; the cost of cinema and concert tickets has doubled over the past four years. But you can still afford to buy an awful lot of the truly excellent Czech beer out of a teacher's wage, if not fund much travelling round the region. (A dual pricing system operates so that those without a Czech passport pay more for hotel rooms and transport.)

Prague has a vibrant nightlife with clubs and cafés, cinema, opera, poetry and dance. There is so much expat culture, that a new arrival who is serious about getting into Czech culture will encounter difficulty. There is also something of a backlash among Czechs against western 'good-for-nothings' who spend Czech currency as if it were Monopoly money. In Prague theft is a serious problem, though walking the streets is still very safe.

In small towns, however, English teachers are still likely to be treated as honoured guests with many offers of hospitality and invitations for example to join skiing trips (which are very cheap), as Hannah Bullock from Oxford discovered in her year out between school and university in the town of Strakonice:

> *I've got some great Czech friends here. A colleague of mine has been very kind (as I've found most Czechs are) and has been like a mentor-cum-grandpa to me, taking me to visit castles, nearby towns, beautiful little villages and to walk in the mountains which border Germany. Most of this would have been very difficult without a car (the trains go very infrequently and at unsociable hours). I've spent many weekends in Prague since it's only one and a half hours by bus. I had to do double takes on hearing English spoken and seeing the* Guardian *being passed round the bars. Now instead of seeing Prague as the opening to Central Europe with its old-fashioned trams and cobbled streets as I did when I first arrived in September, I now think of it as the door back to westernisation.*

One final tip: if you play a musical instrument, take it with you since it's a great way to make local friends.

LIST OF SCHOOLS

ACADEMIC INFORMATION AGENCY (AIA)

Dum zahranicnich sluzeb MSMT, Senovázné nám. 26, 111 21 Prague 1. Tel: (2) 2422 9698. Fax: (2) 2422 9697. E-mail: aia@dzs.cz. Web-site: http://www.dzs.cz
Number of teachers: many teachers needed for state schools throughout the Czech Republic.
Preference of nationality: native speakers.
Qualifications: university degree in relevant subject required (e.g. English or

Linguistics) or BA in other subject plus TEFL/TESL qualification. Previous experience in TEFL highly valued.

Conditions of employment: 10-month contracts September-June. 24 h.p.w.

Salary: 6,000-9,000 Czech crowns per month (net).

Facilities/Support: accommodation provided (free or subsidised). Work and residence permits organised before arrival.

Recruitment: direct application via AIA or Czech Embassy. Deadline for applications is end of April.

AGENTURA EDUCO
Veletrzni 24, 170 00 Prague 7. Tel: (2) 333 70 163 Fax: (2) 203 97 310.

Number of teachers: 6.

Preference of nationality: none.

Qualifications: BA in English. TEFL and teaching experience preferred. Knowledge of economics, business, banking and other fields useful.

Conditions of employment: 1 year contracts possible. From 4 hours per week.

Salary: 120 crowns per teaching unit (45 minutes). Teachers are expected not just to conduct conversation but to teach vocabulary and grammar.

Facilities/Support: no help with accommodation given. No training.

Recruitment: notices in the British Council, Globe Bookstore & Coffeehouse.

AKCENT LANGUAGE SCHOOL
Bítovská 3, 140 00 Prague 4. Tel: (2) 42 05 95/42 01 23. Fax: (2) 42 28 45. E-mail: info.akcent@akcent.cz

Number of teachers: 27-30.

Preference of nationality: none.

Qualifications: BA plus CELTA or equivalent (minimum).

Conditions of employment: 10 months from 1st September. 24 teaching hours (45 minutes) per week. Students aged 5-14 and 14 to adult.

Salary: 9,500-14,000 crowns (gross) per month plus free accommodation (for teachers with at least 1 year of teaching experience).

Facilities/Support: accommodation and travel card provided. Regular training seminars since school is involved in multi-media projects for teacher training. Free weekly Czech language lessons. School runs DELTA courses.

Recruitment: adverts in the *Guardian* and locally. Interviews not essential, but can be held in London or at TESOL conferences in the US.

Contact: Brian O hEithir.

ANGLICTINA EXPRES
Korunní 2, 12000 Prague 2. Tel/fax: (2) 2423 8186/2425 3479. E-mail: anexpres@vol.cz

Number of teachers: 5-10.

Preference of nationality: none.

Qualifications: university degree and some teaching experience preferred.

Conditions of employment: 1 year contracts. Morning and evening work.

Salary: hourly rate.

Facilities/Support: no help with accommodation. Some training available. Materials produced in-house.

Recruitment: direct application. Telephone interviews sufficient.

Contact: Milena Kelly.

BELL SCHOOL
Nedvezská 29, 100 00 Prague 10. Tel: (2) 78 15 342. Fax: (2) 78 22 961.

Number of teachers: 25 (full-time and part-time).

Preference of nationality: British, American.

Qualifications: DELTA or CELTA or equivalent, plus 2 years' teaching experience.
Recruitment: local interviews essential.
Contact: Irena Maskova, Director of Studies.

THE CALEDONIAN SCHOOL

Vltavská 24, 150 00 Prague 5. Tel/fax: (2) 573 13 650. E-mail: jobs@caledonian
school.com; http://www.caledonianschool.com/
Number of teachers: 80.
Preference of nationality: none.
Qualifications: BA plus CELTA or equivalent.
Conditions of employment: 10 month contracts from mid-September. 20-24 45-minute
lessons p.w. School teaches adults and young adults, in-school and in-company.
Salary: 13,500 crowns per month for qualified teachers. Free local transport pass.
Contract completion bonus.
Facilities/Support: accommodation usually offered in Hotel Dum ('Teachers' House')
for 3,400 crowns per month or school arranges a shared flat. School arranges and pays
for flats for teachers who teach at out-of-Prague sites. Monthly teacher development
workshops held. Library has over 500 EFL titles, photocopiers and free e-mail and
internet access for teachers. Social committee organises excursions and events for
staff.
Recruitment: direct application. School hires year round. North Americans can
contact Toronto office: 6 Greenmount Court, Toronto, Ontario M8Y 1Y1 (416-231-
9546/fax 416-231-1730).
Contact: Paul Michel, Director of Studies.

CALIFORNIA SUN SCHOOL

Na Bojisti 2, Prague 2. Tel: (2) 294817/961 80 103/961 80 104/295681. Fax: 92)
822271.
Number of teachers: 20.
Preference of nationality: none.
Qualifications: TEFL certificate and preferably some teaching experience.
Conditions of employment: 6-month contracts in first instance, 10 months thereafter.
30 h.p.w. between 9am and 9pm, or maximum 27 h.p.w for those who teach business
classes.
Salary: 7,500-12,000 crowns per month net plus 3,000 crown bonus at end of 6 month
contract and 10,000 crown bonus at end of second 10-month contract.
Facilities/Support: housing provided for 75% of staff; if school's housing is full,
accommodation allowance is paid. Work permit process handled by school for a 2,000
crown fee, which is deducted from wages over 2 months and refunded after 6 month
contract is completed. New teachers give lessons which are evaluated by senior
staff.
Recruitment: mainly via International TEFL College of Ireland (see *Training:
Abroad*). Interviews not essential.
Contact: Josh Stevenson, Assistant Director.

DAVID'S AGENCY

Stefánikova 2888, 760 01 Zlín. Tel: (67) 37505.
Number of teachers: 5.
Preference of nationality: none.
Qualifications: university degree and TEFL.
Conditions of employment: 10 month contracts. Hours are 8am-noon and 1pm-
4.30pm.
Salary: 15,000 crowns (gross) less about 25% for tax and social security.
Facilities/Support: accommodation arranged for 3,000 crowns per month. Assistance
with work permit process. Training given in Czech language and culture.
Recruitment: via adverts in the *Guardian*. Interviews compulsory and are held in

England in the summer (David's Agency, c/o 18 Low Mill, Lancaster Road, Canton, Lancaster LA2 9HX).
Contact: David Catto, Director.

ENCOUNTER ENGLISH
Azalková 12, 100 00 Prague 10-Hostivar. Tel/fax: (2) 758773.
Number of teachers: 15-20 full-time and 4 part-time.
Preference of nationality: British, North American.
Qualifications: 4 week TEFL course (e.g. CELTA, Trinity) and 1 or 2 years' experience.
Conditions of employment: 10 month contracts (September to June). 24 h.p.w. maximum. No weekend work.
Salary: 8,500 crowns (net) depending on qualifications and experience.
Facilities/Support: accommodation is provided and paid for. All utilities except phone paid by school. If school is given power of attorney, it carries out all work permit procedures. Regular seminars and workshops held.
Recruitment: ads in the UK press, e.g. *Guardian* and direct application.
Contact: Stephen Brierley, General Manager.

ENGLISH HOUSE
Vysehradská 2, 128 00 Prague 2. Tel/fax: (2) 293141.
Number of teachers: 15.
Preference of nationality: British preferred for convenience.
Qualifications: EFL certificate and some experience required.
Conditions of employment: 10 month contracts September-June. Lessons are 45 minutes, held Monday-Friday between 8am and 8pm.
Salary: approximately 13,000 crowns per month.
Facilities/Support: accommodation provided, public transport pass provided and paid. Professional development workshops held twice a month.
Recruitment: personal interview necessary, possible either in London or Prague.
Contact: Jaroslava Fricová, School Manager.

ENGLISH LANGUAGE SERVICES/ELS
Rooseveltova 9, 301 14 Plzen. Tel/fax: (19) 723 6699. Mobile: 0603 412 454. E-mail: els@pm.bohem-net.cz. www.kadel.cz/els
Number of teachers: 2.
Preference of nationality: English, Scottish, Canadian.
Qualifications: standard TEFL and good all-round education.
Conditions of employment: 1 academic year. 30 h.p.w.
Salary: 18,500 crowns (gross) and 8,500 crowns net after deductions for rent, social security and tax.
Facilities/Support: flat provided. Full assistance with work permits. Training provided.
Recruitment: directly or via agency. Phone interviews sufficient.
Contact: Brian Windsor, Director.

ET CETERA LANGUAGE SCHOOL
Dusni 17, 110 00 Prague 1. Tel: (2) 231 3062. Fax: (2) 89 44 84.
Number of teachers: 4-5.
Preference of nationality: none.
Qualifications: TEFL/TESOL/2 years' teaching experience.
Conditions of employment: 1 year contract. Usually 20 h.p.w. (minimum 16, maximum unlimited).
Salary: 150 crowns per lesson.
Facilities/Support: assistance given with accommodation. No training.
Recruitment: direct application and local interviews.

INTERNATIONAL HOUSE PRAGUE

Lupácova 1, 130 00 Prague 3. Tel: (2) 697 4513/900 02 685. Fax: (2) 231 8584. E-mail: ihprague@telecom.cz. Also International House Brno, Sokolska 1, 602 00 Brno. Tel: (5) 41 24 04 93. Fax: (5) 41 24 59 54. E-mail: ihbrno@mbox.vol.cz
Part of ILC Group.
Preference of nationality: must be native speaker of English.
Qualifications: minimum CELTA (grade A or B).
Conditions of employment: 1 year contracts.
Facilities/Support: accommodation provided. Full-time and part-time CELTA courses offered.
Recruitment: via Staffing Unit at IH in London or locally.
Contact: Jim Chapman, EFL Operations Director.

INTERTEXT SERVIS KAREL NAVRATIL

Anglická 24, 360 09 Karlovy Vary. Tel/fax: (17) 323 0436.
Number of teachers: 2.
Preference of nationality: none (e.g. British, American, Canadian).
Qualifications: BA plus CELTA/TESOL, plus preferably some teaching experience.
Conditions of employment: 1 year contracts. 16-20 h.p.w. Teachers expected to teach vocabulary and grammar (Cambridge English) and to conduct conversations.
Salary: 80 crowns net per teaching hour (45 minutes).
Facilities/Support: assistance given with accommodation. On-going assistance with lesson planning.
Recruitment: direct application, personal contact.
Contact: Karel Navrátil, Director.

LANGUAGES AT WORK

Na Florenci 35, 110 00 Prague 1. Tel/fax: (2) 248 11 379. E-mail: employment@mbox.vol.cz; http://www.vol.cz/atwork
Number of teachers: 20 full and part-time.
Preference of nationality: none, but must be native speaking.
Qualifications: preferably CELTA or equivalent, or with teaching experience, particularly in ESP since certain clients require business, computer or other knowledge.
Conditions of employment: 1 year contracts. Approximately 20 h.p.w. (more if requested).
Salary: 135 crowns per hour, 130 crowns until work permit received. Pay rise of 5-10 crowns given each semester. 22% deductions from full-time teachers' salaries.
Facilities/Support: local travel benefits, luncheon vouchers, internet and other benefits. Assistance with finding accommodation. School arranges translations, etc. for work permit application. Monthly methodology seminars.
Recruitment: interviews conducted in Prague. Initial contact welcomed by e-mail. Candidates not available for interview must write a short essay and describe a teaching scenario.
Contact: Mark Benfer, Director of Studies.

SPUSA EDUCATION CENTER

Navrátilova 2, 110 00 Prague 1. Tel: (2) 2223 1702.. Fax: (2) 2223 2530. (SPUSA is an acronym for Society of Friends of the USA.)
Number of teachers: 25.
Preference of nationality: none.
Qualifications: TEFL or equivalent certificate and preferably at least one year's teaching experience.
Conditions of employment: 1 year contracts. 20-25 45-minute lessons p.w. On- and off-site teaching of mainly adults.

Salary: 145 crowns per hour.
Facilities/Support: advice given on finding accommodation. Help with work and residence permits. Health and dental insurance provided. Training workshops held.
Recruitment: direct application. Applicants must submit references, sample lesson plans and copies of diplomas and teaching certificates.
Contact: Lynda Mallinger, Director of Studies.

STATNI JAZYKOVA SKOLA BRNO
Kotlárská 9, 611 49 Brno. Tel/fax: (5) 412 49 001. Tel: (5) 412 48 999.
Number of teachers: 5-7.
Preference of nationality: British.
Qualifications: must have TEFL qualification.
Conditions of employment: 1 academic year (September-June). Approximately 20 h.p.w.
Salary: about 10,000 crowns per month (gross) less 30% in deductions.
Facilities/Support: assistance with finding accommodation, full help with work permits and training available at staff meetings.
Recruitment: liaise with other schools.
Contact: Marie Pilarová, Deputy Head.

STATNI JAZYKOVA SKOLA PRAGUE
Skolsá 15, 116 72 Prague 1. Tel (English Department): (2) 222 32 237. Fax: (2) 222 32 236. E-mail: sjs@sjs.cz. Separate state language school with similar conditions at Buresova 1130, 182 00 Prague 8—Ladvi (2-85 88 028).
Number of teachers: 12.
Preference of nationality: none.
Qualifications: BA in English, TESOL, CELTA or equivalents or teaching experience.
Conditions of employment: 10 months from September 1st. 19 45-minute classes per week between 8am and 8pm.
Salary: starting salary 8,800 crowns per month (gross) plus at least 2 bonuses a year.
Facilities/Support: centrally located accommodation can be arranged for about 4,000 crowns a month (school contributes 500 crowns towards rent). Subsidised meal coupons. 6 free Czech lessons a week (or other language).
Recruitment: contact by mail or in person. Interviews not always necessary, though trial lesson at school preferred.
Contact: Eva Zahradnícková, Head of the English Department (Prague 1); Ruth Vacková, Head of the English Department (Prague 8).

Other Schools to Try
Note that these schools (in alphabetical order according to town) did not confirm their teacher requirements for this edition of *Teaching English Abroad*. Upper case entries marked with an asterisk had entries in the last edition (1997); addresses without asterisks have been taken from various sources, such as British Council lists and the *Yellow Pages*.
Albion Travel, Milady Horákové 14-16, Brno (tel/fax 5-452 40 911)
Berlitz, Starobrnenská 3, Brno (5-422 13 729)
Brno English Centre, VUT Kravi hora 13, 602 00 Brno (tel/fax 5-4121 2262)
Colourful English, námesti Svornosti 8, Brno (5-412 13 306)
Easy English, Botanická 13, Brno (5-742318)
European Language Institute, Ceská 15, Brno (tel/fax 5-422 13 221)
International House Brno, Sokolska 1, 602 00 Brno (5-41 24 04 93)
Secretarial and Language Institute, Stefánikova 36a, Brno (5-412 10 842)

Ability Language School, Lipova Laznia Mountain Spa Resort (tel/fax 2-627 21986). Summer school.

Till English Academy, Cs. Armady 10, 710 00 Ostrava (602-527391/fax 69-226929)

Aliance, Malická 4, 301 11 Plzen

Dum Technicky, Sady Petatrlcátníku 6, 301 24 Plzen

JAP, Slovenská alej 24, 307 04 Plzen

Jazyková skola Evropa, Tylová 15, 301 25 Plzen 1

School of English, Skroupova 3, 301 36 Plzen 1

Státní jazyková skola, Jungmannová 1-3, 301 36 Plzen 1

Language Link, Kopeckého sady 15, 301 36 Plzen

IMB Jazykové Centrum, Purkynova 21, 301 36 Plzen

*AKADEMIE J.A. KOMENSHKEHO, Trziste 20, Mala Strana, 118 43 Prague 1. Main office of network of adult education centres throughout the Czech Republic where native speaker English teachers are needed including gap year students.

Ability Jazyková Agentura, Levského 3203, 13-16 hod, Prague 4 (tel/fax 2-401 07 71).

Aha Jazyková Agentura, Kourimská 11, 130 00 Prague 3 (Vinohrady) (2-673 15 737/fax 2-717 32 127/e-mail aha@ini.cz

Alpha Omega Jazyková Skola, Bubenská 27, 170 00 Prague 7 (tel/fax 2-8757 88).

Berlitz Language Centre, Vlkova 12, 130 00 Prague 3 (2-277101/270559)

Cosmolingua, Zdarilá 8, 140 00 Prague 4 (Nusle) (2-612 25 690/1; e-mail: praha@cosmolingua.cz)

Elvis Jazyková Skola, Dacického 8, 140 00 Prague 4 (tel/fax 2-420044/e-mail info@elvis.cz

English Link, Na Beránce 2, 160 00 Prague 6 (2-360380/fax 2-781 7625)

Exellent, Stepánská 13, 120 00 Prague 2 (tel/fax 2-291063)

European Language Institute, Na Porici 17, Prague 1 (tel/fax 2-248 12 474)

International Training Solutions Ltd., Thamova 24, 186 00 Prague 8

Kolumbus Language Club, Zahrebska 9, 120 00 Prague 2 (900 58 481).

Linguarama, Srobárova 1, 130 00 Prague 3 (2-744889)

Lingua Viva, Spálená 57, Prague 1 (2-291933/fax 2-249 21 051).

*LONDON SCHOOL OF MODERN LANGUAGES, Francouzská Ulice 30, 120 00 Prague 2 (2-242 53 437/fax 2-242 54 259). 50 teachers.

Prague Language Centre, V Jame 8, 110 00 Prague 1 (2-262355/fax 2-262901/e-mail plc@mbox.vol.cz)

Vista Welcome, Konevova 210, 130 00 Prague 3 (tel/fax 2-697 7492).

Hungary

English is compulsory for all Hungarian students who wish to apply for college or university entrance and university students in both the Arts and Sciences must take courses in English. Apart from the much-hated Russian, the second language of Hungary was traditionally German, a legacy of the old Austro-Hungarian Empire. But in most contexts German has been overtaken by English.

The Hungarian education system has much to be proud of, not least the efficacy with which it retrained its Russian teachers as English teachers after the return to democracy in 1989. The network of bilingual secondary schools *(gimnazia)* have produced a large number of graduates with a sophisticated knowledge of English. The vast majority of private language schools are owned and run by Hungarians rather than expats. Because of the calibre of Hungarian teachers of English, native speakers do not perhaps have the cachet that they have in other central European countries. Furthermore, the Hungarian language is so difficult for non-Hungarians to master, many schools prefer native Hungarians as English teachers.

Despite this, a demand for qualified native speakers continues unabated, especially in the business market. The invasion of foreigners in Budapest was never as overwhelming as it was (and is) in Prague, but still Budapest has a glut of teachers, among them some who have fled over-crowded Prague. The opportunities that do exist now are mostly in the provinces. Even in the more remote parts of the country, formal academic qualifications are important. It is a legal requirement that the bilingual schools employ a native speaker as lector. Most *gimnazia* liaise with the Fulbright Commission or the *Central European Teaching Program* and take on Americans, though Britons are also eligible.

Teachers are poorly paid in Hungary, aside from in the top-notch private schools and the British Council. Although the wage in forints has risen over the past two years, the exchange rate has dropped by more than a third. Rents in Budapest are high and take a major proportion of a teacher's salary; some schools help by subsidising accommodation, or it may be possible to arrange accommodation in return for English lessons. Low as the salaries may seem, native speakers can console themselves with the thought that they are usually better paid than Hungarian university lecturers.

FIXING UP A JOB

Very few jobs in Hungary are advertised in the UK and only one or two sending organisations (notably Services for Open Learning) include Hungary in their list of destinations. In the US, recruitment of teaching assistants takes place via a programme at Beloit College in Wisconsin called *Central European Teaching Program*. The programme offers 'cultural immersion through teaching' and is open to anyone with a university degree, and preferably some experience of TEFL and overseas teaching/study experience. CETP liaises with the relevant government department in Hungary to place teachers in state schools throughout the country.

InterExchange in New York has an English teaching programme in Hungary, though the number of participants is small. It cooperates with Diákközpont (DIK) in Hungary to arrange year-long teaching positions in private language schools; the fee for placement is $450.

After Arrival

The British Council in Budapest may be willing to advise personal callers. You can request their list of nine Dual Language Secondary Grammar Schools and consult the 'Book of Lists' from the *Budapest Business Journal* which contains about 40 addresses of private language institutes. The regional resource centres in Györ, Miskolc, Pécs and Szombathely may be more helpful. They should have a list of primary and secondary schools which teach English in the region.

The United States Information Service (Szabadság tér 7-9, 1054 Budapest; 1-302 6200) does not run its own English teaching programme but provides some assistance to Hungarian teacher training efforts with, among other things, the loan of English language materials, for example *FORUM,* the USIS publication for teachers of English, and English language TV series like *Crossroads Café* and *Family Album USA*. The former USIS library of English teaching materials is now available at the Pest County Pedagogical Institute in Budapest at Városház u. 7. (1-117 6570). The latter is open 1.30-4.30pm Monday and Thursday and 8.30am-12.30pm on Wednesday. Outside Budapest, another ELT Resource Centre can be found at the OKI Pedagogical Institute in Veszprém at Óváros tér 21, 8200 Veszprém (tel/fax 88-327725).

A personal approach to potential employers will certainly have more chance of success than writing speculative letters, although anyone in Hungary on a tourist visa will find it difficult to change status (see below). Introducing yourself in the staff room has led to more than one job offer in the past. Steve Anderson returned to the places where he had taught on the CETP scheme in the spring of 1998 and came away convinced that initiative would be rewarded:

> *I believe it's still possible to hook up work upon arrival simply by walking the beat. Of course the trick is to get out of Budapest, where the supply of MATESOL and other substantially qualified teachers runs at a surplus. The provincial cities and town*

(particularly in the impoverished northeast close to the Ukrainian border) would still welcome an energetic and dedicated native-speaking teacher. A student from the university in Szeged in southern Hungary assured me that I could obtain work as a part-time English lecturer after arriving, solely on the basis of my two years' EFL experience in Hungary and my one semester of an MATESOL. Apparently many teachers work their way into full-time positions after proving themselves by this method. Numerous native speaking teachers (from the US, Canada, UK and Australia) have passed through his university to teach for a bit.

State Schools

Native English speakers are sought by many state schools. English is available to pupils at the Dual Language Secondary Schools (a small percentage of the total), in the Gimnázium schools (more academic 'grammar schools', with 20% of total pupils), in technical and vocational schools *(szakközépiskola)* and in ordinary secondary schools throughout the country. The World Bank Program for the Development of Eastern Europe supports about 60 schools in the country and there are many perks for native speaker teachers employed by them such as field trips outside the school.

In the early days of the post-Communist period, the Hungarian Ministry of Education actively sought native speaker teachers for schools throughout the country, mainly through the English Teachers' Association of Hungary. This is the way Brian Komyathy, who describes himself as a New York suburbanite, fixed up his job a few years ago at a vocational school of economics, foreign trade and banking in Szolnok in central Hungary. However the placement of foreign teachers has mostly been delegated now to the foreign organisations mentioned above.

I found out after the fact that my query to the English Teachers' Association was forwarded (along with 24 others) to my current employer. They selected eight finalists whom they contacted, and when the dust settled, I was seen to have gone the distance. The eight Hungarian teachers of English here liked my credentials. I was rather surprised at how effortlessly I was able to arrange the job considering my lack of any previous teaching experience, only a BA in East European and Russian studies. Apparently the department (who have all been to Russia) thought I might have had some common experiences and would fit in as one of the gang, so to speak.

Most positions in Budapest schools are filled from the pool of available expats. The university towns of Debrecen, Miskolc, Szeged and Pécs are all better bets. You might be able to arrange at least part-time work assisting in English classes for university students. A further advantage is that universities normally can provide cheap housing in students' halls of residence.

Private Schools

Private institutes have mushroomed, primarily to meet the needs of the business community but also for children whose parents are keen for them to supplement the English teaching at state schools. It is estimated that there are over 100 private language schools in Budapest alone and 300 around the country, both very fluid numbers since schools open and close so quickly. Many private schools use native speakers as live commercials for the schools, though nowadays they want to advertise the qualifications of their teachers too.

Anyone with a recognised TEFL Certificate has a good chance of finding at least some hourly teaching after arrival in Budapest or elsewhere. British and American accents are both in demand. *International House* offers one-year contracts for qualified teachers of both adults and children and (according to Dennis Bricault) 'a wonderful social and professional atmosphere'.

To find the less well established schools on the spot, check the 'Book of Lists' mentioned above, try to decipher the Yellow Pages, keep your eyes open for the flyers posted in the main shopping streets or check out the English language weeklies. To find out what new institutes have opened or expanded, look at Hungarian papers like *Magyar Nemzet* or the free ads paper *Hirdetes* to see if any courses in *Angol* are being advertised at *Nyelviskola* (language schools).

Private tutoring provides one way of supplementing a meagre salary. Freelance teachers may find a developing market for their linguistic expertise in companies. Many executives need English for business as Hungary seeks to integrate with the economies of the West and attract foreign investors. The Department of Commerce, for example, employs teachers to train bankers, traders and top electrical engineers. Many professionals now need English as part of their work and are both able and prepared to pay for it. If you have a contact at International House in Budapest or Eger, you might enquire whether you can attend the fortnightly Angol Club which holds social events attended by learners and teachers, or perhaps the Executive Club for company clients. This would be a good place to meet potential private students.

REGULATIONS

Hungary was the first country in the former Eastern Bloc to clamp down on the untrained casual English teacher and to bring in work permit regulations. Now it is necessary to arrange the paperwork before leaving your country of residence which makes the task of finding a teaching job considerably harder. Deportation is said to be a real possibility for those who continue to teach for more than 90 days without a labour permit, though a more likely scenario is that the casual teacher with no prospect of getting a work permit will find it very difficult to find an employer in the first place. A foreign employee cannot get paid (at least not legally) until he or she has a labour permit.

A foreigner who wishes to enter Hungary to work must possess a special working visa issued by a Hungarian Embassy or Consulate in the applicant's country of residence. To apply for the working visa, the applicant must have a labour permit (obtained by the Hungarian employer) from the appropriate Hungarian labour office *(Munkaugyi Kozpont)* stating that no Hungarian national is available to do the job. The application for a labour permit must include originals (notarised copies will not suffice) of your university diploma, TEFL certificate (if applicable) and medical report stating that you have no communicable diseases (including HIV). The costs involved in having all these tests done in Hungary is $70-$100.

All documents must be officially translated into Hungarian, which is much more cheaply carried out by the Central Translation Office in Budapest than by the Embassy abroad; the Washington Embassy charges $15 just for the official stamp, never mind the translating service.

Work visas are issued for multiple entries (one year extendable to a maximum of three). Within one month of starting your job, you should go to the local police, accompanied by an official from your place of work to get a temporary residency permit stamped in your passport which is proof that you have both a work permit and a work visa. The fee of 4,000 forints is normally paid by the teacher.

CONDITIONS OF WORK

Salaries vary, but currently teachers in the state sector can expect between 30,000 and 50,000-60,000 forints (net) a month for teaching 20 hours a week. The hourly rate at commercial centres is normally in the range 1,000-1,500 forints while a full-time position should earn a teacher about 50,000 forints (net). It is essential to find out whether pay is net or gross since Hungarians lose about a quarter of their already meagre wages on tax and contributions. Although pay scales are still relatively low, the state sector is a more attractive option than it was a few years ago when it was not uncommon for teachers to hold down two or three jobs just to make ends meet. Brian Komyathy spells out the advantages of working for the state rather than private enterprise:

> I personally would recommend seeking a teaching position in a public school, especially if you're doing it for the experience. At my school, for instance, what made my job of interest to me (in addition to the classroom aspect) was the atmosphere of the school: visitors from abroad, school trips, sporting events, holiday celebrations, student performances, etc. At my school's expense I accompanied students to Budapest and Romania (on a skiing and English camp). Even though I only understood every eighth word, I rather enjoyed attending local festivals and historical

celebrations. (I always showed my face because I felt that I was an unofficial American ambassador.)

Although the wages in money will be low, schools try to shower as many perks as they can on their foreign teacher in addition to free furnished accommodation, e.g. use of a bicycle and travel discounts.

The American Steve Anderson was the first foreigner to work at his school in the 1000-strong village of Vaja in northeastern Hungary close to the Ukrainian border. It was obvious to him that the northeastern reaches of Hungary were most in need of teachers, and he found teaching there more rewarding than he had in a well-resourced school in Western Hungary. Writing recently in *Transitions Abroad* magazine, he reiterates this preference for teaching off the beaten track:

> *Though I initially rode the wave of native English speakers who rolled in to teach in Budapest and other larger cities, I am glad that I jumped ship to work in the poorer provinces. Activities like preparing spicy fish soup over an open fire and swaying to folk songs fiddled by the village gypsy don't happen in less traditional urban centres... The students of Vaja, lacking the luxuries of computers and up-to-date text books, had less developed English skills than those I had encountered the year before. I rewound all the way to the ABCs with my younger class and was forced to develop creative teaching methods I hadn't needed in my more advanced school, where audio and visual materials did the work for me.*

Inexperienced teachers are used by state schools for language and cultural enhancement through conversation classes, while the nitty-gritty teaching of grammar and reading is usually done by Hungarian teachers. This team-teaching approach seems to work well although obviously some of the Hungarian teachers have quite a struggle with English and depend heavily on their 'big shot' foreigner to adjudicate on points of grammar and British versus American usage (which Brian found especially tricky). Don't expect any training facilities; it is more likely to be the other way round with the Hungarian teachers expecting you to do the training, even if you have few qualifications.

Teachers in private schools must expect to teach everything from grammar to conversation, with variable materials. Students are generally keen and no problem to teach. Dennis Bricault, who taught at IH in Budapest for a year, describes pupils as a 'teacher's dream: hard-working, generally competent and with a good idea of what it takes to learn languages'. Some pupils may find modern teaching methods strange as they are used to a more teacher-centred approach, and more creative techniques may take some getting use to.

LIST OF SCHOOLS

ATALANTA BUSINESS AND LANGUAGE SCHOOL
Visegradi u. 9, 1132 Budapest. Tel: (1) 131 4954. Tel/fax: (1) 339 8549. E-mail: atalanta.marketing@atalanta.datanet.hu
Number of teachers: 10.
Preference of nationality: none.
Qualifications: college degree plus TEFL or TESOL certificate.
Conditions of employment: contracts given for length of course, 60 or 100 hours. Full-time teachers work 18 h.p.w.
Salary: 1,100-1,500 forints per hour (net).
Facilities/Support: no assistance with accommodation. Workshops held every other week, and regular lesson observation and feedback. Help given with work permits.
Recruitment: local advertisements and interviews. Candidates can also submit sample teaching materials.
Contact: Eva Malomsoki, Director of Studies.

BABILON NYELVSTUDIO
Károly krt. 3/a IV.em, 1075 Budapest. Tel: (1) 269 5531. Fax: (1) 322 6023. E-mail: bab@mail.datanet.hu
Number of teachers: 3-5.

Preference of nationality: British, American.
Qualifications: BA plus TEFL or TESL certificate and experience.
Conditions of employment: minimum one year. 12-18 h.p.w. taught at 8-11am, 3-5pm and 5-8pm.
Salary: 1,000 forints per hour (net).
Facilities/Support: no assistance with accommodation. Help given with work permits. Training available.
Recruitment: local interviews only.
Contact: Eva Babai, Director.

BELL ISKOLAK
Tulipán u. 8, 1022 Budapest. Tel: (1) 212 4324, 326 8457/326 5257. Fax: (1) 326 5033. E-mail: bellisk@mail.matav.hu
Part of the *Bell* Language Schools.
Number of teachers: 45.
Preference of nationality: British.
Qualifications: BA, CELTA or DELTA and a few years' teaching experience.
Conditions of employment: 20 h.p.w. for full-timers. Also part-time vacancies available. Pupils include young children, secondary school students, adults and business people.
Salary: 1,500 forints for 45-minute lesson. Earnings taxed at rate of 25%.
Facilities/Support: seminars held; training and professional assistance given. Good library and resources.
Recruitment: direct application with CV.
Contact: Eszter Timár, Director of Studies.

BUSINESS POLYTECHNIC
Vendel u. 3, 1096 Budapest. Tel: (1) 215 4900. Fax: (1) 215 4906. E-mail: titkar@mail.poli.hu
Number of teachers: 3.
Preference of nationality: none.
Qualifications: teaching experience in secondary schools.
Conditions of employment: one year in first instance. Hours 8am-2pm.
Salary: negotiable.
Facilities/Support: assistance with accommodation if necessary. Help with work permits and training given.
Recruitment: word of mouth. Local interviews necessary.
Contact: Adrienne Varga, Head of Foreign Language Department.

CENTRAL EUROPEAN TEACHING PROGRAM (CETP)
Beloit College, Box 242, 700 College St, Beloit, Wisconsin 53511, USA. Tel: (608) 363-2619. Fax: (608) 363-2449. E-mail: cetp@stu.beloit.edu. Internet: www.beloit.edu/-cetp
Number of teachers: 90 in schools throughout Hungary (as well as Romania, Poland and Latvia).
Preference of nationality: native speakers of English.
Qualifications: BA or BSc required. Overseas teaching, travel or study experience and/or TEFL/TESL experience preferred. Ability to teach German as well as English in great demand.
Conditions of employment: 10 month contracts from September. 18-22 classes (45 minutes) p.w.
Salary: $150-$200 per month.
Facilities/Support: free accommodation provided. 1-week initial orientation at CETP's Hungarian office (Koszta J u. 5, 6600 Szentes). Periodic workshops and some language training.
Recruitment: advertisements in *Transitions Abroad* magazine, *Student World Traveler*, etc. Phone interviews are sufficient. Placement fee of $1,200.
Contact: Alex Dunlop, CETP Director.

EUROPAI NYELVEK STUDIOJA
Muzeum Krt. 39, 1053 Budapest. Tel: (1) 317 1302. Fax: (1) 266 3889. E-mail: els@mail.datanet.hu
Number of teachers: 5-10.
Preference of nationality: British, American.
Qualifications: DELTA or TEFL Cedrtificate.
Conditions of employment: 15 week contracts (September-January or February-May). 16 h.p.w.
Salary: 1,400 forints per hour (net).
Facilities/Support: no assistance with accommodation or work permits. Training sessions once a month.
Recruitment: word of mouth. Local interviews necessary.
Contact: Ms. Judit Varadi, Director of Studies.

IHH A NYELVISKOLA
International Holiday House, Teleki u. 18, 9022 Györ. Tel: (96) 315444/(30) 363195. Fax: (96) 315665.
Number of teachers: about 20.
Preference of nationality: Australian, British, Canadian, American.
Qualifications: TEFL. Experience an advantage.
Conditions of employment: minimum 1 year. Minimum 18 h.p.w., more hours possible.
Salary: minimum 50,000 forints per month (net).
Facilities/Support: assistance with accommodation and work permits. Compulsory weekly and monthly training sessions.
Recruitment: interviews not essential.
Contact: Ottó László Nagy, Chairman.

INTERNATIONAL HOUSE
Language School & Teacher Training Institute, Bimbó út 7, 1022 Budapest (PO Box 95, 1364 Budapest). Tel: (1) 212 4010. Fax: (1) 316 2491.
Number of teachers: 35.
Qualifications: minimum Cambridge/RSA CELTA.
Conditions of employment: 1 year contracts. 26 lessons per week. Students from age 6, but majority are adults, including in-company business teaching. 9 weeks paid holiday plus return flight to London on completion of contract.
Salary: 78,400 forints per month (net).
Facilities/Support: assistance given with finding accommodation. In-service teacher development.
Recruitment: through direct application and IH, London. Interviews essential.

IS PROSPERO LANGUAGE SCHOOL LTD.
Sas u. 25, 1051 Budapest. Tel: (1) 331 6779. Fax: (1) 331 2150. E-mail: isprospero@mail.matav.hu
Number of teachers: 6.
Preference of nationality: British or American.
Qualifications: EFL and/or Business English qualifications plus some experience in business.
Conditions of employment: 6 month contracts, renewable. About 20 h.p.w.
Salary: negotiable.
Facilities/Support: assistance with accommodation and work permits if required. Training available.
Recruitment: CV and interview. Interviews sometimes available in UK or, if not, by telephone.
Contact: Gyöngyi Köteles, Director of Studies.

KARINTHY FRIGYES GIMNAZIUM

Thököly utca 7, Pestlorinc, 1183 Budapest. Tel: (1) 290 4316. Fax: (1) 291 2367.
E-mail: ba@karinthy.hu
Number of teachers: 4-6.
Preference of nationality: none (must be native speaker of English).
Qualifications: MA (English) or BA plus TEFL experience.
Conditions of employment: 1 academic year contracts. Hours of work from 8am-2pm.
Pupils aged 14-19 studying all academic subjects in English at bilingual school and in
the International Baccalaureate programme.
Salary: average for Hungary.
Facilities/Support: free accommodation provided plus heating/electricity costs. No
training given.
Recruitment: directly or via the Fulbright Commission.

KOLCSEY FERENC GIMNAZIUM

Rakoczi u. 49-53, 8900 Zalaegerszeg. Tel/fax: (92) 311145. E-mail:
suli103@zala.sulinet.hu
Number of teachers: 1 lector.
Preference of nationality: British.
Qualifications: TEFL.
Conditions of employment: one year, extendable. 15-20 h.p.w.
Salary: 50,000 forints (net).
Facilities/Support: assistance with accommodation, work permits and training.
Recruitment: through organisations such as the Soros Foundation. Interviews not
compulsory.
Contact: Judit Magadja, Head of English Department.

LIVING LANGUAGE SEMINAR

(Elö Nyelvek Szemináriuma), Fejér György u. 8-10, 1053 Budapest. Tel: (1) 326
5251/317 9644. Fax: (1) 317 9655.
Number of teachers: 3-5.
Preference of nationality: British, American, Canadian.
Qualifications: a great deal of ESL teaching experience, registered Pitman, Oxford
exam centre. Preparation for Cambridge and local exams, TOEFL, Business
English.
Conditions of employment: contracts from 3 months. Negotiable hours. Mainly
teaching adults (aged 16-40).
Salary: high by local standards.
Facilities/Support: no assistance with accommodation at present.
Recruitment: through adverts. Interviews required.

LONDON STUDIO

Villányi út. 27, 1114 Budapest. Tel: (1) 385 0177. Fax: (1) 385 0177 (ext. 108).
Number of teachers: 10-15.
Preference of nationality: British, American, Canadian, Australian.
Qualifications: MA, BA or Trinity Cert or CELTA (or diplomas).
Conditions of employment: 10 week contracts. Hours are 8-9.30am, 4.30-6pm and 6.30-
8pm plus 8-12am on weekends.
Salary: 1,000-1,500 forints per 45 minute lesson, depending on quality of work and
demonstration lesson.
Facilities/Support: addresses of accommodation agencies are provided. In-house
training once a month.
Recruitment: interview and demonstration lesson in Budapest essential.
Contact: Katalin Sziegl Terescsik, Director of Studies.

NOVOSCHOOL NYELVISKOLA

Ullöi út. 63, 1091 Budapest. Tel: (1) 215 5480. Fax: (1) 215 5488. E-mail: novoschool@mail.matav.hu

Number of teachers: 2-3.

Preference of nationality: British.

Qualifications: university degree and teaching experience in ESL.

Conditions of employment: 1 or 2 years. 5 h.p.w. in first instance, rising to 10 or 20 if satisfactory.

Salary: freelance teachers invoice school for negotiated hourly rate.

Facilities/Support: no assistance with accommodation. Help given with work permits. Workshops held for all teachers.

Recruitment: direct. Interviews are eesential. Applicants observe classes, then teach on trial basis before being taken on.

Contact: Kati Németi, Head of English Section.

TUDOMANY NYELVISKOLA

Vörösvári út. 1 I/1, 1035 Budapest. Tel: (1) 368 1156. Tel/fax: (1) 388 5072. E-mail: info@tudomanynyelviskola.hu. Internet: www.tudomanynyelviskola.hu

Number of teachers: 4-5.

Preference of nationality: British and American.

Qualifications: TEFL/TESL preferred.

Conditions of employment: 10 month contracts. Hours vary.

Facilities/Support: assistance with accommodation not normally given. Training sometimes available.

Recruitment: local interviews essential.

Contact: Tamás Légrádi, Director.

VACI STREET DEVELOPMENT CENTRE

Teréz Krt. 47, 1067 Budapest. Tel: (1) 302 2214. Tel/fax: (1) 353 3274. E-mail: bruce@mail.inext.hu

Number of teachers: 15.

Preference of nationality: none.

Qualifications: TEFL. People with background in theatre preferred.

Conditions of employment: minimum 3 months; many stay for 1 year. 20-28 teaching units (45 minutes) per week. VSDC specialises in Anglo-American corporate training including sales training and specialist courses for hotel and catering industry, information technology, etc.

Salary: varies.

Facilities/Support: advice given on finding accommodation. VSDC handles all requirements for work permits. Weekly training sessions.

Recruitment: CV and interview, occasionally available in London.

Contact: Bruce Anderson, Director.

VARGA KATALIN GIMNAZIUM

Szabadság ter. 6, 5000 Szolnok. Tel: (56) 420810. Fax: (56) 420310. E-mail: molnar@varga-szolnok.sulinet.hu

Number of teachers: 1-2.

Preference of nationality: British or American.

Qualifications: diploma for teaching English/history.

Conditions of employment: 1 year. 20 lessons a week.

Salary: between 30,000 and 60,000 forints depending on age.

Facilities/Support: possible to give help with finding accommodation. Assistance with work permits given.

Recruitment: via organisations like Soros, Fulbright and CETP. Interviews not essential.

Contact: László Molnár, Assistant Principal.

Other Schools to Try

Note that these schools did not confirm their teacher requirements for this edition of
Teaching English Abroad. Addresses have been taken from various sources, primarily
the *Book of Lists* published by the *Budapest Business Journal.*

Ameropa, Móricz Zsigmond krt. 14 IV/1, 1117 Budapest
Arany János Languages School, Csengery u. 68, 1067 Budapest
Berlitz, Váci u. 11/b, 1052 Budapest
Big Ben Languages Studies, Csepreghy u. 4, 1085 Budapest
Budapest Language School for Children, Szász Károly u. 2, 1027 Budapest
Concord, Németvölgyi út. 34, 1126 Budapest
Danubius, Bajcsy-Zsilinszky köz. 1, 1065 Budapest
Dover, Bécsi u. 3, 1052 Budapest
Fast English Alternative Language School, Vigszinház u. 5, 1137 Budapest
Fókusz, Böszörményi út. 8, 1126 Budapest
Foreign Trade Education Center, Falk Miksa u. 1, 1055 Budapest
Interclub Hungarian Language School, Bertalan Lajos u. 17, 1111 Budapest
International Language School, Pf. 64, 1363 Budapest
Katedra Language School, Fövám ter 2-3, 1114 Budapest
Lingua School of English, Szent István krt. 7, 1055 Budapest
LT Lingvearium, Lajos u. 1, 1023 Budapest
Pasaréti Language School, Csévi út. 7, 1025 Budapest
TIT Globe, Múzeum krt. 7, 1088 Budapest
Oxford Nyelviskola, Ikva u. 52, Györ

Bilingual Secondary Schools

Dual Language School, Pf. 125, 8220 Balatonalmádi (88-338990)
Török Ignácz Gimnázium, Petofi Sándor u. 12, 2100 Gödöllo (28-420380)
Katona József Gimnázium, Dózsa György út. 3, 6000 Kecskemét (76-481583)
Apásczai Nevelési Központ Gimnázium, Apáczai Csere János krt. 1, 7621 Pécs (72-441913)
Református Gimnázium, Rákóczi út. 1, 3950 Sárospatak (47-311 039)
Déak Ferenc Gimnázium, József A. u. 118, 6723 Szeged (62-474174)
Ságvári Endre Gimnázium, Rákóczi 49-53, 8900 Zalaegerszeg (92-311145)

Poland

Prospects for English teachers in Poland, western Poland in particular, remain more
promising than almost anywhere else in the world. Even the major cities like Warsaw,
Wroclaw, Kraków, Poznan and Gdansk are promising destinations, especially for
people looking for in-company work. As in the Czech and Slovak Republics there are
numerous possibilities in both state and private schools. School directors are often
delighted to interview native English speakers who present themselves in a
professional manner. The reverence for 'native speakerhood' still runs very high in
Poland. However, as British and American native speakers of English have become
less of a rarity, the EFL public has become more selective. It is no longer possible to
quit at one school, walk next door and start work the next day. The change in visa
regulations which requires foreigners to apply in their home country prevents the
employment situation from being as fluid as it used to be. Yet it still seems that
TEFLers with initiative can create jobs for themselves with hours and a location to
suit.

The craving for English is arguably just as intense as it was immediately after the
collapse of the Communist Party in 1990. The private language school market
continues buoyant despite widespread austerity. Poles seem to have adjusted to their
new era with confidence, especially since the 'new zloty' was introduced in 1995 and

has had a stabilising effect on the economy (though many teachers' salaries are still quoted in US dollars or sterling).

There is a continuing demand for English from the state sector which, due to a shortage of resources, depends very heavily on the steady stream of volunteer teachers supplied by various agencies. The old state exam in English has been replaced by the Cambridge First Certificate creating a large demand for British teachers of English who have some experience of those exams.

Foreign teachers normally find their students unfailingly friendly, open and keen to learn more about the world. Discussion classes are likely to be informed and lively, with students well up to date on developments and very well motivated to practise their English. In some companies, promotion depends on the level of English achieved, which spurs students from the business world to be especially committed. On the other hand, if the company is paying for an employee's lessons, there may be little incentive to attend regularly or with enthusiasm.

FIXING UP A JOB

Interested teachers should not expect to be snapped up by every high quality school to which they apply unless they have at least a TEFL certificate and some sort of teaching experience or a palpable feel for the job.

In Advance

The principal organisations mentioned in the introduction to the chapter recruiting volunteer teachers such as WorldTeach, the East European Partnership and the Peace Corps have withdrawn or scaled down their teaching programmes. Similarly, the Soros Foundation has cancelled its English Teaching Program in Poland as administered by the Batory Foundation. The Anglo-Polish Universities Association (UK North, 93 Victoria Road, Leeds LS6 1DR) continues to recruit native speakers to work at summer language camps (see section below) and also for year-long appointments.

The Education Office of the Polish Embassy can provide information for candidates wanting to teach in Poland. The relevant office is located at the Polish Cultural Institute (34 Portland Place, London W1N 4HQ; 0171-636 6032/fax 0171-637 2190). Obviously this office cannot act as an employment agency but it can attempt to refer enquirers to appropriate organisations.

Placements in state schools were once overseen by the Ministry of National Education at Al. J. Ch. Szucha 25, 00-918 Warsaw, but the Ministry is no longer involved in this activity. The Director of the department of International Cooperation suggests that teachers should apply directly to headteachers of Polish schools. Lists of addresses are available from the regional offices of superintendents of education *(Kuratoria)*; these addresses are posted on the internet at http://www.waw.pl./kuro-p.htm.

Teacher training colleges *(Nauczycielskie Kolegium Jezyków Obcych* or NKJOs) continue to recruit native speaker teachers. A couple of years ago, the Language Methodology Advisory Centre (JODM) attached to the teacher training college in Walbrzych had set up a network of communication between qualified native speaker teachers and state secondary schools and teacher training colleges (NKJOs). Applications sent to JODM were circulated to schools which had registered a need for teachers. Recent confirmation that this system was still operating was not forthcoming; (Att: Rajmund Matuszkiewicz, JODM, ul. Kombatantow 20, 58-302 Walbrzych).

International House has a big presence in Poland with schools in Bielsko-Biala, Bydgoszcz, Katowice, Kielce, Koszalin, Kraków, Lódz, Opole, Poznan, Torun and Wroclaw, some of which are listed in the Directory. The Bell Educational Trust has an Associate Network of schools in Poland in Gdansk, Gdynia, Bydgoszcz and Szczecin (see entry for *ELS Bell*), in Warsaw (U.E.C. Bell, Plac Trzech Krzyzy 4/6, 00-499 Warsaw), Poznan and Kraków (see *Gama Bell*). These high profile ELT organisations are founding members of PASE, the Polish Association for Standards in English which promotes ethical practices in the private sector.

The TEFL pages of the *Guardian* and *TES* probably carry more advertisements for schools in Poland than for any other country. Often these ads provide a contact address in the UK where interviews can be scheduled over the summer. Contacting private schools ahead of time may produce some interest, though in most cases they will want to interview you before making any commitment. Commercial recruitment agencies like *TEFLNet* and *IPG* are often asked to fill vacancies in private language schools. The Beet Language Centre in Bournemouth (Nortoft Road, Charminster, Bournemouth, Dorset BH8 8PY; 01202 397721/397609/fax 01202 309662) is an established UK language school which annually places about 15 teachers in Poland. Applicants must have a first degree and a Certificate or Diploma in TEFL.

On the Spot

Semesters begin on October 1st and February 15th, and the best time to arrive is a month or two beforehand. After arrival, try to establish some contacts, possibly by visiting the English department at the university. Although some school directors state a preference for British or American accents, many are neutral.

Private language schools catering for all kinds of English teaching sprang up everywhere as soon as private enterprise was legally possible. The Warsaw Yellow Pages carry several pages under the heading *Jezykowe Kursy, Szkolenia*. The very busy British Council in Warsaw (near Central station) and the smaller British Council Libraries in Kraków, Wroclaw, Gdansk and seven other cities may be able to assist personal callers. The Gdansk office has a list of the dozen biggest private language schools. In Kraków ask for the comprehensive list of language schools ('Jezyki Obce') in the region compiled annually by a Kraków newspaper (*Gazeta W Krakowie*) for the benefit of Polish readers wanting to compare courses. After obtaining some addresses, would-be teachers should dutifully 'do the rounds' of the *Dyrektors*.

When you fix up interviews with private language schools, it is often very useful to have an interpreter present, since even the directors of such schools do not always speak fluent English. In some cases, you will be offered a certain number of hours but these will only materialise if enough paid-up clients materialise first.

If you base yourself in Warsaw and wish to advertise your availability for private English tuition, try placing a notice just to the right of the main gate of Warsaw University or in one of the main dailies, *Gazeta Wyborcza* or *Zycie Warszawy*. A further idea is to visit the Irish pub on ul. Miodowa near the castle which many English speakers use as their watering-hole.

Most Polish teachers of English work 'on the side' and it may be possible to work in partnership with one of them as a teaching aid, earning a reasonable wage for speaking as instructed (and incidentally picking up some teaching ideas for future use). Freelancing is very popular, and there has been a huge increase in the late 1990s in demand for tailor-made one-to-one courses. Banks are very likely clients and often pay very well by Polish standards. For this work, teachers should have enough ELT awareness to be able to devise their own syllabus.

Academic Institutes

As mentioned above, NKJOs (foreign language teacher training colleges) of which there are 60, are eager to hire qualified, experienced teachers, yet they cannot pay a very high salary. For many years the British Council has recruited qualified and experienced native speakers for its *Studia* operations. These are university institutes of language learning run in partnership between the British Council and universities in Warsaw, Wroclaw, Gdansk, Kraków, Poznan, Lódz, Katowice, Gliwice and Szeczecin (see entries for some). Conditions are similar to those for Polish teachers—salaries are paid in zloties and are sufficient to live on by local standards.

Virtually every institute of higher education (universities, medical academies, technical universities, economics academies, art schools, etc.) has a *Studium Jazyków Obcych* (Foreign Language Department) which is where the students who aren't language majors fulfil their foreign language requirements. The learners are less advanced and possibly less motivated in English than at the NKJOs, and they may be prepared to accept less well qualified native speaker assistants while offering the attractions of an academic setting.

Holiday Language Camps

The Anglo-Polish Universities Association (APASS) organises 'Teaching Holidays in Poland' when English native speakers spend between three and seven weeks in Poland as paid or voluntary teachers. ELT experience is of course welcomed but not essential. A detailed information pack is available from mid-March onwards from APASS at a cost of £3 plus 9in X 6in s.a.e. (32p stamps). Telephone calls to the organisation (0113 275 8121) can be accepted 8-10am and 4-6pm. There is an administrative fee. Reports have been received that details of these summer placements are finalised not long before departure, so be prepared to endure some suspense.

Many private language teaching organisations run short-term holiday courses which require native speakers, including several in the Directory (*English School of Communication Skills, ELS Bell*, etc.). Will Gardner was full of praise for the camp where he worked one summer:

> *I spent one month working for ESCS at their summer camp on Poland's Baltic Coast. The camps were well organised and great fun. As an experienced teacher who has worked in several different countries for a range of schools, I would just like to say what a pleasure it was to work with such a well organised group of people and for a school that completely lived up to its promises. The school supplied a wide range of resources to assist teachers, although a lot of emphasis was placed on originality. The focus was always on communication and fun. The camp facilities were perfect for the situation. Food and accommodation were supplied and the weather was beautiful. Although the students were attending lessons daily, a holiday atmosphere prevailed over all activities.*

One possible contact address in the US was spotted in the 1998 listings from Volunteers for Peace. A camp in Siennica (50km southeast of Warsaw) was looking for volunteer teachers; interested people should write to Earl & Annmarie Adreani, 77 Gayland Rd., Needham, MA 02192.

REGULATIONS

A work visa (Visa 06) must be applied for in your country of origin, as for the Czech Republic, Hungary and Slovakia. The Polish Consulate in London will state the requirements over the phone (0171-580 0476). The required documents must be presented in person to a Polish Consulate: a promisory work permit from your Polish employer, your passport, two photos, a completed application form and the current fee for a work visa of £104. In order for your employer to obtain permission to employ a foreign teacher, he or she will have to submit originals or notarised copies of your degree diploma and TEFL Certificate (if applicable) with official translations. Most schools will assist with the documentation and the majority promise to reimburse all or part of the cost on completion of a contract.

CONDITIONS OF WORK

Generally speaking, private language schools in Poland offer very reasonable working conditions, with fewer reports of profit-mongers and sharks than in other countries experiencing a TEFL boom. Instead of hearing complaints from teachers of employers, it tends to be more often the other way round, as the Director of Studies of a private language school makes clear:

> *My boss, who has been employing British native speakers for seven years and who has proved to be a very patient person, could provide you with some hair-raising stories of teachers signing their contracts and withdrawing at the very last minute (having probably found a more lucrative job in Japan), teachers returning a couple of days late after the Christmas break without presenting any adequate excuse (or not returning at all), not to mention the state of flats and equipment which, after being used for nine months, is often left in a wrecked condition.*

Wages are not high but they go further than they used to. If your accommodation is reasonably priced and you resist the temptation to shop and party to excess, it is even possible to save. The terms of service are seldom exploitative. It is not uncommon for overtime to be paid to teachers for hours worked in excess of the contracted number (typically 24). Erica Jolly and Paul Robinson describe the situation in Gdansk:

> *The big schools in and around Gdansk all seem similar. They are well equipped but don't pay that well. Class sizes are around 12-15 students and hours are usually a minimum of 18 teaching hours per week. The director in charge of teaching is an experienced EFL teacher and teacher-trainer herself, and is always available to help and advise. My only criticism is the propensity towards paperwork: each teacher is obliged to complete forms after each lesson giving details of everything covered, comments, etc.*

The current average gross salary in the private sector is £7-£10 an hour or 2,000-2,500 zloties (£350-£400) per month. The standard deduction is 21% for taxes and contributions. The range of monthly net wages in zloties quoted by schools listed in this chapter was 1,100-1,950, whereas wages quoted in dollars or pounds generally seemed higher. As long as teachers have rent-free housing and fairly ascetic inclinations, this is enough to live on, though almost all foreigners supplement their basic income by doing some one-to-one tutoring. The cost of living has been steadily rising; beer, vodka and eating out at milk bars remain cheap but groceries (especially fruit and vegetables) are sometimes as expensive as they are in Britain. One unforeseen expense Erica mentioned was the high cost of replacing windows on their car which was broken into on several occasions. Her conclusion was that it would be better to stick to public transport if spending a year in Poland.

Heidi Rothwell-Walker enjoyed company teaching, which was a contrast with the basic adult education she had been doing in Britain:

> *I was expected to work any time from 7am to 6pm. Sometimes the early hours (especially in the long winter) can get you down, but you will be rewarded financially for starting at 7am. There was a lot of travelling and waiting at bus stops, but working conditions in the companies were excellent. Not every company gave you access to a white board, overhead projector or cassette player but they could be made available upon request.*

Once you are working either in the public or private sector, you may be approached with various proposals, from 'verifying' English translations of scientific research papers or restaurant menus, to coaching actors and singers preparing for English performances and doing dubbing or voice-overs for films and TV.

As throughout Eastern Europe, accommodation is a major problem, though there are fewer complaints about the high rents and low quality than elsewhere. If you don't mind living with a family in what will almost certainly be cramped conditions, it is possible to get free accommodation in exchange for giving English conversation lessons.

Despite a considerable amount of disorganisation at many schools, no one complains of a lack of hospitality from the Poles. Once they get to know the teacher, students will offer whatever services they can from mending shoes to giving large quantities of home-preserved fruit. Marta Eleniak especially enjoyed her experience teaching children:

> *Teaching in the primary school was really enjoyable as the little kids make you feel so appreciated by giving you flowers, drawing pictures for you and performing songs, poems or dances for you. They always wanted to continue after the bell had gone. One class was so keen that they invited themselves for a lesson even though it was my break.*

All of this makes a refreshing contrast with the lot of the EFL teacher in many other parts of the world. Poles even seem to have the ability to crack jokes in English when their English is very elementary, so lessons are not usually dull. On the whole they are also very well-motivated and hard-working, including adolescents. The number of

Polish women looking for Western husbands has declined, at least according to the manager of a big Warsaw language school (who has just married a Pole).

State Schools

Anyone who likes kids, wants to do good, feel needed and suffer a little will enjoy a year in a state school. Novice teachers can be useful at public schools, though many find it a rude awakening. Shortages of materials and basic classroom equipment are less common than they were five years ago, but classroom facilities in many cases are still sadly lacking. Even the best-hearted of Polish teachers is generally so overworked and underpaid that they are not in a position to spend time advising foreign teachers. A large measure of independence and self-reliance is therefore essential. Novices who are not prepared for all this soon become miserable and embittered, resulting in a lot of unnecessary bad feelings on both sides.

Jobs attached to universities usually offer stability and a light workload, say 12-15 classroom hours a week during the two 15-week semesters. The salary is paid over 12 months and includes full health insurance, housing perks and discounts on train travel. Bear in mind that if you are tutoring some of them privately, this income will vanish over the summer vacation.

LEISURE TIME

Even if the flat that is provided has cable television, there are sights to see, pubs to visit, museum, theatres and parks to enjoy. Films are usually in English with Polish subtitles. Travelling is fairly cheap and easy. The transport system in Warsaw and some other cities looks complicated at first glance but is an fact straightforward. People in shops and so on can seem rude and abrupt, though this should not be taken personally. Be prepared to be stared at for the first few weeks, since you will certainly stick out.

Heidi Rothwell-Walker is convinced that she made the right decision when she chose to work for a school in Poland rather than at one of the other schools around the world that offered her a job:

> *Poland can seem a bit of a backwater, but it's a tremendous experience. It'll change your thinking completely and you'll either love it (like 98% of people) or hate it, but you must try it. I have just renewed my contract for another year because I have been very impressed by them and am very happy here.*

LIST OF SCHOOLS

AGENCJA LEKTOR SCHOOL OF ENGLISH
ul. Sloneczna 39, 11-700 Mragowo. Tel/fax: (89) 741 4141. E-mail: lektor@mragowo.net
Number of teachers: 2-3.
Preference of nationality: British.
Qualifications: BA (preferably English) plus CELTA or equivalent. Experience with children preferred.
Conditions of employment: 9-10 month contracts.
Salary: 1,500 zloties per month (gross) plus up to 50% bonuses.
Facilities/Support: furnished accommodation provided including utilities.
Recruitment: newspaper adverts. Interviews not essential.
Contact: K. Mlynarczyk.

ALBION LANGUAGE SERVICES
ul Noakowskiego 26, 00-668 Warsaw. Tel/fax: (22) 628 8992. E-mail: languages@albion.com.pl
Number of teachers: 5.
Preference of nationality: none.
Qualifications: interesting teaching methods, friendly attitude required.
Conditions of employment: open-ended.

Salary: approx. US$10 per 45 minutes.
Facilities/Support: assistance with accommodation and visas.
Recruitment: direct. Local interview essential.
Contact: Dorota Krajewska, Owner.

AMERICAN ACADEMY OF ENGLISH
Ul. Slowackiego 16, Katowice 40-094. Tel/fax: (1) (32) 253 0272/3/4. E-mail: aae@silesia.top.pl. Parent institution is the US-based Polish-American Foundation for Cultural Exchange.
Number of teachers: 32 for AAE branches throughout Poland.
Preference of nationality: North American.
Qualifications: university degree (English or related subject preferred).
Conditions of employment: one-year contract. 22 h.p.w. Monday to Friday. Lots of evening teaching.
Salary: 1,600 zloties per month (gross).
Facilities/Support: apartment provided. Medical insurance and other benefits. $400 contribution to air fare from US. Free Polish lessons.
Contact: Carl H. Johnson, Associate Director.

BEST
Zespól Lektorów BEST, ul. Pestalozziego 11/13, 80-445 Gdansk. Tel/fax: (58) 344 3474. E-mail: bestudu@ikp.atm.com.pl
Number of teachers: 22.
Preference of nationality: none.
Qualifications: minimum Cambridge/RSA Certificate required. Experience teaching abroad preferred.
Conditions of employment: $9\frac{1}{2}$ month contracts (including 2 week induction). 20 teaching hours plus 2 standby hours p.w. plus 2 teachers' meetings per month. Teaching children, teenagers, adults and business English from beginner to advanced.
Salary: 1,950 zloties per month (net).
Facilities/Support: assistance with finding accommodation and obtaining work permits given. Pre-service training course and regular teachers' meetings.
Recruitment: ads in *Guardian*. Interviews essential and can be arranged in London or via telephone/e-mail at BEST's expense.
Contact: Ewa Krupowicz, Director of Studies.

BERLITZ POLAND
ul. Miedziana 11, 00-835 Warsaw. Tel: (22) 652 0848. Fax: (22) 652 0909.
Number of teachers: approx. 100 for 7 centres in Poland.
Preference of nationality: British, American, Australian.
Qualifications: good college education, open personality, energetic.
Conditions of employment: freelance basis.
Salary: 3,000-5,000 zloties per month (gross) less approx. 16% taxes, 20% for social security if needed.
Facilities/Support: no assistance with accommodation. Detailed help given with work permits.
Recruitment: local interview essential.
Contact: Mrs. Aleksandra Tomaszewska, Country Instructional Supervisor.

BRITISH INTERNATIONAL SCHOOL OF ENGLISH
ul. Grodzka 51, 31-001 Kraków. Tel: (12) 422 86 09. Fax: (12) 422 7934.
Number of teachers: 25 full curriculum primary and secondary school teachers.
Preference of nationality: British.
Qualifications: fully qualified only. Experience in teaching preferred.
Conditions of employment: one year contracts.
Salary: £9 per lesson (45 minutes).
Facilities/Support: assistance with accommodation may be given. Training once a week.

Recruitment: direct application and telephone interviews.
Contact: Andy Harris, Headmaster.

CAMBRIDGE SCHOOL OF ENGLISH

ul. Zakroczymska 6, 00-225 Warsaw. Tel: (22) 831 0955. Fax: (22) 635 6614.
Number of teachers: 35.
Preference of nationality: none.
Qualifications: CELTA and university degree. Experience in lieu considered.
Conditions of employment: 9 month contracts. Working hours are 3pm-8pm plus 2 mornings.
Salary: about £100 per week (net).
Facilities/Support: guaranteed accommodation which costs a quarter to a third of the salary. Help with work permits including free coach trip to London at Christmas to collect permit from Polish Embassy. Weekly training seminars. One senior staff per 5 teachers.
Recruitment: via adverts in *Guardian* and sister school in England, Greenwich School of English. Interviews not always essential.
Contact: David Watson, School Manager.

CELT—CENTRE OF ENGLISH LANGUAGE TRAINING

Konarskiego 2, 30-049 Kraków. Tel: (12) 415 1732.
Number of teachers: varies.
Preference of nationality: none.
Qualifications: any teacher training course.
Conditions of employment: one-year contracts. Afternoon and evening work.
Salary: average hourly rate less 20% deductions.
Facilities/Support: no assistance with accommodation or work visas.
Recruitment: interviews essential.

CONRAD S.C.

Osrodek Nauczania Jezyków Obcych, Orlowicza 8/104, 10-684 Olsztyn. Tel/fax: (89) 542 72 75.
Number of teachers: 2-3.
Preference of nationality: British, American.
Qualifications: BA/MA in Humanities (English); CELTA/TEFLA.
Conditions of employment: 10-12 month contracts. Minimum 25 lessons (45 minutes) p.w. Hours mainly 3-8pm with possibility of some morning and early afternoon sessions.
Salary: minimum £500 per month (£425 net).
Facilities/Support: accommodation provided within 15 minutes walk of school for rent of £120. Work permit arranged. School contributes about £250 to cover teacher's social security.
Recruitment: adverts in *Guardian* and private contacts. Interviews essential and sometimes possible in the UK. Prospective teachers invited to teach at summer camp in Zakopane for last two weeks of July. No fee charged, no wage paid; travel from UK reimbursed (up to 1,140 zloties) if teacher signs a one-year contract.
Contact: Krzysztof and Joanna Kowalscy, Owners.

EF ENGLISH FIRST

Smolna 8 p XVIII, 00-375 Warsaw. Tel: (22) 826 8206. Fax: (22) 826 0871. Also Marszakkowska 1, 00-624 Warsaw (22-828 1915). E-mail: ef-1@ef.com.pl. Also schools in Wroclaw and Budposzsz.
Number of teachers: 20.
Preference of nationality: none.
Qualifications: minimum TEFL Cert. Experience a major advantage.
Conditions of employment: 9 month contracts. Teaching between 7.30am and 9pm plus Saturday mornings.
Salary: US$1,000 per month (net) plus bonuses.

Facilities/Support: assistance with accommodation and work permits. Training available.
Recruitment: newspaper ads. Interviews in Warsaw or London (EF, 5 Kensington Church St, London W8 4LD; 0171-878 3500).
Contact: Neil Hammond, Academic Support Coordinator (Warsaw Office).

ELS-BELL SCHOOL OF ENGLISH
ul. Polanki 110, 80-308 Gdansk. Tel/fax: (58) 554 8382. In association with Bell Educational Trust of Cambridge.
Number of teachers: 20 for several centres in Gdansk, Gdynia, Bydgoszcz and Szczecin.
Preference of nationality: British and American.
Qualifications: CELTA or equivalent plus university degree. Experience preferred.
Conditions of employment: September to June. Up to 25 lessons a week (45 minutes each). Annual workload is 680 hours, teaching mainly afternoons and evenings. Also run summer camps for young learners (aged 9-18).
Salary: 1,950 zloties net, plus end-of-contract bonus of one month's salary.
Facilities/Support: assistance with accommodation. Cost of obtaining work permits is reimbursed by school. In-house teacher development programme. Centre also runs CELTA and DELTA courses.
Recruitment: ads in *Guardian* and on internet. Interviews necessary, occasionally by phone. Interviews sometimes take place in London.
Contact: Ludka Kotavska, Head of Schools.

ENGLISH LANGUAGE CENTRE
University of Silesia, Plac Sejmu Slaskiego 1, 40-032 Katowice. Tel: (32) 256-1296. Fax: (32) 255-2245. E-mail: britc@homer.fil.us.edu.pl
Number of teachers: 5.
Preference of nationality: British, Irish.
Qualifications: CELTA plus experience.
Conditions of employment: 1 year renewable contracts (September till the end of June). 21 h.p.w.
Salary: approximately 2,500 zloties per month (tax free for first two years).
Facilities/Support: free accommodation in teachers' hostel. Access to British Council training seminars. Paid holidays.
Recruitment: CVs and applications welcome by post. Interviews in Poland or UK.

ENGLISH SCHOOL OF COMMUNICATION SKILLS—KRAKOW, TARNOW & NOWY TARG
ul. Bernardynska 15, 13-100 Tarnów. Tel/fax: (14) 213769. E-mail: personnel@escs.pl
Number of teachers: 60 for 3 schools in southern Poland. Also hold summer courses and summer camps at Polish seaside.
Preference of nationality: English as mother tongue.
Qualifications: degree level of education plus EFL methodology certificate or ESCS's own training course offered in September.
Conditions of employment: one-year contracts. 20 h.p.w. 600 teaching hours per school year (October-June) plus 36 project hours. Teaching all ages (6-60). Pre-selected course books, standardised tests and many extracurricular activities for students (baseball, drama club, video club, etc.)
Salary: hourly rate; base salary 2,000 zloties per month; varies according to experience and qualifications.
Facilities/Support: seminars and workshops held. Teacher resource centre includes videos, cassettes and supplementary material. Photocopying and computers on-site.
Recruitment: via universities. Interviews held whenever possible. Applications should be sent to the Personnel Department.
Contact: Steven Greber, Director.

ENGLISH UNLIMITED

Podmlynska 10, 80-855 Gdansk. Tel/fax: (58) 301 3373. E-mail: kamila@eu.com.pl

Number of teachers: 10-15 for seven centres round the Tri-City (Gdansk, Gdynia and Sopot) and in Poznan.

Preference of nationality: none; must be native speakers.

Qualifications: Cambridge/RSA Cert. or Dip. plus experience of overseas teaching.

Conditions of employment: 9 month contracts from September. Hours of teaching normally 4.30-8pm. Courses offered in ESP (e.g. business English).

Salary: £300-£350 per month (net).

Facilities/Support: accommodation arranged. Training provided.

Recruitment: adverts in the *Guardian*. Interviews in Poland or UK essential.

Contact: Kamila Anflink, Director of Studies.

EUROPA 2000

Szola Jezyków Obcych, ul. Dabrowskiego 24, 40-032 Katowice. Tel: (32) 255 10 53. Also: Szkola Jezyków Obcych, ul de Gaulle'a 8, 43-100 Tychy (227-7051 ext 144/126). E-mail: e2000sm@silesia.top.pl

Number of teachers: 2-4.

Preference of nationality: British, American.

Qualifications: MA, BA, experience in English teaching and leading courses.

Conditions of employment: 1-3 years. Usual hours 3pm-8pm.

Salary: £7-£10 per hour less 21% income tax.

Facilities/Support: assistance with finding accommodation and obtaining permits given. Insurance provided.

Recruitment: word-of-mouth. Interviews not essential.

Contact: Edyta Stasiak-Ulfik, Language Centre Manager.

GAMA-BELL SCHOOL OF ENGLISH

ul. Sw. Krzyza 16, 31-023 Kraków. Tel: (12) 421 97 55/421 97 22. Fax: (12) 421 73 79. E-mail: gamabell@bc.krakow.pl

Number of teachers: 10.

Preference of nationality: British.

Qualifications: BA plus CELTA.

Conditions of employment: 9-month contracts. 20 h.p.w. Students from age 10.

Salary: from £5 per hour.

Facilities/Support: assistance with finding accommodation given only to teachers on long-term contracts. Monthly teacher development seminars and workshops (organised by school and by IATEFL Poland).

Recruitment: interviews essential.

Contact: Elzbieta Jarosz, Director of Studies.

GREENWICH SCHOOL OF ENGLISH

ul. Gdanska 2/3, 00-567 Warsaw. Tel: (22) 833 2431. Fax: (22) 833 36 02.

Number of teachers: 30.

Preference of nationality: British.

Qualifications: degree/further education to BA standard. Accredited teaching certificate.

Conditions of employment: one academic year (28th September until 25th June) or more. Varying hours, approximately 20 h.p.w.

Salary: £92-£130 p.w. depending on experience. £150 paid towards flight to Poland.

Facilities/Support: accommodation found by school, normally in shared flats. Rent is approximately $250. Assistance with work permits (before teachers arrive in Poland). Regular programme of lectures, seminars and observations.

Recruitment: adverts in the *Guardian*. Interviews essential and held in various locations in the UK in July.

Contact: Agata Zurowska-Tuchowska, Owner.

INTERNATIONAL HOUSE—BIELSKO BIALA
Ul. Krasinskiego 24, 43-300 Bielsko Biala. Tel: (33) 11 02 29.
Number of teachers: 25.
Preference of nationality: none.
Qualifications, conditions of employment, etc.: same as for International House Katowice (next entry).

INTERNATIONAL HOUSE—KATOWICE
Ul. Gliwicka 10, 40-079 Katowice. Tel: (32) 59 99 97. Fax: (32) 59 84 04. E-mail: ihih@silesia.top.pl. Internet: http://www.silesia.top.pl.-ihih/katowice
Number of teachers: 25-30.
Preference of nationality: none.
Qualifications: minimum CELTA or equivalent.
Conditions of employment: 9 month contracts. 20 contact hours per week, plus one standby slot and attendance at workshops and meetings. Students are all ages and there are several in-company contracts.
Facilities/Support: accommodation and return flights from London are provided. Weekly teacher training workshops, monthly training conferences, computer training, etc. Assisted DELTA and Young Learners Certificate courses available.
Recruitment: via IH Central Department (London) or direct to the school.
Contact: Nick Davids, Director of Studies.

INTERNATIONAL HOUSE—KRAKOW
ul. Pilsudskiego 6, lp, 31-109 Kraków. Tel: (12) 421 9440/422 6482. Fax: (12) 421 8652.
Number of teachers: 40.
Preference of nationality: none.
Conditions of employment: one year contracts. 24 contact hours per week. Students from nine years up. Classes may include in-company Business English for suitably qualified/experienced teachers.
Salary: basic 1,250 zloties (net) per month.
Facilities/Support: assistance given with accommodation. Fortnightly training workshops plus regular developmental observations. In-house intensive courses for teaching young learners and Business English. Support for those wishing to take the DELTA course run annually.
Recruitment: locally or via IH Central Department (London) and other training centres.
Contact: Peter Moran, Director of Studies.

INTERNATIONAL HOUSE—OPOLE
Ul. Kosciuszki 17, 45-062 Opole. Tel/fax: (77) 54 66 55.
Number of teachers: 20.
Preference of nationality: none.
Qualifications, conditions of employment, etc.: same as for International House Katowice.
Contact: Barbara Flisiuk.

INTERNATIONAL HOUSE—WROCLAW
Ul. Ruska 46a, 50-079 Wroclaw. Tel/fax: (71) 723698. E-mail: ih@id.pl
Number of teachers: 20.
Preference of nationality: none.
Qualifications: minimum CELTA or equivalent.
Conditions of employment: same as for International House Katowice.
Facilities/Support: school runs CELTA courses with attractive terms for those who are later employed by IH in Wroclaw, Katowice, Opole or Bielsko Biala. In-house teachers' support includes initial induction; subsidised Cambridge Young Learners certificate course, DELTA and Teaching Business English.
Contact: Malgorzata Szule.

JDJ SERVICE
ul. Gronowa 22, pol. 615-621 Vlp, 61-655 Poznan. Tel: (61) 820 3159. Fax: (61) 821 3109. E-mail: jdj-hqs@ikp.atm.com.pl

Number of teachers: up to 20 for schools in Poznan, Szczezin and Bialystock.

Preference of nationality: British, American, Australian, New Zealand; must be native speaker.

Qualifications: minimum degree plus Trinity Cert or CELTA.

Conditions of employment: 3 months to 1 year. School is open 9am till 7pm. Usually morning, afternoon or evening shifts. Some split shifts possible.

Salary: 25-50 zloties per teaching hour (gross).

Facilities/Support: school finds accommodation prior to teacher's arrival and gives assistance in finding long-term accommodation. School provides paperwork and translation necessary for work visa in country of origin. Fee refunded at end of 1 year contract. In-house workshops.

Recruitment: interviews carried out by Anglo World Central London (3-4 Southampton Place, London WC1A 2DA; 0171-404 3080/fax 0171-404 3443).

Contact: Suzanne Spence, Academic Director (Poznan) or Carole Patilla (Anglo World Central London).

LEKTOR SZKOLA JEZYKOW OBCYCH
ul. Olawska 2, 50-123 Wroclaw. Tel/fax: (71) 343 2599/725292.

Number of teachers: 30.

Preference of nationality: British, American.

Qualifications: Certificate in TEFL required.

Conditions of employment: one-year contracts. 2 90-minute sessions per evening (4pm-5.30pm and 5.40pm-7.10pm). Students are young adults.

Salary: from 40 zloties/£7-£8 per hour.

Facilities/Support: assistance with finding accommodation and obtaining work permit.

Recruitment: personal interviews essential.

Contact: Katarzyna Tarnowska.

LINGUARAMA POLSKA
ul. Sniadeckich 17, 00-654 Warsaw. Tel: (22) 628 7291. Fax: (22) 628 7293. E-mail: warsaw@linguarama.com

Number of teachers: 50 (in Warsaw, Kraków and Poznan).

Preference of nationality: EU citizens.

Qualifications: CELTA.

Conditions of employment: 9 month contracts. Split shifts, before and after business hours.

Salary: £547 or £582 per calendar month depending on grade.

Facilities/Support: assistance with accommodation and work permits which must be obtained in country of birth.

Recruitment: via Linguarama Group Personnel in England (01420 80899).

Contact: Simon Thompson, Manager.

LINGUA STUDIUM JEZYKOW OBCYCH
Ul. Jasnogórska 6, 42-200 Czestochowa. Tel/fax: (34) 324 3368.

Number of teachers: 4.

Preference of nationality: British.

Qualifications: degree in modern languages/literature plus CELTA or Trinity Cert (TESOL).

Conditions of employment: initial contract for academic year. 24 lessons p.w. (45 minutes) mainly afternoons and evenings.

Salary: 1,100 zloties per month net.

Facilities/Support: furnished accommodation, rent and utility bills paid by the school. All the necessary permits and National Insurance provided. In-service teacher training. Access to the latest ELT publications.

Recruitment: adverts in the *Guardian*. Detailed CV and references may be sufficient when interview cannot be arranged.
Contact: Beata Marszalek, Director of Studies.

MTA LANGUAGE CENTRE
Pl. Teatralny 6, Wroclaw. Tel: (71) 72 13 34.
Number of teachers: 4.
Preference of nationality: none.
Qualifications: Cambridge/RSA Certificate/Diploma, TOEFL and other certificates welcome.
Conditions of employment: 2 month contracts. 16-20 h.p.w.
Salary: £600 per month less 20% taxes.
Facilities/Support: assistance with finding accommodation and obtaining work permits given.
Recruitment: interviews not always essential.

NKJO—ELBLAG
ul. Czerniakowska 22, 82-300 Elblag. Tel: (55) 324797. Fax: (55) 326188.
Number of teachers: 2.
Preference of nationality: none.
Qualifications: university degree preferably in linguistics or British studies plus TEFL qualification.
Conditions of employment: 2 year contracts. 12 h.p.w.
Salary: depends on qualifications.
Facilities/Support: assistance with accommodation. Training given.
Recruitment: via voluntary agencies abroad and direct application.
Contact: Aleksandra Arceusz, Director.

NKJO—KRAKOW
ul. Kanonicza 14, 31-002 Kraków. Tel: (12) 422 7955. Fax: (12) 422 6306/423 2318.
Number of teachers: 3.
Preference of nationality: British, American, Canadian.
Qualifications: minimum MA in education, applied linguistics or English literature, plus diploma in TEFL and at least one year's experience of teaching in secondary school or college.
Conditions of employment: 12 month contracts from October 1st. 26 contact h.p.w. Variable hours between 9am and 8pm.
Salary: about £3,000 per year.
Facilities/Support: only 2 university flats available for which the rent would be about £1,000 per year to be shared between two. Computer facilities, etc. available.
Recruitment: British Council and direct application. Local interviews encouraged.

NKJO—LESZNO
pl. Kosciuski 5, 64-100 Leszno. Tel/fax: (65) 520 3607.
Number of teachers: 3.
Preference of nationality: British, American, Canadian.
Qualifications: MA or BA in the arts with EFL training and some experience.
Conditions of employment: minimum stay one year. 12-18 h.p.w.
Salary: 1,200 zloties per month.
Facilities/Support: free accommodation in dormitory or shared flat. Some training through the University of Poznan to which this NKJO is affiliated.
Recruitment: via Ministry of Education, voluntary organisations and direct application. Interviews not essential.
Contact: Anna Geremek.

NKJO—WROCLAW

ul. Skarbowców 8A, 53-025 Wroclaw. Tel: (71) 339 8551. Fax: (71) 618251.
Number of teachers: 5 out of a staff of 30 in the English Department.
Preference of nationality: British, American or other.
Qualifications: BA, MA or PhD in TEFL, British and American literature, history or languages. Sufficient experience of teaching English at higher level, e.g. institutes of higher education.
Conditions of employment: one-year contracts. Full-time contract is 12 h.p.w. (mornings only).
Salary: 800 zloties per month (net).
Facilities/Support: assistance with finding accommodation and work permit given. Possibility of attending professional development conferences, etc.
Recruitment: local interviews essential.
Contact: Anna Karp, Director.

OXFORD STUDY CENTRE

ul. 25 Czerwca 60, 26-600 Radom. Tel/fax: (48) 360 2166. E-mail: bahar@friko.2.onet.pl
Number of teachers: 10-15 native speakers out of a staff of 100.
Preference of nationality: British, but will accept others.
Qualifications: CELTA or equivalent plus degree. Experience preferred.
Conditions of employment: September to June; 2 year contracts also possible. Minimum 22 h.p.w.
Salary: from 1,450 zloties per month (net). Paid overtime 18 zloties per hour.
Facilities/Support: high quality accommodation with all amenities provided but teachers pay the rent. Free private medical insurance. All paperwork for work permits done by school and paid for at end of contract. Teacher development programme. Subsidies for further qualifications like DELTA available for teachers who commit themselves to stay on.
Recruitment: e-mail, newspaper and magazine adverts. Face-to-face interviews preferred but phone interviews possible.
Contact: Grant Kempton, Director of Operations.

POLANGLO

Szkola Jezyków Obcych, ul. Nowowiejska 1/3, 00-643 Warsaw. Tel: (22) 825 7733. Fax: (22) 825 3747.
Number of teachers: 5.
Preference of nationality: British.
Qualifications: BA plus DELTA.
Conditions of employment: minimum 8-12 h.p.w for one semester. General and business English for adults.
Salary: 38-42 zloties per 45 minute lesson.
Facilities/Support: no help with accommodation or work permit; candidates must already have work permit.
Recruitment: local adverts. Local interviews essential.
Contact: Jolanta Dobrowolska, Director.

PROGRAM-BELL

ul. Fredry 7, pok. 22-26, 61-701 Poznan. Tel: (61) 853 6972. Fax: (61) 853 0612.
Number of teachers: 4-5.
Preference of nationality: British, American.
Qualifications: Cambridge/RSA Cert. or Dip. with experience of teaching young children.
Conditions of employment: 9 month contracts. 16 h.p.w. Pupils of all ages including classes for 7-10 year olds. Summer and winter language camps also organised.
Facilities/Support: assistance given with accommodation. Good choice of teaching materials.
Recruitment: newspaper adverts. Interviews held in London in March.

PROLOG
Szkola Jezykow Obcych, ul. Kosciuszki 24, 30-105 Kraków. Tel/fax: (12) 227228.
E-mail: prolog@pp.net.pl
Number of teachers: 3-4.
Preference of nationality: British.
Qualifications: graduates with TEFL Certificate and one year's experience.
Conditions of employment: 9 month contracts. 25 lessons (19 hours) p.w. mainly in the evenings, with some morning classes.
Salary: approximately 1,500 zloties per month (net).
Facilities/Support: assistance with accommodation and work permits. Teachers encouraged to attend teacher training sessions in Kraków. Good range of teaching materials available including video, video camera and other technical resources.
Recruitment: word-of-mouth. Interviews may sometimes be arranged in Canterbury and Birmingham as well as locally.
Contact: Mariusz Siara.

STAIRWAY SCHOOL OF ENGLISH
Ulica Dunajewskiego 6/415, 31-133 Kraków. Tel/fax: (48) 422 1836.
Number of teachers: 12-15.
Preference of nationality: none, though must be willing to collect work permit in country of origin.
Qualifications: minimum one year's experience, plus preferably TESOL Cert or CELTA plus degree. Must be talented and committed.
Conditions of employment: October to June. Majority of classes between 4pm and 9pm with some morning classes. Between 20 and 28 lessons p.w. (45 minutes).
Salary: 25 zloties per 45 minute period (net). School takes care of deductions.
Facilities/Support: assistance with accommodation and work permits. Regular teacher development sessions.
Recruitment: adverts in UK educational press. Unsolicited applications welcome from March to October. Interviews can be held in UK in July/August.
Contact: Tim Murphy, Joint Owner and Director of Studies.

SUCCESS
Osrodek Nauczania Jezyków Obcych, ul. Agawy 5/9, 01-158 Warsaw. Tel: (22) 623 39 40. Fax: (22) 20 55 03.
Number of teachers: 1.
Preference of nationality: British.
Qualifications: TEFL background.
Conditions of employment: 9 month contracts from October. Pupils from primary school age.
Salary: negotiable.
Facilities/Support: no assistance given with accommodation.
Recruitment: personal contact. Local interviews essential.

SZANSA
Prywatny Zaklad Oswiatowy, ul. Lubowska 6a, 60-433 Poznan. Tel: (61) 848 8176.
Number of teachers: 1.
Preference of nationality: American preferred, British possible.
Qualifications: experience in teaching children.
Conditions of employment: part-time work only (a few hours a week).
Salary: average hourly rate.
Facilities/Support: travel costs reimbursed.
Recruitment: interviews held locally; candidates should be living in Poznan already.
Contact: Ewa Dziejma, Manager.

TARGET PROESSIONAL ENGLISH CONSULTANTS
Ulica Polna 50 7p, 00-644 Warsaw. Tel: (22) 660 7054. Fax: (22) 660 7029. E-mail: targeted@it.com.pl
Number of teachers: 40-50.
Preference of nationality: English as native language.
Qualifications: CELTA or equivalent necessary.
Conditions of employment: 9-12 months. 25-30 h.p.w.
Salary: £450-550 per month (gross).
Facilities/Support: assistance with accommodation and loan of first month's rent. School does all paperwork and covers costs of obtaining work permit. Some training available.
Recruitment: via recruitment agencies.
Contact: Michael Gardom, General Manager.

WORLDWIDE SCHOOL
ul. Danilowiczowska 9/21, 00-084 Warsaw. Tel: (22) 827 1269/828 0653.
Number of teachers: 15-20.
Preference of nationality: none.
Qualifications: CELTA plus experience. Also experience in-company or a business background are an advantage.
Conditions of employment: 10 months. 20-25 h.p.w.. Some early mornings.
Salary: £7.50 per hour plus benefits and bonus.
Facilities/Support: assistance with accommodation and work permits (for which school pays). Continuous training and development. Opportunities to attend outside seminars and conferences.
Recruitment: local and through UK interviews. Interviews offered in UK twice a year (July and August).
Contact: Steve Sutton, General Manager.

YES SCHOOL OF LANGUAGE
ul. Reformacka 8, 35-026 Rzeszów. Tel/fax: (17) 852 0720. Fax: (17) 62 65 06. E-mail: yes@rz.onet.pl
Number of teachers: 10 full-time, plus 14 positions on summer camps.
Preference of nationality: British.
Qualifications: university degree and CELTA (or equivalent) required. At least one year's experience is usually required. For summer camp, most important quality is a lively personality.
Conditions of employment: 10-month contracts (September to June). Evening timetable 4.30pm-8pm Monday to Friday. Occasional daytime hours. Students from age 6, at all levels up to CPE.
Salary: 25 zloties per 45 minute lesson net (approximately £4.50).
Facilities/Support: assistance with finding accommodation given. Fee for work permit paid by school for full-time teachers. Video and audio facilities.
Recruitment: adverts in teacher training colleges, internet and direct applications. Interviews not always necessary when applicants have good references and experience. Interviews may be held in the UK during the summer.
Contact: Danuta Balanda, Managing Director.

YORK SCHOOL OF ENGLISH
ul. Bursztynowa 20-22, 31-213 Kraków. Tel: (12) 415 1818/415 1444.
Number of teachers: 7 (full-time).
Preference of nationality: British, also American, Canadian, Irish.
Qualifications: minimum BA or MA (preferably in languages). TEFL certificate (UCLES, Trinity). 1-3 years' teaching experience in EFL.
Conditions of employment: one year (September to June). 25 h.p.w. mainly afternoons/evenings.
Salary: 2,600 zloties a month (about $7 per 45 minutes).

Facilities/Support: accommodation in school flat for two teachers to share (rent is 200 zl</zloties plus electricity). Help given with permits; fees refunded.
Recruitment: adverts in the *Guardian*. Interviews carried out in UK. Regular workshops, conferences and staff meetings.
Contact: Ewa Krupska.

Other Schools to Try

Note that these schools did not confirm their teacher requirements for this edition of *Teaching English Abroad*. Upper case entries marked with an asterisk had entries in the last edition (1997); addresses without asterisks have been taken from various sources, such as British Council lists and the *Yellow Pages*. No attempt has been made to transcribe Polish accents accurately.

NKJO—BIALYSTOK, ul. Liniarskiego 3, 15-420 Bialystok (tel/fax 85-424371). 6 teachers.
EUROPEAN COLLEGE, ul. Konarskiego 4, 85-066 Bydgoszcz (52-22 10 80). 5 teachers, British or Irish preferred.
College of Linguists/Wyzsza Szkola Lingwistyczna, ul. Zwirki i Wigury 9/11, 42-200 Czestochowa (tel/fax 34-365 48 59/324 4859; e-mail: cel@cel.czest.pl). Group of language schools in constant need of English teachers.

Berlitz, ul. Waly Piastowskie 24, 80-855 Gdansk
Empik Szkola Jezyków Obcych, ul. Dlugi Targ 28/29, 80-830 Gdansk
Fluent Szkola Jezyków, ul. Fiszera 14, 80-231 Gdansk
Premiere School of English, ul. Trubadur¢w 4, 80-205 Gdansk
Maryland Kursy i Obozy Jezydowe, Slaska 66b, 80-389 Gdansk
Oswiata Lingiwista, Malczewskiego 51, Gdansk
London School, ul. Abrahama 27/1, Gdynia

Bénédict School, Ul. Sienkiewicza 23, 40-039 Katowice
English Club, Kielce (fax 41-368 1384/e-mail panpol@complex.com.pl
STUDIUM JEZYKOW OBCYCH PROJECT, ul. Szwolezerów 5B/10, 66-400 Gorzów Wlkp (95-320559/fax 95-322058). 2 teachers.
COSMOPOLITAN PRIVATE LANGUAGE SCHOOL, Ul. Katowicka 39, 45-061 Opole (tel/fax 77-548773). 5-6 teachers.
INTERNATIONAL LANGUAGE SCHOOL, ul. Krakowska 51, 45-075 Opole (tel/ fax 77-53 15 97). 7 teachers.
School of English, ul. P. Skargi 74A m 14, 95-200 Pabianice
Stamford School of English, ul. Boh. Monte Cassino 10, 81-775 Sopot
Proficiency Szkola Jezyków Obcych, ul. Grottgera 6/8, 81-809 Sopot
Stanley's Szkola Jezyków Obcych, al. Niepodleglosci 817/2, Sopot
UNIVERSITY OF SZCZECIN, College of English, Al. Piastów 40B, 71-065 Szczecin (91-4333161/fax 91-4331466). 1 teacher with MA/PhD in Humanities plus teaching experience.
Brytania School of English, Tarnów (14-670 3811).
NKJO—WALBRZYCH, ul. Kombatantów 20, 58-302 Walbrzych (tel/fax 74-78695). 2-3 teachers.

A & B American and British School of English, Swietokrzyska 1, 00-360 Warsaw
AMERICAN ENGLISH SCHOOL, Foksal 3/5 pok. 18, Warsaw (22-827 2654).
Angloschool, ul. Popieluszki 7, 01-786 Warsaw (22-663 8883/fax 22-639 8124)
Archibald Szkola Jezyka Angielskiego, Szpitalna 8/19, Warsaw
BRITISH COUNCIL WARSAW STUDIUM, Warsaw University of Technology, ul. Filtrowa 2, 00-611 Warsaw (tel/fax 22-25 82 87). 10-12 teachers.
English Language College, Mokotowska 12, Warsaw
English Language School, ul. Mazowiecka 12 IIIp, 00-048 Warsaw
Lang L.T.C., al. Niepodleglosci 217 m. 8, 02-087 Warsaw (22-825 3940/825 1648/fax 22-825 2273/e-mail clientserv@lang.com.pl). 15 teachers. US $12 per hour gross.
LEXIS Szkola Jezyków Obcych, Marszalkowska 60, Warsaw

Linguae Mundi Szkola Jezyków Obcych, Zlota 61, 00-819 Warsaw
Lingua Nova Szkola Jezyków Obcych, Básniowa 3 pok. 8, Warsaw
Lingwista, Marszalkowska 83, 00-683 Warsaw
MAart Language College, Nowy Swiat 1, 00-496 Warsaw
New School of English, Madalinskiego 22, Warsaw
Peritia Szkola Jezyków Angielskiego, Bednarska 2.4, 00-310 Warsaw
Universal English College (UEC Bell), Plac Trzech Krzyzy 4/6, 00-499 Warsaw (22-625 4792/faz 22-629 5865/e-mail: uec@ikp.atm.com.pl
Warsaw Study Centre, ul. Raszynska 22, 09-026 Warsaw
*ENGLISH LANGUAGE CENTRE, University of Wroclaw, Kuznicza 21, 50-138 Wroclaw (71-402955)

Romania

The downfall of Ceaucescu in 1989 and the collapse of communism in Eastern Europe led to Romania seeking closer links with the West. English was little taught before (French was the second language) but now there is a growing demand as the country seeks to attract foreign investment and to modernise antiquated industries. Unfortunately the weak state of the Romanian economy, legacy of the ruinous Ceaucescu era, means that there is insufficient money to devote to language teaching to meet the demand and in fact the state education system is in a dire state. The Ministry of Education (Strada Gen Berthelot 28-30, 70749 Bucharest; 1-615 7430/614 2680/614 4588/fax 1-312 4819) does not recruit EFL teachers directly, though it cooperates with the British Council to improve standards of local teachers and place volunteers.

For now, Romanians get by with Romanian teachers, satellite broadcasts and teach-yourself tapes. A lucky few receive tuition from a native speaker and some school children benefit from having volunteer teachers and assistants placed in their schools. Anyone seriously intent on teaching in Romania and does not care about remuneration should be able to find an opening. Paul Converse from Oregon travelled in the country one summer a few years ago:

> *I doubt that anyone could make any money teaching English but they would certainly get a free place to live and food and appreciation. When I was in Felenc, the entire village wanted me to stay and teach English.*

The British Council has been very active in promoting English in Romania at all levels. It opened the first joint venture school with the Soros Foundation in Iasi. The British Council Romania web-page has a link to 'Volunteer Teachers' and 'English Language Centres'. The Council works with volunteer placement organisations like *Services for Open Learning* and the *Central Bureau* (see chapter introduction). SOL teachers in Romania are often asked to teach a subject such as geography alongside English. The American organisation *Central European Teaching Program* (Beloit College, 700 College St, Beloit, WI 53511) supplies teachers to schools, particularly in the Hungarian-speaking areas of Transylvania. The Cultural Counsellor at the Romanian Embassy in London (Arundel House, 4 Palace Green, W8 4QD; 0171-937 8125) deals with education and can advise on contacting the Ministry of Education or regional education departments, by whom all teaching jobs in state schools must be processed. The national Inspector of English, Mrs. Anda Maxim, is in charge of all pre-university English education.

In 1996, the Romanian Association for Quality Languages Services (QUEST) was established. The addresses of its seven founder members and one other are available from the British Council in Bucharest or from QUEST's office at the Prosper-Ase Language Centre (prosper1@rolink.iirucro; address below). Under the heading *Limbi Straine—Cursuri* in the Yellow Pages there are about 24 addresses including six *Casa de Cultura*. For the most part, even these established schools must rely on borrowing a few hours of a native speaker's time here and there from state-employed foreigners. They simply can't afford to provide accommodation or anything apart from a local salary.

Although private enterprise now accounts for almost a third of Romania's GDP, there are very few private language schools in Romania at present. International House has a small presence: its school in Timosoara (birthplace of the 1989 revolution) was the first private language school in the country when it opened in 1992. Linguarama has announced that it intends to open a school in Bucharest in 1999/2000. Other Western companies are developing a presence in Romania: McDonald's has opened two restaurants in central Bucharest, and has plans to expand to other cities. At the Coca-Cola operation in Timisoara, for example, a Canadian woman has been teaching business English to employees. A new Hilton hotel is being built in Bucharest and a stock exchange was launched in 1995, all of which will in due course create more demand for commercial English.

Wages will be equivalent to those earned by Romanian teachers, from £50 a month. Of all the countries to which SOL sends teachers, Romania is the only one where the estimated monthly wage falls below £100. Accommodation is normally provided; if it isn't, it takes a good part of a teacher's salary. Rent for a one-bedroom flat in a provincial city can even take all of a local salary, though teachers may receive an extra allowance to help cover this. Plumbing, heating and standards of construction do not match those of Western European countries. Resident foreign teachers are eligible to obtain an AVIZ card, which in theory entitles them to pay the Romanian rate for hotels, etc. (a quarter of the tourist rate) though many hoteliers insist on charging the higher rate. Obviously it is possible to live on the salary earned but not if a teacher indulges in western luxuries in high-price supermarkets catering to privileged Romanians.

Pupils are lively and curious about life in the West, and children are often up-to-date with the latest Western fashions and music from MTV. Photocopiers are scarce and paper is in short supply, if available at all. Outside British Council supported projects and universities, language laboratories and videos are rare teaching aids. Teachers would be advised to take as many teaching materials as possible, e.g. magazine articles, postcards, language games, photos, pictures. Information about the teacher's home town always goes down well.

If going to Romania to teach, request the information sheet 'Work Permits for Foreign Citizens' from the Romanian Embassy. Teachers must apply for a work permit from the Ministry of Employment and Social Protection; the current processing fee is US$200. As usual applicants will have to provide a raft of documents including originals of their teacher training certificate and university degree, documentation from the local or national police indicating that they have no criminal record, a medical certificate and contract. If going to Romania on a preliminary visit, Britons must purchase a visitor visa valid for three months (fee £33) while US nationals can enter without a visa for up to one month.

INTERNATIONAL HOUSE TIMISOARA
Bl. Republicii 9, 1900 Timisoara. Tel/fax: (56) 190593. E-mail: rodica@ihlctim.sorostm.ro.
Number of teachers: 7 in Timisoara and at new teaching centre in Arad 40kms away.
Preference of nationality: none.
Qualifications: tertiary education degree plus CELTA (minimum grade B). Experience of teaching young learners and/or business English preferred.
Conditions of employment: one year contracts starting August to October. 24 h.p.w. including Saturday mornings.
Salary: from $120 (in local currency) plus US$50 a month.
Facilities/Support: free accommodation in flats; utilities paid for by school (except phone). Return flight paid. One-week orientation. No social security paid.
Recruitment: normally through International House, London.
Contact: Hannah Walker.

OPEN DOORS SCHOOL OF ENGLISH
Str. L. Blaga 4, 1900 Timisoara. Tel: (56) 092 302 201. Fax: (56) 194252. E-mail: michelle@online.ro
Number of teachers: 5.
Preference of nationality: none.
Qualifications: university degree and a recognised TEFL/TESL qualification.
Conditions of employment: 10 or 11 months from September. 25 h.p.w. maximum.
Salary: depends on experience.
Facilities/Support: accommodation is provided free; teachers only pay for telephone. School pays translation costs for work permit application, and contributes DM50 per

month worked towards a flight allowance, paid at the end of the contract. Training seminars conducted at school.
Recruitment: via teacher training programmes, internet and word of mouth.
Contact: Michelle Penta, Director.

Other Schools to Try

Prosper-Transilvania Language Centre, Str. Carpatilor, 2200 Brasov
Prosper-ASE Language Centre, Suite 4210 et. 2, Calea Grivitei 2-2A, Bucharest
Access Language Centre, Str. Tebei 21, 3400 Cluj (e-mail ovidiu@access.soroscj.ro).
CLASS, B-dul Mircea cel Batran 103, 8700 Constanta
International Language Centre, Str. Moara de Foc 35, et. 8, 6600 Iasi
RALEX Linguistic Centre, Str. Buna Vestire 35, 1000 Ramnicu-Valcea
Yes Language Centre, Colegiul Pedagogic Andrei Saguna, Str. Gen. Magheru 34, 2400 Sibiu

Russia

At the time of writing, Russia is undergoing its worst political and economic crisis since 1991. Businesses everywhere are closing temporarily or permanently, or (at best) reducing services as they wait and see what will happen. As a business like any other, English Language Teaching has been affected by the crisis. While Russia was still enjoying its boom period, the schools which catered to corporate clients or the nouveau riche charged high fees which could not be sustained through the current period of austerity. These have been among the first to close their doors, followed by many more language schools which have been forced to close or shrink.

With Russia and the rouble so beset with financial troubles, fewer Russians are studying English. This has resulted in the loss of employment to hundreds of English teachers, and people have been wondering what future can there be for TEFL in a Russia where few can afford the luxury of lessons with a native speaker. But many remain optimistic, including Robert Jensky, Director of Language Link Russia:

> *There will always be employment for native English teachers in those companies for which quality English language tuition at an affordable price was always a priority. Those schools which have earned such a reputation will survive and will weather the current financial crisis. Russians are, after all, a remarkably resilient people, and with the advent of rouble stability will come a return to the classroom, and the need for qualified English language teachers will be as great as before.*

Many Russians maintain a passionate interest in English, especially among students at secondary school and university. Many are already fairly competent in the language and want not only to improve their linguistic skills but to become more conversant with western culture, particularly American music. Paper qualifications in ELT are not of much interest to the average young Russian. One estimate has been made that of the more than 150 language schools in Moscow, only about 20 employ native speaker teachers, two thirds of whom are probably working without qualifications.

Apart from the qualified teachers working for the major foreign-owned language chains like *Benedict, Language Link* and *EF English First,* the majority of English teachers in Russia and its Republics, including the Baltics, the Central Asian Republics and Ukraine, have come through voluntary placement organisations or are students of Russian with an interest in the language and culture.

FINDING A JOB

Few schools can afford to advertise and recruit teachers abroad. But anyone with contacts anywhere in the region or who is prepared to go there to make contacts should be able to arrange a teaching niche on an individual basis, always assuming money is no object. Most educational institutes are suffering such serious financial hardships that they can't attract local teachers let alone Western ones. Only in a handful of cases (like the Institute of International Law and Economics in Moscow) are qualified EFL teachers employed and paid accordingly, e.g US$15-$20 per class.

The British Council in Moscow, St. Petersburg, Nizhny Novgorod and Ekaterinburg should be able to send lists of the institutes of higher education and English language gymnasiums in their region. There is a Student Liaison Officer at the British Council in Moscow to whom Britons teaching and living in Russia can turn for advice.

Those who are not deterred by the prospect of earning virtually nothing can contact the International Department of the Education Committee in Moscow who are responsible for the allocation of teachers to state schools. In order for an individual to be considered, he or she should be able to provide a relevant qualification, a health certificate and references.

Private lessons will be less easy to fix up than they were a few years ago when 'New Russians', those who were made relatively rich by the change to a free market, were willing and able to pay up to an outrageous US$30 an hour for one-on-one tuition, sometimes even in hard currency. While spending six months as a student of Russian in the beautiful and historic town of Yaroslavl, Hannah Start found private pupils very easily. She decided to accept only high school students to diminish the risk of crime; apparently if you are teaching in your own accommodation, it is wise to refrain from displaying any expensive Western items.

The main language chains recruit heavily abroad; both *Language Link* and *Benedict* have active departments in the UK which screen and interview candidates (see entries) for their schools throughout Russia. *EF English First's* several schools in Moscow and elsewhere in Russia rely heavily on EF in London (5 Kensington Church St, London W8 4LD; 0171-795 6645/fax 0171-795 6625) who were recently promising qualified EFL teachers US$1,100 a month plus return flight, medical insurance and visa costs. *Saxoncourt Recruitment* fills vacancies in Moscow and Siberia on behalf of IH-affiliated schools, among others, while *Nord Anglia* recruits for its member school, Polyglot (address at end of section).

A thriving English language press has established itself in Moscow and St. Petersburg. Check adverts in the *Moscow Times, Moscow Tribune* and the weekly *St. Petersburg Press.* Look out also for the free ads paper *Iz Ruk v Ruki* in about 15 towns in Russia.

UK Organisations

A number of voluntary and cultural exchange organisations place English language assistants in the former Soviet Union primarily *East European Partnership* and the *Central Bureau* (addresses in the introduction to this chapter). These are recommended since they are a way of getting something organised in a country which is notoriously disorganised. In addition to the ones listed, *GAP Activity Projects* has a sizeable programme in the region and both *i to i International Projects* and *Teaching Abroad* run schemes by which paying volunteers are placed mostly in state schools.

The Central Bureau's Assistants Scheme, open only to candidates who have studied Russian, is now well established in sending students to linguistic universities and paedagogical institutes (outside Moscow, St. Petersburg, Yaroslavl and Voronezh). In addition to the negligible wage paid to all university employees, the Central Bureau pays a monthly top-up of about £100 to enable assistants to have a decent standard of living (though with price increases, even this is barely enough).

Chris Jones had a wonderful year as a teaching assistant in Nizhny Novgorod (seven hours from Moscow) with the Central Bureau and his experiences are representative of others' who have gone through a mediating organisation to teach in the Russian state system:

> *I had no relevant teaching experience, but the fact that I had been to Russia several times before seemed to be a big selling factor; I obviously knew what I was in for.*

During the interview, discussion concentrated on how you thought you would cope with living in Russia for nine months.

My institution was very conscious of not over-burdening me with work and I regularly had to press for more hours. I was expected to concentrate on phonetic and conversational practice but was allowed almost to do my own thing once they realised that I was competent. I used articles from newspapers and magazines for listening and reading comprehensions and made extensive use of popular songs.

There were problems with resources. There were only two video recorders in my university and these had to be booked well in advance. Hand-outs are virtually unheard of in university teaching in Russia and getting photocopying done for lessons was very difficult. Certainly all copies had to be handed back in at the end of each lesson and saved for other groups to use. Sometimes I paid for photocopies myself, as the official channel for using the photocopier (there was only one) involved much wearisome justification to those in authority.

US Organisations

Several organisations in the USA offer volunteers the chance to teach English at any level from university to businesses. The Teaching Intern program run by Project Harmony (6 Irasville Common, Waitsfield, VT 05673; 802-496-4545/fax 802-496-4548) arranges for recent college graduates and experienced teachers to work in host schools and institutions in Russia and Odessa in the Ukraine for six months or a year. The placement fee of $2,150 includes everything including airfares from the US but not health insurance which costs an extra $35 a month. Accommodation is provided, normally sharing with a host family. Project Harmony has offices in St. Petersburg, Moscow and Petrozavodsk.

Adventures in Education Inc. is another cultural exchange organisation which runs a similar voluntary teaching scheme called Petro-Teach (named for St. Petersburg, where placements are made, rather than for the petro-chemical industry of Russia). The application programme begins in February/March for year-long placements beginning on September 1st. The public and private schools where participants teach are located throughout central St. Petersburg and host families are scattered around the city. An intensive pre-teaching Russian course and on-going lessons in Russian is given at the Institute of Foreign Languages. Further details of the programme are available from Adventures in Education Inc. 630-B Main St, Port Jefferson, NY 11777 (414-472-1831; e-mail: sherlocw@uwwvax.uww.edu)

The American Slavic Student Internship Service & Training Corporation (ASSIST) offers a variety of internships for both experienced and inexperienced teachers. It offers a stipend equal to the average Russian wage and a good support network. Internship programme fees range from about $2,700 for a one-month programme to more than $8,000 for a one-year placement including return travel, visas expenses, etc. Details are available from ASSIST, 221 E. Market St, Box 254, Iowa City, IA 52245 (e-mail cmattisn@blue.weeg.uiowa.edu).

WORKING AND LIVING CONDITIONS

Anyone who has seen television news programmes will be aware of the privations of life in Russia, where in some cases teachers and other professionals have been forced to grow vegetables in order to survive. The unregulated housing market makes it very difficult for foreign teachers to find independent accommodation. Employers normally arrange accommodation for their teachers in small shared flats, with host families or in student hostels where conditions are very basic. Many teachers lodge with landladies, of whom there is no shortage considering how many widows there are trying to make ends meet on vanishingly small pensions.

With a serious shortage of teaching aids in many places, resourcefulness will be necessary as Hannah Start demonstrated. She happened to find a cucumber and some milk one day in a shop and so hastily organised an impromptu English afternoon tea. Not surprisingly, the younger generation seems more willing to embrace new communicative teaching methods than the older one, according to Elena Smirnova of the English School Sunny Plus:

Adults cause headaches. They get upset with grammar. Many of them can't easily accept modern methods of teaching. The progress is very slow. For many weeks they can't understand a teacher. They demand changing him. Their pronunciation is terrible, but during classes they keep silent.

Regulations

For people participating in established international exchanges, the red tape is usually straightforward. Russia at the moment is a place where the rules change weekly. In the commercial sector, work permits are more problematic, mainly because so few Russian companies have put their tax affairs in order, which is a prerequisite for obtaining permission from the Federal Migration Service (FMS) to employ foreigners legally. The vast majority of businesses and schools operate outside the law, since the black economy accounts for most of the transactions in Russia. Teachers should be wary of language teaching companies which refuse to give contracts bearing an official stamp.

Only after an employer receives permission to invite foreigners is he or she allowed to become a sponsor of work visas. After a telex has been sent to the Ministry of Foreign Affairs, an invitation can be sent to the applicant to present at the Russian Consulate together with the application for a Multiple Entry Visa, the required fee of £100 and proof of an HIV test (for all visitors intending to stay for more than three months). Foreigners are then given a three-month visa which can later be turned into a work permit, provided the employer posts a sizeable bond. A number of visa agencies are able to obtain one-year multiple entry visas for clients, but these cannot necessarily be turned into work permits unless the employing company on the visa form has prior permission to employ foreigners.

Numerous foreigners do work without proper authorisation, but run a constant risk of being fined or even deported. Rhys Sage became suspicious of an employer who sent him the wrong visa:

> *After a fiasco in Latvia, it has become apparent to me that if a company is not willing to obtain the proper visa then they must be up to something dodgy. When I negotiated my contract with a school in Novosibirsk, they accepted some pretty excessive demands on my part which made me suspicious that the contract was worthless. This, combined with the fact that they sent me a visa form for a transit visa claiming it was a work visa, resulted in my complete loss of interest in them. A transit visa means nothing. It just means that you have permission to cross Russia, and therefore you have no redress if the employer decides to withhold your wages.*

LIST OF SCHOOLS

AMERICAN ACADEMY OF FOREIGN LANGUAGES—MOSCOW
17 Bolsahya, Cheremushkinskaya, Moscow. Tel: (095) 127 23 91. Fax: (95) 129 14 11. E-mail: aafl@co.ru
Number of teachers: 20 full-time and several part-time.
Preference of nationality: native speaker with awareness of differences between American and British English.
Qualifications: TEFL certificate and/or 2 years' teaching experience. Prefer teachers with business background (e.g. marketing, finance, law or public relations). Knowledge of Russian needed for teaching some groups.
Conditions of employment: renewable every 3 months. Hours vary, between 6 and 20 p.w. Maximum 30 h.p.w. Peak hours before 10am and after 6pm.
Salary: generally between US$10 and $20 per hour less local income tax.
Facilities/Support: assistance with accommodation and work permits.
Recruitment: teachers normally hired locally after advertising in local English language press, in trade magazines and on the internet. Interviews not essential; phone interviews given to establish whether teacher is personable, outgoing and enthusiastic.
Contact: Kathleen Zableina, Director.

AMERICAN ACADEMY OF FOREIGN LANGUAGES—ST PETERSBURG
11A Pervaya, Krasnoarmeyskaya, Office 52, St. Petersburg. Tel/fax: (812) 316 41 48. E-mail: young@solaris.ru
Number of teachers: 6-10.
Preference of nationality, qualifications and conditions of employment as above.
Contact: Jerry Yonge, Director.

BENEDICT SCHOOL
Sibirskaya 31, Office 10, Novosibirsk 630004. Tel/fax: (3832) 173875. E-mail: Admin@sks.nsu.ru. Web-site: www.netcom.co.uk/-ice/intro.htm1.
Number of teachers: 5 native speakers out of 30.
Preference of nationality: British, American, Canadian.
Qualifications: TEFL background including the Benedict TEFL training. 1 year's experience preferred of teaching intermediate to advanced students, teenagers and some business English.
Conditions of employment: minimum one semester (3 month) stays, though two or three semesters preferred, after trial period of 6 weeks. Hours normally in morning and evening (6pm-8pm, Monday to Saturday).
Salary: US$7 per hour (net) which may increase after 6 months. Return airfare from UK paid (maximum $500).
Facilities/Support: shared flat provided for US$50 a month rent, or host families in some cases. Assistance with visas. Good range of teaching materials because school is regional distributor for OUP, CUP and Longman. Orientation meeting on arrival, and pre-course observations.
Recruitment: directly or via UK agency: International Educational Centre Ltd., 74 Baxter Court, Norwich NR3 2ST (tel/fax 01603 763378).

BENEDICT SCHOOL
23 ul. Pskovskaya, St. Petersburg 190008. Tel: (812) 113 85 68/114 10 90. Fax: (812) 114 44 45. E-mail: benedict@infopro.spb.su. Web-site: www.netcom.co.uk/-ice/intro.htm1.
Number of teachers: 40-60 for Russia including 18-20 for St. Petersburg (main franchise holder) and others in Novosibirsk (see above), Tomsk, Murmansk and Kemerovo.
Preference of nationality: British, American, Canadian, Australian.
Qualifications: no TEFL background needed for Work-Study programme. TEFL graduates needed for teaching.
Conditions of employment: 3-12 months. 15-25 h.p.w.
Salary: US$400-800 per month (net).
Facilities/Support: work permits not needed for Work-Study Programme; otherwise assistance given. In-hour training courses (10-30 lessons) result in international Benedict teachers' certificate.
Recruitment: directly or via UK agency, IEC Ltd. (address at end of previous entry).
Contact: Natalya Rostovtseva, Managing Director.

BKC – INTERNATIONAL HOUSE
Tverskaya Ul, Dom 9A, bld 4, 103009 Moscow. Tel: (095) 234 0314. Fax: (095) 234 0316. E-mail: bkc.ih@23.relcom.ru. Web-site: http://www.bkc.ru.
Number of teachers: 70 throughout Russia, including 50 in Moscow.
Preference of nationality: any English-speaking country.
Qualifications: CELTA, Trinity Cert (grade B or above) or US MA(TESL).
Conditions of employment: 36 teaching weeks and 5 weeks paid holiday. 25 contact h.p.w.
Salary: $500+ net according to qualifications and experience, plus accumulating bonus paid on completion of contract. Airfare allowance made.
Facilities/Support: free shared flats provided. All bills except telephone paid by school.

Visa department helps teachers arrange a business visa; visa costs are refunded after 3 months of contract. Monthly seminars and regular observations.

Recruitment: via internet, agencies, press adverts and direct applications. Telephone interviews are possible.

Contact: Anna Naumova (Recruitment Manager) or Jan Madakbas (Director of Studies).

EF ENGLISH FIRST
125 Brestskaya 1st Street, 5th Floor, 125047 Moscow. Tel: (095) 937 3886. Fax: (095) 937 3889.

Number of teachers: 25 for 15 schools (11 in Moscow, others in St. Petersburg, Nizhny Novgorod, Ekaterinburg and Vladivostok).

Preference of nationality: British or North American (due to work permit restrictions).

Qualifications: minimum university degree and certificate in EFL/ESL.

Conditions of employment: 9 month contracts. Teaching between 7.30am and 9pm plus some Saturday mornings.

Salary: US$1,100 plus bonuses.

Facilities/Support: help with finding accommodation. Visas/work permits provided. Paid holidays. Flights paid. Orientation upon arrival and ongoing training. Emergency medical insurance. Russian lessons. Well-equipped schools.

Recruitment: directly through Moscow office or through English First offices in London and Boston (see *Finding a Job*).

Contact: Bernard Shearer, Academic Director (Moscow Office).

ENGLISH SCHOOL SUNNY PLUS
PO Box 23, 125057 Moscow. Tel: (095) 151 2500 (3-7pm). E-mail: sunnyplus@glasnet.ru. Web-site: www.sunnyplus.ru

Number of teachers: 10.

Preference of nationality: British, American, Canadian.

Qualifications: university degree and teaching experience. Ideally, TEFL qualification, good experience and excellent communication skills.

Conditions of employment: 3 months between September and end of June. 4-24 h.p.w. Teaching hours 3-9pm Monday to Friday. Classes for children from age 8, adolescents and adults.

Salary: negotiable.

Facilities/Support: give advice on finding accommodation and visa support. Director of Studies provides in-house training.

Recruitment: interviews essential.

Contact: Serguei Smirnov, Deputy Director.

LANGUAGE LINK SCHOOLS
Novoslobodskaya ul. 5, bld. 2, 103030 Moscow. Tel/fax: (095) 232 0225/234 0703. E-mail: jobs@language.ru. Web-site: http://www.language.ru

Number of teachers: 200 throughout Russia (Moscow, St. Petersburg, Volgograd, Siberia, Urals, etc.)

Preference of nationality: British, also American, Canadian and Australian.

Qualifications: university degree and CELTA or Trinity Certificate/Diploma required.

Conditions of employment: 6 or 9 month (40 week) contracts. 25 teaching h.p.w., normally $4\frac{1}{2}$ a day, 5 days a week. Adult classes, children's classes and in-company.

Salary: US$550-$850 (net) depending on location and experience. Return airfare (maximum $560) and local transport paid. 4 weeks of paid holiday (for teachers on 9 month contracts).

Facilities/Support: all teachers provided with free accommodation in 1-room flat (or 2-room flat for 2 teachers). Paid medical services and full visa/work permission support. Academic support via on-site Director of Studies, inset training, seminars and presentations.

Recruitment: interviews and selection mostly carried out by Language Link in London (21 Harrington Road, London SW7 3EU; 0171-225 1065). Teachers applying from outside UK must be interviewed in Russia.
Contact: Robert Jensky, Director.

RUSSIAN-AMERICAN CENTER
Tomsk Polytechnic University, Room 319, Lenin Avenue 30, 634034 Tomsk. Tel: (3822) 41 55 29. Fax: (3822) 27 90 80/27 91 90. E-mail: push@rac.tpu.edu.ru/ knp@tpu.ru/ovp@tpu.ru
Number of teachers: 1.
Preference of nationality: American, British or any.
Qualifications: experience in teaching languages to foreign students with emphasis on pronunciation.
Conditions of employment: one semester. Conditions vary according to individual contract.
Salary: US$5 per hour.
Facilities/Support: assistance with accommodation given and training if necessary.
Recruitment: candidates normally recommended by US or UK partners. Interview not essential.

Other Schools to Try

Breitner Language School, Leninsky Prospekt 29, Moscow 117313
Polyglot International Language Academy, Block 5, 19 Novoyasenevsky Prospect, Moscow 117593 (095-281 2860/e-mail polyglot@glasnet.ru).
*RUSSIAN INSTITUTE OF SOCIAL COMMUNICATIONS (RISC), Dimitri Ulianovna St 26, 117036 Moscow (095-129 2397/fax 95-124 4639). 5 teachers.
System-3 Language & Communication, Kantemirovskaya St 16 No. 531, Moscow 115522
Linguistic University, Minina 31A, 603155 Nizhny Novgorod
Linguistic Gymnasium 13, Bolshaya Pechyorskaya 63B, 603155 Nizhny Novgorod
Linguistic Gymnasium 67, Sofia Perovskaya 1, 603014 Nizhny Novgorod
Lyceum 40, Varvarskaya 15, Nizhny Novgorod
Pedagogical Gymnasium, Gaugelya 30, Nizhny Novgorod
Lingva, 7th Linie 36, Vassilyesvski, Ostror, 199004 St. Petersburg
*ST. PETERSBURG UNIVERSITY OF HUMANITIES & SOCIAL SCIENCES, Department of Foreign Languages, 15 Fuchika Str, 192238 St. Petersburg (tel/fax 812-269 1925).
Express English, e-mail davebish@chat.ru. Advertising EL vacancies in Western Siberia.
*LINK SCHOOL OF LANGUAGES, 15/81 pl. Lenina, 394000 Voronezh (732-55 23 31).

Baltics

Arguably the most westernised part of the old Russian Empire, the Baltic countries of Lithuania, Latvia and Estonia are looking towards a future as part of Western Europe.

LATVIA

Of the three Baltic states, Latvia has changed the least, with no commercial language schools and few TEFL possibilities with state organisations. Qualified ELT teachers should make contact with the English Language Teachers Association of Latvia, 11 Novembra Krastmala 29, 1050 Riga. The only recent advertisement for TEFL vacancies in Latvia invited experienced teachers to send their CV to Cicero Languages International (42 Upper Grosvenor Road, Tunbridge Wells, Kent TN1 2ET).

Even voluntary opportunities are few and far between. The Volunteers for Latvia programme which used to be administered by the Latvian National Council in Great Britain (53 Goodhard Way, West Wickham, Kent BR4 0ER) no longer exists. The International Exchange Center (2 Republic Square, 1010 Riga, Latvia; tel: 2-327476; fax: 2-331920/783 0257; e-mail: iec@mail.eunet.lv) invites volunteers of any nationality to work as counsellors on children's summer camps (where English is taught among many other things) in Latvia and also in Russia and Ukraine, provided they have a basic knowledge of Russian or Latvian. There is a registration fee of $50.

Rhys Sage worked at a summer camp through the IEC one summer and, despite finding the food and working conditions barely tolerable, returned to the same camp several summers later after receiving a faxed invitation from the camp director:

> *I spent two months as an English teacher. Well, that's what they called it. I was merely a token English speaker and was not allowed to do any actual teaching or any real assisting. It was a typically Soviet experience where people were not expected to do anything but were paid and criticised for anything they actually did.*

The British Council in Riga points out that English is taught in state-run Children and Youth Culture Centres. They also provide addresses of a few English language schools which occasionally employ native speakers:

Public Service Language Unit, 3/1 Smilsu Str, 1838 Riga (721 2251/fax 721 3780)

English Language Centre 'Satva', Office 8, 79/85 Dzirnavu Str, 1011 Riga tel/fax 722 6641)

International Centre R & V, 10 Meistaru Str, 1050 Riga (tel/fax 722 4750)

Mirte, 23 Raina Bulv. 1050 Riga (tel/fax 722 2284)

Jurmala Language Centre, 4 Ogres Str., 2000 Jurmala (2-761188)

The Latvian Embassies in London and Washington can send detailed information about visas. Since 1996 it has been possible for people engaged in educational work (including teachers) to apply for a 'special visa' without having to obtain an invitation from the Department of Citizenship and Immigration. This is valid for up to a year and costs $10. The process is somewhat easier than it was when Rhys Sage tried to obtain a resident permit after being offered a job by the Defence Academy in Riga:

> *I was given a huge list of things to get, including documents which absolutely do not exist other than in the minds of Latvian bureaucrats. Depending on who you ask and in which office, the regulations vary. In the end I left Latvia as my 90 days were up and I really didn't feel like staying illegally. As a tourist, it's possible to stay in Latvia for no more than 90 days in a calendar year. There is a great quantity of work in Latvia for English teachers, but the difficulties of obtaining a visa are almost insurmountable.*

Rhys Sage went on to explain that the lack of a visa was only one in a catalogue of woes;

> *I arrived in November expecting, as agreed with the Rektor of the military academy, a room and meals, 120 Lats per month, a visa and health insurance. The room turned out to be an old KGB prison cell with bars over the windows. The shower had black mould up the walls and green slime on the duckboards. A favourite dish served in the mess hall was sauerkraut which was like compost. I was not surprised that most of my students were inattentive, sleepy and generally lacklustre given the diet they had. In the end I spent most of my time hunting for real food. I was never provided with chalk so had to borrow it from the other teachers. There were photocopiers but no paper.*

LITHUANIA

There is more scope for teachers in Lithuania, to which *Travel Teach* and several other placement organisations send volunteers. Lithuanian schools are so keen to have native speakers that qualifications are not necessary, only a university degree. The Lithuanian Embassy in Washington distributes a list of programmes including teaching programmes. The key organisation is the American Partnership for Lithuanian Education (APPLE), PO Box 617, Durham, CT 06422, USA (203-347-7095/fax 203-347-5837). Prospective teachers looking for placement in the state system at secondary or tertiary level are invited to send their resumes to the director, Ms. Vaiva Vebraite-Gust.

It is also possible to approach the Ministry of Education & Science directly, as recommended by John Morgan from Dorset:

> *The best way to fix up a teaching post is to go to Vilnius yourself and see the person responsible for placing English language teachers. I did this last year and the supervisor rang some schools to arrange interviews for me. The pay is not good (about $20 a week) so private lessons are necessary (and the school may help you to arrange these). Living with a family is the cheapest accommodation and easiest to arrange.*

He enjoyed his stint in a state school more than teaching in companies which he had done the previous year through Travel Teach, when the hours were unsocial and the clients liable to be more demanding.

Alan Reekie is another Briton who has taught in Lithuania through the Ministry of Education:

> *Successful applicants receive free accommodation either with a family or in a flat, a Lithuanian teacher's salary and a week's course of lectures on teaching in Vilnius. I am teaching 14-18 year olds who are fairly eager to learn, though because they only have an examination when they leave at 18, it can be harder to motivate the lower forms. Everyone is friendly which seems to be the case in most of Eastern Europe. I would say that the possibility of getting work is very good. An American I have met here found work within a few weeks of arriving here on spec (however he claims to be telepathic so this may have helped).*
>
> *The teaching hasn't been too hard so far, as the schools accept enthusiasm instead of skill. It also helps when your lessons are only 15 minutes long due to a heating failure. This is quite a good programme for people with no experience of teaching or travelling abroad, as you don't have to worry overly about the logistics, at the same time gaining some experience of dealing with the inevitable problems—like my landlady.*

The scheme is coordinated by the Department of Foreign Relations at the Ministry (Volano Gatve 2/7, 2691 Vilnius; 2-622483/fax 2-612077). A letter from the Ministry or a school in Lithuania makes it possible to acquire a special visa which in the case of teachers and aid workers is free of charge.

The British Council will send a list of 17 English language schools in the capital Vilnius including International House.

AMERICAN ENGLISH SCHOOL
Pylimo 20, 2001 Vilnius, Lithuania. Tel/fax: (2) 791011/2.
Number of teachers: 4.
Preference of nationality: none.
Qualifications: 3 years teaching' experience.
Conditions of employment: 4 days per week (afternoons mainly). Other conditions negotiable. Pupils aged 8-16 and adults.
Salary: US$6-8 per hour.
Facilities/Support: preliminary training provided.
Recruitment: trial class to be taught before appointment.
Contact: Egle Kesyliene, Director.

EF ENGLISH FIRST
Kosciuskos g.11, 2000 Vilnius. Tel: (2) 791616. Fax: (2) 791646.
Number of teachers: 10.
Preference of nationality: British or North American.

Qualifications: minimum university degree and certificate in TEFL/TESL.
Conditions of employment: 9 month contracts teaching between 7am and 9pm and some Saturday mornings.
Salary: local equivalent of US$500 a month plus bonus.
Facilities/Support: assistance with finding accommodation. Visas provided. Paid holidays. Orientation on arrival and ongoing training. Local medical insurance. Variety of resources.
Recruitment: directly to school or through English First offices in London or Boston.

SIAULIAI UNIVERSITY, LITHUANIA
P. Visinskio Street 25, 5400 Siauliai, Lithuania. Tel/fax: (1) 432592. E-mail: spi@siauliai.omnitel.net
Number of teachers: 3.
Preference of nationality: British or American.
Qualifications: experience of teaching communicative English, Business English or British studies.
Conditions of employment: 1-2 year contracts. 16 h.p.w. Students aged 18-25.
Salary: depends on experience and scientific degree.
Facilities/Support: room in student hostel available free of charge. Some training and visa assistance provided.
Recruitment: adverts in *TES* and direct application.
Contact: Vita Kusleikiene, Coordinator of University International Relations Office.

Other Schools to Try

The America Center, Pranciskoniu 3/6, 2001 Vilnius
English Language Teaching Centre, Rinktines 28a, Vilnius 2051
Foreign Language Courses, Kauno 1a, Vilnius
Janinos Zukienes, Foreign Language Courses, Taikos 157, Vilnius 2017
Kalba Ltd, Foreign Language Courses, Kalvariju 3, Vilnius 2005
Korepetitorius, English and German Language Courses, Maisiogalos 34-28, Vilnius
Lingue et Commercium, Foreign Language and Commercial School, Studentu 39, Vilnius 2034
Partners for International Education & Training Lithuania, Akmenu g. 1-3, 2009 Vilnius
Poliglotas, Foreign Language Courses, Ozo 17-12, Vilnius
A. Sakalienes Foreign Language School, See and Learn, Zirmunu 37, Vilnius 2012
Soros International House, Ukmerges 41, Vilnius
Vilnius Pedagogical University, International Relations Department, Studentu 39, 2034 Vilnius
Vilnius University, Educational Advising Center, Universiteto 3, 2734 Vilnius

Educational Information Center, Laisves al. 53, 2nd Floor, 3020 Kaunas
Klaipeda International School of Languages, Zveju 2, Klaipeda 5800 (tel/fax 6-311 1190; e-mail mark.uribe@klaipeda.omnitel.net). Recent advertisements for enthusiastic teachers.

ESTONIA

Estonia is arguably the most progressive of the three Baltic countries, and the British Council in Tallinn will send a list headed 'Major Language Schools in Estonia' with 29 addresses of universities and private language schools; most are reproduced below but without contact names and telephone/fax numbers. There are no major organised placement schemes from Britain or the States.

After her sister had worked in Estonia with a Christian organisation, Sarah Wadsworth applied to four schools in Estonia and was offered jobs in three of them. She chose to teach at a specialist music school in the country town of Rapla. She recommends looking in *Opetaja Lent*, the teachers' newsletter, for employment leads in state schools. International House in Tallinn employs nine ELT instructors, and the Peace Corps places English teachers in state schools.

Like so many of the former states of the USSR, the visa requirements are confusing as Sarah found. Getting the work and residence permits took a great deal of time and patience, as well as costing about £60. The main problem was finding out what papers were needed.

INTERNATIONAL LANGUAGE SERVICES
Pikk 9, Tallinn EE0001. Tel: 646 4258. Fax: 641 2476. E-mail: ilsinfo@online.ee. Web-site: http://www.online,ee/ilsinfo
Number of teachers: 5-10.
Preference of nationality: none.
Qualifications: minimum CELTA or Trinity Cert; experience preferred.
Conditions of employment: 9 month contracts. 24 45-minute lessons per week.
Salary: about 8,200 kroons/US$600 per month (gross) less 26% deductions.
Facilities/Support: free flat provided. All procedures for work permits handled by school. Regular seminars and teacher development programme.
Recruitment: internet and English language press. Phone interviews.
Contact: Phil Marsdale, Director.

Other Schools to Try

Nosylienes School, Kudirkos Skg. 11, Marijampole (tel/fax 43-76946). 3 teachers. 20 litas per lesson.
ALF Training Centre Ltd. Rävala pst. 4, Tallinn EE0001
HEDI, Tina 16a, Tallinn EE0001
International House, Pikk 69, Tallinn EE0101
Ko-Praktik, Tondi 1, Tallinn EE0013
Kullerkupp, Pärnu mnt. 57, Tallinn EE0001
Language Learning Service, Tonismagi 3, Tallinn EE0001
LEX, Uus 19, Tallinn EE0001
Lingo Ltd., Väike-Kuke 16, Pärnu, Tallinn EE0001
Mainor Language Centre, Kuhlbarsi tn. 1, Tallinn EE0101. Also Kreutzwaldi 48a Tartu EE2400
Multilingua, Mere pst.4, Tallinn EE0001
Old Town Language Centre (Helo), Pühavaimu 7, Tallinn EE0001
Sugesto, Barva mnt. 6-8, Tallinn EE0001
Tallinn Language School, Rendla 22, Tallinn EE0001
Tallinn Pedagogical University, Language Centre, Narva mnt. 29, Tallinn EE0101
Tallinn Technical University, Language Centre, Akadeemia tee 1, Tallinn EE0026
TEA, Liivalaia 28, Tallinn EE0001

Concordia International University, Kaluri tee 3, Viimsivald, Harjumaa EE3006
Audentese, Sopruse pst. 2, Tartu EE2400
Dialoog, Turu 9, Tartu EE2400
Folkuniversitet, Lai 30, Tartu EE2400
Studium Munga 18, Tartu EE2400
Tartu Language School, Lai 22, Tartu EE2400

Ukraine

The vast republic of the Ukraine has a serious shortage of English teachers and many other things besides. In addition to the British organisations mentioned at the beginning of this chapter which send volunteers to Ukraine, several emigré organisations in the US recruit volunteers, warning that teachers must be prepared to accept a modest standard of living. *Project Harmony* (see description in the section on Russia above) and *Bridges for Education* have active programmes in Ukraine; participants pay $2,150 to teach for six months or a year (including flights from the US). Volunteer teachers who take their own chalk, paper clips, sellotape and other materials are usually glad that they did.

There is some commercial ELT activity, so that recruitment agencies like *Skola* amd *Saxoncourt* in London advertise vacancies in Ukraine from time to time. Since the ELT market is in its infancy, the prospect for tough motivated teachers to rise quickly is excellent.

The British Council in Kyiv has compiled lists of English language institutes of various kinds. In fact it is planning to open an English teaching centre itself in 1999.

LIST OF SCHOOLS

AMERICAN ACADEMY OF FOREIGN LANGUAGES KIEV
89 Chervonoarmeyska, Office 9, 252006 Kiev, Ukraine. Tel/fax: (44) 268 50 95. E-mail: melissa@aafl.kiev.ua
Number of teachers: 6-8.
Preference of nationality: native speaker with awareness of differences between American and British English.
Qualifications: TEFL certificate and/or 2 years' teaching experience. Prefer teachers with business background (e.g. marketing, finance, law or public relations).
Conditions of employment: renewable every 3 months. Hours vary, between 6 and 20 p.w. Maximum 30 h.p.w. Peak hours before 10am and after 6pm.
Salary: generally between US$10 and $20 per hour less local income tax.
Facilities/Support: assistance with accommodation and work permits.
Recruitment: teachers normally hired locally after advertising in local English language press, in trade magazines and on the internet. Interviews not essential; phone interviews given to establish whether teacher is personable, outgoing and enthusiastic.
Contact: Melissa MacDonald, General Director.

INTERNATIONAL INSTITUTE OF LINGUISTICS AND LAW
Gorky St 130, 006 Kiev, Ukraine. Tel: (44) 269 2093. Fax: (44) 269 4753.
Number of teachers: none to date.
Qualifications: experienced teachers.
Conditions of employment: one year contracts. 12-24 h.p.w.
Salary: US$7-10 per 90-minute class.
Facilities/Support: no assistance with accommodation or work permits.
Recruitment: with assistance of the Embassy.
Contact: Ludmila Ivanivna Shumigora, First Vice Rector.

LONDON SCHOOL OF ENGLISH
Central Post Office, PO Box 'B' 158, 242001 Kyiv, Ukraine. Tel/fax: (44) 241 8654/ 8927. E-mail: admin@lse.kiev.ua
Number of teachers: 14. Planning to open business school in Odessa in 1999.
Preference of nationality: none.
Qualifications: minimum CELTA or Trinity Cert; experience not essential.
Conditions of employment: 11 month contracts. 22½ contact hours per week.
Salary: US$700-$800 per month plus $300 for accommodation.
Facilities/Support: accommodation provided within 40 minute commute from school. Invitations sent to home country so candidates can get work permit from Ukrainian embassies abroad.

Recruitment: adverts in *Guardian*, via Saxoncourt Recruitment and by word of mouth. Interviews held in UK in summer.
Contact: Sean Harty, Director/Owner.

MONARCH INTERNATIONAL LANGUAGE ACADEMY
8 Vorovskogo Str, Kyiv, 252000 Ukraine. Tel: (44) 212 0206. Fax: (44) 212 5683.
Number of teachers: 6.
Preference of nationality: British, American.
Qualifications: TEFL certificate/experience of teaching adults.
Conditions of employment: choice of short-term 3 month or 1 year contracts. 24-28 h.p.w.
Salary: negotiable.
Facilities/Support: assistance with accommodation and work permits.
Recruitment: interview essential, locally or in UK with Nord Anglia Education plc.
Contact: Russova Yelena, Chief Coordinator.

UKRAINIAN-AMERICAN HUMANITARIAN INSTITUTE
Wisconsin International University—Ukraine, 9 Pyrogov St, Kyiv 252030, Ukraine. Tel/fax: (44) 216 0666. Tel: (44) 274 1916.
Number of teachers: 4-5.
Preference of nationality: American and British.
Qualifications: MA in ESL/EFL preferred, BAs accepted. Business administration background useful.
Conditions of employment: 1 semester (15 weeks) or one academic year (30 weeks). Flexible hours.
Salary: US$10-20 per hour (net) depending on the course and degree.
Facilities/Support: assistance with accommodation and in-service training for ESL and Business English teachers.
Recruitment: via foreign universities, agencies and word of mouth. Interviews sometimes possible in USA. If not, teachers can be hired on the basis of their CV.
Contact: Prof. Yulia Romanovskaya, Head of Academic Department.

UKRAINIAN NATIONAL ASSOCIATION (UNA)
2200 Route 10, PO Box 280, Parsippany, NJ 07054, USA. Tel/fax: (973) 292-9800. Co-sponsor in Ukraine is PROSVITA.
Preference of nationality: American, Canadian, European native speakers of English.
Qualifications: qualified teachers.
Conditions of employment: voluntary positions. 4 weeks of conversational instruction between May and August. 5 days a week, 4 hours a day. Teachers may be sent to any of the *oblasts* (provinces) to teach beginning, intermediate and advanced conversational English. Students are older adolescents and adults from variety of backgrounds.
Salary: no stipend. Room and board provided in a homestay.
Facilities/Support: books and teaching materials provided. One-day workshop and reunion organised.
Recruitment: $25 non-refundable application fee.
Contact: Oksana Trytjak, Project Coordinator.

UNION FORUM
10 Ternopilska St, PO Box 10722, 290034 Lviv. Tel/fax: (322) 759488.
Number of teachers: 1-2 for international summer camp.
Preference of nationality: British and others.
Qualifications: experience of teamwork with young people aged 18 and above.
Conditions of employment: 2 weeks in July/August. 5 hours per day.
Salary: none (basic board and lodging at recreational site provided).
Facilities/Support: assistance with travel information.
Contact: Valeriy Nefedov, Coordinator.

Russian Republics

Even some of the most exotic sounding ex-USSR republics like Kazakhstan and Uzbekistan are developing an ELT industry. The spur in some cases has been the influx of businesses connected with the Caspian oil industry, which has particularly affected Kazakhstan and Azerbaijan and to some extent Turkmenistan. In response to the increased demand, the Peace Corps is planning to send a substantial number of volunteer English teachers to Kazakhstan within the next year. Already there are some opportunities with international companies for professional ELT teachers where the salaries are on a par with those of the oil-rich states of the Middle East as Richard McGeough, a 28 year old teacher from Britain, explains:

> *My primary motivation for coming to Baku was the salary my post offered, which was £15,000 a year. The students are highly motivated, well-educated and almost embarrassingly hospitable and generous. I'm working in newly modernised premises now, but until recently we had to contend with alternately unheated and unventilated classrooms and regular power cuts in winter. Baku can be too quiet sometimes, although an acquaintance of mine who lived in Ashkhabad, Turkmenistan for two years says that Baku is like Paris compared to there. What Baku lacks in beauty it makes up for in interest. The centre of Baku—the Oil Town and the Old Town— is rustic and charming, and not at all what I'd expected of the old USSR. Having lived in Istanbul before, historical Baku was like a return to the 1950s before ugly modern apartment buildings were put up.*

However, most English teaching is still delivered by the state; for example the list of English Language Institutions sent by the British Council in the Uzbek capital Tashkent comprises only state universities and paedagogical institutes (i.e. teacher training colleges). *i to i International Projects* (see introductory chapter on Finding a Job) sends paying volunteers to teach in Uzbekistan for a fee of £895 excluding travel.

The beginnings of a private EFL industry are evident in Georgia. The Information & Education Officer at the British Council in Tbilisi sent the following addresses in Georgia:

International Language Academy, 17 Chavchavadze Avenue, Tbilisi 380079
International House Tbilisi, 2 Dolidze St, Tbilisi 380015. (This IH school employs only one or two native speakers).
Public Service Language Centre, 8 Rustaveli Avenue, Tbilisi
Nike, English and Computer Teaching Firm, 8 Jambuli St, Tbilisi 380008
Byron School of Tbilisi, 2 Griboedov St, Tbilisi

The British Council in Kazakhstan can send a long list of institutes which are likely to offer English language courses and therefore might be interested in employing part-time or full-time teachers of English. Most are state-owned but there is a growing number of private ones. University faculties often have their own international relations office; for example Pavlodar University is looking for highly educated native speakers to spend an academic year in Pavlodar (Gorky Str. 102/4, 637003 Pavlodar; 3182-326714/fax 326797; or 64 Lomov Str. 64, 637003 Pavlodar; tel/fax 3182-451110/e-mail rector@psu.pvi.kz).

WEBB ACADEMY
148 Vidadi St, 370000 Baku, Azerbaijan. Tel/fax (12) 973047. Tel: (12) 941345.
Number of teachers: 3-5.
Preference of nationality: British.
Qualifications: minimum CELTA with or without experience.
Conditions of employment: 1 year renewable contracts (Sept-July). To teach mixture of students from high school pupils to professionals and housewives.
Salary: on application.

Facilities/Support: accommodation, flight, medical insurance, holiday pay and visa are all provided.
Recruitment: direct application or via UK contact: Mrs. Webb, 4 Chesterfield Close, Canford Cliffs, Poole, Dorset BH13 7DL; tel/fax 01202 709516.
Contact: Berenice Webb.

KAZAKH STATE UNIVERSITY OF WORLD LANGUAGES
200 Muratbaev Str, Almaty 480072, Kazakhstan. Tel: (3272) 672363/674473.
Number of teachers: 4-5.
Preference of nationality: British or American.
Qualifications: MA or PhD.
Conditions of employment: one academic year. 14 h.p.w.
Salary: $100 per month less 5% for taxes.
Facilities/Support: room in dormitory provided. Assistance with work permits given.
Recruitment: via USIS and the British Council. Interviews essential.
Contact: Kunanbayeva Salima, Rector of the University.

Slovak Republic

As the poor cousin in the former Czechoslovakia, the republic of the Slovaks has been somewhat neglected not only by tourists but by teachers as well. As one language school director put it:

> *Many teachers are heading for Prague, which is why Slovakia stands aside of the main flow of the teachers. That's a pity as Prague is crowded with British and Americans while there's a lack of the teachers here in Slovakia.*

The density of private language schools in the capital Bratislava and in the other main cities like Banska Bystrika makes an on-the-ground job hunt promising.

Unfortunately, the government agency which placed teachers in the state education system and in some private language schools is no longer doing so. The Slovak Academic Information Agency (SAIA) began ELT teacher placements when the Slovak Republic became independent in 1993, and cancelled its involvement in July 1998.

Language Link (21 Harrington Road, London SW7 3EU; 0171-225 1065) is affiliated with the *Akadémia Vzdelávania,* the largest semi-private language school in Slovakia (see entry), and actively recruits ELT teachers from the UK. Another contact based in Yorkshire, who recruits for the same organisation, advertises Slovak vacancies in the educational press throughout the summer (details in entry).

American ELT teachers can look to the *City University* based in Washington state for placements in Slovak schools. The three campuses of the City University (in Bratislava, Trencin and Poprad) cater mainly to Slovak students of business who receive intensive English language training alongside their business administration studies.

The Slovakian Embassy can send details of how to apply for a residence permit, valid for one year but renewable. It warns that the entire process takes between three and four months. The procedures are similar to those for the Czech Republic, including a requirement that all documents be officially translated, and that the applicant submit a medical certificate, evidence of accommodation, police clearance and so on. Many employers guide their teachers through the process and pay the fee (currently £91.50).

As well as the British Council in Bratislava, there are English Teaching Resource Centres in Banska Bystrica and Kosice. The main English language newspaper is the *Slovak Spectator* published every other Thursday. Occasionally the classified column carries an advert of interest to people looking for teaching work; one such is Pro Sympatia (Pribinova 23, 810 11 Bratislava; 7-381 0170/381 0313) which was looking for native speakers to provide individual language courses throughout Slovakia. You might also consider advertising your availability to give private tuition. The cost is 200 koruna for up to 20 words plus 23% VAT; contact Krizkova 9, 811 04 Bratislava (7-396336).

The wages quoted by some schools may seem negligible. But if a monthly salary of £185/$300 sounds low, remember that a beer costs 12 koruna/20p and a restaurant meal is 100 koruna (less than £2) plus many schools provide free accommodation. The wages are enough to fund an average lifestyle and do the odd spot of travelling. Budapest, Vienna and Prague are all within easy reach. Slovakia also offers good conditions for mountain walking along thousands of miles of hiking routes (up to an altitute of 2,500 metres) and for mountain cycling.

LIST OF SCHOOLS

AKADEMIA VZDELAVANIA
Gorkého 10, 815 17 Bratislava. Tel: (7) 531 0042. Fax: (7) 3531 0040. E-mail: hviscova@aveducation.sk
Number of teachers: more than 100 posts in dozens of adult education centres and schools throughout Slovakia.
Preference of nationality: mainly British.
Qualifications: CELTA or other TEFL qualification. Energy, enthusiasm and an interest in people required.
Conditions of employment: 1 academic year. Contract is for 40 h.p.w. of which 25 hours should be spent in school. Adult teaching only.
Salary: 7,000 koruna per month in first year; 8,500 koruna in second year. (Note these wages are paid in Bratislava; deduct 500 koruna for other towns.)
Facilities/Support: paid accommodation provided in shared houses or flats. Short pre-service training course is compulsory. Price of return coach fare from London paid at end of contract.
Recruitment: via Language Link in London (address above) or Mrs. P. J. Taylor, 1 Somerset Road, Harrogate, North Yorkshire HG2 0LY (01423 523829). Interviews take place throughout the year.

CITY UNIVERSITY SLOVAKIA
Language Assistance Programs, 919 SW Grady Way, Renton, WA 98055, USA. E-mail: jflaherty@cityu.edu. Bratislava site: Odbojarov 10, 832 32 Bratislava (tel/fax: 7-566 7646. Trencin site: Bezrucova 64, 911 01 Trencin (tel/fax: 831-529337).
Number of teachers: from 30.
Preference of nationality: North American but all native speakers considered.
Qualifications: MATESL or equivalent preferred plus 6 months teaching experience and ability to teach all levels and skill areas. Minimum qualification is BA plus TEFL certification and international living experience.
Conditions of employment: 9 month contracts from 15th September to 15th June. Full-time timetable equivalent to 20 h.p.w. in the classroom plus 4 hours scheduled office hours.
Salary: from US$325 per month plus free housing and return airfares.
Facilities/Support: housing provided (on or off campus) and also medical/dental insurance. Orientation session for all instructors held at beginning of school year. Large English-language library.
Recruitment: all hiring takes place, mainly in the early summer, through Human Resources Department, City University, 335 116th Ave SE, Bellevue, WA 98004 (425-637-1010 ext 4011 or 3973/fax 425-637-9689/e-mail: sanderson@cityu.edu).

THE ENGLISH CLUB
Pri Suchom mlyne 36, 811 04 Bratislava. Tel: (7) 5477 2106. Fax: (7) 5477 2411.
Number of teachers: 5-8.
Preference of nationality: none.
Qualifications: university degree.
Conditions of employment: 10 month contracts (September to June).
Salary: 13,000 crowns (net).
Facilities/Support: assistance with accommodation and work permits.
Recruitment: based on CVs and applications.
Contact: Martin Oravec, Director/Owner.

ENGLISH LEARNING CENTRE
Slovenského 18, 040 01 Kosice. Tel/fax: (95) 644 1701. E-mail: elc@dodo.sk
Number of teachers: 2-3.
Preference of nationality: British.
Qualifications: TEFL experience or as lector.
Conditions of employment: 1 year contracts, renewable. 6 hours a day.
Salary: 13,000-15,000 koruna per month.
Facilities/Support: assistance with accommodation and work permits, insurance and taxes.
Recruitment: via advertisements. Interviews in UK or locally.
Contact: Dr. Silvia Kalaposová, Director.

EUROTREND 21
Starohorská 2, 813 32 Bratislava. Tel/fax: (7) 394350. E-mail: eurotrend21@isnet.sk
Number of teachers: 3.
Preference of nationality: none, as long as they speak grammatically correct English. No assistance given with work permits.
Conditions of employment: 12 month contracts. Daytime teaching hours.
Salary: US$4-7 per hour (gross), depending on experience and results.
Facilities/Support: advice can be given on finding accommodation. No training.
Recruitment: personal interviews only.
Contact: Magda Nagyová, Managing Director.

KRAMAR'S SCHOOL OF ENGLISH
Sladkovicova 105, 953 01 Zlate Moravce. Tel/fax: (814) 21856. E-mail: kramar@ netlab.sk
Number of teachers: 2 (couple preferred).
Preference of nationality: British or North American.
Qualifications: university degree (literature, English or history preferred), TEFL Certificate, few years' experience preferred.
Conditions of employment: minimum 1 academic year. 26-28 lessons a week (lasting 45 minutes). Hours are mainly 3pm to 8.15pm Monday to Thursday, but may be weekend work. Pupils are grouped 7-13 and 13 plus.
Salary: 11,000 koruna (net) plus return flight from London.
Facilities/Support: free accommodation in a rented house, 10 minutes walk from the school. Assistance with work permits but no training. Free return coach tickets London-Nitra twice a year.
Recruitment: adverts, internet, personal contact with other language schools and agencies. Telephone interviews possible. Zlate Moravce is 70 miles east of Bratislava. Interviews are sometimes held in UK.
Contact: Mr. Boris Kramar, Headmaster.

PTK-ECHO
Presovska 39, 821 02 Bratislava. Tel: (7) 55 41 57 97. Fax: (7) 55 56 22 37. E-mail: ptksr@internet.sk
Number of teachers: 4-6.

Preference of nationality: none.
Qualifications: ESL teachers, teachers of Business English with knowledge of Slovak economy.
Conditions of employment: 10-12 month contracts. 20 h.p.w.
Salary: US$10 per lesson.
Facilities/Support: assistance with accommodation and work permits. Training available.
Recruitment: direct. Local interviews only.
Contact: Ada Chadimova, Manager/Co-owner.

PROFESSIONAL COMMUNICATION AND ENGLISH PROGRAMS
**Palfy Kastiel, Svaty Jur. 90021 Bratislava. Tel: (7) 597 0451. Fax: (7) 597 0455.
E-mail: ainovacommunications@ainova.sk**
Number of teachers: 2-3.
Preference of nationality: none.
Qualifications: minimum TEFL certificate. Experience of teaching business English preferred.
Conditions of employment: 1 year contracts, 80 teaching hours per month.
Salary: £400-£420 per month less 25% for deductions.
Facilities/Support: help given in finding accommodation. Training occasionally available.
Recruitment: via adverts in *Guardian* and locally. Interviews held in UK if possible.
Contact: Ruth Kershaw, Director.

Other Schools to Try

Note that these schools (in alphabetical order according to town) did not confirm their teacher requirements for this edition of *Teaching English Abroad*.
Albion English School, Skuteckého 8, 974 00 Banska Bystrica (tel/fax 88-743434)
English Teaching Centre, Skuteckeho 11, 974 00 Banska Bystrica
RK Centrum Universa sro, Skuteckeho 30, 974 00 Banska Bystrica

American Language Institute, Drienova 34, PO Box 78, 820 09 Bratislava
Berlitz, Na Vrsku 2, 811 01 Bratislava
Esperlingua, Jazykova Skola, Obchodna 42, 811 06 Bratislava
Eurolingua Jazykova Skola, Drienova 16, 821 03 Bratislava
Europe House Jazykova Skola, Mikoviniho 1, 831 02 Bratislava
Eurotrend, Starohorska 2, 801 01 Bratislava
Jazykova Skola MTD, Metodova 2, 821 08 Bratislava
Lengua Agency Jazykova Skola, Galbaveho 3, 841 01 Bratislava
Logos Centre, Karpatska 2, 811 05 Bratislava
Perspektiva, Ursulinska 11, 812 93 Bratislava
Pro Sympatia, Centrum Studia Cudzich Jaykov, Pribnova 23, 810 93 Bratislava
Top School of Languages Pistek, Galandova 2, 811 06 Bratislava

Bakschool, Independent Language School, Postova 1, 040 01 Kosice
Effective Language Centre, Biela 3, 040 01 Kosice
English Learning Centre, Zuzkin Park 2, 040 01 Kosice
Fan Action Language Studio, Juzna trieda 13, 040 01 Kosice
Flosculus, Drevny trh. 5, 040 01 Kosice (tel/fax 95-622 5149/e-mail flos@ke.pubnet.sk).
     Language teachers for summer camps and longer periods
Ivega Learning Center, Moldarvska 8, 040 01 Kosice
Lingua Centrum, Szakkayho 1, 040 01 Kosice
Nevequelle, Maurerova 18, 040 22 Kosice
New Life Center, Zuzkin park 4, 040 01 Kosice
Quentin, Magurska 13, 040 01 Kosice
Sophist, Juzna trieda 50, 040 01 Kosice
The Word Company, Alzbetina 47, 040 01 Kosice

S-Klub, Vojenska 28, 934 01 Levice

Vzdelavacia nadacia ASPEKT, Akademicka 4, 949 01 Nitra 1
Jazykova Skola Euro, Nabrezna 30, 940 75 Nove Zamsky
Lingua Jazykova Skola, Zahradnick 2, 931 01 Samorin
Mestske Kulturne Stredisko, Nam slobody 11, 909 01 Skalica
London House, Krusovska 2093, 955 01 Topolcany
BEA English Studio, Anglicka Jazykova Skola, Hlavna 17, 970 01 Trnava

MIDDLE EAST

Oil wealth has meant that many of the countries of the Middle East have long been able to afford to attract the best teachers with superior qualifications and extensive experience. Most employers can afford to hire only professionals and there are few opportunities for newcomers to the profession.

The main exception is Turkey where thousands of native speaker teachers find work. Despite its adherence to Islam, Turkey does not fit comfortably into a chapter on the Middle East. Despite its aspirations to join the European Union, neither does it fit logically into a section on Western Europe. But whatever its geographical classification, Turkey is a very important country for EFL teachers, whatever their background, and is treated at length later in this chapter.

On the one hand the wealthy countries of Saudi Arabia, Bahrain, Oman and the Gulf states generally employ teachers with top qualifications. On the other hand, countries like Syria and Jordan may have more casual opportunities. There is growing interest in learning English among the Palestinians scattered throughout the Arab World, and native speaker teachers in this context are likely to be working on a voluntary basis rather than for expatriate salaries.

As Lebanon surges forward in a frenzy of reconstruction after its tragic 17-year civil war, the demand for English is increasing (see section below). Some countries are still off-bounds, namely Iraq, but the recent thawing of relations between Tehran and London may mean that opportunities might arise in Iran in the coming years. As Joe Hancock from North Wales reported from the town of Bojnurd in northeastern Iran, there is no shortage of demand for English in this country which is full of 'friendly, helpful and respectful people':

> I called in at the local English school to ask if I could assist with conversational English and was immediately asked if I could take a 40-hour English course starting tomorrow. After that they wondered if I could go to Tehran to teach, as they require five expat teachers there. Qualifications were mentioned but not dwelt on. I couldn't accept since my work permit is with the petrochemical company I work for. As a courtesy I asked my employer if I could teach in my spare time (four hours a week) but they forbade it saying that once the school advertised that they had an English native teacher, they would have queues around the block.

Teachers who sign contracts in a strict Islamic country should be aware of what they are letting themselves in for. People spend a year or two of their lives in Saudi Arabia for the money not for the fun (certainly) nor for the experience (unless they are students of Arab culture). When the amount of money accumulating back home is the principal or only motivation, morale can degenerate. The situation can be especially discouraging for women.

Yet not everyone is gasping to get home (or even to Bahrain) to freely available alcohol, etc. A surprisingly high percentage of teachers is recruited locally from a stable expatriate community.

FIXING UP A JOB

Unless you are more or less resident in the Middle East, it is essential in most cases to fix up a job in advance. Casual teaching is not a possibility in most countries for a number of reasons, including the difficulty of getting tourist visas, the prohibitively high cost of staying without working and the whole tradition of hiring teachers. There are a few countries which can be entered on a tourist visa (i.e. Qatar, Yemen and the

United Arab Emirates) if you want to inspect potential employers, but this would be an expensive exercise. Visa difficulties vary from country to country. In Jordan, for example, schools which would like to hire foreign teachers claim to be unable to do so due to work permit restrictions.

Single women, no matter how highly qualified, are at a serious disadvantage when pursuing high-paying jobs in Saudi Arabia and other strict Islamic countries. The majority of adverts specify 'single status male' or, at best, 'teaching couples'. Another requirement often mentioned in job details which excludes many candidates is experience of the Middle East, in acknowledgment of the culture shock which many foreigners encounter in adapting to life under Islam.

Job adverts regularly appear in the *TES, Guardian, TESOL Placement Bulletin* and *International Employment Gazette*. The largest display ads in the British education press are quite often for Middle East vacancies, many placed by recruitment agencies on behalf of high-spending Saudi clients.

The British Council has Teaching Centres in Bahrain (Manama), Israel (Tel Aviv, West Jerusalem and Nazareth), Oman (Muscat and Salalah), Saudi Arabia (Riyadh, Jubail, Jeddah and Dammam), Damascus in Syria and the West Bank & Gaza (East Jerusalem). ELS Language Centers/Middle East has eight Centres in the region: Al Ain, Dubai and Abu Dhabi (UAE), two centres in Jeddah (one for men, one for women) plus one in Riyadh in Saudi Arabia, Doha (Qatar) and Kuwait City, with plans to expand into Syria, Jordan, Oman and Turkey in the near future. These centres employ 20 full-time teachers and many part-time teachers to teach American English (see entry).

There are also American Language Centers in Amman, Damascus and Sana'a. Surprisingly, there isn't a single International House school in the entire region. It is worth writing to the Embassies (particularly of Saudi Arabia and Oman) who occasionally recruit directly on behalf of their Ministries of Education or Defense. The Saudi Embassy in London (30 Charles St, London W1X 7PM) occasionally advertises for teachers with high academic qualifications, as does the Saudi Arabian Defence Office (22 Holland Park, London W11 3TD).

If trying to fix up employment directly with a company in the Middle East, try to be sure that you have a water-tight contract. Even with many years of experience of the region, Peter Feltham experienced difficulties:

> I am an Arabist and have worked in Bahrain, Oman, Saudi Arabia and Egypt on a 'creative job-search' basis, sometimes with extreme success but mostly with disastrous consequences. For example, in Bahrain, I found that about two-thirds or three-quarters of all job offers had not been thought through, and were bogus. I spent between £1,000 and £2,000 in air fares following up bogus job offers and came to the conclusion that this was partly due to the lack of moral implications of failing to tell the truth within Islam.

Predictably, there is not a great deal of input by the voluntary agencies. However the Peace Corps sends a number of English teachers to civil service oriented language schools as well as secondary schools and universities, particularly in Yemen.

Recruitment Agencies

In theory, being hired by an established recruitment agency in your own country should offer some protection against the problems described in the quotation above. However this is not always the case. A couple of years ago an educational consultancy with an office in Toronto recruited a large number of EFL teachers to work for the United Arab Emirates military. When a dispute arose between client and recruiter, the teachers were the ones to suffer since they weren't paid promised salaries and their contracts were not honoured.

ILC Recruitment in Hastings (White Rock, Hastings, East Sussex TN34 1JY) recruit for the ILC school in Kuwait and were recently advertising a salary of 9,000 Kuwaiti dinars (about £1,765) a month, but only for candidates with a DELTA or equivalent plus extensive experience including ESP. In addition to agencies like *English Worldwide* listed in the Introduction, here is a short list of agencies, organisations and corporations which have recently been seen advertising (mostly high level) EFL vacancies in the Middle East:

Brunel Energy UK Ltd., 28-32 Cadogan St, Glasgow G2 7LP. ELT professionals for oil industry company in the Middle East and North Africa.

C.C.L. Recruitment International, 298 High St, Dovercourt, Harwich, Essex CO12 3PJ. Tel: 01255 506001. Fax: 01255 506002.

QTS, 36 High Ash Drive, Leeds LS17 8RA. Tel: 0113 269 6636. Fax: 0113 269 6636. Fully qualified, British trained infant, junior and secondary teachers for Middle East schools.

Robaco Global, 8 Nesburn Road, Barnes, Wearside SR4 7LR. Fax: 0191-551 9102. E-mail: Robaco@dial.pipex.com. Recruit for posts abroad, including the Middle East.

LEISURE TIME

The majority of teachers live in foreigners' compounds provided by their employers. Most of these are well provided with sports facilities like tennis courts and swimming pools. In some locations, such as Jubail in Saudi Arabia, water sports are a popular diversion. Some have described expat life in the Middle East as a false paradise.

The principal pastimes are barbecues, reading out-of-date copies of the *International Herald Tribune,* playing with computers (which are cheaply available) and complaining about the terrific heat and the lack of alcohol. (Saudi Arabia and Kuwait are completely dry states.) Others of course try to learn some Arabic and make local friends, always taking care not to offend against Islam. The constraints of living under Islam are well known. For example in some countries anyone found drinking or smoking in a public place during the month of Ramadan could face a jail sentence, large fine and/or deportation.

Contracts often include two or even three free leave tickets per year, which need not be to your home. (Apparently Bangkok is a popular destination for expats seeking R & R.) This is therefore a good chance to see the world at your employer's expense.

BAHRAIN

Bahrain is among the most liberal of the oil states, and one which attracts foreigners, including women because of its tolerance of women in the workplace. The *British Council* may be of assistance in referring a TEFL-qualified teacher to private clients, whether companies, individuals or secretarial colleges. Unlike in Saudi Arabia, it is possible to teach mixed classes of men and women.

In 1997/8 the volunteer teacher placement agency *i to i* was offering one year contracts in Bahrain but that destination has since been dropped.

ISRAEL/OCCUPIED TERRITORIES

Because of the large number of English-speaking Jews who have settled in Israel from the US, South Africa, etc. there are many native speakers of English working in the state education system and no active recruitment of foreign teachers. There are a number of private language schools, though again few native speakers from outside Israel seem to find jobs with them. Even an Israeli, Shahin Sarsour, who had earned a TEFL Certificate from Transworld Teachers in San Francisco, could not find a job as an English teacher. One might have expected some volunteers on kibbutzim to be involved in teaching English to Hebrew-speaking kibbutzniks, but in fact this does not seem to happen.

The British Council maintains a large presence in Israel and has Teaching Centres in Tel Aviv, Jerusalem and Nazareth, which recruit qualified EFL teachers mainly from the local English-speaking population.

Although the Intifada ended with the granting of self-rule to Palestinians on the West Bank, hostility and occasional outbursts of violence persist between Israeli soldiers and Palestinians. If the peace process can be maintained, opportunities in the Occupied Territories would in all likelihood increase. As well as its own teaching centre in East Jerusalem in the Al-Nuzha Building, 2 Abu Obeida Street (PO Box

19136), the British Council has offices in Gaza City (14-706 Al-Nasra Street, Al-Rimal; PO Box 355), in Hebron (Ein Sarah Street; PO Box 277) and in Nablus (Harwash Building, Radidia Main Street; PO Box 497).

The charity UNIPAL (Universities' Trust for Educational Exchange with Palestinians, BCM UNIPAL, London WC1N 3XX; 0191-386 7124) operates an educational and cultural exchange with Palestinian communities in the West Bank, Gaza and Lebanon. Volunteers teach English to Palestinian children aged 12-14 from mid-July to mid-August. Volunteers much be at least 20 and contribute about £350 for airfare and insurance, while UNIPAL covers the other costs. TEFL training is not a pre-requisite but would be useful. Applications close at the end of February. Other longer-term opportunities might also be available to teachers with the CELTA or equivalent.

KUWAIT

Prior to Iraq's invasion of Kuwait there were up to 1,000 English teachers in Kuwait (though most of them were out of the country at the time of the invasion, since it was the summer vacation). Efforts have been made to revive all the operations (many of them managed by expats rather than Kuwaitis), but the overall numbers have diminished, partly because the big money days are over.

Educational standards are variable, as encountered by B. P. Rawlins in Kuwait:

> *There are simply too many schools in Kuwait acting like pigs at a trough, all of them out there for the money. They dare not criticise any anti-social behaviour by pupils, parents or adult students for fear of losing fees in a competitive market. Professionalism is viewed with hostile suspicion in some quarters.*

This negative view is not subscribed to by all who have spent time in the region. Many agree that English learners in Kuwait, as throughout the Arab world, can be a pleasure to teach because they are so eager to communicate, and so unhesitant to speak English in class.

The British Council in Kuwait keeps an up-to-date list of the many international and English medium schools in the country.

LEBANON

As mentioned earlier, Lebanon is struggling valiantly to recover from its long and painful war, and is looking to a prosperous future in which English will overtake French in popularity, much to the chagrin of the French who are pouring in vast resources to prop up their language and the archaic Lebanese baccalaureate, still compulsory in schools. English is gaining ground due to its status as the international language of business and to a strong tradition of Lebanese emigration to the United States and Australia. The British Council in Beirut is increasingly active, and Council in London (part of the Council on International Education Exchange) has sent a few teachers experienced in business and TEFL to the Academy of English in Jounieh on 12-month contracts; ring 0171-478 2009 for more details.

Increasingly it will be worthwhile investigating possibilities in this tiny but fascinating country. While accompanying her husband on a short-term contract in Lebanon, Anne Cleaver (an early-retired teacher) easily found work (albeit voluntary) at a new Special Needs Centre just outside Beirut:

> *Even during my short period there, I was tentatively offered a full-time post at a neighbouring school and even an opening in Abu Dhabi. There is a real eagerness to learn English in Lebanon. I found Lebanese educationalists, parents and children most welcoming and enthusiastic. Being a British teacher there made me feel more valued, I regret to say, than back in the UK.*

OMAN

The British Council in Muscat does not maintain a list of English language institutes in Oman but can send a copy of the relevant *Yellow Pages*. The main English teaching centres in addition to *Polyglot* in the Directory are:

Capital Institute, PO Box 936, Ruwi 112 (709336/fax 701070)

College of Administrative Sciences, PO Box 710, Ruwi 112 (751572/fax 751570). Intensive English courses for students at this private college of higher education.

Al-Ghosnain Training Institute, PO Box 1016, Ruwi 114, Oman (601102/fax 605521/ web-site http://www.weboman.com/ghosnain)

Another possibility is to write to the government of Oman before departure. Sometimes the Military Attaché's Office at the Oman Embassy (64 Ennismore Gardens, London SW7 1NH) can prove helpful. Try also Educational Services Overseas Ltd. (PO Box 2398, Ruwi, Postal Code 112, Sultanate of Oman; fax: 565573) who, in the summer of 1998, were advertising for male English language trainers with a PGCE in TEFL or a Cambridge DELTA to teach in the interior of Oman on behalf of the Ministry of Education (PO Box 3, Ruwi).

CfBT Education Services recruits EFL instructors for the Government of Oman Colleges of Education (teacher training colleges), interior locations and for Petroleum Development Oman (PDO) based in the capital. With more than 60 employees in-country, CfBT also maintains a project office in Muscat (PO Box 2278, PC 112 Medinat Qaboos; 504938/fax 692537).

After returning from many years of teaching English in Italy to settle down in a renovated barn in South Wales, Sandeha Lynch soon recovered his wanderlust and couldn't resist a six-month contract in Salalah, Oman, which he describes as the best place to be in all Arabia, both summer and winter:

> I'll be going back at the end of August, early, because I want to get sight (and photos) of the Dhofar region while the monsoon is still greening everything. In Thesiger's day, according to his book Arabian Sands, they all hiked about on camels, but now the camels are herded in Toyota Landcruisers.

On a more pedestrian note, he comments that despite a fast-expanding EFL market, there's no room at all for visiting jobseekers, since a tight hold is kept on tourist visas. Many of the private language schools are run by Indian ex-pats.

SAUDI ARABIA

The decline in oil prices during the past 18 years means that fabulously high salaries are no longer earned by EFL teachers in the Kingdom of Saudi Arabia. But expatriate packages are still very attractive, with substantial salaries, free air fares and accommodation plus generous holidays and other perks.

Teaching in a naval academy or petrochemical company while living in a teetotal expatriate ghetto is not many people's idea of fun, especially after a request for an exit visa has been denied. The rare woman who gets a job as a teacher (at a women's college) may live to regret it when she finds that she is prohibited by law from driving a car and must not appear in public without being covered from head to foot.

A sprinkling of companies advertise in the educational press, including the following:

Arabian Careers Ltd., 115 Shaftesbury Avenue, Cambridge Circus, London WC2H 8AD. Tel: 0171-379 7877. Fax: 0171-379 0885. E-mail: recruiter@arabiancareers.com. Web-site: http://www.arabiancareers.com. Male teachers only for Saudi military hospitals.

AVS Recruitment, 223 Southampton Road, Paulsgrove, Portsmouth PO6 4QA. Tel: 01705 354422. Fax: 01705 354001.

British Aerospace Operations Ltd., Systems and Services, Mill Lane, Warton Aerodrome, Warton, Preston, Lancs. PR4 1AX. Tel: 01772 854714. To Saudi Arabia.

Harrison Jones Associates, Buckingham House East, The Broadway, Stanmore, Middlesex HA7 4EB. Trained primary school teachers for Saudi Arabia.

US-based recruiters are most likely to advertise in the *TESOL Placement Bulletin* or other specialist press. The Hassan A. K. Algahtani Sons Co. of Saudi Arabia (PO

Box 195, Al-Khobar 31952) has a US representative based in California: Cheryl Ryan, 1187 Coast Village Road, No. 1-164, Santa Barbara, CA 93108 (fax 805-966-3974; e-mail: cryan@saudijobs.com; web-site: http://www.saudijobs.com).

Professional teachers tempted by the money should bear in mind the drawbacks, as Philip Dray did:

> *I decided against Saudi Arabia. The money was most appealing, but I couldn't think myself into a situation where there was no nightlife, limited contact with women and no culture or history. A year may seem short when you say it fast, but you could get very depressed in a situation like that. Money is nearly everthing but it can't buy you peace of mind. So I opted for a job at a school for boys in the U.A.E. which, from the description, sounds sociable, inviting and accessible.*

After Philip's arrival at the Oasis Residence in Dubai, he was well pleased with his decision, since living conditions in his luxury apartment complex complete with pool, steam room, squash court and gym, were just as lavish as he would have been given in Saudi. High salaries can also be earned in the United Arab Emirates.

Caution must be exercised when considering job offers from the Kingdom of Saudi Arabia. We have heard from several American teachers who have been badly burned by a Saudi employer. Carl Hart, writing from Dammam, cautions against 'unscrupulous bait and switch recruiters' who promise fabulous salaries and benefits knowing full well that when you arrive in the country, the salary and benefits will be significantly less than expected:

> *You'll grudgingly accept the job anyway, thus earning the recruiter his commission. Don't even think of leaving for the Kindgom unless you have an iron-clad contract signed by all parties involved, clearly stating the exact salary and benefits you are to receive and when you will receive them. But even a signed contract guarantees nothing. Virtually everything I was promised by the American who recruited me in the US and is incorporated into my contract with a government ministry was a lie. My salary is 6,500 riyals instead of the promised 9,600 riyals. My summer vacation is 45 days instead of 60, and a promised two-week salary settlement allowance and Chicago-Washington airfare reimbursement have not and will never be given. Be aware that work experience is based upon the number of full years of experience after you receive your highest degree (partial years count for nothing).*
>
> *One more caution: the wheels of Saudi bureaucracy turn verrrry slowly, so absolutely do not quit your present job until you have a contract signed by them. I naïvely believed the recruiter when he told me that my wife and I would be in Saudi Arabia 'within three weeks'. Four and a half months later we were still waiting, unemployed and sleeping on the floor of our empty apartment, an experience which sorely tested my sanity and plunged us deep into debt. Nevertheless I'm glad I came. Saudi may not offer the cultural thrill of some other nations, but accommodation and working conditions are excellent and it's a clean modern country, far safer than my old neighbourhood in Chicago. If you can live without beer and ham sandwiches for a while, it's a great place to save money and work on your magnum opus.*

Despite his reservations, Carl decided to stay on and after two years landed a much better job with a foreign-owned rather than a Saudi company which prompted him to write in a far more positive vein:

> *Saudi Arabia is modern and cosmopolitan and not at all the oppressive sun-baked hotbed of religious fanaticism that some imagine. The overwhelming majority of people here are amazingly normal and not at all rabidly anti-Western. There are jobs with good salaries here—some upwards of $47,000 a year. The important variables are location (will you be in a major city or a military base in the middle of the desert?), housing (will it be a spacious home in a Club Med-like compound or three guys in a trailer?) and vacation (from as little as three weeks a year to as much as three months a year).*

Morris Jensen working for *Elite Training Services* is another teacher who points to the good things about Saudi Arabia including the hospitality, ease of finding lucrative private work, excellent sports facilities, shopping and accessibility of places of interest in the Middle East. He also acknowledges the problems, such as the religious and cultural clashes which arise in the classroom and the frustrating bureaucracy. Among the documents required for a work permit are a medical certificate notarised by the Foreign and Commonwealth Office in London, an authorisation from the Saudi Ministry of Foreign Affairs, copies of diplomas, a contract of employment and accompanying letter from the sponsoring company. The fee of 50 riyals payable before leaving your home country is only the beginning. Your passport is held by your sponsoring employer while you carry around an official copy as identification, at least until you are issued with an *iqama* (resident visa). Every time you want to leave the country you must request an exit and re-entry visa which is given at the discretion of your employer. Some foreign workers have reported having to pay more than £130 for an exit visa.

SYRIA

The opportunities in neighbouring Syria are better established. The Education Adviser at the small British Council office in Damascus is willing to advise individual enquirers and has a list of half a dozen ELT institutions in Syria. The British Council cautions that:

> *Teachers wishing to teach here should make sure of their positions before arrival. They should obtain sponsorship from the prospective employer for residence purposes and have an agreed written contract.*

There's an enthusiastic demand for private tuition, though Syria is a poor country and only a small proportion of the population can afford it. The American Language Center (c/o USIS, PO Box 29, Rawda Circle, Damascus; 11-332 7236/fax 11-333 4801) employs about 40 native speakers for a minimum of three months in its programme of American English courses for adults. Anyone with a TEFL background has a good chance of getting some part-time hours with them. Occasionally they run their own training programme for EFL teachers. They may also know of individuals who want private tutoring in English.

To enter Syria, you should have an entrance visa from the Syrian Embassy in your country, and you must also obtain an exit visa every time you leave. (The journey from Damascus to Beirut takes four hours and costs about $5.) If you do teach for one of the schools, it is normally possible to obtain a resident visa after arrival, which entitles you to stay in hotels at local prices (one quarter of the tourist price in some cases).

YEMEN

Many people consider Yemen to be the most beautiful and interesting of all Middle Eastern states. Mary Hall is working there at present for an aid agency but is familiar with the teaching scene:

> *There are more and more places teaching English here, the two main ones being YALI (Yemen American Language Institute) and the British Council, both of whom recruit mostly qualified teachers from England or the US. The others hire any old bod who turns up, not many of whom are qualified TEFL teachers. Unfortunately they don't pay very well. If there is a Yemeni boss, the wages are even less and often not regularly forthcoming. I had a lodger who was teaching at one place for a pittance as the boss took money out of her wages to pay for her lodgings, even after she moved in with me. I think she was getting a couple of dollars an hour. This is something you sort of get used to. It can be very cheap living here, with rent about $50 a month or less if you're not fussy. You can get a three month visa if you pay and are HIV-negative.*

The Ministry of Education might be willing to place a university graduate with at least a year's teaching experience in a state school between October and June. Half the salary is paid in US dollars and half in Yemeni riyals. Contact the English Adviser in the Planning and Supplies Sector, Public Schools at the Secondary Level, Sana'a (fax 1-274568).

Travel restrictions have been imposed in response to the spate of foreigner-kidnappings; in 1998 11 people were abducted in four months, including a British Council English teacher and his family.

LIST OF SCHOOLS

ELS LANGUAGE CENTERS—MIDDLE EAST
PO Box 3079, Abu Dhabi, United Arab Emirates. Tel: (2) 651516. Fax: (2) 653165. E-mail: Elsme@emirates.net.ae

Number of teachers: 20 full-time plus many part-time in eight centres throughout the Middle East.

Preference of nationality: American and Canadian, though other nationalities are sometimes accepted.

Qualifications: MA in TEFL/TESL and 2 years' experience preferred. Minimum Cambridge/ELS Language Centers TEFL Certificate with 3 years' experience.

Conditions of employment: 1 or 2 year contracts and also summer internship (trainee) programme (2-3 months). 30 contact h.p.w. for full-time teachers, 20 h.p.w. for interns.

Salary: varies according to qualifications, experience and location, e.g. range in Al Ain (UAE) is US$21,0000-24,000 per year tax free plus benefits such as housing, airfares and medical insurance.

Facilities/Support: accommodation provided, though teachers may choose to find their own within their housing allowance. Work and residency permits arranged in all countries, usually involving a medical examination and blood test and a notarised copy of the teacher's degree and qualifications. Standard orientation for all new teachers and monthly workshops.

Recruitment: through TESOL USA and TESOL Arabia, and also via the internet. Telephone interviews sometimes sufficient. Face-to-face interviews arranged at annual TESOL clearinghouse and sometimes in UK or North America.

Contact: James Ward, Director of Education.

Bahrain

BRITISH COUNTIL—BAHRAIN
Sheikh Salman Highway, PO Box 452, Manama, Bahrain. Tel: 261555. Fax: 258689. E-mail: Mary Stansfeld@bc.bahrain.sprint.com

Number of teachers: 11.

Preference of nationality: British.

Qualifications: minimum DELTA or equivalent plus 2 years' overseas EFL experience.

Conditions of employment: 2 year contracts. 36 h.p.w. (24 contact hours). Saturday to Wednesday. Most teaching between 3pm and 9pm.

Salary: 600 dinars per month (net) plus 20 dinar travel allowance.

Facilities/Support: accommodation arranged for 350 dinars.

Recruitment: via British Council Recruitment Unit in London.

Contact: M. B. Stansfeld, Teaching Centre Manager.

Kuwait

INSTITUTE FOR PRIVATE EDUCATION
PO Box 6320, 32038 Hawalli, Kuwait. Tel: 573 7811/2. Fax: 574 2924.
Anglo Kuwait joint venture under British management.

Number of teachers: about 50.

Preference of nationality: British, Irish, American, Canadian, Australian.

Conditions of employment: open contracts. 40 h.p.w. of which up to 30 are contact hours. 6 weeks paid leave per year plus standard insurance and annual gratuity.

Salary: £14,000-18,000 per year.

Facilities/Support: furnished, air-conditioned accommodation and flights provided. Regular schedule of in-service training.

Recruitment: through press adverts or through TecQuipment (TQ), Bonsall St, Long Eaton, Nottingham NG10 2AN (0115-972 2611/fax 0115-973 1520). Recruitment booklet available. Staff never hired without interview which is held in UK, Kuwait or Egypt (via the American University in Cairo).

LANGUAGE CENTRE
Kuwait University, PO Box 2575, 13026 Safat, Kuwait. Tel: 481 0325. Fax: 484 3824.
Number of teachers: 10-15 each semester.
Preference of nationality: American, British.
Qualifications: MA in TEFL/TESL or Applied Linguistics plus minimum 3 years' experience.
Conditions of employment: one year renewable contracts. 15 contact h.p.w.
Salary: 532-623 dinars per month tax-free based on experience.
Facilities/Support: free furnished accommodation or housing allowance. Return air fares and 8 weeks' summer leave provided.
Recruitment: adverts in US and UK, where interviews are conducted.
Contact: Dr. Yahia Ahmad, Director.

Oman

POLYGLOT INSTITUTE
PO Box 221, Ruwi, Oman. Tel: 701261. Fax: 794602.
Number of teachers: 10 including part-time teachers.
Preference of nationality: none.
Qualifications: degree and CELTA or equivalent plus 5 years' experience.
Conditions of employment: 2 year contracts. 30 contact h.p.w.
Salary: 550-600 rials per month (net).
Facilities/Support: accommodation provided. Modern CALL room and good range of resources.
Recruitment: by word of mouth. Interviews essential.

Saudi Arabia

ELITE TRAINING SERVICES
PO Box 11015, Jubail Industrial City 31961, Saudi Arabia. Tel: (3) 341 5514. Fax: (3) 341 1336.
Number of teachers: 7.
Preference of nationality: none.
Qualifications: minimum CELTA or equivalent plus 5 years' experience (2 abroad).
Conditions of employment: contracts from 6 weeks to 1 year (usually the latter). 25 contact h.p.w. plus 12 hours admin.
Salary: about £1,300 per month (net).
Facilities/Support: free furnished accommodation provided. Assistance with work permits. No in-house training.
Recruitment: ads in the *Guardian* or *TES*; personal recommendation. Interviews sometimes carried out in UK.
Contact: Trevor Hopkins, Managing Director.

ENGLISH LANGUAGE CENTER
King Fahd University of Petroleum & Minerals, Dhahran 31261, Saudi Arabia. Tel: (3) 860 2395. Fax: (3) 860 2341. E-mail: elcrecru@kfupm.edu.sa
Number of teachers: 80.
Preference of nationality: American, British, Canadian, New Zealander, Australian.
Qualifications: MA in TEFL/TESL/Applied Linguistics or full-time postgraduate diploma in TEFL plus minimum 2 years' overseas experience.
Conditions of employment: 2 year contracts. 20-25 h.p.w. Pupils aged 17-20.
Facilities/Support: accommodation provided. Contract completion bonus.

Recruitment: through adverts in the *Guardian*. Send cover letter and résumé to Dean of Faculty & Personnel Affairs. Personal interviews required.
Contact: Dr. Fahd A. Al-Said, Dean of Educational Services.

ENGLISH LANGUAGE CENTER
Hail Community College, Hail, Saudi Arabia. Tel and fax: as above. Hail College is a branch of King Fahd University.
Number of teachers: 40.
Preference of nationality: American, British, Canadian, New Zealander, Australian.
Qualifications: minimum BA and 1 year overseas EFL teaching experience plus one of the following: ELT certification, BA in English language teaching/TEFL or closely allied field, or 4 additional years of teaching experience abroad.
Conditions of employment and facilities: as above.
Recruitment: through adverts in the *Guardian*. Send cover letter and résumé to Dean of the College. Personal interviews essential.

EUROPEAN CENTRE FOR LANGUAGES & TRAINING
PO Box 60617, Riyadh 11555, Saudi Arabia. Tel: (1) 476 1218. Fax: (1) 479 3328.
E-mail: anojaim@compuserve.com
Number of teachers: approx. 100 full-time.
Preference of nationality: none.
Qualifications: DELTA/Trinity Diploma/MA (Applied Linguistics).
Conditions of employment: 3, 6, 10 or 12 month contracts. $27\frac{1}{2}$ contact hours p.w. 40 hours per 5 day week.
Salary: £1,540 per month (net). Increments for qualifications and length of service.
Facilities/Support: free accommodation and work permits.
Recruitment: direct hire by adverts. Interviews essential. UK contact Al-Rajhi Co., 16 Connaught Street, London W2 2AF (tel 0468 512266).

RIYADH SCHOOLS FOR BOYS AND GIRLS
PO Box 1541, Riyadh 11441, Saudi Arabia. Tel: (1) 402 8411. Fax: (1) 405 1944.
Number of teachers: at least 9.
Preference of nationality: native speakers.
Qualifications: B.Ed., BA in English, MA in English or M.Ed. with TEFL experience or Diplomas.
Conditions of employment: 1 academic year. Maximum 24 h.p.w. Teaching hours 7am-2.30pm.
Salary: from £1,350 per month (tax-free).
Facilities/Support: housing allowance provided.
Recruitment: adverts in UK educational press followed up by interviews with their representative.
Contact: Abdulrahman Al-Mohaimeed, English Supervisor.

Yemen

MODERN AMERICAN LANGUAGE INSTITUTE (MALI)
PO Box 11727, Sana'a, Yemen. Tel/fax: (1) 241561.
E-mail: MALI1.edu@Y.NET.YE
Number of teachers: between 5 (winter) and 10 (summer).
Preference of nationality: American, British.
Qualifications: minimum college degree. Prefer experienced ESL/EFL instructors. Should be enthusiastic, motivated and willing to adapt to a different culture.
Conditions of employment: minimum 2 months; maximum 1 year renewable.
Salary: US$400-$600 per month depending on experience.
Facilities/Support: single room accommodation provided. Assistance given with residence visas. Subsidised Arabic language instruction available upon request.
Recruitment: phone interviews sometimes sufficient.

Other Schools to Try

Bahrain

Al Maalem Centre, PO Box 20649, Manama (553808/fax 554240)

Awal Training Institute, PO Box 82110, Riffa

Bahrain Training Institute (BTI), PO Box 32333, Isa Town, Bahrain (tel/fax 683416)

Bahrain Computer & Management Institute (BCMI), PO Box 26176, Manama (293493/ 290787; fax 290358)

The Cambridge School of English, PO Box 20646, Manama (532828/fax 530227)

Capital Institute, PO Box 22521, Manama (740744/fax 720060)

Child Development, PO Box 20284, Manama (728000/fax 722636)

Daar Al Merifa, PO Box 3174, Manama (722183/fax 722283)

Delmon Academy, PO Box 10362, Manama (294400/293777/fax 292010)

Global Institute, PO Box 11148, Manama (740940/fax 720030)

Gulf Academy, PO Box 10333, Manama (721700/fax 722636)

Gulf College of Hospitality and Tourism, PO Box 22088, Muharraq (320191/fax 332547)

Gulf School of Languages, PO Box 20236, Manama (290209/fax 290069)

Polyglot School, PO Box 596, Manama (271722/fax 273050)

Jordan

*YARMOUK CULTURAL CENTRE, PO Box 960312, Amman (6-671447). 30 teachers in summer, 12 in winter, mostly on freelance, part-time basis.

Kuwait

Amideast—532 7794

British Institute of Training and Education (BITE)—263 6952

ELS Military School of Languages, PO Box 5104, Salmiya 20062, Kuwait (fax 573 3005)

Kuwait American Cultural Center/Kuwaiti American Center of Education—266 2700

New Horizon—244 9797

Qatar

Arizona English Language Center, PO Box 7949, Doha

Language Institute, PO Box 3224, Doha

ELS Language Center, PO Box 22678, Doha

Syria

American Language Center, c/o US Embassy, PO Box 29, Damascus

Al Razi English Language Centre, PO Box 2533, Damascus

Al Kindi English Language Centre, 29 May Street, Damascus

Damascus Language Centre, PO Box 249, Damascus

Al-Kudssi Institute, PO Box 5296, Aleppo

UAE

Al Farabi Language Centre, PO Box 3794, Dubai

Dar Al Ilm School of Languages, PO Box 9399, Dubai

IEI, PO Box 52714, Dubai

Institute for Australian Studies, PO Box 20183, Dubai

International Language Institute, PO Box 3253, Sharjah

Polyglot Language School, PO Box 1093, Dubai

Higher Colleges of Technology, PO Box 47025, Abu Dhabi, UAE

*AL-WOROOD SCHOOL, PO Box 46673, Abu Dhabi (2-448855/fax 2-449732). 11 teachers with degree and teaching qualification (e.g. PGCE).

Yemen

*THE AMERICAN SCHOOL, PO Box 16003, Sana'a, Yemen (1-417119/fax 1-415355). 14 teachers (not necesssarily American).

Yemen-American Language Institute (YALI), c/o US Information Agency, American Embassy, Sana'a, Yemen (1-203251/fax 1-203364)

Sana'a International School, PO Box 2002, Sana'a, Yemen

Turkey

Of all the feedback this book receives about all the countries covered, Turkey is the country which has elicited the most. Recruitment agencies and major language school groups are keen to have their teacher vacancies publicised, and the major organisations in the field are included here. People who have taught English in Turkey are just as eager to share their experiences and it must be said that not all of them have been happy ones. By describing the problems which many have encountered on short teaching contracts in Turkey, it is to be hoped that readers can guard against them. Every single one of the teachers who has complained about employers breaking their promises, run-down accommodation, sexual harassment and so on, has concluded by saying that Turkish people are wonderful and the country fascinating.

Prospects for Teachers

Turkey's ambition to join the European Union, together with a remarkable expansion in tourism during the last two decades of the 20th century, means that Turkey's prosperous classes are more eager than ever to learn English. The boom in English is not confined to private language schools *(dershane)* which have continued to mushroom in the three main cities of Istanbul, Ankara and Izmir. In order to prepare students for an English language engineering, commerce, tourism or arts course, many secondary schools hire native speaker teachers. Hundreds of private secondary schools *(lises)* consider as one of their main priorities the teaching of the English language. Similarly at the tertiary level, some universities, both private and public, use English as the medium of instruction.

Turkey is a good choice of destination for fledgling teachers of any nationality. Not only are there a great many jobs, but these jobs are often part of a package which includes free accommodation and free air fares (London-Istanbul) on completion of a contract. Virtually all of these employers want to see a university degree and a TEFL Certificate of some kind, preferably the Cambridge/RSA CELTA or equivalent. Both a degree and a specialist qualification are required by the Turkish Ministry of Education before it will approve a work permit (see *Regulations* below).

The bias in favour of British English over American is not particularly strong. Many schools claim to have no preference and yet because they advertise in the UK press and are more familiar with British qualifications, there is a preponderance of British teachers. Also the new requirement that work visas be applied for in the country of origin will make matters more difficult for teachers from the US, Australia, etc.

FIXING UP A JOB

In Advance

The British Council in Istanbul, Izmir and Ankara have lists of private language schools and *lises*. The up-to-date list of ELT institutions supplied by the British Council in Izmir contains about 25 addresses plus about the same number of *lises* and universities. Obviously the list in Istanbul is even longer: 50 language schools, 64 *lises* and nine universities with EFL departments, all in the Istanbul area. The British Council also issues a free one-page 'Information for Foreign Teachers' for prospective and practising teachers.

Bilkent University School of English Language (BUSEL) in Ankara regularly recruits EFL/EAP instructors through *CfBT Education Services* or direct. This privately funded English medium university offers excellent facilities and career opportunities together with campus accommodation, fares, etc. Applicants will need to possess as a minimum an honours degree, CELTA and two years' relevant experience.

Many of the recruitment agencies included in the introductory chapter *Finding a Job* have contacts in Turkey, though most of the traffic seems to be from Britain rather than America. A new British agency with a Turkish director, Mrs. Nilgun Adan, acts as a recruiter for both language schools and *lises*. TRASPA UK Teacher Recruitment Agency (43B Lydford Road, Maida Vale, London W9 3LX; 0181-960 6602/fax 0181-960 0593) sends hundreds of native speaker English teachers each year to language schools as well as primary and secondary schools. Obviously such an agency welcomes people with a PGCE or B.Ed. though there are plenty of openings for people with the two essential qualifications: a university degree and a TEFL certificate.

An agency fulfilling a similar role is Noah's Ark, Paines Close, Maidwell, Northants. NN6 9BJ. Not long ago, another agency called Türkteach Educational Services operated in Bradford, but it has now become untraceable.

Other organisations can place young people on summer camps in Turkey where the emphasis is on teaching English. For example the *Koparan Summer Camp* operates every year at a purpose-built resort near Erdek on the Sea of Marmara, relying on about 40 native speakers. The Turkish workcamps organisation *Genctur* (see entry) takes on young people to work on their language camps; as well as helping with English teaching, assistants participate in social activities, drama, music, sports and crafts. All expenses are paid except air fares. Saday Educational Consultancy (Bayer caddesi nejat bay att. 68-21, Kozyatagi-Istanbul; 216-464-3905) places a large number of British students in Turkish families merely to speak English. They receive free room and board of course plus pocket money of £20 a week. *i to i International Projects* supply EFL teachers to a group of language schools in Izmir; most of the teachers it sends are recruited from its own training courses (see Introduction).

Among the main indigenous language teaching organisations in Turkey are *English Fast* (who employ about 100 native speakers), *Kent English* and *The English Centre* all with branches in Istanbul, Ankara and Izmir. *Dilko*, *Interlang* and *Antik English* are all well established. But even these language chains have come in for criticism over the years, with words like 'cowboy,' 'unprofessional' and 'untrustworthy' being bandied about by disappointed teachers.

Many ads for Turkish schools appear in the *Guardian* and *TES* in the spring and right through the summer. If you are considering accepting a job with an advertiser, ask for the name and telephone number of a previous teacher for an informal reference. An even better indication is if they have been able to keep their teachers for two or more years. If the school is reluctant to provide this kind of information, be suspicious. It may also be worth phoning the British Council office in the relevant city, since they keep a file of complaints about language schools.

On the Spot

Although not the capital, Istanbul is the commercial, financial and cultural centre of Turkey, so this is where most of the EFL teaching goes on. On the negative side, there may be more competition from other teachers here and also in Izmir than in Ankara or less obvious cities like Mersin and Diyarbakir. The best starting place in Istanbul is undoubtedly the British Council as Stephen McKeown discovered:

> The helpful British Council will give you a list of English schools in Istanbul. The addresses read like chemical formulae but you soon get used to them. We were offered jobs by every school we went to and were promised wages of between two and four times the national average.

You may also find yourself drawn back to the British Council after you have landed a job. The modest joining fee entitles you to use the Council's Teaching Centre with a reference collection of ELT books, video cassettes, seminars, etc.

Given the huge demand for native speaker teachers, Turkey is one country where scouting out possibilities on the ground can pay off, rather than signing a contract at a school you have never seen. After Bruce Lawson had a terrible experience with a private language teaching organisation in Istanbul ('their contract was a fiction that Tolstoy would have been proud of'), he concluded that he could have earned half as much again if he had been hired by a school which hired its teachers in Turkey.

Tim Leffel and Donna Marcus from New Jersey were amazed by the contrast between job-hunting in Greece (where Americans encounter visa problems even when they have a Cambridge/RSA Certificate as Tim and Donna had) and Turkey:

> There's a huge demand for teachers (any nationality really) in Istanbul. We lined up work on our second day of interviews. We interviewed at three schools and all of them offered us positions. We chose English Fast in Bakirköy because there were two jobs available in the same place and we were allowed to wear anything within reason (no ties, no new clothes to buy). They were satisfied that we could only commit ourselves for four months. We did see a lot of applicants turned away, even when there was a need for new teachers, because they lacked TEFL credentials.

Fewer and fewer schools are willing to employ people with no formal TEFL background.

Freelance

The standard Ministry of Education contract prohibits private teaching outside the bounds of the signed contract. In fact, unless you are blatantly pinching students from the institution which employs you, most employers turn a blind eye. University English departments might be a place to look for private pupils. The top rate of pay is about £10 an hour.

REGULATIONS

For the past ten years, teachers were permitted to enter Turkey as tourists (after paying the £10 fee for a visitor visa on arrival like everybody else) and then change their status after starting work. That has changed, and it is now necessary to apply before arrival as the Vice Consul at the Turkish Consulate General in London (0171-589 0360) clearly explains:

> Anyone who intends to work in Turkey has to obtain a work visa before departing for Turkey. Otherwise, he/she will not be permitted to take up employment in the country, unless he/she chooses to work illegally. Applications from teachers are usually processed quicker than the other professions. We believe that an application made four weeks before the intended departure would be sufficient. Applications to the Ministry of Education should be done by the prospective employer in Turkey on behalf of the teachers. Written approval of the Undersecretariat for the Treasury also has to be obtained by the Turkish employer.

The fee for a work visa is £60 at present. Teacher agencies undertake some of the bureaucratic steps for employers and employees, though for an extra fee. For example TRASPA UK charge the employer an extra £40.

Because there is still some confusion about the new regulations, it is not clear at what point a teacher has to submit their degree and ELT certificates. The Turkish employer needs to send permission from the Ministry of Education that he or she is authorised to employ foreign teachers and a document from the Undersecretariat for the Treasury. Once these have arrived, the teacher takes them along with the original contract of employment and completed forms in person to the Consulate to apply for a work visa, preferably six weeks before the proposed departure. (Note that the work and residence permit does not allow you to leave and re-enter the country without paying for a new tourist visa.)

This new system will make it impossible for employers to get away with failing to apply for the proper papers. By not officially registering their teachers, employers did not have to pay taxes or contributions. Also they could keep the teachers' original documents as a kind of ransom against the teacher leaving, as happened to a succession of teachers, most recently Mell Carey. As requested, he submitted his documents to his employer in Istanbul and then didn't see them for a year and never did receive the promised work visa.

There were always those who accepted work in language schools while on a tourist visa, and this number may now rise with the increased complications in getting a work visa. If working on a tourist visa, you must renew it every three months, either at the immigration office (where you will have to show that you have the means to support yourself; for example having a Turkish friend undertake to support you would help) or more usually by leaving the country and obtaining a new tourist visa, which costs £10 in sterling at the point of entry. Normally people cross the border to Greece, though a trip to Northern Cyprus is more pleasant. If you do this too many times the border officials may well become suspicious. If you have overstayed, you become liable for a hefty exit fine of US$250.

All salaries in Turkey are quoted net of deductions which amount to about 25% for contributions and tax. If the school makes social security contributions on your behalf, you will have medical cover from your first day of work. The scheme pays all your doctor's bills and 80% of prescriptions. Once again it is prudent to confirm that your employer keeps any promises he makes. More than one teacher has realised at a critical moment that, despite assurances, insurance premiums have not been paid by the school.

A complication for people who intend to teach English in a *lise* or secondary school is that the Ministry of Education insists that teachers of English have a university degree in English and preferably a PGCE or a B.Ed. with English as a main subject. Barry Wade's degree in philosophy with a minor in English was deemed inadequate to teach English at an Istanbul secondary school, despite what he had been told by an agent in England, and he was fobbed off with having to work for less money at a private language school instead.

CONDITIONS OF WORK

The normal deal is a one-year contract with air fare out and back from London, free or subsidised shared accommodation and a monthly salary in Turkish lire equivalent to £350-£400 in private language schools, £500-£650 in primary and secondary schools. Hourly employment is not as widely available as in many other countries.

It is probably a mistake to expect Western attitudes towards employees to prevail. In Turkey the manager is the boss and in many cases does not feel it incumbent on him to work efficiently or to look out for the welfare of his staff. Yet some people in the ELT business believe that the situation is gradually improving, among them the Director of Studies at Antik English in Istanbul:

> *I have worked for approximately four years in Turkey, in Istanbul and in a small remote town in the south. Prospective teachers always hear many horror stories about working in Turkey and to an extent they are well founded. In the past, schools and employers openly abused teachers' rights. But this is definitely changing. There are many good, up-and-coming organisations which can be trusted. Teachers should ask around, be careful about contracts and conditions, and not agree to the first job they are offered without checking out the school, its size, reputation, etc.*

This may well apply to the established chains, but there are still many dodgy operators and swashbuckling and unscrupulous employers. Although one individual's personal experience is not always a good basis for generalising, there has been a lot of duplication in the litany of complaints made about language schools in Turkey which focus on contracts being ignored, late payment of wages (especially irritating when high inflation means that a pay packet in lire is worth considerably less from one day to the next), assigning inflated marks to students to keep or attract custom, and so on. So it is important to remember that some teachers have a marvellous time, as Raza Griffiths had at the first school he worked for, which was in the town of Ordu on the Black Sea coast:

> *It would be no exaggeration to say that as a native English person in a region of Turkey unused to foreigners, I enjoyed celebrity status, with lots of inquiring eyes and lots of invitations to dinner. Although the town did not exactly have a thriving cultural life as we would understand it, this was more than compensated for by the sociableness of the people and their deep desire for communication.*

> *Because it was a private school money was not in short supply and the facilities were excellent with videos, computers, etc. The free furnished flat I was given was large and very comfortable, and there was a free school minibus service that took teachers to the school. On either side of the school there were hazelnut gardens, behind there were mountains and in front the Black Sea, all quite idyllic, especially in summer. The other teachers (all Turkish) were very welcoming from day one, despite the fact that I was less experienced and was getting four times their salary. My salary was the equivalent of £400 per month but went down to about £325 due to spiralling inflation; I could live very comfortably on this and still have a lot left over for spending on holidays and clothes.*

Because of the wild inflation, most schools quote salaries in sterling or dollars and promise quarterly or bi-annual exchange rate adjustments. Always check whether your salary is to be inflation-linked or pegged against a foreign currency and how often it will be adjusted; October and March pay reviews are common. But even if you are unlucky and see your wages plummet on paper, the important things like beer, doner kebabs and bus tickets remain the same price in lire.

Contracts are usually for 9, 10 or 11 months, but if you decide to renew for a second year you are normally paid over the summer holiday. Do not put too much faith in your contract. Rabindra Roy described his as a 'worthless and contradictory piece of paper.' Private language schools will expect you to work the usual unsocial hours and may chop and change your timetable at short notice, while *lises* offer daytime working hours plus (sometimes onerous) extracurricular duties such as marking tests, attending school ceremonies, etc.

The standard holiday allowance for teachers is four weeks. At inferior schools, national holidays must be taken out of this annual leave, including Muslim holidays like Seker Bayrami, usually celebrated at the end of Ramadan and Kurban Bayrami. Both of these festivals last three days and it is customary to make the bridge to a full week.

The Pupils

The major schools are well equipped with TVs, videos, language labs and course materials. But better than the back-up facilities is the enthusiasm of the pupils who are usually motivated, conscientious and well-behaved, and enjoy role play and group discussions. The friendly openness of young Turks may cause a foreign teacher to forget that Turkey is still an Islamic country where dress is conservative and women, no matter how promising, do not normally go on to higher education. 'Willing if unimaginative' was one teacher's description of her students. One undesirable aspect of Turkish education is that many *lises* are too strongly oriented to exam preparation and university entrance.

Student behaviour differs radically depending on what kind of institution you teach in. Private secondary schools tend to be populated with spoiled and immature kids who do not always respect their teachers. Joan Smith found this hard to stomach at the private school in Kayseri where she taught:

> *Turkish parents indulge their children something rotten. Rich spoilt students abound in my classroom and discipline goes out the window. Foreign teachers are regarded as inferior and are given even less respect than the Turkish teachers.*

Joan did not think that she should have to tolerate some of the innuendos her male students were getting away with, but had little hope of justice if they and their friends denied her allegations.

Others' experiences have been very different. Dick Bird, a veteran EFL teacher in Turkey and elsewhere, describes some of his female and other pupils:

> *I have found women students defer to a far higher level of male chauvinism than would be acceptable anywhere in the West. Turkish women also seem to have exceptionally quiet voices and I can't help feeling that this irritating characteristic is somehow related to their role in society—a case of being seen but not heard until you are very very close perhaps? Sometimes my students know too much grammar to be able to express themselves freely. As their own language is radically different to Indo-*

European languages they have a lot of difficulty adapting to the sentence structure of English: they regard relative clauses as a perversion and are baffled, if not mildly outraged, by the cavalier way English seems to use any tense it fancies to refer to future actions but is puritanically strict about how one may describe present and past events. Another difficulty Turks have is that we EFL teachers like to use a lot of words in our meta-language (i.e. language about language e.g. adjective, verb) which do not have cognates in Turkish as they do in other European languages, for example a teacher may inform their students that 'will' expresses probability, not intention; this will be readily understood by an elementary level Spaniard but is total gibberish to a Turk (as I suspect it is to a great many native speakers of English).

Dick's analysis of Turkish EFL students ends with a light-hearted description of their irrepressible energy and enthusiasm:

Whenever the class is asked a question they would fain prostrate themselves at their teacher's feet were it not that years of instilled discipline keep them penned by invisible bonds within the confines of their desks until the ringing of the bell, whereat pandemonium breaks loose as a thousand berserk adolescents fling themselves across the (highly polished) corridor floors and down the (marble) steps headlong into the playground. (This phenomenon may help to explain why fire drills are not a regular feature of Turkish school life.)

Paul Gallantry, Director of Studies at Dilko English in Bakirköy, agrees that Turkish students are fun to teach but identifies a few of the problems he has encountered:

They have several major problems with English, especially mastering the definite article, the third person singular and the present perfect, none of which exist in Turkish. On the whole, their pronunciation is good, but they do have difficulty with words that have three consonants back to back. (My own surname Gallantry inevitably gets pronounced 'Galilantiree'.) If I have to be critical of my students, it is that they neither listen to, nor read, instructions; five minutes into an exercise there is always someone asking 'What am I supposed to do?'. Also a recurring problem is that some students merely come to a language school in order to use it as a social club. They're more interested in meeting someone of the opposite sex than learning English, and this can have a demoralising effect in class.

Accommodation

If accommodation is provided as part of your contract, it may be located close to the school in a modern flat which you will have to share with another teacher or it may be some way away, possibly in an undesirable neighbourhood. Fortunately not many teachers are assigned accommodation as gruesome as Philip Dray's in Izmir:

Cockroaches, centipedes, noisy neighbours, a filthy shower room and a fitted kitchen circa 1920, I was slowly adjusting to it all. But one day, while I was having a shower, I saw a rat looking at me from the ventilation shaft and I knew that my patience had run out. I asked for a new flat but they said they couldn't get a new one before May. So, relucantly (as there were some very nice people at the school) I had to leave.

If the school doesn't provide a flat they will certainly help you find one and act as go-between with the landlord. Most provide some kind of rent subsidy, since rents in Turkey are high relative to the cost of living. The situation in over-crowded Istanbul is especially tight. It is usual to bargain over the rent as if you were buying a second-hand car. Flats are advertised through *Hurriyet* newspaper, or there are estate agencies called *emlak* but these tend to charge a month's rent. Rents often seem steep at the outset which may be because they are fixed for a 12 month period. Foreigners are usually considered an attractive proposition as they tend to be undemanding tenants.

In Istanbul, the nicest flats are along the Bosphorus where the air is clean, the views stunning and a lot of the buildings are older properties with a lot of character; this is why they have been snapped up by well-heeled diplomats and multi-nationals. Rents are lower on the Asian side of the city. Although the Asian side has less charm (actually it has no charm at all), it has less pollution and many people prefer it. At the risk of multiplying horror stories, Bruce Lawson describes his situation a few years ago when housed on the Asian side:

> *The apartment is a jerry-built five-storey block of 16 rooms which are tiny; six rooms don't have windows. The heating rarely works (it's important to note that Istanbul is very cold in winter), there are no cooking facilities so you eat out, which is expensive, and the place is crawling with cockroaches, the bedding is squalid and very smelly. The area is notorious for prostitutes making it dangerous for women. One colleague of mine (she's leaving tomorrow) has been groped every day in broad daylight. The rent-free accommodation is a misnomer, as a sum is deducted from your wages for utilities, although a bill is never produced.*

Ian McArthur chose the opposite situation; his school was in a suburb on the Asian side, but he chose to stay in a cheap hotel in Sultanahmet, partly for the social life:

> *I had to commute (from Europe to Asia in fact) for an hour in the morning and evening, but the marvellous views of the sunrise over the domes and minarets from the Bosphorus ferry whilst sipping a much-needed glass of strong sweet tea, made the early rise worth it.*

LEISURE TIME

Even if you are earning a salary at the lower end of the scale, you should be able to afford quite a good life, especially if you eat a lot of bread, drink local wines and use public transport. Basic meals and food, transport, hotels and cinemas (most films are subtitled rather than dubbed) are still very reasonable, especially away from the seaside and Istanbul. If out and about, be aware that the police sometimes carry out spot checks for ID, so you should carry some around with you, even if it is only a good photocopy of your passport.

Dick Bird points out the advantages of living in Ankara:

> *It's safer than any European capital (except maybe Reykjavik) and although it may not hum at night, there are enough discos etc. to keep you going for a year, plus very cheap classical concerts and cinemas. And the air pollution is not as bad as it was.*

Travel in Turkey is wonderfully affordable. The efficiency, comfort and low cost of Turkish bus travel put the coach services of most other countries to shame. There is very little crime in Turkey. Women will have to learn to handle pestering, which is usually best ignored. Paul Gallantry tries to put the problem into perspective:

> *While Turkey is generally an exceptionally safe place, women teachers can expect a certain amount of harassment from a minority of Turkish men, who seem to believe that all foreign females are prostitutes. This attitude leaves a lot of teachers with a thoroughly negative attitude towards Turkey and Turkish people as a whole, which is unfair.*
> *Turkey generally is a great place to live and work. It's a fascinating country, full of contradictions, as befits a land that is the bridge between East and West. Turkey is the ideal country for anyone starting their EFL career.*

LIST OF SCHOOLS

ACTIVE ENGLISH
Atatürk Bulvari 127/701, Selcan Han. Bakanliklar, 06640 Ankara. Tel: (312) 418 7973/418 4975. Fax: (312) 425 8235.
Number of teachers: 18-20.
Preference of nationality: British, American, Canadian, Australian.
Qualifications: teaching certificate in English preferably or any university degree plus Cambridge/RSA Cert.
Conditions of employment: minimum 8 month contract, otherwise negotiable. 92 hours per month guaranteed. Evening and weekend work. 1 day off per week.
Salary: depends on qualifications and experience.

Facilities/Support: accommodation provided. All books, teachers' manuals, tape recorders, etc. provided by the school.
Recruitment: interviews in Turkey or in London. Send or fax detailed CV and photograph.
Contact: G. C. Ince.

AKADEMI SCHOOL OF ENGLISH
Akkoyunlu Cad. No 22 (P.K. 234), Diyarbakir 21100. Tel: (412) 224 2297/8/9. Fax: (412) 228 8020.
Number of teachers: 3-4.
Preference of nationality: British/American/Canadian.
Qualifications: minimum 4 year degree and CELTA or TEFL Cert (or equivalent).
Conditions of employment: minimum 1 year contracts. 26 h.p.w.
Salary: approximately £700-£900 per month net of all taxes, social security, etc.
Facilities/Support: free air fares. Free furnished shared accommodation provided. Orientation given.
Recruitment: adverts in UK press and recruitment agencies.

ANTIK ENGLISH
Bakirköy branch: Kirmizi Sebboy Sok. No. 10, Istanbul Cad., Bakirköy, Istanbul. Tel: (212) 570 4847/(216) 349 9920. Fax: (212) 583 7934/336 2220. E-mail: ANTIK@prizma.net. Other Istanbul branches in Taksim and Kadiköy.
Number of teachers: 40-50.
Preference of nationality: all native English speakers, but new regulations make it easier for Britons.
Qualifications: degree or further education to HND level plus TEFL Certificate.
Conditions of employment: 9 or 12 month contracts or possibly 3 months over summer period. 5 days on/2 days off (not consecutive). Evening and weekend work expected.
Salary: US$800-$1,050 depending on experience.
Facilities/Support: shared accommodation provided. School assists with work permits. Regular workshops and observations.
Recruitment: via adverts in the *Guardian* and *EL Prospects* and links with training centres and agencies. Interviews regularly conducted in London, Birmingham and Glasgow.
Contact: Michelle A. Maguire, Director of Studies.

BEST ENGLISH
Bayindir Sokak No. 53, Kizilay, Ankara. Tel: (312) 417 1819/417 2536. Fax: (312) 417 6808. E-mail: besteng@alnet.net
Number of teachers: 30.
Preference of nationality: none.
Qualifications: first degree plus CELTA or equivalent plus experience (overseas experience preferred).
Conditions of employment: 1 year renewable contracts. Teaching load is 26 h.p.w. Variable hours between 9am and 9pm, 7 days a week, with 2 days off a week. Students mostly young adults.
Salary: varies according to qualifications and experience.
Facilities/Support: shared accommodation provided but not paid for. Partial payment of health insurance. One way airfare paid on completion of one year plus three weeks paid leave; return airfare and four weeks paid leave if teacher renews contract. In-house training.
Recruitment: adverts and direct application. Interviews held in UK and Ankara.

BEYKENT UNIVERSITY

Foreign Language School, Beykent Beylikdirisu, 34900 Istanbul. Tel: (212) 872 6432. Fax: (212) 872 2489. E-mail: herguneg@superonline.com or: gherguner@beyu.edu.tr
Number of teachers: 10.
Preference of nationality: none.
Qualifications: MA in TEFL, degree in language and/or DELTA.
Conditions of employment: 12 month contracts. Full-time hours are 9am-6pm; 24 contact hours p.w.
Salary: £650-£850 per month (net) paid in lire. Exchange rate adjusted every four months.
Facilities/Support: shared accommodation offered. Advice given on new visa regulations.
Recruitment: via adverts in *Guardian* and *TES*. Interviews held in London.
Contact: Dr. Gulten Herguner, Director.

BRITISH ENGLISH

Cami Duragi Palazoglu Sok. No. 12/2-3-4-5-6, Sisli, Istanbul. Tel/fax: (216) 418 8982. Branches also at Saskinbakkal and Kadiköy.
Number of teachers: 20.
Preference of nationality: British, American/Canadian and Australian.
Qualifications: first degree (arts and language preferred) plus CELTA or Cert TESOL. One year's experience outside Europe a valuable asset.
Conditions of employment: 9 month contracts. 20-30 h.p.w.
Salary: £180 plus 60,000,000 Turkish lire for basic 20 hours. TL2,000,000 paid per hour of overtime. TL20,000,000 per quarter for supplement.
Facilities/Support: free shared accommodation provided or private accommodation at half rent. Monthly training workshops.
Recruitment: via adverts in the *Guardian*. Interviews held in London once a year but mostly by phone/fax.
Contact: Ashley Perks, Director of Studies.

CUKUROVA UNIVERSITY CENTER FOR FOREIGN LANGUAGES

Balcali-Adana. Tel: (322) 338 6084 (switchboard), ext. 2921 for the Centre for Foreign Languages.
Number of teachers: 4-5.
Preference of nationality: British, American.
Qualifications: BA or MA in TEFL or Linguistics. Teaching experience in intensive programmes.
Conditions of employment: 1 year renewable contracts. 12 contact h.p.w. 6 h.p.w in office plus regular meetings for staff development.
Salary: approximately TL300,000,000 per month (net).
Facilities/Support: no accommodation or training provided.
Recruitment: interviews held in Turkey.

DILKO ENGLISH

Hatboyu Caddesi No. 16, 34720 Bakirköy, Istanbul. Tel: (212) 570 1270. Fax: (212) 543 6123. E-mail: dilko@superonline.com. Branches also in Kadiköy, Besiktas and (most recently) Saskinbakkal (Bagdat Caddesi, Kazim Ozalp Sokagi No 15, daire 4, 81070 Saskinbakkal; 216-359 3365).
Number of teachers: up to 30 in Bakirköy and 25-30 in other branches.
Preference of nationality: native speakers.
Qualifications: TEFL certificate or diploma and a 4-year university diploma.
Conditions of employment: 9 month contracts (signing of agreement is compulsory). Minimum 24 h.p.w., maximum 30, including weekend and evening classes. Minimum one day off p.w. Mostly adults, including ESP groups, plus junior groups (ages 11-15) using the *Open Doors* series.

Salary: varies according to qualifications and experience. Some paid in US dollars in first year, all paid in dollars if teacher renews contract.
Facilities/Support: free accommodation minus utilities bills. Workshops held at least once a month.
Recruitment: direct application mostly; sometimes use agents in England who can interview in London.

DILMER LTC
Unlu Cad. 7, Heykel, Bursa. Tel: (224) 222 4673. Fax: (224) 223 1163.
Number of teachers: 12.
Preference of nationality: British.
Qualifications: BA, CELTA (or equivalent) and 1 year's experience preferred.
Conditions of employment: 1 year contracts. 26 h.p.w. Pupils aged from 11.
Salary: salary adjusted every 4 months.
Facilities/Support: free flights and accommodation.
Recruitment: through adverts in *Guardian*. Interviews sometimes in London or, if not, by phone.

THE ENGLISH ACADEMY
1374 Sokak No. 18/4, Selvili Is Hkz. Cankaya (Izmir). Tel: (232) 446 2520. Fax: (232) 425 3042.
Number of teachers: 12-16.
Preference of nationality: British, Australian, New Zealand, Irish, American, Canadian.
Qualifications: minimum CELTA (preferably grade A or B) plus 1 year's experience (preferably two).
Conditions of employment: 9-12 month contracts. 24 h.p.w. working split shift with 2 consecutive days off.
Salary: good local salary according to qualifications and experience.
Facilities/Support: flight paid up to £200. Accommodation provided. Ongoing workshops.
Recruitment: via adverts in the *Guardian*. Half of candidates are interviewed either in UK or Izmir.
Contact: Mr. Morgan Finnegan, Founding Director.

THE ENGLISH CENTRE—ANKARA
Selanik Caddesi No. 8, Kat. 5, Kizilay, Ankara. Tel: (312) 435 3094/435 2503. Fax: (312) 434 2738.
Number of teachers: 10-12.
Qualifications: degree and CELTA or equivalent.
Conditions of employment: standard contract is 11 months plus holiday; 6-month contracts considered. 24 h.p.w. Mostly adult students but some children's classes.
Salary: £300-£400 per month.
Facilities/Support: Istanbul-London air fare and accommodation provided. Training given.
Recruitment: direct application by fax/letter/telephone.
Contact: Tim Harlock, Director of Studies.

THE ENGLISH CENTRE—ISTANBUL
Rumeli Caddesi 92, Zeki Bey Apt. 4, Osmanbey, Istanbul. Tel: (212) 247 0983/225 9172/252 9173. E-mail: englishcentre@superonline.com
Number of teachers: 45.
Preference of nationality: British.
Qualifications: degree and CELTA essential; DELTA and/or experience preferred.
Conditions of employment: 12 month contracts. 24 contact hours p.w. and 1 hour teacher development meeting. 2 consecutive days off per week. Some in-company teaching and some young learners' classes.

Salary: basic salary TL200,000,000 per month. Increments offered for experience and qualifications. Twice annual salary reviews (to compensate for Turkish inflation).
Facilities/Support: free accommodation and flights provided. Assistance with DELTA course. Full-time teacher trainer for lesson support. Well-equipped resources room.
Recruitment: adverts in the *Guardian* and on the internet. Interviews in London or Istanbul.
Contact: Bernadette Philipson, Director of Studies.

THE ENGLISH CENTRE—IZMIR
Cumhuriyet Bulvari No. 125, Kat. 1/D/1, Alsancak, Izmir. Tel: (232) 463 8487/464 3275. Fax: (232) 464 3144.
Number of teachers: 4-6.
Preference of nationality: none.
Qualifications: BA plus TEFL Certificate.
Conditions of employment: 1 year contracts. 25 h.p.w.
Salary: approximately £300 per month. Regularly revised for inflation.
Facilities/Support: free accommodation. Detailed lesson plans provided. Regular training sessions for teachers.
Recruitment: adverts in UK papers. Interviews not essential.
Contact: Ibrahim Tascan, Director.

ENGLISH FAST
Zuhuratbba Cad. 42, Bakirköy, Istanbul. Fax: (212) 561 3231.
Language school group with 5 branch schools: 3 in Istanbul, 1 in Ankara, 1 in and Izmir: 440 Sokak No. 5, Konak-Izmir.
Number of teachers: about 100.
Preference of nationality: none.
Qualifications: must have university degree. EF offers free teacher training course followed by 1 year teaching contract to successful participants.
Conditions of employment: 30 h.p.w. Students are mostly young adults aiming to take TOEFL.
Salary: $800-$1,600 (net) depending on qualifications and experience, paid monthly in local currency.
Facilities/Support: rent-free shared accommodation or monthly housing allowance. Flight allowance yearly ($1,800 for US-based staff, £250 for UK staff). Emphasis on in-service teacher training.
Recruitment: adverts in UK press.
Contact: Charles Napier.

ENGLISH STAR
Sehit Fethi Bey Cad. No. 79/7, Pasaport, Izmir. Tel: (232) 441 1686. Fax: (232) 483 7851.
Number of teachers: 5-6.
Preference of nationality: British.
Qualifications: minimum university degree plus TEFL certificate. Teaching experience preferred.
Conditions of employment: 1 full year contract. Hours between 9am and 9pm. Guaranteed 60 hours per month.
Salary: hourly rate.
Facilities/Support: assistance with accommodation.
Recruitment: via adverts in the *Guardian* or locally. Phone interviews sufficient.
Contact: Ms. Funda Akgül, School Owner/Director of Studies.

ENGLISH WEST
Cumhuriyet Bulv. No. 36/3, Konak, Izmir. Tel: (232) 425 9208. Fax: (232) 441 8514.
Number of teachers: 8-10.
Preference of nationality: British.

Qualifications: minimum university degree and a teaching certificate.
Conditions of employment: one year contracts. 25 h.p.w. (usually 5 days p.w.).
Salary: from £360 per month (net).
Facilities/Support: free accommodation provided. Support from Director of Studies.
Recruitment: interviews not essential.
Contact: Mr. Nihat Aksoy, Company Director.

EURO CENTER OZEL
Erman Yabanci, Dil Kursu, Mithatpasa Cad. No. 102, Kat. 4, 45300 Salihli. Tel: (236) 712 2330/715 0731. Fax: (236) 713 0612.
Number of teachers: up to 3.
Preference of nationality: none, but must have clear pronunciation.
Qualifications: teaching qualifications and experience essential.
Conditions of employment: minimum 1 year. Varying timetable, usually between 8.30am and 5pm.
Salary: from TL150,000,000 (net).
Facilities/Support: assistance with accommodation and work permit.
Recruitment: ads on notice boards. Interviews not required.
Contact: Lütfiye Yaman, School Owner.

EVRIM SCHOOL OF LANGUAGES
Cengiz Topel Caddesi 8, Camlibel, 33010 Mersin. Tel: (324) 233 9541/233 4825. Fax: (324) 237 0862.
Preference of nationality: British, American.
Qualifications: minimum 2 years' experience of teaching, preferably to foreign students. Clear speech and colourful personality are important.
Conditions of employment: 9 month contracts. 30 h.p.w. between 8am and 9pm.
Salary: minimum US$500 per month.
Facilities/Support: in-service training sessions using videos and cassettes every Monday for 90 minutes.
Recruitment: interviews in Mersin or in London (late June/early July).
Contact: G. Durrnaz, Prinicipal.

EYUBOGLU LISESI
Namik Kemal Mah. Dr. Rüstem Eyüboglu Sok. 1, Umraniye 81240, Istanbul. Tel: (216) 329 1614. Fax: (216) 335 7198.
Number of teachers: 18.
Preference of nationality: British, American, Australian, New Zealand, Canadian.
Qualifications: 4-5 years experience, teaching certificate required.
Conditions of employment: 2 year contracts. 24 h.p.w.
Salary: $1,200-1,600 per month (net) according to qualifications and experience; increment of $100 p.m. for MA or IB experience, $200 for PhD.
Facilities/Support: accommodation provided free of charge. Residence permit procedures handled by the school. Intensive training provided.
Recruitment: personal interview necessary.
Contact: Sema K. Ozkaya.

FONO PRIVATE ELEMENTARY SCHOOL
Gündogdu Caddesi 49, Merter, 34016 Istanbul. Tel: (212) 641 9900. Fax: (212) 584 2742.
Number of teachers: 3 English teachers out of staff of 15.
Preference of nationality: British.
Qualifications: must be qualified to teach elementary school.
Conditions of employment: 1 year contracts. 25 lessons per week. Children aged 7-15.
Salary: twice what local teachers are paid.
Facilities/Support: assistance given with accommodation. No training.
Recruitment: adverts in *TES*. Interviews not essential.

GEDIZ PRIVATE COLLEGE
Seyrek Beldesi, Menemen, Izmir. Tel: (232) 844 7444. Fax: (232) 844 7441. E-mail: baysoy@gediz.kiz.tr
Number of teachers: 2.
Preference of nationality: British or American.
Qualifications: must be university graduate.
Conditions of employment: 1 year contracts. 18 45-minute class hours per week.
Salary: $800-$1,000 per month.
Facilities/Support: no assistance with accommodation.
Recruitment: interviews can sometimes be arranged in Britain.
Contact: Ender Sensolsun, Head of English or Hilal Talay, Principal.

GENCTUR
Istiklal Cad. Zambak Sok. 15/5, Taksim 80080, Istanbul. Tel: (212) 249 215. Fax: (212) 249 2554. E-mail: workcamps@genctur.com.tr
Number of teachers: 2-3.
Preference of nationality: British, American, Irish.
Qualifications: experience with children, workcamp and/or teaching experience. Ages 20-30. Must be calm, patient and fit.
Conditions of employment: 2 week summer camps at Aegean resort village. English taught by games and songs.
Salary: free board and lodging.
Recruitment: via partner voluntary organisations abroad (e.g. International Voluntary Service, Old Hall, East Bergholt, Colchester CO7 6TQ, UK). CV and 2 references needed; interviews not necessary.

INKUR ENGLISH LANGUAGE INSTITUTE
Ankara Caddesi, Yalihamam Sokak No. 8, Izmi, Kocaeli. Tel: (262) 321 5325. Fax: (262) 322 5391.
Number of teachers: 5-10.
Preference of nationality: British, American, Australian.
Qualifications: university degree and TEFL certificate.
Conditions of employment: 9 month contracts. 28 contact h.p.w.
Facilities/Support: free accommodation provided. Help with work permits.
Recruitment: advertisements (e.g. in *Guardian*), recommendations and direct applications. Interviews sometimes held in Britain.
Contact: N. G. Dogan, Director.

INTERLANG
Istanbul Cad. Halkçi Sok, Yalçinlar Han. No. 4, Bakirköy, Istanbul. Tel: (212) 543 5795/543 9915. Fax: (212) 542 7854.
Number of teachers: 40 (in 3 schools).
Preference of nationality: British, Australian, New Zealand, Canadian, American.
Qualifications: university degree and TEFL certificate.
Conditions of employment: 9-12 month contracts. 5 days p.w.
Salary: competitive. Guaranteed salary.
Facilities/Support: rent-free accommodation and flight benefits given. Resources include TV and video, computer facilities, photocopiers, etc. Regular teacher training workshops and ongoing teacher development. (Interlang is an RSA/CELTA centre.)
Recruitment: interviews held in London in July/August. Otherwise faxed application and telephone interviews acceptable.
Contact: Mhairi-Anne Barr, Director of Studies.

ISIK LISESI
Tesvikiye Cad. No. 152, Tesvikiye, Istanbul. Tel: (212) 246 6047. Fax: (212) 240 1349.
Number of teachers: 10+.

Preference of nationality: British, American, Canadian.
Qualifications: English degree and teaching certificate.
Conditions of employment: 1 year contracts. About 20 teaching h.p.w.
Salary: £600 per month basic plus extra for years of experience and overtime hours.
Facilities/Support: assistance with accommodation and work permits.
Recruitment: locally or through an agency in UK. Interviews can be held in UK.

ISTANBUL LANGUAGE CENTRE
Yakut Sok. no. 10, Bakirköy, Istanbul. Tel: (212) 571 8284-94. Fax: (212) 571 82 95. E-mail: ilm@ilm.com.tr
Number of teachers: 40 in 4 branches.
Preference of nationality: British, American.
Qualifications: university degree and TEFL certificate.
Conditions of employment: 9-12 month contracts. 28 h.p.w.
Salary: $500 (paid in Turkish lira).
Facilities/Support: furnished shared accommodation provided. Training available (Trinity TESOL Cert course offered).
Recruitment: via adverts in the *Guardian* and agency in the UK. Interviews can be held in UK.
Contact: Odman N. Eroglu, School Owner/Founder.

KARYA
Dr. Esat Isik Caddesi 110, Moda, 81310 Kadiköy, Istanbul. Tel: (216) 349 9849. Fax: (216) 349 9853. E-mail: karya@karya.com.tr
Number of teachers: 16.
Preference of nationality: none.
Qualifications: minimum university degree and CELTA or equivalent. Experience preferred.
Conditions of employment: 9 or 11 month contracts. 26 h.p.w. (mostly evenings and weekends). 5 days per week. Students are mostly well motivated adults.
Salary: approximately £400-£500 per month.
Facilities/Support: accommodation available and assistance with work permits. Paid flights. Regular teacher meetings and workshops held.
Recruitment: via adverts in the *Guardian*, word-of-mouth, notice board in British Council, etc.. Interviews essential (held in London in the summer as well as locally at other times).

KENT ENGLISH—ANKARA
Mithatpasa Caddesi No. 46 Kat. 3,4,5, 06420 Kizilay, Ankara. Tel: (312) 434 3833/ 433 6010. Fax: (312) 435 7334. E-mail: kenteng@hitit.ato.org.tr. Also branch in Bolu: Izzet Baysai Caddesi No. 42, Kat. 3,4,5, Bolu.
Number of teachers: 30+ in Ankara, 5+ in Bolu.
Preference of nationality: British, American, Canadian, Australian, New Zealand, etc.
Qualifications: minimum BA plus CELTA or equivalent.
Conditions of employment: 1 year contracts. Minimum 24 contact h.p.w. Most students aged 20-35.
Salary: hourly rates start at TL2,160,000 (overtime paid at higher rate).
Facilities/Support: subsidised, fully-furnished accommodation. Flight refunded and teacher training available.
Recruitment: telephone or local interviews.
Contact: Ismail Sahin, Director.

KENT ENGLISH—ISTANBUL
Bahariye Arayicibasi Sok No. 4, 81300 Kadiköy, Istanbul. Tel: (216) 347 2791/347 2792/346 3981. Fax: (216) 348 9435.
Number of teachers: 6.
Preference of nationality: British, American.

Qualifications: degree and TEFL Cert. required. Priority given to teaching experience. Mostly adults.
Conditions of employment: 8, 10 or 12 month contracts. Weekend hours: 9.30am-5pm; weekday hours: 9.30am-12.30pm and 7-9pm.
Salary: £500 per month.
Facilities/Support: accommodation provided. Work permits arranged. Some training provided. Paid vacation, bonus, gifts and one-way ticket to UK provided at end of contract.
Recruitment: adverts and personal recommendations. Interviews essential and are held in the UK.

THE KOÇ SCHOOL
P.K. 38, Pendik-Istanbul 81481. Tel: (216) 304 1003. Fax: (216) 304 1048.
Number of teachers: 40.
Preference of nationality: none.
Qualifications: degree and teaching certification in subject field required.
Conditions of employment: 2 year contracts. Teaching hours 8am-4pm.
Salary: $15,000-$40,000 per year (net).
Facilities/Support: housing provided for faculty hired overseas. Training provided. School takes care of paperwork for work permits.
Recruitment: primarily at recruitment fairs. Interview essential.

KOPARAN LANGUAGE SCHOOL
Istiklal Cad. No. 34, Bandirma 10200. Tel: (266) 714 1414. Fax: (266) 714 5050.
E-mail: koparan@escort.net.tr
Number of teachers: 2 or 3 for academic year, 40 in summer.
Preference of nationality: British for long-term staff; no preference for summer camps.
Qualifications: university degree and recognised TEFL certificate essential.
Conditions of employment: 1 year contracts (Sept-Jun). Maximum 26 h.p.w. 35 h.p.w. including meetings and preparation. Summer contract from mid-June (group flight from London) for 10 weeks. Camp is located at purpose-built resort on the Sea of Marmara.
Salary: TL equivalent of £300 per month. Pocket money of £20 per week for summer staff.
Facilities/Support: accommodation provided. Flights reimbursed (including summer flights) at end of contract.
Recruitment: via adverts in the *Guardian*. Often recruit year-round staff from summer crew. Telephone interviews. Summer contact in UK: Patsy Rowden, 100 Nelson Road, Whitstable, Kent CT5 1DZ (01227 261666) mornings only.
Contact: Karen Atis, Director of Studies.

LONDON LANGUAGES INTERNATIONAL (LLI)
Abide-i Hurriyet Caddesi, Kat. 1, Mecidiyeköy, Istanbul. Tel: (212) 211 7445. Fax: (212) 211 7441.
Number of teachers: 8-11.
Preference of nationality: British.
Qualifications: degree, TEFL, teaching experience required.
Conditions of employment: 1 year contracts. Up to 30 h.p.w. Most students are business people.
Salary: up to £750 per month (net).
Facilities/Support: assistance with accommodation and work permits given. Some in-house training.
Recruitment: adverts in the *Guardian*. Interview necessary, sometimes held in UK.

ONDER DIL LANGUAGE SCHOOL
Porsuk Blv. Caglayan Ish. Kat. 6, Eskisehir 26130. Tel: (222) 231 3596. Fax: (222) 233 3356.
Number of teachers: 6.
Preference of nationality: British.
Qualifications: university degree and TEFL certificates.
Conditions of employment: 8-12 month contracts. Mostly evening teaching 6pm-9pm and weekends 9am-6pm. Majority of clients are university students.
Salary: TL equivalent of about US$800 per month (net).
Facilities/Support: free accommodation provided. Orientation on arrival and ongoing help given to inexperienced teachers.
Recruitment: via adverts in the *Guardian,* etc. Telephone interviews.
Contact: Mr. Mustafa Koksal, Principal.

ONLY ENGLISH
Kunduracilar Cad. Dedeoglu Sok. 4/3, Trabzon. Tel: (462) 321 9992. Fax: (462) 321 0223.
Number of teachers: 4.
Preference of nationality: none.
Qualifications: university degree and CELTA plus minimum 1 year's experience.
Conditions of employment: 6 or 12 month contracts. 24 h.p.w. Hours are 5.30pm-9.30pm Monday-Wednesday and 9.30am-7.30pm Saturday and Sunday. Optional overtime often available at a higher rate. Most clients are adults.
Salary: about £250 per month (net).
Facilities/Support: shared flat provided. Free return flights from UK.
Recruitment: via adverts in the *Guardian*. Interviews not essential.
Contact: Ryder Thomas, Director of Studies.

OZEL ORTADOGU LISESI
Spor Cad. No. 26, Yakacik, Istanbul. Tel: (216) 377 2501. Fax: (216) 377 2502.
Number of teachers: 2.
Preference of nationality: British, American, Canadian.
Qualifications: university degree in English or English/American literature plus 2-3 years' experience.
Conditions of employment: 1 year contracts. 24 h.p.w.
Salary: from US$1,100 per month.
Facilities/Support: no assistance with accommodation.
Recruitment: local interview essential.

OZEL TAN LISESI
Yeni Yalova Yolu 12 Km, 16335 Ovaakça/Bursa. Tel: (224) 267 0072 (Pbx). Fax: (224) 267 0071.
Number of teachers: 3.
Preference of nationality: British, American, South African, Australian.
Qualifications: university degree of English faculty.
Conditions of employment: 1 year contracts. 25 h.p.w. (class periods are 45 minutes).
Salary: TL equivalent of £350-£400 per month (net) plus all meals in school canteen.
Facilities/Support: accommodation provided on school premises. Ongoing training meetings and seminars.
Recruitment: telephone interviews.
Contact: Mr. Sami Ipekboyayan, Head of English Department.

SISTEM ENGLISH COURSE
Arifiye Mah. Kibris Sehitleri Caddesi No 18/1, Eskisehir. Tel: (222) 231 2266. Fax: (222) 230 8681.
Number of teachers: 6.

Preference of nationality: none.
Qualifications: can employ newly qualified or experienced teachers.
Conditions of employment: 9 month contracts. 28 lessons per week (50 minutes).
Salary: from TL180,000,000 to TL200,000,000 per month.
Facilities/Support: rent-free shared flat and return ticket London-Istanbul provided. Teacher pays for utilities, normally TL10,000,000. 2 weeks paid holiday in February.
Recruitment: via adverts in the *Guardian*. References are essential but interviews are not.
Contact: Durmus Ari, Director.

Other Schools to Try

Note that these schools (in alphabetical order according to town) did not confirm their teacher requirements for this edition of *Teaching English Abroad*. Upper case entries marked with an asterisk had entries in the last edition (1997); addresses without asterisks have been taken from various sources, such as British Council lists and newspaper adverts.

CIZAKCA LISESI, Ihsan Cizakça Lisesi, Ishaniye, Bursa (tel/fax 224-451 4383. E-mail: cizakca@turk.net. 4-5 teachers.

CAGDIL, Altiparmak Cad., 16050 Bursa

Atadil, Koprubasi Cad., Yalbi Sos. No. 2/2, Eskisehir

BOGAZICI OZEL OGRETIM ISLETMESI, Gökfiliz Ishani Kat, 8 Mecidiyeköy, Istanbul (212-274 2070/71)

ITBA, Süleyman Nazif Sokak No. 68, Nisantasi, Istanbul (212-232 8200/fax 212-233 9667). 30 teachers.

MIMAR SINAN OZEL LISESI, Inönü Caddesi, Mimar Sinan Beldesi, Büyükcekmece 34903, Istanbul (212-881 3630/fax 212-883 2125). 10 teachers who must have B.Ed. or BA English and PGCE.

OZEL GOKDIL LISESI, Bostanci, Degirmenyolu Cad (Ankara Asfalti Uzeri, Içerenköy Girisi), Kadiköy, 81120 Istanbul (216-362 9193/fax 216-362 4094). 5 teachers.

OZEL SISLI TERAKKI LISESI, Ebulula Mardin Cad. 12/A, 80620 Levend, Istanbul (212-279 6626/fax 212-281 2380). 7 teachers.

AEGEAN SCHOOL OF LANGUAGES/VIDEO ENGLISH, Cumhuriyet Bulvari 36/2, 35250 Izmir (232-441 1111/fax 232-484 2471). 12 teachers.

CINAR SCHOOL OF ENGLISH, 860 Sokak No. 1, Kat. 4, Konak, Izmir (232-483 7273/fax 232-441 1113). 18 teachers in 2 Izmir branches.

English Club, Cumhuriyet Bulvari 36/5, Konak-Izmir

English House, Kemalpasa Caddesi 90/3, Karsiyaka-Izmir

Practical English, Necatibey Bulvari No. 19, Uz Is Merkezi 1. K2, Cankaya-Izmir

SITA, Kibris Sehitleri Caddesi No. 125, Karal Apt., Alsancak-Izmir

Turkish American Association, Sehit Nevresbey Bulvari No 23, Alsancak-Izmir

English Lab, 1720 Sokak No. 26/2, Karsiyaka-Izmir

Active English, Ibrahim Gökcen Bulvari No. 50/A, Manisa. 40 minutes north of Izmir.

British Academy, 1717 Sokak No. 81/4, Egem Ishani, 35530 Karsiyaka-Izmir

Anadolu Dershaneleri, 859 Sokak No. 3, Saray ishani B Blok, Konak-Izmir

The Sandwich Method, Mustafa Bey Cad. No. 13 D. 14, Alsancak-Izmir

AFRICA

Contradictions abound in a continent as complex as Africa, and one of them pertains to the attitude to the English language. On the one hand the emergent nations of Africa want to distance themselves from their colonial past. Hence the renaming of Leopoldville, Salisbury and Upper Volta to become Kinshasa, Harare and Burkina Faso. On the other hand, they are eager to develop and participate in the world economy and so need to communicate in English.

What makes much of Africa different from Latin America and Asia (vis-à-vis English teaching) is that English is the medium of instruction in state schools in many ex-colonies of Britain including Ghana, Nigeria, Kenya, Zambia, Zimbabwe and Malawi. As in the Indian subcontinent, the majority of English teachers in these countries are locals. But there is still some demand for native speakers in the secondary schools of those countries. The only countries in which there is any significant scope for working in a private language school or institute are the Mediterranean countries of Morocco, Tunisia and Egypt.

The drive towards English extends to most parts of the continent. In March 1999, VSO is opening a new programme to teach English in Rwanda. It is already supporting an ELT programme in Mozambique, Tanzania, Eritrea, Ghana and Nigeria. Nearly a decade ago, newly independent Namibia decided to make English its official language to replace the hated Afrikaans. A demand for hundreds of native speakers, mainly at the advanced teacher-trainer level, was created overnight, which organisations like the Overseas Development Agency and VSO attempted to supply. Across southern Africa, the dominant language of business and commerce and the language of university text books is English, leaving Portuguese-speaking Mozambique out in the cold, which is why there are so many EFL teachers posted there by Skillshare Africa and VSO.

To balance the picture, it must be said that in some countries (such as Zimbabwe, Zambia and Nigeria) the demand for English teachers has fallen off in favour of science, maths and technology teachers. And continuing unrest and hostility towards the west in the Sudan means that there are few opportunities for English teachers (in a country whose government once funded hundreds of native English speakers to teach in its schools).

Even in ex-colonies of France (Morocco, Tunisia, Senegal, etc.) and of Portugal (Mozambique), English is a sought-after commodity. For example there are two British Council Teaching Centres in Francophone Cameroon (Yaounde the capital and Douala). The only other British Council Teaching Centre in Sub-Saharan Africa is in Nairobi. But the British Council has an English Language Officer in most African countries who may be willing to advise on local opportunities (or the lack thereof).

Political instability has beleaguered a few of the countries where English is in demand, such as Algeria (which is currently too dangerous for expat teachers to consider) and Liberia from which scores of American teachers had to be evacuated earlier in the decade. The situation is different in North Africa where there is relatively more stability and prosperity. Libya is more like a Middle Eastern country and indeed some oil companies employ highly qualified TEFL teachers on Saudi-style salaries.

Prospects for Teachers

Few language schools exist in most African countries and even fewer can afford to employ expatriate teachers. The British Council maintains offices in most African countries and their assessment of the prospects for teachers tallies with that sent by the Information Manager of the British Council in Mbabane, Swaziland:

> *English language is taught from a very early stage in Swaziland. As a result there are no institutes which specifically teach it. However you may want to consider the university and colleges as institutions which teach English, even though it is at an advanced level.*

Similarly in Namibia, the Language Centre at the University of Namibia (Private Bag 13301, Windhoek) is one of the few centres in the country where English is taught.

A somewhat more promising destination is Cameroon where the ELC Manager at the British Council in Douala (Som's Building, 6 Rue Drouot, Douala, B.P. 12801) says that they take on qualified teachers of English from time to time. Anyone with the CELTA or DELTA would stand a chance of finding work. The main office in Yaounde (which has just moved premises) can be contacted at BP 818 (e-mail british.council@camnet.com) while the address of the Teaching Centre in Douala (the commercial capital of the country) is Immeuble Soms, 6 rue Drouot, Douala. Other teaching institutes in Douala include the American Language Center and the Linguistic Centre, while in Yaounde, the Pilot Centre and the American Center run English courses. Government-run organisations are likely to allow only Cameroonians to teach and most schools are so small and disorganised anyway that they would not be in a position to employ a native speaker.

Because a high proportion of teaching opportunities in Africa is in secondary schools rather than private language institutes, a teaching certificate is often a prerequisite. Missionary societies have played a dominant role in Africa's modern history, so many teachers are recruited through religious organisations, asking for a Christian commitment even for secular jobs.

Apart from work with aid or missionary agencies, there are quite a few opportunities for students and people in their gap year to teach in Africa. Students and other travellers have also stumbled upon chances to teach on an informal basis.

FIXING UP A JOB

Placement Organisations

The following organisations recruit EFL teachers for schools in Africa. These postings are normally regarded as 'voluntary' since local wages are paid usually along with free housing. In some cases a substantial placement fee must be paid. See the chapter *Finding a Job* for further details of the general agencies.

Africa & Asia Venture Ltd., 10 Market Place, Devizes, Wilts. SN10 1HT. Tel: (01380) 729009. Fax: (01380) 720060. E-mail: aventure@aol.com. Places school leavers (primarily) as assistant teachers in primary and secondary schools in Kenya, Uganda, Zimbabwe and Malawi, normally for one term. Programme includes in-country orientation course, insurance, allowances paid during work attachment and organised safari at end of four months. The 1999 participation fee is about £2,075 plus air fares.

BUNAC, 16 Bowling Green Lane, London EC1R 0BD. Tel: 0171-251 2372. Fax: 0171-251 0215. Teach in Ghana programme (see section on Ghana below). Also have Work South Africa programme which allows participants to look for jobs after arrival, including as TEFL teachers.

Concern Worldwide, 248-250 Lavender Hill, London SW11 1LJ. Tel: 0171-738 1033. Fax: 0171-738 1032. Main office is in Ireland (52-55 Lower Camden St, Dublin 2; 1-475 4162). Recruits mostly qualified teachers over 21 for a range of development projects including education in Ethiopia, Mozambique, Tanzania, Uganda and Rwanda.

Daneford Trust, PO Box 11190, London E2 6LB. Tel/fax: 0171-729 1928. Youth education charity which sends students and school leavers resident in London (only) to Botswana, Namibia and Zimbabwe for a minimum of three months. Volunteers raise at least £2,000 towards costs with help from the Trust. Must be committed to ongoing development of overseas experience in local community in UK.

International Cooperation for Development (ICD), Unit 3, Canonbury Yard, 190a New North Road, London N1 7BJ. Tel: 0171-354 0883. This Roman Catholic programme has very occasional professional teaching positions in Namibia and Zimbabwe.

Link Africa, Orwell House, Orwell Road, Cambridge CB4 4WY. Tel: (01223) 506665. Fax: (01223) 578665. Education development charity with programmes in Kenya and South Africa. Short-term placements (6-7 weeks) in July/August for qualified, experienced teachers to teach primary and secondary school children.

Peace Corps, Room 803E, 1111 20th St NW, Washington DC 20526. Tel: 1-800-424-8580 (toll-free). Volunteers teach on 2-year assignments in many African countries.

Project Trust, Hebridean Centre, Ballyhough, Isle of Coll, Argyll PA78 6TE. Tel: (01879) 230444. Fax: (01879) 230357. Sends some school leavers (aged 17-19) to teach (often science rather than English) in schools in Namibia, Egypt, Uganda, Botswana and rural Zimbabwe. Participants must fund-raise to cover part of the cost of the placement, at present about £3,250.

St. David's (Africa) Trust, St. David's House, Rectory Road, Crickhowell, Powys NP8 1DW. Tel/fax: 01873 810665. 3-4 month placements in Ghana and Morocco for a few gap year students to work with needy children.

Students Partnership Worldwide (SPW), Westminster School, 17 Dean's Yard, London SW1P 3PB. Tel: 0171-222 0138/976 8070. Fax: 0171-233 0008/963 1006. E-mail: spwuk@gn.apc.org. Places school leavers for 6-10 months in secondary schools in Tanzania, Zimbabwe, Uganda, South Africa and Namibia.

Skillshare Africa, 126 New Walk, Leicester LE1 7JA. Tel: (0116) 254 1862. E-mail: skillshare-uk@geo2.poptel.org.uk. Registered charity has vacancies for volunteer teachers to work for two years in southern Africa (Lesotho, Botswana, Mozambique, Swaziland, Namibia and South Africa). Pay approximately £500 per month plus flights, accommodation, insurance, etc.

Teaching Abroad, Gerrard House, Rustington, West Sussex BN16 1AW Tel: (01903) 859911. Fax: (01903) 785779. E-mail: teaching_abroad@garlands.uk.com. Work placements in Ghanaian schools (see section below).

VSO, 317 Putney Bridge Road, London SW15 2PN. Tel: 0181-780 7550. Sends teachers to Mozambique, Tanzania, Eritrea, Ghana, Nigeria and Rwanda. Also advertising for secondary school teachers for Malawi with degree and TEFL experience.

Teachers for Africa, 5040 E Shea Blvd, 260, Phoenix, AZ 85254, USA. Tel: (602) 443-1800. Fax: (602) 443-1824. Arranges for American educationalists and others with specialised skills (the majority of participants have graduate degrees) to spend an academic year working in educational institutions in sub-Saharan Africa. Monthly stipend of up to US$1,000.

WorldTeach, Institute for International Development, 14 Story St, Cambridge MA 02138, USA. Tel: (617) 495-5527. Fax: (617) 495-1599. Non-profit organisation which recruits volunteers to teach English for one year in Namibia. Volunteers pay about $3,500 for air fares, orientation and insurance.

Religious Organisations

The following missionary societies place English teachers in Africa; in many cases a Christian commitment is a prerequisite:

Christians Abroad, 1 Stockwell Green, London SW9 9HP. Tel: 0171-346 5950. Fax: 0171-346 5951. Send teachers to Tanzania.

Action Partners, Bawtry Hall, Bawtry, Doncaster DN10 6JH. Tel: 01302 710570. Places qualified teachers in Christian schools in Africa, e.g. Egypt, Nigeria and Sudan.

Africa Inland Mission, 2 Vorley Road, Archway, London N19 5HE. Tel: 0171-281 1184. Also: Box 178, Pearl River, NY 10965. Have a few opportunities from time to time for evangelical Christians to teach English in East African nations, i.e. Kenya, Uganda, Tanzania and the Comoros Islands.

United Society for the Propagation of the Gospel, Partnership House, 157 Waterloo Road, London SE1 8XA. Tel: 0171-928 8681. Fax: 0171-928 2371. A few English teaching vacancies in Malawi, Tanzania and Zimbabwe. Unqualified teachers accepted but must have Christian commitment.

Government Recruitment

The Embassies of some African nations may be able to advise prospective teachers on the likelihood of finding jobs in their country. These days, they rarely become directly involved in recruitment, but will refer enquirers to the Ministry of Education. For example the Zimbabwe High Commission used to recruit teachers itself but now only provides the address of the Ministry of Education. Making direct contact with the Ministry after arrival is bound to be more productive than sending off letters from home. Mary Hall who worked for a year as a nurse in Uganda met quite a few European teachers, some without formal qualifications. She recommends contacting the Ministry of Education in Kampala.

One of the changes that majority rule has brought to South Africa is a decentralisation of government departments such as the Department of National Education. The nine provinces of South Africa are gradually assuming greater responsibility for education, and may be able to assist teachers.

Until recently, the charitable organisation Christians Abroad administered a major educational programme in Malawi in cooperation with the British government. But a change in priorities resulted in the withdrawal of government funding and a cancellation of the programme. However VSO continues to recruit people with a degree and TEFL Certificate for Malawian secondary schools. Volunteers for its new programme in Rwanda need have only a BA and preferably a TEFL certificate but experience is not required.

USIA Programmes

The United States Information Agency (USIA) has English Teaching Programs at its Cultural Centers in a number of African countries (in addition to North Africa treated separately below), though it must be said that this operation has been shrinking and several outlets have been closed in the past few years (e.g. Cameroon), though several are listed in the Directory. Virtually all hiring of teachers takes place locally, so speculative applications from overseas are seldom welcome. American Cultural Centers not listed at the end of this chapter are:

Burkina: American Language Center, 01 B.P. 539, Ouagadougou-01, Burkina Faso. Tel: 30 63 60. Fax: 31 52 73.

Burundi: American Cultural Center, B.P. 810, 20-22 Chee P. L. Rwagasore, Bujumbura, Burundi. Tel: 22 33 12/22 56 46. Fax: 22 45 61.

Congo: USIS English Language Program, B.P. 2053, Brazzaville, Congo. Tel: 83 83 94. Fax: 83 46 90.

Madagascar: English Teaching Program, 4 Lalana Dr., Razafindratandra Ambohidahy, Antananarivo, Madagascar. Tel: 22 02 38. Fax: 22 13 97.

Togo: Centre Culturel Americain, Rues Pelletier et Vauban, B.P. 852, Lomé, Togo. Tel: 212 166. Fax: 217 794.

Zaire: Zaire-American Language Institute, ACC, B.P. 8622, Kinshasa 1, Zaire. Tel: 88 43604, ext. 2497/2155.

If teachers (British as well as American) are prepared to travel to an African capital for an interview, they may well get taken on, as happened to the director of one English Language Program:

> *Work in an American Cultural Center is a great way to start off. I myself did it five years ago and am now running a programme. It allows a person to work in Africa but also provides up-to-date material which teachers in the national programmes are often forced to go without. Classes are small and the hours are not too heavy but can usually be increased depending on the capabilities of the teacher. We also do outside programmes in specialised institutions and thus give teachers experience in ESP (hotels, oil companies, Ministries). People with degrees in EFL are very much in demand.*

Miscellaneous Opportunities

Commercial agencies have few clients in Africa. One exception is *Worldwide*

Educational Services which recruits for English-medium colleges in Egypt, and ELS Language Centres/Middle East, PO Box 3079, Abu Dhabi, UAE (Elsme@emirates.net.ae) which employs native speaker teachers in Cairo and a not-yet-opened operation in Tunis.

At the opposite end of the spectrum, grass roots voluntary organisations may have teaching positions. One community which welcomes volunteers is the village of Galoya in The Gambia. A local landowner Omar Drammeh writes that he is 'ready in position at all times in inviting serious interested volunteers to teach English in the village.' Details are available from Mr. Omar Drammeh, c/o Edirssa Kujabi, Gambia Airways, Banjul International Airport, Gambia (fax +220 472277). Another possibility for teaching in the Gambia is arranged by the Marlborough Brandt Group (Wiltshire World Studies Centre, 1a London Road, Marlborough, Wilts. SN8 1PH).

Eight-month attachments to village primary schools in the district of Mshiri in Tanzania are possible through the auspices of the Village Education Project (Kilimanjaro), c/o Mrs. Branson, Mint Cottage, Prospect Road, Sevenoaks, Kent TN13 3UA. The cost to the volunteers is £1,500 plus insurance.

On the Spot

The best chances of picking up language teaching work on the spot are in North Africa, in Egypt, Morocco or Tunisia (treated separately below). Language schools are thriving in South Africa staffed in large measure by English-speaking South Africans but also by foreigners (see entry for *Cape Studies*) or try Cape Communication Centre (66 Strand Street, Cape Town 8001). Tourists can enter South Africa on a tourist visa for three months, renewable for a further three at an office of the Department of Home Affairs.

Opportunities crop up in very obscure corners of the continent. For example EU nationals are entitled to work in Réunion, a *département* of France between Madagascar and Mauritius. Apparently there is a market for freelance teachers; consider advertising in the papers *Quotidien* and *SIR*.

PROBLEMS AND REWARDS

If teachers in Finland and Chile suffer from culture shock, teachers in rural Africa often find themselves struggling to cope at all. Whether it is the hassle experienced by women teachers in Muslim North Africa or the loneliness of life in a rural West African village, problems proliferate. Anyone who has fixed up a contract should try to gather as much up-to-date information as possible before departure, preferably by attending some kind of orientation programme or briefing. Otherwise local customs can come as a shock, for example finding yourself being bowed to (as Malawians do to anyone in a superior job). On a more basic level, you will need advice on how to cope with climatic extremes. Even Cairo can be unbearably hot in the summer (and surprisingly rainy and chilly in January/February).

One unexpected problem is being accorded too much respect, as Mary Hall describes:

> *A white person is considered to be the be-all and end-all of everyone's problems for whatever reason. It's quite difficult to live with this image...Stare and stare again, never a moment to yourself. I'd like to say the novelty wore off but it never did. Obviously adaptability has to be one of the main qualities. We had no running water, intermittent electricity and a lack of such niceties as cheese and chocolate.*

A certain amount of deprivation is almost inevitable; for example teachers, especially volunteers, can seldom afford to shop in the pricey expatriate stores and so will have to be content with the local diet, typically a staple cereal such as millet usually made into a kind of stodgy porridge, plus some cooked greens, tinned fish or meat and fruit. The cost of living in some African cities like Libreville and Douala is in fact very high, and a teaching wage does not normally permit a luxurious lifestyle.

Health is obviously a major concern to anyone headed for Africa. The fear of HIV-contaminated blood or needles in much of central Africa prompts many teachers to outfit themselves with a complete expat medical kit before leaving home (see Introduction). Malaria is rife and there is an alarming amount of mosquito resistance to the most common prophylactics, so this too must be sorted out with a tropical diseases expert before departure.

The visa situation differs from country to country of course but is often a headache. Whereas in Cameroon it is not really necessary to obtain a work permit, in Ethiopia it is much more problematic.

If all that Africa could offer was a contest with malaria and a diet of porridge, no one would consider teaching there. But anyone who has seen movies like *Out of Africa* or *The English Patient* can imagine how the continent holds people in thrall. A chance to see the African bush, to climb the famous peaks of Kilimanjaro or Kenya, to frequent the colourful markets, these are the pleasures of Africa which so many people who have worked there find addictive.

Egypt

Despite some devastating attacks on tourists by Islamic fundamentalists, there is anything but hostility to the English language in Egypt. Of Egyptians who want to learn English, a large percentage are business people, though there is also a demand among university students and school children. Many young Egyptians who aspire to work in their country's tourist industry want to learn English. Students at tourism training centres like the one in Luxor might be looking for some private tuition from a native speaker.

At one end of the spectrum there are the two British Council Teaching Centres in Cairo and Alexandria and the International Language Institute in Cairo affiliated to International House. At the other there are plenty of dubious establishments. Whereas you will need a professional profile for the former, back street schools will be less fussy. The British Council in Cairo has a list of English medium schools in Cairo plus a short list of TEFL establishments, several of which are in the suburb of Dokki. The Alexandria Teaching Centre was recently advertising for teachers with at least a CELTA or equivalent and two years' overseas experience; starting dates were every other month. Another company advertising for teachers to work in the petroleum industry was the British Language Institute (tel/fax 2-347 0481).

While visiting Cairo, Kate Ferguson from Australia was handed a leaflet advertising jobs with the International Language Learning Institute (ILLI) at 34 Talaat Harb Street in the centre of the city. They were appealing for native speakers of English (as well as French and German) to teach for E£10 per hour. Training, accommodation, medical care and a one-year work permit were all promised free of charge. When Kate went to make initial enquiries, she was surprised to find not a dodgy-looking exploitative business but a professional-looking outfit.

Writing in the fortnightly newspaper *Overseas Jobs Express,* David Stanford describes his job-hunt:

> *I had had a chance conversation with a teacher in a Jerusalem youth hostel. He told me the demand for qualified and unqualified native speakers was still high in Cairo, so I put my faith in his advice and bought a cheap single from Gatwick to Cairo. On arrival I had £300 in my pocket, more than enough to support myself for the first month. I made a list of schools to contact and found success on the first day. I gave my details to the receptionist at an evening classes institute in central Cairo and in the afternoon I was summoned from my hotel room to see the manager of the institute. He hired me to start on Monday.*

Cairo seems to be a city where work seeks out the casual teacher rather than the other way round. Taxi drivers and hotel staff may ask you, unprompted, if you are available to teach. Most of these are genuine offers but it is best (especially for women) to be cautious. Most job-seekers find that potential bosses are not as interested in their educational background and experience as in how much confidence they can project. It is not unknown for an interview to take place over a game of chess and plenty of glasses of tea so that your general demeanour can be assessed. Jobs seem to be available year-round, so there is no right or wrong time to arrive.

Language schools are not all located in central Cairo but also in the leafy prosperous residential areas like Heliopolis, Maadi or Zamalek. These are also the best areas to look for private clients as Ian McArthur found:

> *In Cairo I sought to work as a private English tutor. I made a small poster, written in English and Arabic, with the help of my hotel owner. I drew the framework of a Union Jack at the top, got 100 photocopies and then meticulously coloured in the flags. The investment cost me £3. I put the posters up around Cairo, concentrating on affluent residential and business districts. I ended up teaching several Egyptian businessmen, who were difficult to teach since they hated being told what to do.*

A simpler way of advertising your availability to teach might be to place an advert in the expatriate monthly *Cairo Today* (24 Syria St, Mohandasin, Cairo; 2-349 0986) or the fortnightly *Maadi Messenger* (Port Said Road and Road 17, Maadi, Cairo; 2-351 2755). The American University, centrally located at the eastern end of Tahrir Square, is a good place to find work contacts. Also try the notice boards at the Community Services Administration (CSA, Road 21, Maadi, Cairo) where a range of adult education courses for expats is offered. If you do decide to advertise your services as a freelance tutor, it might be a good idea to rent a post office box from a business centre (e.g. the IBA Center in Garden City).

It is not only Egyptian businessmen accustomed to being in control who present problems to the teacher. Bryn Thomas describes his Egyptian pupils at the International Language Institute in the northwest suburb of Sahafeyeen (which now teaches only Arabic) as 'rowdy and sometimes a little over-enthusiastic'. Having just obtained a Cambridge/RSA Certificate in London, Bryn went to visit some friends in Cairo and was immediately offered a three-month summer contract where they were desperate for a teacher. He had to adapt his lessons to please both the ebullient Egyptian youths and a group of shy and industrious Somalis. Bryn describes his predicament with such a mixed class:

> *Different religions, different ways of thinking and (as I learnt in my first week at the school) different modes of dress must all be taken into consideration. One of the problems that English students in this area have difficulty with is hearing the difference between B and P. The exercise for this is to hold a piece of paper in front of the mouth and repeat the letters B and P. Since more air is exhaled during the sounding of the letter P than with B, the paper should fly up when P is said, and move only a little with B. The first time I made the students do this we went round the class, first Hamid the engineer from Alexandria, then Mona who was trying to get a job at the reception in the Hilton and then we came to Magda from Mogadishu (the capital of Somalia). All the Egyptians started to laugh—her whole face apart from her eyes was covered with a yashmak. I decided that this should not impede the exercise so if the yashmak moved it was a P, and not a B!*

Wages at the less prestigious schools will probably be around E£900 per month rising to E£2,400 (gross) at ILI Heliopolis. Living expenses are cheap in Egypt and taxes low (5-7%). This may account for the fact that the Cambridge/RSA Certificate course offered by ILI Heliopolis (an IH-affiliate) is one of the cheapest available. Anyone who obtains the CELTA in Cairo is virtually guaranteed a job locally.

Most teachers enter Egypt on a tourist visa (which can be purchased at the airport) and then ask their school to help them extend it. Work permits must be applied for from the Ministry of the Interior. (Unusually, work permits are not processed by Egyptian representatives abroad.)

The paper should flutter when you sound the letter 'p'

AMIDEAST AMERICAN CULTURAL CENTER
English Teaching Program, 3 El Pharana St, Alexandria. Tel: (3) 483 1922. Fax: (3) 483 9644.
Number of teachers: 15.
Preference of nationality: North American.
Qualifications: minimum CELTA or TESOL certification.
Conditions of employment: local hire agreements. 20 h.p.w. Nine 5-week sessions per year. Students are working adults and university students.
Salary: US$8.50-$15 an hour.
Facilities/Support: good teachers' resources. No assistance with accommodation.
Recruitment: on-site recruitment only.

ELS LANGUAGE CENTERS/MIDDLE EAST
PO Box 3079, Abu Dhabi, UAE. Tel: (2) 651516. Fax: (2) 653165. E-mail: Elsme@emirates.net.ae
Number of teachers: 2-3 full-time and some part-time.
Preference of nationality: North American, though others may be acceptable.
Qualifications: MA in TESL preferred but may accept people with BA, CELTA and 3 years' experience.
Conditions of employment: 1 or 2 year contracts. 30 contact hours p.w. Full-time teachers are permitted to give private tuition. Some summer opportunities may be available.
Facilities/Support: accommodation provided. Deductions from salary made for social security contributions and tax. Standardised orientation given to all new teachers.
Recruitment: TESOL conventions and via the internet.

Ghana

As one of the most stable countries in Africa, Ghana supports several organised schemes for volunteer teachers. BUNAC's *Teach in Ghana* is described in the entry below. BUNAC also runs a more general Work in Ghana programme for three to six months on which participants can arrange teaching placements in schools and universities. (Ghanaians all learn English at school.) Teaching Abroad (see chapter *Finding a Job*) sends paying volunteers mainly to village primary schools for short-term attachments. The programme offers various starting dates and durations for a fee of £1,295 excluding flights to Accra.

From the US, volunteers are recruited into the International Teacher Exchange Programme by Student and Youth Services Ghana (395 E Clinton Avenue, Roosevelt, NY 11575; 516-377-1417/fax 516-546-8538). About five participants teach at the privately run Royal Preparatory School in Apam, central Ghana. The school year begins in February. Another programme in Ghana was launched in January 1999 by Cross Cultural Solutions (47 Potter Avenue, New Rochelle, NY 10801; 914-632-0022/ 800-380-4777) whereby volunteers are placed in villages around the town of Ho in the eastern Plains of Ghana to teach English in village schools (among other projects). The programme fee of $1,850 covers all expenses while in Ghana but not airfare.

The British Council in Accra (PO Box 771) lists three English teaching centres:
The Language Centre, University of Ghana, Legon (21-500381)
Institute of Languages, PO Box M67, Accra (21-221052/221092)
Centre of Language and Professional Studies, PO Box 4501, Accra

TEACH IN GHANA
BUNAC, 16 Bowling Green Lane, London EC1R 0QH. Tel: 0171-251 3472. Fax: 0171-251 0215. Web-site: www.bunac.org
Number of teachers: limited number.
Preference of nationality: British only.
Qualifications: less than 26 years of age. Must have graduated in previous two years in English, modern languages, geography, maths, sciences, accounting or design and technology. Some classroom experience required.
Conditions of employment: 9 month positions from August.
Salary: about $50 per month. Total cost of programme is about £1,350 including 12-month return flight.
Facilities/Support: rented accommodation or homestay provided. Back up provided by sponsoring partner organisation Student & Youth Travel Organisation (SYTO) in Accra. Compulsory insurance arranged by BUNAC (included in fee quoted above).
Recruitment: applications must be accompanied by £500 programme deposit. Interviews in UK. Applications forwarded to Ministry of Education in Ghana. Balance of fees must be paid by end of June.

Kenya

Kenya is another country which has a chronic shortage of secondary school teachers. The worst shortages are in Western Province. English is the language of instruction in Kenyan schools, so not knowing Swahili need not be an impossible barrier. However the Kenyan Ministry of Education restricts jobs in the state sector to those who have a university degree, teaching certification and at least one year of professional teaching experience. The few private language institutes that there are in Nairobi (two of which are included in the Directory) are not subject to this restriction. The British Council in Nairobi (which has its own teaching operation) may be able to provide a contact address for the National Association of English Teachers.

According to the Kenyan High Commission in London, all non-Kenyan citizens who wish to work must be in possession of a work permit issued by the Principal Immigration Officer, Department of Immigration, PO Box 30191, Nairobi, before they can take up paid or unpaid work. It is not certain that immigration regulations would be strictly enforced in the case of native English speakers looking for teaching work on the spot. Certainly in the past it was possible to fix up a teaching job by asking in the villages, preferably before terms begin in September, January and April. Be prepared to produce your CV and any diplomas and references on headed paper.

Also ascertain before accepting a post whether or not the school can afford to pay a salary, especially if it is a *Harrambee* school, i.e. non-government, self-help schools in rural areas. A cement or mud hut with a thatched or tin roof will normally be provided for the teacher's accommodation plus a local salary which would be just enough to live on provided you don't want to buy too much peanut butter or cornflakes in the city. Living conditions will be primitive with no running water or electricity in the majority of cases. The Kenyan version of maize porridge is called *Ugali*. In Daisy Waugh's book *A Small Town in Africa* she describes how when she arrived at the village of Isiolo (a few miles from Nairobi) where she had arranged to teach, she was told that they didn't need any teachers and there were no pupils. She patiently waited and five weeks into term, her class arrived.

People who choose to teach in Kenya do it for love not money. In the words of Ermon O. Kamara, PhD, former Director of the *American Universities Preparation & Learning Centre*:

> Candidates must view being in Kenya as a holiday with pay. The cost of living and corresponding local salaries sound quite low to foreigners. Consequently they must think of the opportunities to enjoy Kenya's beaches, mountains and game parks as well as experiencing a new and interesting culture. During weekends and holidays, one can travel the breadth of Kenya. Also the proximity to other countries in East and Southern Africa permits a traveller to see a good deal of our continent.

School vacations take place in December, April and August.

Global Routes in the US offer 12-week voluntary internships to students who teach English and other subjects in village schools in Kenya. There are no specific requirements apart from an ability to afford the programme fee of $3,550 for the summer and nearly $4,000 for the spring and autumn (excluding air fares).

AMERICAN UNIVERSITIES PREPARATION & LEARNING CENTRE

PO Box 14842, (Chiromo Lane, Westlands Road), Nairobi. Tel: (2) 741764. Fax: (2) 741690.

Number of teachers: 4.

Preference of nationality: American, Canadian, British, Australian.

Qualifications: BA (English)/TEFL qualification; experience preferred.

Conditions of employment: 1 year renewable contracts. Daytime only. Students aged 16-40.

Salary: based on local rates.

Facilities/Support: accommodation provided and paid for by school. Training provided.

Recruitment: local interviews if possible or telephone interview.

Contact: Martha Muchori, Director.

THE LANGUAGE CENTER LTD
PO Box 40661, (Ndemi Close, Off Ngong Road), Nairobi. Tel: (2) 569531/569532/570610/570610/570612. Fax: (2) 568207/569533. E-mail: tlc@africaonline.co.ke
Number of teachers: 8-10.
Preference of nationality: British, American.
Qualifications: overseas teaching experience. University education. Cambridge/RSA CELTA and other teaching certificates desirable. Preferably aged 28-36.
Conditions of employment: 1-2 year contracts. 20 hours of work, 8.25am-12.35pm plus optional afternoon/evening work. Majority of students are adults though some children's classes offered.
Salary: based on hourly rate of 425 Kenyan shillings (US$7) for the first year.
Facilities/Support: no assistance with accommodation. Medical insurance, work permit and minimal assistance with airfares at end of contract provided. On-the-job training provided.
Recruitment: through local newspaper adverts, overseas publications and word of mouth.

PEPONI SCHOOL
PO Box 236, Ruiru, Kenya. Tel: 151-54007/54251. Fax: 151-54479. E-mail: peponi@form-net.com
Number of teachers: 16 (out of staff of 21) at this full-curriculum private boarding school.
Preference of nationality: must be conversant with British exam system.
Qualifications: full degree qualification plus teaching certificate and 4 years' experience.
Conditions of employment: by law, 2 year contracts (renewable). 33 40-minute lessons per week and exams and curricular help.
Salary: 80,000-95,000 Kenyan shillings per month (gross) less a third in tax and contributions.
Facilities/Support: on-site accommodation provided. School arranges work permits. Inset training meetings every term.
Recruitment: adverts and interviews in UK.
Contact: D. J. Marshall, Headmaster.

Morocco

Although Morocco is a Francophone country, English is increasingly a requirement for entrance to university or high ranking jobs, and there is increasing demand from the business communities of the main cities. Like so many African countries, Morocco has sought to improve the standards of education for its nationals so that almost all teaching jobs in schools and universities are now filled by Moroccans. But outside the state system there is a continuing demand for native speakers.

The Moroccan Ministry of Labour stipulates that the maximum number of foreign staff in any organisation cannot exceed 50%. It also insists that all foreign teachers have at least a university degree before they can be eligible for a work permit. Work permits are obtained after arrival by applying for authorisation from the Ministère de l'Emploi, Quartier des Ministères, Rabat. You will need copies of your diplomas, birth certificate and so on. Although a knowledge of French is not a formal requirement, it is a great asset for anyone planning to spend time in Morocco.

A number of commercial language schools employ native English speakers. The hourly rate of pay at most schools is between £5 and £7. American Language Centers are located in the main cities of Morocco. They are private institutes but are affiliated to and partially funded by the United States Information Agency. In addition to the three included in the Directory, American Language Centers are listed at the end of this section.

The voluntary organisation St. David's (Africa) Trust mentioned at the beginning of the *Africa* chapter maintains an office in Morocco: 143 Blvd. Ibrahim Roudani, Taroudant 83000 (8-850500).

LIST OF SCHOOLS

AMERICAN LANGUAGE CENTER
Rue des Nations-Unies, Cité Suisse, Agadir. Tel: (8) 821589. Fax: (8) 848272. E-mail: alcagad@marocnet.net.ma
Number of teachers: 3-6.
Preference of nationality: North Americans preferred.
Qualifications: minimum BA. Teaching experience preferable, especially overseas. MA is a plus.
Conditions of employment: 10 month contracts (October-July). Hours of teaching are 6.30pm-8.30pm Monday-Friday and 2pm-5pm Saturday.
Salary: 95-100 dirhams (gross) per hour plus medical insurance and one month paid vacation leave. 24%-44% withheld for taxes.
Facilities/Support: help teachers to find apartment; small housing stipend. Basic furniture provided. Orientation and teaching conference held each November.
Recruitment: internet and word of mouth. Phone interviews acceptable. Interviews can sometimes be arranged in US.
Contact: Tamara Atkinson, Director.

AMERICAN LANGUAGE CENTER
2 Boulevard Mohammed V, Mohammedia. Tel: (3) 326870.
Number of teachers: 2.
Preference of nationality: none.
Qualifications: minimum BA and ESL or EFL teaching.
Conditions of employment: 1 year contracts. Most teaching is in evenings. School cannot guarantee more than 15 h.p.w. (Students sign up for 30 hour course at a time).
Salary: basic rate of 61 dirhams per hour for employee with BA. Increments of 6 dirhams an hour for an EFL/ESL qualification, 10 dirhams for an MA, and 2 dirhams for each year of teaching experience (maximum of 5 years).
Facilities/Support: no assistance given with accommodation.
Recruitment: personal application from people already resident in Morocco. Interviews in US also possible.

AMERICAN LANGUAGE CENTER
4 Zankat Tanja, Rabat 10000. Tel: (7) 761269/766121/767103. Fax: (7) 767255/767447. E-mail: alcrabat@mtds.com
Number of teachers: 20 full-time.
Preference of nationality: none although mostly North American.
Qualifications: BA in arts/letters mandatory; knowledge of French or Arabic highly desirable. MA (TEFL) or TEFL qualification preferred.
Conditions of employment: 1 year renewable contracts. 20-25 h.p.w. full time. Hours of work between 8am and 10pm weekdays, 9am and 9pm Saturdays. Pupils aged from 5, mostly aged 14-35.
Salary: US$10,000-15,000 per year (gross) for October-July school year. Possibility of paid overtime. Paid sick leave and medical insurance provided.
Facilities/Support: free housing provided for 3-4 weeks while permanent accommodation is sought. Pre- and in-service training given. Free-e-mail for teachers.
Recruitment: through TESOL convention and some walk-ins. Personal interviews essential.

BRITISH CENTRE
3 rue Brahim el Amraoui, Casablanca. Tel: (2) 267019/273190. Fax: (2) 267043. E-mail: british.centre.c.@casanet.ma
Number of teachers: 7.
Preference of nationality: none.
Qualifications: CELTA or equivalent plus at least 2 years' experience.
Conditions of employment: 1 year contracts, renewable.
Salary: average 8,000 dirhams per month (net).
Facilities/Support: low-rent studio flats available. Help given with work permits. Regular seminars and workshops.
Recruitment: local interview essential.
Contact: Jeremy Morgan, Director of Studies.

BUSINESS & PROFESSIONAL ENGLISH CENTRE (BPEC)
74 rue Jean Jaurès, Casablanca. Tel: (2) 470279/470176. Fax: (2) 296861. E-mail: bpec@dounia.net.ma
Number of teachers: 4.
Preference of nationality: none.
Qualifications: all qualified and experienced EFL teachers considered. MA plus at least 2 years' teaching experience preferred. Alternatively, minimum CELTA plus 2 years' full-time experience.
Conditions of employment: 2 year renewable contracts. Normal teaching hours 4.30pm-8.30pm Monday-Friday, plus regular Saturday morning classes.
Salary: 8,000 dirhams per month (net) after deductions of 17% tax and 8% social security.
Facilities/Support: advice given on finding accommodation. Housing and furniture allowance.
Recruitment: direct application. Interviews essential (including by phone) and can sometimes be arranged abroad.
Contact: Graham Bancroft, Technical Manager.

EF ENGLISH FIRST
20 rue du Marche, Residence Benomar, Maaris, Casablanca. Tel: (2) 255174. Fax: (2) 255145.
Number of teachers: 5.
Preference of nationality: British, Canadian, Australian, American or Irish.
Qualifications: minimum university degree and certificate in EFL/ESL.
Conditions of employment: 10 month contracts. Up to 27 contact hours p.w. Teaching between 9am and 9pm Monday to Saturday.
Salary: US$900 per month plus bonus.
Facilities/Support: help with finding accommodation. Visas/work permits provided. Paid holidays. Flight costs reimbursed. Orientation on arrival and ongoing training. Variety of resources.
Recruitment: directly through school or through English First offices in London and Boston.

Other Schools to Try

ALC, 1 Place de la Fraternité, Casablanca (2-275270/fax 2-207457).
ALC, 2 rue Ibn Mouaz, B.P. 2136, Fez (5-931608).
ALC, 2 boulevard El Kadissia, Kénitra (7-366884).
ALC, 3 Impasse du Moulin di Guéliz, Marrakesh (4-447259).
ALC, 21 rue Antsirab, 4th Floor, Meknes (5-523636).
ALC, 1 Rue Emsallah, Tangier (9-933616).
ALC, 14 Bab El Oukla, Tetouan (9-963308).
Bénédict School of English, 124 Ave Hassan II, Ben Slimane (3-290-957/fax 3-328472)

Bénédict School of English, Quartier de la Colline, rue 19 No. 79, Casablanca/
    Mohammedia (3-31 5084).
English Institute, 34 Avenue Lalla Yacout, Casablanca
IBA-Langues, 33 rue de Metz, Casablanca 20 100
London School of English, 10 Avenue des F.A.R., Casablanca
Ecole de Langues des F.A.R., Avenue de la Résistance, Rabat
Institute for Language and Communication Studies, 29 rue l'Oukaimeden, Agdal,
    Rabat
International Language Centre, 2 rue Tihama, Rabat (7-709718). One of the main
    centres of English but relies mainly on part-time staff, already resident in Rabat.

Tunisia

Like its neighbour in the Maghreb, Tunisia is turning away from the language of its
former colonial master France. Although many of the young generation speak fluent
French because they have been taught it in school, teenagers share the goal of making
English their second language. People may be interested in paying you for lessons,
even though you plan to be in the country for a relatively short time, as Roger Musker
was in the winter of 1998:

> *I decided to take a month off work as a kind of sabbatical and, if well planned, at no
> cost. I found all young people in Tunisia keen to practise and speak English whenever
> possible.*
>   *I had one good contact in Sousse, who worked for the Tunisian Tourist Agency. I
> wrote to him from England and he replied that he could line up students on my
> arrival, which included himself and his ten year old daughter (who turned out to be
> my best student). At their house I was plied with extremely sweet tea and sticky cakes
> which you are obliged to eat. Altogether I had eight keen fee-paying students
> including a blind telephone operator, a teacher of English on a revision course and
> students from the Bourguiba Institute at Sousse University, which claims to be the
> second oldest university in the world. For the latter it was necessary to get permission
> from the Ministry of Education via the headmaster.*
>   *Every day I tutored 8-10am and 5-7pm. The hourly rate was 15 Tunisian dinars
> (nearly £8), allowing me to just about cover basic costs and at the same time have a
> working holiday. Even without the contact and knowing Arabic, work is there for the
> asking. It just takes initiative. Go to any official institute, the tourism or municipal
> offices, demonstrate your availability and enthusiasm, give them your contact
> number and await replies.*

The University of Tunis also has a Bourguiba Institute of Modern Languages
(Université de Tunis, 47 Av. de la Liberté, 1002 Tunis-Belvedere; 1-282418) though
they do not enter into correspondence with prospective teachers. If in the capital Tunis,
it might also be worth tracking down the USIA-affiliated teaching programme
Amideast (1-790559).

Zimbabwe

When Zimbabwe became independent on 18th April 1980, it inherited an education
system which was unfairly biassed towards the white population at the expense of the
black. Since then the government has worked hard to redress this imbalance by
building more schools and introducing 'hot seating', whereby the same building houses
two schools, one from 7am to noon and an afternoon sitting from noon to 5pm. One
feature which has remained the same is that English remains the principal medium of
instruction.

Zimbabwe has a serious shortage of teachers, particularly at secondary school level. Despite the fact that the government has set up teacher training colleges in an effort to increase the ratio of home-produced teachers, many are still recruited overseas, mainly through the principal voluntary agencies like VSO. Adult night schools have also been established and native speakers may be able to find part-time evening work to supplement their income.

Most of the hiring of English teachers for schools in Zimbabwe is carried out either by the Zimbabwean Government (through their diplomatic representatives overseas, primarily in London) or by voluntary agencies. The Zimbabwe High Commission in London (429 Strand, London WC2R OSA; 0171-836 7755/fax 0171-379 1167) once recruited large numbers of British teachers on three-year contracts to teach English as well as the sciences, maths, geography, French and technical subjects. However now they merely refer enquirers to the Zimbabwe Ministry of Education (PO Box CY121, Causeway, Harare). The main qualification is a degree in the subject to be taught, though naturally they prefer a teaching qualification as well.

It is feasible to go to Zimbabwe on a three-month tourist visa and apply for a work permit as a teacher when you are out there. However, the red tape can be infuriating, especially if your holiday visa is rapidly running out. It is better to fix up a job beforehand if possible.

British and American visitors do not need a visa for holidays in Zimbabwe, but in order to work they need a residence permit and a temporary work permit. These must be arranged directly through the Department of Immigration in Harare with the help of your prospective employer. Overseas candidates who apply direct to the Ministry of Education need the following documents: birth certificate, marriage certificate where applicable, proof of qualifications and previous experience, satisfactory medical certificate including a radiologist's certificate of freedom from active pulmonary tuberculosis. The red tape may seem daunting, but perseverance will produce results.

Secondary school students work towards the Cambridge Overseas Examinations (GCSE and A level). Although by secondary level all lessons are supposed to be in English, many pupils still have problems with the language, especially in the rural areas where their exposure has been limited. Here the teaching often amounts to EFL. Unlike Britain there is no screening process for exam candidates, other than the ability to pay for the exam fee, so you may well find yourself taking a remedial student through a GCSE exam which they have no hope of passing. Adaptability is an essential quality for teachers. Yet students are much more enthusiastic and well-motivated than their British counterparts.

Judy Fletcher worked in Zimbabwe for over three years and summarises her experiences:

> Zimbabwe is a very exciting place to be; things are changing and developing fast. The people are very friendly once you have shown that you are not a 'Rhodi' (a white Zimbabwean who still wishes it was Rhodesia). The music scene is also very exciting, particularly in the township bars, and the landscape wherever you are is stunning. There is a very strong expatriate network, especially in the cities, but for anybody who really wants to experience Zimbabwe rather than an artificially British lifestyle, this should be avoided as much as possible. Venture into the townships and the rural areas, mix with the people who live there, and you will find Zimbabwe a difficult place to leave.

South Africa

CAPE STUDIES LANGUAGE SCHOOL
100 Main Road, Sea Point, PO Box 4425, Cape Town 8000, South Africa. Tel: (21) 439 0999. Fax: (21) 439 3130. E-mail: capestud@iafrica.com. Web-site: http:// www.capestudies.co.za
Number of teachers: 10.

Preference of nationality: any but preferably those with permanent residency in South Africa.
Qualifications: TEFL experience.
Conditions of employment: 3 month contracts. Hours 8.30am-2.50pm.
Salary: R20 per lesson plus R4 per student.
Facilities/Support: assistance with finding accommodation.
Recruitment: personal interview necessary.
Contact: Jens U. Bauch.

Sudan

SUDAN VOLUNTEER PROGRAMME
34 Estelle Road, London NW3 2JY. Tel/fax: 0171-485 8619
Number of teachers: small voluntary programme.
Preference of nationality: native speakers of English resident in Britain. Passport cannot show evidence of travel to Isreal.
Qualifications: graduates and undergraduates with experience of travelling abroad, preferably in the Middle East. TEFL certificate and knowledge of Arabic helpful but not required. Must be able to tolerate anti-malarial drugs.
Conditions of employment: 7 week summer programme and three month winter programme departing late November. Schools and colleges mostly located in Kharoum area.
Salary: modest living expenses provided and insurance covered.
Facilities/Support: volunteers must pay for their airfare (approx. £410) plus other expenses, estimated about £140.
Recruitment: word of mouth mainly. Application form should be accompanied by £5 administrative fee (non-returnable). Selection interviews and compulsory briefing in UK. Candidates must ask two referees to support their application.
Contact: David Wolton.

Tanzania

INTERNATIONAL LANGUAGES ORIENTATION SERVICES
Oysterbay, Karume Road, PO Box 6995, Dar es Salaam, Tanzania. Tel: (51) 667159/450097. Mobile: 0812 786 240. Fax: (51) 112752/4. E-mail: ilos-tz@ud.co.tz
Number of teachers: 75 in six centres countrywise: Dar es Salaam, Arusha, Zanzibar, Mwanza, Morogoro and Iringa.
Preference of nationality: British, American, Canadian, Australian.
Qualifications: bilingual graduates with TEFL experience or speciality.
Conditions of employment: 2 year renewable contracts. Programmes offered range from kindergarten, primary and secondary school to adult.
Salary: US$300 per month (gross) less 10% for tax and contributions.
Facilities/Support: assistance given with furnished accommodation. Paid work permit. Training workshops and cultural/Kiswahili language orientation.
Recruitment: interviews essential and are sometimes held in UK and US.

ASIA

Although the English language is not a universal passport to employment, especially in these times of economic hardship for many individuals and companies in the Far East, it can certainly be put to good use in many Asian countries. Conditions and remuneration will differ wildly between industrialised countries like Japan, Korea and Taiwan with their western-style economies, and those of developing countries like China, Nepal and Thailand, where both wages and the standard of living are lower.

Both Princeton and Stanford Universities run voluntary programmes in various Asian countries including some TEFL teaching. Stanford's Volunteers in Asia programme has been running since 1963. Every year VIA sends more than 40 volunteer English teachers to Indonesia, Laos, Vietnam and China on short and longer term assignments. Details are available from VIA, Stanford University, PO Box 4543, Stanford, CA 94309, USA (650-723-3228/e-mail: via@igc.apc.org/www.volasia.org). For information about the Princeton programme, contact Princeton-in-Asia, 224 Palmer Hall, Princeton, NJ 08544 (609-258-3657/fax 609-258-08544/e-mail pia@phoenix.princeton.edu/www.princeton.edu/-pia). They place about 65 intern teachers in China, Hong Kong, Indonesia, Japan, Korea, Laos, Singapore and Vietnam; applications must be accompanied by a $30 fee and be submitted by the beginning of December.

Recruitment organisations like *Saxoncourt* and *EF English First* are active in the region. A couple of commercial recruitment agencies specialise in placing ELT-trained teachers in Asian countries. For example *APA Consultancy* (Suite 32, Nevilles Court, Dollis Hill Lane, London NW2 6HG; 0181-452 7836) fills a large number of vacancies in Thailand and Taiwan. OEE Recruitment (PO Box 274, Highland, WI 53543, USA; tel/fax 608-929-4994) is a new agency which has just been set up by an American, Peter McGuire, who taught in a range of Asian countries. He has links with language teaching organisations in Taiwan, China, the Philippines and Korea.

Specialist books about teaching in Asia may be of interest, particularly *Teaching in South-East Asia* by Nuala O'Sullivan (In Print Publishing, 1997) which costs £9.95 from Bailey Ltd. (Learoyd Road, New Romney, Kent TN29 8XV). Small advertisements in the US magazine *Transitions Abroad* for a company which promises to advise enquirers on how to teach conversational English in Japan, Taiwan and Korea might be worth following up; the contact number is 517-324-3123.

Perhaps it is symbolic that voluntary and religious organisations are becoming more active in the provision of English in the most prosperous nations. For example at the time of writing the countries for which *Christians Abroad* was most energetically seeking teachers are Japan, Hong Kong and China.

China

A prominent Japanese politician was recently quoted as saying the 21st century belongs to China. One of the ways it is preparing itself for the new millennium is to learn the language of the West. One of the first signs of China's softening towards the West in the late 1970s was the welcome it extended to English language teachers. Two decades later there are thousands of native speakers teaching at academic institutions around the country and a new middle class who aspire to send their children for private tuition. You might have expected the novelty to have worn off, but the People's Republic still welcomes English teachers in large numbers.

The legacy of the Cultural Revolution, when access to foreign culture was forbidden, has left a great many Chinese with an absorbing fascination for the English language and all things Western. One estimate has been given that there are 450 million English language learners in China, due in large measure to the fact that English is compulsory for school pupils from the age of 9. Many street and shop signs in the capital and other major cities are written in English as well as Chinese, though most Beijing citizens can say nothing in English apart from 'Tiananmen Square.' A great many students and teachers are very keen to improve their English to Cambridge Proficiency standard in the hope of being chosen to study overseas. Others are simply curious. But all are eager to learn, even if the style of learning to which they have become accustomed can be difficult for foreign teachers to cope with.

The other major problem which teachers encounter and which can wear down even the most enthusiastic China buff is the bureaucracy. It is top-heavy, all-powerful and often strikingly inefficient. All teachers admit that working in China is exhausting, but most also find the experience fascinating.

Prospects for Teachers

Any educated native speaker of English should be able to find a job at a school, college or university in China. As an example, the recently updated list of English Language Schools from the British Council in Beijing includes about 50 addresses. Having a degree and any teaching experience is useful, but not much importance is attached to TEFL qualifications.

The Chinese government classifies teachers either as Foreign Experts (FEs) or Foreign Teachers (FTs). Foreign Experts are expected to have an MA in a relevant area (English, Linguistics, TEFL/TESOL, etc.) and some teaching experience at the tertiary level. Foreign Teachers are normally less than 25 and have only a university degree. The designated status FE or FT brings various privileges and conditions as described below. It is almost impossible for a non-graduate to work in a university, including students on exchange schemes likes those run by organisations like *GAP Activity Projects* and *Project Trust*. Instead these younger teachers are normally placed in middle schools (public secondary schools, often boarding schools).

A large proportion of foreigners are employed in Beijing but there are many opportunities in the provinces as well, especially for FTs. The more remote the area or the more hostile the climate, the easier it will be to find a job. Many vacancies for both FEs and FTs go unfilled. Specialist recruitment organisations such as Christians Abroad in the UK and ISIS in the US (see below) are notified of more positions than they are able to fill. Demand exists in the hundreds of universities, colleges, foreign language institutes, institutes of technology, teacher training colleges (called Normal Universities) and secondary schools, especially in the provinces. Normal universities often seem to be overlooked when foreign teachers are assigned centrally, so they are a very promising bet for people applying directly or on-the-spot.

Applications can be made through the Chinese Embassy in your country, the State Bureau of Foreign Experts in Beijing (see next section), through various placement organisations and other voluntary bodies, or by applying directly to institutions. Even ordinary secondary schools employ native speakers; applications can be made through provincial education bureaus. Writing direct to the Foreign Affairs Office *(waiban)* of institutes of higher learning may lead to a job offer. Chinese institutes seem to attach more weight to the letter of application than to the curriculum vitae. Also enclose a photo, a photocopy of the first page of your passport, a copy of any education certificates and two references.

Unfortunately the mechanisms for placing teachers and communicating with them can be subject to the same tendency to bureaucratic ineptitude as plagues teachers in China. Once you have been promised a job, schools can be very remiss about keeping in touch, so keep pressing. Often this is because the person with whom you are in contact does not speak much English but doesn't want to lose face.

Any university graduate travelling in China should be able to arrange a teaching contract just by asking around at the many colleges in the towns and cities on his or her itinerary. Even when foreign travellers have not been looking for work, they have been approached and invited to teach English. It has been suggested that standing in a railway station beside a notice advertising your availability to teach English would succeed, though probably more for private tuition than an institutional job. If you fix up a job at FT level on the spot, it may not be for an entire academic year and your pay may be calculated on an hourly basis.

FIXING UP A JOB

If you want a contract fixed up before leaving home, start the application procedure at least six months and preferably a year before your intended departure. Most recruitment is filtered through the Chinese Education Association for International Exchange (CEAIE) in the capital (37 Damucang Hutong, Beijing 100816; tel: 10-660 20 731; fax: 10-660 16 156) which is a non-governmental organisation with 23 local branches in major cities and extensive contacts with institutes of higher education throughout China who wish to invite native speaker teachers.

CEAIE cooperates with Chinese Embassies in the West. For many years the Education Section of the Chinese Embassy in London at 5-13 Birch Grove, Acton, London W3 9SW (0181-993 0279/fax 0181-993 2215) handled teacher recruitment. As of 1999, the task of matching applicants with vacancies at Chinese institutions has been handed over to the Central Bureau for Educational Visits and Exchanges and also to Council (see entry). Details of the application procedure can be obtained from the Chinese Links Officer at the Central Bureau (10 Spring Gardens, London SW1A 2BN; 0171-389 4431/fax 0171-389 4426). The Development Officer is Angela Grimes (e-mail agrimes@central.bureau.org.uk).

The Central Bureau receives information of posts in China in the new year and sends out this information to universities and interested individuals of any age. The Bureau then screens applications and conducts interviews in March for positions mainly as FTs but also as FEs. The minimum requirement is a university degree, though a TEFL certificate and/or teaching experience preferably abroad improve your chances of acceptance. Dossiers of successful interviewees are then forwarded to appropriate institutes in China who then communicate directly with the applicant if they are interested in hiring them. Teachers who accept posts in China attend an orientation in June at which they can find out exactly what will be expected of them.

Contracts are for between six months and two years, normally starting in September. Details of the contract are a matter of negotiation between the teacher and the hiring institution. Many applicants will have to choose among offers as Will Hawkes did:

> *During my last year at university, I obtained a list of Chinese universities and colleges looking to recruit foreign teachers, then faxed my CV and a letter to the ten which suited me most. I received several offers from around China (including a phone call at 3am) and eventually accepted an offer from Qingdao Chemical Institute on the east coast of China. The offer was quite standard: accommodation, unspectacular money... but a friend of mine had taught at this same institute and thoroughly recommended it, so I went and taught English from September 1997 to July 1998.*

The State Bureau of Foreign Experts (SBFE), Friendship Hotel, 3 Bai Shi Qiao Road, 100873 Beijing (tel: 10-849 888 ext. 83500; fax: 10-831 5832) attempts to coordinate the selection of FTs and FEs. It is possible to approach them once you are in Beijing or before arrival, though applications sent directly to them do not always receive a reply.

Whereas the appointment of teachers for post-secondary institutions is carried out by the individual institution (in cooperation with a national government department), hiring teachers at the secondary level is the responsibility of the provincial education bureaux. For a list of addresses of Chinese institutes of higher education, consult the book *Living in China: A Guide to Teaching and Studying in China Including Taiwan* from China Books & Periodicals, Inc., 2929 24th St, San Francisco, CA 94110 (415-282-2994/info@chinabooks.com) which costs $19.95. One major institute which may be worth trying is Yunnan Institute of the Nationalities (Foreign Affairs Office, Kunming 650031, Yunnan; tel/fax: 871-515 4308), which has up to 15 foreign teachers and experts at any one time.

Limited opportunities exist for part-time teaching in Beijing through the Cultural and Education section of the British Embassy (which doubles as the British Council). Properly qualified and experienced teachers of EFL undertake a variety of teaching duties but without any guarantee of a fixed number of hours. Teachers are responsible for their own accommodation and visas. However plans are in place to open a full-scale teaching centre in the near future.

Private Language Training

A couple of years ago, there were no private language schools in China at all. But legislation allowing privatisation in the fields of media and education has prompted a number of language schools to open. Like private schools everywhere, a certain number of these are run by unscrupulous entrepreneurs interested only in profit. A few are run by Korean businessmen, perhaps escaping the economic downturn in their own country. If considering working in the private sector, try to find out the degree of professionalism of the company you are considering. A few have recently been recruiting large numbers of untrained and inexperienced native speakers from the US who are inspired by Christian missionary zeal.

Other private companies are serious about teaching English. Joint ventures with foreign companies often mount an English training programme, like the *Delter Business Institute* (see entry) which is co-run by a Canadian company. Other partnerships are indicated by the descriptions appended on the British Council list of English language schools, for example the Beijing 21 Century American English Training Centre (4th Floor, China Daily Building, 15 East Huixing St, Chaoyang District) is run by the English language paper the *China Daily* and the ESL English Training Agency of the USA. The Beijing-USA College of English (No. 7 Yuhuili Xiao Ying, Anwai Chao Yang District; 6498 9693/e-mail bjuscoe@midwest.com.cn) employs about ten foreign teachers.

Also in the private sector, some hotels and large companies have their own language training facilities for staff, especially if they are joint ventures with Western companies. Most recruitment of teachers by business and industry takes place locally, since they do not offer accommodation. If in Beijing, check classified adverts in the English language bimonthly magazine *Beijing Scene*.

Still, the vast majority of opportunities remains in the state sector, at establishments with names like the 'Workers School of the Workers' District of Xicheng District'. One of the biggest institutions is the Beijing Normal University (e-mail IPO2@BNU.EDU.CN) which hires native speakers with at least a BA (preferably in English) and TEFL experience to provide oral practice for Chinese undergraduates.

Placement Organisations

The following organisations recruit teachers for China from the UK:

The Amity Foundation—Each year this independent Chinese voluntary organisation invites various church-related societies abroad such as the China Forum of the Council of Churches for Britain & Ireland (35-41 Lower Marsh, London SE1 7RL), the Scottish Churches China Group (address below), Christians Abroad (e-mail projects@cabroad-u-net.com) and the National Council of Churches of Christ (475 Riverside Drive, Room 668, New York, NY 10115) to recruit and select teachers of English for two-year contracts beginning each August. Enquiries welcomed from graduates and others suitably qualified (e.g. B.Ed., CELTA) with Christian commitment to live and work in simple conditions. Applications are due between October and December for departures in July. All travel expenses are covered.

GAP, 44 Queen's Road, Reading, Berks. RG1 4BB. Tel: (0118) 959 4914. Fax: (0118) 957 6634. Offer school-leavers six-month attachments to colleges in five provinces.

Project Trust, Hebridean Centre, Ballyhough, Isle of Coll PA78 6TE. Tel: (01879) 230444. Fax: (01879) 230357. Sends volunteers (aged 17-19) to work as teacher-aides in middle schools and teacher training colleges.

Scottish Churches China Group, 121 George St, Edinburgh EH2 4YN. Tel: 0131-225 5722. Fax: 0131-216 6121. E-mail: kirkwrldlnk@gn.apc.org. 12-month TEFL posts in Dali Medical College (Yunnan province) and China Medical University (Shenyang, Liaoning).

Teaching Abroad, Gerrard House, Rustington, W. Sussex BN16 1AW. Tel: 01903 859911. Teaching placements in Fujian Province (at cost of £1,695) and Tibet (£2,995).

University of Luton, Faculty of Humanities, 75 Castle St, Luton, Beds. LU1 3AJ. Tel: 01582 489019. Occasionally recruit for vacancies in foreign language colleges in northern China. Applicants must have at least a TEFL Certificate.

VSO, 317 Putney Bridge Road, London SW15 2PN. Tel: 0181-780 7500. Have quite a large contingent of teachers in China (about 150). Volunteers need a BA in English, languages or other arts subject plus some experience and a Cambridge/RSA Cert. or equivalent. Also opportunities in Mongolia (unsuitable for vegetarians).

The following US organisations are involved in teacher placements in China:

Appalachians Abroad Teach in China, Marshall University, 212 Old Main, Huntington, WV 25755. Tel: (304) 696-6265. Fax: (304) 696-6353. E-mail: cip@marshall.edu.www.marshall. Place about 15 graduates in Shanghai and Beijing schools. Placement fee is $300 plus $200 fee for ESL training course held in West Virginia.

China Teaching Program, Western Washington University—see entry in Directory.

Colorado China Council—see entry.

English Language Institute - China, PO Box 265, San Dimas, CA 91773. Tel: (909) 599-6773/800-366-ELIC. Fax: (909) 592-9906. Up to 400 teachers are placed in colleges and universities across China and Mongolia for 7 weeks in the summer, 10 months or 18 months. Applicants must have Christian commitment, BA (though a few

Teachers in Mongolia have to be meat eaters

undergraduates accepted onto summer programme) and an aptitude for teaching and living in Asia.

ISIS (International Scientific & Information Services, Inc.), 49 Thompson Hay Path, Setauket, NY 11733. Tel: (516) 751-6437. E-mail: tmccoy@suffolk.lib.ny.us. Place about 12 teachers. Prefer applicants to have TEFL training and experience plus experience of travel or work abroad (preferably in Asia or developing countries), but will consider others. One-year contracts start in September or February.

New China Education Foundation—see entry.

WorldTeach, Institute for International Development, 14 Story St, Cambridge, MA 02138. Tel: (617) 495-5527/800-4-TEACH-0. Fax: (617) 495-1599. Non-profit organisation which sends volunteers to teach adults for six months in Yantai. Undergraduates and graduates can participate in Shanghai Summer Teaching programme. Volunteers teach small classes of high school students at a language camp in Shanghai. Volunteers pay about $4,000 for air fares, orientation, health insurance and field support.

CONDITIONS OF WORK

Foreign Teachers are the poor relations of Foreign Experts. They do not have their airfares or shipping costs reimbursed and they normally earn about half of what an FE earns, i.e. 1,500 yuan per month instead of 2,500-3,000 yuan. While FEs are paid by central government, FTs are funded by local education authorities who do not have large budgets. All teachers have their accommodation provided by the host institution, either in on-site residences or in a foreigners' hotel.

Working and living conditions vary from one institute to the next and it is vital to negotiate as much as possible before arrival and to obtain all promises in writing. When you are first notified by your employer in China that you have a job, you should avoid the temptation to write back enthusiastically accepting it. Rather ask for more details such as your status, salary, timetable and other conditions. You could also ask for the names of any current foreign employees whom you can ask for inside information. What is agreed at this stage will set the terms of employment even though it is standard practice not to sign a contract until after two months' probation (if at all).

Will Hawkes was not dissatisfied with his monthly salary of £100:

> *Though my salary was twice as much as the local teachers are paid, for a foreigner it makes for quite tight living. So, like many other foreign teachers, I supplemented this with private individual tutoring which had good rates in Qingdao since it is quite a rich city with a relative lack of foreign teachers.*
>
> *The Foreign Affairs Office of my institute was an important part of my life on campus. As well as being my boss, it organised my accommodation and salary, and was generally responsible for my well-being as a stranger in China. They looked after me very well, even when I had some difficulties at Christmas. State institutions generally treat their foreign teachers well, whereas private ones can have a 'fire and hire' attitude.*

Better wages can be obtained in the big cities of Beijing, Guangzhou and Shanghai, and also in any of the economic zones such as Hainan Island. But Chinese cities have so many drawbacks in terms of crowds and pollution that the higher wages may not prove enough incentive to work there. For quality of life, western China is probably better than the east. Yunnan province has a particularly congenial climate. This area is also reputed to be less money-oriented than the east coast cities, which may have the drawback that it will be more difficult to find paying private students.

Most foreign teachers are expected to teach between 12 and 18 hours a week, which sounds a light load until you find that there may be 50-100 students in these classes. Often there is a heavy load of marking as well and extra duties such as staffing an 'English corner' or English club, or delivering a weekly lecture on Western culture. In fact some teachers end up working a 45-50 hour week. The administration's main ambition is often to maximise your exposure, which may have the effect of minimising your usefulness. Hours of teaching are unpredictable and the teaching days can be very long. Students get up at 6am and work at night in supervised sessions. If you want to keep your weekends free for travel and relaxation, firmly decline teaching hours on Saturday and Sunday, and be aware that it is all too easy to overcommit yourself in the first few weeks.

Terms run from early September to early July, with a three or four week (paid) holiday over Chinese New Year and the spring festival in January/February. Foreign teachers can sometimes arrange to have longer breaks depending on their exam commitments.

The Pupils

'Big noses' (foreigners) are normally treated with great respect. In the early years of Western contact with China, English teachers outside the big cities found themselves lionised, unable to complete the simplest task in public without an enormous audience. But there are not many corners of China these days into which foreigners, whether teachers or travellers, have not penetrated, and so some of the pressure has been taken off.

Slowly, newer paedagogical methods are being accepted by students and administrators alike. Attitudes differ enormously from one situation to another. Where in one place, techniques that smack of innovation are greeted with blank stares, in another, there can be lively class discussions. Adam Hartley found himself in the former situation:

> *Politics were a complete no-no in class and yet politics are so central to life that you find yourself always coming up against a brick wall of silent faces. Class participation of any kind was hard enough to achieve. I was given a class of 100 people (of vastly different standards) for listening comprehension. I was an absolute monkey, playing, rewinding and replaying a cassette with obnoxious voices and muddled questions. I'd play it twice or thrice, ask if they were ready. 'Yes.' Okay, who thinks the answer is A? No one. Who thinks B? 2 people. Who thinks C? 3 hands. And who thinks D? No one. 5 responses out of 100. I'd try it again and again, and only ever got 27 hands in the air for any one question.*
>
> *I had another class of beginners, and spent two hours reading things very very slowly for them to repeat. Immensely dull, unstimulating and tiring work. Again a tape recorder could have done just as good a job as I did.*

Will Hawkes did not find the teaching such hard going:

> *I taught 12 hours a week, each class lasting a mammoth two hours. Chinese students are more familiar with American English and thus British English is very much in demand to balance things out. The English level of my students, who were aged 17-23, was mostly fairly competent, but with extremes of good and dreadful. Getting into university in China is a great privilege, and most students were eager to grasp this opportunity as a route to greater things in life. I found teaching the Chinese a delight: the students were very eager to learn, ask questions, find out how life is in Britain, always looking to learn and not muck around. We discussed a wide variety of material in class and, although some political areas are best left untouched, general debate was enthusiastically devoured about, for instance, the existence of God, cloning, tradition versus modernity and aliens (a real favourite, with many believers).*

In some cases the classroom is not the best place to draw out the students. Extracurricular activities can present a better opportunity for imparting the English language, as Richard Vincent found when he spent a year as a Project Trust volunteer in Southern China:

> *Most of the positive aspects of my year were achieved outside the classroom. The good students will always work all the hours god sends. However the less motivated can become motivated to try and learn. In my case, playing football gave lots of students who had been labelled 'dossers' the chance to speak English, and many of them became the best contributors in class. The emphasis should always be on fun and trying to get them to use the English they know.*

The enthusiasm of the students goes a long way to counteracting the negative aspects. Chinese people are unfailingly polite and friendly outside official and observed situations.

Accommodation

Every university has either a purpose-built hostel or similar. Foreign teachers are generally housed in the best accommodation the university can offer, often referred to as a 'Panda House' (on the analogy that pandas are pampered in zoos). These differ enormously from place to place. In some places (such as Chengdu University of Science & Technology) the accommodation can be airy and comfortable. In other places it is decidedly spartan and in some cases downright depressing, especially if electricity and heat are rationed. Adam describes his lodgings in Linfen:

> *A flat containing very little was provided. A fridge and TV were provided though never used. I wanted chairs, desks, lamps, and after weeks of pushing I got them. 'Next week you shall have them.' Then next week, 'That man is away at a conference now' and so on. I got carpets put in and had a good set-up, except snow and dust managed to filter in through the windows. After a few weeks, the electricity blew, so I couldn't use the desk lamp (which I'd had to buy) or listen to music. It got depressing living under neon light, padding around on dusty carpets wrapped up in a coat to keep warm.*

Many of the deprivations may sound trivial but cumulatively they can be disheartening. On the other hand local Chinese teachers consider the foreigners' accommodation (like their salaries) to be luxurious compared to their own and it may strike you as churlish to complain too vociferously.

HELLO! I THINK WE'RE GOING TO GET ON FAMOUSLY!

"A tape recorder could have done as good a job"

REGULATIONS

If the hiring body notifies the Bureau of Foreign Experts sufficiently early and you are able to sign a contract before leaving home, you might get a working visa prior to entering China. With an invitation letter or fax from the Bureau, you should be able to obtain a long term work visa from the Embassy of the PRC in your country. According to the Embassy in London, the cost of a multi-entry visa valid for six months is £75 for Britons, £45 for Americans, £150/$76 for 12 months. However the bureaucracy is so convoluted and delays so commonplace that the paperwork can seldom be tidied away before leaving home. One of the requirements is a notarized health certificate.

It is more usual to enter China on a tourist (L) visa and then the Foreign Affairs Office (FAO) at your institute will arrange for an Alien Residence Permit (Z visa). Make sure this happens before your visitor visa expires, which is calculated according to the date of entry to China rather than the expiry date of the visa. Otherwise you will be liable to a fine and will have to leave the country to change status. The Visa Office in Hong Kong is located on the 5th Floor, Low Block, 26 Harbour Road, Wanchai. Once outside the country you must be prepared to wait up to a fortnight for the appropriate faxes to be sent from Beijing. With the Z visa you should be eligible for a one-year multiple entry visa, though this seems to be at the discretion of the official at the Beijing Public Service office who may want to see more 'chops' (official stamps), more forms and an extra fee.

When you arrive, be sure that your host institution sorts out the various permits and teachers' cards to which you are entitled. The Foreign Affairs Office should issue you with a green card (residence permit which prevents expensive visa renewal) and an orange card (purchase document) which allows you to make purchases at the same prices as locals. Free health care of a good standard is provided, so few people bother with medical or personal insurance.

LEISURE TIME

Foreigners who teach in Beijing can lead a standard expatriate life if they want to, attending Embassy films and discos and dining in expensive restaurants. Life in the provinces will be very different. There may be no restaurants even to rival the Chinese take-away in your home town; but the locals will be far more interested in you and perhaps even teach you to cook your own Chinese food. If there are several foreigners, communal dining facilities (often segregated) will normally be provided. Glutinous rice, soy beans and cabbage are staples and fresh produce may be in short supply in winter.

Learning Chinese is the ambition of many teachers and is a great asset especially outside cosmopolitan areas. Take a good teach-yourself book and cassettes, since these are difficult to obtain outside Beijing and Shanghai. Mastering Chinese characters is a daunting business, though the grammar is straightforward. Others prefer to study Tai Chi, Wushu or other exotic martial arts.

Be prepared for noise and air pollution even in small towns, though it is usually possible to escape into the countryside by bicycle or bus. Some universities with large contingents of foreign teachers organise excursions in the same way that Israeli kibbutzim do for their volunteers after a few months. Most of the country is open to independent travellers though if you want to travel to Tibet, you will first have to get permission from the Tibet Tourist Bureau. FEs can easily afford to travel, while FTs may find that extensive travels will leave them out-of-pocket. School and college vacations take place over Spring Festival in or around February, when the trains are very crowded and the weather is cold.

Much of the time you will be responsible for your own amusement, so take plenty of reading matter, including *Wild Swans,* an astonishing account of life in the Cultural Revolution. Will Hawkes would urge anybody to do TEFL in China, concluding that the small sacrifice of a few home comforts is entirely worthwhile for the chance to live in a society rich with 5,000 years of history and culture.

LIST OF SCHOOLS

CHINA TEACHING PROGRAM

Western Washington University, Old Main 530A, Bellingham, WA 98225-9047, USA. Tel: (360) 650-3753. Fax: (360) 650-2847. E-mail ctp@cc.wwu.edu. Web-site: http://www.wwu.edu/-ctp

Number of teachers: 30-45 at various institutions of higher education and secondary schools throughout China.

Preference of nationality: none, provided native speaker of English.

Qualifications: BA minimum, teaching experience helpful. Flexibility and sense of adventure needed. Opportunities also available for business and law experts.

Conditions of employment: one academic year contract starting September or February. 12-18 classroom h.p.w.

Salary: 1,000-2,000 yuan per month for Foreign Teachers (30% converted to foreign currency) and 2,000-3,000 yuan for Foreign Experts (with 50-70% conversion rate).

Facilities/Support: accommodation provided. Compulsory 5-week pre-departure summer training course in TESL, Chinese language and culture for candidates who lack TEFL training or experience, at a cost of $1,200. Recommendations for books and materials to take are given.

Recruitment: college career centres, newspaper and magazine adverts and word of mouth. Application deadline is January 31st (or October 31st for placement only starting in spring). Interviews take place in Bellingham or by phone.

Contact: Todd Lundgren, Director.

COLORADO CHINA COUNCIL

4556 Apple Way, Boulder, CO 80301, USA. Tel: (303) 443-1108. Fax: (303) 443-1107. E-mail: alice@asiacouncil.org. Web-site: www.AsiaCouncil.org

Number of teachers: 20-35 per year placed at institutes throughout China, including Mongolia.

Preference of nationality: mostly American.

Qualifications: BA/BSc or higher degree (all majors considered, though English, TEFL, journalism, business, sciences and engineering especially welcome). Good GPA (minimum 2.5) and two strong letters of recommendation needed. Teaching background helpful but not required.

Conditions of employment: 6 months from early spring, 11 months from 30th July. August placements but not February placements are preceded by compulsory 3-week Mandarin Chinese and teacher training programme and orientation. To teach 14-16 h.p.w.

Salary: monthly stipend, free housing in foreign teachers' complex, medical benefits and one month paid vacation offered by Chinese institutions.

Facilities/Support: some schools reimburse air fare home at end of year.

Recruitment: deadline for applications for August start is 15th February. Non-refundable application processing fee of $100. Council fees are $3,900 (including TEFL training, Chinese course and return airfares), $1,350 fee (administration only) for February start.

Contact: Alice Renouf, Director.

COUNCIL

Council UK, 52 Poland St, London W1V 4JQ, UK. Tel: 0171-478 2000. Fax: 0171-734 7322. Also Council Exchanges, 205 E 42nd St, New York, NY 10017, USA. Tel: 888-COUNCIL. Fax: (212) 822-2699. E-mail: infoUK@ciee.org. Web-site: www.ciee.org

Number of teachers: 100 from UK, 75-100 from US, at tertiary institutions in China, mainly in the developed eastern provinces of Jiangsu, Zheijiang, Shandong and Hubei.

Preference of nationality: native speaker of English.

Qualifications: university degree essential; TEFL training or experience preferred.

Conditions of employment: 5 month contracts from February or 10 months from late

August, teaching Chinese college students. 12-18 h.p.w. Extracurricular duties may involve running an English language club.

Salary: standard salary range for Foreign Teachers is equivalent of £100-£200 per month. Possibility of travel stipend.

Facilities/Support: free accommodation, usually on-campus. One-week orientation in Beijing on arrival including basic EFL training before.

Recruitment: deadlines for applications is May 1st for August departures and November 15th for February departures. UK programme fee is £300, flights £360 and training £315.

Contact: Kathryn Verey, Senior Programme Coordinator.

DELTER BUSINESS INSTITUTE

44 Gao Liang Qiao XieJie, 100044 Beijing. Tel: (10) 6223 7558. Fax: (10) 6223 9116. E-mail: bingl@public3.bta.net.cn. Canadian HQ: 1101 St. Alexandre Ave, Montreal, Quebec H2Z 1P8.

Number of teachers: 50 per year.

Preference of nationality: Canadian, American.

Qualifications: university degree, and aged 25-55.

Conditions of employment: 11 month contracts. 20 contact h.p.w./40 h.p.w.

Salary: US$6,000-$20,000 per year (net).

Facilities/Support: free accommodation and work permit arranged.

Recruitment: via Canadian universities and agent. Interviews not essential.

Contact: Bing Liang, Chief Executive Officer.

EF ENGLISH FIRST

No. 167 Tai Juan Road, Shanghai 200031. Tel: (21) 6415 0076. Also for Business English: EF Business Consulting (Shanghai) Co. Ltd., Floor 22, China Merchants Tower, 66 Lu Jiazui Road, Pudong, Shanghai 200120. Tel: (21) 5882 5083. Fax: (21) 5882 3095.

Number of teachers: 10.

Preference of nationality: British, Canadian, Australian, American, Irish.

Qualifications: university degree and certificate in EFL/ESL. Business experience preferable for EF Business Consulting.

Conditions of employment: 12 month contracts. Teaching between 7.30am and 9pm Monday to Friday and some Saturdays.

Salary: US$650 per month plus accommodation allowance.

Facilities/Support: help with finding accommodation. Visas/work permits provided. Paid holidays. Flight costs reimbursed. Orientation on arrival and ongoing training. Chinese lessons. Well-equipped schools.

Recruitment: directly through Shanghai office or through English First offices in London and Boston.

NEW CHINA EDUCATION FOUNDATION

1587 Montalban Drive, San José, CA 95120, USA. Tel: (408) 268-0418.

Number of teachers: 6-10.

Preference of nationality: American, Canadian or British.

Qualifications: college grads with teaching experience preferred.

Conditions of employment: one academic year.

Salary: 1,750 Renminbi yuan per month on average.

Facilities/Support: accommodation provided. Teachers are advised to bring some teaching materials.

Recruitment: through North American colleges and direct contact. Interviews not essential.

Contact: May Hu, Chairperson Teacher Placement.

Hong Kong

Since the former British colony became the Hong Kong Special Administrative Region of the People's Republic of China on June 23rd 1997, many aspects of life and employment have changed. For example there has been a controversial switch in the state education system away from English as a medium of instruction to Cantonese. While three out of four parents want their children to be educated in English, only one in four is being given a place at such a school. A predictable outcome might be that all these aspiring parents will hasten to send their offspring to private language schools to be taught by native speakers. Rather contradictorily, the Hong Kong authorities announced in late 1997 that they wanted to employ 700 native English speakers to teach in the state education system.

On the other hand, much in Hong Kong remains the same, for example there is still a separate currency, and the chances of the Hong Kong dollar being replaced by the Hong Kong renminbi seem very remote at the present time. In fact the HK dollar has remained remarkably stable over the past two years.

The demand for English teachers continues as strong as ever. What has changed is the ease with which British nationals can sort out the red tape. Formerly they were allowed to stay for a year without many formalities. Now it is illegal to enter Hong Kong as a tourist and take up work. However it is possible to visit the city, fix up a teaching job and then apply for a work permit from a neighbouring country. Anyone who manages to find an employer before arrival can seek their sponsorship to obtain a work permit.

FIXING UP A JOB

Recruitment rarely takes place outside Hong Kong, except by the British Council, which has for many years had a large teaching operation in Hong Kong. About six months before the handover, it moved to 3 Supreme Court Road, Admiralty, perhaps girding its loins for the coming changes. The educational press in Britain carries virtually no adverts for Hong Kong language schools, and virtually no language school is willing to reply to enquiries from abroad.

The government scheme to recruit English teachers is administered by the Hong Kong Education Department (Expatriate Teacher Exchange, 13F Wu Chung House, 213 Queen's Road East, Wanchai). A major programme is being set up at the time of writing whereby Christians Abroad would supply a considerable number of English teachers (who must have a Christian commitment) to various organisations in Hong Kong.

It is a different story once you arrive. Adverts abound on travellers' hostel notice boards and in the papers. The bumper Saturday edition of the *South China Morning Post* is the best bet though it doesn't always contain many useful leads. Common sense suggests that schools which are forced to advertise vacancies so regularly must have a very high turn-over of staff, for which there are probably good reasons. Still, this kind of school may provide an acceptable starting point. (The paper is distributed in the UK by the Colin Turner Group, Thatched House, Balfour Road, West Runton, Norfolk NR27 9QJ.)

Look for English Clubs which provide a cheaper alternative for learners than formal English classes. Joe Doughty describes them:

> *The vast majority of teaching jobs on offer at the lower end of the market are in conversation clubs where Chinese students pay a modest fee, which entitles them to attend as often as they like during opening hours for three months. What happens in practice is that there is a constant coming and going in your 'classroom,' which in my*

case was really just a large alcove without a door. This can be off-putting as you are not sure why students are leaving (was it something I said?) Like most things it gets better and you soon get a reasonably regular group of students. There are periodic checks by a member of the admin to see if you are keeping a reasonable number of students enthralled at any one time.

The place to which travellers have gravitated over the years (though far fewer are coming these days) is Chung King Mansions at 40 Nathan Road in Kowloon. It is nearly as famous for its notice board as for its range of cheap (and grotty) accommodation. The notice board often carries easy-come easy-go offers from schools at the bottom end of the market. According to Martyn Owens, who had a longish stint of teaching in Hong Kong (pre-1997), these job notices often come with scribbled footnotes warning other travellers about the drawbacks (usually low pay in the case of teaching jobs). Andrew Monks suggests trying Modern English in Milton Mansions on Granville Road in Tsimshatsui. Another possibility in Tsimshatsui is suggested by Jane Harris:

I worked teaching English (despite my scouse accent) for three weeks before deciding it was not for me, though it paid well (HK$230 for an hour and a half session one-to-one). I'd never done anything remotely like teaching before, but said that I'd worked as a teacher's helper in the UK, and that was good enough to get a job through the AW Centre (6B Lip Send Building, 15 Carnarvon Road; 2367 1945).

The *Yellow Pages* are the alternative source of institute addresses. Phone calls within the city limits are free, so by phoning around you can easily get an idea of the possibilities. Although hiring is continuous, the summer months bring even more openings, while the Chinese New Year in January/February is a bad time. You might also enquire about teaching opportunities in the Vietnamese Refugee Camps administered by the UN. David Hughes met people teaching in this capacity who did not have professional qualifications though he concluded that 'a nice Southern accent helps'.

Job interviews are not necessarily daunting experiences. Martyn Owens describes his initial meeting with an employer:

After ringing, I went to the school to have an interview with the Director. It was quite informal. She seemed to be most interested in my intended length of stay (after she realised I was 'presentable' so to speak) and asked also about my academic qualifications. She didn't expect me to have had any teaching experience and was most impressed when I presented my TEFL certificate (five-day introductory course at the Surrey Language Centre). I'm sure I would have got the job without it, merely on the basis of my willingness to work.

Freelance teaching can prove lucrative provided you are staying in Hong Kong legally. The private tuition market appealed to the New Zealander Brett Muir because, unlike his British counterparts at that time, he couldn't get a work visa. He describes the tactics he used to find clients:

My recommendation is to hire a paging device (really cheap by the month—major companies have offices in the big subway stations) and write an attractive advertisement for placing in the letter boxes of the ritzy apartment estates in Mid Levels, Jardines, Lookout and Causeway Bay suburbs. Although the gates are locked, the Filipina maids are constantly going in and out, so you just walk in with them to post your photocopied ads. In this way you are always on the phone. Generally it is housewives and businessmen who are looking for conversation practice.

Another way to attract clients is to put notices up in busy places like the chain of Welcome Supermarkets, though you will have to keep checking that your notices have not been covered up or removed by the store manager who has a weekly clear-out.

REGULATIONS

Information about the formalities should be requested from the Chinese Embassies in London and Washington. The office in London which was once the Hong Kong Government Office at 6 Grafton St, London W1X 3LB (0171-499 9821) is now a trade mission. UK nationals may stay as tourists in Hong Kong for up to six months. An application for a change of status must be lodged with the HK Immigration Department (Immigration Tower, 7 Gloucester Road, Wan Chai; 2824 6111/fax 2877 7711/2824 1133) but the applicant must be out of the country. As in Taiwan, the established schools should be prepared to sponsor you for a work permit if you can persuade them that you will stay for a reasonable length of time.

CONDITIONS OF WORK

Except for the highly qualified and privileged teachers who teach at the prestigious end of the market, low wages and long hours are the norm. HK$60 an hour is about the best an unqualified part-time teacher can expect to earn. Gavin Staples was in Hong Kong a couple of years ago and describes conditions at one school notorious for its cowboy practices:

> *One school expected its teacher to work 40 hours a week for HK$40 an hour, which is an appalling set-up. Teachers who turn up even slightly late were fined literally by the minute. One person I met teaching here was so embittered that he stood outside the door and poached students to teach privately. Like so many others, the school at which I ended up teaching on a one-to-one basis was run solely for profit. The students were never graded so you had no idea at what level they were, and the school had about eight books and one dictionary. Although I had been promised HK$50 an hour, my first pay packet was for HK$45.*

As is the case in many other places, the longer you stay, the more stable your hours become. Later Gavin was offered some hours by a reputable teaching agency which paid much better, but they could offer him only six hours a week which would rise to twelve hours after three months. Anyone prepared to sign a contract for more than six months can expect to earn more, though if you find that you can't stick it for that long, you may end up forfeiting some wages for breach of contract. One possible justification for the meagre wage is that many schools hand out detailed lesson plans to their untrained teachers which means that lesson preparation time is minimal.

Always try to collect your wages at frequent intervals since some schools have been negligent in this regard. Teachers have no health or social security protection. When Joe Doughty became ill, he was simply fired.

Erratic hours are also a problem, as Leslie Platt found out:

> *My institute was very vague as to what hours I would be working. I would arrive in the afternoon as instructed only to be informed that no students had turned up but that I had better hang around for a few hours just in case one did. If none did, it meant I didn't get paid.*

Accommodation

Needless to say, the kind of language school described here does not offer accommodation to its teachers. Accommodation in the crowded heart of Hong Kong is astronomically expensive, so it will be a problem unless you are prepared to stay in a hostel. Teachers will probably want to avoid the infamous Travellers Hostel in Chung King Mansions, where a bed in a dorm room not much bigger than a broom cupboard starts at HK$75. After taking a look at it, Vaughan Temby decided that the feat of maintaining a working life and dressing smartly while staying there was beyond him and he looked elsewhere. There are many other hostels in the Mansions complex; Vaughan recommends Jinn's Ti Guest House on the 7th floor of B block where he and two friends were paying HK$160 each for a spacious and airy room (after bargaining). From time to time the Hong Kong authorities clamp down on hostels on the grounds of fire risk, and some of the worst ones may be closed down.

The average rent for a room in a decent shared flat is upwards of HK$5,000 a month, which is far more than most teachers can afford, and flats can easily cost £1,000 a month. Good accommodation is available more cheaply on the outlying islands such as Lamma and Lantau, which can be an attractive option in view of the cheap and plentiful public transport including ferry service, though the commute will take anything up to an hour. Here it is possible to find pleasant flats or even houses for about £400 a month.

LEISURE TIME

Not surprisingly, culture shock is kept to a minimum in Hong Kong by the Western affluence and the British bias. Hong Kong is famed as a shoppers' paradise in which the cheap food, clothing and travel help to alleviate the problem of expensive accommodation. But with inflation running fairly high, the cost of living has risen dramatically, and a teacher's wage does not go very far.

Martyn Owens describes the range of leisure activities:

> *Hong Kong buzzes 24 hours a day and is like a film set! Consequently there is much to do—bowling, movies, sports, restaurants, etc. all probably within walking distance. I spent most of my spare time in restaurants with friends; eating out is the most popular pastime among the locals. I also travelled around the New Territories which is a beautiful place.*

LIST OF SCHOOLS

ISLAND SCHOOL
20 Borrett Road, Hong Kong. Tel: 2524 7135. Fax: 2840 1673. E-mail: school@is.esf.edu.hk
Number of teachers: 3 ESL teachers out of staff of 85.
Preference of nationality: international.
Qualifications: graduates, PGCE and 2 years' experience.
Conditions of employment: 2 year contracts. Hours are 8am-3.30pm. Possibility of moving to another of the 15 schools run by the English Schools Foundation.
Salary: HK$29,000-51,000 per month for a mainscale teacher.
Facilities/Support: expatriate contracts pay rent.
Recruitment: adverts in HK and UK in January. Interviews can be held in both countries.
Contact: David James, Principal.

VENTURE LANGUAGE TRAINING LTD
1A 163 Hennessey Road, Wan Chai, Hong Kong. Tel: 2507 4985. Fax: 2511 3798.
Number of teachers: 12.
Preference of nationality: British.
Qualifications: TEFL or similar/English degree. Experience more important than qualifications.
Conditions of employment: 2 year contracts. 20 h.p.w.
Salary: HK$200 per hour; $300 for Business English courses.
Facilities/Support: no assistance with accommodation. Company will sponsor teachers on 2-year contracts for a work permit.
Recruitment: word-of-mouth. Interviews absolutely essential, and can be held in the UK. Local interview essential.
Contact: Susanne Pickering, Director of Studies.

Indonesia

Indonesia is the fifth most populous nation on earth, a fact of which we are all reminded by the news media when political unrest and violence swept the country in May 1998. Many expat teachers chose this moment to leave the country leaving many schools which had had a high proportion of native speaker teachers with far fewer or none at all. The rioting erupted in the wake of the South East Asian economic crisis. Indonesia has experienced one of the most drastic currency devaluations of any country in recent history. Schools which had for years been attracting professional ELT teachers from abroad with generous salaries and benefits packages could no longer do so.

However the dozen or so major language training organisations have survived the crisis. These so-called 'native speaker schools' with multiple branches in Jakarta and the other cities continue to deliver English courses to the millions of Indonesians who still want to learn the language. These organisations can still afford to hire trained foreign teachers and pay them about ten times the local wage. A few have even expanded, including *EF English First* and *EEC*. The wealth that the oil industry has brought to Jakarta and the country generally has not all vanished. The schools that have suffered most have been the small private institutes employing only Indonesian teachers.

FIXING UP A JOB

The CELTA is highly regarded in Indonesia and anyone who has acquired the Certificate has a good change of pre-arranging a job in Jakarta, Surabaya or Bandung. (Although Yogyakarta has a population of half a million and is arguably the most interesting city in Indonesia, the number of language schools is fewer.) While some schools clearly favour either British or North American teachers, others express no preference, and there are also quite a few Australian and New Zealand EFL teachers in Indonesia. The government's only stipulation from the point of view of awarding work permits is that the teachers must be native speakers.

In Advance

Private schools with overseas contacts advertise and recruit internationally. For example *International Language Programs* carry out interviews in London each summer for the 40 or so teaching positions they have in their two branches. Advertisements in the educational press, especially *EL Prospects* appear with some regularity in the spring and summer.

The British Council offices in Jakarta and Surabaya can send lists of ELT institutes in their regions. The Information Department of the Indonesian Embassy in London can send a list of universities and teacher training colleges throughout the country, though these seldom hire EFL teachers applying from abroad.

Colin Boothroyd taught for a major language school in Jakarta and describes the way he arranged the job:

> *I answered an advertisement in the Education section of the Guardian immediately but did not get a response for a month. The response came in the form of a phone call requesting an interview with me. I was interviewed a few days later—a very relaxed affair in a South London pub—and was told on the spot that I would be recommended for a posting. Two weeks later I received a load of information welcoming me to the school. Three weeks later I was on a plane to Jakarta, having picked up a visa at the Indonesian Embassy in London.*

The beauty of Colin's 18-month contract was that it included free flights, an increasingly rare perk these days. Two or three of the main schools in Indonesia do pay a one-way return fare at the end of a successful contract.

The volunteer agencies are fairly major employers of EFL teachers. Both *GAP* and *Project Trust* send school-leavers to teach in remote parts of Indonesia including Timor and Kalimantan. GAP volunteers are normally placed in different faculties of universities to assist the Indonesian teaching staff.

Even if you have missed an opportunity to be interviewed in your home country, it is still worth contacting the major schools by fax or e-mail. Some hire their teachers on the basis of a telephone interview and, in some cases, a taped example of your voice.

On the Spot

More and more teachers are being hired on the spot, which suits the major schools who then don't have to pay for air fares. Local recruits can negotiate shorter contracts, for example six months, unlike teachers recruited abroad who usually have to stay at least 18 months. Most teaching jobs start in July or September/October. Visit the British Council and check adverts in the English language *Jakarta Post* or *Indonesian Observer*. The Centre Supervisor of the British Council in Surabaya is frequently asked to match up teachers already in Surabaya and schools on an unofficial basis.

With a Cambridge or Trinity Certificate and university degree your chances of being offered a job are high. Unqualified applicants would have to be extremely well presented (since dress is very important in Jakarta), able to sell themselves in terms of experience and qualifications and prepared to commit themselves for a longish spell or to start with some part-time work in the hope of building it up.

Local schools staffed by Indonesians abound, many willing to hire a native speaker at local wages. Some can even arrange a work permit. Travellers have stumbled across friendly little schools up rickety staircases throughout the islands of Indonesia, as the German round-the-world traveller Gerhard Flaig describes:

> In Yogyakarta you can find language schools listed in the telephone book or you just walk through streets to look for them. Most of them are interested in having new teachers. I got an offering to teach German and also English since my English was better than some of the language school managers. All of them didn't bother about work permits. The wages aren't very high, about 10,000 rupiahs an hour. It is fairly easy to cover the costs of board and lodging since the cost of living is very low.

Opportunities exist not only in the large cities but in small towns too. Tim Leffel from New Jersey noticed a large number of English schools in the Javanese city of Solo, and others have recommended Bali. At local schools unused to employing native speaker teachers, teaching materials may be in short supply. One of the problems faced by those who undertake casual work of this kind is that there is usually little chance of obtaining a work permit (see below). It is also difficult for freelance teachers to become legal unless you have a contact who knows people in power.

The problem of visas doesn't arise if you teach English on a completely informal basis as Stuart Tappin did:

> In Asia I managed to spend a lot of time living with people in return for teaching English. The more remote the towns are from tourist routes the better, for example Bali is no good. I spent a week in Palembang Sumatra living with an English teacher and his family. You teach and they give their (very good) hospitality.

REGULATIONS

The work permit regulations are rigidly adhered to in Indonesia and all of the established language schools will apply for a visa permit on your behalf. Some even employ a full-time visa co-ordinator. If the job is arranged before you leave home, you should take a letter of sponsorship from your employer to the Indonesian Embassy in London and, subject to current visas requirements beings fulfilled, they will issue you with a business visa valid for a maximum of five weeks at a cost of £30 (£15 for periods less than five weeks). All other work permit arrangements will be taken care of by your school on arrival, after you have provided your CV, TEFL course certificate, photocopies of your passport and application forms. These are sent to the Indonesian Ministry of Education (Jalan Jenderal Sudirman, Senayan, Jakarta Pusat), the Cabinet Secretariat and the Immigration/Manpower Departments. If and when the application is approved, the work permit will be valid for one employer only and will be revoked and the offending teacher deported if work is undertaken outside the terms of the contract.

After your work permit and temporary stay permit have been granted (with a maximum validity of one year), the documentation will then be telexed to the nearest Indonesian Embassy (normally Singapore) where the teacher can have it stamped in his or her passport. Anyone without the necessary professional qualifications is unlikely to be granted the visa; one participant in the GAP scheme for school-leavers had his English-teaching job cancelled at the last moment since the school found that it could not get a visa for him.

Tourists can stay in Indonesia for two months. It is possible to renew one's tourist status by leaving the country every two months (e.g. flying to Singapore, or by ferry to Penang in Malaysia) but the authorities might become suspicious if you did this repeatedly. Anyone found working on a tourist visa will be deported and blacklisted from entering Indonesia in the future. (Also, the employer would find himself in serious trouble.)

CONDITIONS OF WORK

Despite the devaluation of the rupiah, salaries paid by the 'native speaker' schools provide for a comfortable lifestyle including travel within Indonesia during the vacations. Most schools pay 4,000,000-5,000,000 rupiahs per month, after Indonesian tax of 10% has been subtracted. If inflation continues at the present rate, ask about mid-term salary adjustments. Since the cost of living is low, many teachers are able to save considerable sums while enjoying a very comfortable lifestyle. If you complete a two-year contract, enquire about reimbursement for airfares and a possible tax rebate. Note that in 1997 the Indonesian government imposed a new 'skills Tax' on foreigners of $100 a month.

Many schools offer generous help with accommodation, ranging from an interest-free loan to cover initial rent payments or deposits, to free housing complete with free telephone, electricity and servants. It is customary in the Jakarta housing market to be asked to pay the annual rent in a lump sum at the beginning of your tenancy, and so access to a loan from your employer is often essential.

If you happen to work for a school which takes on outside contracts, you may have the occasional chance to work outside the school premises, possibly in a remote oil drilling location in Sumatra, for up to double pay. The majority of teachers, however, conduct lessons at their school through the usual peak hours of 3.30pm to 8.30pm with some early morning starts as well.

The Pupils

Outside the big cities, the standard of English is normally very low, with pupils having picked up a smattering from bad American television. Classes also tend to be large, with as many as 40 pupils, all expecting to learn grammar by the traditional rote methods. According to a VSO volunteer teaching in Western Java (as quoted in the *TES*), 'If I want to do something interesting, the students complain that it isn't in the exam'. As is the case elsewhere in the world, the average age of English learners is getting younger, so anyone with experience of teaching children or teenagers will be appreciated.

Students in Jakarta present fewer problems as Colin Boothroyd describes:

> *The pupils are incredibly enthusiastic and are genuinely appreciative of the opportunity to learn from native speakers. I have never once had a discipline problem whilst I've been teaching here. My classes have varied from 2 to 20 in size. The students are generally unfamiliar with our communicative form of teaching, since kids aren't really expected to think for themselves in Indonesian schools. Students are reluctant to speak about controversial issues (the issues that should really provoke loads of communication) because they are afraid that big brother may overhear something that doesn't suit. Otherwise the students are brilliant.*

LEISURE TIME

Although Jakarta is a hot, dusty, overcrowded, polluted and poverty-stricken city, there is a great deal to see and do, and many teachers enjoy living there. Indonesia is a fascinating country and most visitors, whether short-term or long, agree that the Indonesian people are fantastic. Travel is cheap and unrestricted, and excursions are very rewarding in terms of scenery and culture. Travel by public transport can be time-consuming and limiting for weekend trips, so you might consider getting a motorcycle, although Jakarta's traffic problems make this too dangerous and unhealthy for many. Internal flights are also within the range of most teachers.

Predictably the community of expatriate teachers participates in lots of joint activities such as football and tennis matches, chess tournaments, beach excursions, diving trips and parties. Most teachers have videos but occasionally go out to see an undubbed American film. Eating out is so cheap relative to salaries that many teachers indulge themselves at restaurants most nights of the week.

The pleasant city of Bandung might prove an attractive alternative to Jakarta. It escaped the violent demonstrations which affected so much of the country in 1998 and offers a good quality lifestyle to teachers, with a good mixture of rural and city life.

Bahasa Indonesian, almost identical to Malay, was imposed on the people of Indonesia after independence in 1949 and is one of the simplest languages to learn both in structure and pronunciation. Mastering a vocabulary of about one hundred words should be enough to get by.

LIST OF SCHOOLS

CLT (CENTRE FOR LANGUAGE TRAINING)
Soegijapranata Catholic University, Jl. Menteri Supeno 35, Semarang 50241. Tel: (24) 316028/314065. Fax: (24) 415429/447365.
Number of teachers: 5.
Preference of nationality: British, American, Canadian, New Zealand, Irish.
Qualifications: minimum BA with TEFL/TESL/TESOL or RSA/Cambridge diploma/ certificate.
Conditions of employment: one year renewable contracts. 24 teaching hours per week. Most but not all students are studying at the university.
Salary: 1,500,000 rupiahs per month net.
Facilities/Support: housing allowance of 300,000 rupiahs provided. Perks include 5,000 rupiah-a-day transport allowance, health insurance cover up to 1,500,000 rupiahs, and flights paid (up to value of $900). 2 weeks' free accommodation at university while teacher finds own accommodation.
Recruitment: links with universities in US and UK, personal contacts. Phone interview necessary.
Contact: Dr. Yoseph Budiyana, Director.

EF ENGLISH FIRST
Wisma Tamara 4th Floor, Suite 402, Jl. Jend. Sudirman Kav. 24, Jakarta 12920. Tel: (21) 520 6477. Fax: (21) 520 4719.
Number of teachers: approximately 200 for schools throughout Indonesia including 8 in Jakarta, and others in Surabaya (see next entry), Java (Semarang, Bogor, Bandung, Cirebon), Sumatra (Medan, Palembang, Lampung) and Sulawesi (Ujung Pandang).
Preference of nationality: British, Canadian, Australian, American or Irish (due to work visa restrictions).
Qualifications: minimum university degree and certificate in EFL/ESL.
Conditions of employment: 12 month contracts. Teaching between 7.30am and 9pm Monday to Friday and some Saturdays.
Salary: varies according to location. End-of-contract bonus.
Facilities/Support: assistance with accommodation. Work permits provided. Flight costs reimbursed. Paid holidays. Orientation upon arrival and ongoing training. All schools well equipped with a variety of resources.
Recruitment: directly through Jakarta office or through English First offices in London and Boston (see *Finding a Job*).
Contact: Academic Support Coordinator in Jakarta office.

EF ENGLISH FIRST—SURABAYA
Plaza Surabaya, Jl. Pemuda 33-37, Surabaya 60271. Tel: (31) 548 4000. Fax: (31) 548 3000. E-mail: e1_guru@rad.net.id
Number of teachers: 30-50.
Preference of nationality: British, Canadian, Australian, American or Irish (due to work visa restrictions).
Qualifications: minimum university degree and certificate in ESL/EFL methodology (CELTA or equivalent). Preference given to people with overseas experience.
Conditions of employment: one year renewable contracts. 4 classes per day (1 hour and 20 minutes each) usually timetabled to be in a morning or evening block. Most students are teenagers and young adults.
Salary: fluctuating due to instability of rupiah. Contracts include roundtrip airfare and a month's end-of-contract bonus.
Facilities/Support: housing provided in shared house. Several days of orientation at beginning and ongoing observation, but no formal training. Wide variety of teacher resources available.
Recruitment: internet and via English First offices in London and Sydney. Interviews can be held in London, Sydney or (if necessary) by telephone.
Contact: Craig Stevenson (Director of Courses) or Michael Pranoto (School Director).

ENGLISH EDUCATION CENTER (EEC)
Jalan Let. Jend. S. Parman 68, Slipi, Jakarta 11410. Tel: (21) 532 3176/532 0044. Fax: (21) 532 3178. E-mail: eec@vision.net.id. Web-site: http://www.indodirect.com/eec
Number of teachers: 30 in three schools in Jakarta.
Preference of nationality: American, British, Australian, New Zealand, Canadian.
Qualifications: BA in relevant subject, CELTA and minimum 1 year's overseas TEFL experience.
Conditions of employment: 1-year contracts. Maximum 25½ h.p.w., normally 2-9pm, but some 8.30am-12.30pm schedules. Students of all ages but many are adolescents.
Salary: 5,000,000-6,300,000 rupiahs per month (with rises expected to take account of inflation).
Facilities/Support: assistance given with finding accommodation, including initial loan. Return air fare after completion of 2-year contract.
Recruitment: teachers recruited locally.
Contact: Robert Bayford, Director of Studies.

ENGLISH LANGUAGE TRAINING INTERNATIONAL (ELTI)
Kelompok Gramedia, Jl. Sabirin 6, Kotabaru, Yogyakarta 55224. Tel: (274) 561849. Fax: (274) 561275.
Number of teachers: 1 (though hoping to employ more when national economic crisis is resolved).
Preference of nationality: American, Canadian, British.
Qualifications: 1-2 years teaching experience and/or TEFL Diploma/Certificate.
Conditions of employment: one-year contracts. 18-24 h.p.w. teaching mainly adults.
Salary: average 750,000-1,000,000 rupiahs per month.
Facilities/Support: no assistance with accommodation.
Recruitment: adverts in *Jakarta Post* and embassies. Interviews in Yogyakarata compulsory.
Contact: Ch. Endang Widyastuti, Director of Studies.

EXECUTIVE ENGLISH PROGRAMS (EEP)
Jalan Wijaya VIII/4, Kebayoran Baru, Jakarta Selatan 12160. Tel: (21) 722 0812/720 8864. Fax: (21) 720 1896. E-mail: eepby@pacific.net.id. Also two other branches in Jakarta and one in Bandung (see next entry).
Number of teachers: 40.
Preference of nationality: none.

Qualifications: CELTA/PGCE plus 1 year's experience preferred.
Conditions of employment: 12 or 24 month contracts. Maximum 28 h.p.w. (overtime paid when hours exceed 24). Teaching between 8.30am and 9pm with no more than 8½-hour span in one day.
Salary: 5,000,000 rupiahs per month (net); higher for Diploma/MA holders with minimum 1 year full-time teaching experience. Interest-free housing loans available for teachers hired from overseas, repayable over maximum of 5 months.
Recruitment: local newspaper adverts, direct overseas hire.
Contact: Ted Thornton, Director of Studies.

EXECUTIVE ENGLISH PROGRAMS (EEP)—BANDUNG
Jalan Lombok No. 43, Bandung 40115. Tel/fax: (22) 708254. Tel: (22) 421 1651.
Preference of nationality: none.
Qualifications: university degree and Cambridge/RSA Cert. required; PGCE and/or 1 year's experience preferred.
Conditions of employment: 12 month contracts. 24 h.p.w. between 2pm and 9pm with some morning classes.
Salary: 3,200,000 rupiahs per month (net) with bonus of US$600 on completion.
Recruitment: local newspaper adverts. Local interviews nearly always necessary.
Contact: Mark Hallett, Director of Studies.

INTERNATIONAL LANGUAGE PROGRAMS (ILP)
ILP Centre, Jl. Raya Pasar Minggu No. 39A, Jakarta 12780. Tel: (21) 798 5210. Fax: (21) 798 5212.
Number of teachers: 40 for two branches in Jakarta.
Preference of nationality: none, but most are British.
Qualifications: CELTA or Trinity Certificate plus 2 years' experience preferred.
Conditions of employment: 2-year contracts. 20-25 contact h.p.w. Students aged 8 to adult.
Salary: 4,500,000 rupiahs net plus bonus and flight.
Facilities/Support: housing provided. Regular upgrading workshops held. Well structured syllabus.
Recruitment: some teachers recruited locally but most are interviewed in London in June/July in reply to adverts in *TES/Guardian*.
Contact: Budhianto Hadinugroho.

INTERNATIONAL LANGUAGE PROGRAMS (ILP)—SURABAYA
Jalan Jawa 34, Surabaya 60281, Jawa Timor. Tel: (31) 502 3333. Fax: (31) 503 0106. E-mail: tjahjani@rad.net.id
Number of teachers: 16.
Preference of nationality: none, but must be classified native speaker (to satisfy work permit requirements).
Qualifications: EFL qualification required, preferably CELTA or equivalent.
Conditions of employment: 1-year contracts. 20 h.p.w. teaching 5 days a week, between 2.30/3.45pm and 5/7/9.15pm. Pupils from age 6.
Salary: starting salary is 5,000,000 rupiahs (net) per month.
Facilities/Support: accommodation provided including utilities and servants. Regular workshops held.
Recruitment: adverts in UK or via the internet. UK recruiter can conduct interviews: Bruce McGowen, 14 Park View, Hastings, East Sussex; tel/fax 01424 441015.
Contact: Peter Mudd, Director of Studies.

INTERNATIONAL LANGUAGE STUDIES (ILS)
Jl. Ambengan No. 1-S, Surabaya 60272. Tel: (31) 534 2457. Fax: (31) 532 8369. Also branches at Jl. Jemursari Selatan II/10, Surabaya 60237 (31-841 5829) and Jl. Simpang Darmo Permai Utara No. 5, Surabaya 60226 (31-717697).
Number of teachers: 3-5.
Preference of nationality: British, American, Canadian and Australian.

Qualifications: TEFL/TESL/Diploma of Education plus minimum 1 year's teaching experience.
Conditions of employment: 1 or 2 year contracts, renewable. 100-120 hours per month. Freelance teaching is strictly prohibited.
Salary: 3,500,000-4,000,000 rupiahs per month (net).
Facilities/Support: accommodation allowance provided. Occasional training workshops and seminars held.
Recruitment: adverts in local papers. Interviews not necessary.
Contact: F. O. Dien Koeswanto, Director.

LOGO EDUCATION CENTRE (LEC)
Jl. H.Z. Arifin No. 208-A, Medan 20112, Sumatra Utara. Tel: (61) 534991/552823. Fax: (61) 552325/537231. E-mail: lecmedan@indsat.net.id
Number of teachers: 2.
Preference of nationality: none.
Qualifications: CELTA and/or 1 year's overseas teaching experience. Computer literacy.
Conditions of employment: 12 month contracts. Normally 110 teaching hours per month including up to 5 evenings a week. Lessons held Monday-Friday. Pupils from pre-school age to adult. Freelance teaching is strictly prohibited.
Salary: 20,000 rupiahs per 90 minute lesson. 1,000,000-2,000,000 rupiahs per month. 100,000 rupiahs withdrawn per month and returned to teacher with interest at end of contract. One-way air fare home will be paid on completion of contract.
Facilities/Support: accommodation and utilities provided free in on-site flat. Indonesian language lessons available.
Recruitment: adverts in *Guardian*. Interviews in London or telephone interview will suffice.
Contact: Mr. Chitra Bustaf, Managing Director.

SCHOOL FOR INTERNATIONAL TRAINING (SIT)
Jalan Sunda 3, Menteng, Jakarta Pusat 10350. Tel: (21) 390 6920/337240/336238. Fax: (21) 335671. Plus two branches in Jakarta and one in Surabaya (Jl. Bengawan 10, Surabaya; 31-577141).
Number of teachers: 20.
Preference of nationality: American, Canadian, British, Australian.
Qualifications: BA/MA (TESOL or related subject) plus several years' experience preferred. Experience in Asia or developing countries desirable.
Conditions of employment: 1 year renewable contracts. 108 hours per month (8am-5pm or 1.30-9pm) 5 days work per week.
Salary: varies with qualifications. 4 weeks annual leave, 12 days sick leave, hospitalisation and accident insurance provided.
Facilities/Support: teachers are provided with housing and transport allowance in addition to base salary.
Recruitment: interviews held locally or by telephone. Local newspaper adverts, TESOL *Placement Bulletin*, foreign adverts and through graduate departments of some American universities.
Contact: Fransisca Laij, Director of Studies.

THE BRITISH INSTITUTE (TBI)—BANDUNG
Jalan Diponegoro 23, Bandung 40124. Tel: (22) 421 1556. Fax: (22) 441465.
Number of teachers: 14.
Preference of nationality: none.
Qualifications: minimum CELTA; DELTA preferred.
Conditions of employment: 12 month contracts. 24 h.p.w. 6 weeks holiday per year. Mostly adult classes with some for children and teenagers.
Facilities/Support: regular in-service workshops and observations.
Recruitment: all teachers hired locally after teaching a demonstration lesson.

Other Schools to Try

Note that these schools did not confirm their teacher requirements for this edition of *Teaching English Abroad*. Upper case entries marked with an asterisk had entries in the last edition (1997); addresses without asterisks have been taken from various sources, such as British Council lists.

TRIAD ENGLISH CENTRE, Jalan Purnawarman 76, Bandung 40116 (22-431309/fax 22-431149). Also in Jakarta, Yogya and Surabaya (World Trade Centre Building, Jl. Pemuda 27-31, Surabaya; 31-531 9311). 15 teachers.

AMERICAN ENGLISH LANGUAGE TRAINING (AELT) CENTER, Jl. R.S. Fatmawati 42A, Jakarta Selatan 12430 (21-769 1001/fax 21-751 3304) and Jl. Bulevar Raya TB II, No. 4, Kalapa Gading, Jakarta 14240 (21-452 2928). 30-40 teachers, mostly American but also other nationalities.

ENGLISH LANGUAGE TRAINING INTERNATIONAL (ELTI), Kompleks Wijaya Grand Centre, Blok F 84 A & B, Jalan Wijaya II, Jakarta Selatan 12160 (21-720 6653/6952/fax 21-720 6654). 20 teachers in various branches (including ELTI Yogyakarta, entry above).

OXFORD COURSE INDONESIA (OCI), Jalan Cempaka Putih Tengah 33C-2, Jakarta Pusat 10510 (21-424 3224/421 4542/fax 21-425 4041). Large indigenous language organisation which employs 400 English teachers, all Indonesian, to teach at 60 branches in 22 Indonesian cities.

SCHOOL FOR INTERNATIONAL COMMUNICATION, Jalan Taman Pahlawan 194, Purwakarta (264-201204/201270) and Jalan Baladewa 77A, Bandung (22-631417/616077). 3 teachers.

STRIVE INTERNATIONAL, Setiabudi 1 Building, 3rd Floor/B-1, Jl. H. R. Rasuna Said, Jakarta 12920 (21-521 0690/fax 21-521 0692). Web-site: strive@rad.net.id. 12-14 teachers for on-site and in-company teaching.

TBI/THE BRITISH INSTITUTE JAKARTA, Plaza Setiabudi 2, Jalan HR Rasuna Said, Jakarta 12920 (21-525 6750/fax 21-520 7574). 20 teachers.

ALA Course, Jl. Raya Kupang Jaya 28, Surabaya

Diana Teaching Centre, Jl. RA. Kartini 31, Surabaya

ELTIM English Language Centre, Jl. H. Misbackh No. 5, Surabaya 60264

Executive College, Jl. Dharmahusada 144, Surabaya

Hyper-Visions International, Jl. Manyar Tirtomoyo III/17, Surabaya 60116

Indonesian Australian Language Foundation/UNAIR Language Centre, Jalan Airlangga No. 8, Surabaya (31-502 3332/fax 31-502 3334/e-mail ialf-unair@surabaya.wasantara.net.id). Diploma level teachers preferred.

International Language Training, Kompleks Ruko Platinum, Plaza Blok 2F, Jl. Raya, Sukomanunggal Jaya

Lanta Educational Centre, Kompleks Platinum Plaza, Jl. Raya Sukomanunggal Jaya Blok II C, Surabaya 60188

New Surabaya College, Jl. Jen. Basuki Rachmat 85, Surabaya 60271

New Surabaya College, Kompleks Pertokoan Pondok, Chandra Indah, Jl. Palem, Surabaya

SELC English for Children, Jl. Embong Ploso No. 23, Surabaya

Target English, Jl. Ketintang Selatan 1/23, Surabaya (e-mail targetenglish@hotmail.com)

TOPSII, Jl. Darmo Baru Barat XII/7, Surabaya

Universal Course Jl. Gembili Raya 14, Surabaya

Japan

The once impressive Japanese economy has been stalled in recession for nearly eight years and the stock market is at its lowest level in over a decade. The yen, affected by regional financial turmoil and a serious banking crisis, has depreciated sharply against the US dollar and remains weak. Unemployment has reached post-war record levels. The steady average salary of 250,000 yen per month for full-time teachers has not risen in eight years, although taxes and the cost of living have increased. (When converted into sterling, this wage represents £160 less than it did two years ago.)

The demands and expectations placed on English teachers are increasing. Small schools and major language school chains alike face intensive financial pressure in the face of fierce competition for a shrinking number of students. In many cases they have hurriedly switched their focus to very young learners including pre-school children. Working at a large school is no longer a guarantee of job security. Not long ago, one of the largest chains, the TOZA English Academy, went bankrupt, leaving its teachers unpaid for several months. Japan is no longer the paradise it was once considered to be by TEFL teachers.

But even with a weakened yen, the wage represents about £1,130, which is higher than can be earned by TEFL teachers in other countries. All figures are of course meaningless without balancing them against the local cost of living. If the salaries seem to be lower, so are the setting-up costs described later. (People say that you can't expect to break even and begin to save before you've been in Japan for nearly a year.)

Despite all this, the demand for English continues very strong. For a start, all children must study English for at least three years in junior high school. But just as the demand is strong, so is the supply. University graduates throughout North America have been turning to their college development offices to find out how to organise a teaching job in the Far East. Newcomers who could once count on finding a reasonably convenient job are now having to travel up to two hours to get to work. Schools which once accepted anyone with fluency have become more selective, and it is no longer a case of prospective teachers picking and choosing among employers. Yet there is still very little emphasis on TEFL qualifications. Image is of paramount importance to the Japanese and many employers are more concerned to find people who are lively and a touch glamorous than they are to find people with a background in teaching.

Many language training organisations operate on a huge scale, with many branches and large numbers of staff. Companies like Aeon, GEOS and Nova actively recruit in North America and Britain. These seem to be the employers most willing to consider teachers with no formal training, though all teachers in Japan must have a four-year BA degree (which is an absolute requirement for work visas). Some chains have been described as factory English schools, where teachers are handed a course book and told not to deviate from the formula. Demand for native speaker teachers is so great that they depend on a steady supply of fresh graduates who want the chance to spend a year in Japan. Often new recruits do not have much say in where they are sent and in their first year may be sent to the least desirable locations.

As long as your expectations are realistic, Japan should turn out to be an excellent choice of destination. Native speakers are hired in a surprising range of contexts: in-house language programmes in steel or electronics companies, state secondary schools, hot-house crammers, 'conversation lounges' where young people get together for an hour's guided conversation, vocational schools where English is a compulsory subject, 'ladies' classes' (quaintly so-called) where courses called 'English for Shopping' are actually offered, and also classes of children from as young as two, since it has become a status symbol in Japan to send children of all ages to English classes. In fact studying English for many Japanese is still more a social than an educational activity.

Culture shock grips most new arrivals to Japan. Incoming teachers are often so distracted by the mechanics of life in Japan and the cultural adjustments they have to make to survive that they devote too little energy to the business of teaching. On the other hand, anyone who has a genuine interest in Japan and who arrives reasonably well prepared may find that a year or two in Japan provides a highly rewarding experience.

Prospects for Teachers

Most private language schools in Japan are looking for native speakers of any nationality with a four year BA or BSc in any discipline and possibly some TEFL experience. Although only a minority are looking for professional qualifications in their teachers, there has been a noticeable increase in the number of qualified EFL teachers (especially from Australia) looking for work, and naturally schools prefer to take them over complete novices. Many schools have no set intake dates and so serious applications are welcome at any time of the year. Still the best times to look for work are in March and September before the semesters begin; July and August are fairly dead.

The favoured accent is certainly American and to a lesser extent Canadian. In fact, not many Japanese can distinguish a Scot from a Queenslander, or an Eastender from an Eastsider. What *can* be detected and is highly prized is clear speech. Slow precise diction together with a smart appearance and professional bearing are enough to impress most potential employers.

FIXING UP A JOB

With such a large selection of vacancies at a sub-professional level, it is often possible for university graduates to fix up a job before arrival. Most schools and companies which recruit abroad sort out visas and help with initial orientation and housing. The disadvantage is that their salary and working conditions will probably compare unfavourably with those of teachers who have negotiated their job after arrival; but most new recruits (*nama gaijin* or raw foreigners) conclude that the trade-off is a fair one. Of course the pool of foreign job-seekers already in Japan is large enough that the jobs offering good conditions tend to be snapped up quickly. Many organisations do not welcome speculative applications from outside Japan.

Before tackling the question of how to find a job after arriving in Japan, the possibilities of arranging a contract before leaving home need to be canvassed. The most prestigious programme of them all is the government-sponsored JET programme which offers what many consider to be a 'dream job' for new graduates.

The JET Programme

The Japan Exchange and Teaching (JET) Programme is an official Japanese government scheme aimed at improving foreign language teaching in schools and fostering good relations between the people of Japan and the 34 participating countries. The majority of participants are from the US (contact details below). The prospects for people who wish to become Assistant Language Teachers (ALTs) in English on the JET Programme are excellent and the requirements few. Britain annually recruits around 600 people to the programme and any UK national who is under 35 with a bachelor's degree and an interest in Japan is eligible to apply. The programme has been in existence since 1987 and is now responsible for placing 5,600 native speakers of English for one year in private and state junior and senior high schools throughout Japan, with an increasing emphasis on rural areas.

In the UK the scheme is administered by the Council on International Educational Exchange at 52 Poland Street, London W1V 4JQ; 0171-478 2010/fax: 0171-734 7322; e-mail: JETInfo@ciee.org). Non-British applicants should contact the Japanese Embassy in their country of origin for information and application forms. US applicants can obtain details from any of the 16 Consulates in the US or from the Office of the JET Programme, Japanese Embassy, 2520 Massachusetts Avenue NW, Washington, DC 20008; 202-238-6772/3 or 1-800-INFOJET/fax 202-265-9484/e-mail: eojjet@erols.com.

The timetable for applicants from the UK is as follows: application forms are available in October; the deadline for applications is early December; interviews are held in January and February; an intensive three-day orientation for successful candidates is held in London in mid-July and departures for Japan take place in late July.

Robert Mizzi from Canada knew that the competition for the programme was intense and worked hard on his application, which paid off since he was called to an interview:

> *The interview was probably the most difficult interview I have ever had. It was only 20 minutes, but a painful 20 minutes. Besides the usual 'Why' and 'Tell us about yourself' questions, I was asked to teach a lesson on the spot using dramatic techniques I would use in class. Stunned, I managed to get out of my seat and draw some pictures of the stars and moon on the board, taught them the meaning of those words and then proceeded to ask the interview team to stand up and learn a little dance to the song 'Twinkle twinkle little star'. All I wanted to do was to create an impression and to stand out of the 300 people being interviewed. People remember you best when you are acting like a complete fool. When it is teaching English as a foreign language, the ability to act like a fool is one of the main requirements of the job. Getting Japanese men in suits up and dancing during a job interview with the prestigious JET programme was a half-crazed risk, but a successful one at that.*

Often government-run exchanges of this kind do not offer generous remuneration packages; however pay and conditions on the JET scheme are excellent. In addition to a free return flight, JET participants receive 3,600,000 yen a year (£16,300/$27,500 at the time of writing in contrast to £22,000/$33,300 two years ago). From that gross salary, social and medical insurance fees of approximately 37,000 yen per month are deducted. The salary is standard for all JET participants; there is no cost-of-living bonus for people placed in Tokyo. Contracts are with individual host institutions in Japan, so there can be discrepancies in working conditions. It is the luck of the draw that determines who goes where, although stated preferences will be taken into consideration. Pension regulations mean that JET teachers can reclaim money paid into the national insurance scheme as a lump sum equivalent to about one month's salary.

ALTs are theoretically expected to work a seven-hour day, though quite often teachers are assigned only three or four classes a week. Mark Elliot feels that the JET programme is 'probably the best job in the world' and describes his situation:

> *I live on a wonderful island, three hours ferry ride from Nagasaki, nearer Shanghai than Tokyo. I have next to no classes, but there's lots more to the job than teaching. After all, the programme is much more about meeting people and generally having a good time/enjoying Japan than it is about teaching. If it was a teaching programme, the Ministry of Education would pay the bills rather than Jichisho, the Home Ministry.*

All JET participants teach in partnership with a native Japanese teacher and so there is little scope for taking any initiative in the classroom. In fact quite a few JET teachers complain that they have too little work to keep them occupied. To a large extent it is the hours put in outside the classroom that make the difference.

As Rabindra Roy wrote from Shizuoka-ken prefecture, 'I can think of very few jobs where a freshly qualified graduate with an irrelevant degree and no experience can walk straight into such a big salary for this little work.' He also describes the programme as 'desperately well organised.' But partly because of the variety in locations and schools and partly because Japan is such a weird and wonderful place, it is impossible to predict what life will be like, no matter how many orientations you attend. About half of JET participants renew for a second year which indicates its success. Quite a few stay for a third year which is the maximum. The programme offers a tremendous amount of support and even those who are placed in remote or rural areas are usually within striking distance of other JET participants.

Theresa Bowerman enjoyed her experiences with JET so much that she joined the staff of Council in London on her return:

> *I was employed by the Board of Education of a small city about 45km from the centre of Tokyo, assisted in English classes at the six public junior high schools in my city, and performed various other duties as required, which included at various times joining in after-school club activities, helping out with weekly English clubs at two local elementary schools, running with students as they trained for the school ekiden (marathon), and teaching 'Emergency English' to the city's firemen. I would say that*

the JET Programme provided me with an invaluable opportunity to live and work in a fascinating country and experience a totally different culture and lifestyle.

In Advance

There are many other ways to fix up a job in Japan ahead of time, though these will normally require more initiative (and possibly more qualifications) than signing on with JET. Many Japanese language schools have formed links with university careers departments, particularly in the US and Canada, so anyone with a university connection should exploit it. Another possibility for Americans is to explore the Japanese-American Sister City Program which assists some native speakers to find teaching jobs in the city twinned with theirs.

GEOS, Nova and *AEON* carry out extensive recruitment campaigns in North America, Britain and Australia. *Shane English Schools* confine their recruitment to the UK through their partner, Saxoncourt Recruitment. At present *Christians Abroad* are energetically recruiting TEFL teachers with a Christian commitment for two year contracts in middle and secondary schools. A steady trickle of adverts appear in newspapers, *EL Prospects, TESOL Placement Bulletin,* etc. placed by individual schools in Japan and agents. Quite often schools and groups of schools will appoint a foreign recruiter. For example the large language chain Kent Schools of English was recently advertising in the *Guardian* for EFL teachers to send their CV and photo to a private address in Enfield, Middlesex. Each summer Hilderstone College (St. Peters Road, Broadstairs, Kent CT10 2AQ) recruit for Shumei secondary schools in the Tokyo area. The advertised pay scale is 3.4-4.4 million yen for the year plus free accommodation. The YMCA is a major provider of English in Japan, but no longer recruits outside the country.

Many schools have no need to advertise abroad since they receive so many speculative resumés (the American term for CV is used in Japan). The internet has evolved into a valuable job search tool. Using any of the popular household search engines such as Yahoo, type 'English Teaching in Japan' and dozens of job-related web sites will appear. The free twice-monthly California-based newsletter O-Hayo-Sensei (which means 'Good Morning Teacher') has pages of teaching positions across Japan. Many of these are at the sub-professional level, but there are usually two or three university positions listed in each edition. Check out its web page at www.ohayosensei.com. Another internet address to try is http://www.safejobsinjapan.com (e-mail info@safejobsinjapan.com; 908-252-1883) which was spotted recently advertising free job listings. Other contacts which may prove useful are the book *Make a Mil-Yen: Teaching English in Japan* by Don Best (Stone Bridge Press, PO Box 8208, Berkeley, CA 94707; 1-800-947 7211 or in the UK 0171-724 7773) even if it is a few years old now. More up-to-date information is available on their website (www.stonebridge.com). A two-hour *Work & Live in Japan Video* of a seminar on working in Japan, which covers social and cultural customs, travel tips and corporate work as well as teaching, can be ordered from the Japan Marketing Group, 400 Groveland Ave, Suite 312, Minneapolis, MN 55403, USA (612-871-7889).

A speculative job hunt from abroad has some chance of success for the well-qualified. There are various sources of language school addresses, of varying degress of usefulness. The Japan Information & Cultural Centre of the Embassy of Japan (101-104 Piccadilly, London W1V 9FN; 0171-465 6500) will send out a fact sheet entitled 'Teaching English in Japan' on request together with a list of over 100 addresses (dated April 1997) taken from the *Yellow Pages*. The British Council in Tokyo has an outdated list with no plans to update it in the near future so recommends consulting the English language telephone directory which is on the internet (http://english.townpage.isp.ntt.co.jp). The British Council in Sapporo can send a photocopied list of language schools in the Hokkaido area, but it too is two years out of date. If you are planning to go to Japan in any event, it is a good idea to send your CV to the big schools a few weeks before arrival, make some follow-up calls and hope to arrange some interviews in your first week.

The Monday edition of the English language *Japan Times* carries quite a few ads for

English teachers. It can be consulted (a few days late) at the Japan Information and Cultural Centre or purchased from the Overseas Courier Service (1 Galleywall Road, London SE16 3PB; 0171-237 0399) at a cost of £2.65 per copy or £137.80 for 52 Monday issues. In the UK specialist Japanese bookshops might be able to refer you to the current work-abroad literature (e.g. Japan Centre Bookshop, 212 Piccadilly, London W1; Books Nippon, 64/66 St. Paul's Churchyard, London EC4 8AA; and OCS Books, 2 Grosvenor Parade, Uxbridge Road, London W5 3NN).

Professional teachers can make contact with JALT, the Japan Association for Language Teaching (Urban Edge Building, 4th Floor, 1-37-9 Taito, Taito-ku, Tokyo 110) which runs a Job Information Centre for its members at is annual conference in the autumn.

An unusual opportunity to teach local people is available at a farm in Hokkaido, the most northerly island of the Japanese archipelago, known as Shin-Shizen-Juku (Tsurui, Akan-gun, Hokkaido 085-12; 0154 64-2821), a place well known to the travelling fraternity. The owner Hiroshi Mine welcomes international travellers who want to conduct conversation classes with local businessmen, farmers, housewives, doctors and children, in exchange for board and lodging and pocket money. Mr. Mine organises the classes, provides transport and some teaching materials. Much depends on the personalities of the other volunteers (often just two or three); whereas some travellers perceive it to be a wonderful opportunity and enjoy a warm atmosphere, others find the place bleak and exploitative.

On the Spot

As has been mentioned, any native speaker with a Bachelor's degree certificate has a chance of landing a job as an English teacher on arrival in Japan. The crucial question is how long will it take. The murderous cost of living means that job-hunters spend hundreds of dollars or pounds very quickly while engaged in the time-consuming business of answering ads, sending round CVs, and going for interviews.

Few things could be more intimidating for the EFL teacher than to arrive at Narita International Airport with no job and limited resources. The longer the job hunt takes, the faster the finances dwindle and the more nerve-racking and discouraging the situation becomes. One way to lessen the monumentality of the initial struggle would be to get out of Tokyo straightaway. Although there are more jobs in the capital, there is also more competition from other foreigners, to the point of saturation. Enterprising teachers who are willing to step off the conveyor belt which takes job-seekers from the airport to one of Tokyo's many 'gaijin houses' (hostels for foreigners) may well encounter fewer setbacks. Osaka seems a good bet since it is within commuting distance of the whole Kansai area, including Kobe which is 20 minutes away by train. In Osaka the cost of living is as much as a quarter less than it is in Tokyo. Another promising destination is Sapporo in the north, the fifth largest city in the country. Ken Foye is a reader of this book who chose to teach on Hokkaido, the northern island on which Sapporo is located:

> *I have been teaching here for a year and a half now and I would recommend Hokkaido to anyone, especially those who don't find living in a large urban metropolis very appealing. Here the people seem much friendlier than in Tokyo, the cost of living isn't as high, there's fresh air and the scenery is magnificent. And I probably would not have ended up here if not for your book.*

Tokyo

One of the most often recommended places to start the job hunt in Tokyo is the Kimi Information Center (Oscar Building, 8th Floor, 2-42-3 Ikebukuro, Toshima-ku, Tokyo 171-0014; 3-3986 1604/fax 3-3986 3037/e-mail kimi529@gol.com; http://www.gsquare,or.jp/kimi). Like so many addresses in Japan, it helps to have specific directions which Deborah Cordingley has provided: take the West Exit from Ikebukuro Station, go to Pasela (a main street), turn right and walk straight along for three minutes until you reach the Royal Hotel which is next door. The Kimi Center offers a range of useful services such as photocopying, computer time and a telephone answering service as well as advising on cheap accommodation and reasonable apartments in and around Tokyo. Free Job Opportunities booklets are available. For 315 yen, they will fax your resumé to a school (more for outside Tokyo). Private rooms at nearby Kimi Ryokan (Japanese-style guest house) cost 4,500 yen (£20/$35); the address is 2-36-8 Ikebokoro, Toshima-ku (3-3971-3766).

Other gaijin houses offer dormitory accommodation for about half that price. Try to pick up a list of gaijin houses from the tourist office and look for ones which charge a monthly rather than a nightly rent since these tend to be the ones which attract long-term residents. Among the cheapest is Mickey House (2-15-1 Nakadai Itabashi-ku; 3-3936 8889) whose bed charges start at 38,000 yen per month. A more typical rent is 60,000 yen. Because it is so difficult to rent flats, some teachers continue living in gaijin houses after they find work. Try to find a gaijin house favoured by teachers such as the one which Ted Travis recommended when he sent a post card from Tokyo:

> There is a wonderful new guest house near Iidabashi called Orchid House, convenient for five different stations. They have five floors, lots of facilities and it is very sociable as well as affordable. Newcomers can usually pick up work from those already employed. The majority of people tend to stay between six months and a year, but short-stay travellers are also welcome. The address is 2-1-11 Kasuga, Bunkyo ku, Tokyo 112; tel: 3-5802 4461. The same company has houses in Nakano, Oji, etc.

Many foreigners live and work in the Roppongi district of Tokyo which might therefore be a sensible place to base yourself. A free ads paper called *Tokyo Classifieds* is distributed in this area on Fridays carrying job and accommodation ads. Once you get to know some other teachers, there is always the chance of inheriting their hours when they decide to move on. According to one report from Osaka, teachers actually 'sell' their hours when they are ready to leave. Even tourist offices such as the one at Hibuya station (exit A-3) have free notice boards where private lessons may be sought or offered, as well as accommodation.

Wherever you choose to conduct your job hunt, English language newspapers are the starting place for most. Jobs in secondary schools are advertised from September on. The Monday edition of the *Japan Times* carries fewer ads than it used to but it is still the best source. Note that ads often specify 'female' which usually indicates a job teaching young children. Male applicants for these posts may have to prove that they have prior experience of working with children.

Jobs in the Kansai region around Osaka are listed at the end of the Tokyo classifieds. The main publication in the Kansai area is the monthly magazine *Kansai Time Out* (1-13 Ikuta Cho 1-chome, Chuo-ku, Kobeshi, Hyogo 651-0092) and its homepage called *Japan File*: http://www.kto.co.jp). It carries fewer job ads than it once did, but still has pages and pages of language school ads. Two Tokyo papers *Mainichi Daily News* (Hitotsubashi 1-1-1, Chiyoda-ku) and *Asahi Evening News* (5-3-2 Tsukiji, Chuo-ku) are also worth a look. As usual, the employers which advertise regularly tend to be the ones with the worst reputations and the highest staff turnover.

Amanda Searle describes what she found in the newspapers when she was job-hunting:

> Most companies give little idea in their adverts of the hours and salary, let alone the age and number of students or the textbooks used. They are not very willing to give that information over the phone, explaining that you will get the opportunity to ask questions if you are called for interview. I sent cover letters out with my resumé, explaining that I was looking only for full-time positions which offered visa sponsorship. I sent out about 20 applications and about ten companies contacted me and I went to eight interviews. I ended up being offered two full-time positions and three part-time ones.

The initial phone call is very important and should be considered as a preliminary interview. Since you may be competing with as many as 100 people answering the same ad, you have to try to stand out over the phone. Speak slowly, clearly, and be very *genki* which means lively and fun. You may be asked to fax your CV to them; the cover letter should be short and intelligent, and the CV should be brief and interesting, emphasising any teaching experience. Always carry a supply of professional looking business cards *(meishi)*.

Demonstration lessons now form an integral part of most job interviews in Japan, regardless of one's qualifications. Try to prepare yourself as much as possible if only because travelling to an interview in Tokyo is a major undertaking which can take up to three hours and cost a lot of money; it would be a shame to blow your chances because of a simple oversight. Dress as impeccably and conservatively as possible, and carry a respectable briefcase, since books are often judged by their covers in Japan. Inside you should have any education certificates you have earned, preferably the originals since schools have long since realised that a lot of forgeries are in circulation. Your resumé should not err on the side of modesty.

REGULATIONS

The key to obtaining a work visa for Japan is to have a Japanese sponsor. This can be a private citizen but most teachers are sponsored by their employers. Not all schools by any means are willing to sponsor their teachers, unless they are persuaded that they are an ongoing proposition. Some schools rely on a stream of Canadians, Australians and New Zealanders on working holiday visas which they must obtain in their home countries. The SWAP Japan Programme allows students aged 18-30 to work for six months in the first instance but is extendable to 18 months. To qualify you must prove that you have US$3,000 at your disposal. Further details are available in Australia from any branch of STA Travel and in Canada from any Travel CUTS office; both issue an information booklet *The Swapper's Guide to Japan*. There is no equivalent scheme for Britons or Americans. For information about obtaining a work visa in the US, log on to the Embassy's web-site on www.embjapan.org/via.html.

Other nationalities will have to find a sponsor. If your visa is to be processed before arrival, you must have a definite job appointment in Japan. Your employer must apply to the Ministry of Justice in Tokyo for a Certificate of Eligibility which he or she then forwards to you. You must take this along with a photocopy of it, your passport, photograph and application form to the Embassy in your country. Normally a visa can be issued within three working days, though it can take longer. New regulations stipulate that anyone who works in Higher Education must have an MA in Education or TEFL.

Many Britons and North Americans enter with a temporary visitor's stamp (valid for three months), find a job and sponsor and then apply for a work visa. Documents which will help you to find a sponsor are the original or notarised copy of your BA or other degree and resumé. The temporary visitor's stamp can be extended for another 90 days (for example at Kushiro immigration office) for a fee. In the past, many people worked on this temporary stamp which they kept extending. Now it is unlikely that someone who has stayed in Japan for six months and then leaves the country will be granted landing permission before a reasonable amount of time has elapsed. Those found to be overstaying as tourists can be deported. Furthermore, employers who are caught employing illegal aliens as well as the foreign workers themselves are subject to huge fines, and both parties risk imprisonment.

Finding an employer to sponsor you for a work visa is very important. A number of schools advertising for teachers state in their ads that they are willing to consider only those who already have a work visa. Others are willing to act as sponsors. Sponsors obtain a Certificate of Eligibility inside Japan and then the teacher must leave the country to change their status (typically on a two or three day trip to Korea), a process which can cost as much as $500 if you fly; the processing fee is 50,000 yen. According to Alan Suter the cheapest way is to take a ferry from Kobe to Pusan, Korea.

The work visa is valid for 12 months and renewable annually. When renewing, one of the most important requirements is a tax statement showing your previous year's earnings. It is difficult to obtain a new visa unless you can show that you have earned at least 250,000 yen per month. Cash-in-hand and part-time jobs may be lucrative but they do nothing to help your visa application. If you break your contract with your employer, you will have to find another sponsor willing to act as sponsor the following year. Once in Japan, visa information should be sought from the Ministry of Foreign Affairs (Gaimusho), 2-2-1 Kasumigaseki, Chiyoda-ku, Tokyo 100 (tel: 3-580-3311).

You are permitted to work up to 20 hours a week on a cultural or student visa. Cultural visas are granted to foreigners interested in studying some aspect of traditional Japanese culture on a full-time basis. In this case you must find a teacher willing to sponsor you. Cultural visas are often granted for shodo (calligraphy), taiko (drumming), karate, aikido, ikebana (flower arranging) and ochakai (tea ceremony). At one time these study visas were liberally handed out but nowadays you must produce concrete evidence that you actually are studying.

The tax situation is normally favourable for teachers, provided they are exempt in their home countries. Note that JET salaries are no longer tax-free. Teachers usually have the basic rate of national income tax in Japan (6-7%) withdrawn at source. A further 3% is owing for local taxes, which are the teacher's responsibility only in their second and subsequent years in Japan. The Japanese government offers nationalised health insurance which covers about three-quarters of medical and dental care bills. The cost is about 4,000 yen per month. Many employers accustomed to hiring native speaker teachers may offer more comprehensive private cover for less.

CONDITIONS OF WORK

Despite a widespread feeling that the glory days of ELT in Japan are over, all things are relative and most established teachers in the late 1990s do not find much to complain about. Despite the high cost of living, most teachers seem to be able to save money without having to lead too frugal an existence. Some even save half their salary in their first year by avoiding eating out and going to the cinema. The longer you work in Japan the higher the salary and better working conditions you can command. Rank beginners outside Tokyo and Osaka can earn as little as 230,000 yen a month, but the steady average of 250,000 yen persists almost everywhere. Perks such as increments for higher qualifications, end-of-contract bonuses, free Japanese lessons and travel tickets, etc. are in fairly wide evidence. A tip for those who manage to save a significant sum was passed on by Ted Travis: buying an international postal money order *(yubin kawase)* from any post office is by far the cheapest way to transfer money out of the country.

Teaching schedules can be exhausting, especially if you work for a company which sends its teachers out to office premises (for which a car is sometimes made available). As usual, the timetable may be announced at the last minute, though it is more difficult to opt out in Japan than in other countries because of the dedication Japanese workers show to their firms. (At best a Japanese worker gets ten days of holiday a year and few take their full entitlement for fear of seeming lazy or disloyal to the company.) Some schools remain open all weekend and on public holidays too. Nova for example expects all its teachers to work on Sundays. But the shift system has its merits as Bridgid Seymour-East from New Zealand found out:

> I went to Hiroshima on a six-month working holiday visa and found work at Nova. I worked their part-time shift, 10am-1pm each day and thoroughlyenjoyed it. I got to know the students as the same ones came in at that time and there would only be three or four teachers on duty. Nova is good if you want to meet other teachers, and be able to swap hours or even do a few weeks in another part of the country. Smaller schools are obviously less flexible.

One of the advantages of working in state schools (as JET teachers do) is that they close for holidays, usually three weeks at Christmas and two weeks in August between semesters. Most schools offer one-week holidays (paid or unpaid or a combination of the two) at the beginning of May (the 'Golden Week') and in the middle of August ('O-bon vacation'). Holidays for those lucky enough to work in institutes of higher education are much more generous.

Private tutoring is still lucrative, paying between 3,000 and 6,000 yen an hour. Occasionally you will meet someone who has has been paid $100 just to have dinner with a language learner and converse in English, but these plums are few and far between.

The Pupils

The stereotype of the diligent Japanese pupil has becoming somewhat outmoded. The younger generation of Japanese is not always willing to play by the rules that their elders lay down, and there is increasing tension in schools which may manifest itself in (mildly) unruly behaviour. But mostly teachers find their students eager, attentive and willing to confer great respect on their teachers and in some out-of-the-way places even celebrity status. All teachers are expected to look the part and most schools will insist on proper dress (e.g. suits and dresses). But they do not want a formal approach to teaching.

Adults will have studied English at school for at least six years, and their knowledge of grammar is usually sound. They go to conversation schools in the expection of meeting native speaker teachers able to deliver creative and entertaining lessons. Yet some are crippled by diffidence or excessive anxiety about grammatical correctness. Michael Frost is one teacher who experienced a clash of cultures when trying to encourage discussion in his classroom:

> *It is very difficult for Japanese students to come out and express an individual opinion. The best tactic is to get them in pairs, so that together they can work something out. They are more productive and open in pairs, and it takes the pressure off them. Then get the pairs into fours, to express a mini-group opinion, then work for a total group agreement. The thing to avoid at all costs is to stroll into class, saying, 'OK, today we are going to discuss environmental issues. Tetsuya, you set the ball rolling: What do you think of pollution?' It will not work.*

"Akiko, tell us your views on love and marriage"

It is a popular myth that Japanese students have good reading abilities in English and require only conversation practice. This was not the experience of Nathan Edwards in 1998, a Diploma-qualified teacher from Canada:

I am currently teaching at the Tokyo YMCA College of English, a pioneer in English teaching in Japan, established in 1880. The fact is that both reading and speaking in English present major challenges even to students with years of English instruction in the Japanese school system. It is highly advisable for teachers to bring a good supply of realia with them (various English brochures, used tickets, maps, coins, etc.) and old lesson plans.

Problems can arise in team teaching situations if your Japanese colleague has not attained a high enough level of English. While teaching in the JET programme, Robert Mizzi came to admire Japanese culture, but he did find some aspects of his job frustrating:

A lot of times I cannot introduce a game idea because, literally, it will take 20 minutes for the teacher to understand (never mind the students).

Among the many strange aspects of Japanese culture is one which most foreigners find particularly disturbing. A native speaker who happens to have non-Caucasian features will almost certainly be discriminated against. Bryn Thomas enjoyed many aspects of his job as a conversation facilitator at a language lounge in the middle of Tokyo but was shocked by one incident. When the publicity photos were being taken for the company brochure, a qualified teacher from Hawaii was rudely asked to step aside from the staff portrait.

Accommodation

It is not uncommon for teachers who are hired overseas to be given help with accommodation, which is a tremendously useful perk, even if the flat provided is small and over-priced, with poor insulation and a badly equipped kitchen. If you are on your own, you will be forced to use a rental agency, the majority of whom do not speak English and are not willing to rent to foreigners. Amanda Searle's advice is 'unless you have connections or are looking at 100,000 yen per month accommodation, don't break your heart trying to find a decent place.'

If you do succeed through an agency, you will have to pay a commission of one month's rent as well as a colossal deposit called 'key money' which is often six months rent in advance. Unlike rent deposits in the West you can't expect to recoup it all. Assuming the range of rents is 60,000-100,000 yen per person per month in Tokyo and perhaps 65,000 yen on average in Osaka, that means you might have to pay more than £2,700 upfront. Rents outside Tokyo and Osaka should be nearer 50,000 yen, with an additional monthly payment of at least 10,000 yen for utilities. Well-established schools may be prepared to lend you the key money or (exceptionally) pay it outright.

There are great discrepancies in the accommodation assigned to JET teachers. While some get beautiful no-rent houses, others get one-room apartments with high rent. Robert Mizzi had no complaints about the rent (just US$80 a month) but he didn't get much for his money:

I have no oven, dryer, hot water, shower or heating. A lot of things I had to buy for the apartment and a lot of things I had to give up. (The thrill of having running water certainly is a luxury where I am.)

A further problem is the near total absence of furnished apartments, so you may have to go shopping for curtains and cookers on top of all your other expenses. Again, schools which normally hire foreign teachers may keep a stock of basic furnishings which they can lend to teachers. Amanda Searle found the solution to this problem:

The 'big gomi' provides a great opportunity to get the things you need. Gomi means rubbish and it is collected from the street. The big gomi takes place in August and December when Japanese workers receive a bonus and then go out to replace many of their belongings. I have obtained a desk, heater, TV, radio (complete with instruction booklet safely stowed in the battery compartment) water pot and chair this way. Any electrical applicances considered to be dangerous or broken have their plugs cut off.

If all this sounds too much hassle, perhaps staying in a *gaijin house* long term is not such a bad idea.

Obviously it is to your advantage to live as close to your place of work as possible, but as noted above many teachers are forced to spend a sizeable chunk of their earnings and a lot of time commuting. Ask your employer to pay for your travel, preferably in the form of a monthly travel pass which can be used for your leisure travel as well. If you're in Tokyo, bear in mind that city buses charge a flat fare of 200 yen.

LEISURE TIME

According to some veteran teachers, leisure time and how to spend it will be the least of your worries. Depending on your circumstances, you may be expected to participate in extracurricular activities and social events which it would cause offence to decline—always a major concern in Japan. Although Bryn Thomas enjoyed the sushi which his school provided for teachers still at work at 9pm, he was less keen on the 'office parties when teachers were required to dress up in silly costumes and be nice to the students'. Most teachers are happy to accept occasional invitations to socialise with their Japanese colleagues or pupils, even if it does mean an evening of speaking very very slowly and drinking heavily. Many teachers find the socialising with students fun if expensive. Knowing a *gaijin* is a considerable status symbol for many Japanese, many of whom are willing to pay good money just for you to go to their houses once a week and eat their food.

But it is not like that everywhere. A glut of Westerners in Tokyo means that your welcome may be less than enthusiastic. In fact non-Japanese are refused entrance to some Tokyo bars and restaurants. Many people head straight out of Tokyo for the more appealing city of Osaka. Julie Fast describes the contrast:

> *I am still enamoured of Osaka; it is like a village after Tokyo. I am constantly amazed at the trees we see everywhere. I never realised in Tokyo how much I hated being constantly surrounded by people. I never had personal space in Tokyo. No one does—which explains the distant, sour looks on most people's faces. What a difference in Osaka. Osaka people have the roughest reputation in all of Japan. From a western point of view, they are the friendliest. I have been invited to houses for lunch, children say hello and people in shops actually talk to you. Which proves you can't judge a country by its largest city.*

All cities are expensive. Any entertainment which smacks of the West such as going out to a fashionable coffee house or a night club will be absurdly expensive. However if you are content with more modest indigenous food and pastimes, you will be able to save money. A filling bowl of noodles and broth costs less than £3, though you may never take to the standard breakfast of boiled rice and a raw egg. Staying home to listen to Japanese language tapes or to read a good book (e.g. *Pictures from the Water Trade,* a personal account of life in Japan) costs nothing. Obviously the more settled you become, the more familiar you will be with the bargains and affordable amusements.

Finding your way around is nothing if not a challenge in a country where almost all road and public transport signs are incomprehensible. What use is an A-Z if you can't read the alphabet? Many feel that it is worth making an effort to master at least something of the written language. There are three alphabets in Japanese: *kanji* (ancient pictograms), *hiragana* and *katakana* (the characters used to spell loan words from English). Amanda Searle is just one teacher who feels that *kana* can be learned through independent study so that at least you will be able to read station names and menus. Learning some of the script not only impresses students and shows that you are making an effort to absorb some of the culture, it also helps you to survive.

Japanese addresses are mind-bogglingly complicated too: the numbers refer to land subdivisions: prefecture, district, ward, then building. When in doubt (inevitable) ask a friendly informant for a *chizu* (map). It is also a good idea to get a Japanese person to write your destination in both *kanji* and transliterated into *roma-ji* (our alphabet).

Japanese people will sometimes go to embarrassing lengths to help foreigners. This desire to help wedded to a reluctance to 'lose face' means that they may offer advice and instructions based on very little information, so keep checking. Young people in jeans are the best bets. Outside the big cities the people are even more cordial. Wherever you go, you don't have to worry about crime.

Travel is expensive. For example the bullet train from Tokyo to Sendai, a couple of hundred miles north, costs about £90 one way. Yet the pace of a teacher's life in Tokyo or another big city can become so stressful that it is essential to get on a local train and see some of the countryside. Hitch-hiking in Japan is safer, easier and more enjoyable than in most countries. The risk is not of being left by the roadside or of being mugged but of being taken unbidden to the nearest railway station (which might be a major detour for the hapless driver who feels obliged to do this out of courtesy). Others will buy meals and refreshments and are genuinely interested in foreigners.

The alienness of Japanese culture is one of the main fascinations of the place. It is foolish to become bogged down worrying about transgressing against mysterious customs. The JET literature, for example, may be unnecessarily intimidating in its pointing up of possible cultural *faux pas*. But in fact Japanese people are more tolerant of foreigners than many give them credit for. Rabindra Roy taught in a state school quite happily and no comment was ever passed on his long hair and beard, earrings and bangles. Similarly Claire Wilkinson felt quite overwhelmed after reading the JET literature. One of the many prohibitions mentioned is 'never blow your nose in public', and so the heavy cold with which she arrived made her even more miserable than it would have otherwise. But she soon discovered that the Japanese allow foreigners a great deal of latitude and that she could relax and be herself without causing grave offence.

The price you pay for the tolerance extended to your alien ways is that you will always be treated as an outsider, no matter how adept you become with chopsticks or at using Japanese phrases. In Japan you will never be able to blend in or go incognito. Kristen Ghodsee sums up the potential hazards:

> *I have seen many foreigners leave Japan angry and full of hatred towards the Japanese because they were unable or unwilling to understand Japanese ways. Outside the metropolises, being pointed at, stared at and laughed at is commonplace. Be prepared to sacrifice all vestiges of privacy. You are fair game in Japan because you are different. You can make and save an incredible amount of money, but you must have an incredible amount of patience and self-confidence. The Japanese are wonderful, friendly people if you can get past the surface differences. If you're coming only to make the quick buck (as many do), and are not willing to be open-minded to a radically different culture, you will make yourself miserable and worsen the ever-worsening opinion the Japanese have of foreigners working in their country.*

When it is finally time to move on, an excellent source of ideas for planning your future (and relevant to more than just JET teachers) is *JET and Beyond* edited by Robin Macdonald; details from the Association for Japan Exchange and Teaching (AJET Drop Box, c/o CLAIR, 4F Nissaykojimachi Building, 3-3-6 Kudan Machi, Chiyoda-ku, Tokyo 102).

LIST OF SCHOOLS

AEON INTER-CULTURAL USA
9301 Wilshire Boulevard, Suite 202, Beverly Hills, CA 90210, USA. Tel: (310) 550-0940. Fax: 550-1463. E-mail: aeonla@aeonet.com. Web-site: www.aeonet.com

One of the largest chains of English conversation schools in Japan with 200 branches.
Number of teachers: 500.
Preference of nationality: none.
Qualifications: 4 year degree and fluency in English.
Conditions of employment: 12 month contracts. 36 h.p.w.

Salary: 250,000 yen per month.
Facilities/Support: furnished apartment provided with subsidised monthly rent. 1-week paid training provided in Japan. Return airfare and cash bonus provided at end of contract and other perks.
Recruitment: group and personal interviews held in various US cities. 3 permanent recruiting offices in US (Los Angeles, New York, Chicago) and 1 in Sydney, Australia. Positions start every month. Rolling deadlines. Initial applicants should send résumé and essay entitled 'Why I want to live and work in Japan'. See Web Site http://www.aeonet.com.
Contact: Erik Orre, General Manager.

AMERICA EIGO GAKUIN (American English Institute)
USA Office: PO Box 1672, St. George, UT 84771. Tel: (435) 628-6301. E-mail: rpurcell@infowest.com
Japan Office: Misono-cho 5-2-21, Wakayama City 640. Tel: (734) 360581.
30 locations, mostly in rural locations.
Number of teachers: 45.
Preference of nationality: American, Canadian.
Qualifications: BA/BSc degree.
Conditions of employment: minimum 6 month contracts. 28 contact h.p.w., 5 days p.w.
Salary: 250,000 yen per month.
Facilities/Support: furnished apartments provided (teachers pay rent of 30,000-55,000 yen). Key money paid by company. Teaching materials provided.
Recruitment: via US office. Interviews not essential.

ECC FOREIGN LANGUAGE INSTITUTE
Offices in Osaka (Kinki District: tel: 6-359-0531), Tokyo (Kanto District: tel: 3-5330-1585), Nagoya (Chubu District: tel: 52-332-6156) and Fukuoka (Kyushu District: tel: 92-715-0731).
Number of teachers: 320 at over 120 schools throughout Japan.
Preference of nationality: none.
Qualifications: BA required.
Conditions of employment: 1 year contracts, mostly starting in April but not always. 25 h.p.w. mostly evenings. Sunday plus 1 other day off per week. Opportunities for paid overtime often available.
Salary: from 250,000 yen per month, more in Kanto District. Rate of tax is 6-10% per month.
Facilities/Support: assistance with accommodation. During compulsory 30-50 hour training course, wage is 1,000 yen an hour.
Recruitment: contact one of above numbers upon arriving in Japan. (Applicant information is shared among districts.) Main hiring period is February/March.

ENGLISH ACADEMIC RESEARCH INSTITUTE
Maruyoshi Building 6-2-2, Higashi Ueno, Taito-ku, Tokyo 110. Tel: (3) 3844-3104.
Number of teachers: 1-2.
Preference of nationality: American, British, Canadian, Australian, New Zealand.
Qualifications: college graduates; no teaching experience needed.
Conditions of employment: 1 year contracts. Hours of work 11am-8.30pm.
Salary: US$30 per hour.
Facilities/Support: no assistance with accommodation. No training given.
Recruitment: through newspaper adverts. Local interviews essential.

ENGLISH ACADEMY
2-9-6 Ichibancho, Matsuyama 790-0001. Tel: (89) 931-8686. Fax: (89) 933-1210.
Number of teachers: 9.
Preference of nationality: none, but most are from US/Canada.

Qualifications: BA, teaching experience preferable, and enthusiasm essential. Some computer experience desirable.

Conditions of employment: 18 month contracts. Maximum 25 contact h.p.w. between 1pm and 9pm. Pupils aged 3-70, but most are younger students.

Facilities/Support: assistance with accommodation given. Partial payment of health insurance. Training available.

Recruitment: through direct application. Interviews required but can be held over the telephone.

GEOS CORPORATION

Shin Osaki Kangyo Building 4F, 6-4 Osaki 1 chome, Shinagawa-ku, Tokyo 141. Tel: (3) 5434-0200. Fax: (3) 5434-0201. E-mail: gkyomu@beehive.twics.com. Web-site: http://www.twics.com/-mjm/hiring.html; also http://www.geos.demon.co.uk

One of Japan's largest English language institutions.

Number of teachers: approximately 1,600 teachers for more than 350 schools throughout Japan.

Preference of nationality: Canadian, American, British, South African, Australian, New Zealand.

Qualifications: university bachelor's degree required (any discipline). CELTA or equivalent would be an asset.

Conditions of employment: 1 year renewable contracts. Long-term career commitment preferred. Full-time schedule between noon and 9pm, 5 days a week.

Salary: base salary is 250,000 yen per month less 10% tax. Extra payment available to teachers depending on student sign-up rates, student renewals, group lesson fees and overtime. Up to 100,000 yen travel benefit paid to teachers on completion of contract.

Facilities/Support: correspondence and preparatory courses and working visas provided prior to departure, and ongoing training in Japan including Japanese lessons. Single occupancy furnished apartment provided at a rental rate of about 50,000 yen per month plus 10,000 yen per month for utilities. Commuting pass provided. Health and accident insurance provided. Career positions available such as teacher trainers/curriculum development, publishing staff, hiring offices, homestay coordinators, etc.

Recruitment: all GEOS teachers are hired outside Japan. Positions comence 4-6 months after an offer of employment from GEOS Corporation in Japan. Contact GEOS hiring office in UK: GEOS Language Ltd., Bow Bells House, Bread St, London EC4M 9BQ (0171-822 1783/fax 0171-822 1785/e-mail london@ geos.demon.co.uk) and in North America: GEOS Language Corporation Ontario, Simpson Tower 2424, 401 Bay Street, Toronto, Ontario M5H 2Y4, Canada (416-777-0109/fax 416-777-0110/e-mail geos@istar.ca) Applicants from Australia and New Zealand should contact GEOS in Japan.

HEARTS ENGLISH SCHOOL

2146-3 Shido, Shido-cho, Okawa-gun, Kagawa 769-2101. Tel: (87) 894-3557. Fax: (87) 894-7227. E-mail: hearts@mb.kagawa-net.or.jp. Web-site: http:// service.kagawa-net.or.jp/hearts/heartsmain.html

Number of teachers: 2 full-time, 1 part-time.

Preference of nationality: American, Canadian, British.

Qualifications: BA with TEFL/TESL or teaching experience, preferably teaching children.

Conditions of employment: minimum 1 year contracts. Approx. 25 h.p.w. Teachers design own curriculum. Half of classes are adults, half children.

Salary: 250,000-270,000 yen per month plus bonus.

Facilities/Support: furnished apartment in quiet location at reasonable rent. Health insurance provided at reasonable cost. Weekly Japanese lessons provided.

Recruitment: adverts in *TESOL Placement Bulletin.* Send resumé, cover letter, references and photos.

Contact: Naomi Yoneda, Director.

INTERAC CO. LTD.
Fujibo Building 2F, 2-10-28 Fujimi, Chiyoda-ku, Tokyo 102. Tel: (3) 3234-7857. Fax: (3) 3234-6055.
Number of teachers: 250 in 10 branches.
Preference of nationality: none, though majority are North American, Australian and British.
Qualifications: minimum university degree plus two years business or technical experience.
Conditions of employment: 12 month contracts. Clients include Honda, Hitachi, etc.
Salary: guaranteed monthly minimum of 250,000 yen. 7% deducted in tax plus local taxes paid separately.
Facilities/Support: 35-hour paid training programme is compulsory. Assistance with accommodation given. One-off housing allowance paid. Company acts as sponsor for visas and guarantor for housing and telephone.
Recruitment: mostly recruit locally, though do make recruiting trips to the US and UK in the spring and autumn. Interviews essential.

JAMES ENGLISH SCHOOL
Sendai (Main Branch), Sumitomo Bank Building, 9F, 20-2-6 Chuo, Aoba ku, Sendai 980. Tel: (22) 267 4911. Fax: (22) 267 4908. E-mail: kigawa1007@aol.com
Number of teachers: 70 in 17 branches in the Tohoku region of northern Japan.
Preference of nationality: native English speakers.
Qualifications: minimum Bachelor degree. Teaching qualifications or TEFL/TESL certificate an asset.
Conditions of employment: commitment for 2 years preferred. 20 contact h.p.w. plus preparation time.
Salary: 250,000-260,000 yen basic salary per month.
Facilities/Support: assistance in finding accommodation. 3-day orientation provided.
Recruitment: newspaper advertisements, internet postings. Interviews are held in various North American cities.
Contact: Kigawa-san, School President.

MATSUDO ENGLISH CENTER
Serizawa Bldg. 3F, 17-11 Honcho, Matsudo-shi, Chiba-ken 271. Tel: (473) 66-0987. Fax: (473) 66-0945.
Number of teachers: 7.
Preference of nationality: American, British.
Qualifications: college graduates; must be enthusiastic and motivated.
Conditions of employment: 1 year contracts. 30 h.p.w. Pupils aged from 2. Unique teaching method and materials developed by company president whereby all negativism is eliminated.
Salary: varies according to experience.
Facilities/Support: assistance with accommodation. Training given.
Recruitment: through newspaper adverts. Interviews essential and sometimes held in US.

M.I.L. THE LANGUAGE CENTER
3.F Eguchi Bldg., 1-6-2 Katsutadai, Yachiyo-shi, Chiba-ken 276. Tel: (474) 85-7555. Fax: 85-7875.
Number of teachers: 15.
Preference of nationality: Canadian, American.
Qualifications: BA in relevant subject; teaching experience and TESL qualification preferred. Must be creative, flexible and willing to teach both children and adults.
Conditions of employment: 1 year renewable contracts. Maximum 40 h.p.w. of which 25 are contact hours, between noon and 10pm weekdays. Pupils from age 4.
Salary: 257-265,000 yen per month with 10% raise for second year and bonus on completion of contract.

Facilities/Support: contribution made to initial costs of accommodation, furnishings and telephone line. Training given.
Recruitment: through adverts and agencies. Mainly telephone interviews. Résumés accepted throughout the year.
Contact: Chie Morizuka, Office Coordinator.

NEW DAY SCHOOL
Yamaichi Kokubuncho Building 5F, 2-15-16, Kokubuncho, Aoba-ku, Sendai 980-0803. Tel: (22) 265-4288. Fax: (22) 227-7421. E-mail: newday@sh.comminet.or.jp
Number of teachers: 7.
Preference of nationality: none.
Qualifications: formal training in TEFL, e.g. MA (Applied Linguistics) or Cambridge/RSA Cert. Experience desirable. Should have interest in professional development.
Conditions of employment: 2 year contracts. 20 contact h.p.w. but 40 hours per 5-day week. Variable hours including some morning/evening shifts.
Salary: 270,000-300,000 yen per month for those with an MA, 250,000-270,000 yen per month without.
Facilities/Support: assistance given with accommodation (for MA-qualified teachers). 1 month training period. Up to 50,000 yen towards health insurance.
Recruitment: adverts in professional journals. Candidates must submit an audio tape and then have an interview by telephone.

NOHKAI ELS ENGLISH INSTITUTE
Kobe Harborland Center Bldg. 19F, 1-3-3, Higashi Kawasaki-cho, Chuo-ku, Kobe 650. Fax: (78) 371 5054.
Number of teachers: 40.
Preference of nationality: none.
Qualifications: university degree. TESL/TEFL certification preferred. Experience teaching in Japan and some knowledge of Japanese language would be an asset.
Conditions of employment: 1 year contracts, renewable. 36 h.p.w. 5 days p.w. including most weekends. Pupils are elementary school conversation classes, junior high school listening and high school entrance excam listening courses.
Salary: 250,000-320,000 yen per month, according to qualifications and experience.
Facilities/Support: assistance with accommodation. Rent 50,000-60,000 yen for single teachers, 75,000 yen for couples. Visa sponsorship. 2-3 training days per year. Junior high course materials are developed in-house.
Recruitment: local interview essential.

NOVA GROUP
Carrington House, 126/130 Regent Street, London W1R 5FE. Tel: 0171-734 2727. Fax: 0171-734 3001. E-mail tefl@novagroup.demon.co.uk. Web-site: www.nova-group.com.
Number of teachers: more than 3000 in 300+ Nova schools located throughout Japan. An average school has 8-12 teachers and several Japanese staff.
Preference of nationality: British, American, Canadian, Australian, New Zealand, Irish. Some French, German, Italian and Spanish positions also available.
Qualifications: BA minimum. Additional TEFL qualifications or experience an advantage.
Conditions of employment: 1 year renewable contracts. Maximum class size of 4 students. Mixture of shifts (10am-5.40pm. 11.20am-7pm and 1.20pm-9pm). 35 h.p.w. including conversation room classes. Excellent opportunities for promotion to senior teacher/trainer positions.
Salary: salaries vary with district. Range is from 259,000 yen in Tokyo and environs rising to an average of 284,000 yen after 2-month probationary period. Comparable salaries in Osaka are 250,000 yen and 275,000 yen; other areas vary slightly. Monthly travel expenses are reimbursed.
Facilities/Support: accommodation, health insurance and visa sponsorship arranged.

Orientation given along with initial and ongoing training, regular feedback, teachers' meetings and specialised training workshops.

Recruitment: positions start at various times of the year. Interviews are essential, and are held through Nova offices in the UK, USA, Canada, Australia or Japan. (See accompanying advertisement for addresses of international personnel offices.)

RIDGE INTERNATIONAL
1-20-16 Teraikedai, Tondabayashi, Osaka T584. Tel: (721) 299295. Fax: (721) 299202.
Number of teachers: 5.
Preference of nationality: British only.
Qualifications: university degree (any discipline), CELTA/Trinity Certificate, minimum 1 year's TEFL experience.
Conditions of employment: 1 year contracts, 4 weeks paid holiday. 21 h.p.w. with overtime sometimes available. Sundays and one day off p.w.
Salary: 250,000 yen per month (plus 3000 yen per hour overtime).
Facilities/Support: shared apartment provided. Monthly rent is 40,000-50,000 yen. Contribution to flight to Japan paid (50,000 yen). Daily travel expenses paid.
Recruitment: adverts in UK press. CV and photo sent to Japan. Interviews carried out in the UK by appointed recruiter.
Contact: Mrs. Masako Mine, Director.

SEIHA ENGLISH NETWORK
4F Ashu Building, Daimyo 2-chome, 114 Chuo-ku, Fukuoka. Tel: (92) 733 0205. Fax: (92) 733 6420.
Number of teachers: 20 full-time to teach in network of children's schools.
Preference of nationality: none.
Qualifications: experience with children, degree needed for visa.
Conditions of employment: 1 year contracts. 85-95 hours per month.
Salary: 180,000-250,000 yen per month or 2,200 yen per hour for part-time teachers. Daily travel expenses paid. Bonus of 100,000 yen paid at end of 1 year contract.
Facilities/Support: subsidised rent in company apartments. Visa sponsorship (after arrival). 2 week training session normally given.
Recruitment: newspaper ads. Phone interviews.
Contact: Henry Karkinen, Head Teacher.

SHANE ENGLISH SCHOOL
c/o Saxoncourt Recruitment, 59 South Molton St, London W1Y 1HH, UK. Tel: 0171-491 1911. Fax: 0171-493 3657. E-mail: recruit@saxoncourt.com
Number of teachers: 180 for 100 schools in Chiba-ken (Greater Tokyo) region.
Preference of nationality: British and Irish.
Qualifications: BA, Trinity or Cambridge/RSA Cert. (preferably grade 'B') or some teaching experience needed.
Conditions of employment: 1 year renewable contracts, usually from September or January. Average 25 contact h.p.w. Pupils from age 3. 5-6 week paid holiday.
Salary: from 250,000 yen per month.
Facilities/Support: assistance with accommodation, health insurance and in-house training given. Pre-service Young Learners training course available. Flights reimbursed in some cases.
Recruitment: via Saxoncourt in London. Interviews essential.
Contact: Ian Hardman, Recruitment Manager.

Other Schools to Try

Note that these schools (in alphabetical order according to town) did not confirm their teacher requirements for this edition of *Teaching English Abroad*. Upper case entries marked with an asterisk had entries in the last edition (1997); addresses without asterisks have been taken from various sources, such as newspaper adverts.

MOBARA ENGLISH INSTITUTE, 618-1 Takashi, Mobara-shi, Chiba-ken 297 (475-22 4785/fax 475-24 0194). 3 teachers.

Fukuoka YMCA, 1-1-10 Nanasumi, Jyonan-ku, Fukuoka-shi, Fukuoka-ken 814-01 (92-822 8701)

FOUR SEASONS LANGUAGE SCHOOL, Aoyamashorin 2F, 4-32-11 Sanarudai, Hamamatsu-shi 432 (534-48 1501). 15 teachers.

David English House, Hiroshima (e-mail deh_dp@mxa.meshnet.or.jp)

Language Education Center, 5-9, 1-chome, Kamiyacho Nakaku, Hiroshima 730-0031. Conversation school in the centre of Hiroshima

Hiroshima YMCA, 7-11 Hatchobori, Naka-ku Hiroshima 730 (fax 82-211 0366)

ABC Language Academy, 214 Nakaban-Cho Ono, Hyogo 675-1308

Tajima English Center, 2-6 Motomachi, Toyooka, Hyogo (796-24 8884/fax 796-24 6624).

CLI, Yamaha Building, 4F, Uomachi 1-1-1, Kokurakita-ku, Kitakyushu-shi 802

CA ENGLISH ACADEMY, 2nd Floor, Kotohira Building, 9-14 Kakuozan-dori, Chikusa-ku, Nagoya (52-762 1135/52-762 1137). 2 teachers.

TRIDENT SCHOOL OF LANGUAGES, 1-5-31 Imaike, Chikusa-ku, Nagoya 464 (52-735 1600/fax 52-735 1788). 20 teachers.

Nagoya YMCA, 2-5-29 Kamimaezu, Naka-ku, Nagoya 460 (fax 52-331 6739)

Osaka College, 1-5-6 Tosabori, Nishi-ku, Osaka 550 (fax 6-445 0297). Affiliated to YMCA.

ENGLISH CIRCLES/EC INC., President Bldg. 3rd Floor, West 5, South 1, Chuo-ku, Sapporo 060 (11-221 0279/fax 11-221 0248). 60 teachers

Sapporo International Business College, Sapporo (11-712 1663/fax 11-712 1660)

Sendai YMCA, 9-7 Tatemachi, Aoba-ku, Sendai, Miyagi-ken 980 (fax 22-222 2952)

Cambridge School of English, 2-2-5, Hanawada, Utsunomiya-shi, Tochigi-ken 320

TOYAMA YMCA ENGLISH SCHOOL, 1-3-14 Tsutsumicho Dori, Toyama 930 (764-259001/fax 764-246937). 5 full-time, 15 part-time.

BBA English School, 2-14-6-6 Kita Okinosu, Tokushima City 770-0872 (886-64 2767/fax 886-55 0954)

INTERNATIONAL EDUCATION SERVICES, Rose Hikawa Building, 22-14 Higashi 2-chome, Shibuya-ku, Tokyo 150 (3-3498 7101/fax 3-3498 7113). 70 teachers.

Sakuragaoka Joshi Gakuen, 1-51-12 Takinogawa, Kita-ku, Tokyo 114

Tokyo YMCA, 7 Mitoshiro-cho, Kanda, Chiyoda-ku, Tokyo 101 (fax 3-3293 7013)

Kumano InterCultural Club (KICC), 1-8-13 Horai Singu, Wakayama (735-28 2234/fax 735-28 2230)

ENGLISH CLUB INC., Naritaya Building, 2nd Floor, 1-3-2 Tsukagoshi, Warabi City, Saitama T335 (48-432 7444/fax 48-432 7446). 20 teachers for 7 schools in Saitama Prefecture.

Yokohama YMCA, 1-7 Tokiwa-machi, Naka-ku, Yokohama 231 (fax 45-651 0169)

Korea

Anyone who has witnessed the early morning scramble by students and businessmen to get to their English lessons before the working day begins in Seoul might be surprised to learn that the name for Korea is 'Land of the Morning Calm'. Because Korea's economy (what's left of it) is so heavily dependent on export, English is a very useful accomplishment for people in business. Korean students are often looking to export themselves, mostly to the US to acquire a college education. Both these groups have probably studied English for many years at school but need to practise conversation with native speakers. School and university vacations (July and January) often see a surge in student enrolment at private language institutes. The teaching of children is booming more than ever and there is a huge demand for English teachers to teach in schools (where English is almost universally compulsory).

The devaluation of the Korean won in 1998 and general economic slump have taken their toll among language schools. According to Tim Leffel, some of the big chains like Wonderland (for whom he worked), Pagoda and BCM were in trouble even before the currency crisis, and the future is uncertain. Many institutes have closed and the ones that remain are less likely to offer generous pay and benefits. Many foreign teachers who were there primarily to earn high wages to send home, perhaps to pay off debts, have fled what they perceive to be a sinking ship, leaving major language school chains short of native speaker staff. (Note that in the case of Korea, 'schools' normally refer to the state sector whereas 'institutes' mean private language academies run as businesses.)

The bias is strongly in favour of North Americans, especially Canadians (who are still arriving in numbers due to their troubled economy) and there are still relatively few British TEFLers in Korea. For years advertisements around American university campuses have been luring fresh graduates to the Far East, but in the present climate, fewer are tempted.

William Naquin, a well-qualified American who taught in Kyunggi-Do, sums up the politics:

> *Korea is a divided country. We were quite nervous that war might break out here between the two Koreas. The situation in the north is universallly reported to be extremely bad, with summary executions and food riots. Experts seem to think the North Korean regime will collapse some time in the next two or three years. This could be good for English teachers in Korea, and it could also be very, very bad. The North Koreans have a lot of missiles, nerve gas and chemical weapons, and are led by the most isolated, despotic lunatic and paranoid military strongmen in the world. Prospective teachers need to know that this is one of the most likely flashpoints for war on earth, and that coming here necessarily involves some degree of risk.*

Prospects for Teachers

There are hundreds of language institutes *(hogwons)* in Seoul the capital, Pusan (Korea's second city, five hours south of Seoul) and in smaller cities. The majority of these are run as businesses, where profit is the primary or even sole *raison d'etre*. ELT training is superfluous in the majority of cases. Native-speaker status is normally sufficient to persuade the owner of an institute to hire an English-speaker, though having some letters after your name makes the job hunt easier. Education is greatly respected in Korea and degrees generally matter far more to most potential employers than specialist qualifications. An MA (no matter in which field) counts heavily in one's favour. For those trying to fix up a job ahead of time, institutes are often willing to hire a teacher without an interview, provided they have a university degree and possibly some evidence of experience as well.

In North America, brokers and agents often act on behalf of institutes or groups of institutes to recruit teachers. Typically advertisements placed by such intermediaries request only native-speaker fluency and a BA/BSc. They are being paid by the school owners so should not charge teachers a fee, though some try.

If you wait until you get to Korea, it is exceedingly easy to fix up a job without resorting to an agent, but the visa is more difficult to arrange. A typical scenario is for an American or Canadian to arrange a job through an agent and obtain the visa before leaving home, complete (or not as the case may be) a one-year contract and then move on to the more lucrative freelance market.

FIXING UP A JOB

In Advance

Three years ago, the Korean government introduced an official teacher placement programme in imitation of JET in Japan. EPIK (English Program in Korea) is run by the Ministry of Education and administered through Korean embassies and consulates in the US, Canada, Australia and the UK. In 1998, EPIK placed about 1,200 native speakers (a decrease on the previous year) in schools and education offices throughout the country. The annual salary offered was 1.2, 1.4 or 1.6 million won (depending on qualifications) plus accommodation, round trip airfare, visa sponsorship and medical insurance. Work starting dates are staggered over the summer with application deadlines falling between January and April.

Details of the 1999/2000 programme had not been finalised at the time of writing, so current information should be obtained from the Education Director, Korean Embassy, 60 Buckinham Gate, London SW1E 6AJ (0171-227 5547/fax 0171-227 5503). Americans should contact any of the dozen Korean Consulates in the US. Other nationalities can contact the EPIK office in Korea (Center for In-Service Education, Korea National University of Education, Chongwon, Chungbuk 363-791 (431-230-3943/fax 431-233 6679). EPIK's homepage is http://cc-sun.knue.ac.kr/epik. Note that EPIK does not attract the praise that the JET Programme does. Writing in *Globe* magazine, Mary McEwan from Newcastle suggests checking out a website about EPIK: http://seamonkey.ed.asu.edu/-jonb/EPIK.html.

Judith Night obtained her job in a provincial town in Chollanamdo Province by applying to the recruiting representative of the Korean Ministry of Education in San Francisco (415-921-2251/3). The Ministry can be contacted directly at Yong chon ri, Changsong up, Changsong gun, Chollanamdo 515-800.

As mentioned above, it is not unusual to arrange a job without an interview. One school suggests that would-be teachers send a cassette of their voices or, even better, a video of them teaching a lesson, which would certainly be more memorable and impressive than simply sending a CV.

William Naquin stresses the importance of arranging the details of a written contract before starting work:

> *I found my present position in Korea in the classified section of the Seattle Sunday paper. A couple of Korean-Americans in Los Angeles, calling themselves 'Better Resource,' flew to Seattle two days after receiving my faxed CV. I cannot suggest strongly enough that teachers considering a position negotiated through a US-based broker get everything in writing. My contract was written in exceedingly poor English, and what it failed to stipulate in terms of housing conditions, medical insurance, etc. was only guaranteed orally. The brokers from LA assured me that I would receive full medical and dental insurance and accommodation would be paid for, either single or double occupancy. It was a mistake on my part to take the broker at his word. Living arrangments here are substandard, with three of us sharing a two-bedroom flat.*

William's ability to save $12,000 in one year helped him to tolerate the inconvenience.

Another possibility for anyone with an MA or advanced TEFL/TESL qualifications is to work for the language department of a Korean university (of which there are nearly 100). Universities probably offer the best paid and most stable employment. Serious teachers should enquire at their local Korean Consulate for addresses. Alternatively, interested people can consult the book *Help Wanted: Korea* ($9.95 plus postage from Pilot Books, 800-79 PILOT). Published in 1997 as a guide to finding work and living in Korea, its author is Sam Hawley, a Canadian who spent two years teaching in Seoul (1995-7). It includes an impressively long list of language school addresses (about 250) though of the many invited to register teacher requirements in this book, few replied. Quite a high proportion of addresses proved invalid, possibly because many of these *hogwons* have gone out of business since the book's publication.

The internet is well equipped to keep track of the volatile English language market and many Korean employers rely exclusively on it. More than one web page lists good and bad employers along with lots of horror stories; try Dave's ESL Café (http://www.pacificnet.net/-sperling/jobcenter.html) which has a link to the 'Gray page.'

On the Spot

Every day there are adverts for teachers in the English language newspapers in Seoul, namely the *Korean Herald* and *Korea Times.* A personal approach to language schools in Seoul or Pusan will usually be rewarded with some early morning and evening work within a week or two. Often new arrivals stay in one of the popular yogwons (hostels) and hear on the grapevine about the English teaching scene. The Chongro area of Seoul contains a high concentration of both hostels and language schools and is a suitable area for a door-to-door job search.

Seoul has an extensive subway system which makes it possible to attend interviews at far-flung schools and (if successful) to commute to work without too much difficulty. Unlike in Japan, the subway stations are labelled and announced in English.

REGULATIONS

Anyone working without a visa risks fines and possible deportation. Similarly, the schools which hire freelance foreigners without permits can be closed down by the government. So, if at all possible, obtain a work visa which in almost all cases is available only to people with a 4 year BA or BSc.

It is much easier if this can be done before arrival. If you do find a school which wants to hire you, they should send you a contract, sponsorship documents (valid for a minimum of one year) and copy of their Business Registration Certificate. You must send these together with your CV, two photos, the original of your degree diploma and two copies (plus transcripts for Americans) and a fee of £40 to your nearest Korean diplomatic representative, who will take four to eight weeks to process the visa.

It is normally possible to reduce the time taken by requesting that documents be sent by telex (at your expense). You must collect your visa at the Consulate. Be sure to apply for a multiple-entry visa, which will allow you to leave the country for holidays without hassle. As usual the work visa (E2) is valid only for employment with the sponsoring employer and extracurricular teaching is illegal; Judith Night heard of several teachers who were deported for failing to take this regulation seriously. Apparently Koreans who inform the authorities about illegal workers are rewarded, so working illegally is more risky than ever.

Alternatively, you can enter Korea as a tourist, find a job and then go to Japan, Hong Kong or Taipei while the visa application is being dealt with. (British and American nationals don't need a tourist visa for stays of less than 90 days; Canadians get six months.) Tourist visas cannot be extended. Anyone planning to go to Korea to look for a job and a visa should dig their university diploma out of storage and bring it with them.

Teachers are liable to income tax from their first day of work. The rate of tax for most teachers seems to fluctuate according to earnings between 4% and 11%. Most teachers participate in the Korean National Medical Insurance Union; some employers cover the cost (about 3% of earnings) but most pay half.

The law permits foreigners to send up to two-thirds of their salary out of the country. This is usually effected by wire transfer, which costs money at both ends and causes delay and confusion in most Korean banks. An alternative is possible if you exploit the loophole which allows people leaving the country to buy $2,000 worth of travellers cheques'. Simply go to the airport every month, buy travellers cheques in US dollars and send them home through the mail.

CONDITIONS OF WORK

Discontentment seems to be chronic among English teachers in Korea. So many American teachers have run amok of faulty contracts, that the US Embassy in Seoul issues a handbook offering guidance called 'Teaching English in Korea: Opportunities and Pitfalls' (which can be requested from the American Citizens Services Branch, 82 Sejong Road, Chongro-ku, Seoul, or seen on the internet). The accompanying letter from the American Citizens Services office does not mince words:

> *Despite contract language promising good salaries, furnished apartments and other amenities, many teachers find they actually receive much less than they were promised; some do not even receive benefits required by Korean law, such as health insurance and severance pay. Teachers' complaints range from simple contract violations, through non-payment of salary for months at a time, to dramatic incidents of severe sexual harassment, intimidation, threats of arrest/deportation and physical assault.*

Tim Leffel is one of the most recent in a long line of American EFL teachers who came to the conclusion that 'nearly 100% of the hogwon owners are crooks or unbelievably inept—sometimes both and in Korea both oral and written contracts are a joke'. He passes on the advice to carry a tape recorder to all interviews and meetings. By working for a big chain, he avoided most problems and was given a decent apartment, good wages and lots of support materials. He even got his post-contract $1,000 though he had to return to Korea six weeks afer finishing work to insist on it. (His employer was Wonderland, 1146-3 Ilsan-Dong, Goyang, 411-310 Kyungki-Do; 344-913 0533/fax 911 0544). When there are conflicts over contracts, Tim advises teachers to choose their battles carefully and to remain civilised as long as possible.

The issue of severance pay is a sore point for many teachers. By law, anyone who completes a 52-week contract is entitled to one month's salary as severance pay. (Note that the length of contract offered by EPIK varies from 44 to 50.) Employers have been known to make life quite unpleasant for their teachers near the end of their contracts, so that they're tempted to leave and forego the bonus. The opening remark in Peter McGuire's letter from Andong was 'You wouldn't believe how thrilled I am to be almost finished with a one-year contract here in Korea.' He went on to say that he made it through to the end only because he is a very determined person and the stakes were high, since he was trying to clear debts at home in Wisconsin.

The quality of *hogwon* varies enormously. Some are run by sharks who may make promises at interview which they can't fulfil, and overfill classes to maximise profits. Many schools do not use recognised course books but rely on home-made materials of dubious usefulness. Despite Korea's reputation as a centre for high tech, some schools lack basic video and computer facilities. Few schools at this level offer any training.

It must be said that not all foreign teachers are disppointed. One of them was Patrick Edgington from California who answered a recruiter's ad in a US daily paper and was soon working for Ah IL Foreign Language Institute in Ulsan (482-138 Sebudong Dong-Ku, Ulsan 682-036). While acknowledging that contracts in Korea guarantee nothing, he was lucky enough to find an honest employer who paid him on time and provided a 'cube' apartment above the institute building (which was acceptable, though cold in winter).

The average teaching schedule in Korea is five or six hours a day, taking place in the early morning (6.30am starts are possible), five days a week. Weekend work is less commonplace than in many other countries. The teaching load in universities is often lighter. The problem seems to be that hogwons realise that teachers come to Korea for no more than a year and therefore milk them for every working minute. Kathy Panton's assessment is that the teacher is there to exploit Korea for money, so Koreans turn around and exploit teachers for labour. She topped the record quote in the last edition of this book by working 181 hours in a month including privates and excluding preparation.

Freelance teachers are paid handsomely. Those who go through an agent to find clients (usually on-site at company premises) earn 20,000-25,000 won an hour, whereas if they find the clients themselves they earn as much as twice that. For Tim Leffel, this was the best part of the experience:

> *For my privates, I have nothing but good things to say. Boring people to talk to sometimes, but they always paid in advance and treated me as a professional.*

The majority of Korean language learners are serious (some attend two-hour classes three or four times a week) and want to be taught systematically and energetically, though even those who have been studying for years often show precious little confidence in conversing. They also expect their teachers to direct the action and are not happy with a laid-back 'let's have a chit-chat' approach. Whereas Judith Night (a certified teacher) found her pupils in the public school system 'eager to learn and a joy to teach', Mark Vetare, with no teaching background, found things very hard going, and concluded in the end that TEFL teaching was not for him:

> *The major drawback is teaching the sullen, bored, exhausted, precocious and Mok Dong spoiled children aged 14-16—torture. (Mok Dong means upper mid class whatever that means.) They drain me of energy. What they want is a white monkey to entertain them and make them giggle. Trouble is they provide zero material to work from. No sports, no interests. Their stated hobbies are sleeping, TV and listening to music. Their parents want their kids to move up book by book as if that's a gauge of progress. 'Oh, you're in 10B, great.' Never mind that they still can't speak English.*

Accommodation

As in Japan, a large deposit ('key money') must be paid before an apartment can be rented, but unlike in Japan this is normally refunded at the end of the tenancy. If you don't hear about available flats from your school or other foreigners, check the English language newspaper or find an English-speaking rental agent. Boarding house accommodation costs 220,000-250,000 won per month.

LEISURE TIME

Visitors are often surprised to discover the richness and complexity of Korean history and culture, partly because Japanese culture is far better known. Despite being a bustling metropolis of more than ten million, Seoul has preserved some of its cultural treasures. Assuming your teaching schedule permits, you should be able to explore the country and, if interested, study some aspect of Korean culture such as the martial art Tae Kwon Do. The country's area is small, the public transport good, though traffic congestion at weekends is a problem.

Teachers often find that their students are friendly, though relationships between Western men and Korean women are strongly disapproved of. Anyone homesick for the West will gravitate to the area of Seoul called Itaewon, where fast food restaurants and discos are concentrated, not to mention a jazz club, a decent bookstore and other expatriate forms of entertainment. Americans may find the English language military television station a welcome recreation. Teachers in the provinces will have to become accustomed to a very quiet life as Judith Night discovered:

> *Anyone interested in coming here to have a social life will be very disappointed. In fact, they had better be ready to deal with isolation, because most likely they will be the only foreigner in the town, and the people may never even have met any foreigners before. If I stay in Korea another year, I will choose to live in Seoul, due to missing a social life.*

Although William Naquin was also working a long way from the bright lights, he fared a little better:

> *Insofar as spare time goes, many weekends are spent recovering from 40+ hours in the classroom. During periods when we aren't quite as busy we watch movies, work out at the primitive health club, go to Seoul and drink. Mountain climbing is big here and when the weather is nice our students take us along with them. Portable hobbies such as music, writing and reading are indispensable.*

LIST OF SCHOOLS

BERLITZ KOREA
Sungwood Academy Building 2F, 1316-17 Seocho-Dong, Seocho-Gu, Seoul 137-074. Tel: (2) 3481 5324. Fax: (2) 3481 3921. E-mail: mpbubb@yahoo.com
Number of teachers: 16.
Preference of nationality: none (e.g. USA, Canada, Australia, UK, Ireland, Singapore)
Qualifications: professional attitude and appearance, creativity, some teaching experience, willingness to learn, flexibility
Conditions of employment: 1-2 year contracts. Average of 6 hours per day between 6.45am and 9pm.
Salary: guaranteed minimum 1.4 million won (average 2.7 million won) per month. Taxes deducted about 5% of salary.
Facilities/Support: few apartment spaces available or a housing stipend. Assistance given with work permits. Berlitz Method training.
Recruitment: via internet. Interviews in person or by telephone.
Contact: Michael Bubb, Method Trainer.

DING DING DANG CHILDREN'S ENGLISH
207-8 Bang-i-Dong, Songpagu, Seoul 138-050. Tel: (2) 424 9111. Fax: (2) 424 9115.
Number of teachers: 46 in 18 schools throughout Korea.
Preference of nationality: Canadian preferred, also American.
Qualifications: minimum university degree and experience of working with children, some teaching experience and TESL certification preferred.
Conditions of employment: 1 year contracts. Maximum 30 teaching hours per 6 day week plus 6 office hours.
Salary: 1.2 million won per month. Optional deductions for health insurance of 50,000 won per month.
Facilities/Support: rent-free apartment provided. Help given with work permits.
Recruitment: newspaper ads, internet ads, via North American universities. Telephone interview conducted in all cases.
Contact: Mr. David Wi, President.

ELS INTERNATIONAL/YBM
Head Office, 649-1 Yeoksam-dong, Kangnam-gu, Seoul 135-081. Tel: (2) 552 1492. Fax: (2) 501 2478. E-mail: teach@ybmsisa.co.kr.
Web-site: http://www.ybmsisa.com
Number of teachers: 100+ native English teachers for schools throughout Korea. YBM/ELSI schools are for adults (including possible on-site corporate training); English Conversation Centers (ECC) are for children aged 3-16, plus M-Plus for adolescents and E2 for children.
Preference of nationality: North American; others considered.
Qualifications: minimum requirement is BA/BSc in any field, CELTA and limited experience. Prefer MA TESOL plus 2 years' experience.
Conditions of employment: 12 month contracts. 6 hours teaching per day Monday to Friday. Adult schools open between 6.30am and 10pm, children's between 10am and 9pm (Monday to Saturday). Overtime may be possible.
Salary: 1.1-2.5 million won per month depending on qualifications and whether housing is included in package. Tax deductions of about 10%.
Facilities/Support: furnished shared accommodation provided by institute. Possibility of having airfares reimbursed, if hired abroad, plus relocation allowance and medical insurance. A severance bonus of one month's salary is paid on completion of a contract. Paid one-week orientation on arrival. 10 days paid vacation.
Recruitment: newspaper adverts and the internet. Interviews are essential and can be conducted in US and UK. North American applicants should contact YBM/Sisa

America, PO Box 4679, Cerritos, CA 90703-4679 (fax 310-404-9513). The UK representative is J. Howard, ELS Language Centres, Garrick House, 3 Charing Cross Road, London WC2 (0171-976 1066/e-mail: UK@els.com).

ESS LANGUAGE INSTITUTE
38-1, 1-ka Kwangbok-dong, Jung-ku, Pusan 600-031. Tel: (51) 246-3251. Fax: (51) 241-1988.
Number of teachers: 10.
Preference of nationality: American, British, Canadian.
Qualifications: BA/MA, TESL major and teaching experience preferred.
Conditions of employment: 1 year contracts. 30 h.p.w., 20 or 21 teaching days a month. Weekends and national holidays off.
Salary: BAs earn 1.45 million won per month; MAs earn 1.5 won. (70% of net pay is based on the current exchange rate against the dollar when the rate exceeds 1,000 won to the US$1.) Bonus of one month's pay paid at successful completion of contract.
Facilities/Support: round trip air fare provided. Furnished shared apartment provided for monthly rent of 150,000 won. Medical insurance provided.
Contact: Kim, Dae-sheol, Director.

JS LANGUAGE SCHOOL
1-190, Munwha-Dong, Jung-ku, Daejon. Tel: (42) 252 3500. Fax: (42) 254 6452. E-mail: js@englishcampus.com
Number of teachers: 5-7.
Preference of nationality: North American.
Qualifications: university degree and TEFL certificate.
Conditions of employment: 1 year contracts. 6 teaching hours per day Monday to Friday. Saturday classes are optional.
Salary: 1.3-1.5 million won (gross) less tax of 7%.
Facilities/Support: housing provided; half rent paid. Help given with work permits. Training available.
Recruitment: via recruiting agents or directly. Interview not essential: documents and photo sufficient.
Contact: Jay Jang, President.

LANGUAGE ARTS TESTING & TRAINING
Chung Jung-Ro, PO Box 269, Seoul 120-013. Tel: (2) 363-3291/363-1277. Fax: 313-5620.
Number of teachers: 6.
Preference of nationality: none.
Qualifications: BA with TEFL qualification; experience preferred.
Conditions of employment: 1 year contracts. Morning shift 7.30-10am and evening 6-9pm. All pupils are adults.
Salary: from 1,000,000 won per month.
Facilities/Support: assistance with housing. Some training provided.
Recruitment: through referrals. Interviews in person or by phone.
Contact: Michael C. Marking, Vice President.

LANGUAGE TEACHING RESEARCH CENTER
60-17, 1-ka, Taepyong-Ro, Chung-gu, Seoul 100-101. Tel: (2) 737-4641. Fax: (2) 734-6036. E-mail: LTRC@unitel.co.kr
Number of teachers: 12.
Preference of nationality: none.
Qualifications: university degree. TEFL experience helpful but not essential.
Conditions of employment: 1 year renewable contracts. 5-7 hours per day in split shifts, 5 days per week. Classes for adults and children. All teachers must be willing to teach children aged 7-16.
Salary: from 13,000 won per hour. Total monthly earnings approximately 1.7-2 million won.

Facilities/Support: housing allowance. One-way airfare. Training provided. Medical insurance available. Money transfer scheme (for remitting savings overseas).
Recruitment: local or telephone interviews.

SI-SA-YONG-O-SA - see ELS International.

SOGANG LANGUAGE PROGRAM
Sogang University, 1-1 Sinsu-dong, Mapo-gu, Seoul 121-742. Tel: (2) 716-1230. Tel/fax: (2) 705-8733. E-mail: jhong@ccs.sogang.ac.kr
Number of teachers: 3-5 per month for 15 institutes.
Preference of nationality: North American.
Qualifications: minimum 4 year college or university degree, preferably early childhood education, elementary education or English majors.
Conditions of employment: 1 year contracts, renewable. Mostly teaching children aged 4-15.
Salary: 1.3-1.7 million won per month depending on qualifications. Deductions for income tax, resident tax, 50% of medical insurance contribution and 66% of national pension contribution.
Facilities/Support: contract provides housing (shared with 2 or 3 other teachers). One-week teacher training programme before teaching.
Recruitment: phone interviews sufficient.
Contact: Julietta Hong, Office Manager.

TOP LANGUAGE SCHOOL
1266-14, 1-ka, Dukjin-Dong, Dukjin-Ku, Jonju-City, Jonbuk. Tel: (652) 254-5090. Fax: (652) 74-4266. E-mail: jade72@hotmail.com
Number of teachers: 30-50 for several franchise schools in Jongu-City.
Preference of nationality: American, Canadian, British.
Qualifications: BA/BSc required. No experience needed.
Conditions of employment: 1 year contracts.
Salary: £610-£800 per month (gross); £6,000 per year (net).
Facilities/Support: free housing and round trip airfare provided. Medical insurance paid.
Recruitment: direct; interviews not needed.
Contact: Jasmin Lee.

WORLD LANGUAGE INSTITUTE
19-16 Kumnamro-1 ka, Dung-ku, Kwangju 501-021. Tel: (62) 228-1723/276-3563/ 228-8487. Fax: (62) 226-3562. E-mail: worldedu@hotmail.com
Number of teachers: 6.
Preference of nationality: none.
Qualifications: university degree.
Conditions of employment: 1 year contracts.
Salary: US$1,500 per month (less tax deduction of 7%).
Facilities/Support: assistance with accommodation and work permits. No training given.
Recruitment: interviews not essential.
Contact: Moon Jae-Tack, Director.

YES ENGLISH SCHOOL
Daewon Building, 5th Floor, Daechi-dong 599, Kangnam-gu, Seoul 135-281. Tel: (2) 553-8880. Fax: (2) 553-5764. E-mail: yescho@nuri.net
Preference of nationality: US or Canada.
Qualifications: 4-year university degree, preferably in English or Education.
Conditions of employment: 1 year contracts. Teaching hours between 4pm and 10pm.
Salary: starting at 1.4 million won plus bonus and airfare. Package equivalent to about US$15,000 per year.

Facilities/Support: furnished apartments and working visas provided. 3-5 day orientation/training before teaching starts.
Recruitment: newspaper adverts, university bulletins and internet. Interviews sometimes held in the US.
Contact: Jonathan Huh, General Manager.

Other Schools to Try

Note that these schools were in the last edition of *Teaching English Abroad* (1997) but did not confirm teacher details for this edition.
BEST FOREIGN LANGUAGE INSTITUTE, 98-3 Jungang-Dong, Changwon City, Kyungsangnam Province 641-030 (551-84 9544/fax 551-83-08600. Many teachers for children and adults.
KOREA FOREIGN LANGUAGE INSTITUTE, 16-1 Kwancheol-Dong, Chongro-Ku, Seoul (2-739-8000/fax 2-739-0602). 30 teachers.
PAGODA LANGUAGE SCHOOL, 56-6 2nd St, Jong-ro, Seoul 110-122 (2-267-2915/fax 2-278-7538). One of the major chains employing about 100 teachers for children and adults.
YONSEI FOREIGN LANGUAGE INSTITUTE, Yonsei University, Shinchon-Dong 134, Sodaemun-ku, Seoul 120-749 (2-361-3462). Newly approved CELTA centre which employs about 70 teachers, preferably with an MA in TEFL, Linguistics, English or Education.

South Asia

In contrast to Thailand and Indonesia with their strong demand for native-speaker English teachers, other countries between Pakistan and the Philippines (with a few exceptions) are not easy places in which to find work as an English teacher. Poverty is the main reason why there is a very small market for expatriate teachers. Outside the relatively wealthy countries of Singapore, Malaysia and Brunei, there is no significant range of opportunities to earn money while teaching English. The largest growth area has been in those countries which were cut off from the West for many years, viz. Cambodia, Vietnam and Laos, where a number of joint venture and locally owned language schools have been opened in the past few years employing native speaker teachers.

Elsewhere, the demand may exist but the resources do not. Very few ordinary citizens in much of South Asia can dream of affording the luxury of English conversation classes. Few Westerners could manage on the wages earned by ordinary teachers in India, Nepal, Sri Lanka, Pakistan, etc. However those foreigners prepared to finance themselves and volunteer their time can find eager students by asking around locally.

Mainstream voluntary organisations, especially *VSO*, are active in the region, especially Vietnam and Laos where they recruit teachers to work in teachers colleges and vocational colleges. *GAP, Project Trust* and other organisations for school-leavers send volunteers to India, Nepal, Pakistan and Malaysia. Local voluntary organisations are also active, especially those concerned with improving literacy in women and children.

BRUNEI

Few people can locate Brunei on a map of the world, let alone anticipate that there is an enormous demand for English teachers there. This wealthy oil state on the north shore of Borneo, in which the Sultan famously donated a television to every household in his tiny kingdom, can afford an expensive educational system for its population of just a quarter of a million. The Ministry of Education (Bandar Seri Begawan 1170, Negara Brunei Darussalam; fax 2-240250) has been implementing a bilingual educational system which 'ensures the sovereignty of the Malay language while at the same time recognising the importance of the English language'. The British Council operates its own English Language Centre at 45 Simpang 100, Jalan Tungku Link, Bandar Seri Begawan 3192.

There are currently over 200 primary and secondary EFL teachers working in Brunei in state sector schools. *CfBT* (1 The Chambers, East Street, Reading RG1 4JD; 0118-952 3900) recruits suitably qualified and experienced individuals along guidelines set by the Brunei Ministry of Education. Teachers at the secondary level must have Qualified Teacher Status, e.g. degree plus PGCE with five years' experience. Primary EFL teachers must have a B.Ed. or degree plus PGCE and two years' experience or a Cert.Ed., CELTA and five years' experience. The package includes above average salaries, flights, baggage, accommodation and other benefits.

INDIAN SUBCONTINENT

In former colonies of Britain, principally the Indian Subcontinent, there are many private schools where English is the medium of instruction and a proportion of the educated classes speak English virtually as a first language. The small number of foreigners who do teach in this region do so in the private sector. Native English speakers have arranged to teach in the state sector, simply by entering a school and asking permission to sit in on an English class. Provided they do not expect a wage, some teaching role could probably be found for them. But it can be very challenging and discouraging. Facilities can be brutal with no teaching materials and no space. The majority of local English teachers, who have not really mastered the language, are very badly paid and can be transferred without appeal at any time; it is not too surprising to find that most are very demoralised.

One organisation which has begun to place graduates on a voluntary basis in various educational institutes in South India is *Jaffe International Education Service* (see entry). Another voluntary organisation in India which occasionally sends self-funding volunteers to projects where they teach English is JAC (Joint Assistance Centre, 6-17/3 DLF Qutab Enclave, Phase 1, District Gurgaon, Haryana 122002; fax 124-351308). The monthly cost for board and lodging is £75.

A number of organisations in the UK send volunteers to teach English in India including the main gap placement organisations. For example *Gap Challenge* send school leavers to teach in Goa and Manali for a fee of nearly £1,700 including flights. Teaching Abroad (Gerrard House, Rustington, West Sussex BN16 1AW; 01903 859911) arranges short-term teaching placements in Kerala and Tamil Nadu, South India (£1,195 excluding travel). Postings are mainly to English medium primary schools. i to i International Projects (One Cottage Road, Headingley, Leeds LS6 4DD) sends teaching assistants who have done a TEFL course to schools in Bangalore and elsewhere (£fee of £1,300).

From the US, Cross Cultural Solutions (47 Potter Ave, New Rochelle, NY 10801; 914-632-0022/CCSmailbox@aol.com) organises volunteer vacations in India. Volunteers work alongside grassroots organisations doing a range of tasks including English teaching. The programme fee is about $1,800. A religious organisation KW International (159 Ralph McGill Boulevard, Atlanta, GA 30308; fax 404-523-5420) fill ESL vacancies in India starting in July.

Nepal

Nepal is a more promising destination than India for short-term or casual English teachers. In Nepal it is necessary to pass English exams in order to progress through the educational system in any subject, so the demand for effective tuition is strong. Richard Davies came away from Kathmandu with the impression that anyone could get a job teaching in Nepal. He had made the acquaintance of an Englishman who had simply walked into the first school and got a job teaching children and adults. He was finding the work very rewarding, but not financially, since he earned 1,000 Nepalese rupees a month (less than £10).

The British Council in Kathmandu no longer has an English teaching operation. Americans should make enquires at the American Language Center (PO Box 58, Kathmandu; 1-419933/fax 1-416746). By British Council standards, the plethora of locally run private language schools are poorly resourced and unable to pay a living wage to teachers. However it they are an established school, they may be able to assist in getting foreign teachers long-stay visas (see entry for *Children's Modern School*). Tourist visas (which can be purchased on arrival for $25 cash) are valid for 30 days, whereupon they have to be renewed which is straightforward for the first three months. A four-month visa can be applied for at the immigration office in Thamel, Kathmandu (tel 470650).

A range of organisations makes it possible for people to teach in a voluntary capacity. No indigenous organisations can afford to bestow largesse on foreigners joining their projects, so westerners who come to teach in a school or a village must be willing to fund themselves. Of course living expenses are very low by western standards, though the fees charged by mediating agencies can increase the cost significantly. Here are a few relevant organisations:

Africa & Asia Venture Ltd., 10 Market Place, Devizes, Wilts. SN10 1HT, UK. Tel: 01380 729009. Fax: 01380 720060. Places school leavers as assistant teachers in primary and secondary schools in Nepal, and also India, normally for one term. Programme includes in-country orientation course and organised travel at end of four months. Fee is over £2,000.

Educate the Children, PO Box 414, Ithaca, NY 14851-0414, USA/e-mail: ETCIthaca@aol.com. Project based in Dilli Bazaar, Kathmandu (tel 421011) helps disadvantaged women and children to acquire skills including English. ETC trains volunteers to work in Nepal for 3-6 months. Voluntary instructors work in boarding schools in the Kathmandu Valley and receive room and board. (Outside the Kathmandu Valley it is almost essential to speak Nepali.)

Gap Challenge, Black Arrow House, 2 Chandos Road, London NW10 6NF. Tel: 0181-961 1122. Fax: 0181-961 1551. Send school leavers from Britain to teach in Nepal for a fee, as do the other gap placement organisations in Britain (see introductory chapter *Finding a Job*).

Grahung Kalika, Western Nepal—described below.

Himalayan Explorers Club, PO Box 3665, Boulder, CO 80307, USA. Tel: 303-494-9656/e-mail: himexp@aol.com. Office in Nepal: PO Box 9178, Kathmandu. Volunteer Nepal Himalaya programme sends volunteers to a Sherpa village near Lukla (near Everest) to teach English mainly to mountain porters and guides. Volunteers stay with a Sherpa family. Departures are in September and February, and programme costs are $2,700 (excluding airfares). The HEC also publishes the *Nepal Volunteer Handbook* which includes a very few possibilities for aspiring English teachers.

Insight Nepal—see entry.

Three Star English School, Dhungin, Faika, Kapan, Kathmandu. Fax: 1-470353. School in the Kathmandu Valley which in the past made known its willingness to accommodate volunteer English teachers (no recent confirmation).

Grahung Kalika, a non-governmental organisation, was established in 1996 to assist the teaching of English in Waling, a municipality in the remote West of Nepal. Volunteers are needed to improve the English of both pupils and teachers in local schools. Although qualifications and experience are not necessary, volunteers will need an enthusiastic and inventive approach as resources are basic and teaching conditions often challenging. Volunteers stay with local families for the duration of their placements and are asked to contribute Rs3,000 ($46/£27) per month to their host family, plus Rs2,000 for one month or Rs3,000 for two or more months to help with the project's running costs. Further information and application forms are available from Prem Subedi, Waling Municipality-3, Waling Bazaar (Tapasi Nursery), Synjya, West Nepal; or in the UK from Mark Scotton, the founder of the organisation (enquiries with s.a.e. to 34 Longdale Lane, Ravenshead, Nottingham NG15 9AD, UK).

Rachel Sedley spent six months between school and university as a volunteer teacher at the Siddartha School in Kathmandu, arranged through the UK organisation Fill the Gap (now called Gap Challenge), and conveys some of the flavour of the experience:

> *The sun is shining and the kids are running riot. New Baneshwar is a suburb of Kathmandu, very busy and polluted, but of course so friendly. I do get tired of being a novelty, especially when I'm swathed in my five metres of bright turquoise silk (we wear saris for teaching) but I'm really loving it here. Already after one month, the thought of leaving the kids and my simple lifestyle is terrible. I find it funny that as a Westerner I'm seen to represent infinite stores of knowledge and yet the servant girl is having to patiently teach me to wash my own clothes. And the general knowledge people have of the fundamentals of life makes me feel helpless and incapable.*
>
> *The children are so gorgeous (most of the time) and the Principal's family with whom I am living are lovely. It seems to me unnecessary to come to Nepal through an organisation. Everyone here is so keen to help.*

Rachel's main complaint about her situation was that she was teaching in a private school for privileged children when she had been led to believe that she would be contributing her time, labour and money to more needy children. While there, she met several people from various schools and orphanages who would love to have English volunteers.

Another gap year volunteer with GAP Activity Projects, Hannah Begbie, enjoyed her stint in a village five hours west of Kathmandu. Although she and her GAP partner would have appreciated more feedback from the headmaster of their school (they weren't sure whether or not their efforts succeeded to engage the children's interest by teaching them songs), they realised that his poor knowledge of English made this difficult. She was full of praise for the organisation and back-up offered by GAP. All volunteers in Nepal met up once a month to go on a group rafting or trekking excursion.

Before *Insight Nepal* raised their age limit to 21, 18 year old Giles Freeman from Australia spent three months in Nepal:

> *I would advise that applicants do have some teaching practice before coming. Classes easily reach 60 or 80 in many schools, making it necessary for the patient teacher to know what they are doing. With no teaching experience, this has proved a little hard, but it's a great challenge. All in all it has been extremely rewarding.*

Bangladesh and Pakistan

The need for English in Bangladesh has been replaced at the time of writing by the desperate need for more basic aid, as the country has been devastated by floods. But no doubt, schools will be rebuilt and the Bangladeshi people will carry on as they have had to do so many times before. Many schools are willing to take on native-speaker teachers of English, but the usual problems pertain: lack of remuneration and difficulty with visas. Most opportunities are available only to teachers willing to finance themselves and to work on a three-month tourist visa. Security clearance and visa processing can take months, and is very difficult unless you have someone to push for you. The British Council employs eight qualified teachers at its own Teaching Centre in Dhaka, who are recruited in London. The Centre also employs a number of hourly-paid teachers who are recruited locally but the demand for courses fluctuates so much that steady employment cannot be guaranteed. People who are established in Dhaka (like spouses of expat managers, etc.) manage to earn reasonable part-time wages teaching private classes.

Far fewer gap placement agencies and other educational charities send volunteers to Bangladesh than to Nepal. The Daneford Trust has added Bangladesh to the list of countries to which it sends students and school leavers resident in London. The participation fee for a minimum of three months is at least £2,000; details from the Daneford Trust, PO Box 11190, London E2 6LB (tel/fax 0171-729 1928).

Few private language schools exist in Pakistan, though the British Council has four teaching centres (Islamabad, Lahore, Karachi and Peshawar) which employ highly qualified and experienced teachers. For information about employment with the British Council in Pakistan, contact the Manager of the Teaching Centre in Islamabad (PO Box 1135/e-mail: bc.islamabad@bc-islamabad.sprint.com). The US counterpart is the Pakistan American Cultural Center (PACC) with seven branches throughout the country; the main one is in Karachi at 11 Fatima Jinnah Road.

The organisation Learning for Life (Fenner Brockway House, 37-39 Great Guildford St, London SE1 0EF; 0171-401 9902/fax 0171-261 9291) sends TEFL teachers to a remote mountainous area of Northern Pakistsan for a year. Accommodation and a local salary are provided.

Sri Lanka

In Sri Lanka, attempts have been made to raise the profile of English in order to find some neutral ground between bitterly opposed Tamil and Sinhala language speakers. This has created some demand for foreign teachers, not all of whom are scared off by the threat of terrorism.

For the past couple of years the organisation, *i to i International Projects* based in Leeds has been sending teachers to Sri Lanka. In 1998 the Sri Lankan government gave permission for a further 250 volunteers to be accepted to teach in state schools and orphanages. To become an 'i-venturer' you need a TEFL qualification (i to i run 20-hour courses for those with no previous training) and the ability to cover the placement fee of about £900 as well as insurance and travel costs.

Simon Rowland joined the scheme between school in Cambridge and university in York:

> I am based in a private non-profit making English institute in a town called Binginya. The school, which opened 10 months ago, is run by a local school teacher of English who is very good at English. Additional classes were set up on my arrival for teachers and business people as well as children. The teaching is mostly enjoyable; classes are conducted purely in English (I know no Sinhala) except for when they occasionally communicate in Sinhala, to my disgust and telling off. They are all willing to learn and, I like to think, have mostly improved quite a lot in the three months I've been here.
>
> The house I'm living in next to the school is wonderful, as are the meals which are brought to us from another house. The local people are all so friendly and falling over themselves to help me. I'd recommend rural Sri Lanka to anyone and think I've had a unique experience.

Despite a number of reservations about the level of organisational back-up provided (for example he had no idea where he would be until he arrived in Sri Lanka), Simon had to conclude that without i to i, he would never have been able to have the experience.

LIST OF SCHOOLS

India

JAFFE INTERNATIONAL EDUCATION SERVICE
Kunnuparambil Buildings, Kurichy, Kottayam 686549, India. Tel/fax: (481) 430470.
Placement agency for young foreign volunteers to teach in English medium high schools, hotel management colleges, teacher training centres, vocational institutes and language schools in Kerala State. Also places teachers at summer schools in various locations in India.
Preference of nationality: must be proficient in English.
Qualifications: minimum university degree in subject to be taught.
Conditions of employment: placements vary from 2 weeks to 3 months between July and March. Minimum period of 4 weeks at summer schools (between April 1st and May 31st).

Salary: none.
Facilities/Support: free homestays arranged including food. Possibility of free transport from nearest airport. Sightseeing programme arranged.
Recruitment: applications from January 1st.

ROSE (Rural Organization for Social Elevation)
Social Awareness Centre, PO Kanda, Bageshwar, Uttar Pradesh 263631, India.
Preference of nationality: none.
Qualifications: none required. Experience of teaching or living in developing country useful.
Conditions of employment: grassroots development project which organises range of activities to help this rural community in the Himalayan foothills includes teaching English in the KSS/ROSE office.
Salary: none. Volunteers contribute to their living expenses.
Facilities/Support: accommodation provided in local homes. Hindi instruction available.
Recruitment: further details in UK from HANSI, PO Box 521, Hove, E. Sussex BN3 6HY; e-mail hansi@origin8.demon.co.uk

Nepal

CHILDREN'S MODERN SCHOOL
PO Box 4747, Kathmandu, Nepal.
Number of teachers: 1-2.
Preference of nationality: native English speaker.
Qualifications: university graduates preferred. Must enjoy working with children.
Conditions of employment: minimum 9 months. School day lasts from 9.45am-3.15pm. Weekends free.
Salary: none. Volunteers must be self-supporting.
Facilities/Support: volunteers find local accommodation. School endorses the volunteer's passport and obtains letter from the Ministry of Education for the Department of Immigration. Volunteer must have some references from their own country.
Recruitment: applicants send CVs in first instance. Local interviews essential.
Contact: P. Regmi, Superintendent.

INSIGHT NEPAL
PO Box 489, Pokhara, Kaski, Nepal. E-mail: insight@clcexp.mos.com.np
Number of teachers: 15 volunteers accepted at each of three starting dates.
Preference of nationality: native speakers.
Qualifications: minimum 'A' levels for UK volunteers, high school diploma for Americans. Age limits 21-60. Teaching or volunteering experience desirable but not necessary.
Conditions of employment: placements last 3-4 months starting February, April or August.
Salary: none. Programme participation fee is $800. New short-term option called Global Hands lasts 4-6 weeks and costs $420.
Facilities/Support: accommodation and two meals a day provided, usually as homestay. Programme includes pre-orientation, placement in a primary or secondary school in Nepal to teach mainly English but also other subjects, a one-week village or trekking excursion and 3 days in Chitwan National Park.
Recruitment: application forms, $25 non-refundable application fee, 4 photos and introductory letter should be sent 3 months in advance of proposed starting date.
Contact: Naresh Shrestha, Director.

FRIENDSHIP CLUB NEPAL (FCN)
Post Box 11276, Maharajgunj, Kathmandu, Nepal. Tel: (1) 427406. Fax: (1) 429176.
E-mail: fcn@ccsl.com.np
Number of teachers: 36.
Preference of nationality: native speakers.
Qualifications: minimum university degree.
Conditions of employment: 3-5 hours a day teaching English in schools or colleges.
Saturday is day off.
Salary: none. Volunteer teachers should contribute $150 per month for their keep
(unless they become a project expert). Basic accommodation is provided.
Recruitment: direct application preferred by e-mail. Postal enquiries should include 2
international reply coupons.
Contact: Prakash Babu Paudel, President.

MALAYSIA

For the many Malaysian students who aspire to go to university in the US, Britain or
Australia, intensive English language tuition is an essential part of their training.
Unfortunately the South East Asian financial crisis means that fewer of their families
can afford to send them abroad or even to private English classes than formerly. As
proof of the decline, CfBT Education Services has completely stopped recruiting into
Malaysia, after for many years running numerous projects at schools and colleges such
as the International Islamic University throughout Malaysia.

The government issues work permits only to highly qualified applicants, who have
at least an MA. People caught working on tourist visasa can expect to be fined and
deported.

The British Council has English Teaching Centres in Kuala Lumpur and Penang; the
former offers the CELTA course throughout the year. According to the British
Council in Kuching, institutions in Sabah and Sarawak recruiting teachers from
overseas are almost non-existent, apart from Sarawak University. But the five tuition
centres in Sarawak and nine in Kota Kinabalu (Sabah) on the lists the British Council
distribute might be able to offer short-term employment to those who make their own
way to East Malaysia:

English Language Specialist House, Jalan Rock, 93200 Kuching, Sarawak
International Tuition School, Jalan Haji Taha, 93400 Kuching (PO Box 3062, 93760
   Kuching), Sarawak, Malaysia (82-480780/fax 82-416250). Several branches in
   Kuching area.
Stamford College, Bangunan Binamas, Jalan Padungan, 93100 Kuching
University of Malaysia Sarawak, Centre for Language and Communication Studies,
   Jalan Datuk Mohd Musa, 94300 Kota Samarahan, Sarawak, Malaysia (82-671000 ext
   461/fax 82-672315)
Advanced Management College, 2nd Floor, Block, A Karamunsing Complex, 88000
   Kota Kinabalu, Sabah
Asian Tourism Institution, 2nd & 3rd Floor, 85 Jalan Gaya, 88000 Kota Kinabalu,
   Sabah
International English Centre, Compleks Sunny, Mile 1.5 Tuaran Road, 88100 Kota
   Kinabalu, Sabah
Inti College, Lot 17-20 Putatan Point, Jalan Kompleks JKR, 88200 Putatan, Kota
   Kinabalu, Sabah
Kinabalu College, 3rd Floor Wisma Sabah, 88000 Kota Kinabalu, Sabah
Kinabalu International School, PO Box 12080, 88822 Kota Kinabalu, Sabah
Kolej Ibukota Kinabalu, Jalan Mat Salleh, Sembulan, 88100 Kota Kinabalu, Sabah.
National College, PO Box 14146, 88847 Kota Kinabalu, Sabah
Stamford College, Menara Jubili, Jalan Gaya, 88000 Kota Kinabalu, Sabah
   Some demand may persisit in the business market. Check adverts in the *Malay Mail*
though the best way to learn of possible openings is to get to know Kuala Lumpur's
expatriate community. The Bangsar English Language Centre in KL has employed

foreign teachers to teach Business English in the past (60-1 Jalan Ma'arof Bangsar Baru, 59100 Kuala Lumpur; 3-282 3166-8/fax 3-282 5578).

One aspect of life in Malaysia which can be difficult to accept is that racial Malays are accorded special privileges over other citizens of Chinese, Indian or tribal origins. For example, places at the universities mentioned above are available exclusively to *bumiputeras* or *'bumis'*, which means literally 'sons of the soil', i.e. ethnic Malays. Otherwise teachers normally suffer less from culture shock than they do in Thailand and Indonesia. Kuala Lumpur (KL) is a model of modernity and efficiency when compared to the neighbouring capitals of Jakarta and Bangkok.

ENGLISH LANGUAGE CENTRE
PO Box 253, Kuching (1st Floor, Lot 2065 Block 10, Jalan Kereta Api, Kuching), Sarawak, Malaysia. Tel: (82) 424126. Fax: (82) 236478.
Number of teachers: 4 for two branches in Kuching.
Preference of nationality: British.
Qualifications: Dip/Cert TESL, primary school/business experience.
Conditions of employment: 1 year contracts. 20-24 h.p.w.
Salary: 2,000 ringgits per month (varies according to qualifications). Business English courses are paid at higher rates.
Facilities/Support: no assistance with accommodation. Help given with work permits. Training available.
Recruitment: local interview essential.
Contact: Valerie Mashman, Director of Studies.

SINGAPORE

Malaysia's tiny neighbour clinging to the tip of the Malay peninsula is a wealthy and Westernised city-state in which there is a considerable demand for qualified English teachers on minimum one-year contracts. Once a teacher does get established in a school, freelance teaching is widely available paying from S$30 an hour.

The Recruitment Unit of the Ministry of Education in Singapore (Kay Siang Road, Singapore 248922; 470 9334) is responsible for recruiting teachers of English Language/English Literature on two to three year contracts in secondary schools. Candidates must have a degree in English and relevant teaching qualifications. No teaching experience is necessary. Successful candidates will receive a gross monthly salary in the range S$1,903-S$4,116 plus airfares into and out of Singapore and an end-of-year bonus and gratuities. Further information is available from the Teacher Recruitment Unit of Contact Singapore in London (Charles House, 5 Regent St, London SW1Y 4LR; 0171-976 2090/e-mail: cslondon@singss.demon.co.uk) or in the US (929 Massachusetts Avenue, Suite 02-C, Cambridge, MA 02139; 617-492-9843/e-mail: cscboston@compuserve.com).

QST (Qualified Status) teachers can earn high salaries in schools in Singapore. For example the Lorna Whiston Study Centre (fax 235 7995) was recently advertising posts for primary and secondary English language teachers at a salary of S$37,440-S$72,240 a year (roughly £13,000-£25,000).

The British Council at 30 Napier Road has a teaching operation which hires qualified teachers locally and can provide a list of 72 language schools. Many are located in the ubiquitous shopping centres, especially along Orchard Road, for example Ascada Language Centre (no. 437), Berlitz (501), Bunka Private Language School (403), Children's Language School (442), Goro (268), ILC/Syscom (545), Inoue (230), Sunnyvale (218), Thames (268) and Tien Hsia (277). Note that these are not complete postal addresses. The vast majority of these language centres are Chinese-owned with a high proportion of teachers from Australia. The Singapore branch of the main international chains are as follows:
Berlitz Language Centre, 501 Orchard Road, B1-20, Orchard MRT Station, Singapore 238878 (733 7472).

ILC Language and Busines Training Centre, 545 Orchard Road 11-07, Far East
  Shopping Centre, Singapore 238882 (338 5415).
inlingua School of Languages, 1 Grange Road 04-01 Orchard Building, Singapore
  239693 (737 6666). Other branch in the Clementi Arcade.
*International House,—*see entry for ATT.

Singapore is not a recommended destination for the so-called 'teacher-traveller'
who, without qualifications but with a smart pair of trousers, hopes to be able to
impress a language school owner. Even people who have qualifications cannot count
on walking into a job. However, there are exceptions, and persistent enquiries have
resulted in the offer of hourly work (at about S$25 an hour).

With the necessary documents (copies of education certificates, medical certificate,
etc.), getting an Employment Pass or Work Permit is fairly straightforward if you have
a sponsoring employer. The Singapore High Commission (9 Wilton Crescent, London
SW1X 8BR) will send a fact sheet which explains that people earning less than S$2,000
a month need to apply for a Work Permit from the Ministry of Manpower, 18
Havelock Road, 03-01, Singapore 059764 (538 3033) and those earning above that
figure need an Employment Pass from the Singapore Immigration & Registration

*After 6 months of wandering around
India, it may be difficult to present
the right image*

Department, 5th Storey, 10 Kallang Road, Singapore Immigration Building, Singapore 208718 (361 6100). Those intending to stay longer than the three months which tourists are permitted, should apply for a Long-Term Social Visit Pass from the Consulate; this application must also be supported by a local sponsor.

Bryn Thomas taught for inlingua, but broke his contract half way through the first year:

> *This was the only contract I broke, but then so did many of the other teachers. It wasn't just the school but the place. Singapore may be a great place for a short shopping spree but unless you like living in a shopping mall, the place isn't much fun for an extended visit and certainly not for a 1½ year contract, unless the pay is on a par with the money you can earn in the Middle East or Japan.*

If shopping malls and a repressive regime (for example there are signs threatening to fine you if you fail to flush the loo or eat on the underground) leave you cold, Singapore is perhaps best avoided.

ADVANCED TRAINING TECHNIQUES/ATT
07-01 Tanglin Shopping Centre, 19 Tanglin Road, Singapore 247909. Tel: 235 5222. Fax: 738 1257.
Affiliated to International House,
Number of teachers: 29.
Preference of nationality: British preferred, also American, Australian, Canadian.
Qualifications: BA and PGCE preferred (especially primary school teachers). Cambridge/RSA Dip. or Cert. plus experience.
Conditions of employment: 1 or 2 year contracts beginning at any time of the year. 25 contact hours per week including 2-3 evenings. Has expanding children's department.
Facilities/Support: S$250 per month housing allowance (accommodation not provided by school).
Recruitment: mostly via International House in London.
Contact: Michael Liew Kok Pun.

VIETNAM, CAMBODIA & LAOS

The demand for English in Vietnam, Cambodia and Laos is phenomenal. In the beginning, opportunities were mainly voluntary and in refugee camps. But there is now a booming commercial market supplying English language training, particularly in Vietnam. The lifting of the US trade embargo a few years ago made it possible for foreign firms to move in to Hanoi and to a lesser extent Ho Chi Minh City, all looking for staff with some knowledge of English. The departure of the UN from Cambodia had a similar effect. Many joint ventures require varying degrees of professionalism in their native speaker teachers. In the provinces, there is very little competition to meet the demand for English.

Government agencies (both local and foreign), international aid organisations and religious groups all remain active in the region, offering extensive development and relief assistance including English language programmes. Many of the people wanting to learn English are doing so in order to be able to apply to institutes of higher learning overseas, so anyone with a background in EAP (English for Academic Purposes) will have a distinct advantage.

VSO carries out an energetic campaign to recruit TEFL teachers for the region but still can't fulfil all the requests they receive. They require a degree plus TEFL certificate and minimum 6 months' experience. From the US, the English Language Institute (PO Box 265, San Dimas, CA 91733; 909-599-6773/fax 909-592-9906) whose programme in China is mentioned in that chapter also supplies volunteers with a BA and Christian commitment to colleges and universities in Vietnam and Laos for periods of 7 weeks in the summer, 10 or 18 months otherwise.

Vietnam

The demand for English has exploded in Vietnam. Volunteers and teachers are needed in the private and public sector, especially in academic institutes. Demand is strongest in the south where most of the wealth remains. The British Council in Hanoi can supply a list of 13 English teaching institutions in Hanoi and elsewhere while the Council office in Ho Chi Minh City can send a dozen addresses in HCMC.

The Britain-Vietnam Friendship Society has just wound up its 'Teachers for Vietnam' project in cooperation with the Highland Education Development Organisation in Vietnam. This is due to the number of organisations which have taken on the work of seeking volunteers for teaching in Vietnam. If requested, the BVFS Secretary can pass enquiries on (Flat 2, 26 Tomlins Grove, London E3 4NX).

It may be possible to change a tourist visa into a business visa after finding an employer and leaving the country while the visa is processed. The police are reported to take an interest in the visa status and activities generally of foreigners. The daily Vietnamese paper *Nguoi Vet* publishes its Thursday edition in English, so check for adverts.

LIST OF SCHOOLS

APOLLO EDUCATION CENTRE
191 Tay Son, Dong Da, Hanoi. Tel: (4) 857 0620. Fax: (4) 857 0637. E-mail: Apollo@netnam.org.vn
Number of teachers: 16.
Preference of nationality: none (British, American, Canadian, Australian).
Qualifications: CELTA or equivalent.
Conditions of employment: 1 or 2 year contracts. 22 h.p.w.
Salary: varies according to qualifications and experience.
Facilities/Support: accommodation provided. Visa sponsorship given.
Recruitment: adverts in international press. Interviews available in UK and Thailand.
Contact: Kalid Muhmood, Director of Studies.

B.E.S.T. SERVICES
Better English Skills Today, 81A Nguyen Son Ha St, Ward 5, District 3, Ho Chi Minh City. Tel: (8) 830 0363. Fax: (8) 830 0364. E-mail: best-vn@hcm.vnn.vn
Number of teachers: several also for campus at 391 Nam ky Khoi Nghia St, Ward 7, District 3, Ho Chi Minh City.
Contact: Nguylen thi Ng Anh, Director.

CENTRE FOR FOREIGN LANGUAGES
College of Agriculture & Forestry, Vietnam National University, Ap An Nhon, Xa Tan Phu, Thu Duc District, Ho Chi Minh City. Tel: (8) 896 0109/896 7808. Fax: (8) 896 3349. E-mail: dhthinh@hcm.vnn.vn
Number of teachers: 5.
Preference of nationality: American, British, Australian.
Qualifications: minimum BA plus English teaching credentials.
Conditions of employment: minimum 6 months. 20 classes p.w. (45 minutes).
Salary: minimum US$7 per hour.
Facilities/Support: assistance with finding accommodation. School obtains educational visa for teacher. Training given when possible.
Recruitment: international cooperation with foreign universities. Local interviews not essential.
Contact: Do Huy Thinh (Ph.D), Director.

DUONG MINH LANGUAGE SCHOOL
424 Hai Ba Trung Street, District 1, Ho Chi Minh City. Also 60 Vo Thi Sau, District 1.
Number of teachers: 4-6.
Preference of nationality: American or British.
Qualifications: university degrees and 2 years of teaching experience.
Conditions of employment: 6 month contracts. Approximately 10 h.p.w. in first instance.
Salary: US$10 for $1\frac{1}{2}$ hour session.
Facilities/Support: can advise teachers on finding a guest house or apartment at reasonable cost. No help given with work permits.
Recruitment: local interview essential.
Contact: Mr. Duong Minh, Principal.

MAY 19th FOREIGN LANGUAGES, MARKETING & INFORMATION CENTRE
62 Hang Dau St, Hanoi. Tel/fax: (4) 825 0282.
Number of teachers: 3-6.
Preference of nationality: British, Irish, etc.
Qualifications: native speakers.
Conditions of employment: 6, 12 or 18 months. 12-16 h.p.w.
Salary: US$6 an hour.
Facilities/Support: accommodation provided by school.
Recruitment: directly or via the Ministry of Education & Training.
Contact: Professor Pham Van Vinh, General Director.

Other Schools to Try

Most of these addresses have been provided by the British Council in Hanoi and Ho Chi Minh City:

AIT, 21 Le Thanh Tong, Hanoi
American Language Institute, 87C Tho Nhuom St, Hanoi (4-934 0263)
Centre for External Professionalism & Expertise, Cooperation and Exchange, 14 Le Thanh Tong, Hanor
Hanoi University for Foreign Study, Km 8, Nguyen Trai Road, Hanoi
Language Link, 64 Nguyen Truong To Street, Hanoi (4-829 4844)
United Nations International School, c/o Hanoi-Amsterdam School, Giang Vo, Hanoi
College of Social Sciences & Humanities, Foreign Language Centre, 10-12 Dinh Tien Hoang St, District 1, Ho Chi Minh City
ELT Lotus, 8 Nguyen Cong Trang St, District 1, Ho Chi Minh City
English School 2000, 70 Dinh Tien Hoang St, District 1, Ho Chi Minh City
Ho Chi Minh University of Education, Foreign Language Centre, 280 An Duong Vuong St., District 5, Ho Chi Minh City
International English School, 101C Nguyen Van Cu St, District 5, Ho Chi Minh City
International Grammar School, HCM, 236 Nam Ky Khoi Nghia St, District 3, Ho Chi Minh City
London English School, 82 Ly Chinh Thang St, District 3, Ho Chi Minh City
SEAMEO, 35 Le Thanh Ton St, District 1, Ho Chi Minh City
TESCAN, 35 Le Thanh Ton St, District 1, Ho Chi Minh City
Vietnam America Society, 190 Pasteur St, District 3, Ho Chi Minh City (8-829 4834/fax 8-823 6002/e-mail ctavhvm@netnam2.org.vn. Advertising vacancies in summer 1998; salary from $11,000.

Cambodia

The UN was virtually in charge of Cambodia until 1994 when it withdrew, leaving the market wide open to private enterprise. Although the major aid agencies like VSO still supply the majority of English teachers to Cambodia, the private sector is now flourishing. Foreign ministries and government offices are all keen to sign up for private lessons as are the diplomatic corps and their families as well as the military. The British Council does not maintain an office in Phnom Penh.

After travelling to Cambodia a few years ago, Murray Turner was impressed by the demand for English teachers:

> *In Cambodia they are so desperate for English teachers that I met more Dutch, Germans and Scandinavians teaching English than Brits or Yanks. Cambodia is one of the most beautiful South East Asian countries I visited and the people are among the friendliest.*

Mark Vetare corroborated this on a visit to Phnom Penh:

> *Just rent yourself a moto for the day and have a spin around Phnom Penh. There's virtually a school on every corner. Not all schools employ native speakers (aka monkeys) since many poor Khmer can't afford them. Pay and hours are the main problems for teachers. Time was when you could get four hours a day. Now you've got to stick around for the better times and more hours. Things are becoming more stringent in the 'real' schools. That being said, it's backpacker heaven: young men with long hair, good (but not necessarily native) English and no high level education still get jobs.*

Wages for casual teachers are about $6 an hour in a country where you can live comfortably on $10 a day. Qualified EFL teachers can earn double or even treble that amount. Cambodia still operates on a dollar economy, so few wages are quoted in riels. Visa extensions are harder than they used to be since the authorities are anxious to prevent drug smuggling and sex tourism. Tourists are now being given one-month visas which are non-extendable. Tourist visas obtained in Ho Chi Minh City, have 'Employment Prohibited' stamped on them. Those who want to work should try to get a business visa at the airport, claiming (for example) to be involved in some export business.

Cambodia is still a volatile country, struggling to emerge from the shadow of its past and of its neighbours. Political instability means that it is difficult to feel safe and settled there. Incidents involving firearms are commonplace, and people are regularly robbed at gun point in Phnom Penh.

In addition to *ACE*, whose teacher specifications are included below, there are many other commercial institutes like the American School for Language Arts, Piey Sianouk Raj Academy and Regent College in Phnom Penh. Opportunities can also be created in Kampong Sum, Siem Reap and Batambang.

AUSTRALIAN CENTRE FOR EDUCATION (ACE)
PO Box 860, Phnom Penh, Cambodia. Tel: (23) 724204. Fax: (23) 426608.
Number of teachers: 30.
Preference of nationality: none.
Qualifications: minimum CELTA. EAP experience desirable.
Conditions of employment: contracts for 3-12 months. 18-27 teaching h.p.w. All adult pupils.
Salary: $1,500-$2,200 per month, less tax at 6%. Hourly rate of $12-$16.
Facilities/Support: no assistance with accommodation, but help given with acquiring visas. Staff development workshop held each month. Well stocked teachers' resource centre.
Recruitment: personal interview necessary. Occasionally interviews are held in Australia.

Laos & Burma

Laos was the last country in the region to open its doors to foreigners. When English institutes began opening in the Laotian capital of Vientiane in 1994/5, most were fly-by-night operations. But there are some respectable schools now (in addition to the college whose entry appears below) such as the Lao American Language Center, 152 Sisangvone Road, Saysettha, Ban Naxay, PO Box 327, Vientiane (21-41 4321/fax 21-41

3760). The American owner runs an internship programme for US university students to spend time teaching. These schools can help their teachers to obtain a long-stay visa since the tourist visa is valid for a maximum of two weeks. With a letter of invitation from a sponsoring organisation, you can apply for a one-month visa which can then be extended.

Matthew Williams visited Laos on one of his frequent visa trips from neighbouring Thailand and reported that the hourly rate of pay for teachers was higher than in Bangkok, yet the cost of living was far less. Vientiane is quieter and more free of hassles, not to say more boring, than other cities in Indo-China.

Surprisingly, the new regime in Myanmar (formerly Burma) has retained English as a major language and theoretically there might be scope for teaching the military rulers and businessmen (albeit for negligible wages). But as Mark Vetare says of the country, 'it is truly a place to champion the poor not cater to the murderers and thieves who run the country.' Many organisations recommend boycotting Myanmar completely to avoid bringing any wealth or comfort to the leaders.

The British Council has a list of about 15 English teaching centres in Yangon including Y.E.S. in the YWCA Building and USIS at 14 Tawwin Road (Dagon Township).

VIENTIANE UNIVERSITY COLLEGE
PO Box 4144, Vientiane, Lao PDR. Tel: (21) 414873/414052. Fax: (21) 414346.
Number of teachers: 25.
Preference of nationality: none.
Qualifications: minimum bachelors degree and CELTA. ESP/EAP experience preferred.
Conditions of employment: 1 year contracts. 22 teaching h.p.w.
Salary: from $1,200-$2,000 per month less 10% income tax.
Facilities/Support: assistance with finding accommodation. School arranges and pays for work permit and residence visa. In-house training programme.
Recruitment: personal interview necessary.

Taiwan

Despite continuing efforts by the Taiwanese government to clamp down on unqualified foreign teachers and cowboy institutes, Taiwan remains a magnet for English teachers of all backgrounds. It seems to have escaped the worst of the Asian economic crisis, and therefore has found itself the preferred destination for many 'refugee' teachers, especially from Korea.

Hundreds of private cramming institutes or *bushibans* continue to teach young children and high school students for university entrance examinations. The market for teaching children from about age three is flourishing, so anyone who enjoys working with primary age children, i.e. likes to sing songs, play games and comfort little ones who miss their mums, will have a good chance of finding work. Women are often considered to have an advantage in this regard, and also tend to be preferred by the mothers of female pupils. Employers in this field generally provide detailed lesson plans which means that little time needs to be spent on lesson preparation.

Many well-established legal language schools are prepared to sponsor foreign teachers for a resident visa, provided the teacher is willing to work for at least one year. Only teachers with a university degree (in any subject) are eligible. Taiwanese consumers of English have a clear preference for the American accent because of strong trading and cultural links between Taiwan and the US. However many schools will hire presentable native speakers whatever their accent. Few want their staff to be able to speak Chinese; in fact one teacher reported seeing a sign in a *bushiban* window boasting 'Teachers Not Speak Chinese.' Language teachers and tutors working in Taipei are predominantly American; native speakers of other nationalities tend to gravitate to southern Taiwan.

FIXING UP A JOB

A few of the major organisations hire overseas. The *Hess Educational Organisation* which specialises in teaching primary school aged children has a US office whose function is primarily to send out information to enquirers. Interviews are conducted either in Taiwan or by telephone from Taiwan. The American owner of a new agency called OEE Recruitment (PO Box 274, Highland, WI 53543, USA; tel/fax 608-929-4994; e-mail: leyte@hotmail.com) plans to place candidates with at least a university degree in schools in Taiwan as well as China and the Philippines.

Another agency which has been seen advertising posts to teach children in Taiwan in the past year is Teachers in Asia, 630A Venice Boulevard, Venice, CA 90291 (310-574-7488/fax 310-574-7489/e-mail: danroth@loop.com).

The YMCA in the US runs an organised recruitment programme for Taiwan (see entry for *Overseas Service Corps*). As in Japan, the Y is a major provider of English language courses and is considered a good employer. There is now a small British Council office in Taipei (7th Floor, Fu Key Building, 99 Jen Ai Road, Section 2) but it is unlikely to be of much use to job-seekers.

Many people arrive on spec to look for work. Finding a *bushiban* willing to hire you is not as difficult as finding a good one willing to hire you. If possible, try to sit in on one or two classes before signing a contract. (If a school is unwilling to permit this, it doesn't bode well.)

The best time to arrive is at the beginning of summer (the end of the school year), when Chinese parents enrol their offspring in English language summer schools. Late August is another peak time for hiring, though there are openings year-round. Always check the Positions Vacant column of the English language *China Post* and the *China News* though work tends to result from personal referrals more than from advertising.

Word-of-mouth is even more important in Taiwan than elsewhere because there is no association of recognised language schools. Furthermore there is no English language Yellow Pages.

If you want to meet foreigners who are clued up about the current teaching situation, try visiting well-known Taipei hostels or pubs like the Roxy. A good notice board is located in the student lounge on the sixth floor of the Mandarin Training Center of National Taiwan Normal University at 129 Hoping East Road.

Once you have decided to approach some schools for work, make contact by telephone in the first place, possibly from the Taipei Railway Station or the Northgate GPO Telegraph Office where there are private cubicles. Next you must present yourself in person to the schools. In order to get around Taipei you should invest in the invaluable English language *Taipei Bus Guide* available from Caves Books (corner of Chung Shan Road and Minsheng E. Road) or Lucky Book Store in the university. Take along your university certificate and any other qualifications, and take the trouble to look presentable. Peter McGuire was told point blank that your appearance and how you conduct yourself at interview counts for everything, and concluded that 'all your experience in life or teaching in other countries really doesn't mean a thing here.' David Hughes specifically recommends paying attention to your feet:

> *Bring plenty of socks/tights. You have to leave your shoes at the door of Chinese homes, and it's difficult to appear serious and composed with a toe poking through.*

Anyone with a high level of education (i.e. MA or PhD) might find work attached to one of the scores of universities and colleges, where working conditions are very good. Foreigners are also allowed to work in public high schools, though it is difficult to function without a knowledge of Taiwanese.

Freelance Teaching

Work visas are valid only for employment with the sponsoring employer. However many teachers teach private students, which pays about NT$600 per hour. In a country where foreigners are sometimes approached in bars or on trains and asked to give English lessons, it is not hard to set up independently as an English tutor. Peter McGuire found the dream job of tutoring a travel agent three to six hours a day, seven days a week and then was invited to accompany his client on a trip to Hawaii:

> *Some of my lessons are given at private clubs, saunas, in taxicabs and fine restaurants. Actually, it's kind of unbelievable.*

A helpful hint is to have business cards printed up, calling yourself 'English consultant'. It is even more lucrative if you can muster a small group of students and charge them, say, NT$300 per person. Women normally find this easier to set up than men. The main problem is finding appropriate premises.

Cancelled hours are also a perennial problem. Freelancers will find it prudent to explain to students gently but forcefully that they will be liable to pay if they cancel without giving sufficient notice; most will not object. You can even request one month's fees in advance. Once you are established, other jobs in the English field may come your way such as correcting business faxes, transcribing lyrics from pop tapes or writing CVs and letters of application for Taiwanese students hoping to study overseas.

REGULATIONS

Working on a visitor visa is still possible but risky since the regulations are strictly enforced. Furthermore, without a resident visa, it will be difficult to exchange any excess earnings into dollars. Information on visas should be requested from the Taiwan overseas office in your country of origin. The Taipei Representative Office in the UK is at 50 Grosvenor Gardens, London SW1W 0EB (0171-396 9152/fax 0171-396 9145). You will need the original of your university or college diploma, a medical report from an approved doctor and a signed contract. The procedures are similar for US citizens.

Details may be obtained from the Coordination Council for North American Affairs (CCNAA, 4201 Wisconsin Avenue NW, Washington, DC 20016-2137; 202-895-1800).

If you are entering Taiwan without a pre-arranged contract you should obtain a single entry or multiple entry visa before arrival (£25 or £50) which will permit you to stay longer than the usual non-extendable two weeks which tourists are granted. Once you find a government-approved school willing to sign a contract for at least 20 hours a week, your employer should apply for a resident work visa. This will take four to six weeks and will require the same documents as above: original (not copy) of your degree, a rigorous medical examination involving eight tests (requiring blood, urine and stool samples) at a cost of about US$40. To change your status, you will have to leave the country; a round trip to Hong Kong costs at least NT$6,500 which some schools (like *Line Up*) will pay. If your tourist visa is due to expire before you have arranged a resident visa, you will also have to leave Taiwan to renew your tourist visa, and have a plausible reason why you want to remain in the country. If you claim to need an extension because you are studying Chinese, you can expect a spot test in Mandarin.

Tax

After the work visa has been issued, tax will be withheld from your pay. The tax rate for foreigners who stay in Taiwan for less than 183 days in one calendar year is 20%. After six months, the rate of tax drops to 7%-10%. Once residency is established, it is possible to apply for a substantial rebate. All teachers must file their tax return before March 31st and refunds are issued by the end of August. There is often a small levy (about US$10 a month) for national health insurance *(Lao Bao)*.

CONDITIONS OF WORK

The majority of schools pay NT$400-500 an hour (gross) though occasionally the rate for cushy morning classes drops below NT$400 and unsociable hours are rewarded (if you're lucky) with a premium rate of NT$550. Rates outside Taipei (where the cost of living is lower) tend to be slightly higher due to the relative scarcity of teachers.

As usual some schools are shambolic when it comes to timetabling their teachers' hours. In a profit-driven atmosphere, classes start and finish on demand and can be cancelled at short notice if the owner decides that there are too few pupils to make it economic. When you are starting a new job, ask your employer to be specific about the actual number of hours you will be given. Although exploitation of teachers (and pupils) is not as rife as in Korea, you should be prepared for anything, as Rusty Holmes had to be:

> *The real reason there was such a high turnover rate of staff at one school was because of the supervisor's habit of barging into class at unpredictable moments and accusing the teacher (especially my Scottish colleague) of mispronouncing words, when she herself could barely speak English. The worst incidents occurred when she beat her own children in the face for getting poor grades, when she engaged a parent in a fistfight over a tuition dispute, and when she physically ran her husband out of the school, all right in front of our students.*

Rusty Holmes had gone to Taiwan with the intention of doing some serious teaching of business English to adults (on the basis of his law degree) but was disappointed to find that for most other foreign teachers, it was just a financial refuelling station for further travels:

> *I wound up teaching everyone from two year old Taiwanese babies to 60 year old Japanese businessmen. One of my jobs was in a small remote town on Taiwan's east coast. I had been lured to this God-forsaken place by an ad in the China Post promising 15 hours a week and a work visa. Once I got settled in, the hours dwindled to nine (just enough to break even) and the distant uncle in Taipei was unable to apply for the visa after all. Many teachers either burn out or become so disgruntled with the management that they are more than willing to leave when their tourist visa expires.*

The usual problems which bedevil TEFL teachers occur in Taiwan, such as split shifts, often ending at 10pm, and compulsory weekend work, especially if you are teaching children. Few schools provide much creative training or incentives to do a good job. Like the educational system of China and so many other countries, Taiwanese state schools rely heavily on rote learning, making it difficult to introduce a more communicative approach, especially at the beginner level.

Whereas some schools offer no guidance whatsoever, others leave almost nothing to the teacher. What is termed a 'training programme' often consists of a paint-by-number teaching manual. Here is an extract from the Teacher's Book of one major chain of schools:

> *How to teach ABCs (e.g. the letter K): Review A-J... Using the flash cards, say 'A—apple, B—boy, C—cat... J—jacket'. The whole class repeats after the teacher. Then say, 'A-B-C-D-E-F-G-H-I-J' and have the whole class repeat. Show the letter K flashcard. Say 'K' having the whole class repeat it each time you say it. Say 'K' 4 or 5 times.*

And so on. This certainly makes the inexperienced teacher's job easier but possibly also very boring. Not everyone can be comfortable with such a regimented curriculum.

LEISURE TIME

Flats are predictably expensive in central Taipei so many teachers choose to commute from the suburbs, where living conditions are more pleasant in any case. Rents in the south of the country are cheaper; apartments in Kaohsiung range from about NT$10,000-20,000 a month. There are so many foreigners coming and going, and the locals are so friendly and helpful, that it is not too difficult to learn of flats becoming vacant. You will have to pay a month's rent in advance plus a further month's rent as a deposit; this bond or 'key money' usually amounts to £300-£400.

Not a single visitor to Taipei, which is one of the most densely populated cities in the world, fails to complain of the pollution, second only to that of Mexico City. Not only is the air choked with the fumes and noise of a million motorised vehicles, but apparently chemicals have infiltrated the water table contaminating locally grown vegetables. It is really horrific. The weather is another serious drawback. The typhoon season lasts from July to October bringing stormy wet weather and mouldy clothes. The heat and humidity at this time also verge on the unbearable.

Although the traffic is at best unpleasant and at worst life-endangering, a motorbike is really the only practicable way to get around and some teachers even come to enjoy the experience of weaving in and out of city traffic with reckless abandon. There are buses in Taipei (the fare is about NT$14 within the city), including 'air-con' city buses which cost more but at least allow you to avoid the sweltering heat in traffic jams. Some teachers stay in hostels near the central station and commute to work in a satellite city where wages are higher than in Taipei (e.g. Tao Yuan and Chung Li). Dorm beds start at NT$200 a night.

Taipei is not the only city to suffer from pollution; Taichung and Kaohsiung are also bad. Even Tainan with two-thirds of a million people has some pollution; 100 new cars are registered here every day adding to the problem. (This is a statistic which rather detracts from Tainan's appeal as the most historic city on the island with many old temples, etc.) Kaohsiung on the south-west coast is a large industrial city with a high crime rate but has the advantage of being near the popular resort of Kenting Beach. The geographical advantage of Taichung further north is proximity to the mountains as well as a good climate and cultural activities. The east coast is more tranquil, though some find it dull.

Taipei has a 24-hour social scene which can seriously cut into savings. Heavy drinking is commonplace. Films (which are usually in English with Chinese subtitles) cost about US$9. The serious saver will follow David Hughes' example and join the local library. For the truly homesick there are some English-style pubs with pool tables and darts boards. For Rusty Holmes, the food was a highlight:

Eating out is just as much a pastime in Taiwan as it is in Hong Kong. There are countless little mom-and-pop restaurants which offer delicious and inexpensive food. My favourite is the US$4 black pepper steak. Considering the high price of food in supermarkets, it would be cheaper to eat out than to cook at home. Taiwan is also a fruit-lover's paradise, though most are expensive by American standards. My favourite is the outstanding sugarcane Taiwan produces.

LIST OF SCHOOLS

ELS INTERNATIONAL
12 Kuling St, Taipei. Tel: (2) 2321 9005. Fax: (2) 2397 2304.
Affiliated to ELS International (see introductory section *Finding a Job*).
Number of teachers: 200-300 (9 locations in Taipei plus 2 in Kaohsiung and Taichung).
Preference of nationality: passport holders of USA, Canada, UK, Australia, South Africa, Ireland or New Zealand.
Qualifications: BA/BSc minimum. Relevant qualifications preferred.
Conditions of employment: 1 year contracts. Morning and evening work. Pupils range in age from 13 to 60.
Salary: approximately NT$475 (£11) per hour. Bonuses paid at end of contract, calculated according to number of hours taught.
Facilities/Support: no assistance with accommodation. Training provided.
Recruitment: direct application/walk-ins. Local interviews compulsory. Applicants may be asked to teach a sample lesson. Original of college diploma should be brought.
Contact: Luisa Sia, Academic Director.

GRAM ENGLISH INSTITUTE
116 Yung Ho Road, 4th Fl, Yung Ho City, Taipei. Tel: (2) 2927 2477. Fax: (2) 2926 2183. E-mail: gram@ms7.hinet.net
Number of teachers: scores of teachers for 44 branches throughout Taiwan, including 10 branches in Taipei area.
Preference of nationality: American/Canadian; others considered.
Qualifications: BA or equivalent and 6 months' formal TESL experience essential. Understanding Chinese may be helpful but not essential.
Conditions of employment: minimum 1 year contracts must be signed. Mostly evening and weekend work. Students include both children and adults.
Salary: US$16-18 per hour part-time. US$1,450 per month full-time.
Facilities/Support: accommodation, in-house training, airport pick-up, work permit, bonuses and insurance all provided.
Recruitment: hire exclusively by local interview.

HESS EDUCATIONAL ORGANIZATION
235 Chung Shan Road, Chung Ho City, Sec. 2, No. 419, Chung Ho City, Taipei County. Tel: (2) 3234 6188. Fax: (2) 3234 9488. E-mail: hesswork@hess.com.tw. Web-site: www.hess.com.tw
Number of teachers: 200+ Native Speaking Teachers (NSTs) in more than 90 branches (schools and kindergartens) throughout Taiwan; 100 new teachers hired each year.
Preference of nationality: must have passport from officially recognised English speaking country, i.e. US, Canada, UK, Australia, New Zealand and South Africa.
Qualifications: Bachelor's degree (in any subject) plus desire to work with varied age groups and to experience Chinese culture. Knowledge of Chinese not necessary because each class has a local assistant teacher to help with translation.
Conditions of employment: 1 year renewable contracts. Three contract options. Classes at language school (for 7-15 year olds) are held in afternoons and evenings. Classes at the kindergarten (ages 3-6) are during the day; full-time kindergarten work for those interested in Early Childhood Education.

Salary: NT$500 per hour (gross), with some variation between locations. Tax rate is 20% for first six months then drops to 10%.

Facilities/Support: airport pick-up can be arranged. Paid 5-day initial orientation. Every branch assists NSTs to find housing. Actively assist NSTs to obtain resident visas and work permits. Application process should be started 3 months in advance to allow teachers to get visa before leaving their home country. Discounted group air travel arranged for North American recruits. Branches offer new arrivals follow-up training. Further training sessions at main office in Taipei.

Recruitment: through Hess website, universities, adverts and direct application. Telephone interviews are essential. Quarterly new teacher intakes during first weeks of September, December, March and June. Overseas hiring completed 3 months before arrival to allow time for visa applications prior to departure.

Contact: Eleanor Chong, Human Resources Department.

KANG NING ENGLISH SCHOOL
PO Box 95, Chutung 310. Tel: (3) 594 3322/595 2332. Fax: (3) 594 3222/596 7392.

Number of teachers: 7 for 2 departments (regular and pre-school).

Preference of nationality: American, British, Canadian.

Qualifications: for Regular Department: academic and/or professional TESOL/ Education background, BA or MA degree. For Pre-School Department, BA degree needed, at least one year pre-school teaching experience.

Conditions of employment: 2 year renewable contracts. 25-28 contact h.p.w.; 40 total hours spent at school (teaching, preparing lessons, curriculum and material development, etc.) Shifts in Regular Dept. are 1.30pm-9.30pm Monday-Friday, 10am-3.30pm Saturday and in Pre-School Dept. 7.30am-4pm Monday-Friday only. All ages and levels; pre-school pupils aged 4-6.

Salary: US$1,500 per month. (Living expenses about $350 a month.)

Facilities/Support: round trip air fare provided. Health insurance and 3 months Chinese training also provided. 1 week paid holiday at Chinese New Year and about 10 other days of holiday.

Recruitment: adverts in TESOL *Placement Bulletin*, etc. Interviews essential, and are scheduled every year at the TESOL Conference.

Contact: Serena Wen, Director.

LANGUAGE TRAINING & TESTING CENTER
170 Hsin-hai Road, Section 2, Taipei 106. Tel: (2) 2362 6385. Fax: (2) 2367 1944.
Non-profit educational foundation with 3,400 students.

Number of teachers: about 60.

Preference of nationality: none.

Qualifications: university degree (linguistics or TESOL preferred). Teaching experience.

Conditions of employment: minimum 1 year. 3-5 hours per day between 8am and 9pm. Adult students (government officials, company employees, university students).
Salary: starting rate of NT$495 per hour. Local taxes and partial health and group insurance deducted.
Facilities/Support: no assistance with accommodation. Help with work visas.
Recruitment: personal interview necessary.
Contact: David Ludwig, Coordinator.

LINE UP LANGUAGE SCHOOL
398-1 Chihsien 1st Road, 2Fl, Hsin-Hsing Area, Kaohsiung City. Tel: (7) 235 8015. Fax: (7) 236 4311. E-mail: DeeWinter@hotmail.com
Number of teachers: 40-50.
Preference of nationality: Americans preferred, also Canadians.
Qualifications: Bachelor degree and desire to teach children.
Conditions of employment: 1 year contracts, 18 month minimum preferred. Usual teaching hours are 1.30pm-9.15pm.
Salary: pay rate schedule starts at NT$475 (US$15) per hour, rises to NT$500 after three months with further increments every 6 months. Teachers are paid NT$8,000 for compulsory training period which is handed over at end of year-long contract.
Facilities/Support: assistance with accommodation and work permit. 34 hours of paid pre-service training given. Detailed Information Guide about living and working in Taiwan written by Terence Crowther, Line Up's Executive Director, given to all employees.
Recruitment: word of mouth, scout, newspaper ads. Interviews sometimes conducted in US and UK.
Contact: Dee Winter, Director.

OVERSEAS SERVICE CORPS YMCA
101 North Wacker Drive, Chicago, IL 60606, USA. Tel: 800-872-9622 ext. 343. Fax: (312) 977-9036.
Number of teachers: 25 per year in 9 community-based YMCAs in Taiwan.
Preference of nationality: American, Canadian.
Qualifications: university degree required. Teaching (TESOL/TEFL) experience and training preferred. Must be motivated to share cultures and build international understanding.
Conditions of employment: 1 year contracts starting October 1st. 14-20 contact h.p.w. plus 10 hours in office.
Salary: NT$15,000-18,000 per month. Overtime paid on teaching hours above 20 p.w.
Facilities/Support: return air fare, paid vacation, accommodation and bonus after 12 months. Orientation held in the US in September and another in Taiwan.
Recruitment: application deadline is April 15th. Applicants must be in North America between then and October start date.
Contact: Jann Sterling, Program Assistant.

RICH ENGLISH
No. 7, Alley 7, Lane 113, Min Sheng East Road, Sec. 3, Taipei 105. Tel: (2) 2712 3671. Fax: (2) 2712 3631.
Number of teachers: 5.
Preference of nationality: English, American.
Qualifications: university degree and CELTA. Experience of living abroad useful. Must be aged 30 or less and have clean-cut appearance.
Conditions of employment: 2 or 3 year contracts. Evening hours and 6 hours of work on Saturday or Sunday. Pupils are children.
Salary: £21,000 per year less 6% deductions for taxes.
Facilities/Support: housing assistance, health insurance.
Recruitment: interviews available in Taipei, London and Denver.

SHANE ENGLISH SCHOOL
5F, 41 Roosevelt Road, Section 2, Taipei. Tel: (2) 2351 7755. Fax: (2) 2397 2642. E-mail: sest@ms12.hinet.net
Number of teachers: 30+.
Preference of nationality: English.
Qualifications: TEFL/CELTA/PGCE all accepted.
Conditions of employment: 1 year contracts. About 92 hours per month, 5 days p.w.
Salary: NT$420 per hour.
Facilities/Support: assistance with accommodation, work permits and training.
Recruitment: via Saxoncourt Recruitment in London (fax 0171-836 1789).
Contact: David Roberts, Director of Studies.

TAIWAN ANGLO-FRENCH INSTITUTE
2F, No. 295 Ho Ping E Rd, Sec 2, Taipei. Tel: (2) 2755 5451. Fax: (2) 2755 4627.
Number of teachers: 3.
Preference of nationality: British.
Qualifications: minimum BA degree plus certificate in teaching and 2 years' experience.
Conditions of employment: 1 year contracts, renewable.
Salary: minimum guaranteed NT$42,000 per month (net) for a minimum of 15 h.p.w. Hourly rate is NT$700 (net). Air ticket paid.
Facilities/Support: furnished accommodation provided; institute pays deposit and first month's rent. Help with resident visa.
Recruitment: via adverts in *EL Gazette* and *Guardian*. Local or UK interviews essential.
Contact: Mr. Sanjay Teeluck, Director.

Other Schools to Try

Note that these schools (in alphabetical order according to town) did not confirm their teacher requirements for this edition of *Teaching English Abroad*. Upper case entries marked with an asterisk had entries in the last edition (1997).

Broadlands English Institute (e-mail yenjuping@hotmail.com). Need teachers to work at summer camps (offering US$1,500 for two months and free one way airfare).
Olive Experiment English, 535 Lung An Road, Hsin Chung City 242.
*OXFORD LANGUAGE & COMPUTER INSTITUTE, 8 Fl, 240 Chung Shan 1st Road, Kaohsiung (7-281 2315/fax 7-211 7119) 20 North American teachers.
*TAIPEI LANGUAGE INSTITUTE, Kaohsiung Center, 2F, 507 Chung Chan 2nd Road, Kaohsiung (7-215 2965/fax 7-215 2981). 5 teachers.
Sesame Street School Tainan—e-mail: Teach@Sesame-Street.com.tw
Head start English School Taipei—e-mail: jamil@unet.net.tw
*JORDAN'S LANGUAGE SCHOOL, 97 Chuan Chow St, 1F, Taipei (2-2332 5080/fax 2-2305 1777). 20+ teachers.
*WORD OF MOUTH ENGLISH, 4F-2, 163 Nan King East Road, Sec. 5, Taipei (2-2762 7114/fax 2-2761 8295). 3 teachers.
Gauden Language School Yuanlin—e-mail: gauden@ms11.hinet.net

Thailand

Thais have always prided themselves on being the only Asian nation never to have been under foreign domination. This may be true of their politics but not of the economy, as the Thais learned when a year or so ago there was a massive withdrawal of foreign investment which led to the collapse of the currency and mass unemployment. The IMF had to deliver a rescue package to the tune of US$17 billion.

In fact the economic problems which have engulfed the whole of Southeast Asia started in Thailand, and the country has been reeling ever since.

Against expectations, the opportunities for teachers have risen slightly, especially in schools which teach English to children. Schools are finding it more and more difficult to attract foreign teachers because of the low wages, so there is less competition for work than in the past. Many Thais feel that in these difficult times, the best investment is in their studies, whether at university or in language instruction. English language teachers are still in high demand, especially those willing and able to teach children. The demand for private tuition and company work has declined sharply except among foreign multi-nationals.

The *Bangkok Post* is as full as ever of advertisements for native speaker teachers, perhaps even fuller, since many foreign teachers left the country when the exchange rate plummeted and their wages shrank. A knowledge of English is eagerly sought by almost all urban young people and, in the context of Thailand, 'urban' is almost synonymous with 'Bangkok', which is five times larger than its nearest rival Chiang Mai. The crisis has of course had repercussions in Bangkok, including a dramatically increased crime rate and high levels of anxiety about security among the expatriate population.

Prospects for Teachers

The many English teaching opportunities in Thailand seldom appeal to the serious career-minded EFL teacher. Only a small percentage of recruitment takes place outside Thailand. Even the British Council has concentrated its efforts on finding staff from among the expatriate population already resident. The major schools use foreign recruitment agencies and the internet to make contact with potential teachers, but most organisations depend on finding native-speaker teachers locally, including Thai universities and teachers' colleges, as well as private business colleges which all have EFL departments. No doubt most would prefer a highly qualified and experienced EFL teacher but the fact is that they couldn't afford one before the crisis and they certainly can't now.

This means that there is a preponderance of teacher-travellers on the Thai teaching scene, earning enough money to fund a longer stay or subsequent travels. Thais are exuberant and fun-loving people and their ideas about education reflect this. They seem to value fun and games *(senuk)* above grammar, and an outgoing personality above a teaching certificate. Of course there is a nucleus of professional EFL teachers working at the most prestigious institutes in Bangkok, but the majority of teachers and tutors teach on a casual basis without formal contracts. So anyone determined to teach in Thailand is guaranteed some opportunities, provided he or she is willing to go to Thailand to seek them out and willing to work for a pittance. Most students of English want to learn the language for a purpose such as tourism or business, and a good teacher will find out their motives and tailor the lessons accordingly.

FIXING UP A JOB

In Advance

Two UK recruitment agencies specialise in Thailand. The *Anglo-Pacific (Asia) Consultancy* (Suite 32, Nevilles Court, Dollis Hill Lane, London NW2 6HG; 0181-452 7836) is an educational consultancy which concentrates on recruiting teachers for schools, colleges and universities in Thailand. Teachers are placed every month by APA who welcome graduates with a CELTA or Trinity Certificate but also try to place people with any TEFL background and/or appropriate personalities as long as they have a university degree. Their recruits are given briefing notes on Thailand and a follow-up visit in their schools if possible. *TEFLNet Recruitment* (Yapham Grange, Yapham Mill, York YO42 1PB; 01904 784440) also has details of vacancies in Thailand around the year. They are primarily looking for degree and Certificate-holders but require no experience.

Despite having an address in Chiang Mai, the agency *Search Associates* do not hold their recruitment fairs for experienced elementary and secondary school teachers in Thailand but in Oxford, Dubai, Kuala Lumpur, etc.

On the Spot in Bangkok

Any new arrival in Bangkok would be well advised to spend a week getting his or her bearings and asking as many foreigners living in the city for inside information about possible employers. Many people say that the teaching scene has become so exploitative and life in the city so unpleasant that it is better to leave Bangkok as quickly as you can.

For those who feel strong enough to survive in Bangkok, language schools are very easy to locate, to approach on spec. The best place to start is around Siam Square where numerous schools and the British Council are located (see map, which is courtesy of Richard Guellala). The Council has a list of private and public universities, institutes, teachers' colleges and international schools throughout the country which have English departments and therefore possible openings for a native speaker, but most people rely on the Yellow Pages, which include dozens of language school addresses.

Another excellent source of job vacancies is the English language press, viz. the *Bangkok Post* (with at least five adverts every day) and to a lesser extent the *Nation*. A favourite teachers' hangout is the Hole-in-the-Wall pub on Khao San Road. Or try the Hard Rock Café in Siam Square.

If the Siam Square schools are not short of teachers, which may be the case in the

Spruce up your sock collection

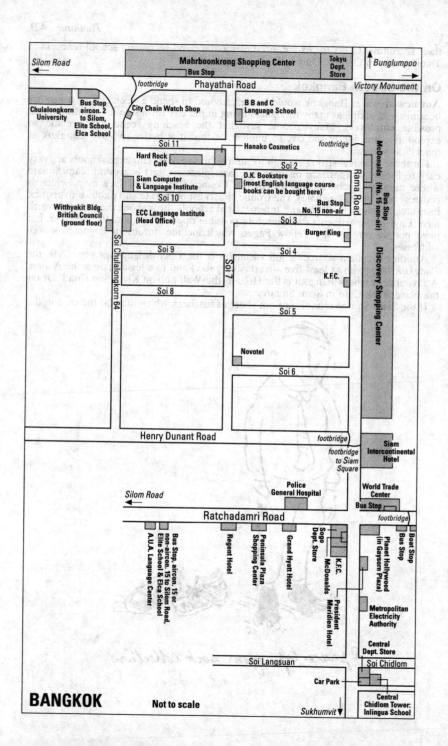

Silom Road

Mahrboonkrong Shopping Center

Tokyu Dept. Store

Bus Stop

Bunglumpoo

footbridge

Phayathai Road

Victory Monument

Chulalongkorn University

Bus Stop aircon. 2 to Silom, Elite School, Elca School

City Chain Watch Shop

B B and C Language School

Soi 11

Hanako Cosmetics

footbridge

McDonalds (No. 15 non-air)

Bus Stop aircon.

Hard Rock Café

Soi 2

Witthyakit Bldg. British Council (ground floor)

Siam Computer & Language Institute

D.K. Bookstore (most English language course books can be bought here)

Bus Stop No. 15 non-air

Soi 10

ECC Language Institute (Head Office)

Soi 3

Burger King

Rama Road

Discovery Shopping Center

Soi 9

Soi 4

Soi Chulalongkorn 64

Soi 7

Soi 8

K.F.C.

Soi 5

Novotel

Soi 6

Henry Dunant Road

footbridge

footbridge to Siam Square

Siam Intercontinental Hotel

Police General Hospital

World Trade Center

Silom Road

Bus Stop

footbridge

Ratchadamri Road

A.U.A. Language Center

Bus Stop, aircon. 15 or non-aircon. 15 to Silom Road, Elite School & Elca School

Regent Hotel

Peninsula Plaza Shopping Center

Grand Hyatt Hotel

Sogo Dept. Store

K.F.C.

McDonalds

President Meridien Hotel

Planet Hollywood (in Gaysorn Plaza)

Boat Stop

Bus Stop

Metropolitan Electricity Authority

Central Dept. Store

Soi Langsuan

Soi Chidlom

Car Park

Central Chidlom Tower: Inlingua School

BANGKOK

Not to scale

Sukhumvit ▼

slack season, you will have to try schools further afield. Travelling around this city of six million is so time-consuming and unpleasant that it is important to plot your interview strategy on a city map before making appointments. Also be sure to pick up a map of the air-conditioned bus routes, particularly if you are contemplating a job which involves travelling to different premises. (Another handy acquisition is a smog mask which costs a few baht.)

It may not be necessary to do much research to discover the schools with vacancies. Many of the so-called back street language schools (more likely to be on a main street, above a shop or restaurant) look to the cheap hotels of Banglamphu, the favourite haunt of Western travellers in the northwest of Bangkok. There is such a high turnover of staff at many schools that there are bound to be vacancies somewhere for a new arrival who takes the trouble to present a professional image and can show a convincing CV. As usual, it may be necessary to start with part-time and occasional work with several employers, aiming to build up 20-30 hours in the same area to minimise travelling in the appalling traffic.

The teaching of children is an expanding area; if you don't want to teach the alphabet, don't accept pupils under the age of five. On the strength of her claim that she had experience of 'working with children,' Alison Eglinton was soon bringing home 6,000 baht (B6,000) per week. (She suggests that anyone teaching young children should master at least one word of Thai: *hong nam* which means toilet.)

When visiting a school, wear your posh clothes and carry CVs and passport photos to clip onto the application forms; otherwise you'll be asked to come back when you have obtained some on the Khao San Road. Don't be surprised if the application form asks some weird questions, such as asking you to give the name, age and profession of every member of your family. You won't be hired on the spot but may well be contacted within a day or two; contact is made by telephone so make sure you are staying in a guest house with a phone. Vaughan Temby recommends the Peachy Guest House (10 Phra Athit Road, Banglamphu) while Bruce Lawson stayed in Sweety Guest House on Soi Post Office, 49 Ratchdamnoen Klang, Banglamphu where an Anglophone member of staff was willing to take messages.

Everyone who has ever had anything to do with teaching English in Thailand emphasises the need to dress smartly, as Bruce Lawson describes:

> *The Thais like their pet farangs (i.e. teachers) to look as much like currency dealers as possible. I bought a suit in Bangkok for £50 especially for the job hunt. Men should take out all earrings and wear a tie, thus risking asphyxiation in the heat and humidity of the hot season. Women should wear a decent skirt, not trousers.*

Ajarn (university graduates) are particularly respected in Thailand and are expected to look respectable. As well as dressing smartly for an interview, try to maintain a reserve manner while still projecting a relaxed and easy-going image. Too many gesticulations and guffawing are considered impolite.

The busiest season for English schools is mid-March to mid-May during the school holidays, when many secondary school and university students take extra tuition in English. This coincides with the hot season. Vacancies continue to be advertised through June, July and August. The next best time to look for teaching work in private schools is October, while the quietest time is January/February.

The noisy Khao San Road is lined with budget accommodation (where a room costs B50-80), many with notice boards offering teaching work and populated with other foreigners (known as *farangs*) well acquainted with the possibilities. They will also be able to warn you of the dubious schools which are known to exploit their teachers. It is best to be suspicious at all times, since there are stories of bogus job adverts being inserted to lure naive new arrivals to hotels to be drugged and robbed.

On-the-Spot in Chiang Mai

According to Anne Kunigagon who has made her home in Chiang Mai, far more people have been coming to Chiang Mai to look for work, since no one wants to live in Bangkok. Teaching opportunities do crop up in branches of the big companies like

ECC and *AUA* and in academic institutes. There are five international schools which do employ English teachers, though most are recruited abroad (e.g. at international teachers' fairs) rather than locally. Murray Turner is one teacher who succeeded in finding work, partly with Annette's help:

> *I am working seven hours a week in Chiang Mai after arriving one week ago. I'm staying at Eagle Guest House [16 Chang Moi Gao Road, Soi 3; tel/fax 53-235387] which is run by Annette who knows everything about language schools (and everything else). I found the job by hiring a bicycle (B100 for five days' hire) and dutifully doing the rounds of the language schools, colleges and kids' schools. Although Chiang Mai is developing rapidly, it is still safe enough and small enough to cycle round, providing you don't venture out between 11am and 2pm (even in winter). I took plenty of passport photos, photocopies of my passport and of my certificate from the one-week TEFL course I'd done (at Pilgrim's in Canterbury).*

The British Council in Chiang Mai (198 Bumrungraj Road) can give you a list of five language institutes, six international schools and three universities. Their handout also explains that they do take on part-time teachers from time to time, normally with the usual British Council qualifications, but sometimes on the basis of a demonstration lesson. They run evening and weekend classes, children's summer schools, Business English courses, English for guides, etc.

Other jobs are available in the school holidays at summer and weekend camps held at resort hotels and attended by rich children from Bangkok. Getting in to these and the summer camps run by the British Council and YMCA is by word of mouth, friends or advertisements. Annette's advice is to be brazen, knock on doors, try hotels, shops catering to tourists, companies which export or have to deal with foreigners, pubs, restaurants, computer shops, large shops in the Night Bazaar area, etc.

On-the-Spot in the Provinces

Teaching opportunities outside Bangkok have almost doubled, however not many foreigners show an interest since the pay is much less than in Bangkok. The estimated four-fifths of teachers who are single males enjoying the nightlife in Bangkok are unwilling to move to a less exciting country town.

Competition for work is almost non-existent in lesser known cities like Nakhon Sawan, Khon Kaen, Udon Thani and Ubon Ratchathani. For a job in a university you will probably have to show a degree or teaching certificate, neither of which will be scrutinised very carefully. The best places are Hat Yai (the booming industrial city in the south and Songkhla (see entry for *Prince of Songkhla University*). Hotels are always worth asking, since many hotel workers are very keen to improve their English. If you find a place which suits and you decide to stay for a while, ask the family who runs your guest house about the local teaching opportunities.

Sometimes the happiest and most memorable experiences take place away from the cities and the tourist resorts. Brian Savage returned to England after a second long stint of teaching in Thailand and describes one of the highlights for him:

> *My most rewarding experience was my week teaching English conversation in a rural high school in Loei province in northeast Thailand. These children had rarely seen and had certainly never spoken to a farang before. My work during that week and a subsequent second visit was really appreciated by the pupils. The first visit came about after I was introduced to a teacher at the Chiang Mai school where I was teaching. If travellers get away from Bangkok and the resorts, they too can have experiences such as this, especially in the friendly towns of the north and northeast. A little voluntary teaching can really boost the confidence of students who are usually too poor to pay to study with native speakers.*

Many Karen tribal refugees have fled from Myanmar (formerly Burma) to the Mae Sod region of northern Thailand. English speakers are much in demand, especially those who are able to stay for more than a couple of months. Advice might be forthcoming from the Karen Refugee Committee, PO Box 5, Mae Sod, Tak 63110 (55-532947/e-mail win3@loxinfo.co.th). Also, the Catholic Office for Emergency Relief & Refugees (COERR), 122-122/1 Soi Naksuwan, Nonsi Road, Chongnonsi, Yannawa,

Bangkok 10120 (fax 2-681 5306) is a local Thai organisation which provides services for refugees and poor Thai villagers. One of its projects is to provide English language teachers for a refugee camp called 'Safe Area for Burmese Students' in Maneeloy Village, Pak Tho District, Ratchaburi Province, Thailand.

REGULATIONS

The vast majority of EFL teachers in Thailand do not have a work visa, a practice to which the authorities have long been turning a blind eye. Foreigners mostly teach on a tourist visa or (preferably) a non-immigrant visa which must be regularly renewed by leaving the country.

Universities and established language schools are more willing than they were to sponsor teachers who have proved themselves successful in the classroom and help them to fill in the 50 or so documents. To be eligible for a work permit you must have a bachelor's diploma or a CELTA (which the Ministry of Education recognises) and a contract. (In the forgery capital of the world, quite a few fictitious university diplomas and even RSA/Cambridge and Trinity Certificates are in circulation.) The entire procedure should take about four months and cost around B2,000. Note that many schools which make vague promises to obtain a work permit for their staff fail to keep their promise because of the expense incurred.

Tourist visas should be applied for in your home country and are valid for an initial 60 days. These can be renewed once inside Thailand for a further month at a cost of B500. If you do not renew before the expiry date you will have to pay B100 for every day you have overstayed when you exit the country. If you make the decision to teach in Thailand before leaving home and can come up with a Thai national willing to write a letter of recommendation on your behalf, apply to the Thai embassy for a non-immigrant visa which allows you to stay 90 days. Failing that, you can apply for a non-immigrant visa at a Thai consulate in a neighbouring country such as Malaysia or Laos, provided you have the necessary papers from your employer; this will be granted in 24 hours.

A non-immigrant visa will have to be renewed every 90 days, again for B500. Most teachers and travellers choose to cross the Malaysian border to Penang (20 hours by train from Bangkok) where a new visa can quickly and easily be obtained from the Thai Consulate. Even people who have done this repeatedly report that there are no problems. The estimated cost of a visa run from Bangkok is well over B2,000; the return train fare in air-conditioned class to Butterworth near Penang is a little less. A possible alternative is to cross into Malaysia at Kota Bharu where there is a small Thai Consulate (closed Fridays). If working in northern Thailand, the obvious place to go is Vientiane in Laos (though you will have to pay for a Laos visa).

As throughout Asia, it is a good idea to look neat and respectable when entering Thailand, especially if you intend to make a habit of it. Those entering from Malaysia should keep an eye open for the sign which reads, 'The following persons will not be allowed entry: hippies, anyone wearing a headband, a waistcoat or silk shorts, anyone barechested, or anyone not wearing undergarments.' In fact Thai border formalities are usually friendly and relaxed.

So far, people teaching on a tourist or a non-immigrant visa have not been required to pay tax. Once a work permit is granted, tax will be withdrawn at a very modest rate, sometimes as low as 2%. Thailand's national health scheme applies to visitors and so not all teachers worry about private insurance.

CONDITIONS OF WORK

In a country where teaching jobs are so easy to come by, there has to be a catch. In Thailand, the wages for *farang* teachers are uniformly low. The basic hourly rate has risen only very slightly over the past six years from B150 to B180 an hour with most decent schools (there are not many) paying B200. Company work pays between B250 and B450 depending on location, but as mentioned earlier the amount of in-company contract work has greatly diminished. The norm is for schools to keep their staff on as part-time freelancers while giving them full-time hours; this is primarily to avoid taxes.

"The following persons will not be allowed entry: hippies, anyone wearing a headband, waistcoat or silk shorts, anyone barechested or not wearing undergarments."

Most language institutes pay weekly in cash, but beware of schools which turn pay day into a moveable feast.

The best remuneration is available from international schools like the *Bangkok Patana School*. Note that the pay at international schools in Bangkok is as much as twice that paid by international schools elsewhere in the country. University and colleges offer around B25,000 a month for a relatively light teaching load.

Few employers help with accommodation which at the present time does not matter much since vacant apartments can be found on almost every street and the rental deposit is very low. According to Helen Welch, newly returned from Thailand in the summer of 1998, many teachers in Bangkok are choosing to live in foreigners' compounds which are, increasingly, patrolled by armed guards. Things are more relaxed in Chiang Mai where a group of people can rent a house or live Thai-style in a studio room with attached bathroom for very affordable rents.

Before accepting a job, find out what teaching materials are in use, if any. A great many schools offer no more than a classroom and a few textbooks lying around, leaving the teacher to design the syllabus, etc. On the other hand there are some schools which have very rigid and unimaginative lesson plans which teachers are obliged to follow.

Thai students are friendly, responsive, eager and a delight to teach. After five years of teaching in Thailand, Richard Guellala offers his view of Thai students:

> *Thais are definitely fun to teach as long as you don't get too friendly with them, as then you'll find yourself in a very awkward situation having lost all credibility. It's best to keep some distance and make them aware during their first lesson that you are in control. Most Thais are false beginners and of lower intermediate levels, and you will find that very few students reach an intermediate level due to lack of motivation and commitment.*

Remember never to touch a student on the head, which is difficult if you are teaching children. In class a show of anger will soon lose the students' respect since the Thais value a 'cool heart' *(jai yen)* and go to great lengths to avoid displays of negative emotion. Calm, smiling and enthusiastic personalities make all the difference.

LEISURE TIME

It has to be said that Bangkok may be an exciting and lively city but it is not beautiful. It has very few parks, bad traffic congestion and polluted air. Bruce Lawson describes the two ways of travelling between Banglamphu and Siam Square:

> *You can travel to work on the cesspool that they call a canal (klong). It's about a five minute walk from Banglamphu on the other side of the Democracy Monument. Get on a boat picking up on the right of the bridge. It costs a few baht and takes just over 10 minutes compared to the 45-minute ride on the non-air con bus. But you swap traffic fumes for the stench of stagnant water full of decomposing rubbish, animals and hideous eight-inch swimming millipedes. So don't fall in.*

There is also a great deal of what some might consider moral pollution, and there is a certain element of the teaching fraternity in Bangkok who are there primarily for the easy availability of sex in the notorious Patpong district (despite the fact that there is a veritable AIDS crisis in Thailand). Helen Welch reports that at least one school has banned all its staff from going into Patpong, for fear of being spotted by a clients or their parents. The ratio of foreign men to women teachers is at least six to one, and many women (although in great demand as teachers) do not enjoy the atmosphere in the city and leave as quickly as they can. Although there are plenty of night clubs and restaurants in Bangkok, there is a dearth of dance and film, and also of sports clubs.

Fortunately for teachers earning a low wage, the more innocent pleasures of Thailand come cheap. Try to learn a little Thai as Bruce Lawson did after getting fried battered banana when he thought he had ordered garlic chicken. He recommends organising word-swaps with students, which will also illustrate to them that they are not the only ones who have to struggle with alien sounds.

Living expenses are not high. Food bought at street stalls is very cheap and tasty, but also brings with it a risk of hepatitis. Apparently there is a national shortage of marmite, so homesick Britons will embrace any new arrival with a supply. Even part-time teachers should be able to afford to travel round the country, visiting jungle attractions like Kanchanaburi, where you can ride an elephant along the banks of the River Kwai, and islands like Koh Samet, Koh Samui and Koh Phangan where life is slow and the beaches are wonderful. Bangkok is also an important hub for travellers and cheap tickets are available to India, etc.

LIST OF SCHOOLS

AMERICAN UNIVERSITY LANGUAGE CENTER
179 Rajadamri Road, Bangkok 10330. Tel: (2) 252 8170-3/650 5040-4 ext. 2208, 2209 or 2114. Chiang Mai branch: AUA, 73 Rajadamnern Road, Amphur Muang, Chiang Mai 50200. Tel/fax: 53-211973.
4 branches in Bangkok and 11 upcountry.
Number of teachers: about 200 in total: 80-90 at main branch, up to 20 at other branches.

Preference of nationality: American and Canadian accents preferred; also British, Australian and New Zealand.
Qualifications: BA in any field or CELTA and completion of high school.
Conditions of employment: 1 year commitment preferred. 4-6 hours teaching daily (no full-time positions). Teaching year consists of 7 6-week terms separated by 1 free week. Courses aimed at professionals aged 18-35.
Salary: starting rate is B189 per hour (net). B15 pay rise every 6 months.
Facilities/Support: participation in pre-service training session (20 hours) is required before teaching hours are assigned. 15,000 titles in resource library. Work permit available after 3 month probation period.
Recruitment: adverts in the *Bangkok Post*, the internet and word of mouth.

BANGKOK PATANA FIRST SCHOOL
2/38 Soi Lasalle, Sukhumvit 105, Bangkok 10260. Tel: (2) 398 0200. Fax: (2) 399 3179.
Number of teachers: 12 ESL teachers.
Preference of nationality: British.
Qualifications: TEFL certificate, good education, experience of working with young children.
Conditions of employment: 1 year contracts. School hours are 7.15am-2.30pm (until 3.30pm on Mondays and Wednesdays).
Salary: B35,000 per month on average (less 6.5% deduction for tax).
Facilities/Support: assistance with accommodation and work permits. 2 1-hour training sessions per week.
Recruitment: adverts in the *Bangkok Post* and *The Nation*. Local interview essential.
Contact: David Meredith, Head of First School.

CHIANG MAI UNIVERSITY
Department of English, 239 Huay Kaew Road, Amphur Muang, Chiang Mai 50200. Tel: (53) 943258. Fax: (53) 943258.
Number of teachers: 30.
Preference of nationality: none.
Qualifications: university degree relevant to teaching English as a second language.
Conditions of employment: 1 year contracts. 12 h.p.w.
Salary: B10,000 per month.
Facilities/Support: no assistance with accommodation. Help given with work permits.
Recruitment: direct applications. Local interview essential.
Contact: Mr. Dheera Chudananda, Head of English Department.

ECC (THAILAND)
430/17-24 Chula Soi 64, Siam Square, Bangkok 10330. Tel: (2) 253 3312. Fax: (2) 254 2243. E-mail: eccthai@comnet3.ksc.net.th; Web-site: http://www.u-net.com/eflweb/schools/ECC/index.htm.
40 branches in Greater Bangkok, 20 elsewhere in Thailand.
Number of teachers: around 500 native speakers (normally recruit 5-10 new teachers each month).
Preference of nationality: none.
Qualifications: must have one of: Bachelor's degree, TEFL qualification, 6 months or more teaching experience, CELTA (preferred).
Conditions of employment: average of 25 h.p.w. 6 days per week between 9am and 9pm. Pupils include children and adults (general, ESP and business classes).
Salary: B19,000-35,000 per month.
Facilities/Support: work permit and insurance provided. Assistance given with finding accommodation. Regular workshops. Cambridge/RSA CELTA course offered five times a year; Introduction to TESOL offered monthly.

Recruitment: adverts in the *Guardian, TES, EL Gazette,* internet web site and qualified walk-ins.

ELITE TRAINING INSTITUTE
2nd Floor, Kongboonma Building, 699 Silom Rd., 10500 Bangkok. Tel: (2) 233 6620/1. Fax: (2) 237 1997. E-mail: elite_training@hotmail.com
Number of teachers: 60-70, some placed in private and government primary and secondary schools.
Preference of nationality: none.
Qualifications: RSA/TOEFL/TOEC and experience in English language teaching.
Conditions of employment: 1 year full-time or 30-40 hour contracts. Full-time teachers work from 8am to 3.30pm Monday to Friday. Hours vary for others.
Salary: B250-B450 per hour (net).
Facilities/Support: assistance given finding accommodation. After 3 month probationary period, full-time teachers are helped to get a non-immigrant B visa.
Recruitment: *Bangkok Post* and internet. Local interviews essential.
Contact: Melanie Austin, Head Teacher.

FUN LANGUAGE INTERNATIONAL (THAILAND) LTD.
275 Lee House, 4/F, Thonglor Soi 13, Sukhumvit 55, Bangkok 10110. Tel: (2) 712 7744-8. Fax: (2) 712 7733. E-mail: engisfun@loxinfo.co.th
Number of teachers: at least 15.
Preference of nationality: British, American.
Qualifications: university degree in Education/English and work experience with toddlers in foreign countries.
Conditions of employment: 1 year contracts. Flexible hours between 9am and 5pm depending on teaching requirements.
Facilities/Support: assistance with accommodation. Help given with work permits after 3 months.
Recruitment: via agency abroad. Telephone interviews occasionally carried out.
Contact: Khun Duangehai Tangsanga, Managing Director.

KING'S COLLEGE OF ENGLISH
Central City Office Tower, Floor 5A, Central City Bangna, Bangna-Trad Road, Prakanang, Bangkok. Tel: (2) 745 6001. Fax: (2) 745 6000.
E-mail: kingth@asiaaccess.net.th
Number of teachers: 40.
Preference of nationality: British, American, Australian.
Qualifications: university degree plus CELTA or equivalent and experience.
Conditions of employment: 1 year contracts. 28 contact h.p.w. 35 hours in school.
Salary: B29,000 per month plus benefits package. Less 5% for deductions.
Facilities/Support: assistance with accommodation and work permits. Training workshop every fortnight.
Recruitment: local adverts and recruitment agency. Interviews not essential.
Contact: Ashley McManus, School Manager.

LANNA INTERNATIONAL SCHOOL
300 Grandview Moo 1, Chiang Mai to Hang Dong Road, Chiang Mai 50100. Tel/fax: (53) 271159.
Number of teachers: 11.
Preference of nationality: none.
Qualifications: appropriate background and training. 2 years' experience.
Conditions of employment: 2 year contracts. Hours are 7.30am to 4pm.
Salary: according to qualifications and experience; normally starts at US$8,000-$9,000 (gross) per year.
Facilities/Support: assistance with accommodation including housing allowance. Help with entry visa before arrival and subsequent procedures.

Recruitment: recruiting fairs and interviews.
Contact: W. D. Morton, Headmaster.

MAEJO UNIVERSITY
Western Languages Section, Faculty of Agricultural Business, Chiang Mai 50290. Tel: (53) 878093. Fax: (53) 498151. E-mail: lalida@maejo.mju.ac.th
Number of teachers: 1 or 2.
Preference of nationality: from English speaking country.
Qualifications: Bachelor's degree (any field) and experience in teaching English/TEFL/ESP.
Conditions of employment: 1 year contracts. 12 h.p.w.
Facilities/Support: assistance with accommodation, though teachers must share at first. Help given with work permits. Occasional seminars on teaching methodology.
Recruitment: word of mouth, ads in newspapers, radio, etc. Local interviews essential.
Contact: Ms. Lalida Puthong, Head of Western Languages Section.

NORTH AMERICAN LANGUAGE SCHOOL
36/1 Ngam Wongwan Road, Bangkok 10900. Tel: (2) 953 0416. Fax: (2) 953 0417. E-mail: northam2000@yahoo.com
Number of teachers: 15-18.
Preference of nationality: none.
Qualifications: university degree preferred; TESOL/CELTA Certificate required. Minimum 2 years experience, preferably in Asia.
Conditions of employment: normally freelance. A few 1 year contracts.
Salary: US$8-16 per hour or from US$850 per month (gross).
Facilities/Support: no assistance with accommodation which is readily available (from US$110 per month). Help given with visa charges and associated travel.
Recruitment: newspaper adverts in Bangkok and via internet. Local interviews essential.
Contact: Phillip W. Venne, Managing Director.

PRINCE OF SONGKHLA UNIVERSITY
Department of Foreign Languages & Linguistics, Faculty of Liberal Arts, Had Yai, Songkhla 90110. Tel: (74) 211030-49 ext. 2780. Fax: (74) 446679.
Number of teachers: 3.
Preference of nationality: none.
Qualifications: BA in English with experience in TEFL/TESL or MA in TEFL/TESL or Applied Linguistics.
Conditions of employment: 1 year contracts. 14+ h.p.w.
Salary: B14,000-18,000 per month. Annual bonus of one month's pay on completion of one fiscal year service.
Facilities/Support: assistance with finding accommodation. Teacher is given transport to the immigration office and labour office to apply for work permit; subsequent steps are taken care of by department secretary. Textbook, teachers' manual, cassettes and worksheets provided. Teacher training sessions held once or twice a year.
Recruitment: personal interview necessary.
Contact: Sutaree Prasertsan, Deputy Head.

SIAM COMPUTER & LANGUAGE INSTITUTE
471/19 Ratchawithi Road, Bangkok 10400. Tel: (2) 247 2345 ext. 370-373. Fax: (2) 644 6974.
Number of teachers: 64 at 35 schools in Bangkok and the provinces.
Preference of nationality: none.
Qualifications: college degree; CELTA or equivalent and experience preferred.
Conditions of employment: 1 year contracts. 6 days per week for full-time. Students of all ages.

Salary: B18,000-20,000 per month plus overtime opportunities. Hourly rates for part-time teachers.
Facilities/Support: no assistance with finding accommodation. Teacher training programme (specialising in teaching children), monthly teachers' meetings, new teacher orientation and training, sound lab and computer lab.
Recruitment: adverts in *Bangkok Post*. Local interviews required.
Contact: Mr. Chalermchai or Mr. Michael.

SIAM COMPUTER & LANGUAGE SCHOOL PHUKET
2 Soi, 7 Phung-nga Road, Muang, Phuket 83000. Tel: (76) 219914-5. Fax: (76) 218720. E-mail: narisara@phuket.a-net.net.th
Number of teachers: 5.
Preference of nationality: none.
Qualifications: ability to teach children aged 6-12.
Conditions of employment: 1 year contracts. Maximum 34 h.p.w.
Salary: from B25,000 per month.
Recruitment: adverts in *Bangkok Post*. Local interview essential.
Contact: Khun Narisara C., Manager/Owner.

STAMFORD COLLEGE
Soi Ju-teeuthit 3, HatYai, Songkhla 90110. Tel: (74) 347203/4. Fax: (74) 347201. E-mail: chain@hatyai.inet.co.th
Number of teachers: 16.
Preference of nationality: none.
Qualifications: minimum degree (or equivalent) plus TEFL certificate or experience.
Conditions of employment: 1 year contracts, renewable. Usual hours between 8.30am and 3.30pm with some evenings. Teachers required to teach 100 hours per month with 80% taking place in daytime. 5 day week including some (but not all) Saturdays. School closed on Sundays. Medical cover, work permit, 3 weeks paid leave plus national holidays are given.
Salary: B26,000 per month (less 5% deductions for tax).
Facilities/Support: assistance with accommodation prior to arrival. Airport pick-ups and orientation. Help with work permits. On-going development programme with regular teachers' meetings, workshops, material evaluation sessions and observations.
Recruitment: through associate schools (20+ in Southeast Asia), the internet and the educational press. Interviews are conducted by telephone.
Contact: David Simons, Director of School Affairs.

TRAINING, CREATIVITY, DEVELOPMENT (T.C.D.) CO. LTD.
399/7 Soi Thongloh 21, Sukhumvit Soi 55, Bangkok 10110. Tel/fax: (2) 391 5670. Tel: (2) 712 8503.
Number of teachers: 35.
Preference of nationality: North American, British or Commonwealth.
Qualifications: TEFL/TESL training preferred, plus as much experience as possible. Preferably aged less than 38.
Conditions of employment: 6 month-1 year commitment preferred. Newcomers start with a few hours a week and build up to 25-35 per week, mostly one-to-one teaching. Prime hours of work between 3.30pm and 8pm. Pupils aged 6-60, most of them Japanese.
Salary: B300-500 per hour.
Facilities/Support: school provides list of cheap housing. Training given. Large ESL resource library.
Recruitment: word of mouth. Local interviews essential. Speculative applications cannot all be answered.
Contact: John F. Moriarty, Owner.

Other Schools to Try

Note that these schools (in alphabetical order according to town) did not confirm their teacher requirements for this edition of *Teaching English Abroad*. Upper case entries marked with an asterisk had entries in the last edition (1997); addresses without asterisks have been taken from various sources, such as British Council lists.

ASBEC, Amnvay Silpa School, 304/1 Sri Ayutthaya Road, Ratchewi, Bangkok 10400

Attawit Commercial College, 280 Sunpawut Road, Bangna, Prakhanong, Bangkok 01260

Berlitz Thailand Ltd., Silom Complex 22F, 191 Silom Road, 10500 Bangkok

British-American Language Institute, Ladphrao, Soi 58-60 Bankapi, Bangkok 10310

CHULALONGKORN UNIVERSITY LANGUAGE INSTITUTE, Prem Purachatra Building, Phaya Thai Road, Bangkok 10330 (2-218 6031/fax 2-252 5978). 15 teachers.

ELCA (English Language Centre of Australia), 313 CP Tower, 26th Floor, Silom Road, Bangkok 10500 (e-mail elcas@loxinfo.co.th)

ELS INTERNATIONAL (THAILAND), 419/3 Rajavithee Road, Phyathai (Opposite Children's Hospital), Bangkok 10400 (2-247 8088/247 8384/245 8953/fax 2-246 4365. 15 teachers for several branches in Bangkok.

ELT—tel 2-966 5753

English for Busy People, 268 Siam Square, Soi 3m, Rama I Road, Patumwan, Bangkok

INLINGUA SCHOOL OF LANGUAGES, Head Office: 7th Floor, Central Chidlom Tower, 22 Ploenchit Road, Pathumwan, Bangkok 10330 (2-254 7029/254 7030/fax 2-254 7098). E-mail: executrn@ksc5.th.com. 40 full-time teachers at several branches in Bangkok and also Phuket (e-mail: inlingua@phuket.a-net.net.th). Advertising recently for corporate teachers and weekend children's teachers.

NAVA—e-mail: Kanittha@ksc15.th.com

Stamford College Group, Stamford Building, Soi Japanese School, Huay Kwang, Bangkok

Text and Talk Consultancy, Phahoihothin Road 32, Bangken, Bangkok

Ake Panya International School, 158/1 Moo 3, Hangdong-Samerng Road, Bangpong, Amphur Muang, Chiang Mai 50230

Australia Centre, 75/1 Moo 4, Tambon Suthep, Amphur Muang, Chiang Mai 50200

CEC, 7th Floor, Kad Suan Kaew Bldg, Huay Kaew Road, Amphur Muang, Chiang Mai 50200

Chiang Mai International School, 13 Chetupon Road, Tambon Watkate, Amphur Muang, Chiang Mai 50000

Nakorn Payap International School, 114 Moo 1, Tambon Nong Pa Krung, Amphur Muang, Chiang Mai 50000

Payap University, 272 Moo 2, Chiang Mai-Lampang Super Highway, Chiang Mai 50000

Tridhos Three Generation School, PO Box 1, Amphur Mae Rim, Chiang Mai 50180

YMCA, 11 Mengrai Rassamee Road, Amphur Muang, Chiang Mai 50200 (53-221819). Also run summer language camps.

ANANDA SHYAMA, 45 Mu 2 Parksong, Ptho, Chumpon 86180. 2-3 volunteers to teach in remote village areas

PATONG LANGUAGE SCHOOL, 95/23 Mu 4 Soi Bangla, Patong Beach, Kathu, Phuket 83150 (76-340373/fax 76-340873).

Rajabhat Institute Udon Thani, Department of Foreign Language, Udon Thani

LATIN AMERICA

Spanning 75 degrees of latitude, the mammoth continent of South America together with the Caribbean islands and the eight countries of Central America, offer a surprising range of teaching opportunities. With the important exception of Brazil where Portuguese is spoken, most South American countries have a majority of Spanish speakers and, as in Spain itself, there is a great demand for English teaching, from dusty Mexican towns near the American border to Punta Arenas at the southern extremity of the continent, south of the Falkland Islands.

The countries of most interest to the travelling teacher are Chile, Argentina, Colombia, Ecuador, Venezuela, Brazil and Mexico. Certain patterns emerged during the research for this book, though sweeping generalisations are of limited value and will not apply to all countries and all situations. Inflation is still a problem for many of the nations of Latin America, especially Colombia and Ecuador, which means that salaries quickly lose their value unless there are frequent adjustments. Although pay scales are often quoted in US dollars, wages are almost always paid in the local currency which in many cases is worth little outside the country.

The economies of Latin American nations are much less volatile than they were at the beginning of the decade. Urban life in the big cities of Argentina or Chile is more like that of Europe than of developing countries. In such cities, the greatest demand for English comes from big business, and because of the strong commercial links between the two American continents, the demand tends to be for American English, though an increasing number of British and Australian teachers are finding work in these countries.

Among the most important providers of the English language are Bi-National Centers and Cultural Centers, the American counterpart of the British Council. There are scores of these centres in Latin America, including over 60 in Brazil and about 15 apiece in Argentina and Mexico. A complete list (under the rather worrying heading 'American Republics' instead of 'Latin America') is available from the United States Information Agency (USIA), Cultural and Binational Centers, English Teaching Fellow Program, 301 4th St SW, Washington, DC 20547. These centres are all engaged in the teaching of English, some on such a large scale that they employ more than 20 teachers. While some want a commitment to stay for two years, others are happy to take someone on for two or three months. While some require only a good command of English (whatever the accent), others want teachers with a BA/MA in TESL from a US university.

Britain also has cultural representatives in nine Latin American nations. The longest established *Culturas Inglesas* are in Argentina, Brazil, Chile, Mexico, Peru and Uruguay, with Costa Rica, Paraguay and Guatemala having joined the list more recently. These Cultural Associations aim to teach English within the framework of British culture and work closely with the British Council and represent the elite end of the market. Normally they require their teachers to have specialised ELT training and experience. Only a few recruit abroad so it is worth making local enquiries on arrival.

Several South American nations have a number of British or American-style bilingual schools and *colegios*. Although this book is not centrally concerned with English-medium schools, which are normally looking for teachers with a PGCE or full teacher accreditation, international schools in South America are mainly for local nationals (rather than expatriates) who want a bilingual Spanish-English education and have a very strong emphasis on English language teaching. Despite the prestige of these schools, some are willing to consider EFL teachers who have not done teacher training. For example many of them accept school leavers participating in gap year projects.

Finally there are private and commercial language institutes from International House (in Brazil and Argentina) through Berlitz (which is strongly represented in Latin America) to the cowboy operations where standards and wages will be extremely low. David Hewitt, a computer programmer from Yorkshire with no TEFL training or experience, was surprised not only to walk into a teaching job in Brazil but also to find himself giving lessons to the director of the school.

In whatever kind of school you teach, or if you just give occasional private lessons to contacts, you will probably find the local people extremely friendly and eager to help. The ethnic diversity and Latin warmth encountered by foreign teachers and travellers throughout the continent usually more than compensate for low wages and (in the big cities) a high crime rate.

Prospects for Teachers

In a land where baseball is a passion and US television enormously popular, American (and also Canadian) job-seekers have an advantage. The whole continent is culturally and economically oriented towards the States. There is a decided preference among language learners for the American accent and for American teaching materials and course books, which explains why so many language institutes are called Lincoln and Jefferson. Business English is gaining ground throughout the region, particularly in Argentina, Chile, Venezuela, Colombia, Brazil and Mexico, and anyone with a business background will have an edge over the competition.

The academic year begins in February or early March and lasts until November/December. In the southernmost nations of Chile and Argentina, January and February are very slack months for language schools; while further north in Bolivia, for example, the summer holiday consists of December/January. The best time to arrive to look for work is a few weeks before the end of the summer holidays. But many institutes run eight to twelve week courses year round and will be eager for the services of a native speaker whatever the time of year.

Very seldom will you find the glut of teachers you find elsewhere in the world, as Nick Branch found:

> English teachers are still much in demand in South America, probably because fewer native speakers visit this region than other parts of the world, due to the perception by many that it is the world's most dangerous/corrupt continent—partly true, but hugely exaggerated in the minds of many. I had no problems at all in South America. One just has to be a little more vigilant than usual.

FIXING UP A JOB

Speculative enquiries from EFL teachers are much less likely to work if sent before arrival than after, although sending a 'warm-up' CV may help your job search. What the principal of a girls' school in Lima wrote to us is echoed by many other institutes. 'Anyone interested in a job is welcome to write to me at any time. If they happen to be in Lima they are equally welcome to come into school.' Unless you are very well qualified or have met your prospective employer before, you are unlikely to be offered a contract while out of the country. This is unfortunate since work visas are best applied for in the country of origin of the teacher (see below).

In Advance

Very few Latin American language schools advertise in the UK press. Even the most prestigious schools complain of the difficulties they encounter recruiting teachers abroad, mainly due to the low salaries they can offer and the very bureaucratic procedures for obtaining a work permit. Some British Council offices in South America keep lists of schools, as do some embassies and consulates in London and

Washington. When 20 year old James Gratton was making plans for his first trip to South America, he wrote to all the embassies in London and received quite a lot of literature, including a number of lists of language schools, for Paraguay, Uruguay, Peru, etc. He claims that the Argentinian Embassy was particularly helpful and friendly. Serious candidates might ask the Cultural Attaché for advice.

LAURELS (the Latin American Union of Registered English Language Schools) currently has over 30 members in Uruguay (all in Montevideo) and 67 member schools in Brazil in most of the important cities. The schools are noted for the high quality of tuition they provide, and are active in cooperating with the British Council in the field of teacher development, particularly in improving services to young and teenage learners. The LAURELS prospectus is updated annually and circulated to institutes considering applying to become members (rather than to prospective teachers). LAURELS may be contacted at International House Goiania, Rua 4, 80 Setor Oeste, Goiania 74110-140, GO, Brazil (62-224 0478/fax 62-223 1846).

Language school chains and organisations which might be of assistance to qualified British TEFL teachers are *International House, Berlitz* and *English Worldwide* which sometimes recruits on behalf of *Culturas Inglesas* and international schools. *Saxoncourt Recruitment* and *IPG* are active in several countries of South America (see chapter *Finding a Job*). School leavers should contact the *Project Trust* (which has links with schools in Brazil, Chile, Guatemala and Cuba), *GAP Activity Projects* (which make TEFL placements in Mexico, Argentina, Paraguay, Ecuador, Chile and Brazil) and *Gap Challenge*.

TEFL training colleges in the US often have close ties with Latin American language schools. The training centres in California like *Transworld Teachers* and *New World Teachers* send large numbers of their graduates to posts in South America.

ELS International has affiliated language schools in Santiago, Buenos Aires, Rio, São Paulo and Curitiba. *Bénédict Schools* are well represented in Ecuador. *EF English First* has been expanding on the continent with schools in Colombia, Ecuador, Mexico, etc.

The *Central Bureau for Educational Visits & Exchanges* arranges for language assistants to work in a number of Latin American countries for a year. Applicants must be aged 20-30 with at least 'A' level Spanish and preferably a degree in modern languages. According to the 'Notes for Applicants' and country-by-country details available from the Assistants Department, posts in Latin America offer greater scope for independent work than is usual on the programme and 'may therefore be of particular interest to those considering a career in TEFL'. Application forms are available from October; the deadline is December of the year preceding placement.

Certified teachers interested in EFL posts might like to contact *Gabbitas Educational Consultants* which send teachers to schools in South America on two or three year contracts, such as Cambridge College in Lima which was recently advertising posts.

PGCE-holders who are committed Christians will be interested to hear that SAMS, the South American Mission Society (Overseas Personnel, Unit 11, Prospect Business Park, Langston Road, Loughton, Essex IG10 3TZ; 0181-502 3502) recruit teachers of English for schools in South America with an Anglican foundation including Colegio San Andres (Asuncion, Paraguay), St. Paul's School (Viña del Mar, Chile) and the *British School* in Puntas Arenas, Chile. In addition to these formal settings, the Church in some areas is establishing high quality English language institutes to provide a service to university students and as a means of forming a bridge into the community.

The Association of American Schools in South America (AASSA, 14750 NW 77 Court, Suite 210, Miami Lakes, FL 33016; 305-821-0345/fax 305-821-4244) coordinates teacher recruitment for its 32 members, all American-international schools in 11 South American countries. Candidates who attend a recruiting fair in December must be state-certified teachers. The placement fee is $300, payable only on being hired, and often reimbursed by the employer.

The *TESOL Placement Bulletin* carries occasional notices of vacancies in South

American schools. A few schools, including some of the biggest Bi-National Centers, attend TESOL Conventions.

Voluntary and international exchange organisations involved in arranging for young people to do some English tutoring include *WorldTeach* with programmes in Costa Rica and Ecuador, *Alliances Abroad* which arranges for fee-paying volunteers to teach in various Latin American countries (the average fee payable is $750 a month); and *World Education Forum* in Costa Rica (see entry in this chapter) which places tutors with host families in Costa Rica and Mexico.

On the Spot

The concept of 'job vacancy' is very fluid in many Latin American language institutes and, provided you are willing to work for local teaching wages, you should be able to create your own job almost anywhere. As throughout the world, local applicants often break into the world of language teaching gradually by teaching a few classes a week. Non-contractual work is almost always offered on an unofficial part-time basis. So if you are trying to earn a living you will have to patch together enough hours from various sources. Finding the work is simply a matter of asking around and knocking on enough doors. For those who speak no Spanish, the first hurdle is to communicate your request to the secretaries at language schools since they invariably speak no English. Try to memorise a polite request in Spanish to pass your CV and letter (in Spanish if possible) to the school director who will know at least some English. Try to charm the receptionist, librarian or English language officer at the British Council, Bi-National Center or any other institute (like the South America Explorers' Club in Peru and Ecuador) which might have relevant contacts or a useful notice board. Check adverts in the English language press such as *The News* in Mexico City or the *Buenos Aires Herald.* English language bookshops are another possible source of teaching leads.

Ask in expatriate bars and restaurants, check out any building claiming to be an 'English School' however dubious-looking, and in larger cities try deciphering the telephone directory for schools or agencies which might be able to use your services. There is more competition as well as more opportunities in the major cities (for example it is said that up to half a million Americans live in Mexico City), so if you are having difficulties rounding up work, you could try smaller towns and cities off the beaten track.

The crucial factor in becoming accepted as an English teacher at a locally-run language school may not be your qualifications or your accent as much as your appearance. You must look as neat and well-dressed as teachers are expected to look, at least when you're job-hunting. Later your standards might slip a little; Nick Wilson who taught for two years in Mexico says that it is easy to spot the English teachers in banks and office buildings; they're the ones wearing jeans, T-shirts and carrying cassettes.

Freelance Teaching

In most Latin American cities, there is a thriving market in private English lessons, which usually pay at least half as much again as working for an institute. It is not uncommon for teachers to consider the language school which hires them as a stepping stone to setting up as a private tutor. After they have familiarised themselves with some teaching materials and made enough contacts among local language learners, they strike out on their own, though this is far from easy unless you can get by in the local language and also have a telephone and suitable premises. Clients can be found by advertising in the quality press, by placing notices on strategic notice boards or by handing out business cards. If the latter, use the local method of address and omit confusing initials like BA after your name: teachers often call themselves 'Profesor' or 'Profesora.'

REGULATIONS

Of course requirements vary from country to country but the prospects are dismal for teachers who insist on doing everything by the book. It is standard for work visas to be available only to fully qualified and experienced teachers on long-term contracts. Often you will have to present an array of documents, from university certificates and transcripts to FBI clearance, which have been authenticated by your Consulate abroad or by the Consulate of the host country. Although many schools will not offer a contract before interview and then will make it contingent on a work permit, the procedures should be started in the teacher's country of origin, which makes the whole business very difficult. All of this can take as long as six months or even a year and involve a great deal of hassle and expense, not least for the employer.

The upshot is that a high percentage of teachers work unofficially throughout Latin America. It is hardly an issue in some countries, for example virtually no one gets a work permit in Costa Rica, not even the long-resident directors of language schools and no one seems to worry about it. Teaching on a tourist visa is a widespread practice in Mexico and Peru. Brazil is much stricter: all exchanges of money are supposed to be accompanied by receipts, which is likely to make life more difficult for casual teachers. There are ways round the regulations, for example to work on a student/ trainee/cultural exchange visa (as in Ecuador or Venezuela).

CONDITIONS OF WORK

The problem of low wages has already been emphasised, and is even worse when inflation is rising. It is customary to be quoted a wage in American dollars (often in the range US$2-4 per hour) and to be paid the equivalent in the local currency. Assuming you are able to save any of your earnings, you will be unable to convert it into a hard currency except on the black market.

Some schools offer perks such as 14-month salaries or return flights to teachers who stay for a two-year contract. Contracts are fairly hard to come by and almost always require a minimum commitment of a year. The advantages are that you are guaranteed a certain income and you have a chance of applying for a work permit.

Teachers without the CELTA or Trinity Certificate are not greatly disadvantaged, partly because this qualification is not as widely known in Latin America as it is in Europe. One exception might be in Uruguay where two institutes offer the Trinity Certificate in TESOL: Dickens Institute (21 de Setiembre 2744, Montevideo) and *English Lighthouse Institute* (see entry at end of Latin America chapter). Many institutes offer their own compulsory pre-job training (to be taken at the teacher's own expense) which provides a useful orientation for new arrivals.

One of the seldom-mentioned perks of teaching in Latin America is the liveliness and enthusiasm of the pupils. Brazilian students have been described as the 'world's most communicative students' and classrooms around the continent often take on the atmosphere of a party. You may also be dazzled by the level of knowledge of Western pop culture, and should be prepared to have your ignorance shown up. Also be prepared to lose their attention if a lesson coincides with a major sporting event.

LEISURE TIME

Whether you are a serious student of Spanish or a frivolous seeker after the excitement generated by Latin carnivals, South America is a wonderful place to live in and travel. Women teachers may find the *machismo* a little hard to take, but will soon learn how to put it in its place. If you want to travel around, the annually revised *South American Handbook* definitely justifies the initial outlay of nearly £25.

Argentina

Argentina has always had a substantial English-speaking population and therefore teaching jobs for unqualified foreigners are relatively scarce. Buenos Aires is a sophisticated city with a high standard of education and a thriving market for business English. Most jobs begin in March/April and last through until Christmas. As in other South American capitals like Santiago, in-company teaching to middle managers and executives in big corporations is booming.

As mentioned earlier, the *Buenos Aires Herald* regularly carries job adverts for English teachers. The newsletter for teachers of English in Argentina and southern South America is called *ELT News & Views* (e-mail me@interlink.com.ar). There is also a useful notice board in El Ateneo, the bookshop at 340 Calle Florida (the main shopping street). Another good contact point is the Instituto de Lengua Espanola para Extranjeros or ILEE where many foreign residents take Spanish classes.

The network of *Culturas Inglesas* which operate under the auspices of the British Council hire only teachers at the British Council standard. Contact names for the following institutes can be obtained from the *British Council Address Book* which is updated quarterly:

Asociacion Bahiense de Cultura Inglesa, Zelarrayan 245, 8000 Bahia Blanca.
Instituto Chaqueno de Cultura Inglesa, Saenz Pena, San Martin 485, 3700 Chaco.
Asociacion Argentino de Cultura Britanica, Av. Hipolito Yrigoyer 496, Cordoba.
Instituto Cultural Argentino de la Plata, Calle 12 No 869, 1900 La Plata.
Instituto Cultural de Mendoza, Necochea 552, 5500 Mendoza.
Cultura Inglesa de Neuquen, Carlos H Rodriguez 439, 8324 Neuquem.
Asociacion Pergamino de Cultura Inglesa, 25 de Mayo 746, 2700 Pergamino.
Asociacion Puntaltense de Cultura Inglesa, Paso 364, 8109 Punta Alta.
Instituto Argentino de Cultural Britanico, Alsina 2s96, 1878 Quilmes.
Instituto Chaqueno de Cultura Inglesa, Don Bosco 256, 3500 Resistencia.
Asociacion Rosarina de Cultura Inglesa, Buenos Aires 1174, 2000 Rosario, Santa Fe
St. John's Language College, Jujuy 210 Sur, 5400 San Juan.
Instituto Cultural Argentina, 25 de Mayo 347, 4000 San Miguel de Tucuman.
Instituto Cultural Anglo Argentino de San Rafael, Avellaneda 250, 5600 San Rafael-Mendoza.
Instituto Cultural Anglo Argentino, Tucuman 367, 4200 Santiago del Estoro.
Asociacion Venadense de Cultura Inglesa, Marconi 631, 2600 Venado Tuerto-Santa Fe.
Asociacion Victoriense de Cultura Inglesa, Abasolo 28, 3153 Victoria.
Instituto Ocampense de Cultural Inglesa, 25 de May 1530, 3580 Villa Ocampo, Santa Fe.

Bi-national centers (Instituto de Intercambio Cultural Argentino-Americano) also offer English courses, as do the three International House schools in the capital (located in Recoleta, Belgrano and San Isidro). To work at one of these, you normally have to have worked for IH before. A large number of full-curriculum private schools prepare students for Cambridge and other exams, such as the Belgrano Day School (Juranmento 3035, 1428 Capital Federal) which has pupils from kindergarten to school leaving age.

Two private institutes to try are American English (Esmeralda 853, P.B. No.9, Buenos Aires) and Centum, Servicios de Idiomas, (Bartlomé Mitre, 4th floor, 1036 Buenos Aires; fax 1-328-5150/328-2385/328-8572) which offers the Trinity College Certificate in TESOL and therefore has a ready supply of qualified teachers. You might also try Links English Language Centre in the centre of Buenos Aires (fax 1-825 5735).

Red Tape

Working papers can be obtained from the National Direction of Migrations by employers, though a school will be willing only for long-term propositions. It will be necessary for the applicant to provide a contract of employment for a minimum of a year, certificate of good conduct from the police authorities in his or her country or countries of residence in the five years prior to applying, birth certificate, all authenticated by the Argentine Foreign Ministry. Teachers generally work on a visitor's visa, leaving the country every three months to renew their tourist visas when they recross the border back into Argentina.

Most teachers are paid hourly by the language institute/s employing them. Self-employed people are obliged to register with the DGI (tax office) and pay approximately 15% of their full-time earnings in tax.

LIST OF SCHOOLS

ASOCIACION ARGENTINA DE CULTURA BRITANICA
Av. HipólitoYrigoyen 496, Córdoba, Argentina. Tel/fax: (51) 691000. E-mail: aacb-cba@satlink.com
Number of teachers: 2.
Qualifications: qualified teachers with at least 3 years' ELT experience.
Conditions of employment: 1 year contract.
Salary: US$15 per hour.
Facilities/Support: teachers normally resident in Córdoba already. In-house training and assistance with work permits given.
Recruitment: CVs and personal interviews.
Contact: Beatriz Gil-Montero, Director.

CAIT (Capacitación en idiomas y traducciones)
Av. Pte. Roque Sáenz Peña 615, Piso 6°, Of. 631/632, 1393 Buenos Aires, Argentina. Tel: (1) 326 3230. Fax: (1) 326 2926. E-mail: cait@ciudad.com.ar
Number of teachers: 15 freelancers.
Preference of nationality: American or British.
Qualifications: TEFL or equivalent and experience in teaching Business English.
Conditions of employment: minimum 1 year (March to December). Teachers are required to have their own tape recorder and to register with the local IRS. School does not insist on exclusivity but expects a firm commitment.
Salary: US$16 per hour.
Facilities: personal computers available to teachers. Teachers are supplied with materials and methodological guidelines. No assistance with accommodation.
Recruitment: local interviews necessary.
Contact: Alejandra Jorge, Director.

Bolivia

Even the poorest of Latin American nations offers reasonable possibilities to EFL teachers, provided you are prepared to accept a low wage. In contrast to the standard hourly wage of $15-$20 per hour in Buenos Aires, the wages paid by language schools in Bolivia are 10-12 bolivianos ($2 at the time of writing). But many teachers touring South America prefer it for cultural reasons. La Paz is a city with a low cost of living and a colourful social mix. The class structure is immediately apparent with the upper class consisting of people of Spanish descent, the middle class or *mestizos* of mixed Spanish/Bolivian ancestry and the underclass of Indians still wearing their traditional costume.

Only a handful of language schools and a couple of *colegios* (private schools) are listed in the La Paz Yellow Pages and they are unlikely to commit themselves to hiring a teacher without meeting them first. The biggest language school in the country is the Centro Boliviano Americano or CBA (Parque Iturralde Zenon 121, La Paz; 2-431379) with three other locations in La Paz plus schools in other cities like Sucre and Santa Cruz. Despite its name it has been trying to increase the number of British native speakers on its staff. Diana Maisel turned down a job offer here because she didn't feel comfortable with the unrelaxed atmosphere, for example police were posted at the door of the school to prevent late entry by tardy students. Instead she accepted work with the Pan American English Centre (Edificio Avenida, Avenida 16 de Julio 1490, 7° piso, Casilla 5244, La Paz; tel/fax 2-340796) where she found the atmosphere much friendlier and more relaxed. Classes rotate teachers every two or three months so that students are exposed to a variety of English accents. It also has a branch in Cochabamba. It was not included in information sent by the British Council in La Paz; they provided the address of Update (Avenida Arce, Esquina Campos, La Paz; 2-332356).

Colegios employ native speakers for their English departments and tend to pay as much as twice as much as the private language schools. Also, the hours of 8.30am-1.30pm are more convenient. Three *colegios* in La Paz are:

Colegio Ingles Saint Andrews, Av. Las Relamas, La Florida, La Paz (2-792484/794041).

Colegio San Ignacio, Av. Hugo Ernest 7050, Següencoma, La Paz (2-783720/784680).

Colegio San Calixto, C/ Jenaro Sanjinés 701, La Paz (2-355278).

Private classes are even more lucrative. The standard rate for beginners is 20 bolivianos, rising to 30 or even 40 bolivianos an hour, but private pupils are even more unreliable than elsewhere in the world. The best place to advertise private English lessons is the Sunday edition of the newspaper *El Diario*.

Jobs can be found outside the capital as well. Judith Twycross received three job offers within a week of arriving in Bolivia's growing city Cochabamba. After Judith's pre-arranged job in Bolivia fell through at the last moment (not an uncommon occurrence), she decided to go in any case. She arrived in January so as to be there a couple of weeks before the beginning of the term. Terms normally last from early February to early September, resuming at the end of September to the beginning of December. With the advantage of a year's teaching experience in Spain and France and a good knowledge of Spanish, she soon found employment:

> *I took with me a letter of introduction and a CV both in Spanish plus a photocopy of my degree certificate. These I photocopied and delivered by hand to the directors of schools and institutes in Cochabamba. I got a list of schools from the Yellow Pages (which you could borrow at a hotel, photocopying kiosk, tourist information office, etc.). I told everyone I met what I was trying to do and received help and advice from hotel managers, taxi drivers and people I stopped on the street to ask for directions.*

Most teachers arrive on a tourist visa and with the help of their employer get a one-year visa (at a cost of $180). Long stay visas are generally not available unless you commit yourself to staying for a minimum of one year. If you do sign a contract and pay a sizeable fee, you should be able to obtain at least a student visa which means you don't have to leave the country at regular intervals to renew your visa.

The British company *i to i* is adding Bolivia to its list of destinations from 1999. The 'i venture' scheme will cost participants £1,300 for an English teaching job to be set up for them.

Brazil

The stabilisation of Brazil's currency over the past two years has encouraged the market for English teaching, which is not confined to the major cities of São Paulo and Rio de Janeiro. There are more than 30 SBCIs *(Sociedades Brasileiras de Cultura Inglesa)* and 60 bi-national centers scattered all over the fifth largest country in the world. Schools in smaller places often notify cooperating institutes in the big cities of any job vacancies for native speakers. But speculative visits to towns of any size would probably be successful eventually. Any of the four British Council offices in Brazil (Brasilia, Recife, Rio and São Paulo) should be able to send a list of Cultura Inglesas and LAURELS member schools.

The distinguishing feature of Brazilian EFL is the high proportion of well qualified Brazilian English teachers. Recruiting teachers from overseas is seen to be unjustifiably costly and also very difficult from the visa point of view. Only individuals with very specialised expertise are invited to work in very senior posts.

The Administrative Director of one of Rio de Janeiro's upmarket schools describes the difficulties:

> *Unfortunately, teaching English is not an area the government considers a priority in issuing visas. There are only two situations in which foreigners can teach in Brazil. Illegally, since there are numerous small schools who can afford to run the risk of hiring illegal foreigners. As a result, pay is usually bad and employment unstable. The alternative is available only to specialists, and is extremely rare. Because we have a web page, I get requests from foreigners all the time. I basically tell them that it is an adventure here, only for the strong of stomach, and you have to be willing to subject yourself to the unsavoury experiences that go along with working without proper papers. I have come across dozens of foreigners who have been promised work-related visas. In 27 years of living in Brazil, I have never, not once, seen this happen. The only cases I know of where a person has taught legally, it has been when they enter the country with visas issued at the Brazilian consulate in their country of residence.*

At the prestigious end of the market, schools like the Culturas Inglesas, bi-national cultural centres and International House schools (the five Britanic Schools in Recife are affiliated to IH, plus there is an IH school in Goiania), do recruit outside Brazil and enable their contracted teachers to obtain permits, though it can take up to six months. International House offers a monthly salary of about 800 Reals, from which you would expect to pay about a quarter in rent.

Otherwise it will be a case of looking around after you arrive, by using the Yellow Pages and expatriate networks. If you want to study Portuguese, you can apply for a student visa which would make it easier to stay on. For example, many foreigners register at the Pontificia Universidade Católica in Rio de Janeiro (Extension Department, Casa 15, Rua Marques Sao Vincente 225, Gávea, 22453-900 Rio; 21-529 9212). This is an excellent place to link up with students and advertise classes if you want to offer private lessons (which pay much better than working for an institute). You can also advertise in local papers like *O Globo*, *O Dia* or *Jornal do Brasil*. People on tourist visas can renew them by taking a trip to neighbouring Paraguay.)

The best time to start work is following *Carnaval* which takes place during the week over Ash Wednesday every February. Bear in mind that the cost of living in the big cities is very high, probably on a par with US cities, so that it is difficult to live on earnings of $8-$10 an hour. Foreigners who do stay usually bring a financial cushion with them or are lucky enough to get private students straightaway.

One way round the visa problems is to join an organised scheme. For example Teaching Abroad (Gerrard House, Rustington, West Sussex BN16 1AW, UK) send people to teach English in Brazil for between one and three months for a fee of £1,195 excluding airfares.

LIST OF SCHOOLS

BRITANNIA SCHOOLS
Central Department, Av. Borges de Medeiros 67, Leblon, Rio de Janeiro (RJ). Tel: (21) 511 0143. Fax: (21) 511 0893. E-mail: sdmale@britannia.com.br. Web-site: www.britannia.com.br20.
Number of teachers: 20 native speaker teachers for schools in Rio de Janeiro, São Paulo and Porto Alegre.
Preference of nationality: British, American, Canadian.
Qualifications: Cambridge/RSA Cert. (Grade 'B') essential, BA and experience.

Conditions of employment: 1-2 year renewable contracts. 25 h.p.w. Students grouped according to age, all in range 16-45.
Salary: varies according to teacher's scale.
Facilities: subsidised assistance with accommodation provided. Training given.

CULTURA INGLESA—BLUMENAU/FLORIANOPOLIS
Rua Marechal Floriano Peixoto 433, Centro, Blumenau 89010-500, SC. Tel/fax: (47) 326 7272; also (48) 224 2696. E-mail: mike@bnu.nutecnet.com.br
Number of teachers: 3.
Preference of nationality: British.
Qualifications: minimum Cambridge/RSA Certificate and 2 years' experience.
Conditions of employment: 1 year contracts. Maximum 24 contact h.p.w. Hours of teaching between 7.15am and 9.40pm and Saturday mornings. Some off-site business teaching.
Salary: US$800-$1000 per month.
Facilities/Support: shared accommodation in a four-bedroomed flat provided free. Flight reimbursement of US$500. Training provided.
Recruitment: through TEFL journals. Interviews and references essential and are occasionally held in Britain.
Contact: Mike Delaney, Cultura Manager.

CULTURA INGLESA DE GOIANIA
Rua 86 No. 07, Setor Sul, Goiania, GO. Tel: (62) 241 4516. Fax: (62) 241 2582. E-mail: cult.ing.sul@persogo.com.br
Number of teachers: 7.
Preference of nationality: British and Irish.
Qualifications: CELTA plus 3 years' experience.
Conditions of employment: 2 year contracts with option to renew for 2 years.
Salary: 1,500 reals (US$1,300 a month) less deductions of approximately 18%.
Facilities/Support: no assistance with accommodation. Help given with work permit (teachers must pick up visas at embassy in London.)
Recruitment: direct application or via agency. Detailed questionnaire sent to candidates' past employers.
Contact: Noel Downer, School Principal.

ENGLISH FOREVER
Rua Rio Grande do Sul 356, Pituba, 41830-140 Salvador-Bahia. Tel: (71) 240 2255. Fax: (71) 248 8706. E-mail: forever@svn.com.br
Number of teachers: 5.
Preference of nationality: British, American, Australian, Canadian.
Qualifications: minimum two years experience.
Conditions of employment: minimum 5 month contract. Around 30 h.p.w. Pupils from 8 years to adults.
Salary: $1,000 per month.
Facilities/Support: accommodation provided at a cost of $250 per month. No assistance with visas. One week in-service training before start of school year and 4 hours training monthly. (School is member of LAURELS.)
Recruitment: via AIESEC (International Association for Students of Economics and Management, 2nd Floor, 29-31 Cowper St, London EC2A 4AP). Interviews not essential, but contact made by phone.
Contact: Dinara de Goes Cavalcanti, Director.

IBI-INDEPENDENT BRITISH INSTITUTE
SHCGN 703, Area Especial 70730-700 Brasilia, DF. Tel: (61) 322 8373/322 0976. Fax: (61) 323 5524. E-mail: ibi@nutecnet.com.br
Number of teachers: 12-15.
Preference of nationality: British.
Qualifications: CELTA (grade A or B), BA, 2 years' experience.

Conditions of employment: 2 year contracts. 22-24 h.p.w. Students of all ages.
Salary: varies according to experience.
Facilities/Support: training/supervision provided.
Recruitment: through contact with former UK teachers. Interviews essential and held in UK.
Contact: Sara Walker, Principal.

INTERLANGUAGES CULTURAL
Rua da Quitanda 20/605, Centro, Rio de Janeiro (RJ). Tel/fax: (21) 224 9413.
Number of teachers: 5.
Preference of nationality: British.
Qualifications: TEFL, experience of working with executives.
Conditions of employment: freelance only.
Salary: varies according to qualifications.
Facilities/Support: no assistance with accommodation or work permits.
Recruitment: direct application. Local interviews.
Contact: Maggie Corson, Coordinator.

NEW START COMUNICACOES Ltda.
Av. Rio Branco 181/702, Centro, 20040-000 Rio de Janeiro, RJ. Tel: (21) 240 5807. Fax: (21) 532 0481. E-mail: newstart@prolink.com.br. Web-site: www.newstart.com.br
Number of teachers: variable, minimum 4.
Preference of nationality: must be native speaker.
Qualifications: TEFL certificate and professional experience in a non-teaching area. Degree in any subject.
Conditions of employment: minimum 6 months.
Salary: minimum US$900 per month (up to $900 is exempt from tax).
Facilities/Support: assistance with accommodation and work permits. Training in basic teaching techniques available.
Recruitment: direct application by CV and telephone. Possibility of interviews in UK.
Contact: Stephanie Crockett, Director of Studies.

Other Schools to Try

The following did not confirm their teacher requirements for this edition. Upper case letters and asterisks indicate that an institiue had an entry in the last edition (1997). Other addresses have been gleaned from British Council lists, etc.

Cultura Inglesa, Av. Barao de Maruim 761, Sao Jose, 49015 040 Aracaju (SE)
Cultura Inglesa, R. Fernandes Tourinho 538, Savassi, 30112 010 Belo Horizonte (MG)
Cultura Inglesa, Av. Guapore 2236, 78975 000 Cacoal (RO)
Cultura Inglesa, 419 R. Humberto de Campos, Vila Celia, 79020 060 Campo Grande (MS)
Cultura Inglesa, 227 Rua 12 de Outubro, 78005 510 Mato Grosso (MT), Cuiaba
Cultura Inglesa, R. Julia da Costa 1500, Bigorilho, 80730 070 Curitiba (PR)
Cultura Inglesa, R. Ponhta Grossa 1565, Vila Progresso, 79824 160 Dourados (MS)
Cultura Inglesa, R. Conde de Porto Alegre 59, 25070 350 Duque de Caxias (RJ)
Cultura Inglesa, Rua Ana Bilhar 171, Aldeota, 60160 110 Fortaleza (CE)
Cultura Inglesa, R. Mal Deodoro 1326, 14400 440 Franca (SP)
*CULTURA INGLESA—CARUARU, Av. Agamenon Magalhaes 634, 55000-000 Caruaru (PE). Tel/fax 81-721 4749. 2-4 teachers.
Cultura Inglesa, Av. Onze 1281, Centro, 38300 000 Ituiutaba (MG)
Cultura Inglesa, Av. Rio Grande do Sul 1411, Bairro dos Estados, 58030 021 Joao Pessoa (PB)
Cultura Inglesa, Av. dos Andradas 536, 36036 000 Juiz de Fora (MG)

CULTURA INGLESA PIEDADE, Av. Bernardo Vieira de Melo, 2101 Piedade, CEP 54.410-010 (81-361 3458/fax 81-361 0467). 3 teachers.

Quick and Easy, Av. Sao Sebastiao 848, Santa Clara, 68005 090 Belém (PA)

**CAMBRIDGE SOCIEDADE BRASILEIRA DE CULTURA INGLESA,* Rua Piaui, 1234 CEP 86020-320 Londrina Paraná (43-324 1092/fax 43-324 0314). E-mail: cambridg@sercomtel.com.br.

ACE American Center of English, Avenida Beira Mar 406, gr. 207, Castelo, 20025-900 Rio de Janeiro (RJ). Tel: 21-220 3345.

Beeline, Avenida 13 de Maio 23, Gr. 429, Centro, 21031-000 Rio de Janeiro (RJ). Tel 21-222 7238/532 5792.

Berlitz Escola de Idiomas, Av. Presidente Vargas 435—S/loja, 20071 003 Rio de Janeiro (RJ)

BRASAS English Courses, Brasil América Sociedade de Ingles, Rua Voluntários de Pátria 190/315, Botafogo, 22270-010 Rio de Janeiro (RJ). Tel: 21-527 1838/fax 21-286 8996/http://www.brasas.com.

Britannia Special English Studies, Av. Borges de Medeiors 67, 22430 040 Rio de Janeiro (RJ)

CCAA Centro de Cultura Anglo Americano, Rua 14 de Maio, 347, Riachuelo, 20950 090 Rio de Janeiro (RJ)

**CENTRO CULTURAL BRASIL ESTADOS UNIDOS,* Avenida T 5, no. 441, Setor Bueno, 74230-040 Goiânia, GO (62-833 1313/fax 62-833 1308). E-mail: ccbeu@international.com.br.

Context Cursos, Rua Marques de Olinda 75, Botafogo, 22251 040 Rio de Janeiro (RJ)

Curso Oxford, Rua Duvivier 28/SL, Copacabana, 22020 020 Rio de Janeiro (RJ)

ELS International, Rua Antonio Viera 24a, Leme, Rio de Janeiro (RJ). Tel: 21-293 4962.

English Center, Rua Toneleiro 219, Copacabana, 22030-000 Rio de Janeiro (RJ). Tel: 21-255 0014.

Feedback, Rua da Quitanda 74, 1 andar, 20011 030 Rio de Janeiro (RJ)

FISK Engllish Schoo, Avenida 13 de Maio 33, SI 306, Centro, 21031-000 Rio de Janeiro (RJ). Tel: 21-220 4110.

IBEU (Instituto Brasil-Estados Unidos), Av. N.S. de Copacabana 690, 5 andar, 22050 000 Rio de Janeiro (RJ) (Caixa Postal 12154). Tel: 21-255 8332/fax 21-255 9355.

Phoenix—Ingles Empresarial, Rua Gal. San Martin 974/102 Leblon, 22631 390 Rio de Janeiro (RJ)

Wizard, Rua Marechal Henrique Lott 120/107, Barra da Tijuca, 22631 390 Rio de Janeiro (RJ)

**BRITANIC INTERNATIONAL HOUSE, RECIFE, Rua Hermógenes de Morais 178, Madalena Recife, PE (81-445 5564/fax 81-445 5481). 7 teachers.*

Yazigi, Rua Frei Solano 30, Lagoa, 22471 250 Rio de Janeiro (RJ)

**SHARING ENGLISH, Rua Souza de Andrade 56, Recife (PE) 52050-300 (tel/fax 81-421 2286). 2 teachers.*

Chile

Chile's economy is flourishing, attracting a great deal of foreign (mainly American) investment. In the 1990s Chile has achieved a remarkable ten percent rate of growth while unemployment is less than 5%. As commercial, touristic and cultural contacts with the outside world have increased in the new democratic Chile, so has the demand for the English language. The most booming market is for business English, though there is also a growing demand for teachers of children.

Of course most of the opportunities are in the capital Santiago where there are more than 30 major language schools, though there are some relevant institutes in the Valparaiso-Viña del Mar area. There will be less competition for teaching vacancies in smaller places like the aptly named La Serena in the dry north of the country.

The prestigious Instituto Chileno-Britanico de Cultura at Santa Lucia 124 in Santiago recruits only highly qualified teachers, and has a good library which incorporates the British Council's resource library for teachers; anyone who pays the modest membership fee can borrow materials, though many schools in Santiago have good libraries themselves. Native speaker teachers are also hired by the Institutos Chileno-Britanico de Cultura in Concepcion, Arica and Viña del Mar (listed below). A further possibility is to teach at English-medium *colegios*, where a longer commitment will be necessary and a reasonable salary paid. Although they employ mainly certified teachers, often hired at recruitment fairs and through international advertising, they do need some native speakers for their English departments.

The commercial institutes in Santiago vary greatly in size, reliability in their treatment of employees and teaching methods. Newcomers to the city quickly learn which are the better schools and gradually acquire more hours with them. Some of the smallest companies do not teach on their own premises at all, but send their teachers out to teach classes in the offices and occasionally the homes of their clients. Most offer a combination of on-site and off-site teaching. In-company teaching usually takes place early in the morning; middle-ranking staff tend to be taught before the official working day begins while directors and higher-ranking executives take their classes at a more civilised mid-morning hour. Most teachers enjoy the variety of off-site teaching rather than classroom teaching which tends to be more textbook-based. Diana Maisel greatly enjoyed teaching small groups of executives from IBM and Ernst & Young when she was in Santiago.

The academic year runs from March to December with a two-week winter holiday in July and one week recess in mid-September. The British Council's Information Office can send a list of 11 private language schools, seven British-Chilean Institutes and 13 British curriculum schools. The Santiago *Yellow Pages* are also a useful source; look up *Escuelas de Idiomas*.

The following schools are among the best known language schools in Santiago. Typically these schools offer a newcomer a few hours and will offer them a full timetable only after a probationary three months.

Berlitz, Av Pedro de Valdivia 2005, Providencia, Santiago. Tel: 2-204 4018. Berlitz has a substantial establishment in Santiago but prefer to interview only candidates who already have a work permit.

British English Centre, Av. Providencia 1308, p.2. Oficina D, Providencia, Santiago. Tel: 2-496165. Prefer teachers who are fluent in Spanish.

Burford, Avda. Pedro de Valdivia 511, Providencia, Santiago. Tel: 223 9357/274 4603. Fax: 2-223 5944. A small 'agency-type' institute which favours British English.

ELADI Instituto Professional, José M. Infante 927, Providencia, Santiago. Tel: 2-251 0365. Fax: 2-225 0958.

Fischer English Institute, Cirujano Guzman 49, Providencia, Santiago. Tel: 2-235 9812/ 235 6667. Fax: 2-235 9810. Contact Adriana Otero Renau. Teaches both on and off-site. Offers plenty of structure in planning lessons.

Impact English, Rosa O'Higgins 259, Las Condes, Santiago. Tel: 2-211 1925/212 5609. Fax 2-211 6165. Contact Señora Pepa. Reputed to offer high rates of pay.

Linguatec, Av. Los Leones 439, Providencia, Santiago. Tel: 2-233 4356. Compulsory one week training course for all accepted teachers which is unpaid but it guarantees the offer of some hours of work on completion. Large branch of US-based teaching organisation which considers itself main rival to Berlitz.

Sam Marsalli, Av. Los Leones 1095, Providencia, Santiago. Tel: 2-231 0652. Hires mainly American and Canadian females.

Tronwell, Apoquindo 4499, 3er Piso, Las Condes, Santiago. Tel: 2-246 1040. Fax: 2-228 9739. Expanding company with high staff turnover. Employ a fairly rigid teaching method (advertise 'Learn English in 120 hours').

Wall Street Institute, San Sebastian 2878, Comuna Condes, Santiago. Tel: 2-332 0330.

Fax: 2-332 0326. They have three branches in Santiago, and one each in Vina del Mar, Rancagua and Antofagasta.

Non-contractual work is usually paid by the hour, starting at less than 3,000 pesos per hour. Most good schools pay more than 4,000 pesos per hour and up to 5,000 pesos to those who have a recognised qualification. The cost of living is higher than in many other places on the continent but not high enough to absorb all of a teacher's earnings. Normally 10% of earnings must be paid in tax, which in some cases can be reclaimed the following year. Diana Maisel started gradually with a few hours from several of the above companies, but after two months was teaching 30-35 hours per week and saving a lot of money (helped by the low rent of 50,000 pesos a month she was paying to lodge with a language school owner). She had sent her CV from England to about 20 schools in Santiago before arrival but got a very discouraging response. Undaunted, she landed in Santiago on her own in early October and easily found work, helped no doubt by her Cambridge/RSA Certificate. Several of the schools she approached recalled that they had already read her CV which she felt worked to her advantage. (A friend from the US with no TEFL training failed to persuade any language institute to hire her and so turned to waitressing instead.)

Red Tape

If you are offered a job before arrival, there are two ways to obtain the appropriate visa permit. Either your employer submits the application at the Ministry of Foreign Affairs in Chile (Direccion de Asuntos Consulares y de Imigracion, Bandera 46, Santiago) or you apply at the Chilean Consulate in your country of origin. You will need a signed and notarised work contract and a full medical report. If granted, the visa will be valid for one or two years. After that you may be eligible for a *visacion de residencia* which allows an unlimited stay.

If you arrive to look for work, you will not be able to get a working visa without leaving the country. If you are able to commit yourself for a year, your employer may be willing to help. Most teachers who stay for shorter periods do not bother trying to change their visa status knowing that the immigration authorities are much less likely to raid language institutes than they are hotels and restaurants where migrant Peruvians work.

Advertising for Private Clients

There are many ways to meet the expatriate community from playing cricket at the Prince of Wales Club to frequenting the English language bookshop Books and Bits at 6856 Avenida Apoquindo. You can advertise for private clients in *El Mercurio,* the leading quality daily. Other newspapers such as *La Epoca* and *La Tercera* have classified ads sections which will cost slightly less than *El Mercurio.* There is a magazine called *El Rastro* consisting of nothing but advertisements into which you can phone in a small ad free of charge (though the response may be less than spectacular). If you need to be written to rather than telephoned it might be useful to take out a Post Box number with the Chilean Correo, particularly if your address is not stable.

A useful option is to find a supermarket which has a noticeboard for small advertisements in their entrance halls. For example the Almac and Jumbo chains of stores have such noticeboards. Almac is located on the corner of Avenida Pedro de Valdivia and Bilbao, while Jumbo is on the corner of Portugal and Diagonal Paraguay. If you can translate between English and Spanish, it will be worth advertising yourself as a translator as well.

LIST OF SCHOOLS

THE BRITISH SCHOOL
Casilla 379, Punta Arenas. Tel: (61) 223381/223233. Fax: (61) 220120/248447. E-mail: cbpa01@ctcreuna.cl
Number of teachers: 9.

Qualifications: university degree and appropriate teaching diploma. Working knowledge of Spanish is essential.
Conditions of employment: 2 year renewable contracts. Hours of work 8am-5pm. Students aged 4-18.
Salary: negotiable.
Facilities/Support: assistance with accommodation, passages, pension.
Recruitment: directly with school.
Contact: John C. McCarry, Headmaster.

INSTITUTO CHILENO BRITANICO DE CULTURA
San Martin 531, Concepción. Tel: (41) 242300. Fax: (41) 234044.
Number of teachers: 5-10.
Preference of nationality: none.
Qualifications: TEFL qualifications and minimum of two years experience.
Conditions of employment: minimum one year (March to December).
Salary: according to qualifications and experience.
Facilities: assistance with accommodation given. Induction programme provided. Prefer teachers to arrive with work permit organised.
Recruitment: local interviews essential.
Contact: Mr. Jorge Pinto, Academic Director.

INSTITUTO CHILENO-NORTEAMERICANO DE CULTURA
Moneda No. 1467, Santiago. Tel: (2) 696 3215. Fax: (2) 697 0365. E-mail: academic@hood.ichn.cl
Number of teachers: 15-20.
Preference of nationality: American, Canadian.
Qualifications: BA in Education or TESL/TEFL and 6 months' teaching experience, or BA in related field with Certificate in TESL/TEFL and 2 years' teaching experience.
Conditions of employment: 1 year contracts starting in March. 30 h.p.w. Peak hours of work early morning and early evening, and some Saturdays. Classes for adults, children, teens, business and academic English.
Salary: equivalent of US$1,100 per month in Chilean pesos.
Facilities/Support: assistance given in obtaining visas. Training provided. Teacher's room with computers, e-mail access and cafeteria privileges.
Recruitment: direct application by mail, e-mail, phone or fax. Applicants should send cover letter, resumé, recent photo, copy of diplomas/certificates and letters of reference from recent employers.
Contact: Jacqueline Abt, Educational Services Director.

INTERNATIONAL BUSINESS CONSULTANTS (IBC)
Presidente Errázuriz 3328, Las Condes, Santiago. Tel: (2) 242 9292. Fax: (2) 233 8143. E-mail: ibc@reuna.cl
Number of teachers: 5-10.
Preference of nationality: none.
Qualifications: minimum CELTA and 1 year's experience. People with solid business background also considered for work with corporate clients.
Conditions of employment: mainly freelance. Contracts normally for 6 months (April to November), though new teachers hired year round.
Salary: 4,500-5,300 Chilean pesos per hour (gross), revised yearly.
Facilities/Support: advice can be given on accommodation. Regular workshops and encouragement of peer support.
Recruitment: walk-ins, word of mouth, recommendations, contacts. Interviews occasionally available in UK.
Contact: Justine Wakefield, Language Consultant.

LET'S DO ENGLISH
Villa Vicencio 361, Office 109, Santiago. Tel: (2) 632 4984. Tel/fax: (2) 633 8535.
Number of teachers: 15-20 a year in Santiago and Temuco.
Preference of nationality: Canadian, American.
Qualifications: experience in TESL/TEFL. Creative, motivated and spontaneous people required.
Conditions of employment: 1 year contracts. 30-40 h.p.w. teaching adults only.
Salary: $1,100 per month (equivalent in Chilean pesos).
Facilities/Support: room and board provided at outset and help given in finding an apartment. Advice given on work visas. Initial training given on school's methods and materials.
Recruitment: most teachers come from New World Teachers in San Francisco. Telephone interviews.
Contact: Yvonne Conde (Director).

POLYGLOT
Villavicencio 361 Of. 102, Santiago. Tel: (2) 639 8078. Fax: (2) 632 2485. E-mail: polyglot@santiago.cl. Web-site: http://www.santiago.cl/polyglot
Number of teachers: 40-50 a year.
Preference of nationality: none.
Qualifications: TEFL or Cambridge/RSA Certificate; university degree; business experience.
Conditions of employment: at least 6 months commitment for freelancers, though 1 year contracts preferred. Teaching hours: 8-10am, 12-3pm and 6-9pm.
Salary: US$8-10 per hour, depending on location.
Facilities/Support: assistance with accommodation and work visas for permanent staff.
Recruitment: adverts. Local interview essential.
Contact: Christoph Flaskamp, Director.

REDLAND SCHOOL
Camino El Alba 11357, Las Condes, Santiago. Tel: 2-214 1265. Fax: 2-214 1020.
Number of teachers: 6.
Preference of nationality: British.
Qualifications: university degree and teaching qualification. In some cases a short TEFL course is sufficient.
Conditions of employment: 1-3 year contract. Classes run 8am-3.30/5pm.
Salary: starting salary about US$9,500 per year. Pupils aged 4-18.
Facilities: free accommodation and utilities provided.
Recruitment: direct contact with British universities and recruiting agencies. Interviews normally take place in the UK.

Other Schools to Try

Instituto Chileno-Britanico de Cultura, Baquedano 351, Arica
Academy of English Studies, Esmeralda 1095, La Serena
Instituto de Ingles Icen SAE, Eduardo de la Borno 222, Paisage Santo Domingo, La Serena (51-224523)
Welcome to English Institute, Paisage Francisco Araya 631, La Serena

Agpen Academy, Av. Lib. B., O'Higgins 949 Of. 2103, Edificio Santiago Centro
American Language Center, Av. Libertador, B. O'Higgins 1941, Santiago
American Language Institute, San Ignacio 277, Santiago
BEA, Salvador 95, 505-515 Providencia, Santiago
Centro Chileno Canadiense, Av. Luis Thayer Ojeda 0191, Of. 601, Tobalaba
English Express, Del Metro Los Leones, Providencia 2133 Of. 703, Santiago
Escuela de Idiomas Language Center, Agustinas 853, Of. 301, Santiago
IBC, Av. Presidente Errázuriz 3328, Las Condes, El Golf, Santiago
Inbusiness, Fidel Oteiza 1971, Ps. 5° Y 7°, Metro P. de Valdivia, Santiago

Lorbeth, Cabo Arestey 2468, Republica, Santiago
OPEC, Casa Central, Agustinas 853 , Of. 1015, Santiago
The Pacific Language Center, Padre Mariano 103, Of. 505, Santiago
Panorámico, Providencia, Los Leones, Santiago
**SANTIAGO COLLEGE,* Los Leones 584, Casilla 130-D, Santiago (2-232 1813/fax 2-232 0755). 13 certified teachers.
**INSTITUTO CHILENO—BRITANICO DE CULTURA,* 3 Norte 824, Casilla 929, Viña del Mar (32-971061/fax 32-686656). 6 Certificate-holders.
English Alive, Av. Vitacura 7125, Vitacura

Colombia

Since most people's only associations with Colombia are with crime and violence, it is not surprising to learn that teaching institutes in that country sometimes have trouble attracting qualified foreign teachers. Foreign teachers are extremely unlikely to become involved in any drug-inspired tensions but are guaranteed to be welcomed by the locals. Memories will be of a local carnival rather than of a neighbourhood shoot-out. With the opening up of trade (called *Apertura*), interest in English has increased, as evidenced by the popularity of English language media like newspapers and radio stations.

Colombia is even more strongly oriented towards the US than elsewhere in South America with an extensive network of Colombian-American Cultural Centers around the country. However Charles Seville from Oxford, who spent a year as an English language assistant at the University de Los Llanos in Villavicencio, was struck by how keen Colombians were to learn British English. There are British Council Teaching Centres in Bogotá and Medellin, catering mainly for the executive market. One ELT organisation which is expanding in the country is EF English First; the main school in Bogotá is at Carrera 13 No. 79-30 (1-611 4194) but there are two others.

It is possible to access the Colombian *Yellow Pages* on the internet (www.quihubo.com) which should provide a starting place for finding school addresses. The main newspaper *El Tiempo* carries numerous adverts for language schools in the capital. There are plenty of local language schools where untrained native speakers can find work, but there are two main disadvantages. Wages and conditions are very poor; many schools offer just a few thousand pesos an hour (possibly about US$2.50), though the schools listed below offer more attractive dollar salaries than that. The second problem is the red tape. As usual, temporary working visas must be applied for in your country of residence. The Colombian Consulate in London sends out clear information about the requirements which include an undertaking by the employer to bear the cost of repatriation if the visa is cancelled and a letter from the Ministry of Work & Social Security testifying that the Colombian employer is not exceeding the legal limit on foreign employees. The visa fee is £128 plus £16 for notarisation charges. If a teacher intends to stay in Colombia longer than six months, he or she must register in person at DAS, the Colombian equivalent of the FBI, within 30 days of arrival. Approval will mean that you are entitled to acquire a *Cédula de Extranjería* (foreigners' ID).

LIST OF SCHOOLS

CENTRO CULTURAL COLOMBO AMERICANO—BARRANQUILLA
Carrera 43, No. 51-95, Apartado Aereo 2097, Barranquilla. Tel: (5) 340 8084.
Fax: (5) 340 8549. E-mail: colombo@b-quilla.cetcol.net.co
Number of teachers: up to 10.
Preference of nationality: none, but must be native speakers.

Qualifications: BA (English or Education) with 2 years' teaching experience or MA (TEFL/TESL) and some teaching experience.
Conditions of employment: 1 year renewable contracts. 6 hours of work a day between 7am and 8.30pm, Monday-Friday. Students aged 5-58 but mostly 18-25.
Salary: from 9,800 pesos per hour plus 2 months' pay and 15 days paid holiday after 1 year.
Facilities/Support: will reimburse one-way airfare from Miami after 4 months and return portion after 1 year. Assistance given with finding accommodation. Some training provided.
Recruitment: interviews not essential. Send resumé.
Contact: Khaitoon M. de Osorio, Academic Director.

CENTRO COLOMBO AMERICANO—MEDELLIN
Cra. 45 No. 53-24, Medellin. Tel: (4) 513 4444. Fax: (4) 513 2666. E-mail: bncmde@medellin.cetcol.net.co
Number of teachers: 150 in programme with 14 US/UK teachers.
Preference of nationality: American, Canadian, British.
Qualifications: BA or MA (Education, Languages, TESOL).
Conditions of employment: 1 year contracts (renewable). 6 contact hours per day. English for children and adults.
Salary: in line with inflation.
Facilities/Support: round trip ticket and visa expenses paid. Housing assistance. Pre-service and in-service training. Medical benefits and Spanish lessons provided.
Recruitment: direct application with CV and 3 letters of recommendation. Selection made through references and phone interview.
Contact: Lai Yin Shem, Academic Director.

CENTRO CULTURAL COLOMBO AMERICANO—CALI
Calle 13 Norte 8-45, A.A. 4525 Cali. Tel: (2) 668 5960/661 4303. Fax: (2) 668 4695.
Number of teachers: 5-10 foreign teachers out of 50-60 for several locations in Cali.
Preference of nationality: American, Canadian.
Qualifications: at least a BA in an English teaching related field and a minimum of 6 months' teaching experience.
Conditions of employment: 1 year renewable contracts. 33 h.p.w. including evening and Saturday work. Students aged 6-60.
Salary: average 800,000 pesos per month.
Facilities/Support: assistance given with finding accommodation. Training provided.
Recruitment: through advertising in newsletters and at conventions. Interviews by phone if necessary.

CENTRO DE INGLES LINCOLN
Calle 49, No. 9-37, Bogotá. Tel: (1) 288 0360. Fax: (1) 287 3806.
Number of teachers: 25.
Preference of nationality: none.
Qualifications: minimum RSA/Cambridge Diploma or equivalent.
Conditions of employment: 10 month contracts. Hours are 7-11am and 7-9pm plus Saturday morning. Extra hours if required.
Salary: $950 per month.
Facilities: no help with accommodation or visas after arrival.
Recruitment: interviews not always essential though they are sometimes carried out in UK.

COLEGIO BRITANICO DE CARTAGENA
Anillo Vial Km. 16, A.A. 20156, Cartagena. Tel/fax: (5) 668 6280.
Number of teachers: handful of ESL positions at full curriculum school.
Preference of nationality: British.

Qualifications: degree in education or occasionally undergraduate in Spanish has year out as classroom support teacher.
Conditions of employment: 1 year contracts.
Salary: local.
Contact: Derek Mullin, Headmaster.

FIRST CLASS ENGLISH LTDA.
Carrera 12 No. 93-78 Piso 4°m Santafé de Bogotá, D.C. Tel: (1) 623 2374/5. Fax: (1) 623 2379.
Number of teachers: 5.
Preference of nationality: American, British or Canadian.
Qualifications: dynamic, energetic, professional and responsible.
Conditions of employment: one-year contracts. Usual hours 7-11am and 6-9pm. Most students are executives. Emphasis on using computers in teaching.
Salary: US$8-12 per hour less 10% taxes.
Facilities/Support: assistance with finding accommodation given. Assist teachers to change visa status. 20-30 hours of training given.
Recruitment: local newspaper ads. Local interviews essential.

OXFORD CENTRE
AA 102420, Bogotá. Tel: (1) 345 1059. Fax: (1) 255 8758.
Number of teachers: at least 10.
Preference of nationality: British.
Qualifications: BA or MA (languages, English, literature).
Conditions of employment: 5 month contracts, starting February or July. 25 classes a week.
Salary: US$600 per month. Teachers with BA or MA in business administration and experience in teaching English will receive a higher salary.
Facilities/Support: bed and breakfast accommodation provided with host families.
Recruitment: through phone interviews and references.
Contact: Javier Sanchez Carrascal, Principal.

Other Schools to Try
CENTRO COLOMBO-AMERICANO, Avenida 19 No. 3-05, Santafé de Bogotá (1-334 7640/334 7643/243 2823; fax 1-282 3372). 20 North American teachers.
INTERNATIONAL LANGUAGE INSTITUTE, Cra. 13 No. 5-79, Castillo Grande, Cartagena (5-66 51 672). 6 teachers.

Ecuador

Compared to its neighbours, Peru and Colombia, Ecuador represents an oasis of political and economic stability. There is a thriving demand for English, particularly American English in the capital Quito, the second city Guayaquil and in the picturesque city and cultural centre of Cuenca in the southern Sierra. The majority of teaching is of university students and the business community whose classes are normally scheduled early in the morning (starting at 7am) to avoid the equatorial heat of the day and again in the late afternoon and evening. Many schools are owned and run by expatriates since there are few legal restrictions on foreigners running businesses.

Damaris Carlisle had no trouble finding work when she arrived in Quito because she had a Cambridge/RSA Certificate and also a friend who was one of the bosses at Lingua Franca. After 18 months she switched employers and worked for the Experiment in International Living, turning down the offer of a contract so that she could take three months off to climb, cycle and explore the region. Although she was content with the wages paid, she says that there is no point in trying to save money since the currency is worth little outside Ecuador. She found Ecuadorian students to be polite and enthusiastic, though a little over-optimistic about what they could achieve.

Wages are not as high as in Chile but higher than in Colombia, and normally allow teachers to enjoy a comfortable lifestyle since the cost of living is low. Accommodation is harder to find in Quito than in Cuenca. Qualified TEFLers should not accept less than 25,000 sucres an hour though the private institutes which accept unqualified teachers pay accordingly less. All teachers (both contract and freelance) have taxes withdrawn at source of between 3% and 8%, with the majority deducting a flat rate of 7%.

Quito is not as large and daunting a city as some other South American capitals and it should be easy to meet longer term expats who can help with advice on teaching. The helpful British Council will give you a list of ELT schools throughout the country and will (unofficially) indicate which offer the best teacher support and modern teaching methods and resources. One possible source of information is the South American Explorers Club clubhouse (membership costs $40). In Quito the Club is at Jorge Washington 311 y Leonidas Plaza (Apartado 17-21-431; tel/fax 2-225228). They keep an informal list of language schools in Ecuador and have a useful notice board.

As throughout the continent, charitable schools for disadvantaged children can always use voluntary help. Nick Branch worked in Quito at Guarderia Maria-Ausiliadora (Don Bosco y Paraiso; 2-51034), a pre-school for disadvantaged children where he did some teaching from the front as well as painting, PE activities and games with the children.

Red Tape

Technically you shouldn't work on a tourist visa but there is little control. Britons are entitled to a stay of six months on a tourist visa whereas Americans can stay 90 days. If possible, teachers should get a 12-IX document in their country of origin, which can be extended by visiting a neighbouring country (usually Colombia). Most employers will help teachers who commit themselves for a reasonable stay to obtain a cultural exchange visa, normally valid for a year. The requirements are as follows: two letters attesting to good character, a notarised copy of a police report, health certificate (including HIV test) and birth certificate, letter of invitation from an Ecuadorian employer, letter of financial support from a backer and a return airline ticket.

LIST OF SCHOOLS

ALPHA ENGLISH PROGRAMS
Salazar 427 y Coruna, Casilla 17-16-18, Quito. Tel/fax: 2-235068. E-mail: alpha@hoy.net
Number of teachers: 6-10.
Preference of nationality: none.
Qualifications: CELTA with good recommendations and preferably some experience.
Conditions of employment: 3, 6 or 9 month contracts, renewable.
Salary: US$600 per month less 3% deductions.
Facilities/Support: assistance with accommodation and work permits. Teacher resource library and training meetings.
Recruitment: professional contacts in UK and US. Interviews sometimes conducted abroad.
Contact: Maureen Massie, Director of Studies/Co-Owner.

BENEDICT SCHOOLS OF LANGUAGES

PO Box 09-01-8916, Guayaquil. Tel: 4-444418. Fax: 4-441642. E-mail: benecent@telconet.net.

Number of teachers: 15 in several branches in Guayaquil (Urdesa, Centro, Garzota, Centenario, Entrerios).

Preference of nationality: British, American, Canadian, Irish.

Qualifications: proficiency in English and teaching certificate or college degree required.

Conditions of employment: minimum of two courses (4 months). Exclusive contract.

Salary: US$5-6 an hour.

Facilities/Support: assistance with accommodation. Pre-service training provided.

Recruitment: local hire.

Contact: Mercedes de Elizalde, General Director.

BENEDICT SCHOOLS OF LANGUAGES

Edmundo Chiriboga N47-133 y Jorge Paez, Quito. Tel/fax: 2-432729. Tel: 2-462972/269542. E-mail: benedict@accessinter.net. Web-site: http://www.virtualsystems.com.ec/benedictq

Number of teachers: 6-8.

Preference of nationality: Welsh, English, American.

Qualifications: good knowledge of grammar. Responsible and hard working. Experience desirable but not a requirement. Young teachers (aged 18-19) can be hired if sufficiently mature.

Conditions of employment: freelance only.

Salary: US$3 per hour.

Facilities/Support: assistance with finding accommodation. In-house training provided.

Recruitment: via the internet. Interviews not essential.

Contact: Mrs. Jesús de Jaramillo, Director.

CENTRO DE ESTUDIOS INTERAMERICANOS/CEDEI

Casilla 597, Cuenca. Tel: 7-839003. Fax: 7-833593. E-mail: English@c.ecua.net.ec

Number of teachers: 18.

Preference of nationality: Americans preferred by students, but all considered.

Qualifications: minimum university degree and TEFL Cert. Experience or elementary education degree for those who wish to teach children.

Conditions of employment: minimum 3 months, preference given to year-long commitments. Courses run from early January to mid-March, early April to early June, mid-June to mid-August and early October to mid-December. Teachers work 3 hours per day (8-9.30am and 6-7.30pm) Monday to Thursday.

Salary: 1.5 million sucres per 50-hour course, equivalent to a monthly salary of approximately US$270.

Facilities: family stays arranged at cost of $185 per month including food or hostel accommodation with access to kitchen at $175 per month.

Recruitment: via CELTA centres in the US. Interviews not essential.

Contact: Sarah Bauer, English Director.

FULBRIGHT COMMISSION

Almagro 961 y Colón (PO Box 17-07-9081), Quito. Tel: (2) 562999/563095. Fax: (2) 508149. E-mail: fulbright@uio.satnet.net

Number of teachers: 15-20.

Preference of nationality: American.

Qualifications: education and experience in language teaching. MA in ESL preferred).

Conditions of employment: 12 month contracts desirable.

Salary: minimum $5 per hour according to qualifications and experience.

Facilities: assistance with finding accommodation. Cultural exchange visas available to full-time teachers. Some training provided.
Recruitment: interviews essential. Letters of recommendation and sample lesson plan should be provided.
Contact: Maria Giovanna Galeano, Administrative Director (Academic Dept).

JEFFERSON BILINGUAL SCHOOLS
PO Box 09-01-4180, Guayaquil. Tel: (4) 853752/873787/870359. Fax: (4) 854274. E-mail: admissions@jefferson.ed.ec
Number of teachers: about 10 native speakers at Jefferson International College, about 5 at Jefferson High School and 1 or 2 at the Primary School.
Preference of nationality: North American or British.
Qualifications: for some posts must be certified primary or secondary trained teachers. For others in English language departments, Certification in TEFL is needed.
Conditions of employment: 1 year contracts. Primary and secondary schools function from 7.30am to 2pm April to January. College facility opens 5pm-10pm May-August, September-December, January-February and March-April.
Salary: full-time salaries roughly US$800 a month (paid in sucres).
Facilities/Support: assist teachers to arrange homestays or apartment accommodation. Help given to teachers who need to obtain work permits in their country of citizenship.
Recruitment: interviews not essential.
Contact: Basil Haylock, Personnel Director.

KEY LANGUAGE SERVICES
Foch 635 y Reina Victoria, Quito (Casilla 17-079770). Tel/fax: (2) 557851. E-mail: kls@hoy.net
Number of teachers: 10-15.
Preference of nationality: any native speaker welcome.
Qualifications: TEFL qualification. Experience preferred. Tidy appearance and professional manner essential.
Conditions of employment: 3 months absolute minimum, 6 months or longer preferred. Mainly off-site business classes offered 7-9am, 12-2pm and 4-8pm.
Salary: 2-3 million sucres per month, according to hours worked.
Facilities/Support: notice board in office carries details of rental accommodation. Advice given on visas. Monthly professional development sessions. Teachers are allocated a paedogogical mentor.
Recruitment: local interview and observation.
Contact: Ida Dolci and Clare St. Lawrence, Directors of Studies.

COLEGIO LOS PINOS
Pedro Dionisio 702, Quito. Tel: (2) 240601/241200. Fax: (2) 434021. E-mail: pinos@pin.k12.ec
Number of teachers: 3.
Preference of nationality: American.
Qualifications: degree in teaching, experience in schools.
Conditions of employment: 1 year contracts, renewable. School day 7.30am-2pm.
Salary: rises in line with inflation.
Facilities/Support: no assistance with accommodation. Certificate given to help apply for work visa.
Recruitment: resumés, references and local interviews.
Contact: Joanne de Falcony, Head of English Department.

NEXUS LENGUAS Y CULTURAS
Jose Peralta 1-19 y 12 de Abril, Cuenca. Tel: (7) 888220. Fax: (7) 888221. E-mail: nexus@cue.satnet.net
Number of teachers: 10.
Preference of nationality: none.

Qualifications: EFL/ESL certificate and experience.
Conditions of employment: 9 months. 18 h.p.w. (full-time).
Salary: 20,000 sucres per hour (based on exchange rate of 5,000 sucres to US$1).
Facilities/Support: no assistance with accommodation. Assistance with cultural exchange visas, visa extensions, etc.
Recruitment: via TEFL institutes and universities.
Contact: Marcela Carrasco, Director.

SOUTH AMERICAN SPANISH INSTITUTE
Amazonas 1549 y Santa Maria, Quito. Tel: (2) 544715. Fax: (2) 226438. E-mail: sudameri@impsat.net.ec
Number of teachers: 15 (depending on number of clients).
Preference of nationality: all native speakers of English.
Qualifications: teacher's degree and experience preferable but not mandatory.
Conditions of employment: minimum 3 months. Full-time hours are 8.30am-5.30pm Monday to Friday. Part-time schedules between 7am and 9pm. Some Saturdays.
Salary: hourly rate from 15,000 sucres (if working less than 19 hours) to 18,000 sucres for Saturday work or if working more than 35 per week ($3-$3.50).
Facilities/Support: advice may be given on accommodation. Help given with cultural exchange visa.
Recruitment: via e-mail, ads in magazines or through universities. Interviews not necessary.
Contact: Mario Cabrera, Staff Manager.

Other Schools to Try

Note that these schools did not confirm their teacher requirements for this edition. Upper case letters and asterisks means that the institute was listed in the last edition. Other addresses have been gleaned from the British Council list and other sources:
Centro Abraham Lincoln, Antonio Borrero 518 y H. Vasquez, Cuenca
Colegio Bilingue Interamericano, Av. Solano y Puente Yanuncay, Cuenca
American Language School, O'Connor 301 y J. Salcedo, Guayaquil
Centro Ecuatoriano Norteamericano, Gral Cordova y Luis, Urdaneta, Guayaquil
Colegio Aleman Humboldt, Los Ceibos, Calle 1era, 216, Guayaquil
Colegio Americano de Guayaquil Academy, Av. Juan Tanca Marengo Km. 6.5, Guayaquil
Colegio Espiritu Santo, Av. Juan Tanca Marengo Km. 2.5, Guayaquil
Colegio Internacional SEK, Via a Salinas Km. 5.5, Guayaquil
Colegio Particular Naciones Unidas, Via a Sanborondon, La Puntilla Km. 1, Guayaquil
Interamerican, Urb. Puerto Azul, Via a la Costa Km. 10.5, Guayaquil
Academia Alianza Americana, Villalengua 187 y 10 de Agosto, Casilla 6186, Quito
Colegio Alberto Einstein, Carcelén Km. 4½, Quito
Colegio Aleman, 6 de Diciembre y Juan Moreno, Espinosa, Quito
Colegio Americano, Carcelén, Quito
Colegio Internacional SEK Ecuador, Orellana y 6 de Diciembre, Quito
Colegio Intisana, Av. Occidental 5329 y Fray, Marcos Joffre, Urb. Cochapamba, Quito
Colegio Isaac Newton, De los Alamos, junto al Martin Cereré, Quito
Colegio La Inmaculada, Av. González Suárez y San Ignacio, Quito
Colegio Spellman de Mujeres, Mercadillo 442, Quito
Colegio Spellman de Varones, Isabel La Católica 256, Quito
College La Condamine, Japón e/ Naciones Unidas y Gaspar de Villaroel, Quito
Escuela Experimental Martin Cerere, De los Alamos s/n, Quito
EXPERIMENTO DE CONVIVENCIA INTERNACIONAL DEL ECUADOR,
   Hernando de la Cruz 218 y Mariana de Jesús, Quito (2-551937/550179/fax 2-550228). 10-15 teachers.
Harvard Institute, 10 de Agosto y Riofrío, Edif. Benalcázar 1000, Piso No. 17, Quito

Instituto Winfield, Orellana 1171 y La Rabida, Quito
Liceo Internacional, Monteserrin, Calle de las Amapolas, Quito
**LINGUA FRANCA,* Casilla 17-12-68, Edificio Jericó, 12 de Octubre 2449 y Orellana,
    Quito (2-546075/fax 2-500734/568664). 6-10 teachers. Recommended for good
    teacher support, etc.
Princeton International Language Institute, 1133 Colon y Amazonas, Quito
Unidad Educativa Part. Angel Polibio Chavez, Ladrón de Guevara, La Vicentina,
    Quito

Mexico

The lure of the United States of America and its language is very strong in Mexico. The
frenzy of American investment in Mexico after the North American Free Trade
Agreement (NAFTA) saw a huge upswing in both the demand for English by
businesses and the resources to pay for it. That boom is now over, but the market for
English is still enormous in universities, in business, almost everywhere. Proximity to
the US and a tendency towards what Australians call the cultural cringe (in Mexico
called *Malinchism* after the lover of Cortès who betrayed her people) means that there
will always be an unquenchable thirst for English taught by native speakers in Mexico.
Foreign teachers are automatically respected and are often promoted almost
immediately.

Companies of all descriptions provide language classes for their employees
especially in the early mornings and evenings (but seldom on weekends or even
Fridays). Roberta Wedge even managed to persuade a 'sleek head honcho in the state
ferry service' that he needed private tuition during the sacred siesta and that busy
executives and other interested employees of a local company needed English lessons
at the same time of day.

It is not surprising that enrolment in English courses is booming when some
employees have been threatened with dismissal unless they master some English. A
vet going to Dubai, a stockbroker doing deals with the New York Stock Exchange,
housewives who have to go to parties with their executive husbands, teenagers with
exam worries, all are keen to improve their English. After each six-year presidential
term of office, the top layers of management in companies (especially oil and banking)
are replaced by new staff who need new training, especially English. The next election
in the year 2000 should boost the demand for English not only in Mexico City and the
border cities to which US industries looking for cheap labour have relocated, but
throughout the country, including the Yucatan Peninsula and other unlikely places, at
least one of which must remain nameless in order to preserve Roberta Wedge's
dreams:

> *After doing a 'taster' ESL course in Vancouver, I set out for Nicaragua with a bus
> ticket to San Diego and $500—no guide book, no travelling companion, no Spanish.
> On the way I fell in love with a town in Mexico (not for worlds would I reveal its
> name—I want to keep it in a pristine timewarp so I can hope to return) and decided
> to stay. I found a job by looking up all the language schools in the phonebook and
> walking around the city to find them. The problem was that many small businesses
> were not on the phone. So I kept my eye out for English school signs. I had semi-
> memorised a little speech in Spanish, 'I am a Canadian teacher of English. I love your
> town very much and want to work here. This is my CV...' Within two days I had a job
> at a one-man school.*

The British Council in Mexico City can provide the addresses of the 25 or so
language centres attached to state universities and also keeps the Yellow Pages which
has a few pages of language schools. The Council does not have an English teaching
centre itself but works closely with the Cultura (Instituto Anglo-Mexicano du Cultura)

which has 12 branches in four cities. Some of their foreign recruitment is the responsibility of *Saxoncourt Recruitment*.

Mexican-American bi-national centres employ hundreds of native speakers, mostly on a local basis. Typically the Instituto Mexicano Norteamericano de Relaciones Culturales de Saltillo (IMARC) in northern Mexico takes on enthusiastic graduates who have experience of working with children to teach young children aged 5 to 8. The school year starts in early August and lasts for 11 months. Letters of enquiry and CVs can be sent to IMARC, Presidente Cardenas 840 Pte., Saltillo, Coahuila 25000 (e-mail: imarc@mexnet.mesas.net). Other US cultural institutes include:

Centro Mexicano-Americano de Cultura, Xola 416, Mexico City 12, DF.

Instituto Cultural Mexicano-Norteamericano de Jalisco, Enrique Díaz de León 300, Sector Juarez, CP 44170, Guadalajara, Jalisco. Tel: (36) 825 58 38. Fax: 825 16 71. Employ up to 25 teachers on minimum 6 month contracts.

Instituto Mexicano-Norteamericano de Relaciones Culturales, Blvd. Navarrete y Monteverde, Hermosillo, Sonora.

Instituto Cultural Mexicano-Norteamericano de Michoacan, A.C., Guillermo Prieto 86, Morelia, Michoacan.

Instituto Mexicano-Norteamericano de Relaciones Culturales de Nuevo Leon, Hidalgo Pte. 76B, Apdo. Postal 2602, Monterrey, 64000 Nuevo Leon. Tel: (83) 340 1583.

Centro Cultural Mexico-Americano, Carranza no. 215 Pte., Apdo. 1337, Tampico, Tam.

A further possibility is to work at English medium schools modelled either on the American or British system. Many of these advertise internationally for certified teachers or recruit through recruiting fairs but, as in Chile, Peru and elsewhere, some are willing to interview native speakers locally to work in the EFL department. Without a TEFL background or at least a solid university education you are unlikely to break into any of these more upmarket institutes.

Gap year students and other inexperienced travellers might want to have a job and accommodation fixed up before arrival. If so, try *Teaching Abroad* in Sussex which runs a teaching programme in Mexico. The fee is £1,295, so teachers cannot break even.

The Private Sector

A host of private institutes supplies language training to business either on their own premises or in-company. The norm is for teachers to freelance and work for a combination of companies. There are also full-time school-based jobs with teaching companies like Harmon Hall and Interlingua which have a national network of branches. Wages are higher (as much as four times higher) at the former, but hours are fewer and less predictable and a lot of time is taken up travelling from office to office. Getting three hours of work a day (early morning and early evening) is easy. Anything above that is much trickier. Freelance teachers must be prepared for frequent holidays cutting into earnings. No institute pays for public holidays, sickness or annual leave. For example attendance goes into a sharp decline after Independence Day on November 20th in the month leading up to Christmas and there are no classes over Easter. Most courses run for three months and there may be a lapse of one or two weeks before another starts. Usually freelancers are paid cash-in-hand with no deductions for tax. Few have working papers (see *Red Tape* below.)

The spectrum of institutes varies enormously. At one extreme there is the employer who pays the equivalent of $3.50 an hour, never pays on time, and who employs only Mexicans with poor English or native speakers who have just arrived with their backpacks and no interest in or knowledge of teaching. The top of the range pays $10 an hour, offers free training and gives contracts that aren't cancelled. These institutes are of course a lot more choosy about their teachers. Whereas a few companies want to control their teachers completely and send inspectors into classes, most leave teachers alone as long as the clients are happy. The typical institute consists only of four people: the owner who gets the contracts, a teacher-coordinator, a secretary and an office boy. According to Nick Wilson from Cumbria, who spent several years teaching freelance in Mexico City, there is a lot of jealousy between the training institutes with mutual accusations of spying, so discretion is advised. He was working for the wife of his director in her own school along with three other teachers she had poached from her unwitting husband. Some institutes try to poach teachers from rival institutes by offering more money.

On arrival in Mexico City, a good place to meet foreigners is the famed Casa de los Amigos, the Quaker-run guest house at Ignacio Mariscal 132 (5-705 0521/705 06461), centrally located near Metro Revolucion. Check adverts in the major Spanish-language daily *El Universal* as well as the English language newspaper *The News*. Rupert Baker answered an advert in *The News* and was invited to attend a disconcertingly informal interview at a restaurant (to which he still wore his tie). He ended up working for six months.

Obviously a TEFL qualification is an advantage though few employers are concerned about whether it is from a 130 hour or a 30 hour course. Business and financial experience is also beneficial, possibly more than a university degree. An ability to make a class interesting and patience are the two key qualities that many employers are looking for. As one of Nick Wilson's bosses said, 'The most important thing is that the students enjoy their classes and *think* that they are learning English; don't just teach or we'll lose customers.' Word-of-mouth recommendations are very important in Mexican culture, and jobs are seldom filled by postal applications.

Michael Tunison contacted half a dozen major teaching organisations from the Yellow Pages and was interviewed by Berlitz and Harmon Hall. Both offered tentative positions based more on his native speaking than his American university degree and journalism background. The starting wage at both schools was the peso equivalent of US$400 per month which seemed typical of the large chains. One problem here is that these organisations do not pay cash-in-hand and therefore they want to hire only teachers with working papers. Another international chain of language schools represented in Mexico is Wall Street Institutes. The Master Franchisee might know of vacancies in the other three centres as well as its own (W.S.I., Polanco 75, Col. Polanco, 11560 Mexico City).

Guadalajara and resorts such as Puerto Vallarta, Cancun, Acapulco and Mazatlan are places where a great many locals need to master English before they can be employed in the booming tourist industry, though wages tend to be lower than in the capital. Several independent US training organisations have set up TEFL training centres in Guadalajara (see *Training* chapter).

Leaving England for the first time, Linda Harrison travelled on a one-way ticket straight from the picturesque Yorkshire town of Kirkbymoorside to the picturesque state of Michoacàn, and suffered severe culture shock at first (despite a professed love for Mexican food developed the year before when she was a student at the University of Central Lancashire). She and a Spanish-speaking friend had pre-arranged jobs at the Culturlingua Language Center (Plaza Jardinadas, Local 24 y 25, Zamora, Michoacàn) which has the distinct advantage of offering its half dozen native speaker teachers accommodation. However it does not offer any pre-service training as Linda found out:

> The director told me that I might as well start teaching the day after I arrived. I stumbled into my first class with no experience, qualifications or books. Twelve expectant faces watched while I nervously talked about England. Twelve faces went blank when I mentioned soap operas.

Zamora is an unpretentious off-the-beaten-track agricultural centre. Culturlingua is always looking for teachers and will consider hiring anyone who is a fluent English speaker and is not painfully shy. The school pays its teachers enough for them to live comfortably and to tour the state of Michoacàn, one of the most beautiful in Mexico. In fact if you get talking to anyone in an out-of-the-way place, sooner or later you will be introduced to the director of the local English institute, as happened to Robert Abblett when he went to work on a remote organic farm near Coatepec, Veracruz. After doing a stint of weeding and planting, the farmer's wife whisked him off to her

English language school where a class of Mexican teenagers fired dozens of questions at him to practise their English and improve their knowledge of British culture.

Stuart Britton spent a couple of years in Mexico living on his teaching, often in a hand-to-mouth fashion. His initial job hunt took place in Ensenada, a tourist town in Baja California:

> *What a strange sensation it was to be in Mexico after the States, but the people I met were so warm and friendly and helpful as soon as I crossed the border, that I felt more at home. I felt that with these warm people around me, I couldn't starve or be eaten up. As far as work, I found a school from a fisherman who had befriended me at the bus station who knew someone etc. etc. and then I finally found a commercial institute, a sort of training school for adults where they teach typing, tourism, English, etc.; there are many of these institutes in Mexico. Mostly the pay is very poor and conditions are basic.*

Working for Yourself

Private lessons are in great demand, and may be given informally in exchange for board and lodging. But it is also possible to teach on a more business-like footing. With so many clients seeking one-to-one tuition through institutes, it is worth considering setting up as an independent tutor and offering private lessons at a rate which undercuts the institutes. Teachers who are tempted to poach students from the organisation they work for should bear in mind that employers who find out have been known to set the immigration department on errant teachers. However it is legitimate to advertise yourself in the press and distribute printed business cards. Elizabeth Reid based some of the material in her book *Native Speaker: Teach English & See the World* on her experiences of teaching in a small Mexican city. She started by developing her own private classes in borrowed premises (a disused shop). She recommends approaching the local community centre (*casa de cultura*), chamber of commerce or public library and offering one free sample class before signing up paying students. To increase goodwill she offered 'scholarships' to a limited number of students who really couldn't afford to pay.

Teaching in companies sometimes produces lucrative spin-offs in the field of translation and editing documents in English. Clients may offer other kinds of work too; for example Nick Wilson was asked to set up a Mexican-British arts foundation through a bank trust by someone he tutored in English.

Regulations

The red tape situation in Mexico is a difficult one. Visitors are not allowed to work or engage in any remunerative activity during a temporary visit. The Free Trade Agreement makes it somewhat easier for Americans and Canadians but still not straightforward. As has been mentioned, established schools are not normally willing to contract people with only a tourist visa, unlike private institutes who often employ teachers on tourist visas for a short period. The most respectable schools may be willing to help full-time contracted teachers with the paperwork but won't pay the cost (estimates vary between $100 and $700). Among the required documents are a CV in Spanish, notarised TEFL and university certificates which have been certified by a Mexican consulate and, if you are already in Mexico, a valid tourist visa. Tourist visas must be renewed every 90 days either by proving at a local government office that you have enough funds to support yourself or (more inconveniently) by leaving the country and recrossing the border to get a further 90 days.

LIST OF SCHOOLS

COLEGIO INTERNACIONAL DE CUERNAVACA
Apartado Postal 1334, Cuernavaca, Morelos, C.P. 62130. Tel: (73) 132905/ 116260/138496. Fax: (73) 117451. E-mail: cintc@infosel.net.mx
Number of teachers: 15 to teach primary aged children at this bilingual kindergarten and primary school.

Preference of nationality: none, only native speaker. (Most materials are American.)
Qualifications: experience and training preferred.
Conditions of employment: 1 year contracts. Hours 7.30am-3pm.
Salary: variable.
Facilities: accommodation arranged. Training provided.
Recruitment: through US universities. Interviews are held by phone or in Santa Ana California in the spring or summer (tel 714-640-7145).
Preference of nationality: none, but American English taught.
Conditions of employment: minimum 6 month contracts. Minimum 5 hours per day. Pupils range in age from 4 upwards.
Salary: US$2-3 per hour plus benefits (25% extra).
Facilities/Support: assistance given finding accommodation. Training provided.
Recruitment: through direct application. Local interviews essential.

Other Schools to Try

ANGLO MEXICAN CULTURAL INSTITUTE, Rio Nazas 116, Colonia Cuauhtémoc, 06500 Mexico (5-208 5547/fax 208 5460). 40 teachers (preferably Britons) for branches in Mexico City, Guadalajara, Puebla and Toluca.
INSTITUTO CULTURAL MEXICANO NORTEAMERICANO DE JALISCO, Enrique Díaz de León 300, Sector Juarez, CP 44170, Guadalajara, Jalisco (36-25 58 38/25 16 71). 20-25 teachers.
UNIVERSIDAD AUTONOMA DE CHIAPAS, Departamento de Lenguas Tuxtla, Blvd. Belisario Dominguez Km. 1081, 29000 Tuxtla Gutierrez, Chiapas (961-50650/fax 961-52392).
UNIVERSIDAD AUTONOMA DE CHIHUAHUA, Facultad de Filosofia y Letras, Lengua Inglesa, Apartado Postal 744, Chihuahua (14-13 54 50/fax 14-14 49 32).
UNIVERSIDAD AUTONOMA DEL EDO DE MEXICO, Centro de Ensañanza de Lenguas, Cerro de Coatepec, a un costado de la Facultad de Geografia, Ciudad Universidad, C.P. 52100, Toluca, Edo. de Mexico (72-15 18 60/fax 12 07 03).
English Unlimited—48-33 12 77/e-mail: eu1slp@teqcorp.com.mx
Language Connect Institute—e-mail: jobs@syrlang.com
Mexican Cross-Cultural Institute, 121 Centro Historico, Queretaro (42-12 34 35; e-mail mcciqro@infosel.net.mx)

Peru

While Ecuador's star has been rising, Peru's has fallen, largely due to the terrorist activities of the Shining Path group, one of whose stated aims is the elimination of foreign influence and whose policy is to attack foreigners. Furthermore, Lima is considered to be one of the most stressful and dangerous South American city in which to live. Continuing low wages and the difficulty of obtaining working papers mean that few professional teachers can be attracted to the private EFL sector. For those who are, it is worth sending a CV to the English Language Officer at the British Council. He will send a list of British schools and language teaching institutes to anyone sufficiently well qualified or alternatively pass the CV to potentially interested institutions such as the five branches of the British-Peruvian Cultural Association (known familiarly as Britanica).

Yet the range of opportunities in Lima is enormous. The stampede to learn English is unstoppable. Many company employees have been told by their bosses to learn English within three months or risk demotion. Some employers organise a course at their place of work, but most expect their staff to fix up private lessons making the freelance market very promising at the moment. In-company training courses in all industries are often offered in English, so knowledge of the language is becoming essential for all ambitious Peruvians. The Peruvian economy is not in dire straits at present, as evidenced by the relative stability of its currency, the new sol.

Many temporary visitors to Peru who lack a TEFL background end up doing some English teaching once they have established a base in the capital, usually earning about $5 an hour at an institute. Some employers offer a free or subsidised training course to new potential recruits, at which native speakers usually excel over the locals whose knowledge of English is often very weak.

James Gratton arrived in Lima to take up what had sounded like a dream job. He had contacted the institutes included on the list sent by the Peruvian Embassy in London and was contacted enthusiastically by one (on the strength of a certificate earned from a one-week intensive TEFL training course in London and nine months of living and teaching in Venezuela the year before.) High wages and many perks were offered, including a promise to meet him at the airport. His new employers' non-appearance at the airport was just the first promise they broke, and the lesson he learned over the next few months was that in Peru (and probably more widely in the continent), you must confirm and reconfirm any arrangements. He lasted only six weeks with this company (and was told that this was a record stay for an expat teacher) but concluded that such bad employers can be used as stepping stones to better opportunities.

A list of 21 bilingual and English medium schools plus a few private schools and universities is available from the Cultural Office of the Peruvian Embassy in London. The list (a couple of years out of date now) is reproduced here:

Private Institutes

Instituto de Idiomas, Camino Real 1037, San Isidro, Lima 27. Tel: (1) 441 5962. Run a good 2-week training course followed by 4 weeks of classroom observation.

Instituto Cultural Peruano Norteamericano/ICPN, Av. Arequipa 4798, Lima 18.

Asociacion Cultural Peruano Britanica, Malecón Balta 740, Lima 18.

Asociacion Cultural Peruano Britanica, Av. Arequipa 3495, San Isidro, Lima (tel/fax 1-421 6004).

Centro de Idiomas di Lima, Av. M. Olguín 215, Lima 33.

Euroidiomas, Av. Santa Cruz 111, Lima 18.

Universities

Pontificia Universidad Catolica del Peru, see entry

Universidad de Lima, Centro de Idiomas, Prolongación Javier Prado Este s/n, Monterrico, Lima.

Universidad Particular Ricardo Palma, Facultad de Traducciones, Avda. Armendáriz 349, Miraflores, Lima 18.

Universidad San Antonio Abad, Centro de Idiomas, Av. de la Cultura s/n, Apartado 367, Cusco.

Colegios

Colegio Markham, (see entry). A serious establishment for serious applicants only.

Colegio British Nursery, Las Flores 399, San Isidro, Lima 27.

Colegio Abraham Lincoln, Fundo Matazango Lote 6, Lima 3.

Colegio Juan XXIII, Detras de Caminos del Inca S/N, San Isidro, Lima.

Colegio Ingles Maria de los Angeles, Paseo Colón 434, Lima 1.

Colegio Santa Maria Marianistas, La Floresta 250, Surco, Lima 33.

Colegio Matter Purissima, Av. Aviación 445, Miraflores, Lima 18.

Colegio Dalton, Av. Petit Thouars 1867, Lince, Lima 14.

Colegio Villa Maria, Av. La Laguna 280, Monterrico-Lima.

Colegio Ingles Santa Sofia, Av. Brasil 2483, Jesus Maria, Lima 11.

Colegio San Silvestre for Girls, Chacaltana 401, Lima 18.

Colegio San Jorge, Gral. Montagne 360, Urb. Aurora, Lima 18.

Colegio San Jose, Av. Jorge Chávez 481, Miraflores, Lima 18.

Colegio Virgen Inmaculada, Av. Morro Solar 110, Valle Hermoso, Monterrico-Lima.

Instituto Franklin D Roosevelt, Av. Javier Prado S/N, San Isidro, Lima 27.

Colegio Reina de los Angeles, Malecón Monte Bello 605, Monterrico-Lima.
Colegio Inmaculado Corazon, Av. Angamos 950, Miraflores, Lima 18.
Colegio John Dewey, Av. Cuba 414, Jesus Maria, Lima.
Colegio Peruano Britanico, Av. Via Lactea 445, Monterrico-Lima. Has been known to offer employment to local enquirers.

Not all the *colegios* are looking for certified teachers, so it is worth approaching them. The hours are more civilised than in a language institute (i.e. 8am-3pm rather than 8.30-10am and 5.30-9pm) and wages are higher. Certified teachers can earn British wages plus a 10% expatriate allowance. One of the pillars of the EFL establishment is Newton College (Av. Ricardo Elías Aparicio 240, Urb. Las Lagunas de la Molina, Miraflores, Lima 12; Apartado 18-0873, Miraflores, Lima 18; tel 14-363211/365345/790470; fax 14-790430). It has about 70 British nationals on staff, half of whom are recruited abroad.

Many institutes are located in the well-to-do port area of Miraflores, where a door-to-door search for work might succeed. Try for example Interaction in English, Manco Cápac 649, Miraflores, Lima 18 (tel 14-462503).

Freelancing

Setting up as a freelance tutor is potentially very lucrative. A standard fee is $10 a lesson, though this can be reduced for clients who want to book a whole course. With wages like that and assuming you have found enough clients, it is not difficult to earn over $1,000 a month (in a country where the minimum wage is $70). James Gratton put a cheap advertisement (written in English) in the main daily *El Commercio* and signed up two clients. This was possible in his case since he was staying at his girlfriend's house where he had free access to a telephone. His new students were both employees of Petro-Peru, and soon other clients contacted James for lessons. He admits that freelancers do lose out to cancellations, though some of his students willingly paid for missed lessons. Freelancing is a continual process of advertising and getting new students to replace the ones that fall by the wayside. James continued giving private lessons for six months and now wonders about the possibility of returning from Northampton to Lima to set up his own small institute.

Regulations

Peruvian work visas are very rare and most people teach on a tourist visa. As in most other countries, a tourist visa cannot be switched to a work visa inside Peru. The immigration authorities on arrival grant either two or three months; one month renewals are granted by the immigration office in Lima up to a total of five months without leaving the country. After that it is necessary to cross the Peruvian border and have your passport stamped for another two or three months, which can be renewed locally as before. One reason which many people use to extend their stay is that they have formed a romantic attachment to a local woman/man. James Gratton felt that the authorities were not interested in rooting out illegal workers. When he approached the immigration office about the requirements for a work visa, they knew he was working but took no steps to stop him.

In his quest for a work visa, James gathered together all the necessary documents, including contract (the duration does not matter particularly), notarised certificates and documents translated into Spanish. All of this cost him a lot of money and time, and he still didn't succeed. He concluded that it would be possible only if you knew someone in the Immigration Department who could give your application a safe passage without having to pay fines (bribes) at every stage. Making key contacts is more important than gathering documentation.

Nick Branch corroborates this conclusion:

> *Getting a work permit for Venezuela is a nightmare. It is far easier to work illegally without one. On no account attempt to get one on your own, since this involves dealing with the DIEX, a truly horrific organisation housed in what resembles a prison and with appalling disorganisation. Two year ago they lost 3,000 passports of*

people applying for work permits. It was later discovered they had been sold on the black market.

The Peruvian Consul in London will send an information sheet entitled 'Non-Immigrant Working Resident Visas' which explains that after the visa has been obtained outside the country it is necessary to present it within a month of arrival at the *Dirección General de Migraciones* at Av. España 700 in Lima. Care must be taken to keep on the right side of the tax office (SUNAT) to which about 15% of earnings are supposed to be paid. James Gratton obtained a tax number even though his passport clearly indicated his status as tourist, but ended up paying virtually no tax.

LIST OF SCHOOLS

FOSTER & FOSTER PRIVATE INSTITUTE FOR ENGLISH
Miguel dasso 139-301 San Isidro, Lima. Tel: 1-949 1902. Fax: 1-442 7520.
Number of teachers: 7+.
Preference of nationality: American.
Qualifications: university degree (in administration, finance, economics, marketing preferred). 1-2 years' experience.
Conditions of employment: 1 year contracts. Normal hours are 7.30-10.30am and/or 6-9pm Monday to Friday plus Saturday mornings.
Salary: $500-$550 per month less 30% deductions.
Facilities/Support: accommodation can be provided for three teachers in flat. No possibility of assistance with work permits.
Recruitment: newspaper adverts. Telephone interviews possible.

MARKHAM COLLEGE
Apartado 18-1048, Miraflores, Lima 18. Tel: (1) 4241 7677. Fax: (1) 4241 7678.
Number of teachers: 25 for British curriculum/IB school for 4-17 year olds.
Preference of nationality: British.
Qualifications: B.Ed./T.Cert/degree/Cambridge/RSA Certificate, etc.
Conditions of employment: 3-year contracts. Many hours on offer.
Salary: above average.
Facilities/Support: assistance with finding accommodation given. Help given with labyrinthine process to get work visa. In-house training available.
Recruitment: adverts in *TES* and recruitment agency (Gabbitas Educational Consultancy). Interviews essential and can be held in UK.

PONTIFICIA UNIVERSIDAD CATOLICA DEL PERU
Centro de Idiomas, Jr. Camaná 956, Lima 1. Tel: 1-431 0052. Fax: 1-431 0052.
Number of teachers: 2.
Preference of nationality: none.
Qualifications: university graduate as ESL teacher. At least 3 years' experience in the field.
Conditions of employment: short contracts only due to strict immigration controls. Classes run from 7am to 21.30pm. Teachers are given lesson outlines, visual aids and tests to set.
Salary: $248 per month (for 3 hours per day), $372 for 4½ h.p.d., and $497 for 6 h.p.d. 10% deduction for taxes.
Facilities/Support: homestay accommodation can be arranged. Free Spanish classes.
Recruitment: direct approach. Interviews not always necessary.

WILLIAM SHAKESPEARE INSTITUTO DE INGLES
Avenida Dos de Mayo 1105, San Isidro, Lima. Tel/fax: (14) 440 1004/968 0107. Tel/fax: (14) 422 1313.
Number of teachers: 6-12.
Preference of nationality: British preferred but others acceptable.

Qualifications: TEFL qualifications or teaching experience in South America. Senior posts demand 5 years' experience.
Conditions of employment: 3 month contracts, renewable. Variable hours according to client demand. Students aged 4-64.
Salary: varies according to experience.
Facilities/Support: training provided.
Recruitment: direct application and passed on from other schools. Adverts in UK newspapers for senior posts. Interviews not essential but can be arranged in UK. Applications should include a recent photograph.
Contact: Glenda Dentone, Principal.

Venezuela

Proximity to the US and the volume of business which is done with *El Norte* mean a strong preference for American accents and teaching materials in Venezuela. Oil wealth abounds in the business community and many corporations hire in-company language trainers through Caracas-based agencies.

But work is not exclusively for Americans, as Nick Branch from St. Albans discovered, nor is it confined to the capital:

> *Merida is very beautiful and a considerably more pleasant place to be than Caracas. The atmosphere and organisation of the institute where I worked were very good. But alas. As with all the English teaching institutes in Merida, the pay is very low. Merida is three times cheaper to live in than Caracas, but the salaries are 5-6 times lower.*

Nick Branch investigated most of the schools and agencies in Venezuela and worked for several of them including one based in the Oriente coastal resort of Puerto la Cruz. Once again the pay was less than in Caracas but advantages like easy access to the Mochima National Marine Park compensated. Opportunities for English teachers even exist on the popular resort island of Margarita.

Check adverts in Caracas' main English language organ, the *Daily Journal*. Most give only a phone number. A typical advert might read:

> *We need English teachers and offer remuneration according to the market, stable incomes, paid training, organization in the work, more earnings according to commissions. Excellent working condition. Work with best team. Punctual payment.*

The last item is worth noting, since many institutes do not pay as much or as often as they promise at the outset. In fact Caracas has more than its fair share of shady characters running language schools, so that newcomers should take their time about signing any contracts. Nick Branch describes what happened after he was hired by a well known institute:

> *The director is a seriously dodgy character. He pays his teachers $100 a month for a 40-hour week (not stated in the offer of employment I received in England). The materials were appalling, written by the school and very outdated and riddled with mistakes. The teacher training was a farce, consisting of a one-day stint run by a relation of the director. Another trainee (a Venezuelan) got up and started his practice class with 'My teacher is a metaphysicist'. Alas, in reality this guy would have had difficulty ordering a bag of King Edwards from his local greengrocer.*

There are plenty of professional and efficient companies as well, though competition from the expat community will be greater to be hired by them. In fact there is less competition for teaching posts than might have been expected, apart from some teachers from neighbouring Guyana (formerly British Guyana). Tensions between these teachers and North American and European teachers have been reported.

Almost no potential employers require a TEFL certificate, although some require teachers to have a degree or at least be on an intellectual par with a university graduate. Almost all schools will tell you that they want you to stay for six months to a year. In reality, few make you sign a contract.

Regulations

Most people work on a tourist visa which is valid for two months but extendable to six. A combined work/study contract (internship in American parlance) is the solution which the *Centro Venezolano Americano* has come up with (see entry) but this is available only to US citizens.

Most long-stay foreigners take brief trips to Curacao or Trinidad and Tobago and get an extension of their tourist visa when returning to Venezuela. Work permits are available only if the employer has obtained approval from the appropriate Ministry and sent the necessary papers to a Venezuelan consulate in the teacher's country of residence. Even with a backer as well established as the British Council, the visa problem looms large. Nick Branch describes the process of getting a work permit in Caracas as a nightmare:

> *On no account attempt to get one on your own, since this involves dealing with the DIEX, a truly horrific organisation housed in what resembles a prison and with appalling disorganisation. Two years ago they lost 3,000 passports of people who were applying for work permits. It was later discovered that they had been sold on the black market.*

Even applying outside the country is unlikely to succeed. James Gratton obtained a definite job offer from a university extension department on Margarita Island (address below) and presented the letter to the Venezuelan Embassy in London. His application was turned down. His main complaint was that you hear a different story from every official. Even renewing his tourist visa at the Immigration Office took a week and involved his having to present a typed letter in Spanish (and why would a bone fide tourist be expected to do that?) Yet he managed to stay legally in Venezuela for nine months, leaving the country when necessary and returning without once being asked to show a ticket home as proof of his intention to leave the country. His most serious problem occurred when one of his employers threatened to report his tourist status to the police if he quit to look for a better job (James did quit and the police were not called.)

CENTRO VENEZOLANO AMERICANO

Av. José Marti, Edf. CVA, Urbanización Las Mercedes, Caracas 1060-A. Also: Apartado 61715 Del Este, Caracas 1060-A. Tel: (2) 993 7911. Fax: (2) 993 6812. E-mail: becarios@sa.omnes.net. Web-site: http://www.cva.org.ve

Number of teachers: 33 interns out of 110 locally hired teachers for approx. 6,000 students. Other branches include Torre Banco Lara, Carmelitas, Piso 14 (2-861 0064/811627/81556) and Merida (61-911436).

Preference of nationality: American, Canadian, Venezuelan.

Qualifications: BA or teachers with EFL/ESL experience. A written and oral test is given to all non-native English speaking applicants.

Conditions of employment: minimum 6 months with renewals up to 2 years. Choice of children's courses (for ages 9-11), teens (12-15) and regular and Saturday courses for adults. Minimum 6 academic hours per day.

Salary: 5,200 Bolivars per 90 minute class. Approx. Bs327,600 per month plus a 100,000 bolivar housing bonus.

Facilities/Support: assistance with obtaining accommodation, health insurance and visas. $3\frac{1}{2}$ week pre-service training course for interns is paid. Free Spanish course. Computer lab and access to cultural centre activities.

Recruitment: mail, fax, e-mail. Telephone interviews.

Schools to Try

Centro de Aprendizaje, Madison, Caracas (2-986 6190/987 6767).

Eduform, Central Polo, Torre 3, Oficina 91, Colinas de Bellomonte, Apto. 69553, Caracas 1050. Specialises in teaching business people.

Emans Language Centre, Caracas and Valencia (2-257 8716/fax 2-257 3668). *Instituto Venezolano Britanico,* Av. Humboldt Mari Carmen, Urb. Bello Monte, Sabana Grande, Caracas/PO Box 51867 (95-25443). On-site and in-company work.

Inversiones English & Spanish for Jobs (ESJ), Av. Libertador, Res. Florida, Apto 5, La Florida (2-712069). Relatively new Caracas company undertaking in-company work.

Loescher Ebbinghaus, La Campina, Centro Comercial, Avenida Libertador, Torre Oeste, 2nd Floor, Off. 2/5 (2-766 5101/2-713680). Other branches e.g. La Trinidad, Calle San José, Quinta Kateriñe, Sorocaima (tel 932459) and in Valencia west of the capital (41-236052). Long hours of preparation at institute are compulsory.

Venusa C.P.S.A., Institute of International Studies & Modern Languages, Av. Urdaneta, Edif. Guilam 49-49 (74-633906/fax 74-633525).

Wall Street Institute, Avda. Francisco de Miranda, Torre Lido piso 11 torre C Ofic. 111c, 113C El Rosal, Caracas (2-953 74 73).

Anglo American Centre, San Cristobel (433116/444410).

Centro de Idiomas Modernas, Valera (314313).

FISA, Puerto la Cruz (81-815734).

Instituto Educativo de Idiomas, C.C. Real, Piso 1, Oficina 17, Porlamar, Isla de Margarita.

Fundacion para la Promotion Desarrollo de la Universidad Oriente, Fundaudo NVA Esparta, Calle Guevara, Quinte Palguarima, Al Frente del Colegio, Las Monjas, Porlamar, Isla de Margarita.

Iowa Institute, Ubicacion Av. Cuatro con Calle 18, Merida (74-526404). Well-run, but low pay.

Central America & the Caribbean

If you keep your ears open as you travel through this enormous isthmus squeezed between two great oceans, you may come across opportunities to teach English, especially if you are prepared to do so as a volunteer. Salaries on offer may be pitiful but if you find a congenial spot on the 'gringo trail' (for example the lovely old colonial town of Antigua in Guatemala), you may decide to prolong your stay by helping the people you will inevitably meet who want to learn English.

As the wealthiest country in Central America. Costa Rica is sometimes referred to as the Switzerland of the region and there are plenty of private language academies in the capital San José. It is government policy to teach English in primary schools which has greatly increased the demand for English teachers. Although state schools can't afford to import expat teachers, they are often willing to accept an offer of voluntary assistance. The school year runs from March 1st to December 1st. Temporary six-month renewable working visas are now issued to teachers working for established employers like the *Instituto Britanico.*

WorldTeach sends college graduates to teach English for nine months in Costa Rica. *World Education Forum* also offers North American students and others an opportunity to work as unpaid part-time English teachers while learning Spanish and living with host families in Costa Rica. The emphasis of this programme is on cultural exchange.

The Jamaican government welcomes qualifying young people from the US and UK to teach in Jamaican schools as part of a student exchange with JOYST (Jamaican Organization for Youth & Student Travel). British nationals should apply through BUNAC (see entry at end of this chaper); Americans should contact *Council* in New York (205 East 42nd St, New York, NY 10017). For general enquiries about the possibility of teaching in Jamaica, contact the Permanent Secretary, Ministry of Education, Youth & Culture, 2 National Heroes Circle, Kingston 4, Jamaica (809-922-1400).

LIST OF SCHOOLS

Costa Rica

INSTITUTO BRITANICO
PO Box 8184, San José 1000, Costa Rica. Tel: 225 0256/234 9054. Fax: 253 1894. E-mail: instbrit@sol.racsa.co.cr
Number of teachers: 15 (variable).
Preference of nationality: British, American, Canadian.
Qualifications: CELTA or equivalent and teaching experience.
Conditions of employment: minimum commitment of 8 months. Split shifts 8-12am and 5-9pm (Monday to Thursday), 9-11am and 6-8pm (Friday) and 8am-12 noon (Saturday). Adult and children's classes (ages 4-16). Children's classes Tuesday to Friday 3-6pm and Saturday 8-11am.
Salary: average $450-$600 a month.
Facilities: no housing allowance. Airport pick-up and first 2 weeks' accommodation provided free. Introductory training and in-service workshops provided.
Recruitment: internally. Local interviews only.
Contact: Tim Groombridge, Director of Teacher Training.

WORLD EDUCATION FORUM
PO Box 383-4005, San Antonio de Belén, Heredia, Costa Rica. Tel/fax: 239 2245. Fax (506) 239-2254.
Number of teachers: 50 on cultural exchange programme.
Preference of nationality: from any English-speaking country.
Qualifications: minimum Bachelor's degree in education (primary or secondary), English, maths, history, science, biology, chemistry or physics.
Conditions of employment: minimum one academic year. Usual hours of teaching 8am-noon or 1pm-5pm (part-time).
Salary: none since this is a voluntary programme.
Facilities/Support: free room and board with families. Tuition in Spanish provided.
Recruitment: send resumés.
Contact: José O. Arauz, Director.

Cuba

PROYECTO CULTURAL E.L.I.
Geissensteinring 46, 6000 Luzern 12, Switzerland. Tel/fax: (41) 360 87 64. E-mail: proyectocultural@compuserve.com. Web-site: www.latino.ch/eli
Number of teachers: 2 at Swiss-Cuban school in Havana founded in 1993.
Preference of nationality: native speakers.
Salary: Cuban standard (teachers should be self-financing).
Facilities: free accommodation in the school or with Cuban families.
Recruitment: all enquiries must be directed to Swiss office.
Contact: Yvo Alexander Wüest-Kim, Director.

Jamaica

TEACH IN JAMAICA
BUNAC, 16 Bowling Green Lane, London EC1R 0BD. Tel: 0171-251 3472. Fax: 0171-251 0215. Web-site: www.bunac.org
Number of teachers: limited.
Preference of nationality: British only.
Qualifications: less than 26 years old. Must have graduated in last two years in maths, English, biology, Chemistry, Physics, accounting, geography, Spanish, French or Design and Technology. Previous teaching experience or experience working with groups of children is desirable, as is experience of living or travelling abroad.
Conditions of employment: 10 months from August to July working in rural secondary schools throughout Jamaica. School hours are 7.30am to 2.30pm.
Salary: from approximately J$100,000 for the year. Jamaican government pays a further tax-free allowance to cover teaching materials and other expenses.
Facilities: accommodation arranged by school either in rented accommodation or in local homes. Limited teaching resources in many schools.
Recruitment: applications through BUNAC. Compulsory interviews in London and possibly elsewhere. Total cost of programme including travel is £1,250.

Paraguay

CENTRO CULTURAL PARGUAYO AMERICANO
Avenida Espana 352, Asuncion, Paraguay. Tel: (21) 24831/24772. Fax: (21) 214544.
Number of teachers: 4.
Preference of nationality: American.
Qualifications: EFL/ESL training and experience of living outside the US.
Conditions of employment: 1 year contracts. Hours of work between 7am and 9pm. Choice of 4 programmes: teaching children (7-11), adolescents (12-15), adults and in-company courses.
Salary: US$5 an hour.
Facilities: no assistance with accommodation. Training provided.
Recruitment: direct application, best times are February and May. Local interviews necessary.

Uruguay

THE BRITISH SCHOOL
Maximo Tajes 6400, 11500 Montevideo. Tel: (2) 603421. Fax: (2) 616338.
Number of teachers: 11.
Preference of nationality: British, for bilingual Spanish/English school.
Qualifications: university degree plus 4+ years of experience.
Conditions of employment: 2 years. 35 h.p.w.
Salary: varies according to qualifications and experience.
Facilities: furnished apartments provided. Assistance given with residence permits (for which are needed a health certificate and birth certificate notarised by Uruguayan Consulate in country of origin). Good library and IT resources.
Recruitment: recruitment agency in London.

ENGLISH LIGHTHOUSE INSTITUTE
Sarandi 1146, Maldonado, Uruguay. Tel/fax: (42) 33893.
Number of teachers: 3-4.
Preference of nationality: Canadian, American, Australian, British.
Qualifications: Bachelor of Education or PGCE in primary education plus a TEFL/TESL Certificate.
Conditions of employment: 9 month contracts (10th March to 10th December). 40 h.p.w. Courses for children, juniors and adults.
Salary: US$1,200 per month less deductions of 10%.

Facilities/Support: accommodation provided; rent of $150 per month plus water, electricity and phone bill deducted from salary.
Recruitment: direct application by fax. Interviews not essential. Couples are welcome.

Other Schools to Try (countries in alphabetical order)

INSTITUTO CULTURAL DOMINICO-AMERICANO (ICDA), Av. Abraham Lincoln 21, Santo Domingo, Dominican Republic (533 4191/fax 533 8809). Many part-time freelance native speakers.

CIS MAM Language School, Boulevard Universitario, Casa No. 4, San Salvador, El Salvador (tel/fax 226 2623). Volunteer teachers to work with members of the Salvadorean opposition. Training provided.

American School of Guatemala, Apartado Postal No. 83, 01901 Guatemala

MODERN AMERICAN ENGLISH SCHOOL, Calle de los Nazarenos 16, Antigua, Guatemala (932-3306/fax 932-0217). 3 North American teachers for minimum of 6 months.

Universidad del Valle de Guatemala, Apartado Postal No. 82, 01901 Guatemala

HAITIAN-AMERICAN INSTITUTE, Angle Rue Capois et Rue St. Cyr, Port-au-Prince, Haiti (22 2947/22 3715). Bi-national center employing quite a few teachers.

NORTH AMERICA

Countless programmes in English as a Second Language (ESL) in the US are subsumed under several distinct programme types, in contrast to the heavy emphasis on 'academy' type EFL or 'workplace' ESP in Europe. Just about every university and college in the major cities has an ESL programme, as do a range of government and charitable organisations. Commercial schools offer a wide variety of classes but tend to focus on survival ESL and EAP (English for Academic Purposes) with writing as a major component. Berlitz and inlingua are representented throughout the USA and are a completely different type of commercial school, concentrating on conversational skills and foreign languages for business people.

There are bilingual/bicultural classes in thousands of high schools across the country. Many require staff who are not only state-certified teachers but also bilingual in exotic languages like Hmong or Gujarati. Most larger cities have at least one free or low-cost workplace literacy/vocational ESL programme which caters for immigrants needing assistance with the basics of English. Some of these programmes operate in outposts (e.g. churches, libraries) and many depend on local volunteers as tutors. Volunteer positions can conceivably lead to better things. Another way of getting your foot in the door is to make yourself available as a substitute (for which you will need a telephone and preferably an answering machine).

Although the demand for ESL teachers is enormous, it is very difficult for foreigners who do not have a 'green card' to obtain the necessary working visa. The J-1 visa is available to university students participating in an approved Exchange Visitor Programme (which are only for the summer) and to researchers and teachers whose applications are supported by their employing institution in the US. Similarly it is extremely difficult to obtain the H-1B 'Temporary Worker' visa which is available for prearranged professional or highly skilled jobs for which there are no suitably qualified Americans, an increasingly unlikely circumstance as more and more Americans are becoming qualified to teach ESL/EFL. Although more US organisations now recognise the Cambridge/RSA Certificate than before, the MA in TESOL still dominates the American EFL scene. *EL Prospects,* the monthly job supplement to the *EL Gazette,* carries some ads for openings in the US, though most of those are academic posts in universities where it might be possible for the employer to overcome the visa problem in the case of highly qualified candidates. Here are a few organisations which were advertising recently:

American Academy of English, 2110 N. Military Road, Arlington, Virginia (703-527-9261/fax 703-527-3858/e-mail info@ameracad.com

ELS Language Centers, 333 N. Glassell, Orange, California (fax 714-538-1899/e-mail eclegg@els.com. Advertising hourly rate of $13.75 for teaching at summer school.

Alhambra Language Systems, California (626-284-9852/fax 626-284 9893).

Torrance Language Systems, California (310-370-5951/fax 310-371-7251).

Even for qualified American teachers, part-time work is the norm, often referred to as being hired as an 'adjunct'. Many contracts are not renewed creating a transient English teaching population. Pay is hourly and varies according to region, e.g $20-30 in Chicago, $25-40 in San Francisco. Part-timers almost never get benefits which means no health insurance or vacation pay. Even full-time teaching openings may be for just nine months with pay as little as $20,000 in the Midwest.

One possibility might be to teach at summer courses or work on summer camps attended by young people from overseas. For example the Council on International Educational Exchange (205 42nd St, New York, NY 10017) recruits ESL instructors for language camps on the east and west coasts, responsible for teaching English language classes to high school age international students in July and August. Even for such short appointments they look for an MA in TESOL or at least a strong background in ESL.

The situation is not dissimilar in Canada, including the difficulty of getting a visa. People with experience might have expected to be able to do some casual one-to-one tutoring of new immigrants, but stiff competition makes this difficult. When David Hughes arrived in Vancouver after a lengthy stint of teaching English in Taiwan, he felt fairly confident that with his experience he would be able to acquire a few fee-paying students from among the huge Chinese population in the area. But he didn't get a single reply to his advert.

ROYAL LANGUAGE TRAINING
2 Cardinal Park Drive, Suite 202 B, Leesburg, Virginia 22075. Tel: (703) 777-9160. Fax: (703) 729-6955. E-mail: Royalint@ix.netcom

Number of teachers: 30 in three locations in Washington DC, Orlando FL and Los Angeles CA.

Qualifications: BA (English major) or TEFL Certificate.

Salary: $10-$15 per hour.

Recruitment: via newspaper adverts.

AUSTRALASIA

While Europeans tend to have a somewhat Eurocentric view of the world, the Antipodean English language industry has built itself into a giant. However the loss of financial confidence in Southeast Asia has seen a sharp decline in the number of fee-paying students going to Australia resulting in a loss of job opportunities for Australian teachers, never mind foreign ones.

Teaching English as a Foreign Language has a very high profile in both Australia and New Zealand. There are no less than 16 Cambridge/RSA Cert. training centres in Australia and five in New Zealand, most of them attached to flourishing English language colleges. There are a further three Trinity TESOL centres in New Zealand, despite its tiny population of about three million. With the decline in students from the

Pacific Rim, more and more Australians and New Zealanders are recognising the value of an EFL qualification for the purposes of working abroad.

For many years there have been very active ESL programmes in all the major Australian cities to cater for the thousands of migrants who have come to Australia since the war. In recent years, the proportion of immigrants coming from Southeast Asia (especially Hong Kong and Vietnam) has nearly overtaken the number accepted from Europe. In addition, Australian universities attract foreign students from China and Southeast Asia, many of whom want English language training before or during their courses. Government-run language teaching programmes operate in universities, colleges of further edition and TAFE (Technical and Further Education) centres.

The ELICOS Association is the national association of institutions, both private and public, accredited to teach English Language Intensive Courses to Overseas Students in Australia. The EA can be contacted at PO Box 30, 43 Murray Street, Pyrmont, NSW 2009 (2-9660 6455/fax 2-9566 2230). The Association is particularly strong in Perth where there are ten ELICOS centres. They have developed national guidelines on the qualifications expected of teachers at ELICOS centres. Teachers must have either a three-year teaching qualification with a TESOL option or a three-year degree plus 800 hours of classroom teaching experience plus an approved TESOL qualification.

The profession is strictly regulated in Australia and standards are high in both the private and public sector. There is a nationally agreed pay scale ('award') for EFL teachers which falls in the range of A$18,000-$30,000 a year. Even highly trained Australian nationals cannot always find jobs. As in the US, a large proportion of local ESL teaching is done by volunteers. Ben Hockley did a four-week training course in Adelaide (now ELLS, English Language & Literacy Services) and gathered that it would be very difficult to find full-time work in Australia. This did not matter to him since he had chosen to do a course which was geared to working abroad, to fulfil his ambition to return to Spain with his Spanish girlfriend to teach.

Unless you are an Australian or New Zealand resident, you must either obtain residency (very difficult unless you have such specialist qualifications that an employer will undertake to support your application) or work on a working holiday visa. In Australia this non-renewable 12-month visa is available to Britons, Irish and Canadians less than 26 years of age who must not work at any one job for more than three months. On the whole, this is unsuitable for the job of English teaching.

There is an exception. Because of the rush of foreign students doing short courses during their autumn and winter holidays, many language schools in Australia and New Zealand do have seasonal requirements in February/March and July/August, and won't expect short-term appointees to have as many qualifications as longer-term staff. Demand for these holiday English courses has increased since the Australian immigration authorities relaxed the restrictions on visas, allowing foreign students to undertake short courses on a tourist visa.

For example International House Queensland (130 McLeod St, Cairns, Queensland 4870) offers short-term opportunities to people on working holiday visas, provided they have the CELTA. The Waratah Education Centre in the Sydney beach suburb of Manly affiliated to International House in 1996. A city centre campus has recently opened. Both employ teachers on a casual basis as well as contracts. The Milner International College of English (379 Hay Street, Perth, WA 6000) has occasional temporary positions for CELTA-holders on a working holiday visa. In New Zealand, try the Auckland Language Centre (PO Box 105033, Auckland; 9-303 1962/fax 9-307 9219).

Currency Conversion Chart

COUNTRY	£1	US$1
Argentina	1.68 peso	1.0 peso
Australia	A$2.86	A$1.68
Austria	19.6 schillings	11.5 schillings
Belgium/Luxembourg	57 francs	33.5 francs
Bolivia	9.5 boliviano	5.6 boliviano
Brazil	2 real	1.2 real
Brunei	2.9 Brunei dollar	1.7 Brunei dollar
Bulgaria	2,780 lev	1,630 lev
Canada	C$2.65	C$1.55
Chile	800 peso	468 peso
China	14 renminbi	8.3 renminbi
Colombia	2,700 peso	1,580 peso
Czech Republic	51 koruna	30 koruna
Denmark	10.6 kroner	6.2 kroner
Ecuador	10,760 sucre	6,300 sucre
Egypt	5.8 Egyptian pound	3.4 Egyptian pound
Finland	8.5 markka	5 markka
France	8.1 franc	5.1 franc
Germany	2.8 DM	1.6 DM
Greece	485 drachma	283 drachma
Hong Kong	13.2 HK dollar	7.8 HK dollar
Hungary	368 forint	215 forint
Indonesia	18,530 rupiah	10,850 rupiah
Italy	2,764 lira	1,618 lira
Japan	230 yen	134.7 yen
Kenya	102 schilling	60 schilling
Korea	12,371 won	1,388 won
Malaysia	6.5 ringgit	3.8 ringgit
Malta	0.63 Maltese lira	0.37 Maltese lira
Mexico	17.6 peso	10.3 peso
Morocco	15.5 dirham	9.1 dirham
Nepal	116 rupee	68 rupee
Netherlands	3.1 guilder	1.85 guilder
New Zealand	NZ$3.40	NZ$2.00
Norway	12.6 krone	7.4 krone
Peru	5.2 new sol	3.0 new sol
Poland	6.1 złoty	3.6 złoty
Portugal	286 escudo	168 escudo
Russia (market rate)	27.3 rouble	15.99 rouble
Saudi Arabia	6.4 riyal	3.75 riyal
Singapore	287 Singapore dollar	1.68 Singapore dollar
Slovakia	63.9 koruna	36.8 koruna
Slovenia	265 tolar	155 tolar
Spain	237 peseta	139 peseta
Sweden	13.5 krona	7.9 krona
Switzerland	2.3 franc	1.35 franc
Taiwan	58 Taiwan dollar	34 Taiwan dollar
Thailand	67 baht	39.5 baht
Turkey	471,000 lira	275,800 lira
USA	1.70 dollar	—
Venezuela (floating rate)	975 bolivar	571 bolivar

Embassies/Consulates
in London and Washington

AUSTRIA: 18 Belgrave Mews West, London SW1X 8HU. Tel: 0171-235 3731.
3524 International Court NW, Washington DC 20008-3035. Tel: (202) 895-6767.
BELGIUM: 103 Eaton Square, London SW1W 9AB. Tel: 0171-470 3700.
3330 Garfield St NW, Washington DC 20008. Tel: (202) 333-6900.
BRAZIL: Consular Section, 6 St. Alban's St, London SW1Y 4SG. Tel: 0171-930 9055.
3009 Whitehaven St NW, Washington, DC 20008. Tel: (202) 745-2828.
BULGARIA: 186–188 Queen's Gate, London SW7 5HL (0171-584 9400/0891 171208).
1621 22nd St NW, Washington, DC 20008. Tel: (202) 387-7969.
CHILE: 12 Devonshire St, London W1N 2DS. Tel: 0171-580 1023.
1732 Massachusetts Ave NW, Washington DC 20036. Tel: (202) 785-3159.
CHINA: Visa Section, 31 Portland Place, London W1N 3AG. Tel: 0171-631 1430.
2201 Wisconsin Ave NW, Washington DC 20007. Tel: (202) 338-6688.
COLOMBIA: Suite 14, 140 Park Lane, London W1Y 3AA. Tel: 0171-495 4233.
1825 Connecticut Avenue NW, Washington, DC 20009. Tel: (202) 332-7476.
CROATIA: 18-21 Jermyn St, London SW1Y 6HP. Tel: 0171-434 2946.
CZECH REPUBLIC: 26-30 Kensington Palace Gardens, London W8 4QY. Tel: 0171-727
4918.
3900 Spring of Freedom St NW, Washington DC 20008. Tel: (202) 363-6315/6.
ECUADOR: Flat 3b, 3 Hans Crescent, Knightsbridge, London SW1X 0LS. Tel: 0171-584
8084.
2535 15th St NW, Washington, DC 20009. Tel: (202) 234-7166.
EGYPT: 2 Lowndes St, London SW1X 9ET. Tel: 0171-235 9719.
2310 Decatur Place NW, Washington DC 20008. Tel: (202) 234-3903.
FINLAND: 38 Chesham Place, London SW1X 8HW. Tel: 0171-235 9531.
3216 New Mexico Ave NW, Washington DC 20016. Tel: (202) 363-2430.
FRANCE: 21 Cromwell Road, London SW7 2DQ. Tel: 0171-838 2000.
4101 Reservoir Road NW, Washington DC 20007. Tel: (202) 944-6200/6215.
GERMANY: 23 Belgrave Square, London SW1X 8PZ. Tel: 0171-824 1300.
4645 Reservoir Road NW, Washington DC 20007. Tel: (202) 298-4000.
GREECE: 1A Holland Park, London W11 3TP. Tel: 0171-221 6467.
2221 Massachusetts Ave NW, Washington DC 20008. Tel: (202) 232-8222.
HUNGARY: 35b Eaton Place, London SW1X 8BY. Tel: 0171-235 2664.
3910 Shoemaker St NW, Washington DC 20008. Tel: (202) 362-6730.
INDIA: India House, Aldwych, London WC2B 4NA. Tel: 0171-836 8484.
2536 Massachusetts Avenue NW, Washington, DC 20008. Tel: (202) 939-9839/9850.
INDONESIA: 38 Grosvenor Square, London W1X 9AD. Tel: 0171-499 7661.
2020 Massachusetts Ave NW, Washington DC 20036. Tel: (202) 775-5200.
ITALY: 14 Three Kings Yard, Davies St, London W1Y 2EH. Tel: 0171-629 8200.
1601 Fuller St NW, Washington DC 20009. Tel: (202) 328-5500.
JAPAN: 101-104 Piccadilly, London W1V 9FN. Tel: 0171-465 6500.
2520 Massachusetts Ave NW, Washington DC 20008. Tel: (202) 939-6800.
KOREA: 60 Buckingham Gate, London SW1E 6AJ. Tel: 0171-227 5505.
2600 Virginia Ave NW, Suite 208, Washington, DC 20037. Tel: (202) 939-5660.
LAOS: 74 Avenue Raymond Poincare, 75116 Paris, France. Tel: 1-45 53 02 98.
2222 S St NW, Washington, DC 20008. Tel: (202) 332-6416/7.
LATVIA: 45 Nottingham Place, London W1M 3FE. Tel: 0171-312 0040.
4325 17th St NW, Washington, DC 20011. Tel: (202) 726-8213.
LITHUANIA: 84 Gloucester Place, London W1H 3HN. Tel: 0171-486 6401.
2622 16th St NW, Washington, DC 20009. Tel: (202) 234-5860.
MALAYSIA: 45 Belgrave Square, London SW1X 8QT. Tel: 0171-235 8033.
2401 Massachusetts Ave NW, Washington DC 20008. Tel: (202) 328-2700.

MALTA: Malta House, 36-38 Piccadilly, London W1V 0PQ. Tel: 0171-292 4800.
MEXICO: 8 Halkin St, London SW1X 7DN. Tel: 0171-235 6393.
    2827 16th St NW, Washington, DC 20009-4260. Tel: (202) 736-1000.
MOROCCO: 49 Queen's Gate Gardens, London SW7 5NE. Tel: 0171-581 5001.
    1601 21st St NW, Washington DC 20009. Tel: (202) 462-7979.
NETHERLANDS: 38 Hyde Park Gate, London SW7 5DP. Tel: 0171-584 5040.
    4200 Linnean Ave NW, Washington DC 20008. Tel: (202) 244-5300.
OMAN: 64 Ennismore Gardens, London SW7 1NH. Tel: 0171-584 6782.
    2535 Belmont Road NW, Washington DC 20008. Tel: (202) 387-1980-2.
PERU: 52 Sloane St, London SW1X 9SP. Tel: 0171-235 6867/1917.
    1700 Massachusetts Ave NW, Washington DC 20036. Tel: (202) 833-9860.
POLAND: 73 New Cavendish St, London W1M 8LS. Tel: 0171-580 0476.
    2224 Wyoming Ave NW, Washington, DC 20008. Tel: (202) 232-4517.
PORTUGAL: Silver City House, 62 Brompton Road, London SW3 1BJ. Tel: 0171-581
    8722/4.
    2125 Kalorama Road NW, Washington DC 20008. Tel: (202) 332-3307.
ROMANIA: Arundel House, 4 Palace Green, London W8 4QD. Tel: 0171-937 8125.
    1607 23rd St NW, Washington, DC 20008. Tel: (202) 232-4747.
RUSSIAN FEDERATION: 5 Kensington Palace Gardens, London W8 4QS. Tel: 0171-229
    8027.
    1825 Phelps Place NW, Washington, DC 20008. Tel: (202) 939-8907/8911/8913.
SAUDI ARABIA: 30 Charles St, London W1. Tel: 0171-917 3000.
    601 New Hampshire Ave NW, Washington DC 20037. Tel: (202) 342-3800.
SINGAPORE: 9 Wilton Crescent, London SW1X 8RN. Tel: 0171-201 1804.
    3501 International Place NW, Washington, DC 20008. Tel: (202) 537-3100.
SLOVAK REPUBLIC: 25 Kensington Palace Gardens, London W8 4QY. Tel: 0171-243
    0803.
    2201 Wisconsin Ave NW, Suite 380, Washington, DC 20007. Tel: (202) 965-5164.
SLOVENIA: Suite 1, Cavendish Court, 11-15 Wigmore St, London W1H 9LA. Tel: 0171-
    495 7775.
    1300 19th St NW, Washington, DC 20007. Tel: (202) 828-1650.
SPAIN: 20 Draycott Place, London SW3 2SB. Tel: 0171-581 5921.
SUDAN: 3 Cleveland Row, St. James's, London SW1A 1DD. Tel: 0171-839 8080.
    2210 Massachusetts Ave NW, Washington DC 20008. Tel: (202) 338-8565.
SWEDEN: 11 Montagu Place, London W1H 2AL. Tel: 0171-914 6413.
    1501 M St NW, Washington, DC 20005.
SWITZERLAND: 16/18 Montagu Place, London W1H 2BQ. Tel: 0171-723 0701.
    2900 Cathedral Ave NW, Washington DC 20008. Tel: (202) 745-7900.
TAIWAN: Taipei Representative Office, 50 Grosvenor Gardens, London SW1W 0EB.
    Tel: 0171-369 9152.
    CCNAA/Coordination Council for North American Affairs, 4201 Wisconsin Ave NW,
    Washington DC 20016-2137. Tel: (202) 895-1800.
THAILAND: 29/30 Queen's Gate, London SW7 5JB. Tel: 0171-589 0173.
    2300 Kalorama Road NW, Washington DC 20008. Tel: (202) 234-5052.
TURKEY: Rutland Lodge, Rutland Gardens, London SW7 1BU. Tel: 0171-589 0360.
    1714 Massachusetts Ave NW, Washington DC 20036. Tel: (202) 659-0742.
UKRAINE: 78 Kensington Park Road, London W11 2PL. Tel: 0171-243 8923.
    3350 M St NW, Washington, DC 20007. Tel: (202) 333-7507.
VENEZUELA: 56 Grafton Way, London W1P 5LB. Tel: 0171-387 6727.
    1099 30th St NW, Washington, DC 20007. Tel: (202) 342-2214.
VIETNAM: 12-14 Victoria Road, London W8. Tel: 0171-937 1912.
    20 Waterside Plaza, New York, NY 10010. Tel: (212) 679-3779.
ZIMBABWE: 429 Strand, London WC2R 0SA. Tel: 0171-836 7755.
    1608 New Hampshire Ave NW, Washington DC 20009. Tel: (202) 332-7100.

For the names of the relevant personnel in the UK, e.g. the Education Attaché, see *The London Diplomatic List* published frequently by the Foreign & Commonwealth Office and held in most libraries.

British Council Offices

ALGERIA: 6 Avenue Souidani Boudjemaa, Algiers. Tel: (2) 605521.*
AUSTRIA: Schenkenstrasse 4, A-1010 Vienna. Tel: (1) 533 2616-80.
BAHRAIN: AMA Centre, (PO Box 452), Manama 356. Tel: 261555.*
BALTIC STATES: Lazaretes lela 3, Riga 226010, Lativa. Tel: (0132) 320468.
　Vilnaius Mokytoju Namai, Vilnaius 39/6, 2600 Vilnius, Lithuania. Tel: (0122)
　616607.
BANGLADESH: 5 Fuller Road, (PO Box 161), Dhaka 1000. Tel: (2) 500 107.*
BELGIUM/LUXEMBOURG: Britannia House, 30 rue Joseph II, 1040 Brussels. Tel: (2)
　219 3600.
BRAZIL: SCRN 708/9, BLOCO F Nos 1/3, (Caixa Postal 6104), 70.740 Brasilia DF. Tel: (61)
　272 3060.
　Av. Domingos Ferreira 4150, Boa Viagem, (Caixa Postal 4079), 51021 Recife. Tel: (81)
　326 6640.
　Rua Elmano Cardim 10, Urca, (Caixa Postal 2237), 22291 Rio de Janeiro RJ. Tel: (21)
　295 7782.
　Rua Maranhão 416, Higienópolis, 01240 São Paulo SP. Tel: (11) 826 4455.
BRUNEI: Hong Kong Bank Chambers, Jalan Pemancha, (PO Box 3049), Bandar Seri
　Begawan 1930, Brunei Darussalam. Tel: (2) 227531.*
BULGARIA: 7 Tulovo St, 1504 Sofia. Tel: 463346.
BURMA (MYANMAR): 80 Strand Road (PO Box 638), Rangoon (Yangon). Tel:
　281700.
CAMEROON: Immeuble Christo, Avenue Charles de Gaulle, (B.P. 818), Yaoundé. Tel:
　211696.*
CHILE: Eliodoro Yanez 832, Casilla 115, Correo 55, Santiago. Tel: (2) 236-1199.
CHINA: c/o British Embassy, Fourth Floor, Landmark Building, 8 North Dongsanhuan
　Road, Chaoyang District, Beijing 100026. Tel: (1) 501 1903.
COLOMBIA: Calle 87, 12-79, (Apartado Aéreo 089231), Santa Fe de Bogotá. Tel: (1) 218
　7518.*
CYPRUS: 3 Museum St, (PO Box 5654), Nicosia. Tel: (2) 44 21 52.
CZECH REPUBLIC: Narodni 10, 12501 Prague 1. Tel: (2) 203751/5.
DENMARK: Gammel Mont 12, 1117 Copenhagen K. Tel: 33 11 20 44.
EAST JERUSALEM & GAZA: 31 Nablus Road, (PO Box 19136), Jerusalem. Tel: (2)
　894392.*
　House 54-279, Orabi St, Al Rimal (PO Box 355), Gaza. Tel: (51) 862461.*
ECUADOR: Av. da Amazonas 1646, Orellana, (Casilla 17-07-8829), Quito. Tel: (2)
　540225.* Costanera 504, Centre Las Monjas y Ebanos, (PO Box 6547), Guayaquil.
　Tel: (4) 388560.*
EGYPT: 192 Sharia el Nil, Agouza, Cairo. Tel: (2) 345 3281-4.*
　9 Batalsa St, Bab Shark, Alexandria. Tel: (3) 482 0199.*
FINLAND: Hakaniemenkatu 2, 00530 Helsinki. Tel: (0) 701 8731.
FRANCE: 9-11 rue de Constantine, 75007 Paris. Tel: (1) 45 55 95 95.
GERMANY: Hardenbergstrasse 20, 1000 Berlin 12 (BFPO 45). Tel: (30) 31 10 99.*
　Hahnenstrasse 6, 5000 Cologne 1. Tel: (221) 20 64 40.
　Rothenbaumchaussee 34, 2000 Hamburg 13. Tel: (40) 44 60 57.
　Lumumbastrasse 11-13, 7022 Leipzig. Tel: (341) 56 47 153.
　Rosenheimerstrasse 116b, Haus 93 (Kustermann Park), D-8000 Munich 80. Tel: (89)
　401832.*
GREECE: Plateia Philikis, Etairias 17, (PO Box 3488), Athens 10210. Tel: (1) 363
　3211.*
　Ethnikis Amynis 9/Tsimiski Corner, (PO Box 50007), 54013 Thessaloniki. Tel: (31) 23
　52 36/7.*
HONG KONG: Easey Commercial Building, 255 Hennessy Road, Wanchai, Hong Kong.
　Tel: 879 5138/831 5138.*
HUNGARY: Benczúr Utca 26, H-1068 Budapest. Tel: (1) 121 4039/1420918.*

INDONESIA: S Widjojo Centre, Jalan Jenderal Sudirman 71, Jakarta 12190. Tel: (21) 522 3250.*
ISRAEL: 140 Hayarkon St, (PO Box 3302), Tel Aviv 61032. Tel: (3) 522 2194-7/524 9798.*
  3 Ethiopia St, (PO Box 32174), West Jerusalem. Tel: (2) 250713.*
  Anis Kardosh St, Nazareth. Tel: (6) 550436.*
ITALY: Palazzo del Drago, Via Quattro Fontane 20, 00184 Rome. Tel: (6) 482 6641/8.*
  Casa Isolani, Strada Maggiore 19, 40125 Bologna. Tel: (51) 225142.*
  Via Manzoni 38, 20121 Milan. Tel: (2) 78 20 16-8.*
  Palazzo d'Avalos, Via dei Mille 48, 80121 Naples. Tel: (81) 414876.*
JAPAN: Cambridge English School, 2-Kagurazaka 1-chome, Shinjuku-ku, Tokyo 162. Tel: (3) 3235 8031.*
  77 Kitashirakawa, Nishi-Machi, Sakyo-ku, Kyoto 606. Tel: (75) 791 7151.*
JORDAN: Rainbow St (off First Circle), Jabal Amman, (PO Box 634), Amman. Tel: (6) 636147/8.*
KENYA: ICEA Building, Kenyatta Ave., (PO Box 40751), Nairobi. Tel: (2) 334811/ 334885.*
KOREA: Anglican Church Annex, 3/7 Chung Dong, Choong-ku, Seoul 100-120. Tel: (2) 737 7157.*
KUWAIT: 2 Al Arabi St, Block 2 (PO Box 345), 13004 Safat, Mansouriya, Kuwait City. Tel: 252 0067/8.*
MALAYSIA: Jalan Bukit Aman, (PO Box 10539), 50480 Kuala Lumpur. Tel: (3) 298 7555/ 230 6304.*
  Wisma Esplanade, 43 Green Hall, (PO Box 595), 10770 Penang. Tel: (4) 630330.*
  Unit 14.01, Level 14, Wisma LKN, 49 Jalan Wong Ah Fook, (PO Box 8), 80700 Johor Bahru. Tel: (7) 233340.*
MALTA: 89 Archbishop St, Valletta VLT 12. Tel: 224707.
MEXICO: Maestro Antonio Caso 127, Col. San Rafael, (Apdo. Postal 30-588), Mexico City 06470 DF. Tel: (5) 566 6144.
MOROCCO: 36 rue de Tanger, (B.P. 427), Rabat. Tel: (7) 760836.*
NEPAL: Kantipath, (PO Box 640), Kathmandu. Tel: (1) 221305.*
NETHERLANDS: Keizersgracht 343, 1016 EH Amsterdam. Tel: (20) 622 36 44.
NORWAY: Fridtjof Nansens Plass 5, 0160 Oslo. Tel: 22 42 68 48.
OMAN: Medinat Qaboos West, (PO Box 7090), Muttrah, Muscat. Tel: 600548.*
  PO Box 18249, Salalah. Tel: 292080.*
PAKISTAN: 20 Bleak House Road, (PO Box 10410), Karachi 75530. tel: (21) 512036/8.
PERU: Calle Alberto Lynch 110, San Isidro, Lima 14. Tel: (14) 70 43 50.
PHILIPPINES: 7, 3rd St, New Manila, Quezon City, Metro Manila. Tel: (2) 721 1981-4.
POLAND: Al Jerozolimskie 59, 00-697 Warsaw. Tel: (2) 628 74 01/3.
PORTUGAL: Rua de São Marçal, 1294 Lisbon Codex. Tel: (1) 347 6141.*
  Casa da Inglaterra, Rua de Tomar 4, 3000 Coimbra. Tel: (39) 23549.*
  Rua do Breiner 155, 4000 Oporto. Tel: (2) 200 5577.*
  Rua Dr. Camilo Dionisio Alvares, Lote 6, 2775 Parede, Cascais. Tel: (1) 457 3414.*
QATAR: Ras Abu Aboud Road, (PO Box 2992), Doha. Tel: 426193.*
ROMANIA: Calea Dorobantilor 14, Bucharest. Tel: (1) 312 0314.
RUSSIA/CIS: Ulyanovskaya Ulitsa, Dom. 1, Moscow 109189. Tel: (095) 297 3499.
SAUDI ARABIA: Olaya Main Road, Al Mousa Centre, Tower B, Third Floor, Office 235 (PO Box 58012), Riyadh 11594. Tel: (1) 462 1818/464 4928.*
  Fourth Floor, Middle East Centre, Falasteen St (PO Box 3424), Jeddah 21471. Tel: (2) 672 3336.*
  Al-Mowajil Building, Dhahran St/Mohammed St, (PO Box 8387), Dammam 31482. Tel: (3) 834 3484.*
SINGAPORE: 30 Napier Road, Singapore 1025. Tel: 473 1111.*
SLOVAK REPUBLIC: Panská 17, 81101 Bratislava. Tel: (7) 331074.*
SPAIN: Calle Almagro 5, 28010 Madrid. Tel: (1) 337 3500.*
  Calle Amigo 83, 08021 Barcelona. Tel: (3) 209 1364.*
  British Institute, Residencia Universitaria Esteban Terradas, Plaza de la Casilla 3, 48012 Bilbao. Tel: (4) 444 6666.*
  Edificio Atalaya, Calle Azhuma 5, 18003 Granada. Tel: (58) 267913.*
  British Institute, Bravo Murillo 25, 35003 Las Palmas de Gran Canaria. Tel: (28) 36 83 00.*

British Institute, Calle del Rosal 7, 33009 Oviedo. Tel: (85) 522 9430.*
British Institute, Goethe 1, 07011 Palma de Mallorca. Tel: (71) 454855.*
Instituto Britanico en Segovia, Trinidad 3, 40001 Segovia. Tel: (11) 434813.*
c/o British Consulate, Plaza Nueva 8b, 41001 Seville. Tel: (5) 422 8873.*
General San Martin 7, 46004 Valencia. Tel: (6) 352 9874.*
SRI LANKA: 49 Alfred House Gardens, (PO Box 753), Colombo 3. Tel: (1) 581171/2.*
SWEDEN: Skarpögatan 6, 11527 Stockholm. Tel: (8) 667 0140.*
THAILAND: 428 Rama 1 Road, Siam Square, Bangkok 10330. Tel: (2) 252 6136.*
198 Bumrungraj Road, Chiang Mai 50000. Tel: (53) 242103.*
TUNISIA: c/o British Embassy, 5 Place de la Victoire, (B.P.229), Tunis 1015 RP. Tel: (1)
259053/353568.
TURKEY: Istaklal Caddesi 251/253, Kat 2-6, Galatasaray (PK 436 Beyoglu 80060),
Istanbul. Tel: (1) 252 74 74-8.
c/o British Embassy, Kirklangic Sokak 9, Gazi Osman Pasa, Ankara 06700. Tel: (4) 428
3165-9.
1481 Sokak, No. 9, Alsancak, Izmir. Tel: (51) 220459.
UKRAINE: Kiev Polytechnic Institute, Room 258, 37 Peremogy Avenue, 20 2056 Kiev.
Tel: (44) 11495.
UNITED ARAB EMIRATES: Saadaqua Tower, Nr. Emirate Sloga Hotel Tourist Club
Area, (PO Box 46523), Abu Dhabi. Tel: (2) 788400.*
Tariq bin Zaid St, Nr. Rashid Hospital, (PO Box 1636), Dubai. Tel: (4) 370109.*
PO Box 1870, Al Ain. Tel: (3) 643838.*
VENEZUELA: Torre La Noria, Piso 6, Paseo Enrique Eraso, Las Mercedes/Sector San
Román, (Aptdo. 65131), Caracas 1065. Tel: (2) 915222.*
YEMEN: House 7, Street 70, (PO Box 2157), Sana'a. Tel: (1) 244121/2.*
ZIMBABWE: 23 Jason Moyo Avenue, (PO Box 664), Harare. Tel: (4) 790627-9.

*Offices marked with an asterisk have their own English Teaching Centres.